CW00516307

Turkish
Pocket Dictionary

Turkish – English
English – Turkish

Berlitz Publishing

New York · Munich · Singapore

Original edition edited by the
Langenscheidt editorial staff

Compiled by Prof. Dr. H.-J. Kornrumpf

Book in cover photo: © Punchstock/Medioimages

Neither the presence nor the absence of a designation
indicating that any entered word constitutes a trademark should be regarded as affecting the legal status
thereof.

Printed in Germany
978-981-246-946-5

Contents
İçindekiler

Abbreviations Used in this Dictionary
Bu Sözlükte Kullanılan Kısaltmalar

The tilde (~, when the initial letter changes into a capital letter or vice versa: ⊋) stands for the catchword at the beginning of the entry or the part of it preceding the vertical bar (|).

Examples: birth (...) ~day = **birthday**

approv|al (...) ~e = **approve**

Bibl|e (...) ⊋iography = **bibliography**

(~) işareti — yazım değişikliği varsa: (⊋) — ya esas sözcüğün tümünü veya onun çizgiye (|) kadar olan kısmını gösterir; örneğin:

birth ... ~day = **birthday**

approv|al ... ~e = **approve**

Bibl|e ... ⊋iography = **bibliography**

a.	also *dahi*
adj.	adjective *sıfat*
adv.	adverb *zarf, belirteç*
Am.	American English *Amerikan İngilizcesi*
ANAT	anatomy *anatomi*
ARCH	architecture *mimarlık*
ASTR	astronomy *astronomi, gökbilim*
AVIA	aviation *havacılık*
b.	bir(i) *someone*
BOT	botany *botanik*
CHEM	chemistry *kimya*
coll.	colloquial *konuşma dili*
conj.	conjunction *bağlaç*
-de	ismin de-hali *locative*
-den	ismin den-hali *ablative*
ECON	economy *iktisat, ekonomi*
EL	electricity, electrical engineering *elektrik, elektro-teknik*

fam.	familiar, informal *teklifsiz, gündelik dil*
fig.	figuratively *mecazî*
GEO	geography, geology *coğrafya, jeoloji*
GR	grammar *gramer, dilbilgisi*
-i	ismin i-hali *accusative*
-in	ismin in-hali *genitive*
inf.	infinitive *mastar, eylemlik*
intj.	interjection *ünlem*
JUR	jurisprudence *hukuk, türe*
MATH	mathematics *matematik*
MED	medicine *tıp*
MIL	military terminology *askerlikle ilgili*
MUS	music *müzik*
n.	noun *isim, ad*
NAUT	nautical terminology *denizcilik*
neg.	negative sense *olumsuz anlam*
PHOT	photography *fotoğrafçılık*
PHYS	physics *fizik*
pl.	plural *çoğul*
POL	politics *siyaset, politika*
prp.	preposition *ön edat, ilgeç*
REL	religion *din*
s.	see *bakınız*
ş.	şey(i) *something*
sg.	singular *tekil*
sl.	slang *argo*
so.	someone *biri*
sth.	something *bir şey(i)*
TECH	technology *teknik*
TEL	telephone, telegraph *telefon, telgraf*
THEA	theatre *tiyatro*
v/i	verb instransitive *geçişsiz fiil*
v.s.	ve saire *and so on*
v/t	verb transitive *geçişli fiil*
vulg.	vulgar *kaba, bayağı*
ZOO	zoology *zooloji*

American Spelling
Amerikan İngilizcesinin Yazımı

İngiltere'de konuşulan İngilizcenin yazımından farklı olarak Amerikan İngilizcesinin (*Am.*'nin) yazımında başlıca şu özellikler vardır:

1. İki sözcüğü birbirine bağlayan çizgi çoğu kez kaldırılır, örneğin co-operate yerine cooperate.

2. **...our** ekindeki u harfi kaldırılır, örneğin: color, humor.

3. **...re** yerine **...er** yazılır, örneğin: center, theater; fakat **...cre** eki değişmez.

4. **...l** ve **...p** ile biten fiillerin türetmelerinde son ünsüz harf ikilenmez, örneğin: travel — traveled — traveling — traveler, worship — worshiped — worshiping — worshiper. Diğer bazı sözcüklerde dahi iki ünsüz harfin birisi kaldırılır, örneğin: waggon yerine wagon, woollen yerine woolen.

5. **...ence** eki yerine **...ense** yazılır, örneğin: defense, offense.

6. Fransızcadan gelen ekler çoğu kez kaldırılır veya kısaltılır, örneğin: dialog(ue), program(me), envelop(e).

7. **ae** ve **oe** yerine çoğu kez yalnız **e** yazılır, örneğin: an(a)emia, man(o)euvers.

8. **...xion** yerine **...ction** kullanılır, örneğin: connection.

9. Söylenmiyen **e**, abridg(e)ment, judg(e)ment v.s. gibi sözcüklerde kaldırılır.

10. **en...** öneki yerine **in...** daha çok kullanılır, örneğin: inclose.

11. *Am.*'de diğer özel yazım biçimleri: staunch yerine stanch,

mould yerine mold, moult yerine molt, plough yerine plow, moustache yerine mustache, cheque yerine check, grey yerine gray, gypsy yerine gipsy, sceptic yerine skeptic, skilful yerine skillful, tyre yerine tire.

12. athough, all right, through yerine altho, alright, thru biçimleri de kullanılabilir.

Pronunciation of the Turkish Alphabet
Türkçe Alfabesinin Söylenisi

A. Vowels and Diphthongs

The vowels are usually short or of medium length. However, there is a number of foreign, mostly Arabic, words with long vowels.

a as **u** in but, sometimes long as **a** in far.
e as **e** in bed.
ı similar to the **a** in along.
i as in hit.
o as in doll or god.
ö as French **œu** in œuvre.
u as in bull.
ü as French **u** in plume.

The diphthongs are as follows:

ay as **uy** in buy.
ey as **a** in make.
oy as **oi** in boil.
uy as French **oui** in Louis.

B. Consonants

The consonants are as in English, except:

c as **j** in jam.
ç as **ch** in chalk.
g as in English, but when followed by **â** or **û** it is palatalized; thus **gâ** is very nearly **g**ya, **gû** like **g**yoo.
ğ with soft vowels (**e, i, ö, ü**) is a consonantal **y**; with hard vowels (**a, ı, o, u**) it is a very guttural but hardly perceptible **g** and very little more than a lengthening of the preceding vowel.
h is always pronounced.
j as French **j** in journal.
k with soft vowels it is frontal like the **k** in kill; with hard vowels

it is backward like the **c** and **ck** in cuc**k**oo; when followed by
â or **û** it is highly palatalized: thus **kâ** is almost like **k**ya
l is much like the English **l**, but before soft vowels and **â** and **û**
it is frontal and similar to the German **l**.
r is much like slight Scottish **r**, but at the end of a word it is
practically unvoiced.
ş as **sh** in she.
v as in vile; after a vowel it may change to the English **w** in we:
e.g. levha, lavta.

C. Circumflex and Apostrophe

The circumflex (düzeltme işareti) denotes:

1. on **a** and **u** the frontal pronunciation of the preceding consonants **g**, **k** and **l** (ikametgâh, kâtip; lûtfen, lûgat are often replaced by lütfen, lügat).
2. the lengthening of a vowel when two words are spelled in the same way: alem (flag), âlem (world).

The apostrophe (kesme işareti) denotes:

1. the separate pronunciation of two syllables: kat'etmek, san'at; in modern spelling, however, it is mostly dispensed with;
2. the separation of suffixes from a proper name or a number: İngiltere'de, 1978'de.

D. Stress

The stress is usually on the final syllable. Important exceptions to this rule are:

1. The stress lies always on the final syllable before the interrogative and negative particles mı, mi, mu, mü and ma, me: geldí mi? Yápma!
2. The suffix -le (from ile) is never stressed: bu surétle.
3. The syllables denoting the tense of the verb (like -yor-, -ir-, etc.) are usually stressed: geliyórum, gidérsin, etc.

Guide to English Pronunciation
İngilizce Söylenişinin Temelleri

İngilizcede 45 ses (fonem) vardır. Bunlardan 12 tanesi ünlü, 9'u iki ünlü ve 24'ü ünsüzdür. Halbuki bunları yazıya çevirmek için alfabede yalnız 26 harf vardır. Bundan dolayı bir harf, bazı durumlarda birden fazla ses için kullanılır; örneğin: far, match, warm, watch, make, arrive gibi sözcüklerde a harfi, birbirlerinden ayrı altı biçimde söylenir. Öte yanda bir ses. birbirlerinden ayrı harflerle gösterilebilir; örneğin: her, girl, fur, learn, worse, colonel sözcüklerindeki ünlü harf aynı biçimde yani uzun ö (ö) gibi söylenir.

Bu sözlüğü kullananlara İngilizce söylenişini kolaylaştırmak için sözlüğün İngilizce-Türkçe bölümünde her maddenin başında olan sözcüğün söylenişi, fonetik bir yönteme göre köşeli ayraçlar içinde gösterilir. Bu yöntemin işaretleri çoğunlukla Türkçe alfabesi harflerinin aynıdır ve Türkçede olduğu gibi söylenir.

Bu sözlükte kullanılan fonetik işaretler şunlardır:

Ses	Türkçesi	İngilizce örnekler
Ünlüler:		
â, aa	lâle, kaabil	far, father
a	a	nut, much
ä	çok açık a'ya benzer yayık bir e	man, mad
e	e	pen, egg
î	î	me, feel
i	i	ship, hint
ı	ı	the, above
ô	uzun o gibi söylenir	all, form
o	o	not, song
ö	uzun ö gibi söylenir	her, girl
û, uu	tufan'daki u'ya benzer	do, shoe
u	u	put, pull

İki ünlüler:

ay	ay	by, life
au	au	out, how
äı	a'ya benzer e ile ı	care, chair
ey	ey	late, may
iı	iı	cheer, fear
ıu	ıu; ou da söylenir	go, foam
oy	oy	boy, voice
uı	uı	sure, poor
yû	yû	new, beauty

Ünsüzler:

b	b	born, rubber
p	p	path, happy
d	d	die, sad
t	t	tie, matter
g	g	gold, dig
k	k	cold; kill
v	v	very, brave
f	f	fine, safe
z	z	zero, maze
s	s	so, gas
j	j	pleasure, occasion
ş	ş	shine, fish
c	c	joke, bridge
ç	ç	church, each
dh	dili üst kesicidişlere dokundurarak söylenen d	that, with
th	dili üst kesicidişlere dokundurarak söylenen t	thank, nothing
h	h	happy, adhere
m	m	make, swim
n	n	name, finish

ŋ	dili damağa dokundurarak genizden söylenen n	si*ng*, E*ng*lish
r	r (dil ağızda yuvarlanarak damağa hafifçe dokundurulur	*r*ed, ve*r*y
l	sözcüğün başında ince, ortasında veya sonunda ise art damaktan çıkarılarak kalın söylenen l	*l*eave; fu*ll*
w	dudakları yuvarlıyarak söylenen v	*w*ill, a*w*ay
y	y	*y*ellow, *y*ear

Vurgulanan heceden önce (') işareti vardır.

Fazla yer harcamamak için İngilizce'de en çok kullanılan eklerin söylenişleri aşağıdaki listede gösterilmiştir. Bir farklılık olmadığı sürece söylenişler, sözlükte bif daha tekrarlanmamıştır.

-ability [-ıbiliti]	-ery [-ıri]
-able [-ıbl]	-ess [-is]
-age [-ıc]	-fication [-fikeyşın]
-al [-ıl]	-ful [-ful]
-ally [-ıli]	-fy [-fay]
-an [-ın]	-hood [-hud]
-ance [-ıns]	-ial [-ıl]
-ancy [-ınsi]	-ian [-iin; yın]
-ant [-ınt]	-ible [-ıbl]
-ar [-ı]	-ic(s) [-ik(s)]
-ary [-ıri]	-ical [-ıkıl]
-ation [-eyşın]	-ily [-ili]
-cious [-şıs]	-iness [-inis]
-sy [-si]	-ing [-iŋ]
-dom [-dım]	-ish [-iş]
-ed [-d; -t; -id]	-ism [-izım]
-edness [-dnis; -tnis; -idnis]	-ist [-ist]
-ee [-î]	-istic [-istik]

-en [-n]
-ence [-ıns]
-ent [-ınt]
-er [-ı]
-ize [-ayz]
-izing [-ayziŋ]
-less [-lis]
-ly [-li]
-ment(s) [-mınt(s)]
-ness [-nis]
-oid [-oyd]
-or [-ı]
-ory [-ıri]
-our [-ı]
-ous [-ıs]

-ite [-ayt]
-ity [-iti]
-ive [-iv]
-ization [-ayzeyşın]
-ry [-ri]
-ship [-şip]
-(s)sion [-şın]
-sive [-siv]
-some [-sım]
-ties [-tiz]
-tion [-şın]
-tious [-şıs]
-trous [-trıs]
-try [-tri]
-y [-i]

A

-a (*dative suffix*) to, towards

aba (*coarse woollen cloth*)

abajur lampshade

abanmak *-e* lean *against*

abanoz ebony

abartmak *v/t* exaggerate

abes useless, trifle

abihayat water of life; elixir

abi (*for* **ağabey**) elder brother

abide monument

abla elder sister

abluka blockade; **~ etm.**, **~ya almak** *v/t* blockade

abone subscriber; subscription; **~ olm** *-e* subscribe to; *-in* **liğinden vazgeçmek** discontinue the subscription of

abstre abstract

abuk sabuk inconsiderate, rash

acaba I wonder if …?

acar clever, cunning; enterprising

acayip strange, wonderful

acele haste, hurry; hasty, urgent; **~** *v/i* haste, hurry

acemi inexperienced; **~lik** inexperience

acente agent; **~lik** agency

acı bitter, sharp

acık grief, sorrow; **~lı** tragic, touching; sentimental

acıkmak feel hungry

acı‖lık bitterness; **~mak** feel pain, hurt; *-e* take pity on; **~nmak** *-e* be pitied

âciz incapable, impotent; **~ kalmak** (*or* **olm.**) *-den* be incapable of, be unable to

acuze old woman; hag

aç hungry; **~gözlü** covetous, avaricious

açı MATH angle

açık open, uncovered; clear; light (*colour*); deficit; **açığa vurmak** *v/t* reveal, disclose; **~ hava** open air; **~ça** *adv.* openly, clearly; **~göz** wide awake, cunning; **~lama** explanation, statement; **~lamak** *v/t* make public, explain; **~lık** open space, interval

açı‖lış opening, inauguration; **~mak** be opened; *-e* open out to

açlık hunger

açmak *v/t* open, begin, unfurl; turn on, switch on, start

ad name, reputation; **~ı geçen** afore-mentioned; **~ına** in the name of, for

ada island; ~ tavşanı rabbit

adak vow; votive offering

adale muscle

adalet justice; ~siz unjust; ~sizlik injustice

adam man, human being

adamak v/t promise, vow

adaş of the same name, namesake

adavet hostility; hate

aday candidate

adçekme designation by lot

addetmek -i ... olarak consider, regard so. to be sth.

Âdem Adam

adet number

âdet custom, habit; MED menstruation; ~â adv. nearly, almost; simply, merely

adım step, pace; ~ ~ step by step

adi common; mean

adil just

adilik commonness; vulgarity, baseness

adlandırmak v/t name, call

adlı named

adl|î judicial; ~iye (administration of) justice

adres address; ~ rehberi address book

Adriyatik (denizi) Adriatic Sea

af pardon; ~ dilemek apologize

afacan unruly, undisciplined

afaki superficial; objective

aferin intj. bravo!, well done!

âfet disaster, calamity; fig. bewitching person

aff|etmek v/t pardon, forgive; ~edersiniz! I beg your pardon!

afiyet health; ~ olsun! may it do you good!, your health!

aforoz REL excommunication

Afrika Africa

afsun spell, charm, incantation; ~cu sorcerer

afyon opium

agraf clip; paper-clip

agrandisman PHOT enlargement

ağ net, web

ağa master, gentleman; ~bey elder brother

ağaç tree; timber; ~lık wooded; wood

ağar|mak become white or pale; ~tmak v/t whiten, clean

ağda syrup

ağı poison

ağıl sheep fold; halo

ağılamak v/t poison

ağır heavy, weighty; serious; strong; ~ yağ, ~ yakıt heavy oil, Diesel oil; ~başlı grave, serious; ~laşmak become heavier, more serious, more mature; ~lık weight, heaviness; fig. nightmare

ağıt lament, mourning

ağız mouth; opening; dialect, manner of speaking; ~lık mouthpiece; cigarette holder

ağla|mak weep (-e or için over); ~tmak v/t cause to weep

ağmak v/i rise

ağrı pain, ache; pains of childbirth

Ağrı dağı Mount Ararat

ağrısız v/i ache, hurt; ~sız without pain

ağu s. ağı

ağustos August

ah intj. ah!, oh!

ahali pl. inhabitants, people

ahbap friend, acquaintance

ahçı s. aşçı

ahdetmek -e promise solemnly, take an oath on

ahenk accord, harmony; ~li harmonious, in accord; ~siz inharmonious

ahır stable

ahiret s. ahret

ahize TEL receiver

ahlâk pl. morals; character; ~î pertaining to morals; moral; ~sız immoral, amoral

ahmak silly, idiotic

ahret REL next world, future life

ahşap wood; wooden

ahu gazelle; ~dudu raspberry

aid|at pl. contribution sg.; allowance; ~iyet interest, concern

aile family; wife; ~vî regarding the family, domestic

ait -e concerning, belonging to

ajan agent; ~s news agency

ak white, clean

akademi academy

akalliyet minority

akarsu running water

akasya acacia

ak|baba vulture; ~ciğer lung(s)

akça whitish, pale; asper; money

Akdeniz the Mediterranean

akdetmek v/t bind, tie; conclude

âkıbet end, consequence, result

akıcı liquid; fluent

akıl reason, intelligence; sense; **aklı başına gelmek** come to one's senses; **aklına gelmek** come to one's mind; ~lı clever, intelligent, reasonable; ~sız stupid, unreasonable

akı|m flowing; current; ~ntı current, stream; ~tmak v/t make flow, let flow, smelt

akide¹ faith, creed

akide² sugar candy

akis contrary, reflex, reflection

akit contract, treaty; marriage

aklî pertaining to mind or reason, reasonable

akmak v/i flow, drip, ooze

akortetmek v/t tune

akraba relative(s)

akreditif ECON letter of credit

akrep scorpion; hour-hand of the clock

aksa|k limping; ~mak v/i limp

akset|mek -e be reflected to; come to the hearing of; ~tirmek v/t reflect, echo

aksır|ık sneeze; ~mak v/i sneeze

aksi contrary, opposite; adverse; ~ **takdirde** other wise, else; ~**lik** contrariness; obstinacy, adverseness; ~**ne** adv. on the contrary; -**in** contrary to

aksiyon ECON share, stock

aksülâmel reaction

akşam evening; ~ **üstü** towards evening; ~**leyin** in the evening

aktarma transhipment; change of train etc.; ~ **yapmak** change the train etc.; ~**k** v/t move, transfer

akt|ör actor; ~**ris** actress; ~**üalite** (film) news-reel

akümülâtör TECH accumulator

al red, crimson

âlâ very good, excellent; **pek ~!** very good!, all right!

alaca of various colours, motley

alacak ECON money owing, credit, claims; ~**lı** creditor

alafranga in the European fashion

alâimisema rainbow

alâka connection, relationship, interest; ~**dar ile** connected with, interested in; ~**dar etm.** -**i** interest (ile in); ~**lı ile** interested in, concerned with

alâmet sign, mark, symbol; ~**i farika** ECON trademark

alan plain, space

alarm alarm

alaşım CHEM alloy

alaturka in the Turkish fashion

alay[1] crowd, procession; MIL regiment

alay[2] joke, derision; ~ **etm.** make fun (ile of)

alaz flame

albay MIL colonel

albüm album

albümin albumen

alçak low, vile, base; ~**gönül-lü** humble, modest; ~**lık** lowness, baseness, meanness

alçal|mak become low; degrade oneself; ~**tmak** v/t lower, reduce; abase

alçı gypsum, plaster of Paris

alda|nmak be deceived; be mistaken; ~**tılmak** be cheated, be defrauded; ~**tmak** v/t deceive, dupe, cheat

aldırmak -**e** take notice of, pay attention to, mind

alel|ade adv. as usual, ordinarily; ~**umum** adv. in general, generally

alem flag; peak of a minaret

âlem world, universe; ~**şümul** universal

alenî public, openly

alerji MED allergy

alet tool, instrument

alev flame; ~**lenmek** flame up, flare

aleyh|- against; -**in** ~**inde bulunmak** be against so. or sth.; ~**tar** opponent

alfabe alphabet

algı perception

alıcı buyer, customer; TECH receiver

alık crazy, imbecile

alıko(y)mak v/t keep back, detain

alım taking; purchase; ~ **satım** purchase and sale

alın forehead

alın|dı ECON receipt; ~**mak** be taken; take offense (-*den* at)

alış taking, buying

alış|kan, ~**kın** tamed, familiar; ~**mak** -*e* be accusmed to, become familiar with; ~**tırmak** v/t accustom, tame; ~**veriş** buying and selling, trade

âli high, trade

âlim scholar

alkım rainbow

alkış applause; ~**lamak** v/t acclaim; ~**lanmak** be greeted with applause

alkol alcohol; ~**izm** alcoholism; ~**suz** non-alcoholic, soft

Allah God; ~~! good Lord!; ~ **aşkına!** for God's sake!; ~ **ısmarladık!** goodbye!

almak v/t take, get, obtain, receive; buy

Alman German; ~**ca** German (language); ~**ya** Germany

Alp dağları, ~ **Alps** pl. Alps

alt n. lower part, underside; adj. lower, inferior; -*in* ~**ına**, ~**ında** under; ~ **taraf** underpart, underside

alternatif alternative; ~ (**akım**) EL alternating current

altı six

altın gold; golden

altmış sixty

altüst etm. v/t turn topsy-turvy

alüminyum aluminium

ama but

amaç target, object, aim

aman pardon, mercy; ~~! for goodness sake!; ~**sız** pitiless, without mercy

amatör amateur

ambalaj packing, wrapping

ambar granary, storehouse, magazine

amca paternal uncle; ~**kızı** girl cousin; ~ **oğlu** male cousin; ~**zade** cousin

amel action, deed; ~**e** worker(s); ~**î** practical; ~**iyat** pl. practical deeds, operations; MED surgical operation

Amerika America; ~ **Birleşik Devletleri** United States of America, U.S.A.; ~**lı**, ~**n** American

amil doing, active; factor

amir commander, superior

amiral admiral

amortis|man ECON amortization; ~**ör** TECH shock absorber

amper EL ampere

ampul EL light bulb

amudî perpendicular, vertical

an a moment, instant; **bir** ~ **evvel** as soon as possible

ana mother; ~ **baba** parents pl.; ~ **okulu** kindergarten

Anadolu Anatolia, Asia Minor

anafor eddy, back current; *fig.* illicit gain

anahtar key; switch

analiz analysis

anamal ECON capital

anane tradition; **~vî** traditional

anarşi anarchy

anason BOT aniseed

anatomi anatomy

anayasa constitution; **~yurt** mother country

ancak but, only, however

ançüez anchovy

andaç gift, souvenir; **~ırmak** *v/t* bring to mind

angaje etm. *v/t* engage, employ; **~man** engagement, employment

angarya, **~e** forced labour

Anglikan Anglican; **~izm** Anglicanism

anık *-e* apt, ready to

anıt monument, memorial

anî sudden, unexpected

anket enquiry

aulam meaning; **~mak** *v/t* understand; conceive

anlaşılır comprehensible, clear, intelligible; **~ma** agreement, understanding; **~mak** *-in* hususunda (or hakkında) come to an agreement on; **~mazlık** misunderstanding

anlatmak *v/t* explain, expound, narrate; **~yış** understanding; intelligence

anmak *v/t* call to mind, remember

anne mother

anonim anonymous; **~ ortaklık**, **~ şirket** ECON joint stock company

anormal abnormal

ansızın *adv.* suddenly, without warning

ansiklopedi encyclopedia

ant oath, vow; **~ içmek** take an oath

anten ZOO, TECH, antenna

antepfıstığı BOT pistachio

antifriz TECH antifreeze

antika antique(s)

antlaşma pact, treaty

antre entrance-hall, vestibule

antrenman training; **~ör** trainer

antrepo bonded warehouse

apandisit ANAT appendicitis

apartman apartment house; **~ (dairesi)** apartment, flat

apse MED abcess

aptal silly, stupid

aptes REL ablution; **~ almak** perform ablution; **~ bozmak** relieve nature; **~ane** latrine

ara interval; relation, understanding; **~ vermek** *-e* stop, cease; **bu ~da** in the meantime; **~da bir** here and there, sometimes; **~mız iyidir** we are on good terms; **~sına**, **~sında** between, among; **~ya girmek** meddle, intervene

araba carriage; cart; car; **~ vapuru** ferry-boat; **~cı**

coachman; driver

araçı mediator; **~lık** mediation

araç means

aralık space, interval

ara|mak v/t seek, look for; **~nmak** be sought, be searched

Arap Arab; Negro; **~ça** Arabic

arasıra adv. sometimes, now and then

araştırma research, investigation; **~k** v/t search, investigate

aratmak v/t make so. search (-e for)

arazi pl. estates; land sg.

arbede riot, tumult

ardıç BOT juniper; **~ kuşu** ZOO fieldfare

ardınca adv. shortly afterwards

ardiye warehouse; storage rent

arduvaz slate

aren arena

argo slang; technical language

arı¹ clean, innocent

arı² bee; **~ kovanı** beehive

arıza accident; defect; **~lı** defective, full of obstacles

arızî accidental

arife eve

arka n. back, back part; **-in ~sına, ~sında** behind; **~ya** one after the other; **~daş** companion, friend; **~lık** back of a chair, etc.

arkeoloji archaeology; **~ müzesi** archaeological museum

arma NAUT rigging; armorial bearings pl.

armağan present, gift

armut pear

Arnavut Albanian; **~ça** Albanian (language); **~luk** Albania

arpa barley; **~cık** sty; foresight of a gun

arsa building-ground, building-site

arsız impudent, insolent

arslan s. aslan

arşın (Turkish yard, ab. 27 in./ 72 cm)

arşiv archives

art n. back, back part; **~çı** MIL rearguard; **~ı** MATH plus

artık n. rest, remnant; adj. remaining, left over; adv. finally; more; **~yıl** leapyear

artır|ım economy, frugality; **~ma** ECON sale by auction; **~mak** v/t increase, augment

art|ış increase, augmentation; **~mak** v/i increase, rise

artist artist

arz¹ earth, land

arz² width, breadth; representation; petition; **~etmek** v/t present, submit; express

arzu wish, desire; **~ etm.** v/t wish, desire

arzuhal petition

asa stick, baton

asab|î nervous; **~iyet** nervousness

asal sayı odd number

asansör lift, elevator

asayiş repose; public peace

aseton CHEM acetone

asfalt asphalt; asphalt highway

asgarî smallest, minimum; ~ fiat minimum price

asıl n. foundation, base; source, origin; adj. essential, real

asıllı hanging, suspended; ~mak -e be hung on, be suspended to

asılsız without foundation

asılzade nobleman, aristocrat

asır century; age, time, epoch

asi rebellious; rebel, insurgent

asil noble

asistan assistant

asit CHEM acid

asker soldier; ~î military; ~lik military service

askı hanger; ribbon

asla (with negation) never, in no way

aslan lion

aslî fundamental; essential

asma hanging, suspending; vine; ~ kilit padlock; ~k v/t hang (-e upon); suspend; put off

asrî modern, up-to-date

astar lining; ~lamak v/t line

asteğmen MIL second lieutenant

astronomi astronomy

Asya Asia

aş food; ~ kabı mess-tin

aşağı adv. down, below; adj. low, inferior; ~yukarı more or less, about; ~da below; ~ya down(wards); ~lamak v/t lower, degrade

aşçı cook

aşı inoculation; graft; vaccine

âşık in love (-e with); lover

aşıkkemiği knuckle-bone

aşılamak v/t inoculate, vaccinate; infect

aşındırmak v/t wear out, corrode; ~mak wear away, be corroded

aşırı excessive; exaggeration; beyond; every second; ~mak v/t -den pass over; steal, rob from

aşikâr clear, evident

aşk love, passion; Allah ~ına! for God's sake!, is that true?; ~ınıza! your health!

aşmak v/t pass over or beyond; exceed, surpass

aşure (sweet dish of cereals, sugar, etc.)

at horse; ~ meydanı hippodrome; ~a binmek ride a horse

ata father; old man; ~lar sözü proverb

atak reckless; boastful

atalet idleness, inertia

atamak v/t appoint

atardamar ANAT artery

atasözü proverb

ataşe attaché

atelye studio; workshop

ateş fire; heat, fever; ~ almak catch fire; ~ etm. v/t fire; ~e

vermek *v/t* set on fire; **~böceği** firefly, glowworm; **~çi** stoker, fireman; **~leme** EL ignition; **~lemek** *v/t* light; **~lenmek** catch fire

atfetmek *v/t* attribute (*-e to*)

atıl|gan dashing, bold; **~mak** be thrown (*-e at*), be discharged; attack (*-e so.*)

atı|m discharge, shot; **~ş** firing

Atina Athens

atkı shawl

atlamak *v/i* jump (*-den* over); *v/t* skip, omit

atlas atlas; satin

atlayış jump

atlet athlete; undershirt

atlı mounted on horseback; rider

atmak *v/t* throw, throw away, drop; fire, discharge

atmosfer atmosphere

atom atom; **~ bombası** atomic bomb

av hunting, shooting, fishing; game, prey

avadanlık artificer's set of tools

avam *pl.* common people; **♀ Kamarası** the House of Commons

avan|s ECON advance *of money*; **~taj** profit, gain

avare vagabond, good-for-nothing

avarya NAUT average

avcı hunter; MIL rifleman; **~lık** hunting

avdet return; **~ etm.** *v/i* return

avize chandelier

avlamak *v/t* hunt, shoot, fish for

avlu courtyard

Avrupa Europe; **~lı** *n., adj.* European; **~lılaşmak** become Europeanized

avuç hollow of the hand; handful

avukat advocate, lawyer

avunmak be consoled (**ile** with)

Avustralya Australia; **~lı** *n., adj.* Australian

Avusturya Austria; **~lı** *n., adj.* Austrian

avutmak *v/t* distract; delude; quieten

ay moon, crescent; month

ayak foot, leg; **~ parmağı** toe; **~ta** on foot, standing; **~kabı** footwear; shoe; **~landırmak** *v/t* stir up, incite to rebellion; **~lanmak** rise in rebellion; **~lı** having feet; **~sız** having no feet; **~takımı** rabble, mob; **~yolu** latrine

ayar standard *of fineness*, accuracy; regulating, adjusting; **~ etm.**, **~lamak** *v/t* test, regulate, adjust

ayartmak *v/t* lead astray, seduce

ayaz dry cold; clearness *of the air*; **~lamak** become cold

ayazma REL sacred spring

aybaşı ANAT menstruation

aydın bright, clear; **~lanmak** brighten up, become clear; **~latmak** *v/t* illuminate; explain; ~lık light; clearness, brightness

ayet REL verse of the Koran

aygır stallion

aygıt apparatus

ayı ZOO bear

ayık sober; ~lamak v/t clean off; select

ayılmak recover from fainting, etc.

ayıp shame, disgrace; ~lamak v/t find fault with, censure

ayır|mak v/t separate, sever; divide; select; ~t etm. v/t distinguish, discern (-den from); ~tmak v/t put aside, reserve

ayin REL rite, ceremony

aykırı -e contrary to, not in accordance with

aylak unemployed, idle

aylık monthly; n. monthly salary

ayna mirror; ~lı having a mirror

ayn|en adv. without any change, textually; ~ı identical; the same

ayraç GR bracket

ayran (drink made with yoghurt and water)

ayrı apart, separate; different; ~ca adv. separately, in addition; ~k separate; ~lmak -den separate oneself from, depart from, leave; ~m difference

ayşekadın (fasulyesi) French beans

aytutulması eclipse of the moon

ayva BOT quince

ayyaş drunkard; ~lık drunkenness

az little; few; seldom; ~ kaldı all but, almost; ~ yağlı low fat (foods)

aza pl. limbs, members; sg. member

azal|mak diminish, be reduced; ~tmak v/t diminish, reduce

azam greater, greatest

azamet greatness, grandeur; ~li magnificent, imposing

azamî greatest, maximum; ~ sürat maximum speed

azar reproach, reprimand; ~lamak v/t scold, reproach

Azerî belonging to Azerbaijan; Turk of Azerbaijan

azgın furious, wild

azık provisions pl.

azınlık minority

azışmak grow vehement

azil dismissal, removal

aziz dear, precious

azletmek v/t dismiss

azmak¹ n. dry well, puddle

azmak² v/i be in flood; be unmanageable

azmetmek -e resolve upon

azot CHEM nitrogen

B

baba father; **~lık** paternity; **~yiğit** brave, virile

Babıâli the Sublime Porte

baca chimney, funnel

bacak ANAT leg, shank

bacanak brother-in-law (*husband of one's wife's sister*)

bacı negro nurse; elder sister

badana whitewash; **~ etm.**, **~lamak** v/t whitewash

badem almond; **~ şekeri** sugar almonds; **~cik** ANAT tonsil

bagaj luggage, baggage

bağ¹ bond, bandage; GR conjunction

bağ² vineyard; **~bozumu** vintage; **~cılık** viniculture

bağdaş sitting cross-legged; **~mak ile** agree, get along with

bağım dependence; **~lı ~e** dependent on; **~sız** independent; **~sızlık** independence

bağıntı relation(ship) (*~e to*)

bağır breast, bosom

bağırmak shout, yell

bağırsak intestine

bağış gift, donation; **~lamak** v/t donate; forgive

bağlaç GR conjunction

bağla|ma connecting, coupling; **~mak** v/t tie, bind, connect, fasten; **~nmak ~e** be tied to; be obliged to; **~ntı** connection; liaison; link (*in Internet sense*)

bağlı ~e bound to, tied to; dependent on

bahane pretext, excuse

bahar¹ spring

bahar² spice; **~at** pl. spices; **~lı** spiced, aromatic

bahçe garden; **~li** having a garden

bahçıvan gardener

bahis discussion; inquiry; **~konusu** theme, subject of discussion

bahrî maritime, naval, nautical

bahriye navy; **~li** sailor

bahsetmek *-den* discuss, speak of

bahş|etmek v/t give; **~iş** tip, bakhshish

baht|iyar lucky, happy; **~sız** unfortunate, unlucky

bakan minister; **~lar kurulu** cabinet, council of ministers; **~lık** ministry

bakı|cı attendant; **~lmak ~e** be attended to, be looked after

bakım attention, upkeep; point of view; **bu ~dan** from this point of view; **~sız** neglected

bakınmak v/i look about

bakır copper

bakış look; care

baki permanent, everlasting

bakir virgin, untouched; **~e** virgin, girl

bakiye remainder; ECON arrears, balance

bakkal grocer; ~iye grocery shop

bakla broad-bean, horse bean

baklava (*sweet pastry made of flake pastry, nuts, and honey*)

bakmak -e look at, examine; look after, see to; **bana bak!** look here! hi!

bakteri bacterium; ~yoloji bacteriology

bal honey; ~ arısı bee

balast ballast

balçık clay

baldır ANAT calf

baldız sister-in-law (*sister of the wife*)

balgam MED mucus, phlegm

balık fish; ~ ağı fishing-net; ~ tutmak v/i fish; ~ yumurtası hard roe; ~çı fisherman

baliğ olm. -e amount to, reach

balina whale

Balkan yarımadası the Balkan Peninsula

balkon balcony

ballı honeyed

balo ball, dance

balon balloon

balotaj POL ballotage

balta axe; ~lamak v/t cut down with an axe; cut away; *fig.* sabotage

Baltık denizi the Baltic Sea

balya ECON bale, packet

balyoz sledge-hammer

bambaşka utterly different

bambu bamboo

bamya BOT gumbo

bana me, to me; ~ **gelince** as to me; ~ **kalırsa** as far as I am concerned

bandıra flag

bando MUS band

bank ECON bank; bench; ~a ECON bank; ~amatik ATM; ~not banknote

banliyö suburb; ~ treni suburban train

bant EL, MED band, tape; ~ izole EL insulating tape

banyo bath; ~ yapmak, ~ almak take a bath

bar bar

baraj barrage, dam

baraka hut, shed

barbunya ZOO red mullet; BOT (*a kind of bean*)

bardak glass, goblet

barem POL classification of salaries

barfiks (*sport*) horizontal bar

barın|ak shelter; ~mak -e take refuge in, take shelter in

barış peace, reconciliation; ~çı peace-loving; ~mak make peace; ~tırmak v/t reconcile

barikat barricade

bariz prominent, manifest

baro JUR bar

barometre barometer

barsak s. bağırsak

barut gunpowder

baş|amak tape, stair; tread; round; ~ı TECH printing; ~ıcı printer; ~ık low

basım printing, impression; **~ evi** printing house

basın press, newspapers; **~ toplantısı** press conference; **~ç** PHYS pressure

basiret understanding, insight; caution

basit simple, plain, elementary

basketbol basketball

bas|kı press, stamp; oppression; **~kın** sudden attack, raid; **~ma** printed cotton; printed goods; **~mak** -e press on, tread on; v/t print; **~tırmak** v/t have printed; suppress, crush

baston stick

basur MED haemorrhoids

baş head, top; beginning; main; **~ ağrısı** headache; **~ göstermek** appear, arise; **~ vurmak** s. **başvurmak; tek ~na** adv. alone; **~ta** at the head, at the top; **~tan** again, from the beginning; **~tan ~a** entirely, completely

başak BOT ear

başar|ı success; **~lı** successful; **~mak** -i succeed in, accomplish

başbakan Prime Minister; **~lık** Prime Ministry

başıboş untied, free

başka other, another; different (**-den** from); **bundan ~** besides this

başkan president, chief; **~lık** presidency

baş|kent capital; **~komutan**

commander-in-chief; **~konsolosluk** Consulate General; **~kumandan** s. **komutan; ~lamak** -e start, begin; **~langıç** beginning, start; **~lıca** main, principal; **~lık** headgear; headline; ARCH capital; **~parmak** thumb; **~piskopos** archbishop; **~şehir** s. **kent**

başvur|mak -e apply to; **~u** application, referring (-e to)

batak n. bog, marsh; adj. marshy; **~hane** gambling den; **~lık** marshy place

batarya MIL, EL battery

batı west

batıl false, vain, useless

batılı POL adj., n. Western (-er)

bat|ırmak v/t sink, submerge; **~mak** v/i sink (-e into), go to the bottom; penetrate

battaniye woollen blanket

bavul suitcase, trunk

bay gentleman; Mr.

bayağı common, ordinary; mean

bayan lady; Mrs., Miss

bayat stale, not fresh

baygın faint; unconscious; **~lık** swoon, fainting

bayılmak faint, swoon

bayındır prosperous, developed; **~lık** prosperity; **2lık Bakanlığı** Ministry of Public Works

bayır slope; hill

bayi vendor

baykuş ZOO owl

bayrak flag, standard; **bayrağı çekmek** hoist the flag; **bayrağı indirmek** lower the flag; **~tar** standard-bearer

bayram religious festival; holiday; **~lık** adj. fit for a festival; n. present given on a festival

baytar veterinary surgeon

baz CHEM base

bazļan, ~en sometimes; **~ı** some, a few; **~ı defa, ~ı kere** sometimes

be! hi! I say!

bebe baby; **~k** baby; doll; ANAT pupil of the eye

becerikļli capable, clever; **~siz** incapable, clumsy

becermek v/t do skillfully

bedava gratis, for nothing

bedļbaht unfortunate, unhappy; **~bin** pessimistic; **~dua** curse, malediction; **~dua etm.** -e curse

bedel substitute, equivalent (-e for); price

beden trunk, body; **~ eğitimi** physical training; **~î** bodily, corporal

bedhah malevolent, malicious

beğenmek v/t like, approve; admire

beher to each, for each, per

bek (football) back

bekâr bachelor; unmarried

bekļçi watchman, sentry; night-watchman; **~lemek** v/t await; watch; hope for

~len(il)mek be expected; **~letmek** v/t cause to wait

bel[1] waist; loins

bel[2] spade

belâ trouble, misfortune, calamity

Belçika Belgium; **~lı** adj., n. Belgian

beledļî municipal; local; **~iye** municipality

belge document, certificate, **~lemek** v/t confirm, prove

belirļlemek v/t determine; **~li** determined; **~mek** v/i appear, become visible; **~siz** indefinite, undetermined; **~ti** sign, symptom; **~tmek** v/t state, make clear

belki perhaps, maybe

belļlemek v/t 1. commit to memory, learn by heart; 2. dig with a spade; **~li** evident, clear; **~li başlı** clear, definite

ben[1] ANAT mole

ben[2] I; **~cil** selfish; **~cilik** ego(t)ism

benek spot, speck; **~li** spotted

benim my; mine; **~semek** v/t make one's own; identify oneself with

benlik egotism; personality

bent paragraph; ARCH dam, aqueduct

benzeļmek -e resemble, be like; **~şmek** resemble each other; **~tmek** v/t compare (-e with); mistake (for)

benzin petrol, gasoline, benzine; **~ borusu** petrol pipe; **~ pompası** pump feeding

petrol *into carburetor*
beraber together
beraet acquittal; ~ **etm.** be acquitted
berat patent, warrant; ~ **gecesi** REL (*Moslem feast, celebrating the night of the revelation of his mission to Mohammed*)
berbat ruined, spoilt; filthy
berber barber
bere¹ beret
bere² bruise, dent
bereket blessing; abundance; ~**li** fertile; fruitful;~**siz** infertile; bringing no good luck
berelemek -*i* cause bruises on
berhava destroyed, annihilated; ~ **etm.** *v/t* destroy; blow up
beri the near side, this side; ~ -*den* since; ~**de** on this side
berk hard, firm
berrak clear, limpid, transparent
bertaraf aside, apart, out of the way; ~ **etm.** *v/t* put aside, do away with
berzah GEO isthmus
besi nourishing, nutrition; fattening
besle|me feeding, nourishing; foster-child; ~**mek** *v/t* feed, nourish; ~**yici** nutritious
bestekâr MUS composer
beş five
beşeriyet human nature; humanity; mankind
beşik cradle

betimlemek *v/t* describe
beton concrete; ~**arme** TECH reinforced concrete
bey gentleman; Mr. (*used after the first name*); husband
beyan declaration, explanation; ~ **etm.** *v/t* declare, explain; ~**name** manifesto, declaration
beyaz white; ~**latmak** *v/t* whiten, bleach
beyefendi sir
beygir horse; ~**gücü** TECH horsepower
beyhude (*yere*) *adv.* in vain
beyin brain; intelligence; ~ **sarsıntısı** MED concussion of the brains; ~**sektesi** MED cerebral apoplexy
beyit verse
bez¹ cloth, duster
bez² ANAT gland
bezelye BOT pea(s)
bıçak knife; ~**lamak** *v/t* stab, knife
bıçkı two-handed saw
bık|kın disgusted, bored; ~**mak** -*den* tire of, get bored with
bırakmak *v/t* leave, quit, abandon; put off
bıyık moustache; ZOO whiskers
biber pepper; **kara** ~ black pepper; **kırmızı** ~ red pepper (pod); ~ **dolması** stuffed peppers
biçare poor, wretched
biçim cut, form, shape; ~**siz** ill-shaped

biç|ki n. cutting-out; **~mek** v/t cut, cut out; reap

bidon n. can

biftek beefsteak

bilakis on the contrary

bilanço ECON balance sheet

bilardo billiards

bilcümle all; in all; totally

bildir|i communiqué; **~im** declaration; **~mek** v/t make known (-e to)

bile even; together with

bileği (taşı) whetstone

bilek wrist

bilemek v/t sharpen, whet

bileş|ik composed; **~ik faiz** MATH compound interest; **~mek** CHEM be compounded (ile with)

bilet ticket; **~ gişesi** ticket window; **~çi** conductor, ticket collector

bilezik bracelet

bilgi knowledge; **~n** learned man, expert; **~siz** ignorant

bilhassa adv. especially, in particular

bili|m knowledge, learning; science; **~nç** conscience; **~nmek** be known; **~rkişi** JUR expert

billur cristal, cut-glass

bilme|ce riddle, enigma; **~k** v/t know, recognise; be able to inf.

bin thousand; **~ bir gece** the Arabian Nights

bina building, edifice; **~en** -e on account of, according to; **~enaleyh** consequently, therefore

binbaşı MIL major; commander

bin|dirmek v/t cause to mount; load; -e collide with, run into; **~ici** rider, horseman; **~mek** -e mount, ride; go on

bir one; **~den** adv. suddenly; together; **~denbire** adv. suddenly; **~i(si)** one of them; someone

bira beer

birader brother

birahane beer-house

bir|az a little; **~birine, ~birini** one another; **~çok** many, a lot; **~den(bire)** s. bir; **~er** one each; **~ey** n. individual

birik|inti accumulation, heap; **~mek** v/i assemble, collect; **~tirmek** v/t collect, amass; save up

birkaç a few, some

birleş|ik united; **~mek** v/i unite, meet (ile with); **~tirmek** v/t unite, connect

birlik unity, union; association; **~te** adv. together, in company

birtakım a quantity, some

bisiklet bicycle; **~ yolu** cycle track

biskü vit biscuit

bit louse

bitap exhausted, feeble

bitaraf impartial, neutral

bitevi(ye) all. of a piece, uninterruptedly

bit|ik exhausted; **~im** ending,

end; ~irmek v/t finish, complete, terminate, eat up; ~işik touching; neighbouring; ~iştirmek v/t join, unite, attach; ~ki plant
bitlenmek be infested with lice; get lice
bitmek come to an end; be completed; be exhausted
bitpazarı rag-fair
biyoloji biology
biz we; ~im our
Bizans Byzantium
bizzat in person, personally
blok block; POL bloc
blöf bluff
bluz blouse
bobin PHYS, EL reel, spool, coil
bodrum cellar
bodur short, dwarf
boğa bull
boğaz throat; mountain pass; strait; 2içi the Bosphorus; ~lamak -i cut the throat of; 2lar the Straits (Bosphorus and Dardanelles)
boğma|ca MED whooping cough; ~k. 1. n. node, joint; 2. v/t choke, strangle
boğu|k hoarse; ~lmak be choked, be drowned; ~m node; knot; ~şmak fly at one another's throats
bohça wrapping cloth, bundle
bok excrement; ordure
boks boxing; ~ maçı boxing match; ~ör boxer
bol wide, loose; ample; ~laş-

mak become wide or loose; be abundant; ~luk wideness, looseness, abundance
Bolşevik Bolshevist
bomba bomb; ~lamak v/t bomb; ~rdıman bombardment, bombing
bomboş quite empty
bonbon bonbon, sweetmeat
boncuk bead
bon|file sirloin steak; ~marşe department store; ~o bond; cheque; ~servis certificate of good service, written character
bora tempest, hurrican
borazan trumpeter; trumpet
borç debt; obligation; ~ almak -den borrow from; ~ vermek lend (-e -i so. sth.); ~lu -e indebted to, under obligation
borda ship's side
bordro payroll
borsa ECON bourse, stock-exchange; ~cı ECON stockbroker
boru tube, pipe; trumpet
bostan vegetable garden
boş empty; unoccupied; unemployed; ~ta unemployed; ~una adv. in vain; ~ vakit, ~ zaman free time; ~almak be emptied; become free; ~altmak v/t empty, pour out
boşa|mak v/t divorce; ~nmak be divorced (-den from)
boşboğaz garrulous, indiscrete; ~lık idle talk
boşluk emptiness; vacuum

botanik *n.* botany; *adj.* botanic(al)

boy length; stature; size; ~unca along

boya dye; paint, colour; ~cı shoe-black; dyer; ~hane dye-house; ~lı dyed; painted; ~mak paint; dye

boykot boycott; ~ etm. *v/t* boycott

boy|lam GEO longitude; ~lu of high stature

boynuz ZOO horn

boyun neck; GEO pass; ~duruk yoke

boyut *match.* dimension

boz grey

boza (*drink made of fermented millet*)

boz|durmak *v/t* cause to spoil, cause to deteriorate; *money:* have changed; ~gun(luk) defeat, rout

bozkır steppe

bozmak *v/t* spoil, ruin, destroy; *money:* change

bozuk destroyed, spoilt, broken; ~ para small change

boz|ulmak be spoilt, be destroyed; break down; ~uşmak break with one another

böbrek ANAT kidney

böbürlenmek be arrogant, boast

böcek insect, bug

böğür side, flank *of the body*

böğürmek bellow

böğürtlen BOT blackberry

bölge zone, district; ~sel regional

bölme partition; dividing wall; ~k *v/t* separate, divide (-e into)

böl|ü MATH divided by; ~ük MIL company, squadron; ~üm dividing; chapter; ~ünmek -e be divided into

bön silly; naive

börek (*pastry or pie*)

böyle so; thus; such; in this way; ~ce, ~likle thus, in this way

branş branch, department, field of work

briket briquette

bronşit med. bronchitis

broş brooch

bu this; ~ kadar that much; that's all; ~nlar *pl.* these; all this; ~nun için for that reason, therefore; ~nunla beraber however, inspite of this

bucak corner, angle; POL subdistrict

buçuk half (*after numerals*); bir ~ one and a half

budak twig, knot *in timber*

budala silly, imbecile; ~lık stupidness

budamak *v/t* lop, trim

bugün today; ~kü of today; ~lük for today

buğday wheat

buğu steam, vapour; ~lanmak be misted over

buhar steam, vapour; ~ makinesi steam-engine; ~lı steamy, vaporous

buhran crisis
buhur incense
buji TECH spark plug
buket bouquet
bukle lock, curl
bukle lock, curl
bulan|dırmak v/t render turbid *or* muddy; turn *the stomach*; **~ık** turbid; cloudy, overcast; **~mak** become cloudy; **midesi ~mak** become nauseated; **~tı** nausea
bulaş|ık smeared over, soiled; MED contagious; *n.* dirty kitchen utensils; **~mak** become dirty; **~tırmak** v/t smear; infect
Bulgar Bulgarian; **~istan** Bulgaria
bulgur boiled and pounded wheat
bul|maca crossword puzzle; **~mak** v/t find; invent; **~undurmak** v/t make available; **~unmak** be found; be present; be; **~uş** finding; invention, idea; **~uşmak** meet
bulut cloud; **~lanmak** become cloudy; **~lu** cloudy, overcast
bulvar boulevard
bunak dotard
bunal|ım crisis; **~mak** be stupefied, be suffocated (*-den* with)
bunun *s.* bu
bura|da here; **~dan** from here; **~sı** this place, here; **~ya** to this spot, here
burç[1] tower
burç[2] ASTR sign *of the Zodiac*

burgu orger, gimlet; corkscrew; **~lamak** v/t drill, bore
burjuvazi POL bourgeoisie
burkmak v/t sprain, twist
burmak v/t twist, wring; castrate; **burun ~e** sneer at
burnuz bathrobe
burs scholarship
burun nose; GEO promontory, cape
buruş|mak be wrinkled, creased; **~turmak** v/t crease, wrinkle; **~uk** puckered, wrinkled
buse kiss
but thigh
buy|ruk order, command; **~rultu** order, decree; **~urmak** v/t order; condescend to *inf.*; **~urun(uz)!** please!
buz ice; frozen; **~ dolabı** refrigerator; **~dağı** iceberg; **~kıran** ice-breaker; **~lu** iced; **~ul glacier**
büfe buffet, bar
bük|lüm *n.* twist, curl, fold; **~mek** v/t twist, spin, curl; **~ülmek** be twisted, be bent; **~ülü** bent, twisted
bülbül nightingale
bünye structure, constitution
bürç *s.* burç
büro office, bureau; **~krasi** bureaucracy, red tape
bürü|mcük raw silk gauze; **~mek** v/t wrap, cover up
bürünmek *-e* be filled with; wrap oneself in
büsbütün altogether, quite
büst bust; portrait.

bütçe ECON budget

bütün *adj.* whole, entire; all; *n.* whole; **~lük** entirety, universality

büyü incantation, corcery; **~cü** sorcerer, magician

büyük great; large; high; elder; **≗ Millet Meclisi** POL Grand National Assembly;

~anne grandmother; **~baba** grandfather; **~elçi** POL ambassador; **~lük** greatness; largeness

büyülemek *v/t* bewitch

büyü|mek *v/i* grow, grow up; **~tmek** *v/t* bring up; enlarge

büzülmek contract; shrink

C

cadde main road, street

cadı witch, hag

cahil ignorant

caiz lawful, permitted

cam glass, pane; **~cı** glazier

camekân *s.* camlık

cami mosque

cam|lamak *v/t* cover with glass; **~lı** glass-covered; **~lık** hotbed, hothouse; shop-window

can soul; life; darling, friend; **~ı sıkılmak** be bored (-e by); be annoyed

canavar monster, brute

can|kurtaran life-belt; **~landırmak** *v/t* animate, invigorate; **~lanmak** come to life, become active; **~lı** alive; lively; **~sız** lifeless; dull

cari *adj.*, ECON current

casus spy; **~luk** espionage

cavlak bald, naked

cay|dırmak *v/t* cause to renounce, make *so.* change his purpose; **~mak** change one's mind; renounce (-den

sth.)

cazibe attractiveness, attraction; **~li** attractive

cazip *s.* cazibeli

CD CD; **~-çalar** CD player; **~-ROM** CD-ROM

cebbar tyrannical; tyrant

cebir. 1. MATH algebra; **2.** force, violence; **~ kullanmak** use force

cebr|en *adv.* by force; **~î. 1.** compulsory, forced; **2.** MATH algebraic

cefa ill-treatment, cruelty

cehennem REL hell

ceket jacket, coat

celbetmek *v/t* attract; summon

celp(name) JUR summons

celse sitting, session

cem|aat community, group, congregation (*a.* REL); **~etmek** *v/t* collect; add up (*a.* MATH); **~î** MATH addition; GR plural; **~iyet** meeting; association; society

cenaze corpse; funeral; **~**

cinsiyet

alayı funeral procession
cendere press, roller press
cengâver warlike, brave
cengel jungle
cennet REL paradise
centilmen gentleman; ~ce
gentleman-like
cenu|bi southern; ~p south
cep pocket; ~ sözlüğü pocket
dictionary; ~ telefonu mobile phone, Am. cellphone
cephane MIL ammunition
cephe front; forehead
cerahat MED pus
cereyan flowing, current,
course; ~ etm. happen, flow,
pass
cerrah surgeon; ~lık surgery
cesaret boldness, daring; ~
etm. -e dare
ceset corpse
cesur bold, daring, coura-
geuos
cetvel list, schedule; ruler
cevahir pl. jewel(s); ~ci jeweller
cevap answer, reply; ~ vermek -e answer to, reply to;
~landırmak v/t answer sth.
cevher essence, substance,
nature; ~li talented; set with
jewels
ceviz BOT walnut
ceylan ZOO gazelle, antilope
ceza punishment, fine; ~ çekmek serve a sentence (-den
for); ~evi prison; ~landır-
mak v/t punish; ~lanmak
be punished
cezbetmek v/t attract, draw

cezir GEO ebb
cezve pot for making Turkish
coffee
chat odası chat room
cılız thin, delicate
cılk rotten; inflamed
cırıldamak, cırlamak creak,
screech
cıvata bolt, screw
cıvık wet, sticky; ~lanmak become wet or sticky
cıvıldamak twitter, chirp
cızıldamak, cızırdamak sizzle
cibinlik mosquito-net
cici 1. good, pretty, nice; 2.
toy, plaything
ciddi earnest, serious; ~iyet
seriousness
ciğer ANAT liver; lung(s); darling
cihan world, universe
cihaz apparatus, equipment;
ANAT system; trousseau
cihet side, direction
cilâ polish; varnish; ~lamak
v/t polish
cilt skin, hide; volume; ~çi
bookbinder; ~lemek v/t bind
a book; ~li bound (book); in
... volumes; ~siz unbound
cilve coquettery, charm; ~li
graceful; coquettish
cimnastik gymnastics
cimri parsimonious
cin genie, demon, spirit
cinas play upon words, pun
cinayet crime
cins species, class, kind; sex;
~el, ~î generic, sexual; ~iyet

sex; sexuality

ciro ECON endorsement

cisim body, substance

cismanî corporeal, material

civa CHEM mercury, quicksilver

civar neighbourhood, environs

civciv chicken

coğrafya geography

compact disk compact disc, CD

conta TECH joint

coş\|kun boiling over; exuberant; excited; ~luk overflowing; enthusiasm

coş\|mak become violent; be enthusiastic; ~turmak v/t inspire, fill with enthusiasm

cömert generous; ~lik generosity

cuma Friday; ~rtesi Saturday

cumhur people, populace; ~başkanı President of the Republic; ~iyet republic; ~iyetçi republican; ~reisi s. ~başkanı

cüce dwarf

cülus accession to the throne

cümle total, whole; system; GR phrase, sentence

cüppe robe with full sleeves and longskirts

cüret boldness, daring; ~kâr, ~li bold, daring

cürüm crime, felony; cürmü meşhut JUR caught in the act

cüz part, section

cüzam MED leprosy

cüzdan wallet, portfolio

cüzî trifling, partial

Ç

çabalamak strive, struggle

çabucak quickly

çabuk quick, agile; ~laştırmak v/t accelerate; ~luk speed, haste

çadır tent; ~ direği tentpole; ~ kurmak pitch a tent

çağ time, epoch, age; ~daş contemporary

çağıldamak burble, murmur

çağırmak v/t call, invite (-e to)

çağ\|lamak burble, murmur; ~layan cascade

çağrı invitation; ~lmak -e be

invited to

çakal ZOO jackal

çakı pokcet-knife

çakıl pebble; ~ döşemek pave with pebbles

çakır\|diken burdock, burr; ~keyif half-tipsy

çakmak[1] v/t drive in with blows; light; fig. know (-den about sth.); be 'ploughed' (in ANAT examination, etc.); şimşek ~ flash (lightning)

çakmak[2] n pocket-lighter; ~taşı flint

çal|ar saat alarm clock; **~dırmak** v/t cause to play or steal; loose by theft; **~gı** musical instrument

çalı bush, shrub; **~lık** thicket

çalınmak be struck or stolen

çalışkan industrious, hard working; **~ma müsaadesi** working permit; **~mak** v/i work, strive; study (-e sth.); **~tırmak** v/t make work, make run

çalka(la)mak v/t shake; rinse, wash out; churn; stir

çalmak v/i ring, strike; -e knock on, give a blow to; ring; v/t steal; instrument: play; **zili ~** ring the bell

çam BOT fir; pine; **~fıstığı** pine kernel

çamaşır underclothing; washing; **~hane** laundry room

çamur mud, clay; **~lu** muddy; **~luk** gaiter; (auto) mudguard

çan bell; **~ kulesi** belfry

çanak earthenware pot; **~ anten** satellite dish

çangırdamak clang, jangle

çanta bag, case; **el ~sı** handbag

çap diameter, bore, calibre

çapa hoe, mattock; anchor; **~lamak** v/t hoe

çapkın vagabond, rascal; rake; **~lık** profligacy; debauchery

çapraşık intricate, tangled

çapraz crossing, crosswise

çapul booty, spoil; raid, sack

çardak hut, pergola

çare remedy, means; **~ bulmak** find a remedy

çark wheel of a machine

çarmıh cross for crucifying; **~a germek** v/t crucify

çarp|ı MATH ... times; **~ık** crooked, bent; slanting; **~ınmak** struggle; **~ıntı** palpitation; **~ışma** collision; clash; **~ışmak** collide; fight; **~ma** blow, stroke; MATH multiplication; **~mak** -e strike, knock against; collide with; MATH multiply (-i ile sth. with)

çarşaf sheet of a bed; veiled dress

çarşamba Wednesday

çarşı bazaar, street with shops

çatal fork; forked; **~lanmak** bifurcate, fork

çatana NAUT small steamboat

çatı framework; roof; **~ arası, ~ katı** attic

çatır|damak v/i chatter, clatter; **~datmak** v/t make chatter; **~tı** clattering; chattering

çatışmak clash, collide (ile with)

çatla|k split, cracked; **~mak** v/i crack, split; **~tmak** v/t split, crack

çatmak v/t fit together; sew coarsely; animal: load; -e scold, rebuke; -e win the favour of so.

çavdar BOT rye

çavuş MIL sergeant

çay¹ stream

çay² tea; **~danlık** teapot

çayır meadow, pasture; **~lanmak** v/i graze, pasture

çehre face, countenance

çek ECON cheque

çek|ecek shoehorn; **~ici** attractive

çekiç hammer

çeki|liş drawing of lots, etc.; **~lmek** withdraw, retire (-den from); **~m** GR inflection, declination, conjugation; **~nmek** -den beware of; refrain from

çekirdek stone, pip

çekirge ZOO grasshopper, locust

çekişmek v/i quarrel; dispute

çekme PHYS attraction; **~ halatı** tow rope; **~ taşıdı** recovery vehicle; **~(ce)** drawer, till; **~k** v/t pull, draw; suffer; send a telegramme; take a photograph

çelebi adj. educated; gentleman

çelenk wreath

çelik steel

çelim form, shape

çelişmek be in contradiction

çeltik BOT rice

çember yoop, ring, circle; **~lemek** v/t hoop; MIL encircle

çene ANAT jaw; chin

çengel hook

çent|ik notch; **~mek** v/t notch; mince

çepel gloomy, dull; muddy

çerçeve frame; **~lemek** v/t frame, put in a frame

çerez tidbits, snack

Çerkez Circassian; **~ tavuğu** (chicken with walnut)

çeşit sort, variety, sample; **~li** various, assorted

çeşme fountain

çeşni taste, flavour

çete band; **~ harbi** guerilla warfare

çetin difficult; harsh

çetrefil confused; bad (language)

çevik nimble, agile

çevir|en translator; **~mek** v/t turn round; change, translate (-e into)

çevre circumference; surroundings; **~ dostu** eco-friendly, environmentally friendly

çevr|elemek v/t surround, encircle; **~i** forced interpretation; whirlpool, whirlwind; **~ilmek** be turned round; be changed, be translated (-e into)

çeyiz bride's trousseau

çeyrek quarter of ANAT hour

çıban boil, abscess

çığ avalanche; **~ır** track left by an avalanche; fig. path, way

çığlık cry, scream

çık|ar yol way out; **~armak** v/t take out, extract; remove, take off; derive, deduce; **~artmak** v/t let remove, let extract; **~ıntı** projection;

~ış exit, sortie; leaving; ~ış vizesi POL exit visa; ~mak come out; appear; get about; be dislocated; -e start; mount; ~maz blind, dead end

çıl|dırmak v/i go mad; ~gın mad, insane

çınar plane-tree

çın|gırak small bell; ~lamak ring; sing

çıplak naked, bare

çırak apprentice; ~lık apprenticeship

çırp|ınmak flutter, struggle; ~mak v/t strike, tap, pat; rinse

çıt|çıt snap fastener; ~ırdamak, ~lamak v/i crackle; ~latmak v/t cause to crackle

çiçek flower, blossom; MED small-pox; ~lenmek bloom, blossom

çift pair; couple; ~ sayı even number; ~ priz EL two-pin plug; ~ sürmek plow; ~ tıklamak double-click; ~çi farmer; ~e paired, doubled; ~leşmek v/i mate; ~lik farm

çiğ¹ raw, unripe

çiğ² s. çiy

çiğdem BOT crocus

çiğnemek v/t crush; chew

çiklet chewing-gum

çikolata chocolate

çil spot, freckle; speckled

çile¹ trial, sufferance

çile² hank, skein

çilek strawberry

çilingie locksmith

çimdik pinch; ~lemek v/t pinch

çimen turf, grass plot; ~lik lawn, meadow

çimento cement

Çingene gypsy

çini tile; tiled

çinko CHEM zinc

çiriş paste, size; ~lemek v/t smear with paste

çirkin ugly; unseemly

çiş urine

çit¹ fence

çit² chintz

çivi nail; ~lemek v/t nail

çiy dew

çizgi line, mark, scratch; ~li marked with lines; striped

çizme top boot; ~k v/t draw; sketch; strike off

çoban chepherd

çocuk infant, child; ~luk childhood; childishness

çoğal|mak v/i increase, multiply; ~tmak v/t increase, augment

çoğul GR plural; ~nluk majority

çok much, many; very; ~ taraflı multilateral; ~luk abundance; crowd

çolak with one arm; crippled in one hand

çoluk çocuk household, family; pack of children

çorak arid, barren

çorap stocking(s)

çorba soup

çök|ertmek v/t make kneel; cause to collapse; ~mek collapse, fall down; **diz** ~**mek** kneel; ~**üntü** debris; sediment, deposit

çöl desert, wilderness

çömlek earthen pot

çöp dust, rubbish; ~ **tenekesi** dustbin, garbage can; ~**çü** dustman

çörek (*a kind of sweetened cake*); disc

çöz|mek v/t untie; solve; ~**ülmek** be untied; MIL withdraw

çözüm solution; ~**lemek** v/t analyze

çubuk shoot, twig; cigarette holder

çukur hole, hollow, ditch, cavity

çul hair-cloth; ~**luk** zoo woodcock

çuval sack

çünkü, çünki because

çürük rotten, spoilt; ~**lük** rottenness, putrefaction

çürü|mek rot, decay; ~**tmek** v/t cause to rot, let decay

D

da, de, ta, te also, too

-da, -de, -ta, -te in; on; at

dadı nurse

dağ[1] brand, mark, cautery

dağ[2] mountain; ~**cı** alpinist

dağ||lmak scatter, be dispersed; be distributed; ~**tm** distribution; ~**tmak** v/t scatter, disperse; distribute

dağlamak v/t brand, cauterize

dağlı[1] branded, scarred

dağlı[2] mountaineer; ~**k** mountainous

daha more (*-den* than); further; yet; **bir** ~ once more

dahi also, too

dâhi genius

dahil inside; included

dahilî internal, inner

daim||a always, perpetually; ~**î** constant, permanent

dair *-e* concerning; about; ~**e** circle; department, office; limit

dakika minute

daktilo typist; typewriting; ~ **(makinesi)** typewriter

dal branch, bough

dalamak v/t bite

dalavere trick, intrigue

daldırmak v/t plunge; layer

dalga wave; undulation; ~**kıran** breakwater; ~**lanmak** become rough; wave; ~**lı** covered with waves; rough

dalgıç diver; ~**n** plunged in thought, absentminded

dalkavuk sycophant, parasite

dallanmak become branched, ramify

dalmak *-e* plunge, dive into

dalya dahlia

dam roof

dama game *of draughts*

damacana large bottle, demijohn

damak palate

damar ANAT vein; GEO seam

damat son-in-law

damga stamp, mark; ~ pulu revenue stamp; ~lamak *v/t* mark with a stamp; ~lı stamped, marked

damıtmak *v/t* distil

damla drop; ~lık dropper; ~mak *v/i* drip; ~tmak *v/t* pour out drop by drop; distil

-dan, -den, -tan, -ten from; than

dana ZOO calf; ~ eti veal

danış|ma information; ~mak consult (*-e -i so.* about *sth.*), ask for; 2 tay Council of State

Danimarka Denmark; ~lı *n., adj.* Danish

dans dance; ~ etm. dance; ~ör dancer

dantel(a) lace

dar narrow, tight; with difficulty

dara ECON tare

darağacı gallows

daral|mak become narrow; shrink; ~tmak *v/t* make narrower, reduce

darb|e blow, stroke; ~ımesel proverb

darboğaz *fig.* bottle-neck

dargın angry, irritated

darı BOT millet

darıl|gan easily offended;

~mak be offended (*-e* with); get cross

darla|ştırmak, ~tmak *v/t* make narrow, restrict

darmadağan in utter confusion

darphane *n.* mint

dava JUR lawsuit; trial; claim; ~ açmak bring a suit of law (*-e* against); ~cı claimant, plaintiff; ~lı defendant

davar sheep *or* goat(s)

davet invitation; summons; ~ etm. *v/t* invite, summon (*-e* to); ~iye card *of invitation*; ~li guest

davran|ış behaviour, attitude; ~mak behave, take pains

davul drum

dayak prop, support; beating; ~ yemek get a thrashing

dayamak *v/t* support, lean (*-e* against)

dayanık|lı lasting; enduring; ~sız not lasting, weak

dayan|ışma solidarity; ~mak *-e* endure; lean on; rely on

dayı maternal uncle

de *s.* da; -se de even if, although

-de *s.* -da

debdebe pomp, display

dede grandfather

dedikodu tittle-tattle, gossip

defa time, turn; birkaç ~ on several occasions; çok ~ often

defetmek *v/t* drive away, expel

defile 42

defile fashion show

defin burial, interment

defne BOT bay-tree, laurel

defnetmek v/t bury

defolmak go away

defter register; book; list; ~dar accountant

değer n. value, worth, price; adj. -e worthy of; ~lendirmek v/t appraise; estimate; utilize; ~li valuable; ~siz worthless

değil not

değin -e until

değirmen mill; ~ci miller

değiş exchange

değişik changed, different; varied; ~lik alteration; variation

değişmek v/i change, alter, vary; ~tirmek v/t change, exchange, alter

değme every, any; ~k be worth; reach, touch (-e sth.)

değnek stick, rod

dehşet terror; ~li terrible

dek -e s. değin

dekar (measure of land: 0.247 acres)

deklanşör trigger (photo)

dekor THEA stage scenery

dekovil narrow gauge railroad

delâlet guidance; indication; ~ etm. -e guide to; show, indicate

deli mad, insane

delik hole, opening

delikanlı youth, young man

delil guide; proof, evidence; ~

göstermek adduce proofs

deli|lik madness; ~rmek go mad, become insane

delmek v/t pierce, hole

dem breath; time; alcoholic drink

demeç statement, speech

demek say, tell; mean; ~ ki this means to say that

demet sheaf, bunch, faggot; ~lemek v/t tie in bunches

demir iron; anchor; ~ almak weigh anchor; ~ atmak cast anchor; ~baş furnishings, inventory; ~ci blacksmith; ~lemek v/i anchor; v/t bolt and bar a door; ~yolcu railwayman; ~yolu railway

dem|lenmek be steeped (tea); ~lik teapot

demokra|si democracy; ~t democrat; ~tik democratic

-den s. -dan

denaet meanness, baseness

deneme trial, test; ~k v/t test, trial

denet|(im) control; ~lemek v/t control

deney CHEM test

denge equilibrium; ~li balanced; ~siz out of balance

denilmek be said; be called

deniz sea; ZOO shrimp; ~böceği ZOO shrimp; ~altı submarine; ~aşırı overseas; ~ci seaman, sailor; ~cilik navigation; sailing

denk bale; balance; ~lem MATH equation; ~leştirmek v/t bring into balance

denmek s. **denilmek**

densiz lacking in manners, tactless

depo depot, warehouse; ~zito ECON deposit, security

deprem earthquake

depreşmek s. **tepreşmek**

derbent defile, pass

dere valley; stream; ~beyi feudal lord; ~otu BOT dill

derece step, stair; degree

dergi magazine, periodical

derhal adv. at once, immediately

deri skin, hide, leather

derin deep, profound; ~leştirmek v/t deepen (a. fig.); ~lik depth, profundity

derkenar marginal note

derlemek v/t gather, collect

derman strength, energy; ~sız week, feeble

dernek association

ders lecture, lesson; ~hane class-room

dert pain, suffering; grief, trouble

deruhte etm. v/t undertake, take upon oneself

deruni internal; cordial

derviş beggar, dervish

derya sea

desen design; drawing

desise trick, intrigue

destan story, legend, epic

deste handle; hilt; bunch; packet

destek beam; prop, support; ~lemek v/t prop up; support

destur permission; ~! by your leave! make way!

deşelemek v/t scratch up

dev giant; demon

deva medicine, remedy

devam continuation, permanence; ~ etm. last; -e continue; follow; ~lı continuous; ~sız inconstant, not persevering

deve camel; ~kuşu ostrich

develop etm. v/t develop (photo)

deveran rotation; circulation

devir rotation, cycle, circuit; period, epoch

devirmek v/t overturn, reverse

devlet state, government; ~çi favouring state control; ~leştirmek v/t nationalize

devr|e cycle; generation; period; ~en adv. by continuation of the present contract; ~etmek v/t transfer (-e to)

devri|k turned over; ~lmek be overturned; ~m revolution; transformation

devriye police round, patrol

deyi|m phrase, expression; ~ş way of speaking

dezenfekte etm. v/t disinfect

dı|ı ANAT rib; MATH side of a triangle

dış outer, exterior; outside; ~ taraf outside

dışarı outside; exterior; out; ~da outside; abroad; ~dan from the outside; from abroad; ~ya abroad; towards the outside

Dışişleri *pl.* POL External Affairs

Dicle GEO Tigris

didiklemek *v/t* tear to pieces; search

didinmek toil, wear oneself out

didişmek quarrel, bicker (ile with)

deferansiyel TECH differential gear

difteri diphteria

diğer other, another; different; next

dijital digital; ~ fotoğraf digital photo; ~ fotoğraf makinesi digital camera

dik upright, straight; steep; ~ kafalı obstinate

diken thorn, sting; ~li thorny, prickly; ~li tel barbed wire

dikey MATH vertical

diki̇li sewn, stitched; set up; ~lmek be sewn, be planted; stand stiff; ~ş sewing, stitching; seam; ~ş makinesi sewing machine

dikkat attention; care; ~ etm. -e pay attention to; be careful with; ~le *adv.* with care; ~li attentive, careful; ~siz careless; ~sizlik carelessness

dikmek *v/t* sew, stitch; set up; plant

diktatör dictator; ~lük dictatorship

dikte dictation; ~ et(tir)mek *v/t* dictate

dil tongue; language; ~ balığı zoo sole; ~bilgisi grammar;

~bilim linguistics

dilek wish, desire; request; ~çe petition, formal request

dilemek *v/t* wish, desire; özür ~ ask pardon

dilen|ci beggar; ~mek beg

dilim slice, strip

dilsiz dumb, mute

dimağ brain, intelligence

din religion, faith

dinç vigorous, robust; ~leştirmek *v/t* strengthen, invigorate; ~lik robustness, good health

din|dar pious; ~daş coreligionist

dindirmek *v/t* cause to cease, cause to stop

dingil axle

dini pertaining to religion

dinle|mek *v/t* listen to, hear, pay attention to; ~nme yeri road house; ~nme yurdu recreation home; ~nmek rest; become quiet; ~yici listener

dinmek cease; leave off

dinsiz without religion

dip bottom, lowest part; ~çik butt *of a rifle*

diploma diploma, certificate; ~sè diplomacy; ~t diplomate

dipsiz bottomless

dirayet comprehension, intelligence

direk pole, pillar, mast

direk|siyon steering-wheel; ~tör director

diren|iş resistance; ~mek insist (-de) on

diri alive, fresh; ~lmek come to life; ~ltmek v/t bring to life; ~m life

dirsek elbow; bend

disiplin discipline

disk TECH disk; discus; ~ atma throw the discus; ~ sürücü disk drive

dispanser MED dispensary

distribütör EL distributor

diş tooth; cog, clove; ~ fırçası toothbrush; ~ macunu toothpaste; ~çi dentist; ~çilik dentistry

dişi female; ~l GR feminine

dişli toothed; cogged

divan. **1.** sofa, divan; **2.** collection of poems; **3.** POL council of state

divane insane; crazy

diyafram ANAT, PHYS diaphragm

diyanet religious affairs pl.

diye saying; ~lek dialect

diz ANAT knee; ~ çökmek kneel; ~ kapağı knee cap

dizanteri MED dysentery

dizel Diesel

dizi line, row, string; ~ilmek -e be arranged in; be strung on; ~mek v/t arrange in a row; string

dizüstü bilgisayar laptop

doçent lecturer, assistant professor

doğa nature; ~l natural

doğan ZOO falcon

doğma birth; by birth; ~k be born; ASTR rise

doğrama work of a carpenter; ~cı carpenter; ~k v/t cut into pieces

doğru straight, upright; right, true, honest; ~dan ~ya directly; ~ca direct, straight; ~lamak v/t confirm; ~lmak become straight; ~ltmak v/t put straight; correct; ~luk straightness; honesty, truth

doğu east; eastern

doğum birth; ~ günü birthday; ~lu -de born in

doğurmak v/t give birth to, bring forth; ~tmak v/t assist delivery

dok NAUT dock

doksan ninety

doktor doctor; physician; ~a doctorate

doku tissue

dokuma weaving; woven; ~cı weaver; ~k v/t weave

dokun|aklı touching, biting, harmful; ~mak. **1.** be woven; **2.** -e touch, injure; ~ulmazlık POL immunity

dokuz nine

dola|mak v/t twist, wind (-e on); ~mbaç(lı) winding, sinuous

dolandırıcı swindler; ~lık swindle

dolandırmak v/t cheat, swindle, defraud

dolap cupboard; waterwheel; merry-go-round

dolaş|ık tortuous, confused; ~mak go around, walk about, make a roundabout

dolaştırmak 46

way; ~tırmak *v/t* make *so.* go around; *-i -e* show *so.* over *sth.*

dolayı *-den* on account of, due to; *conj.* as, because

dol|durmak *v/t* fill; complete; fill up; ~gun full; filled; high (*wages*); ~ma stuffed, filled; ~ma kalem fountain-pen; ~mak become full; be completed; ~muş filled, stuffed; a taxi all seats of which use to be engaged; ~u *adj.* full, filled; solid; *n.* hail; ~unay full moon

domates tomato(es)

domuz pig, swine

don¹ frost

don² pair of drawers

donanma fleet; navy; illumination; ~k be illuminated

donat|ım MIL outfit, equipment; ~mak *v/t* ornament, illuminate

dondurma ice cream; ~cı ice-cream vendor; ~k *v/t* freeze

don|mak *v/i* freeze; set; ~uk matt, dull

dopdolu chockful

dost friend; lover; ~ane, ~ça friendly; ~luk friendship; favour

dosya dossier, file

doy|mak be satiated; ~maz insatiable; ~urmak *v/t* satiate; satisfy

dök|me casting; cast; ~mek *v/t* pour; scatter; cast; ~ülmek be poured; be cast; fall out; disintegrate; drop off

döküm dropping; cast; enumeration *of* ANAT account; ~hane TECH foundry

döküntü remains; debris

döl seed, germ; race, stock; ~lemek *v/t* inseminate, fertilize

dön|dürmek *v/t* turn round, reverse; ~em period *of* time; ~er kebap *meat roasted on a revolving vertical spit*; ~me turning; conversion; REL Jewish convert to Islam; ~mek *v/i* turn back; return; change; ~ük turned (*-e* to); ~üm. **1.** turn, revolution; **2.** (*surface measure: 0.23 acre or 920 m²*); ~üş return(ing); ~üştürmek *v/t* change, transform (*-e* into)

dört four; ~gen, ~kenar quadrangle; ~nala at a gallop

döşe|k mattress; ~me floor covering, pavement; ~meci upholsterer; ~mek *v/t* spread; pave

döviz slogan, device; ECON foreign currency

döv|mek *v/t* beat; hammer; thrash; ~üşmek fight, struggle with one another

dram THEA drama

dua prayer, blessing; ~ etm. pray, bless

duba NAUT barge, pontoon

dubara trick, fraud; ~cı trickster, cheat

duçar olm. *-e* be subject to, be exposed to

dudak lip

duhuliye entrancefee, ticket

duka duke; **~lık** duchy, dukedom

dul widow(er); widowed

duman smoke, mist; **~lanmak** become smoky *or* cloudy (*a. fig.*); **~lı** smoky, misty

durak *n.* stop, halt; **~lamak** *v/i* stop, pause

dur|durmak *v/t* stop, cause to wait; **~gun** stagnant; stationary; **~gunluk** stagnation, standstill; **~mak** *v/i* stop; cease; stand; remain; **~um** position; attitude; **~uş** posture, attitude; **~uşma** JUR hearing *of a case*

duş shower-bath; **~ yapmak** take a shower

dut mulberry

duvar wall; **~cı** mason, bricklayer

duygu perception; feeling; sense; **~lu** sensitive, impressionable; **~suz** insensitive, apathetic

duy|mak *v/t* feel; perceive; learn; hear; **~um** perception; sensation; **~urmak** *-e -i* let *so.* hear *or* learn *sth.*; **~uş** impression; feeling

düdük whistle, pipe, flute

düello duell

düğme button; knob; **~lemek** *v/t* button up

düğüm knot, bow; **~lemek** *v/t* knot

düğün feast (*wedding or circumcision*)

dükkân shop; **~cı** shopkeeper

dülger carpenter, builder

dümen NAUT rudder; **~ci** helmsman

dün yesterday; **~den**, **~kü** of yesterday

dünür father-in-law (*as a relation between the fathers of a married couple*)

dünya world; earth; this life

dürbün telescope; field glasses

dürmek *v/t* roll up

dürt|mek *v/t* prod, goad; **~üşmek** push *or* prod one another

dürüst straightforward, honest

düstur principle, code of laws

düş dream

düş|ey perpendicular; **~kün** fallen, decayed; addicted (*-e* to); **~künlük** decay; poverty

düşman enemy, foe; **~lık** enmity, hostility

düş|mek fall down (*-e* upon); fall to one's lot; **~ük** fallen, drooping; low (*price*); GR misconstrued

düşünce thought, reflection; anxiety; **~li** thoughtful; worried; **~siz** thoughtless, inconsiderate

düşün|mek *v/t* think of; remember; ponder over; **~ülmek** be thought *or* planned

düşürmek *v/t* cause to fall, cause to drop; bring down

düz flat, level, smooth; **~el-**

mek be arranged; be improved; ~eltmek v/t make smooth; put in order; arrange

düzen order, regularity, trick, lie; ~lemek v/t put in order; ~li orderly, tidy; ~siz out of order

düzgün smooth, level; regular

düzine dozen

düz||lem MATH plane; ~lemek v/t smooth, flatten; ~lük flatness, plainness; ~mek v/t arrange; invent; forge

DVD DVD; ~-ROM DVD--ROM

E

-e s. **-a**

ebe midwife

ebed||î eternal, without end; ~iyet eternity

ebeveyn parents

ebleh imbecile, stupid

ebru(lu) marbled (paper)

ecel REL appointed hour of death; appointed term

ecnebi foreign; foreigner

eczacı chemist, druggist; ~lık pharmacy (profession)

ecza(ha)ne pharmacy, chemist's shop

eda payment, execution; tone, manner

edat GR particle

edeb||î literary; ~iyat literature

edep||li well-behaved, with good manners; ~siz illmannered, rude

edi||lgen GR passive; ~lmek be done, be made; ~nmek v/t get, procure

Edirne Adrianople

efe elder brother; village hero

efendi master; Mr. (after the first name); ~m yes, sir! I beg your pardon?

efsane fable; idle tale

ege master, guardian; ~menlik sovereignty

egzos(t) TECH exhaust

eğe file; ANAT rib; ~lemek v/t file

eğer if, whether; when

eğil||im inclination; ~mek v/i bend, incline

eğirmek v/t spin

eğit||im education; ~mek v/t educate; ~men educator

eğlen||ce diversion, amusement; ~celi amusing, diverting; ~dirmek v/t amuse, divert; ~mek be amused, amuse oneself

eğmek v/t bend, incline

eğreltiotu BOT bracken, fern

eğreti false, artificial; makeshift, temporary

eğri crooked, bent; ~lik crookedness, dishonesty; ~lmek become bent, incline;

~ltmek v/t make crooked, bend, twist

ehemmiyet importance; ~li important; ~siz unimportant

ehil family, household; -in ehli ol. be endowed with, be versed in

ehlî tame, domesticated

ehliyet capacity, competence; ~name certificate of competence; driving license; ~siz incapable, incompetent

ehven cheap(est)

ejder(ha) dragon

ek joint; addition, supplement; GR suffix, affix, prefix

eki|li planted, sown; ~m sowing; October

ekin crops; ~ biçmek reap, harvest

ekip team, crew, gang

e-kitap e-book

ekle|m ANAT joint; ~mek v/t join, add (-e to); ~nmek -e be joined to, be added to; ~nti annex

ekmek[1] v/t sow; scatter

ekmek[2] n. bread; ~çi baker

ekonomi economy

ekran TECH screen

eksantrik mili TECH excentric rod

ekselans Excellency

ekser[1] large nail, spike

ekser[2] majority; ~i most; ~iya adv. generally, mostly; ~iyet majority

eksi MATH minus

eksik deficient, lacking; ~ ol-

mayın! thank you very much!; ~lik deficiency, defectiveness; ~siz without defect; complete, perfect

eksil|mek v/i decrease; be absent; ~tmek v/t diminish, reduce

eksper expert

ekspres express train or steamer

ekstra extra, first quality

ekşi sour, acid; ~mek become sour; be upset (stomach); sl. be disconcerted; ~msi sourish

ekvator GEO equator

el[1] country; people

el[2] hand; forefoot; handle; ~ çantası hand-bag; ~ koymak -e seize; monopolize; ~ topu hand-ball; ~ yazısı handwriting; manuscript; ~de etm. v/t get hold of, obtain; ~e almak v/t take charge of; ~e geçmek come into one's possession; ~i açık generous; ~ine bakmak depend on (-in so.)

elastik(î) elastic

elbet(te) certainly, decidedly

elbise pl. clothes; clothing; ~ askısı coat-hanger

elçi envoy, ambassador; ~lik embassy

eldiven glove

elebaşı ringleader, captain

elek sieve

elektrik electricity; ~ akımı electric current; ~li electric

elem pain, suffering

eleman element; personnel
elemek v/t sift, sieve
eleştir|ici n. critic; adj. critical; adj. critical; ~im, ~me criticism; ~mek v/t criticize
elhasıl adv. in short, in brief
ellemek v/t feel with the hand
elli fifty
elma apple; ~ ağacı apple tree
elmas diamond
elti sister-in-law (relationship between the wives of two brothers)
elveda farewell, good-by
elver|işli useful; profitable; ~mek suffice; be suitable
elzem indispensable
emanet deposit, anything entrusted to so.; ~ etm. v/t entrust (-e to)
emare sign, mark; token
emcik teat, nipple
emek work, labour; trouble; ~li retired; pensioner; ~liye ayrılmak retire, be pensioned off; ~lilik retirement; ~siz free from labour; easy; ~tar old and faithful, veteran
emel longing, desire
emin safe, secure, sure; ~ olm. -e be sure of
emir order, command
emlâk pl. lands, possessions, real estates; ~ alım vergisi purchase tax on real estate
emmek v/t suck
emniyet security, safety; police; ~li safe, reliable; ~siz

insecure, unsafe; ~sizlik lack of confidence
empprime print fabric
emretmek v/t order, command
emsal pl. similars, equals; ~siz peerless, unequalled
emtia pl. ECON goods
emzi|k nipple, teat; baby's bottle; ~rmek v/t suckle
en¹ n. width, breadth
en² adv. most (superlative); ~ az(dan) at least; ~ güzel most beautiful
encam end; conclusion, result
endam body, shape, figur
endaze (linear measure, ab. 65 cm)
endişe throught, anxiety; ~li thoughtful, anxious
endüstri industry
enerji energy; ~k energetic
enfes delightful, delicious
enflasyon ECON inflation
engebe unevenness of ground; ~li steep and broken
engel obstacle; difficulty; ~ olm. -e hinder, prevent; ~lemek v/t hinder, hamper
engerek ZOO adder, viper
engin¹ ordinary, common
engin² vast, boundless; ~ deniz the open sea
enginar BOT artichoke
enik whelp, cub, puppy
enişte husband of ANAT aunt or sister
enkaz pl. ruins, debris; wreck
enl|em GEO parallel; ~i wide,

broad

ense back of the neck, nape

ensiz narrow

enstantane snapshot

enstitü institute

entari loose robe

entegrasyon integration

enteresan interesting

enterne etm. v/t intern

entrika intrigue; ~cı schemer, trickster

epey(ce) a good many; fairly

e-posta n. & v/t e-mail; ~ adresi e-mail address

er¹ early; soon

er² man, male; MIL private; ~at pl. non-commissioned officers and private soldiers

erbap expert, specialist

erbaş MIL non-commissioned officer

erdem virtue

ergen marriageable; unmarried; ~in mature, adult; ripe

erguvan judas-tree; purple; ~i purple

erik plum

eril GR masculine

erimek v/i melt, fuse; pass away

erişmek -e arrive, attain; reach the age of marriage

eritmek v/t melt, dissolve; squander

erk power; authority

erkek man, male; husband; ~lik masculinity; manliness

erken early

erkin free, independent

ermek -e reach, attain

Ermeni Armenian; ~ce Armenian (*language*)

ersiz without husband

ertelemek v/t postpone

ertesi the following day, *etc.*; ~ gün the following day

erzak pl. provisions; food

esans CHEM essence, perfume

esas n. foundation; principle; *adj.* basic; ~en *adv.* fundamentally, in principle; ~ı fundamental, essential; ~lı based, founded; sure; ~sız baseless, unfounded

esen hearty, robust; ~lik health, soundness

eser sign, trace; work *of art, etc.*

esham ECON share

esir captive, prisoner of war

esirgemek v/t protect, spare; Allah ~sin! may God protect us!

esirlik captivity

eski old; ancient; out of date; ~ püskü old and tattered things; ~ci oldclothes man, cobbler; ~mek be worn out; ~tmek v/t wear out

eskrim (*sport*) fencing; ~ci fencer

esmek v/i blow; *fig.* come into the mind (-*e of so.*)

esmer brunette, dark complexioned

esna|da: o ~da at that time; -diği ~da *conj.* while; ~sında in the course of, during

esnaf pl. tradesmen, artisans

esnek elastic; ~lik elasticity

esnemek yawn

esrar hashish

esrimek become ekstatic; get drunk

estağfurullah! don't mention it!, not at all!

eş one *of a pair*; husband; wife; partner

eşek donkey; ass; ~ **arısı** wasp, hornet

eşik threshold; bridge *of a violin etc.*

eşit equal, equivalent; ~**lik** equality

eşkıya *sg. u. pl.* brigand(s)

eşsiz matchless, peerless

eşya *pl.* things, objects; luggage; furniture

et meat; flesh

etek skirt; GEO foot *of a mountain*; ~**lik** skirt *of a woman*

eter CHEM ether

etiket label, ticket; etiquett

etiket label, ticket; etiquette; ~**lemek** *v/t* label

etimoloji etymology

etken GR active

etki effect; ~**lemek** *v/t* affect, influence; ~**li** effective, influential

etkin active; effective; ~**lik** activity; efficiency

etmek do, make

etraf *pl.* sides, ends; surroundings; *-in* ~**ında** around; ~**lı** detailed

et|siz without meat; weak; ~**suyu** gravy, meat broth

ettir|gen GR causative (*verb*);

~**mek** *v/t* cause to do

etüt study, essay

ev house, home, dwelling; ~ **idaresi** household; ~ **kadını** housewife; ~**cil** domesticated

evet yes

evkaf *pl.* REL pious foundations; estates in mortmain

evlât child(ren), descendant(s)

evlen|dirmek *v/t* marry, give in marriage (*-e* to); ~**me** marriage; ~**mek** marry (**ile** *so.*)

evli married

evrak *pl.* documents, papers; ~ **çantası** brief-case, portfolio

evren universe

evvel ago; first; *-meden* ~ *conj.* before; **bir an** ~ as soon as possible; ~**â** firstly; ~**ce** previously, formerly; ~**ki**, ~**si** first, former; ~**ki** (~**si**) **gün** the day before yesterday

eyalet province

eyer saddle

eylem action

eylemek *s.* **etmek**

eylül September

eyvah alas!

eyvallah thank you!; good bye!; all right!

ezan REL call to prayer

ezber by heart; ~**lemek** *v/t* learn by heart

ezcümle for instance

ezelî without beginning, eter-

nal
ezilmek be crushed, oppressed
eziyet injury, pain, torture; ~li

fatiguing, painful
ezme something crushed, paste, purée; ~k v/t crush, pound, bruise

F

faal active, industrious; ~iyet activity, energy
fabrika factory; ~cı, ~tör manufacturer
facia tragedy, disaster
fahişe prostitute
fahri honorary
faide s. fayda
fail agent; GR subject
faiz ECON interest; birleşik ~ compound interest; ~e vermek v/t lend at interest
fakat but, only
fakir poor, pauper; ~lik poverty
fakülte faculty of a university
fal omen; fortune; ~a bakmak tell a fortune
falaka bastinado
falan so and so, such and such; and so on
falcı fortune-teller
familya family (a. BOT)
fan dergisi fanzine
fanila flannel; undershirt
fantezi fancy (goods)
faraz|a supposing that; ~î hypothetical
fare mouse; rat; ~ kapanı mouse-trap
farfara empty-headed, braggart; ~lık idle brag, frivolity

fark difference, distinction; -in ~ına varmak become aware of, perceive; -in ~ında olm. be aware of; ~etmek v/t distinguish; perceive; ~lı different, changed; ~sız indistinguishable, without difference
farmason s. mason
farz REL precept; supposition; ~etmek v/t suppose; ~edelim let us suppose
Fas Morocco
fasıl chapter, section
fasıla separation; interval, interruption; ~ vermek -e interrupt, break; ~sız continuous, uninterrupted
fasikül fascicle, section of a book
fasulye BOT bean; taze ~ string beans
faşi|st Fascist; ~zm Fascism
fatih conqueror
fatura ECON invoice
favori whiskers
fayans tile
fayda use, profit, advantage; ~lanmak -den profit by, make use of; ~lı useful, profitable; ~sız useless, in vain
fayton phaeton

fazilet merit, superiority; ~**kâr**, ~**li** virtuous, excellent

fazla remainder; superfluous; more, too much; ~**laşmak** v/i increase

feci painful, tragic

fecir dawn

feda ransom; sacrifice; ~ **etm.** v/t sacrifice; ~**kâr** self-sacrificing, devoted; ~**kârlık** self-sacrifice, devotion

federa||**l** federal; ~**syon** federation, association; ~**tif** s. ı̂

felâket disaster, catastrophe; ~**zede** victim of a disaster

felç MED paralysis; **çocuk felci** infantile paralysis

felek firmament; destiny

Felemenk Holland; ~**li** n., adj. Dutch

felsef||**e** philosophy; ~**î** philosophical

fen technics, art; natural sciences

fena bad, unpleasant; ~**laşmak** become worse, deteriorate; ~**laştırmak** v/t make worse, worsen; ~**lık** evil, bad action

fener lantern, street-lamp, lighthouse

fennî scientific, technical

feragat abandonment, renunciation; ~ **etm.** -**den** renounce, give up

ferah spacious, open; joy, pleasure; ~**lanmak** become spacious, cheerful; ~**lık** spaciousness, cheerfulness

ferdî individual

fer'î secondary; accessory

feribot NAUT train or car ferry

fermejüp snap-fastener

fermuar zip-fastener

fert person, individual

feryat cry, wail

fes fez

fesat depravity, corruption; ~**çı** mischief-maker, conspirator

feshetmek v/t annul, cancel

fesih abolition, cancellation

fethetmek v/t conquer

fetih conquest

fetva REL decision on religious matter given by a mufti

feveran boiling, effervescence

fevkalâde extraordinary

feyezan overflowing, flood

feza ASTR space, universe

fıçı cask, barrel; ~**çı** cooper

fıkara pl. the poor; ~**lık** poverty

fıkırdamak s. **fokurdamak**

fıkra paragraph; passage

fındık BOT hazel-nut; ~ **faresi**, ~ **sıçanı** ZOO common house-mouse

Fırat Euphrates

fırça brush; paint-brush; ~**lamak** v/t brush, dust

fırıldak ventilator; spinning-top; ~**(n)mak** spin round

fırın oven; bakery; ~**cı** baker; who looks after a furnace

fırka POL party; MIL division

fırla||**mak** v/i fly off, fly out; ~**tmak** v/t hurl, shoot

fırsat opportunity, chance

fırtına gale, storm; **~lı** stormy
fısıl|damak v/t whisper; **~tı** whisper
fıskıye jet of water, fountain
fıstık BOT pistachio nut
fışırdamak gurgle, rustle
fışkır|mak v/i gush out, spurt out; **~tmak** v/t spurt, splash
fıtık ANAT hernia, rupture
fıtr|at creation, nature; **~î** natural, innate
fiat s. fiyat
fidan BOT plant, sapling; **~lık** nursery
fide BOT seedling plant
figüran THEA super
fihrist index, catalogue, list
fiil act, action, deed; GR verb; **~î** actual, real
fikir thought, idea; mind, opinion; **~siz** thoughtless
fil elephant
filan s. falan
fildişi ivory
file net
fileto fillet
filim s. film
filinta carbine, short gun
Filistin Palestine
filiz tendril, young shoot; **~lenmek** sprout, send forth shoots
film film; movie; **-in ~ini** almak film; X-ray; **~ yıldızı** film star
filo NAUT fleet, squadron; **~tilla** flotilla
filozof philosopher
filtre filter, sieve; **~ etm.** v/t filter

final n final (sport); MUS finale
finanse etm. v/t finance
fincan cup; EL porcelain insulator
fingirdemek behave coquettishly
firar flight, desertion
firkete hair-pin
fiske flip with the fingers; pinch; **~lemek** v/t give a flip to
fistül fistula
fiş slip of paper, card; EL plug
fişek cartridge, rocket
fitil wick, fuse
fitne instigation, disorder
fiyat price, value
fizik physics
flama NAUT pennant
flaş flash-light
flavta flute
fleş s. flaş
flört flirt
flüt flute
fodra lining, padding
fokurdamak v/i boil up, bubble
folklor folklore
folye foil
fonksiyon MATH function
for forward (football)
forma forme, folio; uniform, colours; **~lite** formality; red tape
formül formula; **~er** formulary
forvet s. for
fosfor phosphorus
fotoğraf photograph; **~ makinesi** camera; **-in ~ını çek-**

mek *v/t* photograph; ~çi
photographer
frak tail-coat
francala white bread; roll
Frans|a France; ~ız French;
~ızca French (*language*)
fren brake
frengi syphilis
Frenk (Western)European;
Üzümü BOT red currant
frenlemek *v/t* brake
frikik free kick (*football*)

friksiyon friction
fuar ECON fair, exposition
fukara(lık) *s.* fıkara(lık)
funda shrub, thicket
furgon luggage-van
futbol football; ~ maçı football match
fuzulî meddling, superfluous
füme smoked; ~ etm. *v/t*
smoke
füze rocket, missile

G

gaddar cruel, perfidious; ~lık
cruelty, perfidy
gafil careless, inattentive; ~
avlamak *v/t* catch unawares
gaga beak; ~lamak *v/t* peck
gâh sometimes
gaile anxiety, trouble; ~li worried; ~siz carefree
gaip absent; invisible
galebe victory; ~ etm., ~ çalmak *-e* conquer, overcome
galeri gallery
galib|a probably, presuma-
bly; ~iyet victory
galip victorious, superior
gam¹ MUS scale
gam² anxiety, grief
gammaz sneak, informer;
~lamak *v/t* calumniate, denounce; ~lık spying
gangren MED gangrene
ganimet spoils, booty
gar railway station
garaj garage

garanti guarantee
garaz malice, grudge; ~kâr
selfish, spiteful; ~sız unprej-
udiced, unbiased
garbî western
gardı|fren brakeman (*rail-
way*); ~rop wardrobe; cloak-
room
gardiyan guard, attendant
gargara gargling, gargle; ~
yapmak gargle
garip strange; curious
garnizon MIL garrison
garp West; Europe
garson waiter
gaseyan MED vomiting
gasıp usurpation
gaspetmek *v/t* seize by force
gâvur *n.* Non-Moslem;
giaour; *adj.* obstinate, merciless; ~luk quality of being
a Non-Moslem; fanacism,
cruelty
gaye aim, object, end; ~t end,

limit; extremely

gayret zeal, energy; ~li zealous, persevering; ~siz slack, without enthusiasm

gayrı now; *neg.* no longer

gayri (*negative prefix*); ~ **kabil** impossible

gaz[1] gas, petroleum

gaz[2] gauze

gazete newspaper; ~ci journalist; news-vendor; ~cilik journalism

gazi REL fighter for Islam; victorious Moslem general

gazino casino, restaurant

gazlı containing gas

gazometre gasometer

gazoz fizzy lemonade

gebe pregnant; ~lik pregnancy

gebermek perish, die

gebre BOT caper-tree

gece night; ~ **gündüz** day and night; ~ **yarısı** midnight; ~**kondu** house *set up in one night without permission*; shanty; ~**leyin** by night; ~**lik** pertaining to the night; night-dress

gecik|me delay; retardment; ~**mek** be late; ~**tirmek** *v/t* delay, be slow in doing *sth.*

geç late; ~ **kalmak** be late

geçe -*i* past (*time*); üçü on ~ 10 minutes past three

geçen past; last; ~**en(ler)de** recently; ~**er** current (*money, etc.*); ~**erli** valid; ~**ici** passing, temporary; ~**ilmek** -*den* be passable

geçim getting on with one another; livelihood; ~**siz** unsociable, quarrelsome

geçin|dirmek *v/t* support, maintain; ~**inmek ile** live by, exist, subsist on

geçirmek *v/t* infect (-*e* with); transport; spend, pass

geçiş change, transfer; ~**li** GR transitive; ~**siz** GR intransitive; ~**siz** GR intransitivity

geç|it pass, ford; ~**mek** *v/i* pass (-*den* along, over, *etc.*); expire, pass away; *v/t* skip, leave out; ~**miş** past; GR past tense; ~**miş olsun!** I wish you a speedy recovery!

gedik breach, notch, gap; ~**li** MIL regular non-commissioned officer

geğirmek belch, eructate

gelecek future; ~ **zaman** GR future tense

gelenek tradition

gelgit tide, flood-tide

gelin bride; daughter-in-law

gelince -*e* as for, regarding

gelincik BOT poppy

gelir income, revenue; ~ **vergisi** income tax

geliş coming, happening; ~**igüzel** *adv.* by chance, at random; ~**me** development; ~**mek** *v/i* develop, grow up; ~**mekte olan ülke** developing country; ~**miş** developed; ~**tirmek** *v/t* develop

gel|mek come; -*e* suit, fit; seem, appear; ~**ip almak** *v/t* fetch, pick up

gem

gem bit *of a horse*; ~ **vurmak**
-*e* curb

gemi ship; ~**ci** sailor

gen *biyoloji* n. gene; *adj.*
broad, vast; untouched
(*ground*)

genç young; youngster; ~**leşmek** become youthful; ~**leştirmek** *v/t* rejuvenate; ~**lik**
youth

gene again, moreover

genel general; ~ **af** amnesty; ℥
Müdür CEO (= *chief executive officer of a company*);
~**ge** circular; ~**kurmay** General Staff; ~**leşmek** become
general; ~**likle** *adv.* generally

general MIL general

genetik. 1. *n.* genetics; **2.** *adj.*
genetic; ~ **mühendisliği** ge-
netic engineering

geniş wide, vast, extens ve;
~**le(n)mek** *v/i* widen, extend,
become spacious; ~**letmek**
v/t expand, enlarge; ~**lik**
width; abundance

gensoru POL interpellation

geometri geometry

gerçek true, actual; really;
~**ten** truly, really; ~**leşmek**
turn out to be true; ~**leştirmek** *v/t* certify, verify; ~**lik**
truth, reality

gerçi *conj.* although

gerdan neck, throat; ~**lık**
necklace, neckband

gereç necessaries, material

gereğince in accordance
with

gerek necessary, needed; req-

uisite; ~ ... ~ whether ... or;
~**çe** statement of reasons; ~**li**
necessary, required; ~**lik** necessity; ~**mek** be necessary;
be suitable (-*e* for); ~**tirmek**
v/t necessitate, require

gergef embroidery frame

gergin stretched, strained;
~**lik** tension

geri behind, back, backward;
~**ye bırakmak** *v/t* put off,
postpone; ~**ci** reactionary;
~**lemek** recede, be slow

gerili stretched, taut

gerilik backwardness

geril|im PHYS, EL tension;
~**mek** be tightened; be
spread

gerinmek stretch oneself

germek *v/t* stretch, tighten

getir|mek *v/t* bring, produce;
~ **meydana** ~**mek** *v/t* create;
~**tmek** *v/t* cause to be
brought

geveze talkative, chattering;
~**lik** babbling, gossip

gevrek brittle, crackly; biscuit

gevşe|k loose, slack; ~**mek**
become loose, become
slack; ~**tmek** *v/t* loosen,
slacken

geyik ZOO deer, stag; ~ **boynuzu** antlers *pl.*

gez¹ MIL back-sight

gez² plumbline

gez|dirmek *v/t* lead about,
conduct, cause to walk
about; ~**gin** widely trav-
elled; ~**i** excursion; ~**inmek**

go about, stroll; *internette*: surf the net; **~inti** walk, stroll; **~mek** go about, travel; *v/t* inspect

gıcıklamak *v/t* tickle; *fig.* make suspicious

gıcırda|mak *v/i* creak, rustle; **~tmak** *v/t* make creak, gnash

gıda food, nourishment; **~lı** nutritious; **~sız** not nutritious

gıdıkla|mak *v/t* tickle; **~nmak** *v/i* tickle

gıpta longing, envy

gırtlak throat

gıyaben *adv.* by default

gıybet backbiting; **~çi** slanderer, backbiter

gibi similar, like; **bunun ~** like this

gid|er ECON expenditure, expense; **~ermek** *v/t* remove, cause to go; **~ilmek** be frequented, visited; **~iş** going, leaving; **~işmek** itch

gidon handlebar *of a bicycle*

girdap whirlpool

girinti recess, indentation

giriş entry, entrance; **~mek** *-e* set about, undertake

Girit (adası) GEO Crete

girmek *-e* enter, go into; begin, join, participate

gişe ticket-window, paydesk

git|gide *adv.* gradually; **~mek** *-e* go to; suit, fit; **hoşuna ~mek** like, be fond of; **~tikçe** *adv.* by degrees, gradually

giy|dirmek *v/t* clothe, dress *so.*; **~im** clothing, dress; **~in-**

~mek dress oneself; **~mek** *v/t* wear, put on

giz|lemek *v/t* hide, conceal; **~lenmek** hide oneself; **~li** hidden, secret; **~lice** secretly; **~lilik** secrecy

gliserin glycerine

glüten CHEM gluten

gol goal; **~ atmak** kick a goal

goril zoo gorilla

göbek navel; belly; **~lenmek** become paunchy

göç migration; **~ebe** nomad; **~mek** move off; **~men** immigrant; refugee; **~menlik** migration; **~ürmek** *v/t* cause to move off (*-e* to)

göğüs breast, chest

gök sky, heavens; **~gürlemek** *v/i* thunder; **~ gürlemesi, ~ gürültüsü** *n.* thunder; **~çe** blue; pleasant; **~deldi, ~delen** skyscraper; **~taşı** turquoise; **~yüzü** firmament

göl lake, pond

gölge *n.* shadow, shade; **~lendirmek** *v/t* shade; **~li** shaded, shady; **~lik** shady spot; arbour

gömlek shirt; skin *of a snake*

gömmek *v/t* bury, hide *by* burying, inter

gömülü buried, underground

gönder|en sender; **~ilmek** *-e* be sent to; **~mek** *v/t* send (*-e* to)

gönenç comfort, luxury

gönül heart; feelings; affection; **~lü** willing; volunteer; **~süz** unwilling; without pride; ~süzlük disinclination; modesty

gör|e -e according to, respecting, considering; ~enek custom, fashion

görev duty, obligation; ~lendirmek v/t charge, entrust (ile with)

gör|gü experience; good manners *pl.*; ~mek v/t see; visit; ~ü view, panorama; ~ülmek be seen *or* visited *or* examined

görümce sister of the husband; sister-in-law

görün|mek appear, be visible; ~üm outward appearance; ~ürde *adv.* in appearance; in sight; ~üş appearance, view

görüş mode of seeing, point of view

görüşmek ile meet, become acquainted with; discuss (-*i* sth.)

göster|ge TECH indicator; ~i show, demonstration

gösteriş appearance, aspect; demonstration; ~li stately, imposing; ~siz poor looking

göster|mek v/t show (-*e* to so.); Allah ~mesin! God forbid!

göt *vulg.* behind, arse

götür|mek v/t take away, carry off; ~ü *adv.* in a lump sum; ~üm endurance, patience

gövde body, trunk; whole carcass

göynük burnt; ripe

göz eye; hole, opening; drawer; ~den düşmek fall into disesteem; ~e almak v/t venture, risk; ~e çarpmak strike the eye; ~ akı the white of the eye; ~ alıcı striking, dazzling; ~ kapağı eyelid; ~ kararı judgement by the eye; ~ yaşı tear; ~altı police supervision; ~bebeği ANAT pupil *of the eye*; ~cü watchman, sentinel; ~de favourite, pet

gözet|im watch, supervision; ~lemek v/t observe, spy upon

göz|etmek v/t mind, look after; watch; ~evi eyesocket; ~lemek v/t watch for, wait for

gözlük spectacles; ~ camı spectacle lens; ~çü optician

göz|süz blind; ~taşı copper sulphate; ~üpek brave, bold, daring

gram gram(me)

gramer grammar

grev strike; ~ hakkı freedom of strike; ~ci striker

gre(y)pfrut BOT grapefruit

gri grey

grip influenza

grup group

gudde ANAT gland

guguk ZOO cuckoo

gurbet absence from home

gurul|damak v/i rumble; ~tu rumbling

gurur pride, vanity; ~lu arrogant, vain

güya *s.* güya

gübre dung, manure; ~lemek
v/t dung, manure

gücenmek -e be offended
with, hurt by

güç¹ strength, force

güç² difficult; ~leşmek v/i
grow difficult; ~leştirmek
v/t render difficult, complicate, impede

güçlü strong, powerful

güçlük difficulty, pain

güçsüz weak, feeble

güdü motive, incentive

güdümlü controlled

güherçile CHEM saltpetre

gül rose; ~ fidanı rosebush; ~
yağı attar of roses

güldürmek v/t make laugh

güllâç (sweet made with wa-
fers, cream, etc.)

gül|mek laugh, smile; ~üm-
semek smile; ~ünç ridicu-
lous; ~üşmek laugh together

gümbür|demek v/i boom,
thunder; ~tü booming noise,
crash, thunder

gümeç honeycomb

gümrük customs; ~ kontrolü
customs control; ~ memuru,
~çü customs officer

gümüş silver; ~lemek v/t silver plate

gün day; sun; light; ~den ~e
from day to day; ~ün birin-
de one day

günah sin, fault; ~kâr sinner,
culpable; ~sız without sin

gün|aşırı every other day;
~aydın! good morning!;

~batısı west; ~çiçeği sunflower; ~delik adj daily; n.
daily wage; ~dem agenda;
~doğusu southeast wind;
east; ~dönümü ASTR solstice

gündüz daytime, by day; ~ün
adv. by day

güneş sun; ~lenmek bathe in
the sun; ~lik sunny place;
sunshade

gün|ey south; ~lük 1. daily; ...
days old; sufficient for ...
days; 2. CHEM frankincense,
myrrh

gür abundant; strong (voice);
rank; ~büz sturdy, healthy

güreş wrestling; ~çi wrestler;
~mek wrestle (ile with)

gürlemek v/i make a loud
noise, thunder

güruh group, lot

gürüldemek thunder

gürültü loud noise, uproar;
~lü noisy, tumultuous;
~süz noiseless, quiet

gütmek v/t drive ANAT animal

güve clothes-moth

güveç earthenware cooking
pot; vegetables and meat
cooked in this pot

güven confidence, reliance;
~lik security; ~mek -e trust
in, rely on; ~sizlik lack of
confidence

güvercin pigeon

güverte NAUT deck

güvey bridegroom, son-in-
-law

güya as if, as though

güz autumn, fall

güzel beautiful, pretty, nice; ~**leşmek** become beautiful,

nice; ~**leştirmek** v/t beautify; ~**lik** beauty, goodness

H

habbe grain, seed

haber knowledge, information; ~ **almak** -*den* receive information, learn from; ~ **vermek** -*e* inform, give notice; ~**ci** messenger; ~**dar olm.** -*den* know, possess information about; ~**leşmek ile** correspond with; ~**siz** not informed (-*den* about)

hac REL pilgrimage to Mecca

hacet need, necessity

hacı Hadji (*one who made the pilgrimage to Mecca*); ~**lar yolu** ASTR the Milky Way

hacim volume, capacity

hacir JUR putting under restraint

haciz JUR seizure

haczetmek v/t JUR seize

haç cross, crucifix; ~**lamak** v/t crucify; ~**lılar** pl. the Crusaders

had limit, boundary; ~**dini bilmek** know one's place

hâd sharp; acute (*illness*)

hadde wire-drawer's plate; ~**hane** TECH rolling-mill

hademe servant *at* ANAT office, *etc.*

hadım eunuch

hadi *s.* haydi

hadise event, incident

hadsiz unbounded, unlimit-

ed

haf half-back (*sport*)

hafıza memory

hafif light; easy; flighty; ~**lemek** become lighter, easier; ~**leştirmek**, ~**letmek** v/t make lighter, easier; ~**lik** lightness, ease of mind; ~**meşrep** flighty, frivolous

hafiye detective, spy

hafriyat pl. excavations

hafta week; ~**larca** for weeks on end; ~**lık** weekly, per week; n. weekly wages

haham REL Rabbi; ~**başı** Chief Rabbi

hain traitor; treacherous; ~**leşmek** become *or* act treacherous; ~**lik** treachery, perfidy

haiz olm. -*i* possess, obtain

hak¹ truth, right, justice; right, true; ♀ God

hak² engraving, erasing

hâk earth, soil

hakaret insult, contempt; ~ **etm.** -*e* insult

hakem arbitrator, umpire

hakikat truth, reality; truly, really; ~**en** adv. in truth, really

hakikî true, real; sincere

hâkim judge; ruler; ruling, dominating; ~ **olm.** -*e* rule over, dominate; ~iyet sovereignty, domination; ~lik the office of a judge

hakketmek v/t engrave, erase

hakkı|nda concerning, with regard to; ~yle adv. properly, rightfully

haklı right, who is right

haksız unjust, wrong; ~lık injustice, wrong

hal[1] condition; state; quality, attribute; present time; GR case; o ~de, şu ~de in this case, therefore, consequently; -diği ~de conj. although

hal[2] melting; solution

hal[3] covered market-place

hala paternal aunt

hâlâ at the present time; now, just

halâs salvation; ~kâr saviour, deliverer

halat rope

halbuki conj. however, nevertheless, whereas

halef successor

halel defect, injury

halen adv. now, at present

Halep Aleppo

hal'etmek v/t dethrone

halı carpet; ~cı carpet maker; ~cılık manufacturing of carpets

hâli -den free from

haliç GEO strait, estuary; 2 the Golden Horn

halife Caliph

halim mild, gentle

halis pure, genuine

halita alloy

halk people, crowd

halka ring, hoop, circle; link; ~lı ringed, linked

halkçı POL populist; ~lık populism

halkoyu POL plebiscite

halletmek v/t solve, dissolve, analyse

halojen lambası halogen reflector

halsiz weak, exhausted

halter bar-bell (sport); ~ci weight-lifter

ham unripe; raw, crude

hamak hammock

hamal porter, carrier

hamam Turkish bath

hamarat hard-working

hamd|etmek -e give thanks to God; ~olsun! Thank God!

hamız acid

hami protector; guarding

hamil bringing; bearer; ~e pregnant

hamle attack, onslaught

hammadde raw material

hamur dough, leaven; quality of paper; ~suz unleavened (bread)

han[1] Khan, sovereign

han[2] caravanserai; commercial building

hançer dagger

hançere ANAT larynx

hands-free hands-free (car phone, device)

hane house; subdivision; square of a chessboard; ~dan family, dynasty

hangar hangar

hangi which?; ~si which of them?

hanım lady; ~efendi madam

hani where?; you know!; well

hantal clumsy, coarse

hap pill

hapis confinement, prison; ~hane prison

hapsetmek v/t imprison, confine

harabe ruin

haraç tribute

haram REL forbidden by religion

harap ruined, devastated; ~ olm. be devastated, fall into ruin

hararet heat; fever; ~li heated, feverish

harbiye MIL war academy

harc|amak v/t expend, spend, use; ~ırah travelling expenses

harç¹ mortar, plaster

harç² expenditure; customs duty; ~lı liable to duty; ~lık pocket-money; allowance

hardal mustard

hareket movement, act, behaviour; departure; ~ etm. -den depart from; ~siz motionless

harem the women's apartments, harem

harf letter; ~i ~ine adv. word for word

harıltı loud and continuous noise

harici external, foreign

hariç n. outside, exterior; adj excluded

harika wonder, miracle

haris greedy, avaricious

harita map, plan; ~cılık cartography

harman threshing of grains; harvest time; threshing floor; blend; ~ dövmek thresh; ~lamak v/t blend

harmoni MUS harmony

harp war; battle, fight; ~ gemisi warship; ~ malulü invalid, disabled soldier; ~ okulu military college

hars culture, education

hartuç cartridge

has -e special, peculiar to

hasar damage, loss; ~a uğramak suffer loss or damage; ~at pl. losses

hasat reaping; harvest

hasebiyle by reason of, because of

haset envy, jealousy; ~çi envious, jealous

hâsıl resulting; ~ olm. result, be obtained (-den from); ~ı adv. in a word

hasır rush mat; ~ koltuk wicker chair

hasis stingy, vile; ~lik stinginess, vileness

hasret regret, longing

hasretmek v/t restrict, consecrate (-e to)

hassas sensitive, delicate; ~iyet sensibility, touchiness

hasta sick, ill; ~ düşmek fall ill; ~bakıcı hospital attendant, nurse; ~lanmak fall ill

hastalık illness, disease; **~lı** ailing, in ill health

hastane hospital

haşarat *pl.* insects, vermin

haşarı dissolute, naughty

haşhaş BOT poppy

haşin harsh, rough

haşiş hashish

haşiye marginal note, post-script

haşlama boiled (*meat*); **~k** *v/t* boil; sting (*insect*)

haşmet majesty, pomp; **~li** majestic

hat line, mark

hata mistake, fault; **~ya düş-mek** err

hatır thought, idea, memory; consideration; **~ın ~ına gel-mek** occur *to one's mind*; **~ından çıkmak** pass out of one's mind

hatıra memory, remem-brance; souvenir; **~t** *pl.* memories; memoirs

hatırla|mak *v/t* remember; **~tmak** *-e -i* remind *so.* of

hatırşinas considerate, oblig-ing

hatip preacher, orator

hatta *adv.* even, to the extent that

hattat calligrapher

hav down (*feather*); nap

hava air, weather, wind, at-mosphere; desire, whim, fancy; **~ alanı** airport; **~ kor-sanı** hijacker; **~ kuvvetleri** *pl.* Air Force; **~cı** aviator; airman; **~cılık** aviation;

~dar airy; **~gazı** coal-gas; **~i** aerial; fanciful; **~i fişek** rocket; **~küre** atmosphere; **~lanmak** be aired, venti-lated; fly

havale assignment, bill of ex-change; **~ etm.** *v/t* transfer, refer (*-e* to); **~name** order for payment, money order

havali environs, neighbour-hood

havan mortar; **~ eli** pestle; **~ topu** mortar, howitzer

havari REL Apostle

hava|sız airless, badly venti-lated; **~yolu** airline

havi *-i* containing; **~ olm.** *-i* contain

havlamak bark

havlu towel

havra *Rel.* synagogue

havuç BOT carrot

havuz artificial basin, pond dock; **~lamak** *v/t* dock

havyar caviare

havza river-basin; sphere, do-main

hayal spectre, phantom, fan-cy, imagination; **~i** fantastic, imaginary

hayat[1] covered court; court-yard

hayat[2] life, living; **~ sürmek** live a life

haydi! come!; be off!

haydut brigant; **~ yatağı** brig-ands' den; **~luk** brigandage

hayhay! certainly!; by all means!

hayır[1] no!

hayır² good, prosperity, excellence; ~ **dua** blessing, benediction; ~**hah** benevolent; ~**lı** good, auspicious; ~**lı yolculuklar!** have a good trip; ~**lı olsun!** good luck to it; ~**sız** good-for-nothing; ill-omened

haykır|ış shouting, bawling; ~**mak** shout, cry out

haylaz idle, lazy; ~**lık** laziness

hayli much, many; fairly

hayran astonished, perplex; ~ **olm.** be astonished, perplexed; -*e* admire

hayret amazement, stupor; admiration; ~**te bırakmak** *v/t* astound; ~**te kalmak** be lost in amazement

haysiyet honour, dignity; ~**li** self-respecting; ~**siz** without dignity

hayvan animal; ~**at bahçesi** zoological garden; ~**ca** *adv.* bestially; stupidly; ~**î** animal, bestial

Hazer denizi Caspian Sea

hazım digestion; ~**sız** indigestible; irritable

hazır present, ready, prepared; ~ **ol!** MIL. attention!; ~**dan yemek** live on one's capital; ~**cevap** quick at reply; ~**lamak** *v/t* prepare; ~**lanmak** prepare oneself; be prepared; ~**lık** readiness, preparation; ~**lop** hard-boiled (*egg*)

hazin sad, melancholy

hazine *s.* hazne

haziran June

hazmetmek *v/t* digest; *fig.* swallow

hazne treasure, treasury; reservoir, cistern; ~**dar** treasurer

hazret REL Saint; 2**i Peygamber** the Holy Prophet (Mohammed); ~**leri** (*after a title*) His Excellency

hece syllable; ~**lemek** *v/t* spell; ~**li** having ... syllables

hecin ZOO dromedary

hedef mark, target; object, aim; ~ **tutmak** -*i* aim at

hediye present, gift; ~ **etm.** *v/t* give as a present (-*e* to)

hekim doctor, physician; ~**lik** profession of a doctor

helâ closet, privy

helâk destruction, death

helâl REL permitted, lawful

hele above all, especially; at least

helezon snail, spiral

helikopter AVIA helicopter

helva (*sweetmeat made of sesame oil and honey*)

hem and also, too; ~ ... ~ (**de**) both ... and, as well as; ~**en** at once; just now; about, nearly; exactly; ~**en** ~**en** almost, very nearly; ~**şeri** fellow townsman; compatriot; ~**şire** sister; hospital nurse

hendek ditch, moat, trench

hendese geometry

hengâme uproar, tumult

henüz yet, still

hep all, the whole; ~**si** all of it

or them

her every, each; ~ **biri** each one; ~ **gün** every day; ~ **halde** in any case; for sure; ~ **hangi** anybody; ~ **ne** whatever; ~ **ne kadar** however much; although; ~ **yerde** everywhere; ~ **zaman** every time, always

hercümerç confused, disordered

herhangi *s.* her hangi

herif fellow, rascal

herkes everyone

hesap counting, reckoning, calculation; account; bill; ~ **etm.** *v/t* calculate; count; ~ **tutmak** keep accounts; ~ **vermek** *-e* give *so.* an account (**hakkında** of *sth.*); **hesaba katmak** *-i* take into account; ~**lamak** *v/t* reckon, estimate; ~**laşmak** settle accounts; ~**lı** calculated; ~**sız** countless, uncertain

heves desire, inclination; ~**kâr**, ~**li** *-e* desirous of, eager for

heybet awe, majesty

heyecan excitement, enthusiasm; ~**lı** excited, enthusiastic

heyet commission, committee

heyhat! alas!

heykel statue; ~**tıraş** sculptor

hezeyan talking nonsense

hezimet utter defeat, rout

hıçkır|**ık** hiccough, sob; ~**mak** have the hiccoughs, sob

hıdrellez beginning of sum-

mer (*May 6th*)

hıfzıssıhha hygiene

hınç hatred, grudge

hır *sl.* row, quarrel; ~**çın** ill-tempered

hırdavat small wares, ironmongery; ~**çı** pedlar, ironmonger

hırıl|**damak** growl, purr; ~**tı** growling, snarling

Hıristiyan Christian; ~**lık** Christianity

hırlamak growl, snarl

hırpalamak *v/t* ill-treat, misuse

hırpani in tatters

hırs inordinate desire, greed

hırsız thief; ~**lık** theft, thieving

hırs|**lanmak** *-den* get angry at; get greedy of; ~**lı** angry; avaricious

hısım relative, kin

hışıldamak *v/i* rustle

hışır unripe (*melon*)

hışırdamak *v/i* rustle, grate

hıyanet treachery, perfidy

hıyar BOT cucumber

hız speed, impetus; ~ **almak** get up speed; ~**landırmak** *v/t* accelerate; ~**lanmak** gain speed; ~**lı** quick, fast; violent

hibe JUR gift, donation

hicr|**et** emigration; REL the Hegira; ~**î** of the Hegira era

hiç no, nothing; never; (*without negation*) ever; ~ **olmazsa** at least; ~**bir şey** nothing at all; ~**bir yerde** nowhere;

~biri nobody, none
hiddet violence; anger; ~lenmek -e be angry with; ~li angry
hidrojen CHEM hydrogen
hikâye narration, story; ~ etm. v/t narrate, tell
hikmet wisdom; inner meaning
hilâf contrary, opposite; -in ~ına contrary to, against
hilâl crescent
hile trick, wile; fraud; ~ci, ~kâr wily, deceitful; ~li fraudulent
himaye protection, defence
himmet effort, zeal; benevolence
hindi zoo turkey
Hindistan India; 2 cevizi BOT coconut
Hint|li n., adj. Indian; 2yağı CHEM castor oil
his sense, perception
hisar castle, fortress
hisse share; allotted portion; ~dar shareholder; ~li having shares, divided into portions
hissetmek v/t feel, perceive
hitabe address, speech; ~t oratory
hitam conclusion, completion; ~ bulmak come to an end
hitap addressing, address; ~ etm. -e address so.
hiyerarşi hierarchy; ~k hierarchic(al)
hiza line, level
hizmet service, duty, employ-

ment; ~ etm. -e serve, render service; ~çi servant; ~li employee
hoca hodja; teacher; ~lık teaching
hodbin selfish, egotistical
hokka inkpot; ~baz conjurer, cheat; ~bazlık cheating, trickery
Hollanda Holland; ~lı Dutch
homo|gen homogeneous; ~seksüel homosexual
homurdanmak grumble (-e at)
hoparlör loudspeaker
hoplamak jump about (-den for)
hoppa flighty, flippant; ~lık levity, flightiness
hor contemptible; ~ görmek -i look down upon
horlamak[1] v/t treat with contempt
horlamak[2] snore
horoz zoo cock, rooster; ~ibiği cockscomb (a. BOT); ~lanmak strut about
hortlak specter, ghost
hortum zoo trunk; TECH hose
horuldamak snore
hostes hostess
hoş pleasant, agreeable; ~ geldiniz! welcome!; ~ bulduk! (answer) thank you!; ~lanmak -den like; ~nut contented, pleased
hovarda spendthrift; rich lover; ~lık dissoluteness
hoyrat coarse and clumsy
hörgüç zoo hump

höyük hill, mound

hububat *pl.* cereals

hudut limits; frontier

hukuk JUR law; **Roma** ~**ü** Roman Law; **ticaret** ~**u** commercial law; ~ **devleti** constitutional state; ~**çu** jurist; ~**î** legal, juridicial

hulâsa extract; summary; ~**ten** *adv.* in short

hulul entering, penetrating

hulya day-dream

humma fever; typhus; ~**lı** feverish (*a. fig.*)

huni funnel *for pouring liquids*

hurafe silly tale, superstition; ~**perest** superstitious

hurda old iron, scrap metal; ~**cı** scrap dealer

hurma BOT date; ~ **ağacı** date palm

husul occuring, appearance; ~ **bulmak**, ~**e gelmek** be accomplished, attained

husumet enmity, hostility

husus particularity; matter; **bu** ~**ta** in this matter; ~**unda** with reference to; ~**î** special; private; ~**iyet** peculiarity

hutbe REL Friday sermon *in the mosque*

huy disposition, temper, habit; ~**lu**, ~**suz** bad-tempered

huzme PHYS bunch *of rays,*

etc.

huzur presence; repose; ~*in* ~**unda** in the presence of

hüccet argument, proof

hücre cell

hücum attack, assault; ~ **etm.** *-e* attack

hükm|etmek *v/t* rule, dominate; decide on; believe, assume; ~**î** judicial; nominal

hüküm rule, authority; command, edict; JUR sentence; decision; ~ **giymek** be condemned; ~ **sürmek** reign; prevail; ~**dar** monarch, ruler

hükümet government, state, authority

hükümsüz no longer in force, null

hüner skill, ability, talent; ~**li** skilful, talented

hüngürdemek *v/i* sob

hür free

hürmet respect, veneration; ~ **etm.** *-e* respect, honour; ~**li** venerable, respectable; ~**sizlik** irreverence, want of respect

hürriyet freedom, liberty

hüsnü|hal good conduct; ~**niyet** good intention, goodwill

hüviyet identity; ~ **cüzdanı** identity card

I

ıhlamur BOT lime-tree; ~ çiçeği lime-blossom

ıkınmak v/i grunt, moan

ıklim s. iklim

ılgar gallop; foray, raid

ılgın BOT tamarisk

ılı|ca hot spring; ~k tepid; ~m moderation, temperance; ~nmak become lukewarm

ırak¹ distant (-den from)

Irak² Irak

ırgat workman

ırk race, lineage; ~çılık racialism

ırmak river

ırz honour, chastity; -in ~ına geçmek violate

ısı heat; warm; ~nmak grow warm

ısır|gan BOT nettle; ~mak v/t bite (-den into)

ısıtma heating; ~k v/t heat

ıskala MUS scale

ıskarta discard (in card games)

ıskat annulment; rejection

ıskonto ECON discount

ıslah improvement, reform; ~ etm. v/t improve, reform

ısla|k wet; ~nmak become wet, be wetted; ~tmak v/t

wet; vulg. flog, beat

ıslık whistle; ~ çalmak whistle; ~lamak v/t boo

ısmarlama ordered; ~k v/t order; Allaha ısmarladık! good-bye!

ıspanak BOT spinach

ısrar insistence; ~ etm. -de insist on

ıssız lonely, desolate; ~lık desolate place, desolation

ıstampa inking-pad

ıstavroz REL cross, sign of the cross; ~ çıkarmak cross oneself

ıstakoz ZOO lobster

ıstılah technical term

ıstırap distress, anxiety

ıstok ECON stock, store

ışık light, lamp; ~landırmak v/t illuminate, light up; ~ölçer photometer

ışılda|k searchlight; ~mak shine, sparkle

ışın gleam, flash

ıtır perfume, aroma; ~ çiçeği BOT geranium

ıtriyat pl. perfumes

ızgara n. grill, grate; adj. grilled

ızrar causing harm

i

iade restauration, giving back; ~ **etm.** *v/t* give back, return

iane help, subsidy, donation; ~ **toplamak** collect subscriptions

ibadet worship, prayer; ~ **etm.** *-e* worship

ibare sentence, clause; ~**t olm.** *-den* consist of

ibik zoo comb

iblis REL Satan, devil

ibra discharge, acquitting

ibraz display, presentation; ~ **etm.** *v/t* **document**: present

ibre needle, pointer

ibret example, warning

ibrik kettle, ewer

ibrişim silk thread

icap requiring, demand; **icabında** in case of necessity; ~ **etm.** *v/i* be necessary; *v/t* necessitate, require

icar letting, leasing; ~ **etm.**, ~**a vermek** *v/t* let out, lease

icat invention; fabrication; ~ **etm.** *v/t* invent, fabricate

icbar compelling, constraining; ~ **etm.** *v/t* compel

icmal summary, resumé

icra execution; performance; ~ **etm.** *v/t* carry out, perform; ~**at** *pl.* performances; acts

iç inside, interior; inner; ~**inde** in, within; ~**ine** into; ~**bü-**

key MATH concave

içecek drinkable; drink

içeri inside, interior; in; ~**de** in; ~**den** from the inside; ~**ye** to the inside; ~**si** its interior; ~ **girmek** *v/i* enter

içgüdü instinct

içim mouthful; taste; ~**li** pleasant to the taste

için for, on account of; in order to; **bunun** ~ for this reason

içindekiler *pl.* contents

içirmek *v/t* cause to drink

içişleri *pl.* POL Internal Affairs

içki drink, liquor; ~**li** licensed to sell alcoholic drinks

içlenmek *-den* be affected, overcome by

içmek *v/t* drink; **tütün** ~ smoke *tobacco*

içten *adv.* sincere, from the heart

içtima assembly; ~**î** social

içtinap avoidance; ~ **etm.** *-den* avoid; abstain from

iç tüzük statutes; ~**yüz** inner meaning, real truth

idam execution; ~ **etm.** *v/t* execute, put to death

idame continuance

idare management; administration; economizing; ~ **etm.** *v/t* administer, manage, handle; ~**ci** good manager, organizer; **~hane** office; **~li** economical; efficient; **~siz** wateful

idbar adversity

iddia claim, pretension; **~ etm.** *v/t* claim; **~cı** obstinate; **~lı** pretentious; disputed

idman training, sport

idrak perception, intelligence; **~ etm.** *v/t* perceive; reach, attain

idrar urine

ifa performance, fulfilment; **~ etm.** *v/t* execute, fulfil

ifade explanation, expression; **~ etm.** *v/t* express, explain

iffet chastity; **~li** chaste; honest

iflâs bankruptcy; **~ etm.** go bankrupt

ifrat excess

ifraz separating; secretion

ifşa divulgation, disclosure; **~ etm.** *v/t* devulge, reveal

iftar REL breaking one's fast

iftihar laudable pride

iftira slander, forgery; **~ etm.** *-e* slander

iğ spindle

iğde BOT wild olive, oleaster

iğilmek *s.* eğilmek

iğmek *s.* eğmek

iğne needle, pin, thorn; injection; **~lemek** *v/t* fasten with a pin (*-e* to)

iğren|ç disgust, loathing; repulsive; **~mek** *-den* feel aversion against

iğreti *s.* eğreti

iğri *s.* eğri

iğril|mek, **~tmek** *s.* eğrilmek, eğriltmek

ihale ECON adjudication

ihanet treachery; **~ etm.** *-e* betray

ihata surrounding; **~ etm.** *v/t* surround, comprehend

ihbar communicating, notification; **~ etm.** *v/t* convey (*-e* to); notify (of)

ihlâl spoiling, infraction

ihmal negligence; **~ etm.** *v/t* neglect; **~ci** negligent, careless

ihracat *pl.* exports

ihraç ECON exportation; **~ etm.** *v/t* export

ihraz etm. *v/t* obtain, attain

ihsan kindness, favour

ihtar reminding, warning; **~ etm.** *v/t* remind, warn of; **~da bulunmak** *-e* warn, remind *so.*

ihtifal commemorative ceremony

ihtikâr profiteering; **~cı** profiteer

ihtilâf difference, disagreement

ihtilâl embezzlement; **~ etm.** *v/t* embezzle

ihtimal probability, possibility

ihtimam care, carefulness

ihtira invention; **~ etm.** *v/t* invent

ihtiras passion, greed

ihtiraz precaution, avoidance; **~ etm.** *-den* guard

ilerlemek

against, avoid

ihtisas¹ sentiment; affection
ihtisas² specialization; **~ sa-hibi** specialist
ihtişam pomp
ihtiva etm. v/t contain, include
ihtiyaç want, necessity; **~cı olm.** -*e* be in need of
ihtiyar¹ old
ihtiyar² choice, selection; **~î** optional, voluntary
ihtiyarlamak grow old; **~lık** old age
ihtiyat precaution; reserve; **~î** precautionary; **~sız** incautious, imprudent
ihtizaz vibration
ihya bringing to life; **~ etm.** v/t animate; enliven
ikame setting up, establishing; substitution
ikamet residence, dwelling; **~ etm.** -*de* dwell, stay in; **~ tezkeresi** residence permit; **~gâh** place of residence, domicile
ikaz rousing, warning
ikbal good fortune, success
iken conj. while; when
iki two; **~de bir** one in two, every other; frequently; **~si** both of them; **~lemek** v/t make two, make a pair; **~lik** consisting of two; disunion; **~nci** secondary
ikindi REL the time of the afternoon prayer
iki|yüzlü having two faces; hypocrite; **~z** twins; twin

iklim GEO climate, region
ikmal completion; **~ etm.** v/t complete, finish
ikna etm. v/t convince, persuade
ikram showing honour, kindness; **~e** show honour to; v/t offer *sth.* (-*e* to); **~iye** bonus, gratuity; prize *in a lottery*
ikrar declaration, confession
ikraz loan; **~ etm.** v/t lend
iktibas quotation, adaptation
iktidar power, ability; POL party in power, government
iktifa etm. be content (**ile** with)
iktisadî economic
iktisap acquisition, gain; **~ etm.** v/t acquire, gain
iktisat economy
il province; country
ilâ up to, towards, until
ilâç remedy; medicine
ilâh god; **~e** goddess; **~î** divine; **~iyat** theology
ilâm JUR decree in writing
ilân declaration, notice; advertisement; **~ etm.** v/t declare, announce
ilâve addition, supplement; **~ etm.** v/t add (-*e* to)
ile with, by means of; and
ileri forward part, front; forward; fast (*clock*); advanced; **~ci** progressive
iler(i)de in front; in future
ilerigelenler pl. notables
ilerle|mek v/i advance, pro-

gress; **~tmek** v/t cause to advance; **~yiş** progress

ilet|ken tranferring; PHYS conducting; **~mek** v/t carry off, send; PHYS conduct

ilga abolition, annulment

ilgi interest; **~lendirmek** v/t arouse one's interest; **~lenmek** be interested (**ile** in); **~li ile** interested in, connected with; **~nç** interesting; **~siz** not interested

ilhak annexation; **~ etm.** v/t annex

ilham inspiration

ilik[1] marrow

ilik[2] buttonhole; **~lemek** v/t button up

ilikli[1] buttoned

ilikli[2] containing marrow

ilim knowledge; science

iliş|ik -e connected with, attached to; connexion, relation; **~ki** relation, connection; **~kin** -e concerning, regarding; **~mek** -e interfere with; be fastened to; **~tir-mek** v/t fasten (-e to); attach

ilk first, initial; **~ defa** (for) the first time; **~bahar** spring; **~çağ** ancient times pl.; **~e** substance; principle; **~el** elementary; primitive; **~okul** primary school

illâ, ille whatever happens; by all means; or else

illet disease, defect; cause, reason

ilmî scientific

ilmik loop, noose

ilmühaber identity papers; certificate

iltica etm. -e take refuge in

iltifat favour

iltihak joining, adherence

iltihap MED inflamation; **~lan-mak** become inflamed

iltimas request; protection, patronage; **~lı** who gets a job by favouritism, favoured

iltizam favouring; POL farming of revenues; **~ etm.** v/t take the part of, favour

ima allustion, hint; **~ etm.** -e allude to, hint at

imal manufacture; **~ etm.** v/t make, produce; **~âthane** factory, workshop

imam REL leader of the ritual prayer, Imam; **~bayıldı** (a dish of eggplants with oil and onions)

iman belief, faith; **~sız** unbelieving; atheist

imar improvement, cultivation; **~ etm.** v/t improve, render prosperous

imaret soup-kitchen for the poor

imbik retort, still

imdat help, assistance; **~ freni** emergency brake; **~ kapısı** emergency exit

imge image

imha distruction, effacement; **~ etm.** v/t obliterate, destroy

imkân possibility, practicability; **~sız** impossible

imlâ spelling, orthography

imparator Emperor; **~içe**

Empress; **~luk** Empire

imrenmek *-e* long for, desire

imsak temperance, diet; REL hour at which the daily Ramazan fast begins

imtihan trial, test; examination; **~ etm.** *v/t* examine

imtiyaz privilege, concession; **~lı** privileged, autonomous

imza signature; **~ etm.** *v/t*, **~ atmak** *-e* sign; **~lamak** *v/t* sign

in den, lair

inadına *adv.* out of obstinacy

inak dogma

inan belief, trust; **~ç** belief, confidence; **~dırmak** *-i -e* cause *so.* to believe *sth.*; **~lır** credible; **~mak** *-e* believe, trust

inat obstinacy; **~çı** obstinate, pig-headed

ince slender, thin, fine, slight; **~lemek** *v/t* examine; **~ltmek** *v/t* make fine, slender, refine; **~saz** MUS Turkish orchestra *of stringed instruments*

inci pearl; **~ çiçeği** BOT lily of the valley

incik[1] ANAT shin

incik[2] bruised; sprain

İncil REL Gospel, New Testament

incinmek be sprained; be hurt, offended *(-den by)*

incir BOT fig; **~ ağacı** fig-tree

incitmek *v/t* hurt; touch; offend

indî subjective, arbitrary

indir|ilen dosya *n.* download; **~im** lowering, reduction; **~mek** *v/t* cause to descend, lower; download

inek cow

infaz execution, carrying out

infilâk explosion

İngiliz English(man); **~ anahtarı** spanner; **~ce** English *(language)*

İngiltere England

inha memorandum

inhina curving, bend

inhiraf deviation

inhisar monopoly

inhitat decline, degradation

inil|demek echo, resound; **~ti** echo; moan, groan

inisiyatif initiative

iniş descent, slope; landing

inkâr denial, refusal; **~ etm.** *v/t* deny, refuse

inkılâp revolution; **~çı** revolutionary

inkıraz decline, extinction

inkişaf development; **~ etm.** *v/i* develop

inlemek moan, groan

inme descending; fall *of the tide;* MED apoplexy, stroke; **~k** *v/i* descend, land; fall *(price)*

insaf justice, fairness; **~lı** just, equitable; **~sız** unjust, unfair

insan human being; man; **~iyet,** **~lık** humanity; humankind; **~üstü** superhuman man

insicam coherence, harmony

insiyak instinct
insiyatif s. inisiyatif
inşa construction, creation; ~
etm. v/t construct, build; ~at
pl. building sg.; works
inşallah if God pleases; I
hope that
internet Internet, net; ~te gezinmek surf the net
intibak adaptation, adjustment
intihap choice; POL election; ~
etm. v/t choose; POL elect
intihar suicide; ~ etm. commit suicide
intikal transition, transfer
intikam revenge; ~almak
-den take revenge on
intişar publication, dissemi-
nation
intizam regularity, order;
~sız irregular, disordered;
~sızlık disorder
intizar expectation; curse
inzibat disciplin; MIL military
police
ip rope, cord, string
ipek silk; silken; ~ böceği zoo
silkworm; ~li of silk
iplik thread, sewing-cotton
ipotek mortgage
iptal rendering null and void;
~ etm. v/t annul
iptida beginning; ~i primitive,
elementary
iptila addiction (-e to)
irade will, command; decree
İran Persia; ~lı Persian
irat income, revenue
irfan knowledge, culture

iri huge, voluminous; ~baş
zoo tadpole; ~leşmek be-
come large; ~lik largeness;
size
irin pus, filth; ~lenmek suppurate
irk|ilmek become stagnant;
MED swell, tumefy; ~inti
stagnant pool
İlanda Ireland; ~lı Irish
irmik semolina
irs inheritance
irsal sending; ~ etm. v/t send
irsî hereditary
irtibat connection; communication
irtica going back, reaction
irtidat REL apostasy from Islam
irtifa elevation; altitude
irtikâp bribery, corruption; ~
etm. v/t commit, perpetrate
is soot
İsa Jesus
isabet hitting the mark; thing
done right; ~ etm. -e hit; fall
to one's share
is'af compliance
ise however, as for; when, if; ~
de although
ishal purging, diarrhoea
isim name; GR noun; ~lendir-
mek v/t name, call
iskambil playing card; (kind
of card game)
iskân settling, inhabiting; ~
etm. v/t settle, inhabit
iskandil NAUT soundinglead
iskarpela carpenter's chisel
iskarpin low shoe

iskele NAUT landing-place, quay; port; larboard

iskelet skeleton

iskemle chair, stool

İskenderiye Alexandria; ~un Alexandrette

İskoç Scotch; ~ya Scotland; ~yalı Scottish, Scotsman

iskonto ECON discount

iskorbüt scurvy

İslâm Islam; ~iyet the Moslem world

İslanda Iceland

islenmek become black with soot

islim steam

ismet chastity, innocence

isnat imputation; ~ etm. v/t ile accuse so. of, charge so. with

İspanya Spain; ~lı Spanish

İspanyol Spanish; Spaniard; ~ca Spanish (language)

ispat proof, confirmation; ~ etm. v/t prove, confirm

ispinoz ZOO chaffinch

ispirto alcohol

israf wasteful expenditure; ~ etm. v/t waste, squander

İsrail Israel

istasyon station

istatistik statistics

istavroz s. ıstavroz

istek wish, longing; ~li interested; bidder; candidate; ~siz unwilling; apathetic

iste|m volition; ECON demand; ~mek v/t wish for, desire, want

isteri MED hysteria

istibdat despotism, absolute rule

isticar hiring; ~ etm. v/t take on hire

isticvap interrogation

istida demand, petition; ~ etm. v/t demand, request

istif stowage, arrangement of goods; ~ etm. v/t pack, stow

istifa resignation; ~ etm. -den resign from

istifade profit, advantage; ~ etm. -den benefit, profit by

istif|çi packer, stevedore; ~lemek v/t stow, pack; hoard

istihbar asking for information; ~at bürosu information office

istihdaf etm. v/t aim at, pursue

istihdam employment; ~ etm. v/t take into service, employ

istihkâm fortification; military engineering

istihlâk consumption

istihsal producing; production; ~ etm. v/t produce, obtain

istihza ridicule, mockery

istikamet direction

istikbal future

istiklâl independence; ☨ Marşı the Turkish National Anthem

istikrar stability

istikraz loan; ~ etm. v/t borrow

istilâ invasion; ~ etm. -e invade

istim steam

istimal using, making use of

istimdat asking for help

istimlâk JUR expropriation; ~ **etm.** v/t expropriate

istinaden -e based on

istinat relying (-e upon); ~ **etm.** -e rely on, lean on

istintak JUR interrogation cross-examination; ~ **etm.** v/t interrogate

istirahat repose; ~ **etm.** rest, take one's ease

istirdat restitution

istirham asking a favour; petition; ~ **etm.** -den-i petition, ask so. for sth.

istiridye ZOO oyster

istismar etm. v/t exploit

istisna exception; ~ **etm.** v/t exclude; ~î exceptional

istişare consultation; ~ **kurulu** advisory council

istizah POL interpellation; ~ **etm.** v/t ask for an explanation, question

İsveç Sweden; ~li Swedish

İsviçre Switzerland; ~li Swiss

isyan rebellion; ~ **etm.** rebel

iş work, action; business, occupation; affair; ~ **başında** at one's work; ~im var I am busy; ~alan employee

işaret sign, signal, mark; ~ **zamiri** GR demonstrative pronoun; ~ **etm.** -e mark; indicate; ~lemek v/t mark, denote

iş|başı foreman; ~birliği cooperation; ~bölümü division of labour

işbu this, the present

işçi workman, labourer; ~lik occupation or pay of a workman

işemek v/i urinate

işgal occupation; ~ **etm.** v/t keep busy; MIL occupy

işgüder POL chargé d'affaires

işgüzar efficient

işit|ilmek be heard; ~mek v/t hear, listen too

işkembe paunch, tripe

işkence torture; ~ **etm.** -e torture

işkil doubt; suspicion

işle|k good flowing; busy; ~me handiwork; embroidery; ~mek v/t work, manipulate, work up; carve, engrave; -e penetrate; ~meli embroidered; ~nmek be worked up; ~r functioning

işletme working, running; administration, management; ~k v/t cause to work, run, operate

işporta open basket; ~cı peddler

işsiz unemployed; ~lik unemployment

iştah appetite, desire; ~sız without appetite

işte look!; here!; now, thus

iştikak derivation; ~ **ettirmek** v/t derive (-den from)

iştirak participation; ~ **etm.** -e participate in

iştiyak longing

işveren employer

it dog

itaat obedience; ~ **etm.** *-e*
obey; ~**li** obedient; ~**siz** dis-
obedient

italya Italy; ~**n** Italian; ~**nca**
Italian (*language*)

itfaiye fire-brigade

ithaf dedication; ~ **etm.** *v/t*
dedicate (*-e* to)

ithal import; ~ **etm.** *v/t* import; ~ **gümrüğü** import duty; ~**ât** *pl.* imports

itham imputation, accusa-
tion; ~ **etm.** *v/t* accuse (ile
of)

itibar esteem, regard, credit;
~**etm.** *-e* esteem, show consideration; ~ **nazarına almak** *-i* consider, take into
account; ~**dan düşmek** be
discredited; ~**en** *-den* from,
dating from; ~**î** nominal, theoretical

itikat belief, creed

itilâf agreement, understanding

itimat confidence, reliance; ~
etm. *-e* rely on, have confidence in; ~**name** POL letter
of credentials

itina care, attention; ~**sız**
careless, inattentive

itiraf confession, admission; ~
etm. *v/t* confess, admit

itiraz objection; ~ **etm.** *-e* object to

itişmek push one another

itiyat habit

itizar apologizing, excuse

itlâf destruction; waste

itmek *v/t* push

ittifak concord; alliance

ittihat union

ittihaz etm. *v/t* procure; take

ittisal being in contact

ivdirmek *v/t* hasten; ~**edi(lik)**
haste; ~**mek** be in a hurry

iye possessor, owner; ~**lik zamiri** GR possessive pronoun

iyi good, well; the good; **en
~si** the best of it; ~**ce** well,
rather good; ~**leşmek** get
better, improve; ~**leştirmek**
v/t improve; ~**lik** goodness,
kindness; ~**mser** optimistic

iyot CHEM iodine

iz footprint, track, trace

izafet (terkibi) GR nominal
compound; ~**î** relative; nominal

izah explanation; ~ **etm.** *v/t*
manifest, explain; ~**at** *pl.* ex-
planations

izale removing

izci tracker; boy-scout

izdiham crowd

izdivaç matrimony

izhar display, manifestation; ~
etm. *v/t* show, display

izin permission, leave; ~ **vermek** *-e* grant leave, give permission; ~**li** on leave; with
permission; ~**siz** without
permission

izlemek *v/t* trace

izole etm. *v/t* EL, PHYS insulate, isolate

izzet might, glory, honour

J

jambon ham
jandarma police soldier, gendarme
jant TECH rim *of a wheel*
Japon Japanese; **~ca** Japanese (*language*); **~ya** Japan
jelatin gelatine

jeolo|g geologist; **~ji** geology
jest gesture
jet AVIA jet-plane
jilet safety-razor; razorblade
jimnastik s. cimnastik
jüri JUR jury

K

kaba large, coarse, rough, vulgar; **~dayı** rough fellow, bully
kabahat fault; offence; **~li** guilty; **~siz** innocent
kabak 1. BOT pumpkin; marrow; **2.** *fig.* bald, close-shaven; worn out (*tyre*)
kaba|kulak MED mumps; **~laşmak** become coarse *or* vulgar; **~lık** sponginess; coarseness
kabar|cık MED bubble, pimple, pustle; **~ık** swollen, blistered, puffy; **~ma** flood-tide, high-water; **~mak** swell, become fluffy, be raised; **~tı** swelling; **~tma** *adj.* embossed, in relief; *n.* relief
kabız MED constipation
kabil -*e* capable of, possible for
kabile tribe
kabiliyet capability, possibility; **~li** intelligent, skilful;

~siz incapable
kabine POL cabinet; small room
kabir grave, tomb
kablo EL cable
kabotaj NAUT cabotage, coast navigation
kabristan cemetery
kabuk bark, rind, peel, skin, shell, crust; **-in kabuğunu soymak** peel, skin; **~lu** having a shell, *etc.*
kabul acceptance; reception; consent; **~ etm.** *v/t* accept, receive, consent to
kaburga ANAT thorax; rib; NAUT frame *of a ship*
kâbus nightmare
kabz|a handle, hilt; **~ımal** ECON middleman
kaç how many?, how much?; **saat ~?** what is the time?; **~a?** what is the price?
kaçak fugitive, deserter; contraband; **~çı** smuggler;

81   **kakmak**

~çılık suggling

kaçamak flight, evasion, sub-
   terfuge; ~lı evasive

kaçık crazy; ladder *in a stocking*; ~lık craziness

kaç|ınılmaz inevitable;
   ~ınmak *-den* abstain from,
   avoid; ~ırmak *v/t* make *or*
   let escape, drive away; miss;
   smuggle; ~ışmak *v/i* disperse, flee in confusion;
   ~mak flee, run away (*-den*
   from); escape

kadar 1. as much as, as big as;
   like, about; **beşyüz** ~ about
   five hundred; 2. *-e* up to, until; *-inceye* ~ *conj.* until; **yarı-
   na** ~ until tomorrow

kadastro land survey

kadavra corpse, carcass

kadayıf (*various kinds of
   sweet pastry*)

kadeh glass, cup; wineglass

kadem foot; pace

kademe step, stair, rung; degree; ~li stepped

kader destiny, fate, providence

kadı Moslem judge, Cadi

kadın woman; matron; ~budu
   (*meat ball with eggs and
   rice*); ~göbeği (*sweet dish
   made with semolina and
   eggs*)

kadife velvet

kadim old, ancient

kadir¹ *adj.* powerful, capable
   (*-e* of)

kadir² worth, value

kadran TECH face, dial

kadro staff, roll, cadre

kafa head; nape; intelligence;
   ~dar intimate, likeminded;
   ~lı having a head; intelligent

kafes cage, lattice, grating; ~li
   latticed

kâfi sufficient, enough (*-e* for)

kafile caravan, convoy

kâfir REL misbeliever, Non-
   -Moslem

kafiye rhyme

Kafkas (dağları) Caucasus

kaftan robe, caftan

kâğıt paper; letter; ~ **para** paper money

kağnı two-wheeled ox-cart

kâhin soothsayer, seer

kahkaha loud laughter

kahraman hero, gallant; ~lık
   heroism

kahr|etmek *v/t* overpower; *v/i*
   be distressed; ~olmak be de-
   pressed; ~olsun! to hell with
   him!

kahvaltı breakfast

kahve coffee; Oriental coffee-house; ~ **değirmeni** cof-
   fee-mill; ~ci coffeemaker;
   ~rengi brown

kâhya steward, majordomo

kaide base, rule, principle

kâinat universe

kak¹ dried fruit

kak² puddle, pool

kakao cocoa

kakırdamak rattle, rustle,
   crackle; *sl.* die

kakışmak keep nudging (**ile**
   so.)

kakma repoussé work; ~k *v/t*

push, nail, encrust
kaktüs BOT cactus
kala -*e* to (*time*); **saat ona beş** ~ five minutes to ten
kalabalık crowd, throng, confused mass
kalafatlamak *v/t* caulk, careen
kalas beam, plank
kalay tin; **~cı** tinshmith; **~lamak** *v/t* tin; **~lı** tinned
kalbî cardiac; cordial
kalbur sieve; **~dan geçirmek**, **~lamak** *v/t* sieve, sift
kalça ANAT hip
kaldıraç TECH lever; **~ım** pavement, causeway; **~mak** *v/t* raise, erect, lift; remove; abolish
kale fortress, castle; goal; **~ci** goalkeeper
kalem reed; pen; paintbrush; office; **~e almak** *v/t* write, draw up; **~tıraş** pencil sharpener
kalender unconventional
kalfa assistant master; qualified workman
kalın thick, stout, coarse; **~laşmak** become thick or stout; **~lık** thickness
kalınmak stay, stop
kalıntı remnant, remainder
kalıp mould, form, model; **~lamak** *v/t* form
kalıt inheritance
kalıfiye qualified
kalite quality
kalkan shield
kalkın|dırmak *v/t* cause to re-

cover; lead towards progress; **~ma** recovery; progress, development; **~mak** *v/i* recover, rise
kalkış rising; departure
kalkışmak -*e* try *to do sth.*
kalkmak rise, get up
kalmak remain, be left
kalori calory; **~fer** central heating
kaloş galosh
kalp[1] 1. *n.* change, transformation; **2.** *adj.* false, spurious, forged
kalp[2] ANAT heart; ~ **sektesi** heart attack
kalpak fur cap
kalpazan counterfeiter
kama dagger, wedge
kamara ship's cabin; 2 House *of Lords or Commons*
kamaş|mak be dazzled; **~tırmak** *v/t* dazzle
kambiyo ECON foreign exchange (office)
kambur *n.*, *adj.* hunchback(ed)
kamçı whip; **~lamak** *v/t* whip; *fig.* stimulate
kamer ASTR moon; **kameralı cep** camera phone
kamış reed, cane
kâmil perfect, complete
kamp camp; camping; ~ **yeri** camping place; **~anya** cropping-season
kamu everybody; public; ~ **hizmeti** public service; ~ **oyu** public opinion; ~ **yararı** public interest; **~laştırmak**

v/t nationalize; **~tay** POL National Assembly

kamyon truck; **~et** small truck, station-car

kan blood; **~ gütmek** continue blood feud; **-in ~ına dokunmak** make one's blood boil

kanaat contentment, conviction; opinion; **~ getirmek** come to the conclusion (*-e* that); **~kâr** contented

Kanada Canada; **~lı** Canadian

kanal canal; **~izasyon** canalization

kanama bleeding; **~k** bleed

kanarya ZOO canary-bird

kanat wing (*a.* ZOO, TECH), leaf *of a door*; **~lanmak** take wing, fly away; **~lı** winged, folded

kanatmak *v/t* make bleed

kanca large hook; **~lamak** *v/t* put on a hook; grapple with a hook

kançılar POL head of the registry office *of a consulate*; **~ya** consular office

kandırmak *v/t* satisfy, convince; take in, cheat

kandil oil-lamp; **~ gecesi** REL the nights of four Moslem feasts *when the minarets are illuminated with oil-lamps*

kanepe sofa

kangal coil, skein

kanı conviction, opinion

kanık content, satisfied; **~sa-mak**, **~sımak** *-e* be satiated by; become inured to

kanıt proof, evidence; **~lamak** *v/t* prove

kanlanmak become soiled with blood; increase one's blood; **~lı** bloody

kanmak be satiated with; believe

kanser MED cancer

kansız MED anaemic; **~lık** anaemia

kantar weighing-machine

kantin canteen

kanun[1] MUS (*a zither-like instrument*)

kanun[2] rule, law; code of laws; **~î**, **~lu** legal, legislative; **~iyet**, **~luluk** legality; **~suzluk** lawlessness

kanyak brandy

kap[1] cape, mantle

kap[2] receptacle; vessel; cover

kapak cover, lid; **~lanmak** *v/i* fall on one's face; capsize

kapa|lı shut, covered, closed; **~mak** *v/t* shut, close, cover up; **~n** trap; **~nış** closing; **~nmak** be shut, closed, covered up

kaparo ECON earnest money

kapatmak *v/t* shut, close; get very cheap

kapı door, gate; **~cı** door-keeper

kapılmak *-e* carried away by

kapışmak *v/t* snatch, scramble for; *v/i* get to grips (**ile** with)

kapital capital; **~ist** capitalist;

~izm capitalism

kapitülasyon POL capitulation

kaplamak v/t cover (-e with); bind, line

kaplan ZOO tiger

kaplıca thermal spring

kaplumbağa ZOO tortoise

kapmak v/t snatch, seize, carry off

kaporta bonnet, hood (auto); NAUT skylight

kapot s. kaput

kapsa|m contents pl.; **~mak** v/t comprise, contain

kapsül capsule

kaptan captain

kaptıkaçtı minibus

kaput MIL cloak; bonnet, hood (auto)

kar snow; **~ topu** snowball; **~ yağmak** snow

kâr gain, profit

kara[1] n. mainland, shore; **~ya çıkmak** go ashore; **~ya oturmak** NAUT run aground, be stranded

kara[2] black, gloomy; **~ağaç** BOT elm; **~basan** nightmare; **~biber** BOT black pepper; **~borsa** black market; **~ca** ZOO roe, deer; **~ciğer** liver; **2deniz** Black Sea; **~fatma** ZOO cockroach; **~göz** Turkish shadow-play; Turkish Punch; **~kol** police-station; **~koncolos** bogy, vampire

karakter character; **~istik** characteristic

kara|kuş ZOO eagle; **~lamak**

v/t blacken, dirty

karanfil BOT carnation

karanlık darkness, dark

karantina quarantine

karar decision, resolution, agreement; firmness; **~ vermek** decide (hakkında upon); **~a varmak** reach a decision; **~gâh** headquarters

kararlaş|mak be agreed (hakkında upon); **~tırmak** v/t decide, resolve on

kararlı settled, decided; **~lık** stability

kararmak become black, dark

karar|name decree; **~sız** unstable, restless; **~sızlık** instability, indecision

karartmak v/t blacken, blackout

karavan caravan, trailer; **~a** MIL mess tin; meal

karayolu overland route

karbon CHEM carbon; **~ kâğıdı** carbon paper

karbüratör TECH carburator

kardan mili TECH cardan shaft

kardeş brother; sister; **~çe** brotherly, fraternal; **~lik** brotherhood

kare square; **~li** in squares, chequered

karga ZOO crow; **~burun** who has a prominent nose

kargaşa(lık) disorder, tumult

kargı pike, javelin

kargı|mak v/t curse; **~ş** cursing

karı wife; woman; **~ koca** wife

and husband, couple

karık n. snow-blindness; adj. snow-blind

karın belly, stomach

karınca zoo ant

karış span

karışık mixed, confused; ~lık confusion, disorder

karış|mak -e interfere, meddle with; ~tırmak v/t mix; confuse

karina bottom of a ship

karlı covered with snow

kârlı profitable, advantageous

karma mixed; ~ eğitim co-education

karmak v/t knead; mix; thrust (-e into)

karmakarışık adj. in utter disorder

karnabahar BOT cauliflower

karne schoolboy's report; book of tickets

karpuz BOT water-melon

karşı -e opposed to, against; -in ~sına, ~sında opposite to, in front of; ~ ~ya face to face

karşıla|mak v/t meet; reply to; oppose; ~nmak be met; ~şmak meet face to face; ~ştırmak v/t confront; compare

karşılık reply, retort; equivalent; ~lı equivalent; reciprocal

karşıt adj. opposite, contrary (-e to)

kart¹ old, hard, dry

kart² card

kartal zoo eagle

karton cardboard

kart|postal postcard; ~vizit visiting-card

karyola bedstead

kasa chest, safe; cashier's office

kasaba small town

kasadar cashier

kasap butcher

kâse bowl, basin

kasık ANAT groin

kasım November

kasınmak shrink; be conceited

kasırga whirlwind, cyclone

kasıt intention, endeavour

kasket cap

kasmak v/t tighten, curtail; oppress

kasnak rim, hoop

kastarlamak v/t bleach

kast|en adv. intentionally, deliberately; ~etmek v/t purpose, intend; mean; ~î adj. deliberate

kasvet depression, gloom; ~li oppressive; gloomy

kaş eyebrow; something curved

kaşar sheep cheese

kaşık spoon

kaşı|mak v/t scratch; ~nmak scratch oneself; itch

kâşif discoverer, revealer

kaşkaval soft cheep cheese

kat fold, layer; coating; story of a building

katalog catalogue

katar file of camels, etc.; train

kategori category

katetmek v/t cut, traverse

katı hard, violent, strong; ~ **yürekli** strong-hearted

katılaş|mak become hard or heavy; ~**tırmak** v/t make hard or strong

katılık hardness, severity

katılmak -e be added to, join

katır zoo mule

katıyağ solid oil, paraffin

kati definite, decisive

katil[1] killing, murder

katil[2] murderer

kâtip clerk, secretary

katiye|n adv. definitely, absolutely; ~**t** definiteness

katkı addition, supplement; ~**da bulunmak** -e be added to

katla|mak v/t fold, pleat; ~**nmak** -e be folded into; undergo, suffer, endure

katl|etmek v/t kill; murder; ~**iam** general massacre

katma addition; ~**değer vergisi** surplus value tax; ~**k** v/t add (-e to), join, mix

katman layer, stratum

katmer a kind of pastry; multiplicity; ~**li** manifold, multiplied

Katolik Catholik; ~**lik** Catholicism

katran tar; ~**lamak** v/t tar; ~**lı** tarred

kauçuk caoutchouc, unvulcanized rubber

kav tinder

kavak вот poplar

kaval shepherd's pipe

kavalye escort; male partner in a dance

kavanoz jar, pot

kavas guard or attendant of ANAT embassy or consulate

kavga brawl, quarrel, fight; ~**cı** quarrelsome; ~**lı** quarreling, angry

kavis bow, arc, curve

kavla|k barkless, peeled off; ~**mak** peel off, fall off

kavra|m concept, idea; ~**mak** v/t seize, grasp; ~**yış** conception, understanding

kavşak junction, crossroads

kavuk quilted turban

kavun вот muskmelon

kavurmak v/t fry; roast

kavuşak s. kavşak

kavuş|mak -e reach, attain, touch, meet; ~**turmak** v/t bring together, unite, join; ~**um** ASTR conjunction

kay MED vomiting

kaya rock

kayak ski

kayalık rocky place

kayb|etmek v/t lose; ~**olmak** be lost, disappear

kayd|etmek v/t enrol, register; ~**ol(un)mak** -e be registered in

kaygan slippery; polished

kaygana omelet

kaygı care, anxiety; ~**lanmak** be worried; ~**lı** worried, anxious

kaygın polished, slippery

kaygısız carefree; **~lık** freedom from care
kayık. 1. *n.* boat, caique; **2.** *adj.* displaced
kayın[1] beech
kayın[2] brother-in-law; **~baba** father-in-law; **~birader** brother-in-law; **~peder** *s.* **~baba**; **~valide** mother-in-law
kayıp. 1. *n.* loss; **2.** *adj.* lost
kayırmak *v/t* protect, care for
kayısı BOT apricot
kayış[1] slipping
kayış[2] strap, belt
kayıt registration, enrolment; restriction; **~ sildirme** cancellation, deletion of a record; **~lamak** *v/t* restrict, limit; **~lı** registered; restricted; **~sız** unregistered; carefree; **~sızlık** indifference, carelessness
kaymak[1] *v/i* slip, slide
kaymak[2] *n.* cream
kaymakam head official *of a district*
kaynak. 1. spring, fountain; source; **2.** TECH weld, welding
kaynamak *v/i* boil, spout up
kaynana mother-in-law
kaynaşmak *v/i* unite, weld (**ile** with); **~tırmak** *v/t* weld together
kaynata father-in-law
kaynatmak *v/t* cause to boil; boil, weld
kaypak slippery; stolen
kaytan cotton *or* silk cord

kaz goose; **~ beyinli** stupid, silly
kaza. 1. accident, mischance; **2.** JUR office and functions of a Cadi; **3.** POL district; **~en** *adv.* by accident
Kazak Cossack
kazalı dangerous
kazan couldron; boiler
kazanç gain, profits; **~dırmak** *v/t* cause to win *sth.*; **~mak** *v/t* earn, win, gain
kazazede ruined, shipwrecked
kazı excavation; **~cı** excavator; engraver
kazık stake, peg, pile; trick, swindle; **~çı** swindler; **~lamak** *v/t* cheat, play a trick on
kazımak *v/t* scratch, eradicate, erase
kazma digging; pickaxe, mattock; **~k** *v/t* dig, excavate; engrave
kebap roast meat
kebze ANAT shoulder-blade
keçe felt; mat
keçi goat
keder care, grief, affliction; **~lenmek** be sorrowful, anxious; **~li** sorrowful, grieved
kedi ZOO cat; **~otu** BOT valeriana
kefalet JUR bail, security
kefaret REL atonement
kefe scale *of a balance*
kefen shroud
kefil JUR bail, guarantor; **~ olm.** stand as surety (**-e** for); **~lik** bail, security

kehle louse; **~lenmek** become lousy

kehlibar amber

kek cake

keke stammering; **~lemek** *v/i* stammer, stutter; **~me** having a stammer

kekik BOT thyme

kekre acrid, sharp

kel *n.* MED ringworm; *adj.* bald, scabby

kelebek ZOO butterfly

kelek *adj.* partly bald, immature; *n.* unripe melon

kelepçe handcuffs; TECH pipe clip

kelepir bargain

keler ZOO lizard; reptile

kelime word

kelle head

kemal perfection, maturity; value, price

keman violin; ARCH bow; **~cı** violinist; **~e** MUS bow *for a violin etc.*

kemer belt, girdle; ARCH arch, vault; aquaeduct

kemik bone; **~li** having bones, bony

kemir|gen ZOO rodent; **~mek** *v/t* gnaw, nibble

kemiyet quantity

kenar edge, border; shore; **~lı** having an edge *or* margin; having a hem

kendi self; **~ ~ne** by himself, all alone; **~ni beğenmek** be arrogant, conceited; **~si** himself; **~liğinden** of one's own accord, spontaneous;

~lik personality

kene ZOO tick

kenet TECH metal clamp; **~lemek** *v/t* clamp together

kenevir BOT hemp

kent town, city

kepaze vile, contemptible; **~lik** vileness, degradation

kepçe skimmer, ladle

kepek BOT bran

kepenk pull-down shutter, wooden cover

keramet REL miracle

kere time; **üç ~** three times

kerempe NAUT rocky promontory

kereste timber; material for making shoes

kerevet wooden bedstead

kereviz BOT celery

kerhane brothel

kerpeten pincers

kerpiç sun-dried brick

kerte notch, score; degree

kertenkele ZOO lizard

kert|ik notch, gash; **~mek** *v/t* notch, scratch, gash

kervan caravan; **~saray** caravanserai

kesbetmek *s.* kesp etm.

kese purse, small bag; coarse cloth bath glove; **~ kâğıdı** paper bag

keser adze

kesif dense, thick

kesi|k cut, broken; curdled; **~lmek** be cut; cease, be exhausted; be cut off; **~m** cutting; section, sector

kesin definite, certain; **~leş-**

mek become certain *or* definite; **~ti** deduction; interruption

kesir breaking, fracture; MATH fraction

kesişmek conclude an agreement, settle an account (**ile** with)

keski bill-hook, coulter

keskin sharp, keen; **~leşmek** become sharp, severe; **~lik** sharpness, incisiveness

kesme *adj.* cut; fixed (*price*); **~k** *v/t* cut, cut off; interrupt; define; diminish; coin

kesp etm. *v/t* earn, acquire

kestane BOT chestnut

kestirmek *v/t* cause to cut, shorten; cause to cease; decide

keşfetmek *v/t* uncover, discover

keşide drawing *in a lottery*

keşif discovery

keşiş REL Christian priest; monk

keşke, keşki would that …!

keşkül sweetened milk *with pistachio nuts and almonds*

keten flax; linen

ketum discreet, keeping a secret

keyfletmek amuse, enjoy oneself; **~î** arbitrary, capricious; **~iyet** condition; quality

keyif health; inclination, whim; tipsy; **~ çatmak** enjoy oneself; **~li** merry, happy; **~siz** indisposed; **~sizlik** in-

disposition; depression

kez time; **bu ~** this time

keza(lik) thus, too

kıble REL direction of Mecca *to which a Moslem prays*

Kıbrıs Cyprus; **~lı** Cypriote

kıç hinder part, behind

kıdem priority, seniority; **~li** senior in service

kıkırda|k ANAT cartilage, gristle; **~mak** rustle, rattle; *sl.* die

kıl hair, bristle

kılavuz guide; NAUT pilot; **~luk** profession of a guide

kılçık fish-bone; string *of a bean*

kılıç sword; **~ balığı** ZOO sword-fish

kılıf case; sheath

kılık shape, appearance, costume

kılınmak be done, performed

kılmak *v/t* render, make; perform

kımılda|(n)mak *v/i* move, shake; **~tmak** *v/t* move, shake

kın sheath

kına henna; **~lı** dyed with henna

kına|mak *v/t* reproach; **~msımak** *v/t* find fault with

kınnap yarn; twine

kıpırda|(n)mak move slightly, vibrate; **~tı** slight quiver

kıp|kırmızı, ~kızıl bright red

kır. 1. *n.* country, wilderness; **2.** *adj.* grey

kıraathane reading room,

coffee-house
kıraç parched, sterile
kırağı white frost
kıral king; **~içe** queen; **~lık** kingdom, kingship
kırat carat; value
kırba water-skin, leatherbottle
kırbaç whip; **~lamak** v/t whip
kırç hoar-frost, rime
kırçıl sprinkled with grey
kırgın disappointed
kırık. 1. adj. broken, cracked; **2.** n. fragment, splitter; **~lık** physical weariness, weakness
kırılmak break, be broken; be offended (-e by)
Kırım (yarımadası) the Crimea
kırıntı crumb, fragment
kırıtmak -e behave coquettish towards
kırk forty
kırkı shears, scissors; **~mak** v/t shear, clip
kırlangıç swallow, martin
kırma n. pleat, fold; adj. folding (gun, etc.); **~k** v/t break, split, fold, lower, destroy; **~lı** pleated
kırmızı red; **~biber** BOT red pepper
kırpık clipped; **~ıntı** clippings; **~mak** v/t clip, trim, shear; wink
kırtasiye stationery; **~cilik** selling of stationery; fig. bureaucracy, red tape
kısa short; **~ mesaj** text-mes-

sage; **~ mesaj göndermek** v/t text; **~ca** adv. shortly, briefly; **~lık** shortness; **~lmak** become short, shrink; **~ltma** abbreviation; **~ltmak** v/t shorten
kısas JUR retaliation
kısık pinched; hoarse, choked; **~lık** hoarseness
kısılmak be pinched; become hoarse
kısım part, portion, piece
kısıntı restriction
kısır barren, sterile; **~laştırmak** v/t render sterile; **~lık** sterility
kısıt JUR putting under restraint
kıskaç pincers; pair of folding steps
kıskanç jealous, envious; **~lık** jealousy, envy
kıskanmak envy, grudge (-den -i so. sth.)
kısmak v/t pinch, cut down, diminish
kısm|en adv. partly, partially; **~et** destiny, lot, fate; **~î** partial
kısrak mare
kıstırmak v/t cause to be pinched, crush
kış winter; **~ lastiği** winter tyre; **~ın** adv. in the winter
kışkırt|ıcı inciter, provoker; **~mak** v/t incite, excite
kışla MIL barracks; **~k** winter quarters; **~mak** pass the winter
kışlık suitable for the winter

kıta continent; MIL detachment

kıtık *n.* tow

kıtır maize grains cracked over a fire, popcorn; **~damak** *v/i* crack(le)

kıt|laşmak become scarce; **~lık** scarcity, dearth

kıvanç pleasure, joy; **~mak** be proud (ile of)

kıvılcım spark

kıvır|cık curly, crisp; **~t** *v/t* curl, twist, coil

kıvr|ak brisk, alert; **~anmak** writhe (*-den* with); **~ılmak** *v/i* curl up, twist about; **~ım** twist; fold

kıyafet appearance; dress

kıyamet REL Resurrection of the Dead; tumult

kıyas comparison

kıyı edge, shore, bank

kıy|ık, ~ımlı minced, chopped up; **~ma** minced meat; **~mak** *-i* mince, chop up; *-e* sacrifice; do an injury to

kıymet value, price, esteem; **~li** valuable, precious; **~siz** worthless

kıymık splinter

kız girl, daughter; virgin; **~ kardeş** sister

kızak sledge, slide

kızamık MED measles

kızar|mak turn red, blush; be roasted; **~tma** roasted, roast meat; **~tmak** *v/t* roast, grill

kızdırmak *v/t* heat, anger, annoy

kızgın hot; angry, excited;

~lık heat, excitement

kızıl red; 2ay POL Red Crescent; **~cık** BOT cornelian cherry

kızışmak get angry, excited

kızlık maidenhood, virginity; **~ adı** maiden name

kızmak get hot; *-e* be angry with

ki that, in order that; who **-ki** (*-kü*) in; of; **Türkiyede'ki İngilizler** the English in Turkey; **bugünkü Türkiye** Turkey of to-day

kibar noble, rich; **~lık** gentility, nobility

kibir pride, haughtiness; **~lenmek** be proud *or* haughty; **~li** proud, haughty

kibrit CHEM sulphur; match

kifayet sufficiency; **~ etm.** be contented (ile with); **~li** adequate

kil clay

kiler store-room; pantry

kilim woven matting, kilim

kilise church

kilit lock; **~lemek** *v/t* lock; **~li** furnished with a lock; locked

kiliz BOT reed

kilo|(gram) kilogram(me); **~metre** kilometre; **~vat** kilowatt

kils limestone

kim who?; whoever

kimlik identity; **~ cüzdanı** identity card

kimse someone, anyone; **~siz** without relations *or* friends

kimy|a chemistry; **~ager** chemist; **~evi** chemical

kimyon BOT cummin

kin malice, grudge, hatred; **~ beslemek** nourish a grudge

kinaye allusion, hint

kinin MED quinine

kip GR form, voice

kir dirt

kira hire, rent; **~ya vermek** v/t let; **~cı** tenant; **~lamak** v/t rent, hire; **~lık** for hire, to let

kiraz BOT cherry

kireç lime

kiremit tile

kiriş violine string; rafter

kir|lemek v/t dirty, soil; **~len-mek** become dirty; **~letmek** v/t dirty, soil; **~li** dirty, soiled

kirpi ZOO hedgehog

kirpik eyelash

kişi person, human being; one; **~lik** special to ... persons; personality; **~sel** personal

kişneme neigh

kitabe inscription; **~t** art of writing, style

kitabevi bookshop

kitap book; **~çı** bookseller; **~lık** library

kit|lemek v/t lock; **~li** locked

klakson motor horn

klasik classic, classical

klasör file

klavye keyboard

kliring ECON clearing

klinik clinical hospital

klişe cliché (a. fig.)

klon clone; **~lama** cloning;

~lamak clone

klor CHEM chlorium

klüp club

koalisyon POL coalition

koca. 1. husband; **2.** large, great; old; **~başı** village headman; **~lı** having a husband; **~(l)mak** grow old; **~man** huge, enormous; **~sız** unmarried; widow

koç ram

koçan corncob, stump; heart *of a vegetable*

kodeks official list of pharmaceutical formulas

kof hollow, rotten; stupid

koğuş dormitory

kok coke

kok|ak smelling, fetid; **~la-mak** v/t smell; **~mak** v/i smell, stink; **~muş** putrid, rotten, *fig.* lazy, dirty

kokoroz BOT ear of maize; maize plant

kokoz *sl.* poor, hard up

kokteyl cocktail

koku smell, scent; *-in* **~sunu almak** perceive the smell of; **~lu** having a special smell, perfumed; **~suz** having no smell

kol arm, foreleg; wing, branch; TECH handle, bar; **~ saati** wrist watch

kola starch; **~lamak** v/t starch and press; **~lı** starched

kolan band, belt, girth

kolay easy; **~laştırmak** v/t make easy, facilitate; **~lık** easiness; means

kolej collage
koleksiyon collection
kolektif collective; ~ **ortaklık** (*or* **şirket**) private firm
kolektivizm collectivism
kolera MED cholera
koli parcel
kol|lamak v/t search, keep under observation; ~**luk** cuff
Kolonya Cologne; ~ **suyu** Eau-de-Cologne
kolordu army corps
koltuk armpit; arm-chair; ~ **değneği** crutch; ~**çu** old-clothes man; ~**lu** having arms (*chair*)
kombin|a ECON combine, factories *pl.*; ~**e** combined
komedi comedy
komik comic; ridiculous
komiser superintendent of police
komisyon commission; ~**cu** commission-agent
komit|a a secret society; ~**e** committee
komodin bed-side table
kompartıman compartment
komplike complicated, complex
komplo plot, conspiracy
komposto stewed fruit
komşu neighbour; ~**luk** being a neighbour
komuta command
komutan MIL commander, commandant; ~**lık** command, authority
komüni|st communist; ~**zm** communism

konak halting-place, stage; mansion, government house; ~**lamak** stay for the night
konca bud
konç leg *of a boot or stocking*
kondoktor, kondüktör conductor
konferans lecture; POL conference; ~ **vermek** give a lecture
konfor comfort
kongre congress
koni cone; ~**k** conic
konmak -*e* be placed on; stop during night at; camp in; be added to
konser concert
konserv|atuvar MUS conservatory; ~**e** canned food; can
konsey POL council
konsolos consul; ~**luk** consulate
kont count
kontenjan ECON quota
kontes countess
kontrat(o) contract
kontrol control; ~ **etm.** v/t control
konu subject, matter, theme; ~**k** guest; ~**ksever** hospitable; ~**lmak** -*e* be put, placed in
konuş|ma lecture; talk; ~**mak** talk (-*i* **ile** about *sth.* with *so.*); ~**ulmak** be discussed (**ile** with)
konut residence, house
kooperatif ECON co-operative (organization); ~**çilik** co-op-

erative system

koparmak v/t pluck, break off

kopça hook-and-eye; **~lamak**
v/t fasten with hook-and-eye

kopmak v/i break in two;
break out

kopya, kopye copy; **~** etm.
v/t, -in **~sını** (**~sini**) çıkarmak copy

kor¹ MIL army corps

kor² ember; redhot cinder

koramiral NAUT vice admiral

kord|ele ribbon; **~on** cord,
cordon

korgeneral MIL lieutenant
general

koridor corridor

korkak timid; coward; **~lık**
cowardice; timidity

korkmak -den be afraid of,
fear

korku fear, alarm; **~lu** fright-
ening, dangerous; **~luk**
scare-crow; banister; **~nç**
terrible; **~suz** fearless;
~tmak v/t frighten, threaten

korna horn of a car, atc.

korner corner (football)

koro MUS chorus

korsa, korse corset

kort tennis court

koru small wood; **~cu** forest
watchman

koru|mak v/t defend, watch
over; **~nma** defence; **~nmak**
-den defend oneself against,
avoid; **~yucu** defender

koskoca enormous

koş|mak v/i run; v/t harness,
put to work; **~turmak** v/t

cause to run, dispatch; **~u**
race; **~ucu** runner

koşul condition, stipulation

kota ECON quota

kotra NAUT cutter

kova bucket; **~lamak** v/t pursue

kovan hive; cartridge-case

kovmak v/t drive away, repel,
persecute

kovuk hollow, cavity

kovuşturmak v/t JUR prose-
cute

koy GEO small bay

ko(y)mak v/t put, place (-e
in), add (-e to); **yoluna ~**
v/t put right, set going

koyu thick, dense; dark; **~laş-
mak** become dense or dark;
~luk density; depth of colour

koyun¹ sheep

koyun² bosom

koy(u)vermek v/t let go

koz BOT walnut

koza cocoon

koza(la)k cone of a tree

kozmetik cosmetics

köçek ZOO camel foal; boy
dancer

köfte meat ball

köhne old, worn, antiquated

kök root, base; origin; -in
~ünden koparmak v/t eradicate; -in **~ünü kurutmak** ex-
terminate; **~lemek** v/t up-
root; **~lenmek, ~leşmek**
take root; **~lü** having roots,
rooted

köle slave; **~lik** servitude

kömür charcoal; coal; **~ ocağı** coal-mine; **~cü** charcoal burner; coal-dealer; **~leşmek** v/i char, carbonize; **~lük** coal-cellar; NAUT bunker

köpek dog

köprü bridge

köpü|k froth, foam; **~rmek** v/i froth, foam

kör blind; **~bağırsak** ANAT appendix

körfez GEO gulf

kör|lenmek, ~leşmek become blind, blunt; **~leştirmek, ~letmek** v/t blind; blunt; **~lük** blindness, bluntness

körpe fresh, tender

körük bellows; **~lemek** v/t fan with bellows

köse with no beard

kösele stout leather

kösnü lust

köstebek ZOO mole

köstek fetter, hobble

köşe corner, angle; **~ başı** street-corner; **~bent** TECH angle-iron; **~li** having corners *or* angles

köşk pavillon, summerhouse

kötü bad; **~ye kullanmak** v/t misuse; take advantage of; **~leşmek** become bad; **~lük** badness; **~msemek** v/t think ill of; **~mser** pessimistic

kötürüm paralysed, crippled; **~lük** paralysis

köy village; **~lü** peasant, fellow villager

kral, ~içe, ~lık s. kıral, kıraliçe, kırallık

kramp MED cramp, convulsion

krank TECH crank; **~ mili** crank-shaft

krater GEO crater

kravat tie

kredi credit

krem cosmetic cream; **~a** cream *of milk*; whipped cream; **~şanti(yi)** whipped cream

kriko TECH lifting-jack

kriz crisis

kroki sketch

krom CHEM chromium

kruvazör NAUT cruiser

kuaför s. **kuvaför**

kubbe dome, cupola

kucak breast, embrace; lap; **~lamak** v/t embrace; include

kudret power, strength; **~li** powerful; **~siz** powerless, incapable

kudu|rmak go mad; **~z** MED hydrophobia, rabies

Kudüs Jerusalem

kuğu ZOO swan

kukla doll; puppet

kuku ZOO cuckoo

kukulete hood, cowl

kul slave, creature

kulaç fathom

kulak ear; **~ vermek** listen (*-e* to); **~ memesi** lobe *of the ear*; **~lık** TECH earpiece, earphone

kule tower, turret

kullanış method of using; **~lı**

serviceable, handy

kullanmak v/t use, employ; drive *a car, etc.*

kulluk slavery, servitude

kulp handle

kuluçka broody hen; **~ya oturmak** sit on the eggs

kulunç colic, cramp

kulübe hut, shed; MIL sentry box

kulüp s. **klüp**

kum sand; gravel (*a.* MED)

kumanda MIL command; **~n** commander

kumar gambling; **~baz** gambler; **~hane** gambling casino

kumaş tissue, fabric; cloth, texture

kumbara money-box; bomb shell

kumlu sandy, gravelly; **~k** sandy (place)

kumral light brown

kumru ZOO turtle-dove

kumsal sand-beach

kundak swaddling clothes; bundle of rags; **~çı** incendiary; **~lamak** v/t swaddle; set fire to

kundura shoe; **~cı** shoemaker

kunduz ZOO beaver

kupa¹ cup, wine-glass

kupa² hearts (*cards*)

kupkuru bone-dry

kupon coupon

kur¹ ECON rate of exchange

kur² courtship, flirtation; **~ yapmak** -*e* pay court to, flirt with

kur'a lot; **~ çekmek** draw lots

kurabiye *cake made with almonds, nuts, etc.*

kurak dry, arid; **~lık** draught

kural GR rule

Kur'an REL the Koran

kurbağa ZOO frog

kurban sacrifice; victim; **~ bayramı** REL The Moslem Festival of Sacrifices; **~ kesmek** REL kill an animal for sacrifice; **~ olayım!** I beseech you!

kurcalamak v/t scratch, rub; meddle with

kurdela s. **kordele**

kuriye courier

kurmak v/t set up, establish; pitch *the tent*; lay *the table*

kurmay MIL staff

kurna basin of a bath *under the tap*

kurnaz cunning, shrewd; **~lık** cunning, shrewdness

kurs¹ disk

kurs² course *of lessons, etc.*

kurşun lead; bullet; **~ kalem** lead pencil; **~î** leadcoloured

kurt¹ wolf

kurt² worm, maggot

kurtar|ılmak be saved, rescued; **~mak** v/t save, rescue

kurt|lanmak become maggoty; *fig.* become impatient; **~lu** wormy; *fig.* uneasy, fidgety

kurtul|mak -*den* escape from, be saved from, get out of; **~uş** liberation, escape

kuru dry, dried, bare; **~ fasulye** kidney beans; **~ kahve**

roasted *or* ground coffee; ~ meyva dried fruit(s)

kurul commission, committee

kurula|mak *v/t* wipe dry, dry; ~**nmak** be wiped dry, dried

kurul|mak be founded, established; *-e* settle oneself comfortably on; ~**tay** assembly, congress

kurulu established; composed (*-den* of)

kuruluk dryness

kuruluş foundation

kurum[1] soot

kurum[2] association, society

kurum[3] pose, conceit

kurumak *v/i* dry, wither up

kurum|lanmak be puffedup; ~**lu** conceited, puffedup

kuruntu strange fancy; illusion

kuruş piastre (*the 100th part of a lira*); ~**luk** being worth … piastres

kurut|maç blotter; ~**mak** *v/t* dry, cause to shrivel

kus|mak *v/t* vomit; ~**turucu** emetic

kusur defect, fault; ~**a bakmayınız!** I beg your pardon!; Excuse me!; ~**lu** defective, incomplete; ~**suz** without defect; complete

kuş bird

kuşa|k sash, girdle; ~**nmak** *v/t* put on, gird on; ~**tmak** *v/t* surround; besiege

kuşbaşı *adj.* in small pieces (*meat, etc.*)

kuşet couchette, bed

kuşkonmaz BOT asparagus

kuşku suspicion, nervousness; ~**lanmak** feel nervous *or* suspicious

kuştüyü feather

kut luck, prosperity; ~**lamak** *v/t* celebrate *sth.*; congratulate *so.*; ~**lanmak** be celebrated; ~**lu** lucky, happy; ~**lulamak** *v/t* offer congratulations to *so.*

kuts|al, ~**î** sacred; ~**allık**, ~**iyet** sanctity

kutu box, case

kutup GEO pole; ~ **yıldızı** ASTR Pole-Star

ku(v)aför ladies' hairdresser

kuvve potency, faculty; strength

kuvvet strength, force, power; ~**ten düşmek** weaken, lose strength; ~**lendirmek** *v/t* strengthen; ~**lenmek** become strong; ~**li** strong, powerful; ~**siz** weak

kuyruk tail; queue; ~**ta beklemek** stand in line

kuyruklu having a tail; ~ **piyano** MUS grand piano; ~ **yıldız** ASTR comet

kuytu snug, hidden, remote

kuyu well, pit, borehole

kuyumcu jeweller, goldsmith

kuzen male cousin

kuzey north

kuzgun ZOO raven

kuzin female cousin

kuzu lamb; ~**m** my dear; ~**dişi** milk-tooth

kübik 98

kübik cubic

küçük small, young; ~**ayı** ASTR Ursa minor

küçül|mek become small, be reduced; ~**tme** GR diminutive; ~**tmek** v/t diminish, reduce

küçümsemek v/t belittle

küf mould, mouldiness; ~ **bağlamak**, ~ **tutmak** become mouldy

küfe large basket

küf|lenmek turn mouldy; fig. become out-of-date; ~**lü** mouldy; out-of-date

küfretmek -e curse, blaspheme

küfür unbelief, blasphemy

kükremek foam with rage; roar (lion)

kükürt CHEM sulphur; ~**lü** sulphurous

kül¹ the whole, all

kül² ashes; ~ **etm.** v/t reduce to ashes; ruin

külâh conical hat; anything conical; trick, deceit

külçe metal ingot, heap

külek tub with handles

külfet trouble, inconvenience; ~**li** troublesome, laborious; ~**siz** easy

külhan stoke-hold of a bath; ~**beyi** rowdy, idle youngster

külliyet totality, entirety; ~**li** abundant

küllü containing ashes

külot riding-breeches pl.; knickers pl.; ~**lu çorap** tights pl.

külrengi ash-coloured

kültive etm. v/t cultivate

kültür culture; ~**el** cultural; ~**lü** civilized, educated

kümbet ARCH cupola, dome

küme heap, mass; hut, hide

kümes poultry-house, coop

künde fetter, hobble

künk earthenware water-pipe

künye personel data

küp¹ large earthenware jar

küp² cube

küpe ear-ring; ANAT dewlap

kür health cure

kürdan tooth-pick

Kürdistan Kurdistan

küre¹ globe, sphere

küre² furnace

kürek shovel; oar; ~ **çekmek** row; ~ **kemiği** ANAT shoulderblade

küre(le)mek v/t clear away, shovel up

küresel spherical; global; ~ **ısınma** global warming; ~**leşme** ECON globalization

kürk fur; fur-coat; ~**lü** of fur, adorned with fur

kürsü reading-stand, pulpit; professorial chair

Kürt Kurd; ~**çe** Kurdish (language)

küskü TECH crow-bar; iron wedge

küskün disgruntled; ~**lük** vexation

küsmek -e be offended with

küstah insolent; ~**lık** insolence

küt adj. blunt, not pointed; n.

the noise of knocking on a door, etc.
kütle heap, block, mass
kütük tree-stump; baulk; log;

ledger, register
kütüphane library
kütürdemek v/i crash, crunch
küvet basin, sink; bathtub

L

laboratuvar laboratory
lacivert lapis-lazuli; darkblue
laf word, talk; empty words, boasting; **~ atmak** -*e* make insinuating remarks to
lağım underground tunnel; sewer; **~la atmak** v/t blast
lahana BOT cabbage
lâhika appendix, additional note
lahit tomb
lahmacun *kind of meat pizza*
lahza instant, moment
lakap cognomen; nickname
lake lacquered
lakırdı word, talk, gossip
lâkin but; nevertheless
lâl *n.*, *adj.* ruby
lâle BOT tulip
lamba cornice, mortise; lamp
lânet curse, imprecation; damnable; **~ okumak** swear and curse; **~lemek** v/t curse
lap flop!, flap!
lapa mush, pulp
lastik *adj.* of rubber; *n.* rubber; galoshes; tyre; **~li** made of rubber; elastic
lata lath
latarna MUS barrel-organ

latif fine, slender, elegant
latife joke, witticism; **~ci** fond of making jokes
Latin Latin; **~ce** Latin (*language*)
lâubali free-and-easy, careless
lav GEO lava
lavabo hand-basin
lavanta lavender-water
lavta[1] MUS lute
lavta[2] MED obstetric forceps; doctor, mid-wife
lâyık -*e* suitable for, worthy
lâyiha JUR explanatory document, bill
layık lay, secular; **~lik** secularism
lâzım -*e* necessary for; requisite
leblebi roasted chick-peas
leğen bowl, basin
Leh Pole; Polish
leh- in favour of, for; **-*in* ~*in de* (~*ine*) olm.** be in favour of
lehçe[1] dialect; language
Lehçe[2] Polish (*language*)
lehim solder; **~lemek** v/t solder; **~li** soldered
Leh|istan Poland; **~li** Polish; Pole

leke stain, mark, spot (*a. fig.*);
~ **etm.** *v/t* stain; **~lemek** *v/t*
stain; try to dishonour; **~li**
spotted, stained; **~siz** spot-
less, immaculate

lenf(a) lymph

lenger large deep dish; NAUT
anchor

leş carcass

letafet charm, grace

letarji lethargy

Levanten Levantine

levazım(at) *pl.* materials,
supplies, provisions

levha signboard

levrek ZOO sea bass

leylak BOT lilac

leylek ZOO stork

lezzet taste, flavour; pleasure; **~li** pleasant to the taste;
delightful; **~siz** tasteless

liberal liberal; **~izm** liberal-
ism

libre pound (*500 gramme*)

lider POL leader; **~lik** leadership

lif fibre; loofah

lig league, union

liman harbour

limon lemon; **~ata** lemonade;
~lu flavoured with lemon

linç lynching

linyit lignite

liposuction MED liposuction

lira *Turkish* lira; **~lık** of the
value of ... liras

liret *Italian* lira

lisan language, tongue

lisans diploma; license

lise high-school

liste list

litre litre (*1.76 pint*); **~lik** holding ... litres

liyakat merit, suitability; **~li**
able, qualified; **~siz** unqual-
ified

lobut club

loca box *at the theatre, etc.*;
Masonic lodge

lodos south-west wind

loğusa woman after childbirth; **~lık** childbed

lojman lodging *for workers
and employees*

lokanta restaurant; **~cı** restaurant keeper

lokavt ECON lock-out

lokma mouthful, morsel; kind
of sweet fritter

lokomotif locomotive, engine

lokum Turkish delight

lonca guild

Londra London

lop round and soft; **~ yumurta**
hard-boiled egg

lor cheese *of goat's milk*

lort lord; **2lar Kamarası** the
House of Lords

lostra shoe polish

losyon lotion; Eau-de-Cologne

loş dark, gloomy, dim

lök awkward, clumsy

lökün putty

lûgat word; dictionary

lütf|en please!, **~etmek** *v/t*
have the kindness of *-ing*; allow

lûtuf kindness, favour; **~kâr**

kind, gratious
Lübnan Lebanon
lüfer zoo bluefish
lügat s. lûgat
lüks n. luxury; adj. luxurious
Lüksemburg Luxemburg
lüle curl, fold, paper-cone; ~taşi meerschaum

lüp: ~e konmak get something gratis
lütf|en, ~etmek s. lûtfen, lûtfetmek
lütuf, ~kâr s. lûtuf, lûtufkâr
lüzum necessity, need; ~lu necessary, needed; ~suz unnecessary, useless

M

maada -den besides, except; bundan ~ besides this, furthermore
maalesef unfortunately, with regret
maarif education, public instruction
maaş salary; allowance
mabet place of worship, temple
mabeyin interval; relation; mabeynimizde between us
mablak spatula; putty knife
Macar Hungarian; ~ca Hungarian (language); ~istan Hungary
macera event; adventure; ~cı, ~perest adventurous, adventurer
macun putty; paste
maç match
maça spade at cards
maçuna TECH steam-crane
madalya medal
madd|e matter, substance, material; paragraph; ~î adj. material
madem(ki) while, since, as

maden mine; mineral; metal; ~ kömürü coal, pitcoal; ~ ocağı mine; ~ suyu mineral water; ~î metallic, mineral
madrabaz ECON middleman
madun adj., n. subordinate
mafiş a kind of very light fritter
mafsal joint
magazin magazine
magneti|k magnetic; ~zma magnetism
mağara cave, pit
mağaza large store; storehouse
mağdur wronged, victim
mağlubiyet defeat
mağlup defeated; ~ etm. v/t defeat
mağrur proud (-e of); conceited
mahalle quarter of a town
mahallebi sweet dish made with rice and milk
mahallî local
maharet skill, proficiency
mahcubiyet bashfulness, modesty

mahcup

mahcup ashamed, bashful
mahdut limited; definite
mahfaza case, box
mahfil place of resort, club; REL private pew in a mosque
mahfuz protected, looked after
mahir skilful
mahiyet reality; nature, character
mahkeme JUR court of justice
mahkûm sentenced, subject (-e to); ~ **etm.** v/t sentence, condemn; **~iyet** condemnation, sentence
mahluk created; creature
mahlut mixed
mahmuz spur; NAUT ram of a ship; **~lamak** v/t spur
mahpus imprisoned
mahreç outlet; origin, source
mahrem confidential, secret
mahrukat pl. combustibles; fuel sg.
mahrum deprived (-den of)
mahrut cone; **~î** conical
mahsul harvest, produce; crop; **~dar** productive, fertile
mahsus -e special, peculiar to, reserved for
mahun mahogany
mahv|edici destroying, crushing; **~etmek** v/t destroy, abolish; **~olmak** be destroyed, ruined
mahya lights strung between minarets during Ramazan to form words or pictures
mahzen underground storehouse, cellar
mahzur objection, inconvenience
maişet means of subsistence, livelihood
maiyet suite, following
majör MUS major
makale article in a newspaper, etc.
makam place, abode; office
makara TECH pulley, reel spule
makarna macaroni
makas scissors, shears pl.; TECH switch, points; **~çı** pointsman; **~tar** cutter-out
makbul accepted; liked
makbuz receipt for payment, etc.
makine machine; engine; ~ **inşaatı**, ~ **yapımı** mechanical engineering; **~li** fitted with a machine; **~li tüfek** machine-gun
makinist engin-driver; mechanic
maksat aim, purpose
maksure private pew in a mosque
maktu cut off; fixed (price)
maktul killed
makul reasonable, wise
makyaj make-up
mal property, possession; wealth, goods; ~ **sahibi** owner
malarya MED malaria
mali financial; ♀ **İşler Müdürü** CFO (chief financial officer)
malik olm. -e possess, own

maliye finance; Ձ **Bakanlığı**
(**Bakanı**) Ministry (Minister) of Finance; ~cı financier; economist

Malta Malta; Ձ **eriği** BOT loquat

maltız¹ brazier

Maltız² *n.* Maltese

malul ill; invalid

malum known; ~unuzdur ki
you know that

malumat information, knowledge; ~ vermek -*e* inform *so.*
(hakkında of *sth.*); ~ım yok I
have no knowledge; ~lı
learned, informed

malzeme necessaries *pl.*; materials

mamafih nevertheless

mamul made (-*den* of); manufactured; ~ât *pl.* manufactures, goods

mamur prosperous, flourishing

mana meaning, sense; ~lı significant; allusive; ~sız
senseless, without significance

manastır monastery

manav fruiterer

manda¹ ZOO water buffalo

manda² POL mandate

mandal latch; catch; clothes
peg; tuning peg *of a violin
etc.*

mandalina BOT mandarin

mandallamak *v/t* shut with a
latch; hang up with a peg

mandıra small dairy

manevî moral, spiritual

manevyat morale

manevra manoeuvre(s); trick

manga MIL squad; NAUT mess

mangal brazier; ~ kömürü
charcoal

mangan(ez) CHEM manganese

mani obstacle, impediment; ~
olm. -*e* prevent, hinder

mânia obstacle, difficulty; ~lı
koşu hurdle race

manifatura textiles *pl.*; ~cı
draper

manikür manicure

manivela TECH lever, crank

manken mannequin; tailor's
dummy

manolya BOT magnolia

mansap GEO river-mouth

mantar BOT mushroom; cork

mantık logic; ~î logical

manto woman's cloak, mantle

manya mania

manzara view, panorama; ~lı
having a fine view

manzum written in rhyme
and metric; ~e row, series;
poem

marangoz joiner, cabinet-maker; ~luk joinery, cabinet-making

mareşal MIL Marshal

margarin margarine

marifet knowlege, skill; ~iyle
by means of

marka mark, trademark; konulan ~ trademark; ~lı
trade-marked

marksizm Marxism

marmelat jam; marmalade
maroken Morocco leather
marş MUS march; starter (auto)
marşandiz goods train
mart March (month)
martaval lie; ~ atmak talk nonsense
martı ZOO gull
maruf well known
maruz exposed (-e to); ~ kalmak -e be exposed to
marya ZOO female animal
masa table, desk; ~ örtüsü table-cloth; ~ tenisi table tennis, ping-pong
masaj massage
masal story, tale, myth
maskara adj. funny; ridiculous; n. buffoon; mask; ~lık buffoonery; shame
maske mask; ~li masked
maslahat business, affair; ~güzar POL chargé d'affaires
maslak stone trough
mason Freemason; ~luk Freemasonry
masraf expense; ~lı expensive
mastar GR infinitive
masum innocent
masun guarded, safe; ~iyet inviolability, immunity
maşa tongs; pincers
maşallah wonderful!; What wonders God hath willed!
mat¹ matt, faint
mat² check-mate
matara waterbottle
matbaa printing-office; ~cı printer
matbu printed; ~a(t) printed matter
matem mourning
matematik mathematics
materyalizm materialism
matine THEA matinée
matkap drill
matlubat pl. demands, debts due
matlup n. debt due; adj. demanded
matrah category of taxed goods, standard
matuf directed, aiming (-e at)
mavi blue; ~msi, ~mtırak bluish
mav(u)na barge, lighter
maya ferment, yeast; fig. essence, origin; ~lanmak ferment; ~lı fermented, leavened
maydanoz BOT parsley
mayhoş slightly acid, bittersweet
mayın MIL floating mine
mayıs May (month); ~ böceği ZOO cock chafer
maymun ZOO monkey; ~cuk TECH picklock
mayo bathing suit
mayonez mayonnaise
mazbata official report, protocol, minutes pl.
mazgal embrasure, loophole
mazı BOT gall-nut; arbor vitae
mazi past, bygone; the past
mazlum oppressed, suffered injure
maznun accused, suspected

memeliler

(ile of)

mazot Diesel oil

mazur excused, excusable; ~ **görmek, ~ tutmak** v/t hold excused

meal meaning, purport

meblağ sum, amount

mebni -e based on; because of

mebus POL deputy, member of parliament

mebzul abundant, lavish

mecal power, ability; **~siz** powerless, exhausted

mecaz metaphor, figurative expression; **~î** figurative, metaphorical

mecbur compelled; ~ **olm.** -e be compelled to; ~ **etm.** v/t compel; **~î** obligatory, forced; **~iyet** compulsion, obligation

meccan|en adv. gratis; **~î** adj. free, gratis

meclis sitting; assembly, council

mecmua review, periodical

mecnun mad, insane

mecra watercourse, canal

meçhul unknown

meddah story-teller

meddücezir GEO ebb and flow, tide

medenî civilised, civil; ~ **hal** state of being married or unmarried; ~ **kanun** JUR civil law; ~ **nikâh** civil marriage

medeniyet civilisation; **~siz** uncivilised

medih praise

medrese REL Moslem theological school

mefhum sense; concept, idea

mefkûre ideal

mefruş furnished; **~at** pl. furniture

meftun -e madly in love with, admiring

meğer but, however, only; **~ki** unless; **~se** s. **meğer**

mehaz source, authority of a book

mehenk touchstone; test

Mehmetçik the Turkish 'Tommy'

mehtap moonlight

mekani|k mechanics; **~zma** mechanism

mekkâre pack-animal

mektep school

mektup letter; **~laşmak** correspond by letter (ile with)

mekûlât pl. comestibles, provisions

melankoli n. melancholy; **~k** adj. melancholy, gloomy

melek angel

melemek v/i bleat

melez cross-breed, half-bred; mixed; **~leme** BOT cross-breeding

melfuf enclosed (-e in)

melhem ointment, salve

melodi melody

memba spring; source, origin

meme teat, nipple, udder; TECH burner, nozzle; ~ **vermek** -e nurse; **~den kesmek** v/t wean; **~liler** pl. ZOO mammals

memleha salt-pit, saltworks
memleket country; home district; ~**li** inhabitant, fellow countryman
memnu forbidden
memnun pleased, glad (-*den* at); ~ **etm.** *v/t* please, make happy
memnuniyet pleasure, gratitude; ~**le** *adv.* gladly, with pleasure
memur official, employee; ~**iyet** official post, duty, appointment; quality and duties of an official
mendil handkerchief
mendirek NAUT artificial harbour
menekşe BOT violet
menetmek *v/t* prevent, forbid
menfaat use, advantage, profit; ~**li** useful, advantageous; ~**perest** self-seeking
menfez hole; vent
menfi exiled, banished; negative
mengene press, clamp, vice
menkul transported; ~**at** *pl.* movables
mensucat *pl.* textiles
mensup -*e* related to, connected with; ~ **olm.** -*e* belong to
menşe place of origin
menteşe hinge
menzil halting-place, stage; range *of a gun*
mera pasture
merak curiosity, whim, great interest; ~ **etm.** -*i* be anxious

about; be curious about; -*e* be interested in; ~**lı** curious, interested (-*e* in); ~**sız** uninterested, indifferent
meram desire, intention
merasim *pl.* ceremonies
merbut -*e* attached to; ~**iyet** dependence
mercan ZOO coral
mercek PHOT lense
merci reference, competent authority
mercimek BOT lentil
merdane TECH cylinder, roller
merdiven ladder, steps, stairs
merhaba Good-day!, hello!
merhale day's journey, stage
merhamet mercy, pity; ~ **etm.** -*e* pity; ~**li** merciful, tender-hearted; ~**siz** merciless, cruel; ~**sizlik** cruelness
merhum deceased
mer'i JUR in force
meridyen GEO meridian
Merih ASTR Mars
meriyet being in force, validity
merkep donkey
merkez centre; ~**cilik** centralization; ~**kaç** centrifugal; ~**lenmek** be concentrated, centralized (-*e* in)
Merkür ASTR Mercury
mermer marble
mermi projectile, missile
merserize CHEM mercerized
mersi thank you!
mersin BOT myrtle
mert manly, brave
mertebe degree, rank, grade

mertlik manliness, courage
mesafe distance, space
mesaha measurement, measure *of land*
mesai pl. efforts, pains; ~ **saatleri** pl. working hours
mesaj message
mesam|at pl. pores; ~**e** pore
mescit small mosque
mesela adv. for instance, for example
mesele question, problem
meshetmek v/t stroke, rub lightly
Mesih REL the Messiah; **2î** Christian
mesken dwelling
meskûkât pl. coins
meskûn inhabited
meslek career, profession; ~**î** professional; ~**siz** without a career; unprincipled; ~**taş** colleague
messetmek v/t occur, rise; -*e* touch
mest¹ drunk
mest² light soleless boot
mesul responsible, answerable (-*den* for)
mesuliyet responsibility; ~**sigortası** liability insurance
meşakkat hardship, trouble
meşale torch
meşe BOT oak
meşgul busy; occupied; ~ **etm.** v/t keep busy, engage; ~**iyet** occupation, work
meşhur famous, well-known
meşhut JUR witnessed
meşin leather

meşrep character
meşru JUR legal, legitimate
meşrubat pl. drinks
meşrutiyet POL constitutional government
met GEO high-tide
meta merchandise, good
metal metal
metanet firmness, solidity
meteor ASTR meteor; ~**oloji** meteorology
methal entrance; beginning
methetmek v/t praise
metin¹ text
metin² solid, firm
metod method, system
metre metre
metres mistress, kept woman
metris MIL entrenchment
metro underground railway, subway; ~**polit** REL Greek Metropolitan
metruk left, abandoned
mevcudiyet existence, presence
mevcut existing, present
mevduat pl. ECON deposits
mevki place, position; class *on a train, etc.*
mevkuf arrested, detained
mevlit, mevlut REL the birthday of the Prophet Mohammed
mevsim season; ~**lik** seasonal; ~**siz** untimely, out of place
mevsuk reliable, authentic
mevzi place, position
mevzu subject, proposition; ~**(u)bahis** subject under dis-

cussion, theme

meyan middle; **bu ~da** among them

meydan open space, public square, ground; opportunity; **~ okumak** -e challenge; **~a çıkarmak** v/t expose to view, publish, discover; **~a çıkmak** come forth, show oneself; **~a getirmek** v/t form, create, bring into view; **~a koymak** v/t produce, bring forward

meyhane wine-shop, tavern

meyil inclination, slope; **~li** inclined (-e towards)

meyletmek be inclined; -e have a liking for

meyus hopeless, despairng

meyve fruit; **(~li)** made of fruit; **~ suyu** fruit-juice

meyyal -e inclined towards, fond of

meyzin s. müezzin

mezar grave, tomb; **~cı** grave-digger; **~lık** cemetery

mezat ECON auction

mezbaha slaughterhouse

meze snack, appetizer

mezhep REL creed; school of thought

meziyet excellence, virtue; talent; value

mezkûr mentioned, aforesaid

mezun -den graduate of; excused from; on leave; authorized; **~ olm.** -den graduated from; **~iyet** leave; authorization

mı s. mi

mıh nail; **~lamak** nail v/t (-e on)

mıknatıs magnet; **~lamak** v/t magnetize

mıntaka zone, district

mırıl|da(n)mak mutter, grumble; **~tı** muttering, grumbling

Mısır Egypt; **2** BOT maize; **~lı** Egyptian

mıskala burnisher

mısra line of poetry

mızıka MUS band; toy trumpet; mouth-organ

mızmız hesitant; querulous

mızrak lance

mi, mı, mu, mü interrogative particle, sometimes adding emphasis

mide ANAT stomach

midye ZOO mussel

miğfer helmet

mihanikî mechanical (a. fig.)

mihmandar host; **~lık** hospitality

mihnet trouble, affliction

mihrak PHYS focus

mihrap niche in a mosque indicating the direction of Mecca

mihver pivot, axis, axle

mikâp cube

mikro|çip micro chip; **~fon** microphone; **~p** microbe; **~skop** microscope

miktar quantity, amount

mikyas measuring instrument; scale

mil¹ silt

mil² pin, peg, pivot

mil³ GEO mile

milâdî pertaining to the birth of Christ, A.D.

milât REL birth of Christ

mili|gram milligram; ~metre millimetre

millet nation; people; ~ meclisi POL national assembly; ~lerarası international; ~vekili POL deputy

millî national; ~ bayram national holiday

milliyet nationality; ~çi nationalist; ~çilik nationalism

milyar milliard; *Am.* billion, a thousand million

milyon million; ~er millionaire

mimar architect; ~lık architecture

mimber pulpit *in a mosque*

minare minaret

minder mattress

mine enamel; dial *of a clock*; ~lemek *v/t* enamel

mineral mineral

mini|k small and sweet; ~mini very small, tiny

minkale MATH protractor

minnet obligation, taunt; ~tar grateful, indebted (-*e* to)

minör MUS minor

minyatür miniature

miraç ascent to heaven; ~ gecesi REL night of Mohammed's ascent to heaven

miras inheritance; ~çı heir (-*ess*)

mirî belonging to the state

misafir guest, visitor; ~hane

public guesthouse *in villages*; ~perver hospitable

misal model, precedent

misilleme JUR retortion; retaliation

misk musk

miskin poor, wretched; abject; MED leprous; ~ hastalığı leprosy

misli ... times as much (*or* many)

misyon mission; ~er missionary

miting meeting

miyavlamak miaow

miyop MED short-sighted

mizaç temperament, disposition

mizah jest, joke, humour; ~çı humorist

mobilya furniture

moda fashion

model pattern, model

modern modern

mola rest, pause; ~ vermek *v/i* rest, pause

molekül PHYS molecule

moloz rough stone; rubble

monarşi monarchy

monoton monotonous

montaj TECH mounting, fitting

mor violet, purple; ~armak become bruised

morfin MED morphine

morg mortuary

Mosko|f Russian; ~va Moscow

mostra pattern, sample

motel motel

motif MUS, *etc.* pattern, motif

motor motor; motorboat; **~lu** having a motor

motosiklet motor cycle

motör, ~lü s. **motor, motorlu**

mozaik mosaic-work; floor made of concrete mixed with marble splinters

mu s. **mi**

muadil equivalent (*-e* to)

muaf *-den* excused from; exempt from; **~iyet** exemption, immunity

muahede pact, treaty

muaheze censure, criticism; **~ etm.** *v/t* blame, criticize

muahhar posterior; subsequent

muamele dealing; transaction; procedure, formality; **~ etm.** *-e* treat

muamma mystery; riddle

muarız opponent; *-e* against, opposing

muasır contemporary

muaşeret social intercourse

muattal isused; idle

muavenet help, assistance; **~ etm.** *-e* help

muavin assistant

muayene inspection, examination; **~ etm.** *v/t* inspect, examine; **~hane** MED consulting-room

muayyen definite, determined

muazzam great, esteemed

mubah REL tolerated, permissible

mubayaa purchase; **~cı** ECON stockbroker

mucibince according to requirements, as necessary

mucip causing, cause, motive; **~ olm.** *v/t* cause

mucir who lets or hires out

mucize miracle, wonder

mudi ECON depositor, investor

mufassal detailed, lengthy

muğlak abstruse, obscure

muhabere correspondence by *letters*; MIL signals *pl.*

muhabir correspondent

muhaceret emigration

muhacir emigrant, refugee

muhafaza protection, preservation; **~ etm.** *v/t* protect, take care of; **~kâr** conservative; **~kârlık** conservatism

muhafız guard, defender; commander of a fort

muhakeme JUR hearing of a case, trial; judgement

muhakkak certain, without doubt

muhalefet opposition; **~ etm.** *-e* oppose, disagree with; **~ partisi** POL opposition party

muhalif *-e* opposing, contrary to

muharebe battle, war

muharip warrior, combatant

muharrik stirring up; moving

muharrir writer, editor, author

muhasara siege; **~ etm.** *v/t* besiege

muhasebe book-keeping, accountancy; **~ci** accountant

muhasım opponent

muhatap: ~ **olm.** be addressed in speach; be reproached (-e with)

muhatara danger; ~**lı** dangerous, risky

muhavere conversation; THEA dialogue

muhayyile imagination, fancy

muhbir who gives information; reporter

muhit surrounding; milieu

muhkem firm, strong, tight

muhlis sincere

muhrip NAUT destroyer

muhtaç: ~ **olm.** -e be in want, in need of

muhtar headman *of a village or quarter*; ~**iyet** autonomy; ~**lık** office of a headman

muhtasar abridged

muhtekir profiteer

muhtelif diverse, various

muhtemel possible, probable

muhterem respected, honoured

muhteşem magnificent, majestic

muhtev|a contents; ~**i** -*i* containing

muhtıra note; memorandum; ~ **defteri** note-book

mukabele reward, retaliation; confronting; ~**bilmisil** JUR retortion; retaliation

mukabil opposite, facing; -*e* in return for; **buna** ~ on the other hand; ~**inde** opposite, in return

mukadderat *pl.* destiny *sg.*

mukaddes sacred, holy

mukavele agreement, contract; ~**name** written agreement, deed; pact

mukavemet resistance, endurance; ~ **etm.** -*e* resist, endure

mukavva cardboard

mukayese comparison

mukim who dwells *or* stays; stationary

muktedir capable, powerful; ~ **olm.** -*e* be able to, capable of

multipleks multiplex (*cinema*)

mum wax; candle

mumaileyh aforementioned

mumya mummy

munis sociable; tame

muntazam regular, orderly; ~**an** *adv.* orderly, regularly

munzam extra, additional

murabaha usury; ~**cı** usurer

murabba square; squared

murahhas delegated; delegate, plenipotentiary

murakabe control, supervision; meditation

murakıp controller

murat wish, intention

musallat: ~ **etm.** -*i* -*e* bring down *sth.* upon *so.*; ~ **olm.** -*e* fall upon, infest

musannif compiler of a book; classifier

Musevî Jew, Jewish

musibet calamity, evil

musiki music

muska amulet, charm

musluk tap; spigot; ~ **taşı**
stone basin *under a tap*
muş NAUT steam launch
muşamba tarpaulin; mackintosh, waterproof
muştu good news
mut luck; happiness
mutaassıp fanatical, bigoted
mutabakat conformity,
agreement
mutabık agreeing (-*e* with)
mutaf maker of goat-hair
goods
mutat customary, habitual
muteber esteemed, of good
repute; JUR valid
mutedil moderate
mutemet reliable; fiduciary
mutfak kitchen; cuisine
mutlak absolute, autocratic;
~**a** *adv.* absolutely, certainly;
~**iyet** absolutism
mutlu lucky, fortunate
muttasıl -*e* joined to; *adv.*
continuously
muvaffak successful; ~ **olm.**
succeed
muvaffakıyet success; ~**li** successful; ~**siz** without success; ~**sizlik** lack of success,
failure
muvafık agreeable, suitable
(-*e* for)
muvakkat temporary, provisory
muvasala communication; ~**t**
arrival

muvazene(t) equilibrium,
balance
muvazzaf MIL. regular
muz BOT banana
muzaf -*e* added, appended to
muzır harmful, detrimental
muzip plaguing, tormenting;
mischievous; ~**lik** teasing;
practical joke
mü *s.* mi
mübadele exchange; barter
mübalağa exaggeration; ~
etm. exaggerate; ~**lı** exaggerated
mübarek blessed, sacred;
bountiful
mübaşir JUR process-server,
usher *of a court*
mücadele dispute, struggle
mücahit REL, *fig.* champion
mücavir neighbour(ing)
mücellit bookbinder
mücerret bare; abstract
mücevher jewel; ~**at** *pl.* jewels, jewellery
mücmel concise; summary
mücrim guilty; criminal
müdafaa defence, resistance;
~ **etm.** *v/t* defend
müdafi defender
müdahale interference, intervention; ~ **etm.** -*e* meddle
with, interfere in
müddeiumumî JUR public
prosecutor
müddet space of time, period, interval; -*diği* ~**çe** *conj.*
as long as, while
müderris teacher; professor
müdevver round, spherical;

transferred

müdür director, administrator; **~lük** directorate, head office

müebbet perpetual, for life

müellif author

müessese foundation, establishment, institution

müessir touching; effective, influential

müeyyide confirming statement; POL sanction

müezzin REL muezzin, who calls Moslems to prayer

müfettiş inspector; **~lik** inspectorship, inspectorate

müflis bankrupt, penniless

müfreze MIL detachment

müfrit excessive; extremist

müfteri slanderer, calumniator

müftü REL Mufti, expounder of Islamic law; **~lük** office and rank of a Mufti

mühendis engineer; **~lik** engineering

mühim important, urgent; **~mat** pl. ammunition sg.

mühlet respite, delay

mühtedi REL who converted to Islam

mühür seal, signet-ring; **~lemek** v/t stamp with a seal; **~lü** sealed

müjde good news

mükâfat recompense, reward; prize; **~landırmak** v/t reward, recompense

mükellef obliged, liable (ile to); **~iyet** obligation, liabili-ty

mükemmel complete, perfect, excellent

mülâhaza consideration, reflection; **~ etm.** v/t observe; consider

mülâkat meeting, interview

mülâyim suitable; gentle

mülhak -e added, annexed to; dependent on

mülk possession, property, landed property

mülkiyet possession, property; **~ zamiri** GR possessive pronoun

mülteci refugee

mümarese skill; training

mümbit fertile, productive

mümessil representative

mümeyyiz distinctive

mümkün possible; **~ olduğu kadar** as far as possible

mümtaz distinguished, privileged; autonomous

münadi herald, public crier

münakalât pl. transport, communication sg.

münakaşa dispute; **~ etm.** v/t discuss, dispute

münasebet fitness; proportion; relation, connection; opportunity; **~siz** unseemly, unreasonable

münasip suitable, proper; **~ görmek** v/t think proper, approve of

münavebe alternation, turn

münderecat pl. contents of a book, etc.

müneccim astrologer

münevver enlightened, educated

münferit separate

münhal solved; vacant

münhani bent, curved

münhasır -*e* restricted to

münzevi retiring to a solitary place; hermit

müphem vague, indefinite

müptelâ -*e* subject to, having a passion for

müracaat application; reference; ~ **etm.** -*e* refer, apply to

mürai hypocrite; ~**lik** hypocrisy

mürebbiye governess

mürekkep. 1. adj. -*den* composed of; **2.** n. ink; ~**li** inky; filled with ink

mürettebat pl. NAUT crew sg.

mürettip compositor, typesetter

mürteci POL reactionary

mürtekip corrupt, taking bribes

mürur passage, lapse of time; ~**uzaman** JUR limitation

müsaade permission; favour; ~ **etm.** v/t permit, consent to; ~ **ederseniz**, ~**nizle** with your permission, if you don't mind

müsabaka competition; race; ~**ya girmek** compete

müsademe collision, encounter

müsadere confiscation; ~ **etm.** v/t confiscate

müsait -*e* favourable to, convenient for

müsamaha indulgence, tolerance; ~ **etm.** -*e* be indulgent towards, tolerate; ~**kâr**, ~**lı** tolerant

müsavi|at equality; ~**i** equal, equivalent

müseccel officially registered; notorious

müsekkin MED sedative

müshil MED purgative

müskirat pl. intoxicants

Müslüman REL Moslem; ~**lık** the Religion of Islam; the Moslem world

müspet proved; positive

müsrif extravagant

müstahdem adj. employed; n. employee

müstahkem fortified

müstakil independent; apart

müstakim straight; upright

müstecir who rents; tenant

müstehcen obscene

müstehzi jeering, mocking

müstemleke POL colony

müstenit -*e* based on, relying on

müstesna excluded (-*den* from); exceptional

müsteşar POL councillor; undersecretary

müsvedde draft, rough copy

müşahede witnessing; observation

müşahhas personified; concrete

müşavere consultation; deliberation

müşavir counsellor

müşerref honoured
müşkül *adj.* difficult; *n.* difficulty; ~**ât** *pl.* difficulties; ~**ât çıkarmak** raise difficulties
müştak derived, derivative
müştemilât *pl.* contents; annexes, outhouses
müşterek common, joint
müşteri customer, purchaser, client
müşür MIL field-marshal
mütalaa studying, observation; opinion; ~ **etm.** *v/t* read, study
mütareke POL armistice
müteahhit contractor; purveyor
müteakıp *-i* following after; subsequent
müteallik *-e* dependent on, concerning
mütecaviz *-i* exceeding, transgressing
müteessir *-den* sorry for, regretful of; influenced by
mütehassıs specialist
mütemadiyen *adv.* continu-

ously, continually
mütenakız contradictory
mütenasip proportional, symmetrical
müteradif synonymous
mütercim translator
müteveccih *-e* turned towards, facing; ~**en** *-e adv.* in the direction of
müthiş terrible, fearful; enormous
müttefik agreeing; allied
müttehem accused, suspected (**ile** of)
müverrih historian, chronicler
müvezzi distributor; postman
müzakere discussion, conference, negotiation
müzayede ECON auction
müze museum
müzehhep gilded, gilt
müzik Western style music
müzmin chronic; ~**leşmek** become chronic

N

nabız pulse; *-in* **nabzını ölçmek** *veya* **tutmak** feel one's pulse
nacak short handled axe
nadan tactless, uneducated
nadir rare, unusual; ~**en** *adv.* rarely
nafaka livelihood; JUR alimony

nafia public works *pl.*
nafile useless, in vain
nağme tune, song
nahif thin, weak, fragile
nahiye ANAT region; POL subdistrict
nahoş unpleasant; unwell
nakarat refrain, repetition
nakd|en *adv.* in cash; ~**î** cash,

in ready money; ~i ceza JUR fine

nakıs deficient; MATH minus

nakız annulment; violation

nakil transport, removal, transfer

nakletmek v/t transport, transfer; narrate; ~i traditional; ~iyat pl. transport sg.; ~iye transport expenses pl.

nakzetmek v/t JUR annul

nal horseshoe; ~bant shoeing-smith; blacksmith; ~bur hardware dealer

nalın pattens, clogs

nallamak v/t shoe

nam name, reputation; ~ına in the name of

namaz REL the Moslem ritual prayer; ~ kılmak perform the ritual prayer; ~gâh open space devoted to prayer

nam|dar, ~lı famous, celebrated

namlu barrel of a gun, etc., blade

namus honour, good name; ~lu honourable, honest; ~suz without honour, dishonest; ~suzluk dishonesty

namzet candidate; ~lik candidacy

nane BOT mint; peppermint; ~ şekeri peppermint drop

nankör ungrateful; ~lük ingratitude

nar BOT pomegranate

narcil BOT coconut

nargile water-pipe, narghile

narh ECON officially fixed price

narin slim, slender, delicate

narkotik narcotic drug

nasbetmek v/t nominate, appoint (-e to)

nasıl how?, what sort?; ~sa in any case

nasip appointment, nomination

nasır wart, corn

nasihat advice, admonition; ~ etm. -e advise

nasip lot, share, portion; ~ olm. -e fall to one's lot

naşir publisher

natıka eloquence

natura nature, constitution

navlun NAUT freight, chartering expenses

naylon nylon

naz coquetry; whims

nazar look, regard, consideration; the evil eye; ~ı itibara almak v/t take into consideration; ~ boncuğu bead worn to avert the evil eye; ~an -e according to, with regard to; seeing that; ~î theoretical; ~iye theory

nazım versification, verse

nazır adj. -e overlooking, facing; n. POL Minister

nazik delicate; polite; courteous; ~âne adv. politely

naz|lanmak be coy; feign reluctance; ~lı coquettish, coy; reluctant

ne¹ what?, what, whatever, how; ~ güzel! how nice; ~

ise anyway; ~ **kadar** how much?; ~ **kadar zaman** how long?; ~ **var ki** but; in fact; ~ **zaman** when?

ne² not; nor; ~ ... ~ ... neither ... nor

nebat plant; ~**at bahçesi** botanical garden; ~**î** vegetable

necat salvation, safety

necefaşı rock-cristal

nedamet regret, remorse

neden for what reason?, why?; *n.* reason; ~**se** for some reason or other

nefer individual, person; MIL private

nefes breath; ~ **almak** breathe, take a breath; ~ **çekmek** take a whiff; *sl.* smoke hashish; ~ **vermek** breathe out; ~**li çalgı** MUS wind-instrument

nefis¹ soul, life, self, essence

nefis² excellent, exquisite

nefiy banishment, exile; negation

nefret aversion (*-den* for), disgust

nefrit MED nephritis

neft naphta

nefyetmek *v/t* banish

negatif negative (*a.* PHOT)

nehir river

nekes mean, stingy

nem moisture; damp; ~**lenmek** become damp; ~**letmek** *v/t* moisten; ~**li** damp, humid

Neptün ASTR Neptune

nere, ~**si** what place?; whatsoever place; ~**de** where?;

~**den** from where?; ~**ye** whither?, to what place?; ~**li** from what place?

nergis BOT narcissus

nesep family, genealogy

nesiç weaving; tissue

nesil generation; family

nesir prose

nesne thing; anything; GR object

neşe gaiety, merriment, joy; ~**lendirmek** *v/t* render merry; ~**li** merry, in good humour; ~**siz** sad, in bad humour

neşet origin

neşir publishing, publication

neşr|etmek *v/t* publish; ~**iyat** *pl.* publications

net net (*weight*); clear, distinct

netice consequence, effect, result; ~**lenmek** come to a conclusion; close (*ile* with); ~**siz** without success, results

nevi species, sort, variety

nevralji MED neuralgia

nevruz the Persian New Year's Day (*March 22nd*)

ney MUS reed, flute

neye *s.* **niye**

nezafet cleanliness

nezaket delicacy; politeness; ~**li** refined; polite; ~**siz** impolite

nezaret supervision, superintendence; Ministry; ~ **etm.** *-e* superintend, direct, inspect

nezif MED haemorrhage

nezle cold in the head; ~ **olm.**

catch a cold

nıkris MED gout

nışadır CHEM sal ammoniac; ammonia

nice how many?; many a ...; ~**lik** state, quantity

niçin why?

nida cry, shout

nifak discord, strife

nihaî final

nihayet n. end, extremity; adv. at last, finally; ~**siz** endless, infinite

nikâh betrothal, marriage ~**lı** married; ~**sız** unmarried, out of wedlock

nikbin optimistic

nikel nickel

nikotin nicotine

nilüfer BOT water-lily

nine grandmother

ninni lullaby

nirengi GEO triangulation

nisan April

nispet relation, proportion; spite; ~**en** adv. relatively; spitefully

nispî proportional; relative

nişan sign, mark; indication; scar; target; engagement; POL decoration, order; ~ **almak** -i take aim at; ~ **yüzüğü** engagement ring; ~**gâh** backsight of a gun; butt, target; ~**lı** engaged

nişasta CHEM stark

nite|kim just as; as a matter of fact; ~**le(ndir)mek** v/t qualify; ~**lik** quality

niyaz entreaty, supplication

niye why?

niyet resolve, intencion; ~ **etm.** -e, -mek ~**inde olm.** intend

niza quarrel, dispute

nizam order, regularity; system; ~**î**, ~**lı** legal; regular; ~**name** regulation; ~**sız** in disorder, illegal

Noel Christmas; ~ **ağacı** Christmas tree; ~ **baba** Father Christmas

nohut BOT chick-pea

noksan adj. deficient, defective; n. deficiency, defect

nokta point, dot; full stop; spot, speck; MIL sentry, post; ~**i nazar** point of view; ~**lamak** v/t dot, mark, punctuate; ~**lı virgül** GR semicolon

norm standard; ~**al** normal

Norveç Norway; ~**li** n., adj. Norwegian

not note; mark in school; ~ **almak** -den take a note of; ~ **vermek** -e pass judgment on, think of; ~**a** POL, MUS note

noter JUR notary; ~**lik** office of a notary

nöbet turn of duty, etc.; watch; MED onset, fit; ~ **beklemek** mount guard; ~**çi** adj. on guard, on duty; n. watchman; ~**leşe** adv. in turn, by turns

nöt(ü)r CHEM, GR neutral

numara number; note, mark; item, event; ~**lamak** v/t number; ~**lı** numbered

numune sample, pattern, model

nur light, brilliance

nutuk speech, discourse

nüans nuance

nüfus pl. people, souls; inhabitants; ~ **cüzdanı** identity card; ~**kütüğü** register of births and deaths; ~ **sayımı** census; ~**lu** having … inhabitants

nüfuz penetration; influence; ~**lu** influential

nükleer nuclear

nükte subtle point, witty remark; ~**li** witty

nümayiş show, pomp; demonstration

nümune s. numune

nüsha specimen, copy

O

o he, she, it; that, those

oba large nomad tent; nomad family; nomad camp

objektif PHOT lens, objective; adj. objective

obruk PHYS concave; n. pit

observatuvar observatory

obur gluttonous, greedy

ocak¹ January

ocak² furnace, kiln, hearth, fireplace; quarry, mine; family; club, local branch of a party, etc.; ~**çı** stoker, chimney-sweep

oda room, office; chamber; ~**cı** servant at ANAT office or public building

odak PHYS focus

oditoryum auditorium

odun firewood, log; ~**cu** wood-cutter; seller of firewood

ofis office

oflamak say 'ugh'

ofsayt offside (football)

Oğlak ASTR Capricorn; 2 ZOO kid

oğlan boy; knave at cards; ~**cı** pederast

oğul¹ son

oğul² ZOO swarm of bees

ok arrow; beam, pole

okaliptüs BOT eucalyptus

okçu archer

oklava rolling-pin

oksijen oxygen; ~**t** CHEM oxyde

okşamak v/t caress, fondle

oku|l school; ~**ma yazma** reading and writing; ~**mak** v/t read; learn, study; ~**muş** educated, learned

okunak|lı legible; ~**sız** difficult to read

oku|nmak be read or recited; ~**tmak** -e -i cause so. to read sth.; instruct so. in sth.; teach so. sth.; ~**tman** lecturer; ~**yucu** reader

okyanus GEO ocean

olacak which will happen

olağan commonly happening, frequent; ~üstü extraordinary

olanak possibility; ~lı possible

olanca utmost, all

olası probable; ~lık probability

olay event, incident

oldukça adv. rather, pretty

olgu fact

olgun ripe, mature; ~laşmak become ripe, mature; ~luk ripeness, maturity

olimpiyat olympic games pl.

olmadık unprecedented

olmak v/i be, become; happen; ripen, mature

olmamış not ripe, immature; ~z impossible

olmuş ripe, mature

olta fishing-line; ~ iğnesi fish-hook; ~ yemi bait

oluk gutter-pipe, groove; ~lu grooved

olum|lu GR positive; ~suz GR negative

olunmak become, be

olur all right; possible; ~ olmaz anybody

oluş nature, condition; genesis, formation; ~um formation

omlet omelette

omurga ANAT backbone; NAUT keel

omuz shoulder; ~ silkmek shrug the shoulders; ~lamak v/t shoulder

on ten

ona to him, her, it

onamak v/t approve

onar|ım repair, restauration; ~mak v/t repair

onay suitable, convenient; ~lamak v/t approve, ratify

onbaşı MIL corporal

onda tenth; ~lık tenth; decimal

ongun flourishing, prosperous

onikiparmak (bağırsağı) ANAT duodenum

online adj. & adv. online; ~ alışveriş online shopping; ~ bankacılık online banking

ons ounce (28.35 gramme)

onu him, her, it; ~n his, hers, its

onur dignity, honour

opera MUS opera; ~tör MED surgeon

ora, ~sı that place; ~da there; ~dan from there, thence; ~ya thither, there

orak sickle; harvest; ~çı reaper

oralı of that place

oramiral NAUT vice-admiral

oran measure, scale; proportion; ~lı proportioned; ~tı MATH porportion

ordinaryüs professor holding a chair

ordu MIL army; ~evi officers' club; ~gâh military camp

org MUS organ

organ ANAT, POL organ; ~ik organic; ~izma organism

orgeneral MIL full general

orijinal original

orkestra MUS orchestra

orkide BOT orchid

orkinos ZOO tunny fish

orman forest, wood; **~cı** forester; **~lık** woodland

orospu prostitute, whore

orta middle, centre; central; **~ parmak** middle finger; **-in ~sından** through; **~dan kaldırmak** v/t remove; **~ya çıkmak** arise, come into being; **~ya koymak** v/t put forward; **~çağ** the Middle Ages pl.; **~elçi** Minister Plenipotentiary

ortak partner, associate; accomplice; **~laşa** adv. in common, jointly; **~lık** partnership; ECON joint-stock company

orta|lamak v/t reach the middle of; divide in the middle; **~m** environment; **~nca. 1.** middle, middling; **2.** BOT hydrangea; **~okul** secondary school

Ortodoks orthodox; **~luk** the Orthodox Church

oruç REL fasting, fast; **~ tutmak** fast; **~lu** fasting

Osmanlı Ottoman; **~ca** the Ottoman Turkish language

ot grass, herb; fodder

otel hotel; **~ci** hotel-keeper; **~cilik** hotel industry

otla|k pasture; **~mak** graze

oto motorcar; **~büs** motorbus; **~krasi** autocracy

otomat automaton; **~ik** automatic

oto|mobil s. oto; **~nomi** autonomy; **~park** car park; **~rite** authority

otur|ak chamberpot; seat, foot, bottom; **~mak** -e sit down on; run aground on; -de sit on, dwell in; settle; **~tmak** v/t seat, place

oturum sitting, session; **~ açmak** log in a. on (to); **~ kapamak** log out (from)

otuz thirty

ova grassy plain, meadow

ovalamak s. uvalamak

ov|mak, ~uşturmak s. uvmak, uvuşturmak

oy opinion; vote; **~ vermek** -e vote for

oya pinking, embroidery; **~lamak** v/t **1.** pink, embroider; **2.** fig. distract one's attention

oydaş who has the same opinion, like-minded

oylama voting, poll; **~k** v/t vote on

oylaş|ım deliberation; **~mak** v/t discuss, deliberate on

oyma sculpture, carving, engraving; **~cı** sculptor, engraver

oymak[1] v/t scoop out; engrave, carve

oymak[2] n. subdivision, tribe

oyna|k playful; unstable; TECH loose, having much play; **~mak** play, dance; be loose; **~tmak** v/t cause to play, move, dance

oysa(ki) yet, however, whereas

oyuk adj. hollowed out; n. cave

oyulga tacking; ~(la)mak v/t tack together

oyun game, play, jest; ~ bozan spoil-sport, kill-joy; ~cak toy, plaything; ~cu player, gambler; dancer

Ö

öbek heap; group

öbür the other; the next but one

öç revenge

öde|mek v/t pay, indemnity; ~nce JUR damages pl., compensation, allowance; ~nek appropriation, allowance; ~nmek be paid; ~nti subscription, fee

ödev duty

ödlek cowardly, timid

ödün compensation

ödünç loan; ~ almak -den borrow from; ~ vermek lend (-i -e sth. to)

öfke anger, rage; ~lendirmek v/t anger, bring into a rage; ~lenmek -e grow angry at; ~li choleric, hotheaded

öge element

öğle noon; ~nde at noon, about midday; ~(n)den önce in the morning; ~(n)den sonra in the afternoon; ~yin s. ~nde

öğren|ci pupil; ~im study, education; ~mek v/t learn; become familiar with; hear

öğret|i doctrine; ~im instruction; lessons; ~mek v/t teach (-e to so.); ~men teacher

öğün portion of a meal

öğür of the same age; familiarized

öğüt advice; ~ vermek -e, ~lemek v/t advise

ökçe heel of a boot

ökse birdlime; ~otu BOT mistletoe

öksür|mek v/i cough; ~ük cough

öksüz motherless; orphan; without friends

öküz ZOO ox; ~gözü BOT arnica

ölç|ek measure, scale; ~mek v/t measure

ölçü measure; dimensions; ~lü measured, temperate; ~süz unmeasured; immoderate; ~t criterion

öldür|mek v/t kill; ~tmek v/t order to be killed; ~ücü mortal, fatal

öl|mek die, fade, wither; ~mez undying, immortal; ~ü dead; corpse

ölüm death; ~ tehlikesi danger of life

ömür life, existence

ön front; foremost; ~de in the front; before; ~ümüzde in front of us; _-in_ ~ünde, ~üne in front of; ~ tekerlek front wheel

önce in front, first; _-den_ before; ilk~, ~den first of all; ~lik payment in advance

öncü MIL vanguard

öndelik precedence, priority

önder leader; ~lik leadership

önek GR prefix

önem importance; ~li important; ~siz unimportant

öner|ge proposal, motion; ~i offer; ~mek _v/t_ propose, motion

öngör|mek _v/t_ provide for; ~ü far-sightedness

ön|lemek _v/t_ resist, face, prevent; ~lük apron; ~söz preface; ~takı GR preposition; ~yargı prejudice; ~yüzbaşı MIL lieutenantcommander

öp|mek _v/t_ kiss; ~ücük kiss; ~üşmek kiss one another

ördek ZOO duck; MED urinal _for use in bed_

örf common usage; sovereign right; ~î conventional; ~i idare JUR state of siege

örgen organ

ör|gü plaited _or_ knitted thing; tress of hair; ~güt organization; ~mek _v/t_ plait, knit; darn

örne|ğin _adv._ for instance; ~k specimen, sample, model, pattern; example

örs anvil

örselemek _v/t_ handle roughly, spoil, rumple

örtmek _v/t_ cover, wrap, veil

örtü cover, wrap; blanket; ~lmek be covered, wrapped; ~lü roofed; covered, wrapped up; concealed; ~nmek cover, veil oneself

örümcek ZOO spider; (~ ağı) cobweb

öt ANAT gall, bile

öte the farther side; other, farther; ~beri this and that, various things; ~denberi from of old; ~ki the other, the farther

ötmek _v/i_ sing; crow

ötürü _-den_ by reason of, on account of, because of

öv|gü eulogy; ~mek _v/t_ praise; ~ülmek be praised; ~ünmek boast (ile with)

övüt|mek _v/t_ grind; _fig._ eat heartily; ~ülmek be ground

öyle so, such, like that; ~ki such as to _inf._; so that; ~likle _adv._ in such a manner; ~yse if so, in that case

öyük artificial hill, mound

öz _adj._ own, real, genuine, essential; _n._ marrow; essence; pith; cream; self; ~ad Christian name; ~dek matter; ~deş identical

özel personal, private special; ~ad GR proper name; ~hayat private life; ~lik peculiarity; ~likle _adv._ particularly, specially

özen care, pains _pl._; ~mek _-e_ take pains about, desire ardently; ~siz careless, superficial

özerk POL autonomous; ~lik autonomy

özet extract; summary; ~lemek v/t sum up, summarize

öz|gü -e peculiar, to; ~gün specific, peculiar

özgür free, independent

özle|m longing; inclination; ~mek v/t wish for, long for;

~tmek -e -i make so. long for

özlü having kernel, pith, etc.; pulpy, substantial

özne GR subject

özümlemek v/t BOT assimilate

özür defect; apology; ~ dilemek ask pardon; ~lü having an excuse

özveri self-sacrifice, self-denial

P

pabuç shoe, slipper; ARCH base(ment); ~cu shoemaker

paça lower part of the trouser leg; zoo trotters

paçavra rag; ~cı rag-picker

padavra shingle, thin board

padişah sovereign, Sultan

pafta metal plate; large coloured spot; GEO section of a map

paha price

pahalı expensive; ~laşmak become high-priced; ~lık dearth

pak clean, pure

paket packet, parcel; package; ~ yapmak -den, ~lemek v/t pack up, make into a parcel

pakt POL pact

palamar NAUT hawser, cable

palamut[1] zoo tunny, pelamid

palamut[2] BOT valonia

palanka MIL redoubt

palavra idle talk, boast

palaz n. zoo young

palmiye BOT palm-tree

palto overcoat

pamuk cotton; ~lu of cotton; wadded

panayır fair

pancar BOT beet

pancur outside shutter

pandül pendulum

panik panic

pankart placard

panorama panorama

pansiman MED dressing

pansiyon boarding house; ~er boarder

pantolon trousers

pantufla felt slipper

panzehir antidote

papa REL Pope

papağan zoo parrot

papalık REL Papacy, the Holy See

paparazzi sg. paparazzi pl. (pl. ~ler)

papatya BOT camomile; daisy

papaz REL priest; king at cards

papiyon bow-tie
papyekuşe surface-coated paper, art paper
para money; Para (40th part of a Piastre); ~ **bozmak** change money; ~ **cezası** JUR fine; ~ **etm.** be worth; ~ **kırmak** earn a lot of money
parabol parabola
parafe etm. v/t initial
paragraf paragraph
parakete NAUT log; long fishing-line
parala|mak v/t tear, cut in pieces; ~**nmak** be torn in pieces; become rich
paralel adj. parallel; n. GEO parallel; parallel bars pl. (sport)
paralı rich; expensive; requiring payment
parantez paranthesis; bracket
parapet NAUT bulwarks; parapet
para|sal ECON monetary; ~**sız** without money; gratis
paraşüt parachute; ~**çü** parachutist
paratoner lightning conductor
paravana folding screen
parazit parasite; atmospherics pl. (radio)
parça piece, bit; segment; ~**lamak** v/t break or cut into pieces; ~**lanmak** be broken into pieces; ~**lı** in parts; allusive, sarcastic
pardesü light overcoat
pardon I beg your pardon!

parıl|damak gleam, glitter; ~**tı** glitter, gleam, flash
park park; car park; ~ **saati** parking meter; ~ **yapmak** park a car; ~ **yeri** parking place; Am. parking lot
parke parquet; small paving stones pl.
parla|k bright, shining; successful; ~**mak** shine, flare; become distinguished
parlamento parliament
parlatmak v/t cause to shine, polish
parmak finger, toe; spoke of a wheel; ~ **izi** fingerprint; ~**lık** railing, balustrade, grating
parola password
pars ZOO leopard
parsa money collected from the crowd
parsel plot of land; ~**lemek** v/t divide into plots of land, subdivide
parşömen parchment
parti POL political party; match, game; ~**li** party member; ~**zan** partisan
pas¹ rust, tarnish, dirt; ~ **tutmak** rust
pas² stake at cards; pass (sport)
pasaj passage; arcade
pasak dirt; ~**lı** dirty, slovenly
pasaport passport
pasif adj. passive; n. ECON liability, debt
paskalya REL Easter; ~ **ekmeği** a kind of sweet bread
pas|lanmak become rusty;

~lanmaz stainless; ~lı rusty, dirty

paso pass *on a railway, etc.*

paspas doormat

pasta¹ fold, pleat

pasta² cake, pastry, tart; ~cı pastry-cook, confectioner; ~(ha)ne confectioner's shop, pastry-shop

pastırma pressed meat

pastörize pasteurized

paşa Pasha (*former title of generals and governors of a province*)

paşmak shoe, slipper

pat¹ *adj.* flat, snub

pat² BOT aster

pat³ thud

patak whacking, beating; ~lamak *v/t* give a whacking to

patates BOT potato

patavatsız tactless

paten skate; roller skate

patenta patent; NAUT bill of health; POL letters of naturalisation

patır|damak make the noise of footsteps; ~tı noise; row, tumult

patik child's shoe; ~a footpath

patinaj skating, slipping

patla|k burst, torn open; ~mak *v/i* burst, explode; ~ngaç, ~ngıç fire-cracker; toy torpedo; ~tmak *v/t* blast, blow up

patlıcan BOT aubergine, egg-plant

patrik REL Patriarch; ~hane Patriarchate; ~lik the office of a patriarch

patron head of a firm *or* business, employer

paviyon pavilion

pay share; lot, portion; MATH dividend; ~da MATH divisor; ~daş participator, partner

paydos cessation from work; break, rest

paye rank, dignity

payitaht residence, capital

payla|mak *v/t* scold; ~şmak *v/t* share, divide up

paytak *adj.* knock-kneed; *n.* pawn *at chess*

payton *s.* fayton

pazar¹ Sunday

pazar² open market, market-place; ~laşmak bargain (ile with); ~lık bargaining; ~lık etm. *s.* ~laşmak

pazartesi Monday

peçete napkin

pehlivan wrestler; *fig.* hero, champion

pehpeh! bravo!

pehriz abstinence, continence; MED diet; ~ tutmak fast; observe a diet

pek hard, firm, violent; very much; ~âlâ! very good!; all right!; ~i! very good!; very well!

pek|işmek become firm; ~mez boiled grape-juice

peksimet hard biscuit

pelerin cape

pelesenk BOT balm, balsam

pelte jelly, gelatine

peltek lisping
pembe rose colour, pink
penaltı penalty kick (*football*)
pencere window
pençe paw; strength, violence; sole *of a shoe*; **~lemek** v/t grasp, claw; **~leşmek** be at grips (**ile** with)
penisilin MED penicillin
pens penny
pens(e) TECH pliers, tweezers *pl.*
pepe stammering; **~lemek** stammer
perakende ECON retail; **~ci** retailer
perçin TECH rivet; **~lemek** v/t rivet, clench; **~li** riveted
perdah polish, gloss; **~ vurmak** -*e*, **~lamak** v/t polish, burnish; **~lı** polished, shining; **~sız** unpolished, dull; matt
perde curtain, screen, veil; membrane; THEA act; **~lemek** v/t screen, veil; **~li** veiled, curtained; having ... acts; **~siz** without veil, shameless
perende somersault; **~ atmak** turn a somersault
perese mason's plumb-line; *fig.* state, condition
pergel pair of compasses
perhiz *s.* **pehriz**
peri fairy; good genius
perişan scattered, routed; wretched, ruined; **~ etm.** v/t scatter; rout; **~ olm.** be

scattered, routed; **~lık** disorder, wretchedness
perma(nant) permanent wave, perm
permi pass *at the railway*; ECON permit
peron platform
persenk refrain, word continually repeated in speech
personel personnel, staff
perşembe Thursday
pertavsız PHYS magnifying glass
peruka wig
pervane ZOO moth; TECH propeller, screw
pervasız fearless, without restraint
pervaz cornice, fringe
pesek tartar *of the teeth*
pestil pressed and dried fruit pulp
peş the space behind; -*in* **~inde dolaşmak (gezmek)** pursue *sth.*; -*in* **~inden koşmak** run after
peşin *adv.* in advance, formerly; *adj.* paid in advance, ready
peşkeş gift
peşkir napkin
peştamal large bath-towel
petek honeycomb; circular disk
petrol petroleum
pey money on account; **~ vermek** pay a deposit
peyda existent, manifest; **~ olm.** appear
peygamber REL prophet

peyk ASTR, POL satellite

peylemek v/t reserve for oneself

peynir cheese

peyzaj landscape (picture)

pezevenk vulg. pimp, procurer

pıhtı coagulated, liquid; **~laşmak** clot, become coagulated

pınar spring, source

pırasa leek

pıratika NAUT clean bill of health

pırıl|damak gleam, glitter; **~tı** gleam, flash

pırlangıç humming-top

pırlanta n. brilliant

pırtı (worn-out) things pl.

pıtır|damak make a tapping sound; **~tı** tapping, crackling sound

piç bastard, offshoot, sucker

pide a kind of flat bread

pijama pyjamas pl.

pikap MUS record-player; pick-up, small truck

pike¹ piqué, quilting

pike² AVIA diving

piknik picnic

pil EL battery

pilaki stew of beans or fish with oil, onions, etc.

pilav pilaf

piliç chick

pilot AVIA, NAUT pilot

pineklemek slumber, doze

pingpong ping-pong, table tennis

PIN numarası PIN number

pinti stingy

pipo tobacco pipe

pir patron saint

pire flea; **~lenmek** become infested with fleas

pirinç¹ rice

pirinç² brass

piruhi stewed dough with cheese or ground meat

pirzola cutlet

pis dirty; foul; obscene; **~boğaz** greedy

piskopos REL bishop

pis|lemek -e relieve oneself on, make a mess on; **~lenmek** become dirty; **~letmek** -i make dirty, soil; **~lik** dirtiness, dirt, mess

pist running track

piston TECH piston; **~ kolu** connecting rod, piston-rod

piş|irim(lik) amount to be cooked at one time; **~irmek** v/t cook, bake; learn very well; **~kin** wellcooked, wellbaked; fig. self-assured

pişman: **~ olm.** -e be sorry for, regretful of; **~lık** regret; penitence

pişmek be cooked, baked; ripen, mature

piyade MIL foot-soldier; infantry; pedestrian; pawn at chess

piyango lottery

piyano MUS piano; **~ çalmak** play the piano

piyasa promenading; ECON market, market price

piyaz onions and parsley add-

ed to a stew; salad *of beans,*
onions, oil, etc.
piyes THEA play
plaj strand, beach
plak gramophone record; ~a
number plate *of a car*
plan plan; ~**lamak** *v/t* plan;
~**ör** AVIA glider; ~**ya** carpenter's plane
plasman ECON investment
plastik plastic
platin platinum
plebisit POL plebiscite
plise pleated
Plüton ASTR Pluto
podra powder
podüsüet suède
pohpohlamak *v/t* flatter
poker poker
polarmak *v/t* PHYS polarize
polemik polemics
poliçe ECON bill of exchange;
insurance policy
poligon MIL artillery range
polis police; policeman
politika politics; policy; ~**cı**
politician; who knows when
to flatter
Polon|ez Pole, Polish; ~**ya**
Poland
pompa TECH pump; ~ **lamak**
v/t pump
ponksiyon MED puncture
ponza pumice (stone)
porselen porcelain
porsiyon portion, plate
porsuk ZOO badger
portakal BOT orange
portatif portable
Portekiz Portugal

portmanto coat stand, coat
hanger
portre portrait
posa sediment; tartar
post skin, hide *with the fur on*
posta post, postal service;
passenger-train, mail train;
~ **pulu** postage stamp; ~**cı**
postman
pot: ~ **gelmek** go wrong; ~
yeri difficulty
postane post-office
potin boot
potrel TECH iron support
potur pleat, fold; pleated;
Turkish breeches
poyra TECH hub; axle end
poyraz GEO north-east wind
poz pose; PHOT exposure; ~
vermek *-e* PHOT expose
pozitif positive
pörsük shrivelled up; withered
pösteki sheep *or* goat skin; ~
saydırmak *-e* give tiresome
but useless work to do
pratik *adj.* practical; *n.* practice; ~**a** *s.* **pıratika**
prens prince; ~**es** princess
prensip principle
prevantoryum sanatorium
for tuberculosis suspects
prim premium
priz EL wall-socket
profes|ör professor; ~**yonel**
professional
program program(me)
proje project
projek|siyon projection; ~**tör**
search-light

prolet|arya proletariat; **~er** proletarian

propaganda propaganda; **~cı** propagator

protestan REL Protestant; **~lık** Protestantism

protesto protest; **~ etm.** *v/t* protest against

protokol protocol

prova trial, test, rehearsal; printer's proof

pruva NAUT prow, bow

psik|analiz psychoanalysis; **~oloji** psychology

puan *s.* **puvan**

puding GEO conglomerate; pudding

pudra *s.* **podra**

pul thin round disk; scale for fishing; stamp; **~cu** vendor of stamps; stamp collector; **~lamak** *v/t* stamp; **~lu** bearing stamps; **~suz** without stamps

pupa NAUT stern

puro cigar

pus mist, haze; blight, mildew; **~arık** hazy; mirage;

~armak become hazy

pusat equipment

puse kiss

puslanmak be misty, hazy

pus|mak crouch down, lie in ambush; **~u** ambush; **~uya yatmak** lie in wait

pusula¹ NAUT compass

pusula² short letter *or* note

put idol; cross; **~perest** idolator

puvan point, score

püf puff *of wind, etc.*; **~kürmek**, **~lemek** *v/t* blow out, puff

pünez drawing-pin

pürçek curl, curly

püre purée, mash

pürtük knob, protuberance

pürüz roughness, unevenness; **~lü** rough, uneven; **~süz** even, smooth

püskül tuft, tassel

püskür|geç TECH atomizer; **~mek** *v/t* blow out, spray, splutter; **~tmek** *v/t* scatter, beat off

R

Rabbi: Ya ~! My God!

rabıt connection, bond

rabıta tie, bond, connection, conformity; **~lı** in good order, regular; **~sız** disordered, irregular

radar radar

radyatör TECH radiator

radyo radio, wireless

radyum radium

raf shelf

rafadan soft-boiled (*egg*)

rağbet desire, inclination; **~li** desirous (-e for); in demand, sought after; **~siz** feeling no inclination

rağmen -e in spite of

rahat n. rest, ease, comfort; adj. at ease, comfortable; ~ **etm.** rest, make oneself comfortable; ~**sız** unquiet, uneasy; indisposed, ill; ~**sızlık** uneasiness; indisposition

rahibe REL nun

rahim ANAT womb

rahip REL monk

rahle low reading-desk

rahmet mercy, compassion; fig. rain; ~**li(k)** the deceased, the late

rakam figure, number

raket tennis-racket

rakı raki, arrack

rakıs dance, dancing

rakik tender, softhearted

rakip rival; ~**siz** unrivalled

rakkas pendulum; ~**e** woman dancer

raksetmek dance, play

ramazan Ramazan (the month of Moslem fasting)

rampa. 1. NAUT boarding; **2.** ramp; loading platform

randevu rendezvous, meeting, date; ~ **evi** secret brothel; ~**cu** keeper of a secret brothel

randıman ECON yield, profit, output

rap rap (music)

rapor report; medical certificate; ~**tör** reporter

raptiye paper-clip

rasat ASTR observation; ~**ha-ne** observatory, meteoro-

logical station

raspa TECH scraper; grater; ~ **etm.** v/t scrape

rastge||le met by hazard; by chance, at random; ~**lmek** -e meet by chance, come across; ~**tirmek** v/t succeed in meeting

rasla||mak -e meet by chance; ~**ntı** chance, coincidence

raşiti||k MED rachitic, rickety; ~**zm** rickets

ravent BOT rhubarb

ravnt round (sport)

ray rail of the railway, etc.

rayiç ECON market price, current value

rayiha smell, aroma

razı -e satisfied, contented with, agreeing to; ~ **etm.** v/t satisfy

realite reality

reçel fruit preserve, jam

reçete recipe, prescription

reçin||a, ~**a** BOT resin

reddetmek v/t reject, repel, refute

redingot frock-coat

refah comfort, luxury

refakat accompaniment; ~ **etm.** -e accompany

referandum POL referendum

refetmek v/t raise, remove, annul

refik companion; ~**a** wife

reform reform

rehber guide; guide-book; ~**lik** guiding

rehin pawn, pledge, security

rehine hostage

reis head, chief, president

rejim POL regime; MED diet

rejisör THEA stage-manager

rekabet rivalry, competition; ~ etm. compete (ile with)

reklam advertisement

rekolte harvest, crop

rekor record; ~cu record breaker

rektör rector *of a university*; ~lük rectorship

relatif relative

remiz sign, nod; allusion

ren[1] ZOO reindeer

Ren[2]: ~ nehri the Rhine

rencide hurt, annoyed

rençper workman, farmhand

rende carpenter's plane; grater; ~lemek v/t plane, grate

rengârenk multicoloured

renk colour; ~li coloured; ~siz colourless, pale

repertuvar THEA repertoire, program(me)

resif GEO reef

resim design, drawing, picture; ceremony; tax, toll; ~ çekmek (*or* çıkarmak) take a photo; ~li illustrated

resmî official, formal; ~ elbise evening dress; uniform; ~ gazete official gazette

ressam designer, artist; ~lık the art of painting

reşit JUR adult

ret rejecting; repudiation

retuş *s.* rötuş

reva lawful, permissible

revaç ECON being in demand,

being current

revani *a kind of sweet made with semolina*

revanş *s.* rövanş

reverans bow, courtesy

revir infirmary

rey rivalry; vote; ~ vermek *-e* vote for

rezalet vileness, baseness

reze hinge

rezene BOT fennel

rezil vile, base

rıhtım NAUT quay; wharf

rıza consent, acquiescence; ~ göstermek *-e* consent to, resign oneself to

riayet observance; respect, consideration; ~ etm. *-e* treat with respect, pay attention to; ~sizlik disrespect, irreverence

rica request; ~ etm. v/t request (*-den* from *so.*)

ringa ZOO herring

risale treatise, pamphlete

risk risk; ~e etm. v/t risk

ritim MUS rhythm

rivayet narrative, tale

riya hypocrisy; ~kâr hypocritical

riyaset presidency, chairmanship

riziko risk

roket rocket

rol role, part

roman novel; ~cı novelist; ~tik romantic

Romanya R(o)umania

romatizma MED rheumatism

Romen Roman; ~ rakamları

pl. MATH Roman numbers
rop robe, dress
rosto roasted; roast meat
rota NAUT ship's course
rozbif roast beef
rozet rosette
rölöve registration
römork trailer; **∼ör** tractor;
NAUT tugboat
Rönesans Renaissance
röportaj report *of a newspaperman*
rötuş PHOT retouchin
rövanş revenge *(sport)*
rugan varnish; patent leather
ruh soul; spirit; essence; energy
ruhan|î spiritual; **∼iyet** spirituality
ruhban REL clergy
ruh|bilim psychology; **∼î** psychic; **∼lu** animated, lively

ruhsat permission, permit;
∼name permit; credentials
ruhsuz inanimate, lifeless
Rum Greek *living in Moslem
countries*; **∼ca** Modern
Greek *(language)*; **∼en** Rumanian; **∼î** *adj. (Turkish
modification of the Julian
calendar)*
Rus Russian; **∼ça** Russian
(language); **∼ya** Russia
rutubet dampness, humidity;
∼li damp
rüsum *pl.* customs, taxes
rüşvet bribe; **∼ almak, ∼ yemek** accept bribes
rütbe degree, grade; rank
rüya dream; **∼ görmek** v/i
dream; **∼sında görmek** -*i*
see in a dream
rüyet seeing, vision
rüzgâr wind; **∼li** windy

S

saadet happiness
saat hour; time; watch; clock;
∼ kaç? what is the time?; **∼
beştir** it is five o'clock; **∼çi**
watchmaker
sabah morning; **∼ları** every
morning; **∼leyin** in the
morning, early; **∼lık** morning dress
saban plough
sabık former, previous, foregoing
sabıka JUR previous conviction; **∼lı** previously convicted

sabır patience; **∼lı** patient;
∼sız impatient; **∼sızlık** impatience
sabih havuz NAUT floating
dock
sabit fixed, stationary, firm;
proved
sabotaj sabotage
sabretmek be patient; -*e* endure
sabun soap; **∼cu** soap-maker,
soap-seller; **∼lamak** v/t soap;
∼luk soap-dish

saç¹ sheet-iron, iron plate; *adj.* made of sheet-iron

saç² hair

saçak eaves of a house; fringe; **~bulut** fleecy cloud, cirrus; **~lı** having eaves; fringed

saç|kıran MED alopecia; **~lı** having hair, hairy

saçma scattering; small shot; *adj.* nonsensical; **~k** *v/t* scatter, sprinkle; **~lamak** talk nonsense, say incongruous things

sada sound; echo

sadaka alms; charity

sadakat fidelity, devotion; **~li** faithful, devoted (-*e* to)

sadaret Grand Vizierate

sade mere, simple; unmixed, pure; plain; **~ce** *adv.* merely, simply; **~dil** guileless, naive; **~leştirmek** *v/t* simplify; **~lik** ingenuousness

sadık faithful, honest (-*e* to)

sadme collision; explosion

sadrazam Grand Vizier

saf¹ row, line, rank

saf² pure; sincere

safa enjoyment, pleasure; peace, ease

safdil simple-hearted, naive

safha phase

safi clear, pure; sincere; net

safiha leaf, sheet, plate

safra¹ NAUT ballast

safra² ANAT bile, gall

safran BOT saffron

safsata false reasoning; sophistry

sağ. 1. alive, safe, sound; **2.** right, right-handed; **~a dönmek** turn to the right

sağanak rainstorm, downpour

sağcı POL rightist, right-wing sympathizer

sağduyu common sense

sağım quantity milked

sağı bird excrement

sağır deaf; giving out a dull sound; **~lık** deafness

sağ|lam sound, whole, trustworthy; **~lamak** *v/t* secure, ensure; **~lamlaştırmak** *v/t* put right, make sound *or* firm

sağlık life; health

sağmak *v/t* milk; take honey from

sağmal, sağman giving milk; **~ inek** milch cow

sağrı rump of ANAT *animal*

sağu eulogy; lamentation

saha space, field area

sahaf dealer in secondhand books

sahan copper pan; **~lık** landing *on a staircase*, platform

sahi sound, true, correct; **~ mi?** is that really so!?

sahibe female owner

sahife *s.* sayfa

sahih *s.* sahi

sahil shore, coast, bank

sahip owner, possessor; **~ olm. -*e*** possess, own; **~siz** ownerless, abandoned

sahne THEA stage

sahra open place; desert

sahte false, counterfeit; ~**ci**, ~**kâr** who counterfeits or forges; ~**kârlık** forgery, counterfeiting

sahur REL meal before dawn *during Ramazan*

sair other; that remains; ~**filmenam** somnambulist

sakal beard; whiskers; ~**ı koyvermek** (or **uzatmak**, **salıvermek**) let the beard grow; ~**lı** bearded; ~**sız** having no beard

sakar[1] white blaze *on a horse's forehead*

sakar[2] ill-omened, unlucky

sakarin saccharine

sakat defected; disabled, invalid; ~**lamak** v/t injure, mutilate; ~**lık** infirmity; defect

sakın beware!, don't!; ~**ca** objection; danger; ~**gan** timid; cautious; ~**mak** -*den* guard oneself from, beware of; be cautious

sakır|damak shiver; ~**tı** shivering

Sakıt ASTR Mars

sakız mastic

sakin *adj.* stationary; *n.* inhabitant

sakit silent; taciturn

sak|lamak v/t hide, keep secret; keep, store; ~**lambaç** hide-and-seek; ~**lanmak** hide oneself; be kept; be concealed

saklı hidden, secret; preserved

saksağan ZOO magpie

saksı flower-pot

saksonya Dresden china

sal NAUT raft

salâhiyet authority, competence; ~**vermek** -*e* authorize; ~**tar** authoritative; competent (-*e* for)

salak silly, doltish

salam salami

salamura brine for pickling

salapurya NAUT small lighter

salata salad, lettuce; ~**lık** cucumber

salça sauce; tomato sauce

saldır|gan aggressor; ~**ım** aggression, attack; ~**mak** -*e* attack, make an attack on; ~**mazlık** POL non-aggression

salep BOT salep; hot drink made of salep

salgın. 1. *adj.* contagious, epidemic; *n.* contagion; **2.** POL temporary tax

salı Tuesday

salık information

salıncak swing; *a kind of* hammock; ~**lı koltuk** rocking-chair

salınmak sway from side to side; be thrown (-*e* at, into); TECH be turned on

salıvermek v/t let go, set free, release

salih suitable for oneself

salim sound, healthy

salip REL cross, crucifix

salkım hanging bunch, cluster; BOT acacia, wistaria

salla|mak v/t swing, shake, wave; ~**nmak** swing about;

fig. totter, loiter about

salmak *v/t* throw, spread, cast (*-e* on); impose; *-e* attack

salon guest-room, dining room, hall

salt *adj.* mere, simple; *adv.* merely, solely

salta¹ standing on the hind legs (*dog, etc.*)

salta² slackening *of a rope*

saltanat sovereignty, rule; *fig.* pomp, magnificence

saltçılık absolutism, autocracy

salya ANAT saliva

salyangoz ZOO snail

saman straw; ~ kâğıdı tracing-paper; ~ nezlesi MED hay fever; ~kapan amber; ~lık barn, granary; ~yolu ASTR the Milky Way

samim|î sincere, cordial; ~iyet sincerity

samur ZOO sable

samyeli poisonous wind, simoon

san reputation, esteem

sana to you, you

sanat trade, craft; art; skill, ability; ~ okulu trade school; ~çı, ~kâr artisan; artist; actor; ~lı artistic

sanatoryum sanatorium

sanayi *pl.* industries; ~leştirmek *v/t* industrialize

sancak flag, standard, POL sub-province

sancı stomach-ache, gripes, stitch; ~mak ache

sandal¹ sandalwood

sandal² sandal (*shoe*)

sandal³ NAUT rowing-boat; ~cı boatman

sandalye chair; *fig.* office, post

sandık chest, coffer, box; cash-box

sandviç sandwich

sangı confused, stupefied

sanı idea, imagination; ~k suspected, accused

saniye second, moment

sanki supposing that; ~ -miş gibi as if, as though

sanmak *v/t* think, suppose

sansar ZOO pine-marten; polecat

sans|ör POL censor; ~ür censorship

santi|gram centigram(me); ~m(etre) centimetre

santral telephone exchange; power-station

santr|for centre forward (*sport*); ~haf centre half (*sport*)

sap stem, handle, stalk

sapa *adj.* off the road

sapak unnatural, abnormal

sapan sling, catapult

sapık abnormal, perverted; crazy

sapılmak turn off (*-e* into)

sapıtmak *v/i* go crazy; talk nonsense

sap|lamak *v/t* thrust, pierce (*-e* into); ~lı having a handle *or* stem

sapmak *-e* deviate, turn to; get into

sapsarı bright yellow; very pale

sapta|mak v/t fix, establish; **~nmak** be fixed

saptırmak v/t make deviate, turn (-e to)

sara MED epileptic fit

saraç saddler, leatherworker

sarahat explicitness

sararmak turn yellow or pale

saray palace, mansion; government house

sardalya ZOO sardine

sarf expenditure, use; **~** etm. v/t spend; expend; **~ınazar** etm. -den disregard, relinquish; **~ıyat** pl. expenses

sargı bandage

sarhoş drunk with; **~luk** drunkenness

sarı yellow; pale; **~çalı** BOT barberry

sarı|k turban; **~lı** wound, surrounded; or wrapped in; throw oneself upon; clasp, embrace

sarılık yellowness; MED jaundice

sarım bandage; EL, PHYS turn of winding

sarı|sabır BOT aloe; **~şın** fair-haired, blond

sarih clear, explicit

sark|aç pendulum; **~ık** pendulous, hanging; **~ınmak** lean over; -e molest, worry; **~ıntı** robbery; molestation; **~mak** -den hang down from, lean out of; -e come down on, attack

sarmak v/t wind; surround; wrap (-e into); **-e** climb (vine)

sarman huge

sarmaş|ık BOT ivy; **~mak** embrace one another

sarmısak BOT garlic

sarnıç cistern, tank

sarp steep, inaccessible; **~laşmak** become steep

sarraf money-changer

sars|ak palsied, quivering; **~ı** shock of an earthquake; **~ık s.** **~ak**; **~ılmak** -den be shaken by; **~ıntı** shock, concussion; **~mak** v/t shake, agitate, upset

sataşmak -e annoy, seek a quarrel with, tease

sathî superficial

satıcı salesman, seller

satıh upper surface, face

sat|ılık on sale, for sale; **~ılmak** -e be sold to; **~ım** sale; **~ın almak** v/t buy

satır¹ line of writing; **~ başı** paragraph (indentation)

satır² large knife

sat|ış selling, sale; **~mak** v/t sell (-e to)

satranç chess

Satürn ASTR Saturn

satvet force, power

sav word; thesis

savana savanna

savaş struggle, fight; war; **~çı** combatant; **~kan** warlike, brave; **~mak** struggle, fight (ile with)

savat engraving in black on

silver, Tula work

savcı public prosecutor; **~lık** office of the prosecutor

savmak v/t drive away, dismiss; get over ANAT *illness*; pass away

savruk awkward, clumsy

savsak negligent, dilatory; **~lamak** v/t put off with pretexts

savsamak v/t neglect

savunma defence; **Millî ₂ Bakanlığı** Ministry of National Defence; **~k** v/t defend

savurmak v/t toss about; blow violently

savuş|mak pass, cease; slip away; **~turmak** v/t escape, avoid

sây endeavour, effort

saya upper part of *a shoe*

sayaç TECH meter, counter

saydam transparent

saye shadow, shade; **~sinde** thanks to; **bu ~de** by this, here by

sayfa page; **~yı çevirmek** turn over the leaf

sayfiye summer house, villa

saygı respect, esteem, consideration; **~larımla** yours faithfully; **~lı** respectful, considerate

saygın esteemed, respected; **~lık** esteem, credit

saygısız disrespectful; **~lık** disrespect

sayı number

sayıklama talk in one's sleep *or* delirium

sayı|lama statistics; counting; **~lı** counted, limited; **~lmak** be counted, numbered, esteemed; **~m** census; **~n** esteemed; dear (*in a letter*); **~sız** innumerable

sayış|mak settle accounts (**ile** with); **₂tay** POL the Exchequer and Audit Department

say|lav POL deputy, member of parliament; **~mak** v/t count, number; count as, respect, esteem; suppose

sayrı ill; **~msak** sham patient

saz¹ MUS musical instrument; Oriental music

saz² BOT rush, reed; **~lık** place covered with rushes

sebat stability; perseverance; **~kâr, ~lı** enduring, persevering; **~sız** unstable, fickle

sebebiyet vermek -*e* cause, occasion

sebep cause, reason; source; **~ olm.** -*e* cause; **~siz** without any reason *or* cause

sebil public fountain

sebze vegetable

seccade prayer rug

seciye character, natural disposition; **~li** of high moral character; **~siz** untrustworthy

seçilmek be picked, chosen

seçim election; **~ hakkı** POL suffrage, franchise

seçkin choice, distinguished

seçme|k choose, select, elect; **~n** elector

sedef mother-of-pearl

sedir[1] *a kind of* divan
sedir[2] BOT cedar
sedye stretcher
sefahat dissipation
sefalet poverty, misery
sefaret POL ambassadorship; embassy, legation; **~hane** embassy, legation; (*building*)
sefer. 1. voyage; campaign; **2.** time, occurance; **~ber** mobilized for war; **~berlik** mobilization; **~tası** food box *with several dishes fastened together*
sefih spendthrift; dissolute
sefil poor, miserable
sefir POL ambassador
seğir|mek tremble, twitch nervously; **~tmek** *-e* run, hasten to
seher time before dawn
sehpa tripod; three-legged stool; gallow
sehven *adv.* inadvertently
Sekendiz ASTR Saturn
seki pedestal; stone seat
sekiz eight
sekmek hop, ricochet
sekreter secretary
seksen eighty
seksüalite sexuality; **~el** sexual
sekte pause, interval
sektirmak *v/t* cause to rebound, ricochet
sektör sector
sel torrent, inundation, flood
selâm greeting, salutation, salute; **~ söylemek** *-e* give

one's regards to; **~ vermek** *-e* greet, salute
selâmet safety, security, soundness
selâmla|ma salutation, welcome; **~mak** *v/t* salute, greet; **~şmak** exchange greetings (**ile** with)
selâm|lık the part of a Moslem house reserved for men; **~(ün)aleyküm!** Peace be on you! (*formal greeting of Moslems*)
self predecessor, ancestor
selim safe, sound
selüloit celluloid
selüloz cellulose
selvi *s.* **servi**
semafor signal
semaver samovar
semavî celestial, heavenly
sembol symbol
semer pack-saddle
semere fruit, profit, result
semir|mek *v/i* grow fat; **~tmek** *v/t* fatten; manure
semiz fat, fleshy; **~lik** fatness; **~out** BOT purslane
sempati sympathy; **~k** sympathetic
semt region, quarter; **~ürres** ASTR zenith
sen you, thou
sena praise, eulogy
senaryo THEA scenario
senat|o senate; **~ör** senator
sendelemek *v/i* totter, stagger
sendika trade union; **~cılık** trade unionism

sene year; ~lik lasting ... years

senet written proof, document, title-deed; ~li based on written proof

senfoni MUS symphony

seni you; thee; ~n thine, your, of you

senli benli familiar, intimate

sentetik CHEM synthetic

sepet basket; wickerwork; ~çi maker or seller of baskets; ~lemek v/t put in a basket; sl. get rid of

sepi dressing for hides; ~ci tanner; ~lemek v/t tan, prepare

serbest free, independent; ~çe adv. freely; ~i, ~lik liberty

serçe ZOO sparrow

ser|dar MIL general, commander-in-chief; ~dengeçti who sacrifices his life

sere span

seren NAUT yard

sergi anything spread for sale; exhibition; ~lemek v/t exhibit

sergüzeşt adventure

seri¹ n. series

seri² adj. quick, swift

serilmek -e be spread out on; fall, drop on

serin cool; ~leşmek become cool; ~letmek v/t cool, refresh; ~lik coolness

serkeş unruly, rebellious

serlevha title, heading

sermaye ECON capital, stock;

~dar capitalist

sermek v/t spread (-e on, over)

serpelemek v/i drizzle

serp|ilmek fall as if sprinkled; grow; ~inti drizzle, spray; repercussion; ~mek v/t sprinkle, scatter (-e on)

sersem stunned, bewildered; ~letmek v/t stunn, stupefy; ~lik stupefaction, confusion

serseri vagrant; loose

sert hard, harsh, severe, violent; ~leşmek become hard, severe; ~lik hardness, harshness, violence

servet wealth

servi BOT cypress

servis service, waiting

ses sound, noise, voice, cry; ~çıkarmak speak; ~ vermek give out a sound; ~lemek v/t hearken, listen to; ~lenmek -e call out to; answer a call

sesli voiced; ~ (harf) GR vocal

sessiz quiet, silent; ~ (harf) GR consonant

set barrier, dam, bank

sevap good deed, meritorious action

sevda love, passion; intense longing; ~lı madly in love

sevgi love, affection, compassion; ~li beloved, dear

sev|ici Lesbian; ~ilmek be loved, lovable

sevim love, affability; ~li lovable, sympathetic

sevinç joy, delight; ~li joyful

sevin|dirmek v/t make happy; cheer, comfort; ~**mek** -e be pleased with
Sevir ASTR Taurus
sevişmek love one another
seviye level, rank, degree
sevk driving; dispatch; ~ **etm.** v/t drive; send; ~**iyat** pl. dispatch sg.
sevmek v/t love, like, fondle
seyahat journey, travelling; ~ **etm.** v/i travel
seyir movement, voyage; looking on; ~**ci** spectator, onlooker
seylâp flood, torrent
seyran pleasure trip, excursion
seyrek rare, sparse
seyr|etmek v/t see, look on; v/i move, go along; ~**üsefer** traffic
seyyah traveller
seyyar mobile, portable; ~**e** ASTR planet
sez|gi perception; intuition; ~**mek** v/t perceive, feel, discern
sezon season
sıcak hot, warm; heat; ~**lık** heat
sıçan zoo rat; mouse; ~**otu** CHEM arsenic
sıçra|mak spring, jump (-e on); ~**tmak** v/t make jump, spring (-e on)
sıfat quality, attribute; GR adjective; ~**iyle** in the capacity of
sıfır zero, nought

sığ shallow
sığamak v/t tuck or roll up
sığın|ak shelter; ~**mak** -e take refuge or shelter with
sığır ox, cow; buffalo; ~ **eti** beef; ~**tmaç** herdsman, drover
sığ|ışmak fit into a confined place; ~**mak** -e go into, be contained by
sıhhat health; truth; ~**li** healthy, sound
sıhh|î hygienic; ~**iye** public health
sık close together, dense, tight; ~**ı** tight, strict, severe; necessity; ~**ıcı** tiresome, boring
sıkıl|gan bashful, shy; ~**mak** be bored; be ashamed (-e to inf.) be pressed (-e into); **canı** ~**ılmak** be bored
sıkıntı annoyance, boredom; lack
sıkış|ık pressed together; ~**mak** be pressed together, crowded; ~**tırmak** v/t press, squeeze (-e into); force, oppress
sıklaşmak be frequent, close together
sıklet heaviness, weight
sıklık density, frequency
sıkma squeezing; ~**k** v/t press, squeeze, tighten
sımsıkı very tight, narrow
sına|at trade, craft; ~**î** industrial
sınamak v/t try, test
sınav examination; ~**lamak**

v/t examine

sındırmak *v/t* defeat, rout

sınıf class; sort, category; **~ta kalmak** fail in one's class

sınır frontier; **~lamak** *v/t* limit; determine; **~lı** limited; determined

sır¹ glaze; silvering

sır² secret, mystery

sıra row, file, rank; order, series; turn; **~diği ~da** *conj.* while; as; **~sı gelmek** *-e* have one's turn; **~sına göre** according to circumstances; **~ca** MED scrofula; **~lamak** *v/t* arrange in a row, set up in order; **~lanmak** stand in line; **~lı** in a row, in due order; **~sız** out of order, improper

sırça glass

sırf *adv.* pure; mere; sheer

sırık pole, stick; **~lamak** *v/t sl.* carry off, steal

sırıt|kan given to grinning; **~mak** *v/i* grin; *fig.* show up

sırma silver-thread

sırnaşık worrying, pertinacious

sırsıklam wet to the skin

sırt back; ridge; **~armak** pile up *(clouds)*; arch its back *(cat)*; **~lamak** *v/t* take on one's back

sırtlan ZOO hyena

sıska dropsical; thin and weak

sıtma MED malaria; **~lı** malarial

sıva plaster

sıvalı¹ plastered, stuccoed

sıvalı² with sleeves rolled up

sıvamak¹ plaster *(-e -i sth. with)*

sıvamak² *v/t* tuck up, roll up

sıvazlamak *v/t* stroke, caress

sıvı *adj.* liquid; **~ndırmak** PHYS liquify, turn into a fluid

sıvışık sticky; importunate

sıyanet preservation, protection

sıyga GR tense, mood

sıyırmak *v/t* tear *or* peel off, strip off, skim off

sıyrı|k *adj.* brazenfaced; *n.* abrasion; **~ntı** scrapings *pl.*; scratch

-sız *s.* **-siz**

sızdırmak *v/t* cause to ooze out, squeeze

sızı ache, pain; **~ltı** complain, lamentation

-sızın *s.* **-sizin**

sızıntı oozings, tricklings *pl.*

sızla|mak suffer sharp pain; **~nmak** moan, lament

sızmak ooze, leak

siber... cyber...

sicil register; **~li** registered; previously convicted

sicim string, cord

sidik ANAT urine; **~kavuğu** bladder

sigara cigarette; **~ içilmeyen** smoke-free *(zone, building)*; **~lık** cigarette-holder

sigorta insurance; EL fuse; **~etm.** *v/t* insure; **~lı** insured

sihir magic, sorcery, charm; **~baz** magician, sorcerer; **~li**

bewitched
sikke coin
sikmek v/t vulg. have sexual intercourse with
silâh weapon, arm; ~ **başına!** to arms!; ~**landırmak** v/t arm; ~**lanmak** arm oneself; ~**lı** armed; ~**sız** unarmed; ~**sızlanma** POL disarmament
sil|ecek large bath-towel; ~**gi** duster; sponge, eraser; ~**giç** wind-screen wiper; ~**ik** rubbed out, worn
silindir cylinder; roller; top hat
silinmek be scraped; rub oneself
silk|elemek v/t shake off; ~**inmek** shake oneself; ~**inti** shaking, trembling; ~**mek** v/t shake, shake off
sille box on the ear, slap
silmek v/t wipe, scrub, rub down, erase; **burnunu** ~ blow the nose
silo silo
silsile chain, line; dynasty
sima face; figure, personage
simge symbol
simit cracknel *in the shape of a ring*; NAUT life-belt
simsar ECON broker; commission agent
simsiyah jet black
sincap ZOO squirrel
sindir|im digestion; ~**mek** v/t digest, swallow
sine bosom, breast
sinek ZOO fly; ~**lik** fly-whisk
sinema cinema

sinir ANAT sinew, nerve; ~**len-dirmek** v/t irritate; ~**lenmek** -*e* become irritated at; ~**li** on edge, nervous; ~**lilik** nervousness
sinmek -*e* crouch down into, be hidden in; penetrate; *fig.* be cowed, humiliated
sinüs MATH sine
sinyal signal; blinker (*auto*)
sipahi MIL cavalry
sipariş ECON order, commission; ~ **almak** take orders; ~ **etm.** v/t order
siper shield, shelter; peak *of a cap*
sirayet contagion, infection
sirk circus
sirke[1] vinegar
sirke[2] nit
sirküler circular
siroko sirocco
sis fog, mist; ~**lenmek** become damp, foggy; ~**li** foggy, misty
sistem system
sistire scraper
sitem reproach
sivil civilian
sivilce pimple
sivri sharp-pointed; ~**lik** sharp-pointedness; ~**lmek** become pointed; *fig.* make rapid progress in one's career; ~**ltmek** v/t make pointed at the end; ~**sinek** ZOO mosquito
siyah black; ~**lanmak** become black
siyas|al political; ~**et** politics,

policy; ~î political

siyoni|st Zionist; ~zm Zionism

siz you

-siz, -sız, -suz, -süz without; ... -less

sizin your; of you

-sizin, -sızın without, before Skandinavya Scandinavia

skeç THEA sketch

smokin dinner-jacket

snop snob

soba stove; ~cı maker or installer of stoves

soda soda; ~ (suyu) soda water

sofa hall, ante-room

sofra dining-table; meal; ~yı kaldırmak clear away; ~yı kurmak lay the table

softa REL theological student; fanatic, bigot

sofu religious, devout; fanatic

soğan BOT onion

soğuk cold; frigid; ~ almak catch a cold; ~kanlı calm, coolheaded; ~luk coldness; cold sweat

soğumak get cold

soğutma|ç TECH cooling system; ~k v/t cool, render cold

sohbet chat, conversation; ~ etm. have a chat

sokak road, street

sokmak v/t drive in, insert; sting, bite; injure, calumniate

sokul|gan sociable, quick to make friends; ~mak -e push into; steel in

sokuşturmak v/t push, slip (-e into)

sol left, left-hand side; ~ak left-handed; ~cu POL leftist

sol|gun faded, withered; ~mak fade, wither

solucan ZOO worm; bağırsak ~ı tapeworm; yer ~ı earthworm

soluk¹ faded, withered, pale

soluk² breath; ~ soluğa out of breath

solu|mak -den snort, pant with; ~ngaç ZOO gill; ~nmak breathe

som¹ solid, massive

som² ZOO salmon

somaki porphyry

somun round loaf; TECH nut

somurt|kan sulky; ~mak frown, sulk

somut concrete

somye spring mattress

son end, result; last, final; afterbirth; ~ derece the uttermost; extremely; ~bahar autumn, fall

sonda TECH bore; MED catheter; ~j TECH test bore; fig. sounding, exploration; ~lamak v/t bore, sound

sonek GR suffix

sonra afterwards, in future; -den after; ~dan later, recently; ~dan görme parvenu; ~ları adv. later; ~sız eternal, without end

sonsuz endless, eternal

sonuç end, result; ~la(ndır)mak v/t conclude; cause;

~lanmak result (ile in)

sop clan

sopa thock stick; *fig.* beating;
~ atmak *-e* give a beating to;
~ yemek get a beating

sorgu interrogation; ~ya çekmek *v/t* cross-examine, interrogate

sorguç plum, crest

sormak[1] ask (*-e -i so.* about
sth.); *-i* inquire about

sormak[2] *v/t* suck

soru question, interrogation;
~lmak be asked

sorum responsibility; ~lu responsible

soru|n problem, question,
matter; ~şturmak *v/t* inquire
about

sosis sausage

sosyal social; ~ sigorta social
insurance; ~ist socialist;
~izm socialism

sosyoloji sociology

Sovyetler Birliği Soviet Union

soy family, lineage; ~adı family name, surname

soygun pillage, spoliation

soylu of good gamily

soymak *v/t* strip, peel, undress; rob, sack

soysuz degenerate; good-
-for-nothing

soytarı clown, buffoon

soy|ulmak be stripped,
peeled; ~unmak undress
oneself; ~ut abstract, incorporeal

söbe oval

söğüt BOT willow

sök|mek *v/t* tear down, rip
open; *fig.* surmount; ~türmek *v/t* cause to tear
down *or* rip open; read
with difficulty; ~ük unstitched, ripped

sömestr semester, halfyear

sömür|ge colony; ~mek *v/t*
devour; *fig.* exploit

sön|dürmek *v/t* extinguish,
disconnect, switch off;
~mek go out (*fire*); be deflated; ~ük extinguished, deflated

söv|gü curse; ~mek *-e* curse,
swear at; ~üşmek swear at
one another

söyle|mek *v/t* say, explain (*-e*
to)

söylen|iş pronunciation;
~mek be spoken *or* said;
~ti rumour

söyle|tmek *-e -i* make *so.* say
sth.; ~v speech, discourse

söz word, speech, rumour; ~
atmak *-e* make improper remarks to; ~cü speaker,
spokesman; ~cük word;
~gelişi *adv.* for instance

sözleşme agreement, contract; ~k agree (ile with)

sözlü agreed together; verbal

sözlük dictionary, vocabulary

sözümona so-called

spam spam (mail)

spatül spatula

spekülasyon speculation

spiker speaker

spor sport, games; ~ alanı sports field, athletic ground; ~cu, ~tmen sportsman, athlete

stadyum stadium (*sport*)

staj apprenticeship; ~iyer apprentice

sterlin Sterling

stilo fountain-pen

stok s. ıstok

stratejik MIL strategics

stüdyo studio

su water, fluid, sap, broth; stream; ~ almak leak; ~ya düşmek fail, come to nought; ~ bendi water reservoir

sual question, inquiry

subay MIL officer

sucu water-seller

sucuk. 1. sausage (*esp. in the Turkish way*); **2.** sweet-meat made of grape juice, nuts, etc.

suç fault; crime; ~lamak v/t accuse (ile of); ~landırmak v/t find guilty; ~lanmak be accused (ile of); ~lu criminal, offender; ~suz innocent; ~üstü adv. JUR red-handed

sugeçirmez waterproof

suiistimal misuse, abuse; ~kast criminal attempt

sukut fall, lapse; ~u hayal disappointment

sula|k watery, marshy; water-trough; ~ma irrigation; ~mak v/t water, irrigate; ~ndırmak v/t mix with water

sulh peace, reconciliation; ~çu, ~perver peace-loving

sulp hard, solid

sultan. 1. ruler, sovereign, sultan; **2.** daughter of a sultan, princess

sulu watery, moist, juicy; *fig.* importunate; ~ boya water-colour

sumen writing-pad

sunî artificial, false

sun|mak v/t offer, present (-e to); ~u ECON offer; ~ulmak -e be presented to

supap TECH valve

sur city wall, rampart

surat face, mien; ~ asmak make a sour face

sure REL Chapter of the Koran

suret form, shape, manner; copy; -in ~ini çıkarmak make a copy of; bu ~le in this way

Suriye Syria; ~li n, adj. Syrian

susak adj. thirsty; n wooden drinking cup

susam BOT sesame

susa|mak be thirsty; -e thirst for; ~mış thirsty

sus|mak be silent, cease speaking; ~malık hush-money; ~turmak v/t silence

susuz waterless, arid; ~luk lack of water

sutyen brassière

SUV SUV (= sports utility vehicle)

suvare evening show, soirée

su|varmak v/t water ANAT an-

imal; ~**yolu. 1.** watermark *in a paper*; **2.** water conduit

-suz *s.* **-siz**

sübye sweet drink *made with pounded almonds, etc.*

sühulet being easy, facility

sühunet heat; temperature

sükût silence

sülâle family, line

sülük zoo leech; bot tendril

sülün zoo pheasant

sümbül bot hyacinth; ~î cloudy, overcast

sümkürmek expel mucus from the nose

sümük anat mucus; ~lü slimy, snivelling; ~lü böcek slug

sünger sponge; ~ kâğıdı blotting-paper; ~taşı pumice stone

süngü bayonet

sünnet rel **1.** the habits of the Prophet Muhammad; **2.** circumcision; ~çi circumciser; ~li circumcised

sünnî rel Sunnite

süprüntü sweepings, rubbish

süpür|ge broom, brush; ~mek *v/t* sweep, brush

sürat speed, velocity; ~li quick, hurried

sürç slip, mistake; ~mek stumble

süre period, extension; ~ce *conj.* as long as, while; ~ç process

sürek duration; ~li lasting, prolonged; ~siz transitory

süreli periodic(al)

Süreyya astr the Pleiades *pl.*

sürfe zoo caterpillar, maggot

sürgü harrow; bolt; trowel; ~lemek *v/t* harrow; bolt

sürgün. 1. pol exile, banishment; exiled person; **2.** bot shoot, sucker; **3.** med diarrhoea

sürme. 1. kohl, collyrium *for painting the eyelids*; **2.** bolt

sürmek *v/t* drive; banish (*-e* to); rub (*-e on*); *v/i* continue; pass

sürme|lemek *v/t* bolt; ~li having a bolt, bolted

sürpriz surprise

sürşarj surcharge

sürt|mek *v/t* rub (*-e* against); *v/i* loiter, wander about; ~ünme tech friction

sürü herd, flock, drove; ~cü drover; driver

sürüklemek *v/t* drag, involve (*-e in*)

sürülmek be rubbed; *-e* be driven to

sürüm econ sale, demand; ~lü in great demand

sürün|gen zoo reptile; ~mek *v/t* rub in *or* on; ~mek *v/i* drag oneself along the ground, live in misery

süs ornament, decoration; ~lemek *v/t* adorn, embellish; ~lenmek adorn oneself; ~lü ornamented, decorated, carefully dressed

süt milk; ~ana, ~anne wet nurse, foster-mother; ~çü milkman

sütlaç rice-pudding

sütleğen BOT euphorbia; **~lü**
milky in milk; **~nine** wet
nurse
sütun column (*a. in a newspaper*); pillar
süvari MIL cavalryman; cavalry
Süveyş Suez; **~ kanalı** Suez

Canal
-süz *s.* **-siz**
süz|geç, ~gü filter, sieve,
strainer; **~mek** *v/t* strain, filter; *fig* look attentively at;
~ülmek. 1. be filtered; **2.**
glide; **3.** become weak

Ş

şadırdamak bubble, murmur
şadırvan reservoir with a jet
or taps
şafak twilight; dawn
şaft TECH shaft
şah¹ Shah
şah²: ~a kalkmak rear up
(*horse*)
şahadet witnessing, testimony; REL death in battle *of a
Moslem*; **~ getirmek** pronounce the Moslem creed;
~ parmağı index finger;
~name certificate
şah|ane royal; magnificent;
~damarı ANAT aorta; **~eser**
masterpiece
şahıs person, individual; **~
zamiri** GR personal pronoun
şahin ZOO peregrine falcon
şahit witness; example; **~lik**
testimony
şahlanmak rear up (*horse*)
fig. become angry and
threatening
şahmerdan TECH beetle; battering-ram
şahs|en *adv.* personally, in

person; **~î** personal, private;
~iyet personality
şair poet
şaka fun, joke, jest; **~ söylemek, ~ yapmak** jest, joke;
~cı joker, jester
şakak ANAT temple
şaka|laşmak joke (**ile** with);
~sız earnest(ly)
şakır|damak rattle, jingle; **~tı**
clatter, rattle
şaki brigand, robber
şaklaban mimic, buffoon
şaklatmak *v/t* crack a whip,
etc.
şakul plumb-line; **~î** perpendicular, vertical
şal shawl
şalgam BOT turnip
şallak naked
şalter EL switch
şalupa NAUT sloop
şalvar baggy trousers
şamandıra float *for a wick*;
NAUT buoy
şamar slap, box on the ear
şamata great noise, uproar
şamdan candlestick

şamfıstığı BOT pistachio nut

şâmil -*i* comprising, including

şamme (sense of) smell

şampanya Champagne

şampiyon champion; ~a championship

şan fame, glory, reputation

şangırdamak crash, make the noise of breaking glass

şanjman TECH gear, shift

şanlı glorious, famous

şans chance, luck

şansız without renown, unknown

şanslı lucky; ~sız unhappy

şansölye POL chancellor

şantaj JUR blackmail, extortion; ~cı blackmailer

şantiye building-site; NAUT wharf, dockyard

şantöz female singer

şap CHEM alum

şapırdamak make a smacking noise; ~tı smacking noise *of the lips*

şapka hat; truck *of a mast*; cowl *of a chimney*; ~sını çıkarmak take off one's hat; ~cı hatter; ~lık wardrobe

şaplamak make a smacking noise

şarap wine

şarıldamak flow *with a splashing noise*; ~tı gurgling, splashing

şarjör cartridge clip *or* drum

şark east; Orient

şarkı song; ~ söylemek sing; ~cı song-writer; singer

şarkî eastern; ~iyat Orientalism

şarlatan charlatan

şart condition; ~lı stipulated; having a condition attached; ~name list of conditions; ~sız unconditional

şasi TECH chassis

şaşaa glitter; splendour

şaşalamak be bewildered, confused

şaşı squinting, squint-eyed; ~lamak squint

şaşırmak *v/t* be confused about; lose, miss; ~tmak *v/t* confuse, bewilder, mislead

şaşkın bewildered, confused; ~lık bewilderment

şaşmak -*e* be perplexed, astonished at; -*i* lose, miss; deviate (-*den* from)

şato castle

şatranç chess

şayan -*e* deserving, suitable for; ~ı dikkat notable, worth attention

şayet perhaps; if

şayia rumour

şaz irregular, exceptional

şeamet evil omen

şebboy BOT wallflower

şebek ZOO baboon

şebeke net; network; gang

şecere genealogical tree

şef chief, leader

şefaat intercession

şeffaf transparent

şefkat compassion, affection; ~li compassionate, affectionate

şeftali BOT peach

şehir town, city; **~lerarası** interurban; **~li** townsman, citizen

şehit REL martyr; Moslem who dies in battle *or* during an accident; **~lik** martyrdom

şehriye BOT vermicelli

şehv|ani lustful, sensual; **~et** lust, sensuality

şehzade prince

şekavet brigandage

şeker sugar; candy; a sweet; *fig.* darling; **~ bayramı** REL Moslem feast after the Ramadan fast; **~ hastalığı** MED diabetes; **~ci** sweet-seller; confectioner; **~kamışı** sugar-cane; **~leme** candied fruit; doze, nap; **~li** sugared, sweetened; **~pare** pastry *over which syrup had been poured*

şekil form, shape; plan; kind; feature; **~ vermek** -*e* form, shape; **~siz** shapeless, without form

şeklî formal

şelâle waterfall

şema outline, sketch, plan

şemsiye parasol, umbrella; **~lik** umbrella-stand

şen joyous, cheerful; **~elmek** become inhabited; **~lendirmek** v/t cheer, enliven; **~lenmek** become cheerful, gay, joyous; become inhabited; **~lik** gaiety, cheerfulness; public rejoicings

şerbet sweet drink, sherbet;

liquid manure

şeref honour; glory; distinction

şerefe ARCH gallery *of a minaret*

şerefiye tax on the increase of land value

şereflen|dirmek v/t honour, do honour to; **~mek** acquire honour, be honoured

şerh explanation; commentary

şeriat REL the Moslem religious law; **~çı** upholder of the religious law

şerik partner, shareholder

şerit ribbon, tape; film

şev n. slope; *adj.* sloping

şevk desire, yearning

şevket majesty, pomp

şey thing; what's his name; **bir ~** something

şeyh sheikh; REL head of a religious order; **~ülislâm** Sheikhulislam (*the highest religious dignitary of the Ottoman Empire*)

şeytan REL Satan, devil; *fig.* crafty man; **~lık** devilry

şezlong chaise longue

şık[1] chic, smart

şık[2] one of two alternatives

şıkır|damak rattle, jingle; **~tı** jingling

şıklık elegance, smartness

şımar|ık spoilt, saucy, impertinent; **~mak** be spoilt, get above oneself; **~tmak** v/t spoil

şıngır|damak crash, make

the noise of breaking glass;
~tı the noise of breaking
glass

şıp noise *of a drop falling;* **~**
diye all of a sudden

şıra must, unfermented
grape-juice

şırıl|damak make the noise of
gently running water; **~tı**
splashing

şırlop eggs served with yogurt

şırvan(ı) loft *over a shop or*
beneath a roof

şiar badge, sign; habit

şiddet strength, violence, severity; **~lenmek** become severe *or* intensified; **~li** violent, severe

şifa restoration to health,
healing; **~ bulmak** recover
health

şifah|en *adv.* orally, verbally;
~î oral, verbal

şifalı wholesome, healing

şifre cipher, code; *-in* **~sini**
açmak decipher; decode;
~li in cipher

Şiî REL Shiite; **~lik** Shiism

şiir poetry; poem

şikâyet complaint; **~ etm.**
complain (*-den* about, *-e*
to); **~çi** complainant

şile BOT marjoram

şilep NAUT cargo boat *or*
steamer

şilin Shilling

şilte thin mattress, quilt

şimal north; **~î** northern,
north

şimdi *adj.* at present, now;

~den henceforth; already;
~ki the present, actual; **~lik**
adv. for the present

şimşek lightning; **~ çakmak**
lighten, flash

şimşir BOT box-tree

şinitsel cutlet, schnitzel

şirin sweet, affable

şirk REL polytheism

şirket ECON company, partnership

şirpençe MED carbuncle, an-
thrax

şirret *adj.* malicious, tartar

şiryan ANAT artery

şiş[1] *n.* swelling; spit, skewer;
~ kebabı meat roasted
on a spit *or* skewers

şiş[2] *n.* swelling; *adj.* swollen

şişe bottle; lamp-glass

şişirmek *v/t* cause to swell,
inflate, pump up; **~kin** swollen, puffed up; **~ko** *sl.* very
fat

şişlemek *v/t* spit, skewer, stab

şişman fat; **~lık** fatness

şişmek swell, become inflat-
ed, swollen

şive accent; idiom; **~siz** with
a bad accent

şlep *s.* şilep

şoför chauffeur, driver

şose macadamized road,
highway

şoven POL chauvinistic; **~lik**
chauvinism

şöhret fame, reputation;
pseudonym

şölen feast, banquet

şömine fireplace

şövalye knight

şöyle adv. in that manner, so; just; such; ~ **böyle** so so, not too well; roughly speaking

şu that; this

şua ray of light

şubat February

şube section, branch (office)

şuh lively; coquettish

şura, ~sı that place, this place; ~da there, here; ~dan from there, from here; ~ya there, thither

şûra council; **Devlet** ₂**sı** POL Council of State

şurup syrup; sweet medicine

şuur comprehension, intelligence; conscience; ~**suz** unconscious

şükran thankfulness, gratitude

şükür thanks, gratitude

şümul comprehending; ~**ü olm.** -e include, embrace; ~**lü** comprehensive

şüphe doubt, suspicion; ~**lenmek** have a suspicion or doubt (-den about); ~**li** -den suspicious of, suspected of; doubtful; ~**siz** doubtless

şüt shot (football)

T

ta¹ even; until; ~ -**e kadar** even until; ~ **ki** so that; in order that

ta² s. da

-ta s. -da

taahhüt undertaking, engagement; ~**lü** registered (letter)

taalluk -e connection with, relation to; ~ **etm.** -e concern

taarruz attack, assault; ~ **etm.** -e attack, assault

taassup REL bigotry, fanaticism

tabak¹ plate, dish

tabak² tanner

tabaka¹ layer; class; sheet

tabaka² tobacco or cigarette box

tabaklamak v/t tan

taban sole; floor, base; bed of a river

tabanca pistol

tabanvay: ~**la gitmek** sl. go on foot

tabela sign of a shop, etc.; list of food; card of treatments

tab|etmek v/t print, ~**ı** print, edition

tabi -e following; dependent on, subject to

tabi|at nature; character, quality; ~**î** natural, normal; adv. naturally

tabiiyet dependence; POL nationality

tabip doctor, physician

tabir phrase, expression

tabiye MIL tactics

tabla circular tray, disk; ash-tray

tabl|et tablet; **~o** picture; tableau; MATH table

tabur MIL battalion; **~cu** MIL discharged from hospital

tabure footstool

tabut coffin; large egg-box

tabya MIL bastion, redoubt

taciz bothering, worrying; **~ etm.** v/t annoy, disturb

taç crown, diadem; BOT corolla; ZOO crest of a bird

tadım the faculty of taste

tadil adjustment; modification (pl. **~ât**)

taflan BOT cherry laurel

tafsil, pl. **~ât** detail; **~ât vermek ~** explain all details to; **~âtlı** detailed

tağşiş ECON adulteration of a product

tahakkuk verification; **~ etm.** v/i prove true, be realized; **~ ettirmek** v/t certify, verify, realize

tahakküm arbitrary power; oppression

tahammül endurance; **~ etm. -e** endure, support

tahammür CHEM fermentation

taharri search; **~ (memuru)** detective, plain-clothes policeman

tahayyül imagination, fancy; **~ etm.** v/t fancy, imagine

tahdit limitation; definition; **~ etm.** v/t limit, circumscribe

tahıl cereals

tahin sesame oil

tahkik verification; investigation; **~ etm.** v/t verify, investigate; **~at** pl. investigations; research sg.

tahkim fortifying; **~ etm.** v/t strengthen, fortify

tahkir insult; **~ etm.** v/t despise, insult

tahlil CHEM analysis

tahlis|(iye) rescuing; **~iye sandalı** NAUT lifeboat

tahliye emptying, evacuation; **~ etm.** v/t empty, discharge

tahmin estimate, conjecture; **~ etm.** v/t estimate, calculate; **~en** adv. approximately; **~î** approximate

tahribat pl. destructions

tahrif distortion, falsification; **~ etm.** v/t falsify, misrepresent

tahrik incitement; **~ etm.** v/t incite, instigate, provoke

tahrip destruction, devastation; **~ etm.** v/t destroy, ruin

tahrir writing, essay; **~en** adv. in writing

tahsil collection; study, education; **~ etm.** v/t acquire; study; **~ât** pl. payments; taxes; **~dar** collector of taxes, etc.

tahsis assignment; **~ etm.** v/t assign **-e**; **~at** pl. allowance, appropriation sg.

taht throne; **~a çıkmak** succeed to the throne; **~tan indirilmek** be dethroned

tahta 154

tahta board, plank; wood; *adj.*
  wooden; ~**biti**, ~**kurusu** zoo
  bed-bug
tahterevalli see-saw
tahvil transforming, conver-
  sion, draft; ~ **etm.** *v/t* con-
  vert, transmute; ~**ât** *pl.* ECON
  securities
taife *s.* tayfa
tak arch, vault
takas ECON clearing
takat strength, power; ~**siz**
  powerless, exhausted
takdim presentation, offer; ~
  etm. *v/t* present, offer, introduce (-*e* to)
takdir appreciation, supposition; ~ **etm.** *v/t* appreciate,
  understand, estimate; -*diği*
  ~**de** in case, if
takdis REL sanctification,
  consecration
takı GR particle, postposition;
  ~**ılmak** -*e* be affixed to, attach oneself to; deride, ridicule
takım set, lot; service, suit;
  squad, team, gang; ~**adalar**
  pl. GEO archipelago *sg.*;
  ~**yıldız** ASTR constellation
takınmak *v/t* attach to oneself; put on, assume ANAT *attitude*
takır|damak make a tapping
  or knocking noise; ~**tı** tap-
  ping, knocking
takibat *pl.* JUR persecution *sg.*
takip pursuit, persecution; ~
  etm. *v/t* follow, pursue
takke scull-cap

takla(k) somersault
taklit imitation, counterfeiting; ~ **etm.** *v/t* imitate, feign
takma attached; false; ~ **diş**
  false tooth; ~ **saç** false hair
takmak *v/t* affix, attach (-*e*
  to), put on
takoz wooden wedge
takrib|en *adv.* approximately,
  about; ~**î** *adj.* approximate
takrir statement, report; JUR
  notification of transference
  of real property
taksa tax, due
taksi taxicab
taksim division, partition,
  distribution; ~ **etm.** *v/t* divide; distribute; ~**at** *pl.* divi-
  sions, parts
taksimetre taximeter
taksir JUR default, omission;
  ~**li** imprudent, guilty
taksit instalment; ~**le** *adv.* by
  instalments
takt tact
taktik MIL tactics
taktir *v/t* distil
takunya clog
takvim calendar, almanac
takviye reinforcement; ~ **etm.**
  v/t strengthen, reinforce
takyit restriction
talâk divorce
talaş sawdust, filings
talaz wave, billow; a being
  ruffled up (*silk*)
talebe student, pupil
talep request, demand; ~ **etm.**
  v/t request, ask for
tali secondary, subordinate

tapınak

talih luck, good fortune; ~li lucky; ~siz unlucky

talik etm. v/t suspend, put off; attach (-e to)

talim instruction, drill; ~ etm. teach, drill sth. (-e to so.); ~atname regulations pl.

talip(li) -e desirous for

talk talc

taltif etm. v/t show favour to; confer on (ile sth.)

tam adj. complete, entire, perfect; adv. completely; exactly

tamah greed, avarice; ~kâr greedy, avaricious (-e for)

tamam n. completion, end; whole; adj. complete, ready; that's right!; ~en, ~iyle adv. completely, entirely; ~lamak v/t complete, finish; ~lanmak be completed, finished

tambur mus oriental guitar

tamim circular letter; generalization

tamir repair, restoration; ~ etm. v/t repair, mend; ~at pl. repairs

tamlama gr compound word; ~nan gr the part of a compound in the nominative; ~yan gr genitive

tampon wad, plug; buffer (railway); bumper (auto)

tamsayı math whole number

tan dawn

tan s. -dan

tandır oven made in a hole in the earth

tane grain, seed, berry; piece; ~cik granule; ~lemek v/t granulate; ~li having grains or berries

tanı MED diagnosis; ~dık acquaintance

tanık JUR witness; ~lamak v/t prove by witnesses; ~lik evidence

tanı|lamak v/t MED diagnose; ~mak v/t know, recognize; acknowledge

tanım definition; ~ harfi GR article; ~lamak v/t describe, define

tanın|mak be known or recognized; ~mış wellknown, famous

tanış|ıklık acquaintance; ~mak make acquaintance (ile with); ~tırmak v/t introduce (ile to)

tanıt proof, evidence; ~mak v/t introduce (-e to)

tank MIL tank

Tanrı God; ♀ god; ♀sız godless, atheist

tansık miracle, wonder

tansiyon ANAT blood-pressure

tantana pomp, magnificence

tanzifat pl. town scavenging service sg.

tanzim putting in order, organizing; ~ etm. v/t organize, arrange; ♀at pl. the political reforms in 1839 and the time following

tapa fuse; cork

tapan harrow, roller

tap|ı worshipped idol; ~ınak

REL temple; ~ınmak, ~mak -e worship, adore

tapon second-rate, worthless

tapu title-deed; ~lamak v/t register *with a title-deed*

taraça terrace

taraf side, direction, part, end; party; ~ından by, from the direction of; ~gir partial, biased; ~lı having sides *or* supporters; ~sız neutral; ~sızlık neutrality; ~tar partisan, supporter

tarak comb; rake, harrow; weaver's reed; crest *of a bird*; gills *of a fish*; ~lamak v/t comb; rake

tara|ma scan; ~mak v/t comb, rake; search minutely; scan (*computers, medically*); ~nmak comb oneself; be combed

tarassut watching, observation

tarayıcı scanner

taraz combings, fibres *pl.*

tarçın BOT cinnamon

tardetmek *s.* tart etm.

tarh¹ flower-bed

tarh² imposition *of taxes*; substraction

tarhana preparation of yogurt and flour *dried in the sun*

tarım agriculture; ~sal agricultural

tarif description, definition; ~ etm. v/t describe, define

tarife time-table; price-list

tarih history; date; ~çi histori-

an; ~î historical; ~li dated

tarik way, road; method; ~at REL religious order

tarla arable field; ~ kuşu ZOO lark

tart expulsion; repulsion; ~ etm. v/t expel; degrade

tartı weighing, weight; balance; ~lı weighed, balanced; ~lmak be weighed

tartışma dispute; ~k v/i argue, dispute

tartmak v/t weigh; ponder well

tarz form, shape, manner

tarziye apology; ~ vermek -e give satisfaction to

tas bowl, cup

tasa worry, anxiety, grief

tasar project, plan; ~ı POL bill, draft law; ~lamak v/t plan, project

tasarruf possession; economy, saving; -in ~unda olm. be in the possession, at the disposal of; ~ sandığı savings bank

tasavvuf REL mysticism

tasavvur imagination, idea; ~ etm. v/t imagine

tasdik confirmation, ratification; ~ etm. v/t confirm, affirm, ratify; ~name certificate

tasfiye cleaning, liquidation; ~ etm. v/t clean, clear up, liquidate; ~hane TECH refinery

tashih correction; ~ etm. v/t correct

tasım syllogism; ~lamak v/t

plan, project

tasla|k draft, sketch, model; **~mak** v/t make a show of, pretend to

tasma collar *of a dog, etc.*, strap

tasnif classification; **~ etm.** v/t classify; compile

tasrif GR declension, conjugation

tasvip approval; **~ etm.** v/t approve

tasvir design, picture; **~ etm.** v/t depict, draw

taş stone; hard as stone; **~çı** stonemason, quarryman

taşı|mak v/t carry, transport, bear; **~nmak** -e be carried to; move to, go very often to; **~t** vehicle

taşkın overflowing

taş|kömür coal, pitcoal; **~la-mak** v/t stone; grind; **~lı** stony, rocky; **~lık** stony place

taşmak v/i overflow, boil over

taşra the outside; the provinces *pl.*

tat taste, flavour, relish; *-in* **tadına bakmak** taste

tatarcık ZOO sandfly

tatbik adaptation, application; **~ etm.** v/t apply, adapt; **~î** practical; applied

tatil suspension of work; holiday, vacation

tatlı *adj.* sweet, drinkable, agreeable; *n.* dessert, sweet; **~laştırmak** v/t sweeten; **~lık** sweetness; kindness; **~msı** sweetish

tatmak v/t taste, try

tatmin etm. v/t satisfy; calm, reassure

tatsız tasteless; disagreeable

tatula BOT datura, thorn-apple

taun MED pest, plague

tav TECH proper heat *or* condition

tava frying-pan; TECH ladle; trough *for slaking lime*

tavan ceiling

tavassut mediation

tavır mode, manner, attitude

tavla¹ backgammon

tavla² stable

tavlamak v/t bring to its best condition; *fig.* deceive, swindle

tavsif description; **~ etm.** v/t describe

tavsiye recommendation; **~ etm.** v/t recommend (*-e* to)

tavşan ZOO hare; **~cıl** ZOO vulture, eagle

tavuk hen; **~göğsü** *sweet dish made with milk and the pounded breast of a fowl*

tavus ZOO peacock

tay ZOO foal

tayfa hand, troup, crew

tayfun typhoon

tayın MIL ration

tayin appointment, designation; **~ etm.** v/t appoint; decide, fix

tayyör tailor-made costume

taze fresh; new; young; **~leşmek** become young *or* fresh; **~lik** freshness, youth

tazı greyhound

tazim honouring, respect

taziye condolence

tatmin indemnification (*pl.* ~at); ~ etm. *v/t* indemnify

tazyik pressure; oppression; ~ etm. *v/t* put pressure on; oppress

te *s.* da

-te *s.* -da

teati exchange

tebaa POL subject *of a state*

tebarüz etm. become manifest *or* prominent

tebdil change, exchange

teberru gift, donation; ~ etm. *v/t* offer as a free gift

tebessüm smile

tebeşir chalk

tebliğ communication, communiqué; ~ etm. *v/t* transmit, communicate

tebrik congratulation; ~ etm. *v/t* congratulate (*-den dolayı* on)

tebriye etm. *v/t* acquit

tecavüz transgression, aggression; ~ etm. *-e* transgress; attack; ~*-i* pass, exceed

tecdit renewal

tecessüs search; inquisitiveness

tecil etm. *v/t* defer, postpone

tecrit separation, isolation; ~ etm. *v/t* free, isolate (*-den* from); ~ kampı POL isolation *or* concentration camp

tecrübe trial, test, experiment; ~ etm. *v/t* try, test, experiment; ~li experienced;

~siz inexperienced

teçhiz equipping; ~ etm. *v/t* equip, fit out

tedafüî defensive

tedarik preparation, provision; ~ etm. *v/t* procure, obtain, provide

tedavi MED treatment, cure

tedavül circulation

tedbir precaution, measure; ~ almak take the necessary measures

tedfin interring, burial

tedhiş terrifying; ~çi terrorist; ~çilik terrorism

tedirgin irritated, troubled; ~ etm. *v/t* disturb, trouble

tediyat *pl.* payments, deposits; ~e payment

tedric|en *adv.* gradually; ~î *adj.* gradual

teessüf regret, being sorry; ~ etm. *-e* regret, be sorry for

teessür emotion, grief

teessüs being founded *or* established

tefe TECH machine for winding silk; ~ci ECON usurer; ~cilik usury

tefekkür reflection

teferruat *pl.* details

tefrik separation, distinction; ~ etm. *v/t* separate, distinguish (*-den* from)

tefrika discord

tefsir interpretation

teftiş investigation, inspection; ~ etm. *v/t* inspect

teğmen MIL lieutenant

tehdit threat, menace; ~ etm.

v/t threaten
tehir delay, postponement; ~ **etm.** *v/t* defer, postpone
tehlike danger; ~**li** dangerous; ~**siz** without danger
tek *n.* a single thing; *adj.* single, alone; ~ **başına** apart; on one's own; ~ **sayı** MATH odd number; ~ **tük** here and there
tekâmül evolution
tekaüt retirement, pension; ~ **maaşı** retirement pay, pension
teke ZOO **1.** he-goat; **2.** shrimp
tekel monopoly
teker(lek) *n.* wheel; *adj.* circular, round; ~**leme** the use of similarly sounding words in folk narratives
tekerrür recurrence; relapse
tekil GR singular
tekin empty, deserted; ~ **olmıyan** haunted; ~**siz** taboo
tekit confirmation; ~ **etm.** *v/t* confirm, repeat
tekke REL Dervish Convent
teklif proposal, offer; obligation; ~ **etm.** *v/t* propose, offer, submit (*-e* to); ~**siz** without ceremony; free and easy; ~**sizlik** unceremoniousness
tekme kick; ~**lemek** *v/t* kick
tekne trough; hull
teknik technical; ~**çi**, ~**er**, **teknisyen** technician
tekrar repetition; again; ~ **etm.**, ~**lamak** *v/t* repeat
teksif making dense

teksir multiplication; ~ **etm.** *v/t* multiply; duplicate; ~ **makinesi** multiplying machine, hectograph
tekstil textiles *pl.*
tekzip contradiction, denial; ~ **etm.** *v/t* deny, contradict
tel wire; fibre; thread; hair; string; ~ **çekmek** send a wire; ~ **enclose** with wire; ~ **örgü** barbed-wire fence
telaffuz pronunciation
telâfi compensation; ~ **etm.** *v/t* make up for, compensate
telakki interpretation, view
telâş confusion, alarm, anxiety; ~**a düşmek**, ~**lanmak** be confused, flurried; ~**lı** flurried, upset
telef ruin, perdition; death; ~**at** *pl.* losses of life
teleferik TECH telpher, cable ropeway
telefon telephone; ~ **etm.** *-e* telephone; ~ **kabinesi** telephone-box; ~ **kartı** phone-card
teles threadbare
telesekreter voice mail; ~**de not bırakmak** leave a message on a voice mail
televizör television set; ~**yon** television
telgraf telegraph; telegram; ~ **çekmek** send a wire
telif composition; reconciling; ~ **etm.** *v/t* write, compile; ~ **hakkı** copyright
telkih inoculation, vaccination

telkin suggestion, inspiration;
~ **etm.** v/t suggest (-e to)

tellal broker, middleman

tellemek v/t adorn with gold
wire or thread; wire

telsiz adj. wireless; n. wireless
telegraphy; ~ **telefon** wireless phone

teltik deficiency; defect; ~**siz**
complete, whole; round
(sum)

telve coffee-grounds

temas contact; ~ **etm.** -e
touch, touch on; ~**ta bulunmak** be in touch (**ile** with)

temaşa walking about to see
things; scene, show; ~ **etm.**
v/t look at

temayül inclination, tenden-
cy (-e towards)

temayüz etm. be distinguished

tembel lazy; ~**lik** laziness

tembih warning; stimulation;
~ **etm.** -e excite; warn

temdit prolongation, extension

temel n. foundation; base;
adj. basic; ~ **atmak** lay a
foundation; ~ **hak** JUR constitutional right; ~**leşmek**
become firmly established,
settle down; ~**li** fundamental; permanent; ~**siz** without
foundation, baseless

temenni desire, wish; ~ **etm.**
v/t desire, request

temerküz concentration; ~
kampı POL concentration
camp

temettü ECON profit; dividend

temin making sure, assurance; ~ **etm.** v/t assure, secure; ~**at** pl. security sg.; deposit, guarantee sg.

temiz clean, pure; honest;
~**lemek** v/t clean; clean up;
clear away; ~**lik** cleanliness,
purety; honesty

temkin self-possession; dignity; ~**li** grave, dignified

temlik JUR disposal, aliena-
tion

temmuz July

tempo time, measure, pace

temsil representation; THEA
performance; ~ **etm.** v/t represent; THEA present; ~**ci**
agent

temyiz distinguishing; JUR appeal; ~ **etm.** v/t distinguish;
JUR appeal; ~ **mahkemesi**
court of appeal

ten the body; ~ **rengi** flesh-
-colour

-ten s. **-dan**

tenakuz contradiction

tenasül reproduction, generation

tencere saucepan, pot

tender tender (railway)

teneffüs respiration; rest; ~
etm. v/i breathe; pause

teneke tin, tinplate; ~**ci** tin-
smith

tenezzüh pleasure walk, excursion

tenezzül fig. condescension

tenha solitary, lonely; ~**lik**

solitude, lonely place

tenis tennis; ~ **alanı** tennis court

tenkıye MED clyster, syringe

tenkit criticism; ~ **etm.** v/t criticize; ~**çi** critic

tensikat v/i reorganisation sg.: combing out of officials, staff reduction

tente awning

tentene lace

tentür CHEM tincture; ~**diyot** tincture of iodine

tenvir illumination; ~ **etm.** v/t illumine; ~**at** pl. lighting of a street, etc.

tenzilât pl. ECON reductions of prices, etc.; ~**li** reduced in price

teori theory; ~**k** theoretical

tepe hill; summit; ~**lemek** v/t thrash unmercifully; fig. kill; ~**li** crested (bird)

tepinmek v/i kick and stamp

tepir hair sieve

tepki reaction; power of repulsion; ~**li uçak** AVIA jet aeroplane; ~**mek** v/i react

tepmek v/t kick

tepreşmek MED return and cause a collapse

tepsi small tray

ter sweat, perspiration

terakki advance, progress; ~**perver** progressive

terane tune; fig. yarn, story

teras s. taraça

teravi REL prayer special to the nights of Ramazan

terazi balance, pair of scales;

ASTR Libra

terbiye. 1. education, training; **2.** sauce; flavouring; ~ **etm.** v/t educate, train; ~**li. 1.** educated, goodmannered; **2.** flavoured; ~**siz** uneducated, ill-mannered; ~**sizlik** bad manners pl.

tercih preference; ~ **etm.** prefer v/t (-den to)

tercüman interpreter, translator

tercüme translation; ~ **etm.** v/t translate (-e into); ~**ihal** biography

tereddüt hesitation; ~ **etm.** hesitate

tereke JUR heritage; legacy

terementi turpentine

terennüm singing

tereyağı fresh butter

terfi promotion, advancement; ~ **etm.** v/i be promoted

terfih etm. v/t bring prosperity to

terhin pawning, pledging

terhis MIL discharge of a soldier

terim (technical) term

terk abandonment; ~ **etm.** v/t abandon, leave; renounce

terkip composition, compound; GR s. izafet

ter|lemek sweat, perspire; ~**li** sweating, perspiring

terlik slipper

terminal terminal (station)

termo|metre thermometre; ~**s**® thermos® flask; ~**stat**

TECH thermostat

ters[1] excrement *of* ANAT *animal*

ters[2] back, reserve; opposite, wrong; contrary; ~ **gelmek** *-e* appear to *so.* to be in the wrong way; ~ **gitmek** go wrong, turn out badly; ~**ine** *adv.* in the reverse way

tersane NAUT dockyard

tersim etm. *v/t* picture, design, draw

terslik contrariness, vexatiousness

tertemiz absolutely clean

tertibat *pl.* installations

tertip arrangement, order, plan; composition; ~ **etm.**, *v/t* organize; arrange; compose; ~**çi** planner, organizer; ~**lemek** *s.* ~ **etm.**

terzi tailor

tesadüf chance event, coincidence; ~ **etm.** *-e* meet by chance, come across; ~**en** *adv.* by chance

tesanüt solidarity

tesbit *s.* tespit

tescil registration

teselli consolation

teshin heating; ~ **etm.** *v/t* heat

tesir effect, impression, influence; ~ **etm.** *-e* affect, influence; ~**li** impressive

tesis laying a foundation; ~ **etm.** *v/t* found, establish, institute; ~**at** *pl.* institutions, establishments

teskere stretcher; bier

teskin etm. *v/t* pacify, calm

teslim delivery; surrender, submission; ~ **etm.** *v/t* hand over, deliver (*-e* to); ~ **olmak** *v/i* surrender

tespih REL rosary

tespit establishing; proving; ~ **etm.** *v/t* establish, confirm, prove

testere TECH saw

testi pitcher, jug

tesviye making level; payment; free pass *given to travelling soldiers*; ~ **etm.** *v/t* level, smooth, plane

teşbih comparison, simile

teşebbüs effort, initiative; ~ **etm.** *-e* start, undertake; ~**e geçmek** set to work

teşekkül formation, organization

teşekkür thanks, giving thanks; ~ **etm.** *-e* thank; ~ **ederim!** thank you!

teşhir exhibiting; ~ **etm.** *v/t* exhibit; ~ **salonu** showroom

teşhis recognition, identification; MED diagnosis

teşkil formation, organization; ~ **etm.** *v/t* form, organize; ~**ât** *pl.* organization *sg.*

teşri JUR legislation

teşrif conferring honour, arrival; ~ **etm.** *v/t* honour by visiting; ~**at** *pl.* ceremonies; protocol *sg.*

teşrih MED anatomy; dissection

teşriî JUR legislative

teşrik: ~**i mesai** joint effort, co-operation

teşvik encouragement, incitement; ~ etm. v/t encourage, incite (-e to)

tetik[1] trigger

tetik[2] adj. agile, quick; prompt

tetkik examination; ~ etm. v/t investigate, examine

tevali etm. v/i follow in ANAT uninterrupted succession

tevcih etm. v/t direct, confer (-e to)

tevdi entrusting; ~ etm. v/t entrust, deposit

tevellüt birth

tevfikan -e in conformity with

tevkif detention, arrest; ~ etm. v/t detain, arrest; ~hane place of custody

Tevrat REL Pentateuch

tevsi etm. v/t enlarge, extend

tevsik etm. v/t prove by documentary evidence

tevzi distribution, delivery; ~at pl. postal deliveries

teyel coarse sewing, tacking; ~lemek v/t sew coarsely, tack; ~li tacked

teyit confirmation; ~ etm. v/t strengthen; confirm

teyp tape recorder

teyze maternal aunt

tez[1] adj. quick; adv. quickly

tez[2] n. thesis

tezahür manifestation; ~at pl. demonstration sg.

tezat contrast

tezek dried dung

tezgâh loom, work-bench; counter; NAUT ship-building

yard; ~tar who serves at a counter

tezhip gilding, inlaying with gold

tezkere note; certificate

tezlemek v/t hasten, accelerate; ~lenmek make haste; ~lik speed, haste

tezvir willful misrepresentation; deceit

tezyin (pl. ~at) adorning, decoration

tıbbî medical; ~iye medical school

tığ crochet-needle, bodkin, awl; ~lamak v/i give a piercing pain

tıkaç plug, stopper; ~lı stopped up, plugged; ~mak v/t stop up, plug; ~nık s. ~lı; ~nmak be stopped up; choke, suffocate

tıkır|damak clink, rattle; ~tı rattling, clinking

tıkış|ık crammed, squeezed together; ~mak be squeezed together

tıkız hard, tight

tıkmak v/t thrust, squeeze, cram (-e into)

tıknaz plump

tıksırmak sneeze with the mouth shut

tılsım talisman, charm

tımar[1] military fief

tımar[2] dressing of wounds; grooming of a horse; pruning; ~hane lunatic asylum

tıngıldamak, tıngırdamak tinkle, clink, clang

tın|ı tone, timbre; ~lamak tinkle, ring (*metal*)

tıp medicine

tıpa stopper, plug, cork

tıpır|damak walk with little noise; tap, throb; ~tı tapping; tripping noise

tıpkı *adj.* same; ~ ... gibi *adv.* exactly like; ~ basım facsimile

tırabzan hand-rail, banister

tıraş shaving; *sl.* boring talk; bragging; ~ etm. *v/t* shave; ~ olm. get a shave; ~çı boring talker, braggart; ~lı. 1. shaved; 2. needing a shave

tırıllamak *sl.* be 'broke'

tırkaz bar behind the door

tırmalamak *v/t* scratch

tırmanmak -e climb

tırmık scratch; rake, harrow; ~lamak *v/t* scratch, rake, harrow

tırnak finger-nail, toe-nail, claw, hoof; NAUT fluke of ANAT anchor

tırpan scythe; ~lamak *v/t* mow

tırtıkçı *sl.* pickpocket

tırtıl ZOO caterpillar; ~lı traktör TECH crawler tractor

tıslamak hiss (*goose*); spit (*cat*)

ticaret trade, commerce; ~ odası ECON chamber of commerce; ~hane business house, firm

ticarî commercial

tifo MED typhoid fever

tiftik mohair

tifüs MED typhus

tik twitching; mannerism

tike piece, patch

tiksinmek -den be disgusted with, loathe

tilki ZOO fox

timsah ZOO crocodile

timsal symbol, image

tin soul, spirit

tip type

tipi blizzard, snow-storm

tirbuşon corkscrew

tire sewing cotton

tirfil BOT clover

tirit bread soaked in gravy

tiriz lath, batten; piping *of clothes*

tiryaki addicted (-*in* ~si to *sth.*)

titiz peevish, captious, hard to please; ~lik peevishness, pedantry

titre|k trembling; ~mek shiver, tremble; ~şim vibration

tiyatro theatre

tiz high-pitched

tohum seed, grain, semen; ~luk kept for seed

tok satiated; closely woven, thick; ~ gözlü contented, not covetous

toka[1] buckle

toka[2] shaking hands, clinking glasses; ~laşmak shake hands (ile with)

tokat slap; ~lamak *v/t* slap

tokmak mallet; door-knocker; wooden pestle

tokurdamak bubble

tokuş|mak collide (ile with);

~turmak *v/t* cause to collide (ile will); clink (*glasses*); cannon (*billiard-balls*)

tolga helmet

tomar roll, scroll

tombak CHEM copper-zinc alloy

tombaz NAUT barge; pontoon

tomruk heavy log, square boulder

tomurcuk BOT bud; ~lanmak put forth buds

ton¹ ton

ton² MUS note

ton³ (balığı) ZOO tunny

tonilato NAUT tonnage

tonoz ARCH vault

top ball, any round thing; gun, cannon; roll of *cloth or paper*; the whole; ~ yekûn total; ~aç top (*plaything*)

topal lame; cripple; ~lamak limp

toparla|k round; *n.* MIL limber; ~mak *v/t* collect together, pack up

top|**atan** BOT ANAT *oblong kind of melon*; NAUT ~çeker gunboat; ~çu MIL artillery; artilleryman

toplam total, sum

toplama MATH addition; ~ kampı concentration camp; ~k *v/t* collect, gather, sum up; clear away; put on weight

toplan|**mak** *v/i* assemble; come together; ~tı assembly, meeting

toplatmak *v/t* seize, confiscate

toplu having a knob *or* round head; collected, in a mass; ~ iğne pin; ~ sözleşme collective agreement; ~ tabanca revolver; ~luk compactness; community

toplum community; ~bilim sociology; ~sal sociology

toprak earth, soil, land; ~altı being in the earth; ~sız landless

toptan ECON wholesale; ~cı wholesaler

topuk heel, ankle

topuz mace, knob

tor net

torba bag; ANAT scrotum

torik ZOO large bonito

torna TECH (turning-) lathe; ~cı turner; ~vida screwdriver

torpido(bot) NAUT torpedo-boat

torpil NAUT mine; torpedo; ~lemek *v/t* torpedo

tortu dregs, sediment

torun grandchild

tos blow *with the head*; ~lamak *v/t* butt

toto pools *pl.*

toy¹ banquet

toy² ZOO great bustard

toy³ *adj.* inexperienced, "green"

toygar ZOO crested lark

toyluk inexperience

toynak hoof

toz dust; powder; *-in* ~unu almak dust; ~armak raise the dust; **~lu** dusty; **~luk** gaiter

töhmet suspicion; guilt

töre custom(s); **~l** moral; ethical; **~n** ceremony, celebration

törpü rasp, file; **~lemek** v/t rasp, file

tövbe REL repentance; **~kâr**, **~li** penitent

trafik traffic

trahom MED trachoma

trajedi tragedy

traktör tractor

Trakya Thrace

trampa ECON barter, exchange

trampete MUS side drum

tramplen spring-board

tramvay tram, streetcar

transfer transfer

transistor TECH transistor; **~lu** equipped with transistor(s)

transit transit

travers sleeper (*railway*)

tren train (*railway, etc.*)

tribün tribune

trişin trichina

troleybüs trolley-bus

trompet trumpet

tropika GEO tropical zone; tropic; **~l** tropical

tröst ECON trust

trup THEA troupe

tufan REL the Flood; violent rainstorm

tugay MIL brigade

tuğ horse-tail, plume; **~amiral** NAUT rear-admiral; **~bay** MIL brigadier; **~general** MIL

brigadier-general

tuğla brick

tuğra monogram *of the Sultan*

tuğyan overflowing; *fig.* rebellion

tuhaf uncommon, curious, odd, comic; **~iye** millinery, clothing accessories *pl.*; **~lık** being odd *or* funny

tul lenght; ASTR longitude

tulum skin *for holding water, etc.*; tube; overall; MUS bagpipe

tulumba pump; fire-engine

tumturak bombast, pompous speech

Tuna (nehri) Danube

tunç bronze

tur tour

turba turf; peat

turfa REL not kosher

turfanda early (*fruit, etc.*), not in its proper season

turi|st tourist, traveller; **~zm** tourism, travelling

turna ZOO crane

turn|e THEA tour; **~ike** turnstile; **~uva** tourney, tournament

turp BOT radish

turşu pickle

turta tart, cake

turunç BOT Seville orange

tuş key *of a piano, typewriter, etc.*

tuta|k 1. handle; 2. hostage; **~m** small handful; **~mak** 1. handle; 2. proof, evidence; **~nak** protocol, report; **~r** total, sum; **~rak**, **~rık** MED seizure, fit

tutkal glue; **~lamak** *v/t* glue; **~lı** glued

tut|ku passion (*-e* for); **~kun** *-e* affected by, given to; **~mak** *v/t* hold, hold on to; catch, seize; stop; hire, rent; amount to; *v/i* take root; adhere; **~sak** MIL prisoner, captive; **~turmak** *v/t* begin, start; run his mind on

tutuk embarrassed, tongue-tied; **~lamak** *v/t* detain, arrest; **~lu** arrested, detained; **~luluk** confinement

tutulma ASTR eclipse; **~k** *-e* be struck with, be mad about

tutum conduct; economy

tutuş|mak catch fire; *-e* start, meddle into; **~turmak** *v/t* set on fire; *-i -in* **eline** press *sth.* into *someone's* hand

tutya CHEM zinc

tuvalet toilet; dressing-table; lavatory

tuz salt

tuzak trap; **~ kurmak** *-e* lay a trap for

tuz|la salt-pan; **~lamak** *v/t* salt, pickle; **~lu** salted, pickled; **~luk** saltcellar; salt shaker; **~ruhu** CHEM hydrochloric acid, spirit of salt; **~suz** unsalted, insipid

tüberküloz MED tuberculosis

tüccar merchant

tüfek gun, rifle

tüken|mek be exhausted, give out; **~mez. 1.** inexhaustible; **2.** *n. a kind of syrup;* **~mez**

kalem ball-point pen

tüket|im consumption; **~mek** *v/t* exhaust, use up

tükür|mek *v/t& spit (*-e* on); **~ük** spittle, saliva

tül tulle

tüm the whole; **~admiral** NAUT Vice-Admiral; **~en** great number, 10.000; MIL division; **~general** MIL major general; **~leç** GR object, complement; **~lemek** *v/t* complete

tümsek GEO small mound

tün night; **~aydın!** good evening!

tünel tunnel

tüp tube

tür species

türbe ARCH tomb, mausoleum

türbin turbine

türe JUR law

türedi upstart, parvenu

türe|mek appear, come into existence; **~tici** inventor; **~tmek** *v/t* produce, invent

Türk Turk; Turkish; **~çe** Turkish (*language*); **~çülük** POL Panturkism

Türkiyat Turkology

Türkiye Turkey; **~ Cumhuriyeti** the Turkish Republic

Türk|leşmek become like a Turk; **~lük** the quality of being a Turk; **~men** Turcoman; **2oloji** turkology

türkü MUS folk song

türlü *adj.* various, of many sorts; *n.* sort, kind, variety;

bir ~ somehow; iki ~ in two ways

türüm genesis, creation

tüt|mek v/i smoke; ~sü fumigant, incense

tütün tabacco; ~ içmek smoke (tobacco); ~cü grower or seller of tobacco

tüy feather; hair; ~lenmek grow feathers; *fig.* grow rich; ~lü feathered; ~süz without feathers; young

tüzel JUR legal; ~ kişi juristic person, corporation

tüzük regulations, statutes *pl.*

U

ucuz cheap; ~luk cheapness

uç tip, point, extremity, end; frontier

uçak aeroplane; ~ bileti air-travel ticket; ~ faciası air disaster; ~savar (topu) MIL anti-aircraft gun

uç|kun spark; ~kur belt, band *for holding up trousers*; ~lu pointed

uçmak fly; evaporate; fade away, disappear

uçsuz without a point

uçucu flying; volatile

uçur|mak v/t cause to fly; cut off; ~tma kite (*toy*); ~um precipice; abyss

uçuş flight, flying; ~ hattı flight route

uçuşmak fly about

ufacık very small, tiny

ufak small; ~ para small change; ~ tefek small, of no account; ~lık small change

ufa|lamak v/t break up, crumble; ~lmak diminish, become smaller

ufkî horizontal

uflamak say 'off'

ufuk horizon

uğra|k frequented place *or* region; ~mak -e stop, touch at; meet with, suffer; undergo; ~şmak be busy, fight (ile with); ~tmak -i -e cause so. to stop at; expose so. to; -i -den dismiss so. from

uğul|damak hum, buzz; howl; ~tu humming, buzzing

uğur good omen; uğru(n)da for the sake of, on account of; ~lu lucky, suspicious; ~suz inauspicious; ~suzluk ill omen

uhde obligation, charge

uhrevî REL pertaining to the next world

ulaç GR gerund

ulak courier

ulamak v/t join (-e to)

ulan hi! man alive!

ulaşım communication, contact; ~mak -e reach, arrive at

ulaştır|ma communication; ~ma Bakanlığı Ministry of

Transport; ~mak v/t cause to reach (-e a place, etc.)

ulema pl. REL. doctors of Moslem religious law

ulu great, high; ~lamak v/t honour

ulumak howl (dog, etc.)

uluorta adv. rashly, recklessly, without reserve

ulus people, nation; ~al national; ~lararası international

ulvî high, sublime

umacı bogy man

um|madık unexpected; ~mak v/t hope, expect

umum adj. general, universal, all; n. the public; ~î general, universal; public

umumiyet generality; ~le adv. in general

umut hope; ~suz hopeless, desperate

un flour

unmak heal, get well

unsur element

unut|kan forgetful; ~mak v/t forget

unvan title; superscription

Uranus ASTR Uranus

uranyum CHEM uranium

urgan rope

us state of mind, reason, intelligence

usan|ç boring, boredom; ~dırıcı boring, tedious; ~dırmak v/t bore, disgust; ~mak become bored, disgusted (-den with)

uskumru ZOO mackerel

uskur NAUT screw, propeller; ~u TECH screw thread, worm

us|lanmak become sensible, well-behaved; ~lu well-behaved, sensible

usta n. master; master workman; adj. skilled, clever; ~lık mastery, proficiency

ustura razor

usturuplu sl. striking, hitting the target, right

usul method, system, manner; ~üne göre adv. duly, in due form; ~cacık, ~la(cık) adv. slowly, gently, quietly

uşak boy, youth; servant, assistant; ~kapan ZOO lammergeier

utan|ç shame, modesty; ~dırmak v/t make ashamed, cause to blush; ~gaç, ~gan bashful, shy; shamefaced; ~mak be ashamed (-den of); -e recoil at, be ashamed of doing

Utarit ASTR Mercury

uvalamak v/t press with the hand, crumble

uv|mak v/t press with the hand, massage, polish; ~uşturmak v/t rub against each other

uyan|dırmak v/t awaken, revive, stir; ~ık awake, vigilant; ~mak awake, wake up, come to life

uyar conformable; ~lamak v/t accomodate, adjust (-e to)

uyarmak v/t awaken, arouse; fig. remind, warn

uydurma invented, false, made-up; ~k v/t make to fit, adapt; ~syon sl. invention, fable

uygar civilized; ~lık civilization

uygulamak v/t apply

uygun -e conformable, in accord to, fitting; ~ bulmak, ~ görmek v/t agree to, approve of; ~ gelmek -e suit; ~luk being appropriate, fitting; ~suz unsuitable

uyku sleep; ~ya dalmak fall asleep; ~suz sleepless

uyluk ANAT thigh

uymak -e conform, fit to; follow, listen to; harmonize with

uyruk POL subject, citizen; ~luk nationality

uysal conciliatory, easygoing

uyuklamak v/i doze

uyum harmony, conformity

uyu|mak sleep; ~rgezen somnambulist

uyuşmak¹ come to an agreement (ile with)

uyuş|mak² become numb, insensible; ~turmak v/t be-

numb, deaden; ~uk numbed, insensible

uyut|mak v/t send to sleep; fig. ease, allay; put off; ~ucu soporific

uyuz MED n. itch, mange; adj. mangy, scabby

uz good, able

uzak distant, remote (-den from); ~laşmak retire, be far away (-den from); ~laştırmak v/t remove, take away (-den from); ~lık distance, remoteness; ~tan from far-off; ~tan kumanda remote control

uza|m largeness, extent; ~mak grow long, extend, be prolonged; ~nmak -e be extended to, stretch oneself out on, extend to; ~tmak v/t extend, prolong; ~y ASTR space

uzlaşmak come to an agreement pr understanding

uzman expert, specialist

uzun long; ~luk length, lengthiness

uzuv ANAT member, organ

Ü

ücret pay, wage, fee, cost, price; ~li paid, employed for pay; ~li memur employee; ~siz unpaid; gratis

üç three; ~ köşeli triangular, three-cornered; ~gen MATH

triangle; ~üz triplets pl.; triplet

üflemek -e blow upon; -i blow out

üfür|mek -i blow; -e cure by breathing on; ~ükçü sorcerer *who claims to cure by breathing on*

üleş|mek divide, share (**ile** with); **~tirmek** *v/t* distribute, share out (**-e** to)

ülfet familiarity, friendship

ülke country

Ülker ASTR the Pleiades

ülkü ideal

ülser MED ulcer

ültimatom POL ultimatum

ümit hope, expectation; **~** **etm.** *v/t* hope, except; **~lendirmek** *v/t* make hopeful; **~li** full of hope; **~siz** hopeless; desperate

ün fame, reputation

üni|forma uniform; **~versite** university

ünlem cry, shout; GR interjection; **~ işareti** GR exclamation mark

ünlemek **-e** call out to

ünlü famous; GR vowel

ünsiyet familiarity (**ile** with)

ünsüz GR consonant

üre|m ECON interest; **~mek** *v/i* multiply, increase; **~tim** ECON production; **~tmek** *v/t* multiply, breed, raise

ürkek timid, fearful; **~lik** timidity

ürk|mek **-den** start with fear from, be frightened of; **~ütmek** *v/t* startle, scare

ürpermek stand on end (*hair*)

ürümek howl; bay

ürün product

üs base, basis

üsçavuş MIL sergeant

üslup manner, form, style

üst *n.* upper surface, top; outside; **-in** **~ün(d)e** in, upon, over; **-in** **~ünden** from above, over; **~ ~e** one on top of the other

üstat master, teacher

üstderi ANAT, BOT epidermis

üsteğmen MIL first lieutenant

üste|lemek **-e** be added to; recur (*illness*); **~lik** *adv.* furthermore, in addition

üstün superior (**-den** to); victorious; **~körü** superficial; **~lük** superiority

üstüvane TECH cylinder

üşen|ç, **~geç**, **~gen** lazy, slothful; **~iklik** laziness, sloth; **~mek** **-e** be too lazy to *inf.*, do with reluctance

üşmek **-e** flock to

üşü|mek catch cold; **~tmek** *v/t* cause to catch cold; *v/i* catch cold

ütü flat-iron; **~lemek** *v/t* iron; singe; **~lü** ironed, singed; **~süz** not ironed

üvey step-; **~ baba** stepfather; **~ evlât** stepchild

üye member *of a council, etc.*; ANAT organ

üzengi stirrup

üzere **-mek** at the point of **-ing**, just about to *inf.*

üzeri|nde **-in** on, over, above; **-in** **~ne** on; upon; about

üzgeç rope ladder

üzgü oppression; cruelty; **~n** weak, invalid

üz|mek *v/t* strain, break; hurt

the feelings of; ~ülmek be
worn out; -e be sorry for, regret

üzüm BOT grape
üzüntü anxiety; dejection;
~lü tedious; anxious

V, W

vaat promise; ~ etm. v/t
promise
vacip necessary
vade fixed term, date; ~li having a fixed term
vadetmek s. vaat etm.
vadi valley
vaftiz REL baptism; ~ etm. v/t
baptize
vagon railway car; ~ restoran
dining-car
vah vah! intj. how sad!; what
a pity!
vahe oasis
vahim serious, dangerous
vahiy REL inspiration, revelation
vahş|et wildness, savageness;
~î wild, savage, brutal
vaiz REL sermon
vaiz REL preacher
vaka event, occurence
vakar gravity, dignity; ~lı
grave, dignified, calm
vakf|etmek v/t devote, dedi-
cate (-e to); ~iye REL deed
of trust of a pious foundation
vakıa adv. in fact; indeed
vakıf pious foundation, wakf
vâkif -e aware, cognizant of
vakit time; -diği ~ conj. when;
~siz inopportune, untimely

vakt|aki conj. when, at the
time that; ~inde in due time;
~iyle adv. in due time; at one
time
vakum PHYS vacuum
valf TECH valve
vali POL governor of a province
valide mother
valiz suit-case
vallahi! intj. By God!
vals waltz
vanilya BOT vanilla
ventilatör ventilator, fan; ~
kayışı ventilator-belt
vapur steamer
var there is, there are; ~ olm.
exist; ~ ol! may you live
long!; bravo!
varak leaf; sheet of paper; ~a
leaf; note, letter
varda! intj. keep clear! make
way!
var|dırmak v/t cause to reach
(-e a place or condition);
~ılmak be reached (-e place);
~ış arrival
varidat pl. revenues
varil small cask
vâris heir
varlık existence, presence,
self; wealth; ~ vergisi property tax

varmak -e arrive at, reach, attain; result, end in

varoş suburb

varta great peril

varyete THEA variety theatre

varyos sledge-hammer

vasat middle; average; ~î *adj.* middle, average

vasıf quality; ~landırmak *v/t* qualify, describe

vasıl olm. -e arrive at, reach

vasıta means; intermediary; vehicle; ~siyle by means of; ~li indirect; ~siz direct

vasi JUR executor; trustee

vasiyet will, testament; ~name written will

vaşak ZOO lynx

vat EL Watt

vatan native country; ~daş compatriot; ~daşlık citizenship; ~perver patriot

vatman tram-driver

vay! *intj.* oh! woe!

vazgeç|irmek -i -den make so. give up *or* abandon *sth.*; ~mek -den give up, cease from, abandon

vazıh clear, manifest

vazife duty, obligation; home-work (*school*); ~lendirmek *v/t* charge, entrust (ile with)

vaziyet position, situation

vazo vase

ve and; ~ saire and so on

veba MED plague, pestilence

vecibe obligation

vecih face; direction; *s.* veçhile

veçhile: bir ~ in some way; bu ~ in this way

veda farewell; ~ etm. -e bid farewell to; ~laşmak say farewell (ile to)

vefa fidelity, loyality; ~dar, ~lı -e faithful, loyal to; ~sız faithless, untrustworthy

vefat death; ~ etm. die

vehim groundless fear

vekâlet attorneyship, representation; POL Ministry; ~name JUR power of attorney

vekil agent, representative; POL Minister of State; ~harç major-domo

velense *a kind of* thick blanket

velet child; bastard

velev (ki) *conj.* even if

velhasıl in short

veli JUR guardian; REL saint; ~aht POL heir to the throne; ~nimet benefactor, patron

velvele noise, clamour

Venüs ASTR Venus

veraset inheritance

verecek debt

verem *n.* MED tuberculosis; *adj.* (~li) tuberculous

veresi(ye) *adv.* on credit

verev oblique

vergi tax; gift; ~ beyannamesi income-tax return; ~li generous

verilmek -e be given, delivered to

verim produce, profit, output; ~li profitable, productive; **~siz** yielding little produce, unfruitful

vermek v/t give, deliver, attribute (-e to); pay

vernik varnish

vesika document

vesile cause, pretext

vesselâm so that's that!

vestiyer cloak-room

veteriner MED veterinary surgeon

vetire process

veto veto

veya(hut) or

vezin weighing, weight; metre (poetry)

vezir Vizier; minister

vezne treasury, pay-office; **~dar** treasurer, cashier

vıcıklamak v/t make sticky

vınlamak buzz, hum

vırılda(n)mak talk incessantly; grumble, nag

vızıl|damak buzz, hum; **~tı** buzzing noise

vicdan conscience; **~lı** conscientious, honest; **~sız** unscrupulous

vida TECH screw; **~lamak** v/t screw; **~lı** having screws; screwed

vilâyet POL province

villa villa

vinç TECH crane, winch

viraj curve of a road

viran ruined; **~e** n. ruin

virgül GR comma

virüs MED, a. computer virus

visamiral NAUT vice-admiral

viski whisky

viskonsolos POL vice-consul

vişne BOT morello cherry

vites TECH gear; **~ kolu** gear lever

vitrin shop-window

Viyana Vienna

vize POL visa

vizita MED visit; doctor's fee

voleybol volleyball

volkan GEO volcano

volt EL volt; **~aj** voltage

votka vodka

vuku occurence, event; **~ bulmak**, **~a gelmek** happen, take place; **~at** pl. events, incidents

vukuf -e knowledge of, information about

vulkanize etm. v/t TECH vulcanize

vurgu GR accent, stress; **~lu** stressed

vurgun(culuk) ECON profiteering

vur|mak v/t hit (-e against); apply (-e to); kill; steal, swindle; **~uş** blow; **~uşmak** fight (ile with)

vusul arrival

vuzuh clearness

vücu|t existence, being; the human body; **~da gelmek** arise, come into existence

web F internet; **~ sitesi** website

www (= world wide web) bir internet adresin başlangıcı

Y

ya¹ *intj.* oh!

ya² (*at the beginning of a sentence*) well; yes, but ...; (*at the end of a sentence*) indeed; there!; after all

ya³ or; ~ ... ~ ... either ... or ...

-ya *s.* **-a**

yaba wooden fork

yaban desert, wilderness; stranger; ~ **domuzu** zoo wild boar; ~ **kedisi** zoo wild cat; ~ı strange; foreign; ~ı untamed, wild; ~ı **gül** bot wild rose

yadırgamak *v/t* regard as a stranger, find strange

yadigâr souvenir; *fig.* scoundrel

yadsımak *v/t* deny

yafta label

yağ oil, fat, grease; ~dan(lık) grease-pot; oil-can

yağdırmak let rain (-e upon); econ glut with

yağış rain; ~ı rainy

yağ|lamak *v/t* grease, oil; ~ı fat, greasy, oily; *fig.* profitable

yağma booty; loot; ~ *v/t* plunder; ~ **etm.** *v/t* plunder; ~cı plunderer, pillager

yağmak *v/t* rain (-e upon)

yağmur *n.* rain; ~ **yağmak** rain; ~lu rainy; ~luk raincoat

yağsız fat-free

yahni meat stew with onions

yahşi pretty

yahu! *intj.* see here!; say!; my goodness!; please!

Yahudi *n.* Jew; *adj.* Jewish; ~lik Judaism; quality of a Jew

yahut or

yaka collar; bank, shore

yakacak fuel; combustibles *pl.*

yakala|mak *v/t* collar, seize; ~nmak be seized; be held responsible

yakı med cautery, plaster

yakıcı burning, biting

yakın *adj.* near (-e to); *n.* nearby place, neighbourhood; ~da *adv.* near; in the near future; recently; ~dan *adv.* closely, from the near; ~laşmak -e approach; ~lık nearness, proximity

yakışık suitability; ~sız unsuitable, unbecoming

yakışmak be suitable, proper (-e for)

yakıt fuel

yakinen *adv.* for certain, doubtless

yaklaş|ık approximate; ~mak -e approach, approximate; ~tırmak *v/t* bring near

yakmak *v/t* light, set on fire; apply

yakut ruby

yalak trough; stone basin

yalamak *v/t* lick, sweep over

yalan lie; false; ~ **söylemek** lie; ~**cı** lier; imitated, false; ~**cılık** lying, mendacity; ~**lamak** *v/t* deny, contradict

yalçın bare, slippery, steep

yaldız gilding; ~**lamak** *v/t* gild; ~**lı** gilt; false

yalı shore, beach; waterside residence

yalım. 1. flame; **2.** blade, edge

yalın single; bare, naked; ~ **hal** GR nominative case; ~**ayak** barefoot

yalıt‖**kan** PHYS, EL isolating, insulating; ~**mak** *v/t* isolate, insulate

yalnız alone; only; ~**lık** solitude, loneliness

yalpa NAUT rolling

yaltak‖**(çı)** fawning, cringing; ~**lanmak** fawn, flatter; ~**lık** flattery

yalvaç messenger, prophet

yalvarmak *-e* entreat, implore, beg

yama patch

yamaç side, slope *of a hill*

yamak assistant

yama‖**(la)mak** *v/t* patch; ~**lı** patched

yaman strong, violent

yamanmak *-e* be patched on; *fig.* be imposed on; foist oneself on

yamuk bent, crooked; MATH trapezoid

yamyam cannibal; ~**lık** cannibalism

yan side, flank; direction; ~

sokak side street; ~ ~**a** side by side; *-in* ~**ına** towards, to; *-in* ~**ında** beside; with; *-in* ~**ından** from

yanak ANAT cheek

yanardağ GEO volcano

yanaş‖**ma** approaching; hireling; ~**mak** *-e* draw near, approach, come alongside; ~**tırmak** *v/t* bring near, let come alongside

yanay profile, side-face

yandaş partisan, supporter

yandık BOT camel-thorn

yangı inflammation; ~**lan-mak** become inflamed

yangın fire, conflagration; ~ **muhbiri** fire-alarm; ~ **sigor-tası** fire insurance

yanık burned, scorched; piteous; burn, scald

yanıl‖**mak** make a mistake; go wrong; ~**tmak** *v/t* lead into error

yanıt *n.* answer; ~**lamak** *v/t* answer

yani that is, namely

yankesici pickpocket

yankı echo; reaction

yanlış *n.* mistake, error; *adj.* wrong, incorrect; ~**lık** mistake, blunder

yanmak burn, be alight; catch fire; be burnt

yansı reflection; ~**lamak**, ~**tmak** reflect

yansız neutral, impartial

yapağı, ~**k** wool *shorn in spring*

yapı building, edifice; ~**cı** *n.*

maker, constructor; *adj.* constructive; ~lı made, built

yapılış construction; structure; ~mak be built, be constructed

yapım construction, building; manufacture; ~evi factory, workshop

yapınmak *v/t* make *or* have made for oneself; *-e* try to *inf.*

yapışkan sticky, adhesive; ~mak *-e* stick to, hang on; ~tırmak *v/t* attach, fasten (*-e* to)

yapıt work *of art, etc.*

yapma *n.* imitation; *adj.* false; ~k *v/t* do, make, construct

yaprak leaf; sheet *of paper*; ~lanmak come into leaf

yaptırmak *v/t* cause to be made, order

yar precipice, abyss

yara wound; *fig.* pain

yaradan REL Creator; ~dılış creation; nature, constitution

yaralamak *v/t* wound, hit; ~lanmak be wounded; ~lı wounded

yarama *-e* be useful, suitable for; ~maz useless; naughty; ~mazlık naughtiness

yaranmak offer one's services (*-e* to)

yarar *adj. -e* useful, serviceable for; *n.* advantage; ~lık capability, courage

yarasa ZOO bat

yaraşıklı suitable; ~mak *-e* harmonize, go well with

yaratıcı creative, creating; ~mak *v/t* create

yarbay MIL lieutenant-colonel

yarda yard

yardak assistant

yardım help, assistance; ~ etm. *-e* help; ~cı helper, assistant; *adj.* auxiliary; ~cı fiil GR auxiliary verb

yargı JUR decision; lawsuit; ~ yetkisi judicial power; ~ç judge; ~lamak *v/t* try, judge; ~tay Court of Appeal

yarı half; ~ ~ya *adv.* fifty-fifty; ~k split, cleft, crack, fissure

yarım half; ~ada GEO peninsula

yarın tomorrow; ~ değil öbür gün the day after tomorrow

yarış race, competition; ~ma competition; ~mak race, compete (ile with)

yarmak *v/t* split, cleave, break through

yas mourning; ~ tutmak be in mourning

yasa law

yasak *n.* prohibition; *adj.* forbidden, prohibited; ~ etm. *v/t* forbid

yasama ~ yetkisi JUR legislative power; ~k *v/t* arrange

yasemin BOT Jasmin

yaslı in mourning

yassı flat and wide; ~lık flatness, planeness; ~ltmak *v/t* flatten, plane

yastık pillow, cushion, bolster; nursery-bed (*garden*)

yaş[1] *adj.* wet, damp; *n.* tears

yaş[2] age; **yirmi ~ında** 20 years old

yaşa|m life; **~mak** *v/i* live; **~ntı** way of life; experience of life

yaşarmak become wet

yaşayış way of living, life

yaşlanmak grow old

yaşlı[1] wet

yaşlı[2] aged

yat NAUT yacht

yatağan heavy curved knife

yatak bed, lair, berth; bed; TECH bearing; **~ odası** bedroom; **~ takımı** bedclothes; **~lı vagon** sleeping-car

yata|lak bedridden; **~y** horizontal

yatı halting place *for the night*; **~lı okul** boarding school; **~rım** ECON deposit; investment; **~rmak** *v/t* cause to lie down; deposit; **~şmak** calm down, become quiet

yat|mak *-e* lie down on, lean towards; go *to bed*; **~sı** time two hours after sunset

yavan with little fat; tasteless

yavaş slow; low, soft (*voice*); gentle, mild; **~** *adv.* gently, steadily; **~lamak** become slow; **~latmak** *v/t* slacken, slow down

yave foolish talk

yaver assistant; MIL aide-de-camp

yavru young; cub, chick

yavuklanmak *-e* become engaged to

yavuz ferocious, resolute

yay bow; TECH spring; ASTR Sagittarius

yaya on foot; pedestrian; **~ gitmek** go on foot; **~ kaldırımı** foot pavement; **~n** on foot; *fig.* without skill

yaygara shout, outcry

yaygın widespread

yayık[1] churn

yayı|k[2] spread out; wide; **~lmak** *-e* be spread on

yayım publishing; publication; **~lamak** *v/t* publish

yayın publication; **~evi** publishing house

yayla high plateau; **~mak** graze *on a high plateau*

yaylı having springs

yaymak *v/t* spread, scatter; broadcast

yayvan broad

yaz summer

yaz|ar writer, author; **~dırmak** *v/t* cause to be written, have registered; **~gı** destiny

yazı writing; handwriting; written article; **~ makinesi** typewriter; **~hane** desk; office

yazık pity; shame; deplorable; **~!** what a pity!

yazıl|ı written; inscribed; **~mak** be written; be registered (*-e in*)

yazım orthography, spelling

yazın¹ literature

yazın² *adv.* in summer

yazışmak correspond (**ile** with)

yazıt inscription

yazlık suitable for the summer

yazma writing; ~ **kitap** manuscript; ~**k** *v/t* write; register, enrol (-**e in**)

-ye *s.* -a

yedek in reserve, spare; ~ **parça** spare part; ~ **subay** MIL reserve conscript officer

yedi seven

yediemin JUR depositary, trustee

yedirmek *v/t* cause to eat, feed

yegâne sole, unique

yeğen nephew; niece

yek|nesak uniform, monotonous; ~**pare** in a single piece

yekûn total, sum

yel wind

yele mane

yelek waistcoat

yelken sail; ~ **açmak** hoist sails; ~**li** *adj.* fitted with sails; *n.* sailing ship

yelkovan minute-hand; weather-cock

yellemek *v/t* blow upon, fan

yelpaze fan; ~**lemek** *v/t* fan

yelpik asthma

yem food; feed; bait

yemek. 1. *n.* meal, food, dish; banquet; 2. *v/t* consume, eat, spend; bite; suffer; ~**lik** serving as a food, edible

yemin oath; ~ **etm.** swear, take an oath (-*in* **üzerine** by); ~**li** sworn in

yemiş. 1. fruit; 2. zoo fig(s)

yem|lemek *v/t* bait; feed; entice; ~**lik** *adj.* suitable for food; *n.* trough, manger; *fig.* bribe

yemyeşil very green

yen sleeve

yençmek *v/t* crush, smash

yenge the wife of one's uncle *or* brother

yengeç zoo crab; ♋ ASTR Cancer

yengi victory

yeni new; recent; ~**den** anew, once again; ~**bahar** BOT allspice; ~**çeri** Janissary; ~**lemek** *v/t* renew, renovate; ~**lenmek** be renewed, renovated; ~**lik** newness; renovation, reform

yenilmek¹ be eaten

yenilmek² be overcome, lose

yenmek¹ *v/t* overcome, conquer

yenmek² be edible

yepyeni brand new

yer earth, ground, place; space, room; ~ **bulmak** take place; ~**de** on the ground; ~**inde** in its place, suitable; ~**ine** instead of; ~**ine getirmek** *v/t* carry out

yer|altı underground, subterranean; ~**el** local; ~**fıstığı** BOT peanut

yerleş|mek -*de* settle down in, become established in;

~tirmek v/t put into place, settle

yer|li local, indigenous, native; ~siz out of place; ~yüzü GEO face of the earth

yeşil green, fresh; ~lenmek become green; ~lik greenness; meadow; greens

yetenek ability, capacity

yeter sufficient, enough; ~li competent, qualified; ~lik competence, qualification; ~siz inadequate

yetim orphan

yetinmek be contented (ile with)

yetiş|mek -e reach, attain; catch (train, etc.); be brought up; suffice; ~tirmek v/t cause to reach; bring up, educate

yetki competence, qualification; ~li competent, qualified; ~n perfect

yetmek -e suffice; reach; attain

yetmiş seventy

yevmiye daily pay

yığılı heaped, piled up

yığın heap, pile; ~ak MIL concentration; ~tı accumulation, heap

yığ|ışmak v/i crowd together; ~mak v/t collect, pile up

yıka|mak v/t wash; ~nmak wash oneself

yıkı|cı destructive; ~k demolished, ruined; ~lmak be demolished, fall down; ~m bankruptcy; ~ntı ruins, debris

yık|mak v/t pull down, demolish; ~tırmak v/t cause to be pulled down

yıl year

yılan zoo snake; ~balığı zoo eel; ~cık MED erysipelas; ~kavi adj. spiral, winding

yılbaşı New Year's Day

yıldırak shining; 2 ASTR Canopus

yıldırım lightning; ~ harbi MIL blitzkrieg

yıldız star; ~çiçeği BOT dahlia

yıldönümü anniversary

yılgı horror, dread; ~n cowed, frightened

yılışık importunate; ~mak grin impudently

yıl|la(n)mak take on years; grow old; ~lık n. annual, yearbook; adj. one year old; for one year

yılma|k -den be afraid of, dread; ~z undaunted

yıpra(n)mak wear out, be worn out, grow old

yırtıcı: ~ hayvan beast of prey

yırt|ık torn, rent, tattered; fig. shameless; ~lmak be torn, rent; ~mak v/t tear, rend; break in (horse)

yiğit hero; young man; adj. courageous; ~lik courage, heroism

yine s. gene

yirmi twenty

yit|irmek v/t lose; ~mek be lost; go astray

yiv groove; TECH thread

yiyecek food

yobaz REL fanatic; ~lık fanaticism

yoğaltım consumption; ~mak v/t consume, use up

yoğun thick, dense; ~luk density, thickness

yoğurmak v/t knead

yoğurt yogurt, yaourt; ~cu maker or seller of yogurt

yok there is not; non-existent, absent; no; ~ etm. v/t annihilate

yoklama roll-call; MIL call-up; examination; ~k v/t search, examine, try, test

yok|luk absence, lack, non-existence; ~sa if not, otherwise; or; but not

yoksul destitute; ~luk destitution

yoksun deprived (-den of)

yokuş rise, ascent; ~ aşağı down-hill; ~ yukarı uphill

yol road, way, street; manner, method; rule; law; ~ açmak -e cause; ~ vermek -e make way to; discharge; ~a çıkmak start, depart; ~una koymak v/t set right; ~unda in order, going well; ~unu şaşırmak lose the way; ~ kesici brigand

yolcu traveller, passenger; ~luk travelling

yol|daş comrade; ~lamak v/t send, dispatch (-e to); ~lu striped; having such and such roads or manners; ~luk provisions for a journey

yolmak v/t pluck, tear out, strip

yolsuz roadless; contrary to law; ~luk irregularity; abuse, misuse

yonca BOT clover, trefoil

yonga chip, chipping

yontmak v/t cut, sharpen; chip

yordam agility, dexterity

yorgan quilt; ~cı quiltmaker

yorgun tired, weary; ~luk fatigue, weariness

yormak[1] v/t tire, fatigue

yormak[2] v/t attribute (-e to)

yortu REL Christian feast

yorulmak[1] be tired

yorulmak[2] be attributed (-e to)

yorum commentary, interpretation; ~lamak v/t explain, comment on

yosma pretty, attractive; coquette

yosun BOT moss; ~lu mossy, covered with moss

yoz virgin (soil), wild

yön direction; ~eltmek v/t direct, turn (-e towards)

yönet|im administration, management; ~mek v/t direct, administer; regulation; ~melik regulation; ~men director

yöntem method, way

Yörük Turcoman nomad

yörünge ASTR orbit

yudum mouthful

yufka n. thin layer of dough; adj. thin, weak

Yugoslavya hist Yugoslavia

yuha *intj.* shame on you!; **∼la-mak** *v/t* hoot down *or* off

yukarı *n.* top, upper part; *adj.* high, upper, top; **∼da** above, overhead; **∼dan** from above; **∼ya** upward

yulaf BOT oats

yular halter

yumak¹ *v/t* wash

yumak² ball *of wool, etc.*

yummak *v/t* shut, close

yumru round thing, boil

yumruk fist; blow with the fist; **∼lamak** *v/t* hit with the fist

yumu|k closed, half-shut; **∼lmak** become closed

yumurta egg; roe, spawn; **∼akı** the white of an egg; **∼sarısı** the yolk of an egg; **∼lık** egg-cup

yumurtlamak *v/t* lay *eggs; fig.* invent

yumuşak soft, mild; **∼lık** softness, mildness

yumuşa|mak *v/i* become soft; **∼tmak** *v/t* soften

Yunan Greek; **∼istan** Greece; **∼lı** Greek; **∼ca** Greek (*language*)

yunusbalığı dolphin

yurdu eye *of a needle*

yurt native country; home *for students, etc.*; **∼sever** patriotic; **∼taş** fellow countryman

yut|kunmak *v/i* swallow one's spittle, gulp; **∼mak** *v/t* swallow, gulp down

yuva nest, home; socket; **∼la-mak** *v/i* make a nest

yuvar ANAT blood-corpuscle; **∼lak** round, spherical; roundness; **∼lamak** *v/t* roll, make round, swallow greedily; **∼lanmak** *v/i* revolve, roll; topple over

yüce high, exalted; **2 Divan** JUR High Court; **∼lik** height, loftiness

yük load, burden; **∼ gemisi** NAUT cargo-steamer, freighter

yükle|m GR predicate; **∼mek** load *v/t* (*-e* on); attribute (*-e* to); **∼nmek** *-e* shoulder; throw oneself against; **∼tmek** *v/t* place, impose (*-e* on)

yüklü loaded; pregnant; *sl.* drunk

yüksek high; loud (*voice*); **∼ mühendis** graduated engineer; **∼ öğretim** higher education; **∼lik** height, elevation

yüksel|mek rise; **∼tmek** *v/t* raise; *fig.* praise

yüksük thimble

yüküm obligation; **∼lü** charged (ile with)

yün wool; woollen; **∼lü** woollen

yürek heart; *fig.* courage, boldness; **∼li** stout-hearted, bold; **∼siz** timid

yürü|k fast, fleet; **2k** *s.* **Yörük**; **∼mek** walk, advance, march; **∼rlük** JUR being in force, validity

yürüt|me görevi JUR

executive power; **~mek** v/t cause to walk; put into force; put forward; ~um execution of ANAT order, etc.

yürüyüş n. march, walk

yüz¹ one hundred

yüz² face; surface; motive, cause; **bu ~den** for this reason; **~ünden** on account of; **~ çevirmek** turn away *(-den* from); **~ kızartıcı** shameful; **~ tutmak** ~ begin, turn towards; **~ vermek** give encouragement, be indulgent

(-e to)

yüzbaşı MIL captain

yüzey face, surface

yüzgeç swimming, floating

yüz|leşmek be confronted (ile with); meet face to face; **~lü** with *such and such* a face *or* surface

yüzmek¹ v/t flay, skin

yüzmek² v/i swim

yüzsüz shameless; **~lük** effrontery, shamelessness

yüzük ring

yüzyıl century

Z

zabıt seizure; protocol; **~name** protocol; minutes pl.

zafer success, victory

zağ keen edge

zahife zoo reptile

zâhir outward, external; clear, evident; **~î** external, outward

zahmet trouble, difficulty; **~ çekmek** suffer trouble *or* fatigue; **~ etmeyiniz!** don't trouble yourself!; **~li** troublesome, difficult; **~siz** easy

zaika the faculty of taste

zakkum BOT oleander

zalim tyrannical, unjust

zam gradation, increase; **~ yapmak** *-e* raise the price of

zaman time, period; **~-diği** ~ conj. when; **o ~** then; **bir ~(lar)** once, at one time; **~aşımı** JUR prescription;

~sız untimely, inappropriate

zambak BOT lily

zamir GR pronoun

zamk gum; **~lamak** v/t gum; **~lı** gummed

zammetmek v/t increase, add

zampara who runs after women, rake

zan opinion

zanaat craft, handicraft

zangırdamak tremble, clank

zani adulterer

zannetmek v/t think, suppose

zapt|etmek v/t seize, take possession of; restrain, master; **~urapt** discipline

zar¹ membrane; film; thin skin

zar² dice

zarar damage, injury, harm; **~ vermek** *-e* cause harm *or*

loss; ~ı yok! never mind!, it
doesn't matter!; ~lı harmful
(-*e* to); ~sız harmless; not
so bad

zarf envelope; cover; cup-
holder; case; GR adverb;
~ında during, within

zarif elegant, graceful; witty;
~lik elegance

zarp striking, blow; ~ mus-
luğu main cock of pipes

zarur|et need, necessity;
want, poverty; ~î necessary,
indispensable

zat essence; person, individual; ~en *adv.* in any case, as a
matter of fact; ~î essential;
personal

zavallı unlucky, miserable

zaviye corner, angle

zayıf weak, thin; slim, slender; ~lamak become thin
or weak; ~latmak v/t weak-
en, enfeeble; ~lık weakness,
debility

zayi lost; ~at *pl.* losses

zayiçe horoscope

zebir ZOO zebra

zebun weak, powerless

Zebur REL the Psalms of Da-
vid

zecir compulsion

zecrî compulsory; coercive

zedelemek v/t bruise; mal-
treat

zehir poison; ~lemek v/t poison; ~li poisonous; poisoned

zekâ intelligence, quickness
of mind

zekât REL alms *prescribed by*

Islam

zeki quick-qitted, intelligent

zelil low, base

zelzele GEO earthquake

zemberek spring *of a watch,*
etc.

zemin earth, ground (*a. of a*
design); *fig.* subject, theme;
~ katı ground-floor

zencefil BOT ginger

zenci negro

zencir *s.* zincir

zengin rich; ~le(ş)mek become rich; ~lik wealth

zeplin AVIA Zeppelin airship

zerdali BOT wild apricot

zerde sweetened rice coloured
with saffron

zerdeva ZOO beech marten

zerre atom; molecule

zerzevat *pl.* vegetables; ~çı
greengrocer

zeval decline, decadence; ~î
reckoned from noon; ~siz
everlasting, permanent

zevce wife

zevk taste, flavour; enjoyment, pleasure; good taste;
-in ~ine varmak appreciate;
~lenmek ile mock at, make
fun of; ~li pleasant, amus-
ing; ~siz tasteless; unpleasant

zevzek giddy, talkative; ~len-
mek say stupid things; ~lik
senseless chatter, silly behaviour

zeyil appendix, addendum

zeyrek intelligent

zeytin BOT olive; ~ yağı olive

oil; ∼lik olive grove
zeytunî olive-green
ziddiyet contrast; *fig.* detestation
zıh edging, border
zıkkım unpleasant food
zımba drill; file-punch; ∼lamak *v/t* punch
zımbırtı twanging noise; *fig.* worthless thing
zımn|en *adv.* tacitly, by implication; ∼î implied, tacitly understood
zımpara emery; ∼ kâğıdı emery paper
zıngı|ldamak, ∼rdamak tremble; wobble
zıpkın NAUT harpoon
zıplamak jump, skip about
zıpzıp marble *for playing*
zırdava *s.* zerdeva
zırdeli raving mad
zırh armour; ∼lı armoured; *n.* NAUT battleship
zırıl|damak chatter continuously; ∼tı chatter, squabble
zırnık CHEM yellow arsenic
zırva silly chatter; nonsense
zıt the contrary, opposite; *-in* zıddına gitmek get on *one's* nerves; ∼ gitmek oppose (ile *so.*)
zıvana short tube; mouthpiece *for a cigarette*
zıya loss
zifos splash of mud
zift pitch; ∼lemek *v/t* daub with pitch
zihin mind, intelligence, memory

zihniyet mentality
zikir remembrance, recollection; REL recitation of litanies *by dervishes*
zikretmek *v/t* mention
zikzak zigzag
zil cymbal; bell; ∼i çalmak ring the bell; ∼zurna blind drunk
zimmet ECON debit side of ANAT *account*; *-in* ∼ine geçirmek *v/t* place to *one's* debit; kendi ∼ine geçirmek *v/t* embezzle
zina adultery, fornication
zincir chain; fetters; ∼lemek *v/t* chain; ∼li chained; provided with a chain
zindan dungeon; ∼cı jailer
zinde alive, active
zira *conj.* because, for
zira|at agriculture; ∼î agricultural
zirve summit, peak
ziya light
ziyade more; surplus; too much; ∼siyle *adv.* to a great degree, largely
ziyafet feast, banquet
ziyan loss, damage; ∼ı yok! no matter!
ziyaret visit; pilgrimage; ∼ etm. *v/t* pay a visit to; ∼çi visitor; ∼gâh REL place to which a pilgrimage is made
ziynet ornament, decoration
zoka artificial bait
zonklamak *v/i* throb with pain
zooloji zoology

zor *n.* compulsion; strength; *adj.* difficult; **~aki** *adv.* under compulsion; by force; **~la** *adv.* with difficulty; by force

zorba who uses force, bully; **~lık** violence, bullying

zorla *s.* **zor**

zorla|mak *v/t* force (*-e* to *inf.*); use force against; try to open; **~şmak** grow difficult; **~ştırmak** *v/t* render difficult, complicate; **~yıcı** compelling

zor|lu strong, violent; **~luk** difficulty; **~unlu** necessary

zuhur appearance, happen-

ing; **~ etm.** appear

zulüm wrong, oppression

zurna MUS *a kind of* shrill pipe

zücaciye glassware, porcelain

züğürt *sl.* bankrupt, 'stony-broke'

Zühal ASTR Saturn

Zühre ASTR Venus; **2vî** MED venereal

zülüf love-lock, tassel

zümre party, group

zümrüt emerald

züppe fop, affected person

zürafa ZOO giraffe

zürriyet issue, progeny

A

a [ey, ı] bir

aback [ı'bäk]: **be taken ~** şaşalamak, şaşırıp kalmak

abandon [ı'bändın] v/t terketmek, bırakmak; **~ment** JUR terk

abash [ı'bäş] v/t utandırmak

abate [ı'beyt] v/t indirmek, azaltmak, hafifletmek; v/i azalmak

abb|ess ['äbıs] REL başrahibe; **~ey** ['ı] manastır; **~ot** ['ıt] başrahip

abbreviat|e [ı'brîvieyt] v/t kısaltmak; **~ion** kısaltma

ABC ['eybi'sî] alfabe

abdicat|e ['äbdikeyt] vazgeçmek, istifa etm. -den; **~ion** istifa

abdomen ['äbdımın] ANAT altkarın, karın

abduct [äb'dakt] v/t kaçırmak

abeyance [ä'beyıns]: **in ~** henüz karara bağlanmamış

abhor [ıb'hô] nefret etm. -den; **~rence** [-ôrıns] nefret, tiksinme; **~rent** tiksindirici

abide [ı'bayd] v/i kalmak, durmak

ability [ı'biliti] kabiliyet, yetenek

abject ['äbcekt] alçak, sefil

able ['eybl] muktedir; güçlü; **be ~ to** inf. muktedir olm. -e, yapabilmek -i

ablution [ı'bluuşın] aptes

abnormal [äb'nômıl] anormal

aboard [ı'bôd] gemide; gemiye

abode [ı'bıud] s. abide; n. ikametgâh, oturulan yer

aboli|sh [ı'boliş] kaldırmak, iptal etm.; **~tion** [äbıu'lişın] kaldırılma, ilga

A-bomb ['eybom] atom bombası

abominable [ı'bominıbl] iğrenç, nefret verici

abortion [ı'bôşın] MED çocuk düşürme

abound [ı'baund] v/i bol olm.

about [ı'baut] aşağı yukarı, hemen hemen; prp. hakkında; -in etrafında; **be ~ to** inf. -i yapmak üzere olm.

above [ı'bav] yukarıda; -in üstünde; -den yukarı, -den fazla; **~ all** her şeyden önce

abreast [ı'brest] yan yana

abridge [ı'bric] v/t kısaltmak, özetlemek; **~ment** kısaltma; özet

abroad [ı'brôd] yabancı ülke-
de, dışarıda

abrupt [ı'brapt] anî; sert

abscess ['äbsis] MED çıban

absence ['äbsıns] yokluk, bu-
lunmayış; ~ of mind
dalgınlık

absent ['äbsınt] yok, bu-
lunmıyan; ~-minded dalgın

absolute ['äbsıluut] katî, kesin

absolut|ion [äbsı'luuşın] gü-
nahların affı; ~ism istibdat,
mutlakçılık

absolve [ıb'zolv] v/t beraet
ettirmek (from -den)

absorb [ıb'sôb] v/t emmek,
içine çekmek

abstain [ıb'steyn] çekinmek
(from -den)

abstention [-'stenşın] çekinme

abstinen|ce ['äbstinıns] per-
hiz, sakınma; ~t perhizkâr

abstract ['äbsträkt] adj. mücerret, soyut; nazarî; n. özet;
v/t çıkarmak, ayırmak

absurd [ıb'sɜd] gülünç, manasız

abundan|ce [ı'bandıns] bol-
luk, zenginlik; ~t çok, bol

abus|e [ı'byûs] n. suiistimal,
kötüye kullanma; v/t kötüye
kullanmak; ~ive tahkir edici

abyss [ı'bis] uçurum

acacia [ı'keyşı] BOT akasya

academ|ic [äkı'demik] aka-
demik, üniversiteye ait; ~y
[ı'kädımi] akademi

accelerat|e [ık'selıreyt] v/t

hızlandırmak; ~or TECH gaz
pedalı

accent ['äksınt] vurgu, aksan;
şive, ağız

accept [ık'sept] v/t kabul
etm.; ~able kabul edilebilir;
~ance kabul

access ['äkses] giriş, MED nöbet; ~ road giriş yolu; have ~
to girebilmek -e; ~ary s.
~ory; ~ible [ık'sesibl] erişilebilir, tırmanılabilir; ~ion
[äk'seşın] ulaşma; tahta
çıkma; ~ory [äk'sesıri] JUR
ferî fail; ferî, ikinci derecede

accident ['äksidınt] tesadüf;
kaza, arıza; ~al [-'dentl] tesadüfî, arızî

acclimatize [ı'klaymıtayz] v/t
alıştırmak

accomodat|e [ı'komıdeyt] v/t
uydurmak, yerleştirmek;
~ion uyma; yerleşme

accompan|iment [ı'kampıni-
mınt] refakat; ~y refakat
etm. -e

accomplice [ı'komplis] suç
ortağı

accomplish [ı'kompliş] v/t
bitirmek, başarmak; ~ed hünerli, usta; ~ment başarı

accord¹ [ı'kôd] v/t uzlaştır-
mak; v/i uymak (with -e)

accord² uygunluk; ahenk; anlaşma; akort; of one's own ~
kendiliğinden; ~ance uygunluk; ~ing to -e göre

account [ı'kaunt] v/i hesap
vermek; sorumlu olm. (for
-den); n. hesap; rapor; hikâ-

ye; sebep; **on no** ~ hiçbir suretle, asla; **on** ~ of sebebiyle, -den dolayı; **take** ~ of hesaba katmak -i; ~**ant** ECON muhasebeci; ~**ing** muhasebe

accredit [ı'kredit] v/t tasdik etm.; yetki vermek -e

accrue [ı'kruu] v/i hâsıl olm., gelmek

accumulat|e [ı'kyûmyuleyt] v/t artırmak, toplamak; v/i artmak, toplanmak; ~**ion** toplama, yığın; ~**or** EL akümülatör

accura|cy [äkyurısı] doğruluk, sıhhat; tam vaktinde olma; ~**te** ['-it] doğru, tam

accursed [ı'kзsid] melûn

accus|ation [äkyu'zeyşın] suçlama, itham; ~**ative** [ı'kyûzıtiv] GR -i hali; ~**e** [ı'kyûz] suçlamak, itham etm. (so. of sth. b-i b. ş. ile); ~**er** JUR davacı

accustom [ı'kʌstım] v/t alıştırmak (**to** -e); ~**ed to** alışık, alışkın -e

ace [eys] birli; fig. çok cesur savaş havacısı

ache [eyk] n. ağrı, sızı; v/i ağrımak, sızlamak

achieve [ı'çîv] v/t icra etm., meydana çıkarmak, elde etm.; ~**ment** başarı

acid ['äsid] CHEM n. asit; adj. ekşi

acknowledge [ık'nolic] v/t kabul etm., tanımak; itiraf etm.; b. ş-in alındığını bildirmek; ~**ment** kabul; tasdik; itiraf

acorn ['eykôn] BOT meşepalamudu

acoustic|(al) [ı'kuustik(ıl)] akustiğe ait; ~**s** pl. akustik sg.

acquaint [ı'kweynt] bildirmek, tanıtmak (so. with b-e b. ş-i); ~**ance** tanışma; malumat; tanıdık; **be** ~**ed with** bilmek -i, haberdar olm. -den

acquire [ı'kwayı] v/t elde etm., kazanmak; ~**ment** edinme; edinilen bilgi, hüner

acquisition [äkwi'zişın] edinme, elde edilen şey, kazanç

acquit [ı'kwit] v/t JUR beraet ettirmek; ~**tal** beraet

acre ['eykı] İngiliz dönümü (0.40 hektar)

acrid ['äkrid] buruk, acı

acrobat ['äkrıbät] akrobat, cambaz

across [ı'kros] karşıda karşıya, öbür tarafa; çapraz

act [äkt] n. fiil, hareket, iş, yapılan şey; JUR kanun; THEA perde; v/i hareket etm., davranmak (**upon** -e göre); THEA rol oynamak; ~**ion** fiil, hareket, iş; faaliyet; etki; JUR dava; MIL muharebe

active ['äktiv] faal, enerjik, canlı; GR geçişli; ~**ity** faaliyet, çeviklik

act|or ['äktı] aktör, artist, rol oynayan; ~**ress** aktris, kadın aktör

actual ['äkcuıl] gerçek, hakikî; **~ity** [äktyu'äliti] hakikat; gerçek durum; **~ly** *adv.* gerçekten

acute [ı'kyût] şiddetli, keskin; keskin akıllı

adapt [ı'däpt] *v/t* uydurmak, tatbik etm.; **~able** uyabilir

add [äd] *v/t* katmak, eklemek, ilâve etm.; MATH toplamak

addict ['ädikt] düşkün; **~ed** [ı'diktid] to **-e** düşkün, *-in* tiryakisi

addition [ı'dişın] ilâve, ek, zam; MATH toplama; **in ~** to *-den* başka; **~al** eklenilen

address [ı'dres] *n.* adres; hitabe; *v/t* *-in* üstüne adres yazmak; hitap etm. **-e ...**; **oneself** to girişmek *-e*; **~ee** [ädre'sî] alacak olan

adept ['ädept] usta, mahir

adequa|cy ['ädikwısi] kifayet, yeterlilik; **~te** ['ı-wit] uygun, münasip

adhe|re [ıd'hiı] yapışmak, yapışık kalmak (**to -**e); **~sive** ['-'hîsiv] yapışkan, yapışıcı; **~sive tape**, **~sive plaster** plaster, bant

adjacent [ı'ceysınt] bitişik, komşu

adjective ['äciktiv] GR sıfat

adjoin [ı'coyn] *v/t* bitişik olm. *-e*

adjourn [ı'cən] *v/t* ertelemek, tehir etm.; **~ment** tehir

adjudicate [ı'cuudikeyt] *v/i* JUR karar vermek (**upon -**e)

adjust [ı'cast] *v/t* doğrultmak,

düzeltmek; ayar etm., uydurmak (**to -**e); **~ment** uydurma, ayarlama, düzeltme

administ|er [ıd'ministı] *v/t* idare etm., tatbik etm.; **~ration** idare, yönetim; hükümet; **~rator** [-treytı] idareci, müdür; JUR tereke idare memuru

admirable ['ädmırıbl] takdire değer

admiral ['ädmırıl] NAUT amiral

admir|ation [ädmı'reyşın] hayranlık, takdir; **~e** [ıd'mayı] *v/t* takdir etm., çok beğenmek; **~er** hayran olan kimse; âşık

admissi|ble [ıd'misıbl] kabul olunabilir; **~on** itiraf; kabul; giriş; **~on fee** duhuliye, girmelik

admit [ıd'mit] *v/t* itiraf etm.; içeriye almak, kabul etm.; **~tance** kabul; giriş; **~tedly** *adv.* itiraf edildiği gibi, gerçekten

admoni|sh [ıd'moniş] *v/t* ihtar etm., tembih etm.; **~tion** [ädmı'nişın] ihtar, tembih

ado [ı'duu] telâş, gürültü

adolescent [ädıı'lesnt] genç, delikanlı

adopt [ı'dopt] *v/t* benimsemek, kabul etm.; evlâtlığa kabul etm.; **~ion** kabul etme; evlât edinme

ador|able [ı'dôrıbl] tapılacak; **~ation** [ädô'reyşın] tapma; aşk; **~e** [ı'dô] tapmak *-e*

adorn [ı'dôn] *v/t* süslemek; **~ment** süs

Adrianople ['eydrü'nıupl] Edirne

adrift [ı'drift] sularla sürüklenen

adroit [ı'droyt] becerikli, usta

adult ['ädalt] büyük, reşit, ergin

adulter|ate [ı'daltıreyt] *v/t* karıştırmak, bozmak; **~ation** karıştırma; **~er** JUR zina işliyen, zâni; **~ess** zina işliyen kadın; **~y** zina

advance [ıd'vâns] *n.* ilerleme, terakki; terfi; ECON avans, peşin; *v/t* ilerletmek; *v/i* ilerlemek; **in ~** *adv.* peşin olarak; **~ booking** önceden rezervasyon; **~d** ilerlemiş, ileri; **~ment** ilerleme; terfi

advantage [ıd'vântic] avantaj, yarar, fayda; **take ~ of** faydalanmak *-den*; **~ous** [äd-vın'teycıs] faydalı, yararlı

advent ['ädvınt] gelme; REL Noel yortusundan önceki dört hafta

adventur|e [ıd'vençı] macera, sergüzeşt; **~er** avantüriye, maceracı; **~ous** maceraya düşkün, cesaretli; tehlikeli

adverb ['ädvəb] GR zarf

advers|ary ['ädvısırı] düşman, muhalif; **~e** ['.-ɔs] zıt, ters, karşı gelen

advertise ['ädvıtayz] *v/t* ilân etm.; **~ment** [ıd'vɔtismınt] ilân, reklam; **~r** ilân eden *veya* reklam yapan kimse;

ilân gazetesi

advice [ıd'vays] nasihat, öğüt; tavsiye; **take ~** sözünü dinlemek

advis|able [ıd'vayzıbl] tavsiye edilir, makul, uygun; **~e** *v/t* nasihat etm., haber vermek *-e*; **~er** müşavir; **~ory board** istişare kurulu

advocate ['ädvıkeyt] *n.* avukat; *v/t* tavsiye etm.

aerial ['äıril] *adj.* havaî; *n.* anten

aero|drome [äırı'drıum] hava alanı; **~nautics** [.-'nôtiks] *pl.* havacılık *sg.*; **~plane** uçak

aesthetics [îs'thetiks] *pl.* estetik *sg.*

afar [ı'fâ] uzak(ta)

affair [ı'fäı] iş, mesele, olay

affect [ı'fekt] *v/t* tesir etm., dokunmak *-e*; **~ation** yapmacık, gösteriş; **~ed** yapma, yapmacıklı; tutulmuş (with *-e*); **~ion** sevgi; düşkünlük; **~ionate** [.-şnit] şefkatli, sevgi gösteren

affinity [ı'finiti] yakınlık, benzeşme

affirm [ı'fɔm] *v/t* tasdik etm.; **~ation** [äfɔ'meyşın] tasdik, teyit; **~ative** [ı'fɔmtiv] müspet, olumlu

affix [ı'fiks] *v/t* bağlamak, takmak, yapıştırmak

afflict [ı'flikt] *v/t* vermek *-e*, eziyet etm. *-i*; **~ed** tutulmuş (with *-e*); **~ion** dert, keder

affluen|ce ['äfluıns] bolluk; **~t** bol

afford [ı'fôd] v/t meydana getirmek, vermek; bütçesi müsait olm. -*e*

affront [ı'frant] hakaret, tahkir

afire [ı'fay] tutuşmuş, yanan

afloat [ı'flut] su üzerinde dolaşan

afraid [ı'freyd] korkmuş, korkar; be ~ of korkmak -*den*

afresh [ı'freş] yeniden, tekrar

Africa [ˈæfrıkı] Afrika; ~n Afrikalı; **n-American** siyah Amerikalı

after ['âftı] -*den* sonra; -*e* göre; -*e* rağmen; sonra; ~ all bununla birlikte; ~ that bundan sonra; ~**effect** sonra görülen sonuç; ~**noon** ikindi, öğleden sonra; good ~**noon!** günaydın!, merhaba!; ~**thought** sonradan gelen düşünce; ~**wards** ['-wıdz] sonra (-dan)

again [ı'gen] tekrar, gene, bir daha; bundan başka; ~ and ~, time and ~ bazan, arasıra

against [ı'genst] -*e* karşı, -*e* rağmen; -*in* aleyhinde

age [eyc] yaş; çağ, devir; of ~ reşit, ergin; **under** ~ küçük, reşit olmıyan; at ['eycid] yaşlı; yıllanmış; ~**d fifty** [eycd-] elli yaşında; ~**less** eskimez

agen|cy ['eycınsı] ajans, acentalık, vekillik; ~**da** [ı'cendı] gündem, ruzname; ~**t** ['eycınt] acente, vekil; casus; âmil

agglomeration [ıglomı-'reyşın] yığılma, toplanma, yığın

aggrandize [ı'grändayz] v/t büyütmek

aggravat|e ['ägrıveyt] v/t zorlaştırmak, fenalaştırmak; kızdırmak; ~**ion** zorlaştırma; hiddet

aggregate ['ägrigıt] adj. toplu, bütün; v/t toplamak

aggress|ion [ı'greşın] saldırma, tecavüz; ~**ive** saldırgan; ~**or** saldıran

agile ['äcayl] çevik, faal

agitat|e ['äciteyt] v/t sallamak, tahrik etm., karıştırmak; ~**ion** heyecan; tahrik; ~**or** kışkırtıcı, tahrikçi

ago [ı'gıu] önce, evvel; **long** ~ uzun zaman önce

agon|izing [ˈägınayzıŋ] eziyet verici; ~**y** ıstıraptan kıvranma, şiddetli acı

agrarian [ı'grärın] ziraî, tarımsal

agree [ı'grî] v/i razı olm., aynı fikirde olm., muvafakat etm.; ~ **to** razı olm. -*e*, kabul etm. -*i*; ~ **with** anlaşmak, bir fikirde olm. b. ile; ~**able** [-î-] uygun, münasip; hoş, nazik; ~**ment** [-î-] anlaşma, sözleşme

agricultur|al [ägri'kalçırıl] ziraî, tarımsal; ~**e** ziraat, tarım

aground [ı'graund] karaya oturmuş

ague ['eygyû] MED sıtma

ahead [ı'hed] önde, ilerde;

ileriye

aid [eyd] *n.* yardım, muave-net; *v/t* yardım etm. *-e*

ailing ['eyliŋ] rahatsız

aim [eym] hedef, amaç; nişan alma; ~ **at** amaçlamak *-i;* nişan almak *-i;* ~**less** gayesiz, hedefsiz

air [äı] **1.** *n.* hava; tavır, eda; melodi; **2.** *v/t* havalandır-mak; **in the open** ~ açıkta; ~**base** MIL hava üssü; ~**bed** deniz yatağı; ~**brake** TECH hava freni; ~**conditioned** otomatik ısıtma ve soğutma tesisatı olan; ~**craft** uçak; ~**craft carrier** uçak gemisi; ~**cushion** şişirme yastık; ~**field** hava alanı; ~ **force** hava kuvvetleri *pl.;* ~ **host-ess** hostes; ~ **lift** hava köprü-sü; ~**line** hava yolu; ~**liner** yolcu uçağı; ~**mail** uçak pos-tası; ~**man** havacı; ~**pipe** TECH hava borusu; ~**plane** uçak; ~**port** hava alanı; ~ **raid** hava hücumu; ~ **raid shelter** sığınak; ~ **route** hava yolu; ~**ship** hava gemisi; ~**sick** hava tutmuş; ~ **termi-nal** *hava yollarının* şehir bü-rosu; ~**tight** hava geçmez; ~**y** havalı, hafif

aisle [aıl] ara yol, geçit

ajar [ı'câ] yarı açık, aralık

akin [ı'kin] to akraba *-e*

alabaster ['älıbâstı] ak mer-mer

alacrity [ı'läkriti] çeviklik; is-teklilik

alarm [ı'lâm] *n.* alarm, tehlike işareti; korku, telâş; *v/t* tehli-keyi bildirmek *-e;* korkut-mak *-i;* ~**clock** çalar saat

alas! [ı'läs] vay!, yazık!

Albania [äl'beynyı] Arnavut-luk

alcohol ['älkıhol] alkol, ispir-to; ~**ic** alkolik, ispirtolu

alderman ['ôldımın] kıdemli belediye meclisi üyesi

ale [eyl] *bir çeşit bira*

alert [ı'lıt] uyanık; **be on the** ~ tetikte olm.

algebra ['älcıbrı] cebir

Algeria [äl'cıırı] Cezayir

alibi ['älibay] JUR *suç işlendiği anda* başka yerde bulun-duğunu ispat etmesi

alien ['eylyın] yabancı

alight [ı'layt] *adj.* ateş, içinde, yanan; *v/i* AVIA inmek

alike [ı'layk] benzer, aynı

aliment ['älimınt] yiyecek, gıda; ~**ary** [ˌ'mentrı] besle-yici, yiyeceğe dair

alimony ['älimnı] nafaka

alive [ı'layv] hayatta, canlı

all [ôl] bütün; her, hepsi, her; **after** ~ nihayet, bununla bir-likte; **not at** ~ asla, hiç; ~ **of us** hepimiz; ~**right** iyi, pekâ-lâ, tamam, ~ **the better** daha iyi ya

alleg|ation [äle'geyşın] ileri sürme, iddia; ~**e** [ı'lec] *v/t* ileri sürmek, iddia etm.; ~**ed** sözde, diye

allegorical [äle'gorikıl] ale-gorik

alleviate [ı'lîvieyt] *v/t* azaltmak

alley ['äli] dar sokak; iki tarafı ağaçlı yol; **blind ~** çıkmaz yol

alli|ance [ı'layıns] ittifak, birlik; **~ed** ['älayd] müttefik

alligator ['äligeytı] zoo Amerika timsahı

allocate ['älikeyt] *v/t* tahsis etm., dağıtmak

allot [ı'lot] *v/t* ayırmak

allow [ı'lau] *v/t* müsaade etm., kabul etm.; razı olm. *-e*; vermek *-i*; *v/i* hesaba katmak (**for** -*i*); **~ance** müsaade; tahsisat; cep parası

alloy ['äloy] CHEM alaşım

all|-round çok cepheli; **2 Saints' Day** REL Azizler günü (*1 kasım*); **~weather** her havaya dayanan

allude [ı'luud] to ima etm. *-i*

allure [ı'lyu] *v/t* çekmek, cezbetmek; **~ment** çekicilik

allusion [ı'luujın] ima

ally ['älay] *n.* müttefik; [ı'lay] *v/i* birleşmek

almighty [ôl'mayti] her şeye kadir

almond ['âmınd] BOT badem

almost ['ôlmust] hemen hemen, az kaldı

alms [âmz] *pl.* sadaka

aloft [ı'loft] yukarıda

alone [ı'lhun] yalnız, tek başına; **leave ~** kendi haline bırakmak *-i*; **let ~** şöyle dursun

along [ı'loŋ] boyunca; **all ~** öteden beri; her zaman;

come ~! haydi gel!; **~side** yan yana

aloud [ı'laud] yüksek sesle

alphabet ['älfıbît] alfabe; **~ical** [-'betikıl] alfabe sırasına göre

already [ôl'redi] şimdiden; zaten

also ['ôlsıu] dahi, da (de, ta, te); bir de; ayrıca

altar ['ôltı] kilise mihrabı

alter ['ôltı] *v/t* değiştirmek; *v/i* değişmek; **~ation** değişiklik

alternat|e [ôl'tınit] *adj.* nöbetleşe değişen; ['-tıneyt] *v/t* nöbetleşe değiştirmek; **~ing current** dalgalı akım; **~ion** değişme; **~ive** [-'tını-tiv] ikinci şık

although [ôl'dhıu] her ne kadar, *-diği* halde, bununla birlikte, gerçi

altitude ['ältityûd] yükseklik

altogether [ôltı'gedhı] hep birlikte, tamamen

alum ['älım] CHEM şap

alumin|ium [älyu'minyım], *Am.* **~um** [ı'luuminım] alüminyum

always ['ôlweyz] daima, her zaman

am [äm, ım] I **~** ben -im

amalgamat|e [ı'mälgımeyt] *v/t* karıştırmak; *v/i* bileşmek; **~ion** karışma; alaşım

amass [ı'mäs] *v/t* yığmak, toplamak

amateur ['ämitı] amatör

amaze [ı'meyz] *v/t* hayrette bırakmak, şaşırtmak; **~e~**

ment şaşkınlık, hayret; **~ing** şaşırtıcı

ambassador ['äm'bäsıdı] POL büyük elçi

amber ['ämbı] kehribar

ambiguous [äm'bigyus] müphem, şüpheli

ambition [äm'bişın] ihtiras; büyük istek; **~ous** hırslı, çok istekli

ambulance ['ämbyulıns] hasta arabası; **~ station** ilk yardım istasyonu

ambush ['ämbuş] n. pusu; v/t pusuda beklemek

ameliorate [ı'mîlyıreyt] v/t iyileştirmek, düzeltmek; **~ion** iyileşme

amen ['ä'men] REL âmin

amend [ı'mend] v/t düzeltmek, ıslah etm.; v/i iyileşmek; **~ment** düzeltme, tadil; **~s** pl. tazminat; **make ~s** kusurunu düzeltmek

America [ı'merikı] Amerika; **~n** Amerikalı, Amerikan

amiable ['eymyıbl] hoş, tatlı

amicable ['ämikıbl] dostça, dostane

amid(st) [ı'mid(s)t] -in ortasında

amiss [ı'mis] eksik, yanlış; bozuk; **take ~** fenaya almak -i

ammunition [ämyu'nişın] cephane, mühimmat

amnesty ['ämnisti] genel af

among(st) [ı'maŋ(st)] -in arasında, arasına; içinde

amortization [ımôtı'zeyşın]

ECON amortisman

amount [ı'maunt] n. miktar, meblâğ, tutar, yekûn; v/i varmak (**to** -e)

amphitheatre ['ämfithiıtı] amfiteatr

ample ['ämpl] geniş, bol; **~ifier** ['.ifayı] TECH amplifikatör; **~ify** ['.ifay] v/t genişletmek, büyütmek

amputate ['ämpyuteyt] MED v/t kesmek

amuck [ı'mak]: **run ~** kudurmuş gibi etrafa saldırmak

amulet ['ämyulit] tilsim

amuse [ı'myûz] v/t eğlendirmek, güldürmek; **~ment** eğlence

an [än, ın] bir

anachronism [ı'näkrınizım] bir olayı ait olmadığı tarihte gösterme

an(a)emia [ı'nîmyı] MED kansızlık

an(a)esthesia [änis'thîzyı] MED anestezi

analogous [ı'näligıs] benzer, kıyas yoluyle olan; **~y** [.-ci] kıyas; benzerlik

analyse, Am. **~ze** ['änılayz] v/t çözümlemek; **~sis** [ı'nälisis] analiz, çözümleme

anarchy ['änıki] anarşi

anatomy [ı'nätımi] anatomi

ancestor ['änsistı] ata, dede; **~ry** ecdat, dedeler pl.

anchor ['äŋkı] n. çapa, gemi demiri; v/i demir atmak, demirlemek

anchovy ['änçvi] ançüez

ancient ['eynşınt] eski, kadim

and [ænd, ınd] ve, ile; daha; ~ so on ve saire

anecdote ['ænıkdıut] fıkra, hikâye

anew [ı'nyû] yeniden, tekrar

angel ['eyncıl] REL melek

anger ['æŋgı] hiddet, öfke

angina [æn'caynı] MED anjin, boğak

angle¹ ['æŋgl] köşe, açı; fig. görüş noktası

angle² n. olta; v/i balık tutmak

Angl|ican ['æŋglikın] Anglikan; ~o-Saxon ['æŋglu'sæksın] Anglosakson, İngiliz

angry ['æŋgri] öfkeli, kızgın; darılmış (at, about -den dolayı); gücenmiş (with -e)

anguish ['æŋwiş] ıstırap, keder

angular ['æŋgyulı] köşeli

animal ['ænimıl] hayvan

animat|e ['ænimeyt] adj. canlı; v/t canlandırmak; ~ed cartoon canlı resimlerden ibaret film; ~ion canlılık, heyecan

animosity ['æni'mositi] düşmanlık

anise ['ænis] BOT anason

ankle ['æŋkl] anat topuk, ayak bileği

annex ['æneks] n. ek; müştemilât pl.; v/t ilhak etm., eklemek, katmak; ~ation [~'seyşın] ilhak

annihilate [ı'nayıleyt] v/t yo-

ketmek

anniversary [æni'vəsıri] yıldönümü.

annotation [ænu'teyşın] haşiye, not

announce [ı'nauns] v/t bildirmek, ilân etm.; ~ment bildiri, ilân; ~r sözcü, spiker

annoy [ı'noy] v/t taciz etm., kızdırmak; be ~ed kızmak; ~ance canını sıkma

annual ['ænyuıl] yıllık

annul [ı'nal] feshezmek, iptal etm.

anodyne ['ænıudayn] uyuşturucu (ilâç)

anomalous [ı'nomılıs] anormal

anonymous [ı'nonimıs] anonim

another [ı'nadhı] başka, diğer, öbür; with one ~ birbirini

answer ['ânsı] n. cevap, yanıt; v/t cevap vermek -e, yanıtlamak -i; sorumlu olm. (for -den); uymak (to -e)

ant [ænt] karınca

antagonis|m [æn'tægınizım] düşmanlık; ~t düşman, muhalif

Antarctic [ænt'âktik] Antarktika

antelope ['æntilup] zoo ceylan

antenna [æn'tenı] zoo duyarga; TECH anten

anthem ['ænthım] ilâhî; millî marş

anti-aircraft gun MIL uçaksavar topu; ~biotic ['_bay'o-tik] antibiyotik

anticipat|e [än'tisipeyt] *v/t* önceden görmek, beklemek; ~ion önceden görme, tahmin, bekleme

anti|cyclone ['änti'saykluın] yüksek basınç alanı; ~dote ['-dıut] panzehir; ~freeze antifriz

Antioch ['äntîak] Antakya

antipathy [än'tipıthi] antipati, sevişmezlik

antiqu|arian [änti'kwäriın] *adj.* antikaya ait; *n.* antikacı, antika meraklısı; ~ary ['-wırı] antikacı; ~e [än'tîk] çok eski, kadim; ~ity [-'tik-witi] eskilik; eski zamanlar *pl.*

antiseptic [änti'septik] antiseptik

antler ['äntlı] zoo geyik boynuzu

anvil ['änvil] örs

anxi|ety [äŋ'zayıti] endişe, kuruntu, merak; ~ous ['äŋksıs] endişeli, meraklı; be ~ous to *inf.* arzu etm. -*i*, can atmak -*e*

any ['eni] bir; her hangi, her bir; bazı, birkaç; hiç; ~ more artık; daha fazla; ~body her hangi bir; ~how her nasılsa; her halde; ~one *s.* ~body; ~thing her hangi bir şey, her şey; hiçbir şey; ~way *s.* ~how; ~where her hangi bir yer(d)e; hiçbir yer(d)e

apart [ı'pât] ayrı, bir tarafta;

başka (from -*den*); ~ment apartman dairesi

apathetic [äpı'thetik] hissiz, ilgisiz

ape [eyp] zoo maymun

aperture ['äpıtyuı] aralık, delik, açık

apex ['eypeks] zirve, tepe

apiece [ı'pîs] her bir; beher

A-plant [ey-] nükleer elektrik fabrikası

apolog|ize [ı'polıcayz] özür dilemek (for -*den*); ~y özür dileme, itizar

apoplexy ['äpıupleksi] MED inme, felç

apostasy [ı'postısi] REL irtidat, dininden dönme

apostle [ı'posl] REL havari; misyoner

apostrophe [ı'postrıfi] GR kesme işareti

apothecary [ı'pothikırı] eczacı

appal(l) [ı'pôl] *v/t* korkutmak, ürkütmek

apparatus [äpı'reytıs] cihaz, makine

apparel [ı'pärıl] elbise

apparent [ı'pärınt] açık belli; görünüşte olan

appeal [ı'pîl] yalvarma, *n.* başvurma; JUR temyiz; *v/i* başvurmak (to -*e*); beğenmek (-*i*); ~ing yalvaran; sevimli, cazip

appear [ı'pıı] *v/i* görünmek, gözükmek, meydana çıkmak; ~ance görünüş; gösteriş

appease [ɪ'pîz] v/t yatıştırmak, teskin etm.

append|icitis [ɪpendi'saytis] MED apandisit; **~ix** [ɪ'pendiks] ek, zeyil

appeti|te ['äpitayt] iştah; **~zing** iştah verici

applau|d [ɪ'plôd] v/t alkışlamak; **~se** [-z] alkış

apple ['äpl] elma; **~pie** üstü hamurlu elma turtası

appliance [ɪ'playıns] alet, cihaz

applica|ble ['äplikıbl] uygulanabilir; **~nt** istekli; **~tion** tatbik; dilekçe, istida

apply [ɪ'play] v/i müracaat etm., başvurmak (**to** -e, **for** için)

appoint [ɪ'poynt] v/t tayin etm., atamak; kararlaştırmak; **~ment** tayin, memuriyet, iş; randevu

apportion [ɪ'pôşın] v/t paylaştırmak

appreciat|e [ɪ'prişieyt] v/t takdir etm., -in kıymetini anlamak; **~ion** değerlendirme, kıymet bilme; ECON kıymet artması

apprehen|d [äpri'hend] v/t yakalamak, tevkif etm.; anlamak; korkmak -den; **~sion** tevkif; anlama; korku; **~sive** çabuk kavrayan; korkan (**of** -den)

apprentice [ɪ'prentis] çırak; stajiyer; **~ship** [-işip] çıraklık; staj

approach [ɪ'prıuç] n. yaklaşma, yanaşma; müracaat; v/t yaklaşmak, yanaşmak, **-e**; **~ road** giriş yolu

appropriat|e [ɪ'prıupriit] adj. uygun, münasip; v/t tahsis etm., ayırmak; **~ion** tahsis

approv|al [ɪ'pruuvıl] tasvip, uygun görme; **~e** v/t beğenmek, uygun görmek

approximate [ɪ'proksimit] takribî, aşağı yukarı

apricot ['eyprikot] BOT kayısı; zerdali

April ['eyprıl] nisan

apron ['eyprın] önlük

apt [äpt] uygun; yerinde; zeki; **be ~ to** inf. -mek eğiliminde olm.; **~itude** ['äptityûd] kabiliyet; uygunluk

aqua|rium [ı'kwäirium] akvaryum; **~tic** [ı'kwätik] suda yaşar; **~tic sports** pl. su sporları

aqueduct ['äkwidakt] su kemeri

aquiline ['äkwilayn] kartal gibi; gaga burunlu

Arab ['ärıb] Arap; **~ia** [ı'reybyı] Arabistan; **~ian** Arabistan'a ait; **~ic** ['ärıbık] Arapça

arable ['ärıbl] sürülebilir

arbitra|ry ['äbitrırı] keyfî; **~te** [-treyt] hakem sıfatıyla karar vermek; **~tion** hakem kararı

arbo(u)r ['âbı] kameriye, çardak

arc [âk] yay, kavis; **~ade** [â'keyd] kemeraltı yolu

arch¹ [âç] kemer, tak

arch² *adj.* saklaban, açıkgöz

arch(a)eology [âki'olıcı] arkeoloji

archaic [â'keyik] kadim, eski

arch|angel ['âk-] başmelek; ~bishop REL başpiskopos; ~duchess arşidüşes; ~duke arşidük

archer ['âçı] okçu; ~y okçuluk

archipelago [âki'peligıu] GEO adalar grubu

architect ['âkitekt] mimar; ~ure mimarlık

archives ['âkayvz] *pl.* arşiv

archway kemeraltı yolu

Arctic ['âktik] kuzey kutbunda bulunan (bölge)

ard|ent ['âdınt] ateşli, heyecanlı; ~o(u)r ateşlilik, gayret

are [â] *s.* be

area ['âırı] saha, alan, bölge; yüzölçümü

Argentina [âcın'tînı] Arjantin

argue ['âgyû] *v/t* ileri sürmek, ispat etm.; münakaşa etm.; ~ment delil; münakaşa; ~mentation delil gösterme

arid ['ârid] kurak, çorak

arise [ı'rayz] *v/i* kalkmak, çıkmak, doğmak (from -*den*)

aristocra|cy [âris'tokrısı] aristokrasi; ~t ['-tıkrät] aristokrat

arithmetic [ı'rithmıtık] aritmetik

ark [âk] tahta sandık; Noah's

2 REL Nuh'un gemisi

arm¹ [âm] kol

arm² *n.* silah; *v/t* silahlandırmak; *v/i* silahlanmak

armament ['âmımınt] teçhizat *pl.*, silahlanma; ~ race silahlanma yarışı

armchair koltuk

Armenia [â'mînyı] Ermenistan

armistice ['âmistis] mütareke

armo(u)r ['âmı] zırh; ~ed zırhlı; ~ed car zırhlı otomobil

armpit koltuk altı

arms [âmz] *pl.* silahlar

army ['âmi] MIL ordu; ~corps kolordu

arnica ['ânikı] BOT arnika, öküzgözü

aroma [ı'rumı] güzel koku

around [ı'raund] -*in* etrafın(d)a; orada burada, oraya buraya

arouse [ı'rauz] *v/t* uyandırmak, canlandırmak

arrange [ı'reync] *v/t* tanzim etm., düzenlemek; ~ment tertip, sıralama, düzenleme

arrears [ı'rıız] *pl.* geri kalan *sg.*; ödenmemiş bo ç

arrest [ı'rest] *n.* tutuklama, tevkif; durdurma; *v/t* tevkif etm., tutuklamak, durdurmak

arriv|al [ı'rayvıl] varış, geliş; gelen kimse; ~e varmak, vâsıl olm. (at -*e*)

arrogan|ce ['ârıugıns] kibir,

gurur; ~t kibirli, mağrur

arrow ['äriu] ok

arsenal ['âsinl] tersane

arsenic ['âsnik] CHEM arsen(ik)

arson ['âsn] kundakçılık

art [ât] sanat; hüner, maharet; fine ~s pl. güzel sanatlar

arter|ial [â'tiiriıl] ANAT atardamara ait; ~ial road anayol; ~y ['âtırı] atardamar

artesian [â'tiziyın] artezyen

artful kurnaz

artichoke ['âtiçıuk] BOT enginar

article ['âtikl] makale; madde; GR tanım edatı

articulate [â'tikyuleyt] v/t dikkatle telaffuz etm.; adj. açık, seçkin

artificial [âti'fişıl] sunî, yapma

artillery [â'tilırı] MIL topçuluk

artisan [âti'zän] zanaatçı

artist ['âtist] artist, sanatkâr; ~ic [â'tistik] artistik

artless sade, saf

as [äz, ız] gibi, kadar; iken; -diği gibi; -den dolayı; -mekle beraber; çünkü; ~ a rule genellikle; ~ if sanki, güya; ~ soon ~-ince; -irmez; ~ well ~ gibi

ascen|d [ı'send] v/i, v/t çıkmak, tırmanmak -e; ~dancy [-dınsi] üstünlük; nüfuz; ♀sion Day REL İsa'nın göğe çıkışı yortusu; ~t çıkış, tırmanma

ascertain [äsı'teyn] v/t soruş-

turmak, öğrenmek

ascetic [ı'setik] REL zahit, münzevi

ascribe [ıs'krayb] v/t atfetmek (to -e)

aseptic [ä'septik] aseptik

ash[1] [äş] BOT dişbudak

ash[2] pl. ~es ['äşiz] kül

ashamed [ı'şeymd]: be ~ of utanmak -den

ash|-bin, ~-can çöp tenekesi

ashore [ı'şô] karada; karaya

ash-tray kül tablası

Asia ['eyşı] Asya; ~ Minor Küçükasya, Anadolu; ~n- -American adj. & n. Asya kökenli Amerikalı; ~tic [eyşi'ätik] Asyalı

aside [ı'sayd] bir tarafa, yana; başka (from -den)

ask [äsk] v/t sormak -e; rica etm. -den; ~ for sormak -i, istemek -i

asleep [ı'slîp]: be ~ uyumak; fall ~ uykuya dalmak

asparagus [ıs'pärıgıs] BOT kuşkonmaz

aspect ['äspekt] görüş, görünüş

asphalt ['äsfält] asfalt

aspir|ation [äspı'reyşın] istek, iştiyak; nefes alıp verme; ~e [ıs'payı] şiddetle arzu etm., elde etmeğe çalışmak (after or to -i)

aspirin ['äspirin] MED aspirin

ass [äs] eşek

assail [ı'seyl] v/t saldırmak, hücum etm. -e; ~ant saldıran

assassin [ı'säsin] katil; ~ate

[-eyt] *v/t* öldürmek; ~**ation** suikast, katil

assault [ı'sôlt] *n.* saldırı, taarruz; *v/t* saldırmak *-e*

assembl|age [ı'semblic] TECH montaj; ~**e** [-bl] *v/t* toplamak, birleştirmek, kurmak; *v/i* toplanmak, birleşmek; ~**y** toplantı; montaj; ~**y** line TECH sürekli iş bandı

assent [ı'sent] *n.* muvafakat; *v/i* muvafakat etm. (to *-e*)

assert [ı'sət] *v/t* ileri sürmek, iddia etm.; ~**ion** öne sürme, iddia

assess [ı'ses] *v/t* tarh etm.; takdir etm.; ~**ment** vergi (takdiri)

assets ['äsets] *pl.* ECON aktifler

assiduous [ı'sidyuıs] çalışkan, gayretli

assign [ı'sayn] *v/t* ayırmak, tahsis etm. (to *-e*); ~**ment** tayin, atama; JUR feragat

assimilate [ı'simileyt] *v/t* benzetmek, uydurmak (to *-e*)

assist [ı'sist] *v/t* yardım etm. *-e*; *v/i* hazır bulunmak (at *-de*); ~**ance** yardım; ~**ant** yardımcı, muavin; asistan

assizes [ı'sayziz] *pl.* jüri mahkemesi *sg.*

associat|e [ı'sıuşıeyt] *v/t* birleştirmek *-i*; *v/i* ortak olm. (with *-e*), katılmak (*-e*); [..it] *n.* ortak; ~**ion** birleşme; kurul; ortaklık

assort|ed [ı'sôtid] çeşitli;

~**ment** tasnif; çeşitler *pl.*

assume [ı'syuum] *v/t* üstüne almak; farzetmek

assumption [ı'sampşın] üstüne alma; farz, zan; kibir, gurur; gasıp; ♀ REL Meryem'in göğe kabulü

assur|ance [ı'şuırıns] temin; güven; söz; sigorta; ~**e** [-u] *v/t* temin etm.; söz vermek *-e*; sigorta etm. *-i*; ~**ed** sigortalı olan

asthma ['äsmı] MED astma, yelpik

astir [ı'stə] harekette, heyecanlı

astonish [ıs'toniş] *v/t* şaşırtmak, hayrete düşürmek; be ~**ed** şaşmak, hayret etm.; ~**ment** şaşkınlık, hayret

astray [ıs'trey]: lead ~ *v/t* baştan çıkarmak

astride [ıs'trayd] bacakları ayrılmış

astro|loger [ıs'trolıcı] müneccim; ~**naut** [ästrınôt] astronot; ~**nomy** [ıs'tronımi] astronomi

astute [ıs'tyût] kurnaz; zekâli

asunder [ı'sandı] ayrı, ayrılmış

asylum [ı'saylım] sığınak, barınak

at [ät, ıt] -da, -de; -a, -e; -in üstün(d)e; yanın(d)a; halinde; ~ five o'clock saat beşte; ~ home evde; ~ the age of yaşında

ate [et] *s.* eat

atheism ['eythiizm] ateizm,

tanrısızlık

Athens ['äthinz] Atina

athlet|e ['äthlit] atlet, sporcu; **~ic** [_'letik] atletik, kuvvetli; **~ics** atletizm

Atlantic [ıt'läntik]: **the ~ Ocean** Atlas Okyanusu

atlas ['ätlıs] atlas

ATM [eyti'äm] *n.* bankamatik

atmosphere ['ätmısfıı] atmosfer; *fig.* hava, çevre

atom ['ätım] atom; **~ bomb** atom bombası

atomic [ı'tomik] atomla ilgili; **~ age** atom çağı; **~ energy** atom enerjisi; **~ pile** reaktör

atone [ı'tıun] *v/i* tarziye vermek (**for** için)

atroci|ous [ı'trıuşıs] vahşi, tüyler ürpertici; **~ty** [_'ositi] gaddarlık

at-seat TV taşıt araçlarında koltuğa takılan küçük televizyon

attach [ı'täç] *v/t* bağlamak, yapıştırmak, takmak (**to** -*e*); **~ oneself to** iltihak etm., takılmak -*e*; **~ed to** bağlı -*e*; **~ment** bağlılık; sevgi

attack [ı'täk] *n.* hücum, saldırma; MED nöbet; *v/t* hücum etm., saldırmak -*e*

attain [ı'teyn] *v/t* ermek -*e*, elde etm. -*i*; *v/i* varmak, yetişmek (**to** -*e*)

attempt [ı'tempt] *n.* teşebbüs, gayret; suikast; *v/t* teşebbüs etm. -*e*, kasdetmek -*e*; denemek -*i*

atten|d [ı'tend] *v/t* hazır bulunmak -*de*, refakat etm. -*e*, bakmak -*e*; *v/i* dikkat etm. (**to** -*e*), dinlemek (-*i*); **~dance** bakım, hizmet; maiyet; **~dant** hizmetçi; **~tion** dikkat; nezaket; **~tion!** MIL hazır ol!; **~tive** dikkatli; nazik

attest [ı'test] *v/t* tasdik etm.; **~ation** [ätes'teyşın] tasdik

attic ['ätik] çatı arası

attitude ['ätityûd] davranış, tavır

attorney [ı'töni] JUR avukat, vekil; **power of ~** vekâletname; **~-general** başsavcı

attract [ı'träkt] *v/t* çekmek, cezbetmek; **~ion** çekme gücü; çekim, alımlılık; **~ive** çekici, alımlı

attribute ['ätribyût] *n.* sıfat; remiz, simge; GR yüklem; [ı'tribyut] *v/t* atfetmek (**to** -*e*)

auburn ['öbın] kestane rengi

auction ['ôkşın] *n.* artırma ile satış; *v/t* artırma ile satmak; **~eer** [ôkşı'nii] tellal

audaci|ous [ô'deyşıs] korkusuz; küstah; **~ty** [ô'däsiti] pervasızlık; küstahlık

audi|ble ['ôdibl] işitilebilir; **~ence** ['_yıns] dinleyiciler *pl.*; huzura kabul; **~torium** [_i'törim] konferans salonu; dinleyiciler *pl.*

aught [öt]: **for ~ I care** bana ne

augment [ôg'mınt] *v/t* artırmak; *v/i* artmak; **~ation**

art(ır)ma
August[1] ['ôgıst] ağustos
august[2] [ô'gast] yüce, aziz
aunt [ânt] teyze; hala; yenge
auspic|es ['ôspisis] *pl.* uğurlu fal; *fig.* himaye; **~ious** [ôs'pişıs] uğurlu
auster|e [os'tıı] sert; sade; **~ity** [-'teriti] sertlik; sadelik, süssüzlük
Australia [os'treylyı] Avustralya; **~n** Avustralyalı
Austria ['ostrıı] Avusturya; **~n** Avusturyalı
authentic [ô'thentik] sahih, güvenilir
author ['ôthı] yazar; sebep; **~itative** [ô'thorititiv] otoriter; yetkili; **~ity** otorite; yetki; etki; uzman; makam, daire; **~ize** ['-ırayz] *v/t* yetki vermek *-e*; **~ship** yazarlık; asıl
autocracy [ô'tokrısi] otokrasi, istibdat
auto|graph ['ôtıgrâf] otoğraf; imza; **~matic** [-'mätik] otomatik; **~mation** TECH otomasyon; **~nomous** [ô'tonımıs] POL özerk; **~nomy** özerklik, muhtariyet; **~psy** ['ôtıpsi] MED otopsi
autumn ['ôtım] sonbahar, güz
auxiliary [ôg'zilyıri] yardımcı
avail [ı'veyl] *v/t* faydalı olm., yaramak *-e*; **~able** mevcut, elde edilebilir; geçer(li)
avalanche ['ävılânş] çığ
avaric|e ['ävıris] hırs, tamah; **~ious** [-'rişıs] haris, tamah-

kâr
avenge [ı'venc] *v/t -in* intikamını almak
avenue ['ävinyû] cadde, iki tarafı ağaçlı yol
average ['ävıric] *n.* orta, ortalama, vasat; *adj.* ortalama; *v/t -in* ortasını bulmak; *-in* ortalaması olm.
aver|se [ı'vɜs] muhalif, karşı (to, from *-e*); **~sion** nefret, hoşlanmayış; **~t** *v/t* çevirmek; önlemek
aviat|ion [eyvi'eyşın] havacılık; **~or** ['-tı] havacı
avoid [ı'voyd] *v/t* sakınmak, çekinmek *-den*; **~ance** sakınma
avow [ı'vau] *v/t* itiraf etm., kabul etm.; **~al** itiraf
await [ı'weyt] *v/t* beklemek
awake [ı'weyk] *adj.* uyanık; *v/t* uyandırmak; *v/i* uyanmak; **be ~** to *-in* farkında olm.; **~n** *v/t* uyandırmak
award [ı'wôd] *n.* hüküm, karar; ödül, mükâfat; *v/t* (mükâfat olarak) vermek *-e*
aware [ı'weı]: **be ~** of bilmek *-i*, haberdar olm. *-den*; **become ~** of öğrenmek *-i*; *-in* farkına varmak
away [ı'wey] uzakta; uzağa
awe [ô] *n.* korku, sakınma; saygı; *v/t* korkutmak; **~ful** ['ôful] korkunç, müthiş; berbat
awhile [ı'wayl] bir müddet
awkward ['ôkwıd] beceriksiz, biçimsiz; sıkıntılı

awning ['ôniŋ] tente
awoke [ı'wuık] s. awake
awry [ı'ray] eğri, yanlış, ters
axe [äks] balta
axiom ['äksiım] aksiyom

ax|is ['äksis] pl. ~es ['-îz]
mihver, eksen; ~le(-tree)
['äksl-] TECH dingil
ay(e) [ay] evet, hayhay
azure ['äzı] mavi

B

babble ['bäbl] v/i saçmala-
mak; n. saçma sapan konuşma
babe [beyb] s. baby
baboon [bı'buun] ZOO Habeş
maymunu
baby ['beybi] bebek; ~ carriage Am. çocuk arabası;
~hood bebeklik çağı
bachelor ['bäçılı] bekâr
back [bäk] n., adj. arka; adv.
arkada, arkaya; geri(ye); yeniden, tekrar; v/t geri yürütmek; himaye etm.; desteklemek; para yatırmak -e; v/i
geri gitmek; ~ tyre arka lastik; ~ wheel arka tekerlek;
~bite v/t iftira etm. -e; ~bone
ANAT omurga, belkemiği; fig.
karakter, metanet; ~fire geri
tepme; ~ground arka plan;
fig. muhit, görgü; ~side kıç;
~stairs pl. arka merdiven
sg.; ~ward geri, arkaya doğru; isteksiz; gelişmemiş
bacon ['beykın] domuz
pastırması
bacteri|um [bäk'terium] pl. ~a
[-iı] bakteri
bad [bäd] fena, kötü, zararlı,
kusurlu; he is ~ly off malî

durumu pek fenadır; want
~ly v/t çok istemek
bade [bäd] s. bid
badge [bäc] nişan, rozet
badger ['bäcı] ZOO porsuk
badminton ['bädmıntın] badminton
baffle ['bäfl] v/t şaşırtmak,
bozmak
bag [bäg] torba, çuval, kese;
çanta; kese kâğıdı
baggage ['bägic] bagaj; ~
check Am. bagaj kâğıdı
bag|gy ['bägi] çok bol;
~pipe(s pl.) gayda; ~piper
gaydacı; ~snatcher el çan-
taları çalan hırsız
bail [beyl] JUR n. kefalet; kefil;
~ (out) v/t kefil olm. -e
bailiff ['beylif] çiftlik kâhyası;
JUR mübaşir
bait [beyt] yem (a. fig.)
bak|e [beyk] v/t (fırında) pişir-
mek; v/i pişmek; ~er fırıncı,
ekmekçi; ~ery fırın, ekmekçi
dükkânı; ~ing powder toz
mayası
balance ['bälıns] v/t tartmak,
dengelemek; n. terazi; baskü-
ye; bilanço, denge; ~ of payments ECON ödemeler den-

gesi
balcony ['bälkıni] balkon
bald [bôld] saçsız, kel; çıplak
bale [beyl] balya, denk
balk [bôk] *n.* kiriş; engel; *v/t* mâni olm. *-e*; kaçırmak *-i*
Balkans ['bôlkıns] *pl.* Balkan (yarımadası) *sg.*
ball [bôl] top; küre; yumak; balo
ballast ['bälıst] balast; safra
ball-bearings *pl.* TECH bilyalı yatak *sg.*
ballet ['bäley] balet
ballistics [bı'listiks] balistik
balloon [bı'luun] balon
ballot ['bälıt] *n.* oy (kâğıdı); *v/i* oy vermek (for için); ~box oy sandığı
ball(-point)-pen tükenmez kalem
ballroom dans salonu
balm [bâm] pelesenk; *fig.* teselli; ~y ['-i] yatıştırıcı
balsam ['bôlsım] pelesenk
Baltic Sea ['bôltik-] Baltik denizi
balustrade [bälıs'treyd] tırabzan, parmaklık
bamboo [bäm'buu] BOT bambu
ban [bän] *n.* yasak; REL aforoz; *v/t* yasaklamak
banana [bı'nânı] BOT muz
band [bänd] bağ, şerit, kayış; topluluk, güruh; bando, müzik takımı
bandage ['bändic] *n.* sargı; *v/t* bağlamak, sarmak
bandmaster MUS bando şefi

bang [bäŋ] *n.* çat, pat, gürültü; *v/t* gürültü ile kapamak
banish ['bäniş] *v/t* POL sürgüne göndermek; ~ment sürgün
banisters ['bänistız] *pl.* tırabzan *sg.*
bank [bäŋk] *n.* kenar, kıyı; bayır; yığın; ECON banka; *v/t* bankaya yatırmak; ~(ing) account banka hesabı; ~er bankacı; ~holiday *bankaların kapalı olduğu tatil günü;* ~ing bankacılık; ~note banknot; ~rate ıskonto haddi; ~rupt ['-rapt] müflis, iflâs etmiş
banner ['bänı] bayrak, sancak
banns [bänz] *pl.* evlenme ilânı *sg.*
banquet ['bäŋkwit] şölen, ziyafet
bapti|sm ['bäptizım] REL vaftiz; ~ze ['-tayz] *v/t* vaftiz etm.; ad koymak *-e*
bar [bâ] *n.* sırık, çubuk, kol; engel, mania; kalıp, parça; bar; JUR baro; *v/t* kapamak; önlemek
barb [bâb] ok ucu, diken; ~ed wire dikenli tel
barbar|ian [bâ'bäriın] barbar; ~ous ['-bırıs] barbarca, vahşi
barber ['bâbı] berber
bare [bäı] çıplak, açık; boş; sade; ~faced yüzsüz, utanmaz; ~foot(ed) yalınayak; ~headed başı açık, şapkasız; ~ly *adv.* sadece; ancak

bargain ['bâgin] *n.* anlaşma; pazarlık, kelepir; *v/i* pazarlık etm. **(for** için)

barge [bâc] NAUT mavna, salapurya

bark¹ [bâk] ağaç kabuğu

bark² *v/i* havlamak

barley ['bâli] BOT arpa

barn [bân] ambar; ahır

barometer [bı'romitı] barometre

barracks ['bârıks] *pl.* MIL kışla *sg.*

barrage ['bâric] baraj, bent

barrel ['bârıl] fıçı, varil; namlu; *(163,7 l; Am. 119,2 l);* ~**organ** latarna

barren ['bârın] kısır; kurak, çorak

barricade [bâri'keyd] *n.* barikat; *v/t* barikatla kapamak

barrier ['bâriı] engel, mania; çit

barring ['bâriŋ] *prp.* hariç, -den maada

barrister ['bârıstı] JUR avukat, dava vekili

barter ['bâtı] ECON *n.* trampa; *v/t* trampa etm.

basalt ['bäsôlt] bazalt

base [beys] *n.* temel, esas; taban, kaide; MIL üs; CHEM baz; *adj.* bayağı, alçak; *v/t* kurmak **(upon** üstüne); ~**ball** beysbol; ~**less** temelsiz, esassız; ~**ment** temel; bodrum katı; ~**ness** aşağılık, alçaklık

bashful ['bäşful] utangaç, sıkılgan

basic ['beysik] *adj.* esas, temel

basin ['beysn] leğen; havuz; havza

basis ['beysis] esas, temel, dayanak

bask [bâsk] *v/i* güneşlenmek

basket ['bâskit] sepet, küfe; zembil; ~**ball** basketbol

bass [beys] ZOO levrek; MUS baso

bastard ['bâstıd] piç

baste [beyst] *v/t* -*in* üzerine erimiş yağ dökmek; teyellemek -*i; fig.* dayak atmak -*e*

bat¹ [bät] yarasa

bat² sopa, çomak

bath [bâth] *n.* banyo; hamam; *v/i* banyo yapmak; ~**e** [beydh] *v/i* (denizde) yıkanmak; yüzmek; ~**ing suit** ['beydhiŋ-] mayo; ~**robe** bornuz; ~**room** banyo (odası); ~**towel** hamam havlusu; ~**tub** küvet

battalion [bı'tälyın] MIL tabur

batter ['bätı] *v/t* şiddetle vurmak -*e*; ~**ed** çarpık; eskimiş

battery ['bätırı] MIL batarya; EL pil

battle ['bätl] muharebe, savaş; ~**field** savaş alanı; ~**ship** zırhlı savaş gemisi

baulk [bôk] *s.* **balk**

bawdy ['bôdi] açıksaçık

bawl [bôl] *v/i* bağırmak, haykırmak

bay¹ [bey] GEO koy, körfez

bay² BOT defne

bay³ doru *(horse)*

bay⁴ havlamak; **keep at ~** sıkıştırmak

baza(a)r [bɪ'zâ] çarşı

be [bî, bi] olmak, bulunmak; **there is** or **are** vardır; **~ to** inf. *-meğe* mecbur olm.

beach [bîç] kumsal, plaj; **~wear** plaj elbisesi

beacon ['bîkın] fener

bead [bîd] boncuk; inci

beak [bîk] gaga; ağız

beam [bîm] n. kiriş, mertek; terazi kolu; ışın; v/t yaymak; v/i parlamak

bean [bîn] вот fasulye

bear¹ [bäı] zoo ayı

bear² v/t taşımak; tahammül etm., katlanmak *-e*; doğurmak *-i*; üstüne almak *-i*; **~ in mind** aklında tutmak; **~ out** desteklemek; **~ up dayanmak (against** *-e***)**

beard [bîıd] sakal; **~ed** sakallı

bearer ['bäırı] taşıyan; hamil; **~ing** tavır, davranma; ilgi; tahammül; тесн yatak; **~ings** pl. yol, yön sg.

beast [bîst] hayvan; canavar; **~ of prey** yırtıcı hayvan

beat [bît] n. vuruş, darbe; devriye; v/t dövmek, vurmak; çalmak; çalkamak; yenmek; **~ it!** defol!; **~en** s. beat; **~ing** dövme, dayak

beauti|ful ['byûtıful] güzel, latif; **~fy** ['-tifay] v/t güzelleştirmek; **~y** güzellik; güzel kimse; **~y parlo(u)r** güzellik salonu; **~y-spot** (yüzdeki) ben; güzel manzaralı yer

beaver ['bîvı] zoo kunduz; kunduz kürkü

because [bi'koz] çünkü, zira, *-diği* için; **~ of** *-den* dolayı, sebebiyle, yüzünden

beckon ['bekın] v/t işaret etm. *-e*

become [bi'kam] v/i olmak; v/t yakışmak *-e*; **what has ~e of him?** o ne oldu? şimdi ne halde?; **~ing** uygun; yakışık

bed [bed] v/t yatırmak, yerleştirmek; n. yatak, karyola; dip; bahçe tarhı; **~ and breakfast** kahvaltı ve yatacak yer; **~bug** tahtakurusu; **~clothes** pl. yatak takımı sg.; **~ding** yatak; **~linen** yatak takımı; **~rid** (*-den*) yatalak; **~room** yatak odası; **~side table** komodin; **~spread** yatak örtüsü; **~stead** karyola, kerevet; **~time** yatma zamanı

bee [bî] zoo arı

beech [bîç] вот kayın ağacı

beef [bîf] sığır eti; **~eater** Londra kalesi bekçisi; **~steak** biftek; **~ tea** sığır eti suyu

bee|hive arı kovanı; **~keeper** arıcı; **~line** en kısa yol

beer [bîn, bîı] n. be

beet [bît] вот pancar

beetle ['bîtl] вот böcek

beetroot pancar; **~ sugar** pancar şekeri

befall [bi'fôl] v/i vuku bulmak; v/t -in başına gelmek

before [bi'fô] önde; önce; -in önünde, önüne; -in huzurunda, huzuruna; -den önce; ~hand önceden; ~ long çok geçmeden, az zamanda

befriend [bi'frend] v/t dostça hareket etm., yardım etm. -e

beg [beg] v/i dilenmek; v/t dilemek, istemek (of -den); I ~ your pardon özür dilerim, affedersiniz

began [bi'gän] s. begin

beggar [bi'begı] dilenci; pop. çapkın

begin [bi'gin] v/t başlamak -e; meydana gelmek; to ~ with ilk olarak; ~ner yeni başlayan, başlayıcı; ~ning başlangıç

begone [bi'gon] intj. defol!

begun [bi'gan] s. begin

behalf [bi'hâf]: on ~ of adına, namına; lehinde

behave [bi'heyv] v/i davranmak, hareket etm.; ~io(u)r [-yı] davranış, tavır

behead [bi'hed] v/t -in başını kesmek

behind [bi'haynd] arkada; -in arkasında, arkasına; geri

behold [bi'huld] v/t görmek; bakmak -e

being ['biiŋ] n. oluş, varlık

belated [bi'leytid] gecikmiş

belch [belç] v/i geğirmek; v/t püskürtmek

belfry [bi'belfri] çan kulesi (sahanlığı)

Belgian ['belcın] Belçikalı;

~um ['-ım] Belçika

belie|f [bi'lîf] inanç; iman; itikat; güven; ~ve [-v] v/t inanmak -e; zannetmek -i; v/i güvenmek, inanmak (in -e); make ~ve v/t inandırmak (so. -e); ~ver inanan, inançlı, mümin

belittle [bi'litl] v/t küçültmek

bell [bel] zil, çıngırak, çan, kampana; ~-flower BOT çançiçeği

belligerent [bi'licırınt] muharip; kavgacı

bellow [bi'belu] v/i böğürmek; ~s [-z] pl. körük sg.

bell-pull zil kordonu; ~push zil düğmesi

belly [bi'beli] karın

belong [bi'lon] v/i ait olm. (to -e); ~ings pl. eşya; pılı pırtı

beloved [bi'lavd] sevilen; sevgili

below [bi'lu] aşağıda; -in altında; -den aşağı

belt [belt] kuşak, kemer; kayış; bağ; bölge

bench [benç] sıra, bank; tezgâh

bend [bend] n. kavis, dönemeç; viraj; v/t bükmek, geriltmek, kıvırmak; v/i bükülmek, eğilmek, çevrilmek

beneath [bi'nîth] s. below

bene|**diction** [beni'dikşın] hayır dua, takdis; ~fable ['-fâktı] iyilik eden, velinimet; ~ficent [bi'nefisınt] hayır sahibi, lütufkâr; ~ficial [-'fişıl] yararlı; hayırlı; ~fit

['‿fit] *n.* yarar, fayda, menfaat; hayır; *v/i* yaramak, faydalı olm. *-e*; *v/i* faydalanmak (by *-den*); ∼volent [bi'nevɪlɪnt] iyi dilekli, hayırhah

bent [bent] *s.* bend; be ∼ on azmetmek *-e*, çok istemek *-i*

benzene ['benzin] CHEM benzol

benzine ['benzin] benzin

bequeath [bi'kwiðh] *v/t* vasiyet etm., terketmek; ∼st [‿'kwest] vasiyet; bağışlama

bereave [bi'riːv] *v/t* çalmak *-den*; (of *sth. -i*); ∼eft [‿'reft] *s.* bereave

beret ['berey] bere

berry ['beri] BOT tane

berth [bɜːth] yatak; ranza

beseech [bi'siːç] *v/t* yalvarmak *-e*

beside [bi'sayd] *-in* yanına, yanında; *-in* dışında; ∼ oneself çılgın; ∼s *-den* başka; *adv.* bundan başka

besiege [bi'siːc] *v/t* kuşatmak

besought [bi'sɔːt] *s.* beseach

best [best] en iyi(ler); at ∼ olsa olsa; make the ∼ of mümkün olduğu kadar yararlanmak *-den*; ∼ man sağdıç; to the ∼ of my knowledge benim bildiğime göre

bestial ['bestyıl] *v/t* vemek, vahşi

bestow [bi'stıu] *v/t* vemek, hediye etm.; bağışlamak (upon *-e*)

bet [bet] *n.* bahis; *v/i* bahse girmek

betray [bi'trey] *v/t* ele vermek; ağzından kaçırmak; ∼al hıyanet, ele verme; ∼er hain.

betroth [bi'trıudh] nişanlamak (*so.* to *AD*); ∼al nişan (*-lama*)

better ['betı] daha iyi; üstün; get the ∼ of yenmek *-i*, üstün olm. *-den*; get ∼ iyileşmek; so much the ∼ daha iyi

between [bi'twin] *-in* arasına, arasında; *-in* arada, araya; ∼decks *pl.* NAUT güverte

beverage ['beviric] içecek

bewail [bi'weyl] ağlamak *-e*

beware [bi'wäi] *v/i* sakınmak, korunmak (of *-den*); *intj.* dikkat, sakın!

bewilder [bi'wildı] *v/t* şaşırtmak; ∼ment şaşkınlık, hayret

bewitch [bi'wiç] *v/t* büyülemek, teşhir etm.

beyond [bi'yond] ileri, ötede, öteye; *-in* ötesine, ötesinde; *-den* ötede; *-in* dışında, üstünde; ∼ doubt *adv.* şüphesiz; it is ∼ me buna akılım ermez

bias ['bayıs] *n.* meyil; peşin yargı; *v/t* etkilemek; ∼(s)ed peşin yargı sahibi

Bible ['baybl] REL Mukaddes Kitap, Tevrat, Zebur ve İncil; ∼ical ['biblikıl] Mukaddes Kitaba ait; Qiography [bibli'ogrıfi] bibliyografya

bicycle ['baysikl] bisiklet

bid [bid] *n.* teklif; *v/t* emretmek; davet etm.; ~ **farewell**
vedalaşmak (to ile); ~**den**
s. **bid**; ~**ding** artırma; emir;
davet

bier [biı] cenaze teskeresi

big [big] büyük, kocaman; iri;
~ **business** ECON büyük ser-
mayeli ticaret; ~ **shot** *sl.* ko-
daman

bigamy ['bigımi] JUR çok
karılı evlenme

bigot|ed ['bigıtid] mutaassıp,
dar kafalı; ~**ry** dar kafalılık

bike [bayk] bisiklet

bilateral [bay'lätırıl] iki taraflı

bilberry ['bilbıri] BOT yaban
mersini

bile [bayl] ANAT safra

bilingual [bay'liŋgwıl] iki dil-
li

bilious ['bilyıs] safralı

bill[1] [bil] **1.** ZOO gaga

bill[2] hesap pusulası; fatura;
JUR kanun tasarısı; *Am.*
banknot; ECON poliçe; ~ **of**
exchange poliçe; ~ **of**
health sağlık raporu

billfold *Am.* cüzdan

billiards ['bilyıdz] *pl.* bilardo
sg.

billion ['bilyın] bin milyar;
Am. milyar

billow ['bilıu] *n.* büyük dalga;
v/i dalgalanmak; ~**y** dalgalı

bimonthly ['bay'manthli] iki
ayda bir

bin [bin] kutu, sandık, teneke

bind [baynd] *v/t* bağlamak;

sarmak; ciltlemek; mecbur
etm.; *v/i* TECH katılaşmak,
donmak; ~**ing** *adj.*
yapıştırıcı; kesin; *n.* cilt (-le-
me); bağlama tertibatı

binoculars [bi'nokyulız] *pl.*
dürbün *sg.*

biography [bay'ogrıfi] hal
tercümesi

biology [bay'olıcı] biyoloji

birch [bıç] BOT huş ağacı

bird [bıd] kuş; ~ **of passage**
ZOO göçmen kuş; ~ **of prey**
ZOO yırtıcı kuş; ~'**s eye view**
kuş bakışı görünüş

birth [bıth] doğum; soy; başlangıç; **give** ~ **to** doğurmak
-*i*; **date of** ~ doğum tarihi;
~**control** doğum kontrolü;
~**day** doğum günü; ~**place**
doğum yeri; ~**rate** doğum
oranı

biscuit ['biskit] bisküvit

bishop ['bişıp] REL piskopos

bit [bit] **1.** gem; **2.** parça, lok-
macık; **3.** *s.* **bite**

bitch [biç] ZOO dişi köpek

bite [bayt] *n.* ısırım; lokma;
diş yarası; sokma; *v/t*
ısırmak; sokmak; yakmak,
acıtmak; ~ **at** ısırmağa çalışmak -*i*

biting ['baytıŋ] keskin; acı

bitten ['bitn] *s.* **bite**

bitter ['bitı] acı, keskin; sert;
~**ness** acılık; sertlik

bitumen ['bityumin] zift, katran

blab [bläb] *v/i* boşboğazlık
etm.

black [bläk] *adj.* siyah, kara, karanlık; uğursuz; *v/i* kararmak; *v/t* karartmak, boyamak; ~**berry** BOT böğürtlen; ~**bird** ZOO karatavuk; ~**boardd** yazı tahtası; ~**en** *v/t* karartmak; *fig.* lekelemek; ~**head** (yüzde siyah) benek; ~**ing** ayakkabı boyası; ~**mail** *n.* JUR şantaj; *v/t* şantaj yapmak -*e*; ~**market** kara borsa; ~ **marketeer** kara borsacı; ~**ness** siyahlık; kötülük; ~**smith** demirci, nalbant

bladder ['blädı] ANAT mesane, sidik torbası, kavuk

blade [bleyd] bıçak ağzı; ot yaprağı; kürek palası

blame [bleym] *v/t* ayıplamak, sorumlu tutmak; *n.* kabahat, kusur; sorumluluk; **be to** ~ suçlu olm. (for ile); ~**less** kabahatsiz, kusursuz

blank [bläṅk] boş; yazısız; manasız; şaşkın; *n.* boş kur'a

blanket ['bläṅkit] battaniye

blasphemy ['bläsfimi] küfür

blast [blâst] *n.* (şiddetli *ve* *ani*) rüzgâr esmesi; boru sesi; patlama; *v/t* berhava etm., yakmak, patlatmak; ~**furnace** TECH yüksek fırın; ~**ing** berhava etme; patlama

blaze [bleyz] *n.* alev; parlaklık; yangın; *v/i* parlamak, yanmak, ışık saçmak; ~**r** spor ceketi

bleach [bliç] *v/t* ağartmak, beyazlatmak

bleak [blik] çıplak; soğuk

blear [blii] *adj.* çapaklı (*göz*); *v/t* kamaştırmak

bleat [blît] melemek

bled [bled] *s.* **bleed**

bleed [blîd] *v/i* kanamak, kanını dökmek; *v/t* *fig.* -*in* parasını sızdırmak; ~**ing** kanama

blemish ['blemiş] *n.* kusur; leke; *v/t* lekelemek

blend [blend] *n.* alaşım; harman; *v/t* karıştırmak; *v/i* karışmak

blent [blent] *s.* **blend**

bless [bles] *v/t* kutsamak; hayır dua etm. -*e*; ~ **my soul!** aman ya Rabbi!; ~**ed** ['ːid] mübarek, kutlu; ~**ing** hayır dua

blew [bluu] *s.* **blow**

blight [blayt] yanma, pas, küf

blind [blaynd] *adj.* kör; *fig.* kısa görüşlü; çıkmaz (*yol*); *n.* perde; kepenk; ~**alley** çıkmaz yol; ~**fold** *adj.* gözleri bağlı; *v/t* -*in* gözlerini bağlamak; ~**ness** körlük

blink [blink] *v/i* göz kırpmak, yanıp sönmek; ~ **the facts** gerçeğe gözlerini yummak

bliss [blis] saadet, bahtiyarlık

blister ['blistı] kabarcık; yakı

blizzard ['blizıd] tipi, kar fırtınası

bloat [blıut] *v/i* şişirmek; tütsülemek; ~**ed** ['ːid] göbeği yağ bağlamış; ~**er** tütsülenmiş ringa balığı

block [blok] *n.* kütük, kaya

parçası; engel; blok; v/t tıkamak, kapamak: ~ **letters** *pl.*
kitap yazısı; ~ **up** v/t kapatmak, tıkamak

blockade [blo'keyd] *n.* abluka; v/t ablukaya almak

blockhouse blokhavz

blond(e) [blond] sarışın

blood [blad] kan; soy; **cause
bad** ~ aralarını bozmak; in
cold ~ soğukkanlı; ~**cur-
dling** tüyler ürpertici; ~**less**
kansız; *fig.* renksiz; ~**poi-
soning** kan zehirlenmesi;
~**shed** kan dökme; ~**shot**
kanlanmış; ~**vessel** ANAT
kan damarı; ~**y** kanlı

bloom [bluum] *n.* çiçek; *fig.*
gençlik, tazelik; v/i çiçek açmak

blossom ['blosım] *n.* bahar
çiçeği; v/i çiçek açmak

blot [blot] ANAT leke; ayıp; v/t
lekelemek, kirletmek, ka-
rartmak; ~ **out** silmek; ~**ter**
kurutma kâğıdı tamponu;
~**ting-**tape sünger kâğıdı

blouse [blauz] bluz

blow[1] [blu] vuruş, darbe;
come to ~**s** kavgaya tutuşmak

blow[2] v/i esmek, üflemek; v/t
üflemek; MUS çalmak; ~ **in**
çıkagelmek, uğramak; ~
one's nose sümkürmek; ~
out v/t üfleyip söndürmek;
v/i dinmek; ~ **up** havaya
uçurmak; ~**n** *s.* blow[2]

blue [bluu] mavi; *fig.* kederli;
~**bell** BOT yabani sümbül;

~**bottle** BOT peygamber çiçeği; zoo mavi sinek; ~**s** *pl.*
fig. melankoli *sg.*

bluff [blaf] *n.* blöf; v/t blöf
yapmak *-e*

bluish ['blu(u)iş] mavimsi

blunder ['blandı] *n.* hata, gaf;
v/i hata yapmak; v/t berbat
etm.

blunt [blant] *adj.* kesmez, kör;
fig. sözünü sakınmaz; v/t
körletmek, körleştirmek

blur [blı] *n.* leke; bulaşık şey;
v/t bulaştırmak, silmek

blurt [blıt]: ~ **out** v/t ağzından
kaçırmak

blush [blaş] *n.* kızarma, utan-
ma; v/i utanmak, kızarmak

boar [bô] zoo erkek domuz

board [bôd] *n.* tahta, levha;
mukavva; masa; yiyecek: kurul; idare; v/t döşemek, kaplamak; yedirip içirmek; binmek *-e*; ~ **and lodging** yiyecek ve yatacak; ♀ of Trade
Ticaret Odası *veya* Ba-
kanlığı; **full** ~ tam pansiyon;
notice ~ ilân tahtası; on ~ gemide; trende; ~**er** pansiyon
kiracısı; yatılı öğrenci; ~**ing
house** pansiyon; ~**ing
school** yatılı okul

boast [bıust] *n.* övünme; v/i
övünmek, yükseklten atmak;
~**ful** övüngen, palavracı

boat [bıut] sandal, kayık; gemi; ~**ing** sandal *v.s.nin* eğlence için kullanılması; ~**man**
sandalcı, kayıkçı; ~**race**
kayık yarışı

bob [bob] *v/t* hafifçe hareket ettirmek; *v/i* oynamak, kımıldamak

bobbin ['bobin] makara, bobin

bobby ['bobi] *coll.* polis memuru

bob-sleigh ['bob–] kızak

bodi|ce ['bodis] korsaj, korse; **~ly** bedenî; *adv.* büsbütün

body ['bodi] vücut, beden; ceset; kurul, heyet, grup; karoseri; **~guard** hassa askeri

bog [bog] batak, bataklık

bogus ['bugəs] sahte, yapma

boil [boyl] *n.* çıban; *v/i* kaynamak; *v/t* kaynatmak, haşlamak; **~ over** *v/i* taşmak; **~ed egg** rafadan yumurta; **~er** kazan

boisterous ['boystırıs] şiddetli, gürültülü

bold [buld] cesur, atılgan; arsız, küstah; **~ness** atılganlık; küstahlık

bolster ['bulstır] yastık

bolt [bıult] *n.* cıvata, sürme; yıldırım; ok; *v/t* sürmelemek; yutmak; *v/i* kaçmak; make a **~** for *-e* doğru atılmak; **~** upright dimdik

bomb [bom] *n.* bomba; *v/t* bombalamak; **~ardment** [.'bâdmənt] bombardıman; **~er** ['~ı] bombardıman uçağı

bond [bond] bağ, rabıta; bono; ECON tahvil; **in ~** antrepoda; **~age** esirlik, esirlik

bone [bıun] kemik; kılçık

bonfire ['bonfayı] şenlik ateşi

bonnet ['bonit] başlık, bere; motor kapağı, kaporta

bonn|ie, ~y ['boni] güzel, zarif; gürbüz

bonus ['bıunıs] ikramiye

bony ['bıuni] kemikleri görünen, zayıf; kılçıklı

book [buk] *n.* kitap; defter; *v/t* ısmarlamak, tutmak, kaydetmek; **~ed up** hepsi satılmış; yer kalmamış; **~binder** ciltçi; **~case** kitap dolabı; **~ing-clerk** gişe memuru; **~ing-office** bilet gişesi; **~keeper** defter tutan, muhasebeci; **~keeping** defter tutma; **~let** broşür; **~seller** kitapçı; **~shop** kitabevi

boom [buum] ECON fiatların yükselmesi, piyasada canlılık

boor [buı] kaba adam

boost [buust] *v/t* arkasından itmek; artırmak

boot [buut] bot, potin, çizme; **~ee** ['.ti] kadın botu

booth [buudh] kulübe, baraka

booty ['buuti] ganimet, yağma

border ['bôdı] *n.* kenar, pervaz; sınır; *v/t* sınırla(ndır)mak; *v/i* bitişik olm.; (on, upon *-e*)

bore[1] [bô] *s.* bear

bore[2] *n.* çap, delgi, boru kutru, sonda; can sıkıcı adam, can sıkıcı iş; *v/t* delmek, sondalamak; *-in* canını sıkmak; **~hole** sonda deliği

boric ['bôrik]; ~ **acid** CHEM bor asidi

born [bôn] *s.* **bear²**; doğmuş; **be** ~ doğmak; ~**e** *s.* **bear²**

borough ['barı] kasaba, küçük şehir

borrow ['boru] *v/t* ödünç almak, borç almak

bosom ['buzım] göğüs, koyun

Bosphorus ['bosforıs] Boğaziçi

boss [bos] patron, şef

botan|ic(al) [bı'tänik(ıl)] botaniğe ait; ~**y** ['botıni] botanik

botch [boç] *n.* kaba iş; *v/t* kabaca yamamak, bozmak

both [buuth] her iki(si); ~ ... **and** hem ... hem de

bother ['bodhı] *n.* canını sıkma, sıkıntı; *v/t -in* canını sıkmak; *v/i* endişelenmek (**about** *-den*)

bottle ['botl] *n.* şişe, biberon; *v/t* şişeye koymak; ~**neck** şişe boğazı; *fig.* dar geçit

bottom ['botım] dip, alt; kıç; temel; ~**less** dipsiz

bough [bau] dal

bought [bôt] *s.* **buy**

boulevard ['buulvâ] bulvar

boulder ['buldı] çakıl; kaya parçası

bounce [bauns] *n.* sıçrama; *v/i* sıçramak

bound¹ [baund] *s.* **bind**; ~ **for** *-e* gitmek üzere olan; ~ **to** *inf.* *-meğe* mecbur

bound² *v/t* sınırlamak

bound³ *v/i* atlamak, sıçramak

bound|ary ['baundırı] sınır; ~**less** sınırsız, sonsuz; **out of** ~**s** yasak bölge

bounty ['baunti] cömertlik; ECON ikramiye, prim

bouquet [bu(u)'key] buket, demet; koku (*şarap*)

bout [baut] MED nöbet; yarış

bow¹ [bau] yay, kavis

bow² [bau] NAUT pruva

bow³ [bau] *n.* reverans; *v/t* eğmek; *v/i* reverans yapmak

bowels ['baulz] *pl.* barsaklar

bower ['bau] çardak, kameriye

bowl¹ [bıul] kâse, tas, kadeh; pipo ağzı

bowl² *n.* top; *v/t* yuvarlamak, atmak

bowler ['bıulı] melon şapka

box [boks] *n.* kutu, sandık; loca; arabacı yeri; kulübe; TECH yuva; *v/i* boks yapmak; ~**er** boksör; ~**ing** boks; **2ing Day** 26 aralık; ~**ing-match** boks maçı; ~**office** tiyatro gişesi

boy [boy] erkek çocuk, oğlan; **2 Scout** izci

boycott ['boykıt] *n.* boykot; *v/t* boykot etm.

boy|-friend erkek arkadaş; ~**hood** çocukluk çağı; ~**ish** (erkek) çocuk gibi

bra [brâ] sutyen

brace [breys] *n.* kuşak, köşebent; *pl.* pantolon askısı; *v/t* sağlamlaştırmak; ~ **up** sıkmak; ~**let** ['_lit] bilezik

bracket ['bräkit] *n.* kol, destek; raf; GR ayraç, parantez; v/t birleştirmek, birbirine bağlamak

brackish ['bräkiş] tuzlumsu, acı

brag [bräg] v/i yüksekten atmak, övünmek; ~gart ['_ıt] palavracı

braid [breyd] n. saç örgüsü; kurdele, örgülü şerit; v/t örmek; kurdele takmak -e

brain [breyn] beyin, dimağ; ~less akılsız; ~wave birdenbire gelen fikir

brake [breyk] n. fren; v/i fren yapmak; v/t frenlemek

bramble ['brämbl] BOT böğürtlen çalısı

branch [brânç] n. dal; kol, şube; v/i dallanmak, kollara ayrılmak

brand [bränd] n. yanan odun; kızgın demir, dağ, damga; marka, cins; v/t dağlamak, damgalamak; ~new yepyeni; ~y kanyak

brass [brâs] pirinç; ~ band bando, mızıka

brassière ['bräsii] sutyen

brave [breyv] adj. cesur, yiğit; v/t göğüs germek -e; ~ry kahramanlık

brawl [brôl] kavga, gürültü

brazier ['breyzıy] mangal

Brazil [brı'zil] Brezilya; ~ian Brezilyalı; ~nut BOT Brezilya kestanesi

breach [brîç] n. delik, kırık; bozulma; v/t kırmak, bozmak

bread [bred] ekmek; ~and--butter letter teşekkür mektubu

breadth [bredth] genişlik, en

break [breyk] n. kırık; ara; arası kesilme; (day) ağartı; v/t kırmak, koparmak, parçalamak; dağıtmak; açmak, yarmak; alıştırmak; mahvetmek; promise: tutmamak; ara vermek -e; v/i parçalanmak, kırılmak; kuvvetten düşmek; (day) ağarmak; ~ away ayrılmak; ~ down v/t yıkmak; v/i bozulmak; ~ off v/i ayrılmak; v/t ayırmak; ~ up v/t parçalamak, kırmak; v/i dağılmak; ~able kırılacak; ~down yıkılma, bozulma; ~fast ['brekfıst] kahvaltı; ~through fig. başarı

breast [brest] göğüs; meme; ~stroke kurbağalama yüzüş

breath [breth] nefes, soluk; out of ~ soluğu kesilmiş; ~e [brîdh] nefes almak; ~ing ['_îdhiŋ] nefes (alma); ~less ['_ethlis] nefesi kesilmiş

bred [bred] s. breed

breeches ['briçiz] pl. pantolon, külot sg.

breed [brîd] n. soy, ırk; v/t doğurmak, üretmek, yetiştirmek; ~er yetiştirici; ~ing üreme, yetiştirme

breeze [brîz] hafif rüzgâr, meltem

brevity ['breviti] kısalık

brew [bruu] v/t yapmak, hazırlamak; v/i bastırmak

üzere olm.; ~ery bira fabrikası

bribe [brayb] n. rüşvet; v/t rüşvet vermek -e; ~ry rüşvet verme veya alma

brick [brik] tuğla; ~layer duvarcı; ~work tuğla işi; pl. tuğla ocağı

bridal ['braydl] gelinlik, geline ait

bride [brayd] gelin; ~groom güvey; ~smaid düğünde geline refakat eden kız

bridge [bric] n. köprü; briç oyunu; v/t köprü kurmak -e; ~ over atlatmak

bridle ['braydl] n. at başlığı; dizgin; v/t gem vurmak, dizgin takmak -e; ~bath, ~road atlılara mahsus yol

brief [brif] kısa; ~case evrak çantası

brigade [bri'geyd] mıl tugay; ~dier [-gı'dıi] tuğbay

bright [brayt] parlak, berrak, neşeli, canlı; zeki; ~en v/t parlatmak, neşelendirmek; v/i parlamak; ~ness parlaklık; uyanıklık

brillian|ce, ~cy ['brilyıns, '-si] parlaklık, pırıltı; ~t adj. çok parlak; çok zeki; n. pırlanta

brim [brim] kenar, ağız; ~ful(l) ağzına kadar dolu

bring [briŋ] v/t getirmek; ~ about v/t sebep olm.; ~ an action dava açmak; ~ along yanında getirmek; ~ forth meydana çıkarmak; ~ up

yaklaştırmak; yetiştirmek; ~ to an end sona erdirmek

brink [briŋk] kenar

brisk [brisk] faal, canlı, işlek.

bristle ['brisl] n. sert kıl; v/t tüyleri ürpermek

Brit|ain ['britn] Britanya; ~ish Britanyalı, İngiliz; ~on ['britn] İngiliz

brittle ['britl] kolay kırılır, gevrek

broach [bruç] v/t delik açmak -e; fig. girişmek -e

broad [bröd] geniş, enli; açık, belli; erkinci, liberal; ~cast n. radyo yayımı; v/t yayımlamak; ~en v/t genişletmek; ~minded açık fikirli

brocade [brı'keyd] brokar

broil [broyl] gürültü, kavga

broke [bruık] s. break; ~n s. break; ~er simsar, komisyoncu

bronchitis [broŋ'kaytis] med bronşit

bronze [bronz] tunç, bronz

brooch [bruç] broş

brood [bruud] n. yumurtadan çıkan civcivler veya kuş yavruları pl.; v/i kuluçkaya yatmak

brook [bruk] dere, çay

broom [brum] süpürge

broth [broth] etsuyu

brothel ['brothl] genelev

brother ['bradhı] kardeş, birader; ~hood kardeşlik; ~-in-law kayınbirader, bacanak, enişte; ~ly kardeşçe

brought [brôt] s. bring

brow [brau] ANAT kaş; alın

brown [braun] kahverengi, esmer; ~ **paper** ambalaj kâğıdı

bruise [bruuz] *n.* bere, çürük; *v/t* berelemek, çürütmek

brush [braş] *n.* fırça; çalı; tüylü kuyruk; *v/t* fırçalamak, süpürmek; hafifçe dokunmak -*e*; ~ **up** tazelemek

Brussels ['braslz] Brüksel; ~**sprouts** ['-l'sprauts] BOT frenk lahanası

brut|**al** ['bruutl] hayvanca, vahşi; ~**ality** [-'tâliti] vahşet, canavarlık; ~**e** [bruut] hayvan, canavar

bubble ['babl] *n.* hava kabarcığı; *v/i* köpürmek, kaynamak

buck [bak] *n.* erkek karaca, geyik *v.s.*; *Am. sl.* dolar; *v/i* sıçramak

bucket ['bakit] kova

buckle ['bakl] *n.* toka, kopça; *v/t* tokalamak, kopçalamak; ~ **on** tokalamak, takmak

buckskin güderi

bud [bad] *n.* tomurcuk, konca; *v/i* konca vermek

buddy ['badi] *sl.* arkadaş

budget ['bacit] bütçe

buffalo ['bâfilu] manda

buffer ['bafı] TECH tampon

buffet ['bafit] büfe

buffoon [ba'fuun] soytarı, maskara

bug [bag] tahtakurusu; *Am.* böcek; ~**gy** *Am.* hafif at arabası; çocuk arabası

bugle ['byûgl] borazan, boru

build [bild] *v/t* inşa etm., kurmak, yapmak; ~ **upon** güvenmek -*e*; ~**er** inşaatçı; inşaat ustası; ~**ing** bina, yapı

built [bilt] *s.* build; ~-**in** gömme; yerleşmiş

bulb [balb] BOT soğan; EL ampul

Bulgaria [bal'gâiri] Bulgaristan; ~**n** Bulgar; Bulgarca

bulge [balc] *n.* bel verme, şiş; *v/i* bel vermek, kamburlaşmak

bulk [balk] hacim, kütle; en büyük kısım; ~**y** hacimli, büyük

bull [bul] ZOO boğa; ~**dog** buldok köpeği

bullet ['bulit] kurşun, mermi

bulletin ['bulitin] günlük haber, tebliğ; ~ **board** *Am.* ilân tahtası

bullion ['bulyın] altın *veya* gümüş külçesi

bully ['buli] *v/t* korkutmak

bum [bam] *sl.* serseri, başıboş

bumble-bee ['bambl-] ZOO hezen arısı

bump [bamp] *n.* vuruş, çarpma; *v/i* çarpmak (**against** -*e*); *v/t* vurmak; ~**er** tampon; ağza dolmuş bardak

bun [ban] kuru üzümlü çörek

bunch [banç] demet, deste, salkım

bundle ['bandl] *n.* bağ, bohça, paket; *v/t* (**up**) çıkınlamak, sarmalamak

bungalow ['baŋgılu] tek

katlı köşk

bungle ['bʌŋgl] n. kötü iş, bozma; v/t bozmak, bulaştırmak

bunk [bʌŋk] yatak yeri, ranza

bunny ['bʌni] tavşan(cık)

buoy [bɔy] şamandıra; ~ant yüzebilir; fig. neşeli.

burden ['bɜːdn] n. yük, ağır iş; ana fikir; nakarat; v/t yüklemek (so. with -e -i)

bureau ['bjuərəu] büro, yazıhane; Am. çekmeceli dolap

burglar ['bɜːglə] gece hırsızı; ~y ev soyma

burial ['beriəl] gömme; ~-ground mezarlık

burly ['bɜːli] iriyarı

burn [bɜːn] n. yanık; v/t yakmak; v/i yanmak; ~er gaz ocağı memesi; ~ing yanan; ~t s. burn

burst [bɜːst] n. patlama; patlak, yarık; v/i patlamak, yarılmak; v/t patlatmak; ~ into flames alevlenmek; ~ into tears ağlamağa başlamak

bury ['beri] v/t gömmek; saklamak

bus [bʌs] otobüs; miss the ~ fig. fırsatı kaçırmak

bush [buʃ] çalı, çalılık

bushel ['buʃl] İngiliz kilesi. (36, 37 l)

bushy çalılık; fırça gibi

business ['biznis] iş, görev, meslek; ticaret; mesele; ~ hours pl. iş saatleri; ~like ciddi, düzenli; ~man iş adamı; ~ tour, ~ trip iş yolcu-

luğu

bust [bʌst] büst; göğüs

bustle ['bʌsl] n. faaliyet; telâş; v/i acele etm.; telâşlanmak

busy ['bizi] faal, iş gören, meşgul; işlek; be ~ -ing, ~ oneself with meşgul olm., uğraşmak -mekle

but [bʌt, bɪt] ama, fakat; ancak; bilakis; şu kadar ki; halbuki; -den başka; the next ~ one birinci değil ikinci

butcher ['buçi] n. kasap; v/t kesmek

butler ['bʌtlə] kâhya; sofracı

butt [bʌt] fıçı; dipçik; hedef; tos; ~ in sl. karışmak -e

butter ['bʌtə] n. tereyağı; v/t tereyağı sürmek -e; ~cup вот düğünçiçeği; ~fly zoo kelebek; ~milk yayık ayranı

buttocks ['bʌtəks] pl. kıç sg.

button ['bʌtn] n. düğme; konca; v/t up düğmelemek, iliklemek; ~hole ilik

buttress ['bʌtris] payanda, destek

buy [bay] v/t satın almak, almak; ~er alıcı

buzz [baz] n. vızıltı, gürültü; v/i vızıldamak

buzzard ['bʌzɪd] zoo bir cins şahin

by [bay] -in yanında, yakınında; ile, vasıtasiyle; tarafından; -e göre; ~ and ~ yavaş; az sonra; ~ and large genellikle; ~ day gündüz; ~ far çok daha fazla; ~ God! vallahi!; ~ itself kendi kendine; **day** ~ **day** her gün; ~**e-bye** ['bay'bay] *s.* **good-bye**; ~**gone** geçmiş; ~ **election** POL ara seçim; ~**name** lakap; ~**pass** dolaştırma;

~**product** yanürün; ~**stand-er** seyirci; ~**street** yan sokak
Byzantium [bay'zantıyım] Bizans

C

cab [käb] kira arabası
cabaret ['käbırey] kabare
cabbage ['käbic] BOT lahana
cabin ['käbin] kamara; kulübe; **three-berth** ~ üç yataklı kamara
cabinet ['käbinit] dolap; POL kabine, bakanlar kurulu; ~-**maker** ince iş yapan marangoz
cable ['keybl] *n.* kablo, palamar; telgraf; v/i telgraf çekmek; ~-**car** teleferik; ~**gram** telgraf
cab|man taksi şoförü; ~**stand** taksi durağı
cackle ['käkl] v/i gıdaklamak
cact|us ['käktıs], *pl.* ~**uses** ['-siz], ~**i** ['-tay] BOT atlasçiçeği, kaktüs
café ['käfey] pastahane
cafeteria [käfi'tiırıi] kafeterya
cage [keyc] kafes; asansör odası
Cairo ['kayırıu] Kahire
cake [keyk] kurabiye, pasta, kek, çörek; kalıp; ~ **of soap** sabun parçası; ~-**tin** kek kalıbı
calamity [kı'lämiti] felâket,

afet
calculat|e ['kälkyuleyt] v/t hesaplamak, tahmin etm., saymak; ~**tion** hesap, tahmin
calendar ['kälindı] takvim
calf [kaaf], *pl.* **calves** [-vz] **1.** ZOO dana; buzağı; **2.** ANAT baldır
calib|re, *Am.* ~**er** ['kälibı] çap
call [kôl] *n.* çağırma; çağrı, davet; uğrama; telefon etme; v/t çağırmak; bağırmak; uyandırmak; adlandırmak; demek; ~ **at** uğramak -*e*; ~ **back** geri çağırmak; ~ **for** istemek -*i*; icabetmek -*i*; ~ **on** ziyaret etm. -*i*, uğramak -*e*; ~ **up** MIL silah altına çağırmak; ~**box** telefon hücresi; ~**er** ziyaret eden kimse; telefon eden kimse; ~**ing** meslek, iş
callous ['kälıs] sertleşmiş, hissiz
calm [kaam] *adj.* sakin, durgun; *n.* sakinlik; v/t yatıştırmak; ~ **down** v/i yatışmak; ~**ness** sakinlik, durgunluk
calor|ie, *Am.* ~**y** ['kälıri] kalori
cambric ['keymbrik] patiska
came [keym] *s.* **come**

camel 220

camel ['kämıl] zoo deve

camera ['kämırı] fotoğraf makinesi, kamera; ~ phone kameralı cep

camomile ['kämıumayl] BOT papatya

camouflage ['kämuflâj] n. kamuflaj; v/t kamufle etm.

camp [kämp] n. kamp; MIL ordugâh; v/i kamp kurmak; ~aign sefer, savaş; ~er kamp yapan kimse; ~ground Am. s. ~ing-ground; ~ing kamp yapma; ~ing-ground kamp yeri

campus ['kämpıs] üniversite veya okul arazisi

can¹ [kän] kap, kutu; konserve kutusu

can² inf. -ebilmek

Canad|a ['känıdı] Kanada; ~ian [kı'neydyın] Kanadalı

canal [kı'näl] kanal, mecra

canary [kı'näıri] zoo kanarya

cancel ['känsıl] v/t silmek, çizmek; kaldırmak, iptal etm.; be ~(l)ed iptal olunmak

cancer ['känsı] kanser

candid ['kändid] samimî, açık

candidate ['kändidit] namzet, aday

candied ['kändid] şekerle kaplanmış

candle ['kändl] mum; ~stick şamdan

candy ['kändi] şekerleme, bonbon

cane [keyn] baston, değnek

cann|ed [känd] Am. kutulanmış; ~ery Am. konserve fabrikası

cannibal ['känibıl] yamyam

cannon ['känın] MIL top

cannot ['känot] inf. -ememek

canoe [kı'nuu] hafif sandal, kano

canopy ['känıpi] gölgelik, tente

cant [känt] ikiyüzlülük, riyakârlık; argo

can't [kaant] s. cannot

canteen [kän'tîn] kantin; MIL aş kabı; Am. matara

canvas ['känvıs] keten bezi, kanava; tuval, yağlı boya resim; ~s v/t -i dolaşarak oy veya sipariş toplamak

cap [käp] kasket, başlık; kapak

capa|bility [keypı'biliti] kabiliyet, yetenek; ~ble muktedir, kabiliyetli, ehliyetli; kabil (of -e)

capacity [kı'päsiti] istiap; yetenek; verim; kabiliyet

cape¹ [keyp] GEO burun

cape² kap, pelerin

caper¹ ['keypı] BOT kebere

caper² v/i sıçramak

capital ['käpitl] n. başkent, hükümet merkezi; ECON sermaye, kapital; GR büyük harf; adj. esas büyük, mükemmel; ~ crime JUR cezası idam olan suç; ~ism kapitalizm; ~ist anamalcı, kapitalist

capitulation [kıpityu'leyşın] teslim; POL kapitülasyon

capricious [kı'prişıs] kaprisli

Capricorn ['käprikôn] ASTR keçi burcu

capsize ['käp'sayz] NAUT v/t devirmek; v/i devrilmek

capsule ['käpsyûl] kapsül

captain ['käptin] NAUT kaptan; MIL yüzbaşı

caption ['käpşn] başlık, serlevha; yazılı tercüme (film)

captivate ['käptiveyt] v/t cezbetmek; ~e tutsak, esir; ~ity [.'tiviti] tutsaklık

capture ['käpçı] n. yakalama, esir alma; v/t tutmak, yakalamak

car [kaa] otomobil, araba; vagon; ~ ferry araba vapuru

caravan ['kärivän] kervan; treyler; ~serai [.sıray] kervansaray

carbine ['kaabayn] karabina

carbohydrate ['kaabıu'haydreyt] CHEM karbonhidrat

carbon ['kaabın] CHEM karbon; (~ paper) kopya kâğıdı; ~ic [kaa'bonik] karbonik

carbuncle ['kaabankl] çıban, şirpençe

carbure|**tter**, ~ (t)**or** ['kaabyuretı] TECH karbüratör

carca|**se**, ~ss ['kaakıs] leş

card [kaad] kart; karton; oyun kâğıdı; ~ index klasör; fişler pl.; ~board karton, mukavva

cardiac ['kaadiäk] MED kalple ilgili

cardigan ['kaadigın] yün ceket

cardinal ['kaadınl] REL kardinal; adj. baş, esaslı; ~ number asıl sayı

care [käı] n. dikkat, bakım; ilgi; merak, üzüntü; v/i ilgilenmek (for ile); endişelenmek (-den); bakmak (-e); take ~ of muhafaza etm. -i; bakmak, dikkat etm. -e; with ~ dikkatle; ~ of evinde, eliyle

career [kı'rıı] meslek hayatı, kariyer

care|**free** kaygısız; ~**ful** dikkatli; ~**less** dikkatsiz, ihmalci, kayıtsız

caress [kı'res] n. okşama; v/t okşamak

care|**taker** kapıcı; ev yöneticisi; ~**worn** kederden bitkin

cargo ['kaagıu] yük, hamule

caricature ['kärikı'tyuı] karikatür

caries ['käiriîz] MED diş çürümesi

carnal ['kaanl] cinsî, şehvanî; dünyevî

carnation [kaa'neyşın] BOT karanfil

carol ['kärıl]: Christmas ~ Noel şarkısı

carp [kaap] ZOO sazan

car-park park yeri

carpenter ['kaapıntı] marangoz, dülger, doğramacı

carpet ['kaapit] halı

carpool n. (tasarruf amacıyla) otomobilleri sıra ile kullanma anlaşması; v/i birlikte aynı arabayla işe, okula v.b. gitmek

carriage ['käric] araba, vagon; taşıma, nakil; nakliye

ücreti; davranış; ~free nakli-
yesiz; ~way araba yolu

carrier ['käri] taşıyan; nakli-
yeci; **aircraft ~** uçak gemisi;
~ **bag** alışveriş torbası

carrion ['kärin] leş; *adj.* leş
gibi

carrot ['kärıt] BOT havuç

carry ['käri] v/t taşımak, götürmek, nakletmek; ~ **on** devam ettirmek; ~ **out** yerine
getirmek

cart [kaat] iki tekerlekli yük
arabası; **put the ~ before
the horse** bir işi tersinden
yapmak

cartoon [kaa'tuun] karikatür;
(animated) ~ miki filmi; ~**ist**
karikatürcü

cartridge ['kaatric] hartuç;
PHOT kartuş, kaset

cart-wheel araba tekerleği;
takla

carv|e [kaav] v/t oymak, hak-
ketmek; *meat*: sofrada kesmek; ~**er** oymacı, hakkâk

cascade [käs'keyd] çağlayan

case[1] [keys] kutu, kasa

case[2] hal, husus, olay; **in that
~** o takdirde; **in ~ of** halinde;
in any ~ her halde

casement ['keysmınt] pencere kanadı

cash [käş] *n.* para, nakit; v/t
paraya çevirmek; bozmak;
~ **down** peşin para; ~ **on delivery** ödemeli; ~**-and-carry**
adj. peşin para ile alınan;
~**ier** [kä'şiı] kasadar, veznedar

casing ['keysiŋ] kaplama

cask [kaask] fıçı, varil; ~**et**
['..it] değerli eşya kutusu;
Am. tabut

Caspian Sea ['käspîın -] Hazer denizi

cassock ['käsık] papaz cüppesi

cast [kaast] *n.* atma, atış; dökme, kalıp; tip, kalite; v/t atmak, saçmak; TECH dökmek;
be ~ down peşin kul kararmak;
~ **iron** TECH dökme demir; ~
steel dökme çelik

caste [kaast] kast, birbirine
karşı kapalı sınıf

castle ['kaasl] kale; şato

castor ['kaastı] tuzluk, biber-
lik

castor oil hintyağı

castrate [käs'treyt] v/t hadım
etm.

casual ['käjyuıl] tesadüfi,
rastgele; ~**ty** kaza; kayıp

cat [kät] kedi

catalog(ue) ['kätılog] katalog, liste

cataract ['kätıräkt] çağlayan

catarrh [kı'tâ] MED nezle

catastrophe [kı'tästırıfı] felâket, facia

catch [käç] v/t tutmak, yakalamak; kavramak; av; yetişmek
-e; *n.* tutma; av; tuzak; kilit
dili; ~ **a cold** nezle olm.. üşümek; ~ **up** yetişmek (**with**
-e); ~**ascatch-can** serbest
güreş; ~**ing** çekici; MED bu-
laşıkcı; ~**word** parola; slogan

category ['kätigıri] cins, kategori

cater ['keytı] v/i tedarik etm., hazırlamak (**for** -i)

caterpillar ['kätıpilı] tırtıl

cathedral [kı'thîdrıl] katedral

Catholic ['käthlik] Katolik; **~ism** [kı'tholisizım] Katoliklik

cattle ['kätl] sığır, davar

Caucasus ['kôkısıs] Kafkas (dağları *pl.*)

caught [kôt] *s.* catch

ca(u)ldron ['kôldrın] kazan

cauliflower ['koliflauı] BOT carnabahar

cause [kôz] *n.* neden, sebep; dava; v/i sebep olm. -*e*; *fig.* doğurmak v/t; **~less** sebepsiz

caut|ion ['kôşın] *n.* dikkat; ihtar; sakınma; v/t uyarmak, ihtar etm.; **~ous** ihtiyatlı, çekingen

cavalry ['kävılri] MIL süvari

cav|e [keyv], **~ern** ['kävın] mağara, in

caviar ['käviâ] havyar

cavity ['käviti] çukur, boşluk

CD [sî'dî] CD; **~ player** CD-çalar; **~-ROM** CD-ROM

cease [sîs] v/i bitmek, durmak; v/t bitirmek; **~less** sürekli, durmadan

cedar ['sîdı] BOT sedir

cede [sîd] JUR terketmek

ceiling ['sîliŋ] tavan; azami sınır

celebrat|e ['selibreyt] v/t kutlamak; **~ion** kutlama

celebrity [sı'lebriti] şöhret

kazanmış şahıs

celery ['seliri] BOT kereviz

celibacy ['selibisi] bekârlık; REL evlenme yasağı

cell [sel] hücre; EL pil

cellar ['selı] kiler, bodrum

cellphone ['selfıun] *Am.* cep telefonu

Celtic ['keltik] Keltlere ait; Keltçe

cement [si'ment] *n.* çimento; tutkal; v/t yapıştırmak

cemetery ['semitri] mezarlık

censor ['sensı] v/t sansür etm.; **~ship** sansür

censure ['senşı] *n.* azar (-lama); v/t azarlamak, tenkit etm.

census ['sensıs] nüfus sayımı

cent [sent] doların yüzde biri; **per ~** yüzde; **~enary** [-'tînıri], **~ennial** ['tenyıl] yüz yıllık; *n.* yüzüncü yıldönümü

centi|grade ['sentigreyd] santigrat; **~metre** santimetre

central ['sentrıl] orta, merkezî; **~ heating** kalorifer; **~ize** v/t merkezîleştirmek

cent|re, *Am.* -er ['sentı] *n.* orta, merkez; v/t ortaya koymak, merkeze toplamak; v/i merkezlenmek; **~re-forward** santrfor; **~re-half** santrhaf

century ['sençuri] yüzyıl

CEO [sî'ıu] ECON (= *chief executive officer*) Genel Müdür

cereals ['sıırıılz] *pl.* hububat; zahire *sg.*

cerebral ['seribrıl] ANAT beyne ait

ceremon|ial [seri'mıunyıl] resmî; *n.* tören; **~ious** törensel; **~y** ['mıni] tören; REL ayin; POL protokol, teşrifat

certain ['sıtn] muhakkak; kesin; emin; belirli; bazı; **~ly** *adv.* elbette, tabiî; **~ty** kesinlik

certi|ficate [sı'tifikit] tasdikname; ruhsat; belge; ilmühaber; **~fy** ['sıtifay] *v/t* tasdik etm., onaylamak; **~tude** ['~tyûd] kesinlik

CFO [sîäf'ıu] ECON (= *chief financial officer*) Mali İşler Müdürü

chafe [çeyf] *v/t* sürtmek, sürterek berelemek; *v/i* sürtünmek; sinirlenmek; **~r** böcek

chaff [çâf] saman tozu

chaffinch ['çäfinç] ZOO ispinoz

chagrin ['şägrin] iç sıkıntısı

chain [çeyn] *n.* zincir; silsile; *v/t* zincirlemek

chair [çä] iskemle, sandalye; başkanlık makamı; kürsü; **~lift** telesiyej; **~man** başkan

chalk [çôk] tebeşir

challenge ['çälinc] *n.* meydan okuma, davet; *v/t* çağırmak; meydan okumak

chamber ['çeymbı] oda; salon; meclis; **2 of Commerce** Ticaret Odası; **~maid** kadın oda hizmetçisi

chamois ['şämwâ] ZOO dağ keçisi; **~leather** ['şämi-] güderi

champagne [şäm'peyn] şampanya (şarabı)

champion ['çämpyın] şampiyon, kahraman; **~ship** şampiyonluk

chance [çâns] şans, talih; tesadüf; fırsat; ihtimal; **by ~** tesadüfen; **take one's ~** talihe bırakmak

chancellor ['çânsılı] rektör; şansölye

chandelier [şändi'lıı] avize

change [çeync] *n.* değiş(tir)me, değişiklik; bozulan para, bozukluk; *v/t* değiştirmek; boz(dur)mak; *train:* aktarma yapmak; *v/i* değişmek; **for a ~** değişiklik olsun; **~ one's mind** fikrini değiştirmek; **~able** kararsız; değişebilir; **~less** değişmez

channel ['çänl] kanal; yol; **the 2** GEO Manş Denizi

chaos ['keyos] karışıklık; kaos

chap [çäp] çocuk, arkadaş

chapel ['çäpıl] küçük kilise; **~lain** ['~lin] papaz

chapter ['çäptı] bölüm, kısım

charakter ['käriktı] karakter, seciye; şöhret; vasıf; harf; THEA şahıs; **~istic** karakteristik, tipik; **~ize** *v/t* tanımlamak; vasıflandırmak

charcoal ['çâkıul] mangal kömürü

charge [çâc] *n.* yük, hamule; şarj; hamle; görev, memuriyet; bedel, ücret; itham;

yüklemek, doldurmak; suç-
lamak (**with** ile); *price:* istemek; hücum etm. *-e;* **free of**
~ karşılıksız; **in** ~ **of** ile vazi-
feli; **take** ~ **of** yüklenmek, üstüne almak *-i*

chariot ['çäriıt] iki tekerlekli
araba

charit|able ['çäritıbl] hayırse-
ver; **~y** hayırseverlik

charm [çâm] *n.* büyü; muska;
fig. çekicilik; *v/t* büyülemek;
teshir etm.; **~ing** çekici

chart [çât] NAUT harita

charter ['çâtı] *n.* berat, imtiyaz; *v/t* kiralamak; ~ **plane**
charter uçağı

charwoman ['çâwumın] temizleyici kadın

chase [çeys] *n.* av, takip, ko-
valama; *v/t* avlamak, kovala-
mak

chasm ['käzım] yarık, uçurum

chassis ['şäsi] şasi

chast|e [çeyst] iffetli, temiz;
~ity ['çästiti] iffet, saffet

chat [çät] *n.* sohbet; *v/i* sohbet
etm., konuşmak; ~ **line** *cinsel*
nitelikli konuşmalar için aranan *ücretli telefon hattı;* ~
room chat odası

chatter *v/i* çene çalmak, çatırdamak; **~box** boşboğaz, geveze

chauffeur [şufi] şoför

cheap [çîp] ucuz; değersiz;
bayağı; **~en** *v/t* ucuzlatmak;
v/i ucuzlamak; **~ness** ucuz-
luk

cheat [çît] *n.* hile, düzen; hile-
ci; *v/t* aldatmak, dolandır-
mak

check [çek] *n.* engel, durdurma; kontrol; fiş, marka; *Am.*
çek; *v/t* önlemek, durdurmak; karşılaştırmak, kontrol
etm.; ~ **in** *Am.* oteldefterine
kaydolmak; ~ **out** *Am.* otel-
den ayrılmak; **~ed** kareli;
~room gişe; *Am.* vestiyer

cheek [çîk] yanak; yüzsüzlük;
~y yüzsüz

cheer [çiı] *n.* alkış, 'yaşa!' sesi;
neşe; *v/t* alkışlamak, neşelendirmek; ~ **(on)** yüreklen-
dirmek; ~ **(up)** teselli etm.;
~ful neşeli, şen; **~io!** ['·ri'iu]
Allaha ısmarladık!; **~less**
neşesiz, kederli; **~y** neşeli

cheese [çîz] peynir

chemical ['kemikıl] kimyasal;
~s *pl.* kimyasal maddeler

chemist ['kemist] kimyager;
eczacı; **~ry** kimya

cheque [çek] çek

chequered ['çekıd] kareli

cherish ['çeriş] *v/t* aziz tutmak; gütmek

cherry ['çeri] BOT kiraz

chess [çes] satranç oyunu;
~board satranç tahtası;
~man satranç taşı

chest [çest] sandık, kutu;
ANAT göğüs

chestnut ['çesnat] kestane;
kestane renginde

chew [çuu] *v/t* çiğnemek;
~ing-gum çiklet

chicken ['çikin] piliç, civciv;

~pox ['_poks] MED su çiçeği hastalığı

chief [çif] büyük, en önemli; *n.* baş, şef; **~tain** ['_tın] kabile reisi

chilblain ['çilbleyn] MED soğuk şişliği

child [çayld], *pl.* **~ren** ['çildrın] çocuk; **~hood** çocukluk; **~ish** çocukça; **~less** çocuksuz; **~like** çocuk ruhlu

chill [çil] *n.* soğukluk algınlığı; soğuk; *v/t* soğutmak; üşütmek; **~ out** *v/i coll.* dinlenmek, rahatlamak; **~y** soğuk, serin

chime [çaym] *n.* ahenkli çan sesi; *v/i* çal(ın)mak; **~ in with** uymak *-e*

chimney ['çimni] baca; **~sweep(er)** baca temizleyici

chin [çin] çene

China ['çaynı] Çin; **Ω** porselen, çini

Chinese ['çay'nîz] Çinli; Çince

chink [çink] yarık, çatlak

chip [çip] *n.* çentik; küçük parça, kırıntı; *v/t* yontmak, çentmek

chirp [çɜp] cıvıldamak

chisel ['çizl] *n.* çelik kalem; *v/t* oymak, yontmak

chivalr|ous ['şivılrıs] mert, kibar; **~y** şövalyelik, mertlik

chlorine ['klôrîn] klor

chocolate ['çokılit] çikolata

choice [çoys] seçme, tercih; tercih hakkı

choir ['kwayı] koro

choke [çıuk] *v/t* tıkamak, boğmak; *v/i* tıkanmak, boğulmak

cholera ['kolırı] kolera

choose [çuuz] *v/t* seçmek; tercih etm.

chop [çop] *n.* darbe; parça; pirzola; *v/t* doğramak, yarmak

chord [kôd] kiriş, tel

chose [çɔuz], **~n** *s.* **choose**

Christ [krayst] Hazreti İsa; **Ωen** ['krisn] *v/t* REL vaftiz etm., isimlendirmek; **Ωening** vaftiz

Christian ['kristyın] Hıristiyan; **~ name** öz ad; **~ity** [_i'äniti] Hıristiyanlık

Christmas ['krismıs] Noel; **~ Eve** Noel arifesi; **~tree** Noel ağacı

chronic ['kronik] MED müzmin, süreğen; **~le** tarih, vakayiname

chuck [çak]: **~ out** *v/t* kapı dışarı etm.

chuckle ['çakl] kendi kendine gülmek

chum [çam] arkadaş

church [çɜç] kilise; **~yard** *pl.* kilise avlusu; mezarlık

churn [çɜn] *n.* yayık; *v/t* yayıkta çalkamak; köpürtmek

chute [şuut] çağlayan; paraşüt

cider ['saydı] elma şarabı

cigar [si'gaa] yaprak sigarası, puro; **~ette** [sigı'ret] sigara

cinder ['sındı] kor, köz; **Ωella** [_'relı] Sinderella; **~track** atletizm pisti cine|-camera ['sini-] film çekme makinesi; ~ma ['sinimi] sinema

cinnamon ['sinimi] tarçın

cipher ['sayfi] n. sıfır; şifre; v/t şifre ile yazmak

circle ['sɜkl] n. daire, halka, çevre; grup; THEA balkon; v/t devretmek, kuşatmak

circuit ['sɜkit] dolaşma; dolaşım; devre; short ~ EL kontak

circular ['sɜkyulı] dairevî; ~ (letter) sirküler

circulat|e ['sɜkyuleyt] v/i dolaşmak; v/t dağıtmak; ~ion dolaşma; deveran; dağıtım mikdarı

circum|cise ['sɜkımsayz] v/t sünnet etme; ~cision sünnet; ~ference [sı'kamfırıns] çevre; ~flex ['sɜkımfleks] GR düzeltme işareti; ~scribe ['-skrayb] v/t -in etrafını çizmek; sınırlamak -i; ~stance hal, durum, keyfiyet

circus ['sɜkıs] sirk; meydan

cistern ['sistın] sarnıç

citadel ['sitıdl] kale, hisar

cite [sayt] v/t JUR celbetmek; zikretmek, anmak

citizen ['sitizn] hemşeri; vatandaş; ~ship vatandaşlık

city ['siti] şehir; site; ~ guide şehir planı; ~ hall belediye dairesi

civil ['sivl] sivil; nazik; iç, dahilî; ~ ceremony medenî nikah; ~ rights pl. vatandaşlık hakları; ~ service devlet hizmeti; ~ war iç savaş; ~ian sivil şahıs; ~ity nezaket; ~ization medeniyet; ~ized uygar, medenî

clack [kläk] tıkırtı

clad [kläd] s. clothe

claim [kleym] n. iddia; istek, talep; v/t iddia etm.; istemek; ~ant iddialı

clammy ['klämi] soğuk ve ıslak, yapışkan

clamo(u)r ['klämi] gürültü, patırtı; ~ous gürültülü

clamp [klämp] kenet, köşebent

clan [klän] kabile, klan

clandestine [klän'destin] gizli, el altından

clank [kläŋk] n. tınlama, çınlama; v/i tınlamak, çınlamak

clap [kläp] n. vuruş, el çırpma; v/t çırpmak

claret ['klärit] kırmızı şarap

clari|fy ['klärifay] v/t tasfiye etm.; aydınlatmak; ~ty açıklık

clash [kläş] n. çarpışma (sesi); v/i çarpışmak

clasp [kläsp] n. toka; el sıkma; v/t sıkmak, kavalamak, bağlamak; ~knife çakı

class [klâs] n. sınıf, tabaka; kategori; tasnif etm.

classic ['kläsik] klasik yazar; adj. klasik; mükemmel; ~al klasik

classif|ication [kläsifi'keyşın] tasnif, sınıflandırma; ~y ['-fay] v/t sınıflandırmak

class|-mate sınıf arkadaşı; **~room** dersane; **~struggle,** **~war** sınıflar mücadelesi

clatter ['klätı] n. takırtı; v/i takırdamak

clause [klôz] madde, şart; GR cümlecik

claw [klô] hayvan pençesi; pençe tırnağı

clay [kley] kil, balçık

clean [klîn] adj. temiz, pak; v/t temizlemek; **~ out** temizlemek; **~ up** düzenlemek; bitirmek; **~(li)ness** ['klenlinis, 'klinnis] temizlik; **~se** [klenz] v/t temizlemek

clear [klıı] adj. berrak, açık, sarih, aşikâr; ECON net; v/t temizlemek, açmak; kurtarmak; boşaltmak; **~ away** kaldırmak; **~ up** v/t halletmek; v/i açılmak; **~ing** açık saha; ECON kliring; **~ness** berraklık, açıklık

cleave [klîv] v/t yarmak; v/i çatlamak; bağlı olm. (**to** -e)

clef [klef] MUS anahtar

cleft [kleft] yarık; s. cleave

clemency ['kleminsi] şefkat, yumuşaklık

clench [klenç] v/t sıkmak

clergy ['klöci] REL rahipler sınıfı; **~man** papaz, rahip

cleric ['klerik] rahip; **~al** rahiplere ait; kilisenin siyasete karışmasına taraftar

clerk [klâk] kâtip

clever ['klevı] akıllı, becerikli, marifetli; zarif

cliché ['klîşey] klişe

click [klik] n. şıkırtı, çatırtı; v/i şıkırdamak

client ['klayınt] müşteri

cliff [klif] kayalık; uçurum

clima|te ['klaymit] iklim; **~x** ['_-mäks] dönüm noktası, zirve

climb [klaym] n. tırmanma; v/i, v/t tırmanmak (-e); **~er** dağcı; BOT sarmaşık

clinch [klinç] kucaklama

cling [klin] yapışmak (**to** -e)

clinic ['klinik] klinik

clink [klink] v/t tokuşturmak

clip [klip] n. kırkım; klips; pens; mandal; v/t kırpmak; **~ping** gazete kupürü

cloak [kluk] manto, palto, pelerin; **~room** vestiyer; bagaj gişesi

clock [klok] masa saati; duvar saati; **two o'~** saat iki; **~wise** saat yelkovanlarının döndüğü yönde

clod [klod] toprak parçası, kesek

clog [klog] n. kütük; engel; v/t engel olm. -e

cloister ['kloystı] manastır

clon|e [klun] n. klon; v/t klonlamak; **~ing** n. klonlama

close [klus] adj. yakın, bitişik, dikkatli; sık, sıkı, dar; n. son; v/t kapamak, bitirmek; v/i kapanmak, sona ermek; **~ down** v/t kapamak; v/i kapanmak; **~ in on** -in etrafını çevirmek; **~d** kapalı

closet ['klɔzit] oda; dolap; helâ

clot [klɔt] *n.* pıhtı; *v/i* pıhtılaşmak

cloth [klɔθ] kumaş; bez; masa örtüsü; **lay the ~** sofrayı kurmak; **~e** [kluːdh] *v/t* giydirmek, örtmek; **~es** [-z] *pl.* elbise(ler); **~es-hanger** elbise askısı; **~es-line** çamaşır ipi; **~ing** giyim; elbise

cloud [klaud] *n.* bulut; *v/t* bulutla örtmek; bulandırmak; *v/i* bulutlanmak; **~y** bulutlu; bulanık

clove[1] [kluːv] karanfil (*bahar*)

clove[2] **~n** *s.* cleave

clover ['kluːvɪ] yonca, tirfil

clown [klaun] palyaço, soytarı

club [klab] **1.** çomak, değnek; **2.** kulüp; **~s** (*s pl.*) ispati, sinek

clue [kluː] *fig.* ipin ucu

clumsy ['klamzi] beceriksiz, acemi

clung [klaŋ] *s.* cling

cluster ['klastı] *n.* demet; salkım; küme; *v/i* toplanmak

clutch [klaʧ] *n.* tutma, kavrama; TECH debriyaj; *v/t* yakalamak, tutmak

coach [kuːʧ] *n.* vagon; araba; hoca, antrenör; *v/t* hazırlamak, alıştırmak

coagulate [kɔˈægjuleyt] *v/i* koyulaşmak, pıhtılaşmak

coal [kɔul] kömür

coalition [kɔuˈlışın] POL koalisyon

coal|-mine, **~pit** kömür ocağı

coarse [kôs] kaba; bayağı

coast [kɔust] *n.* kıyı, sahil; *v/i* sahil boyunca gitmek; **~guard** sahil muhafızı

coat [kɔut] *n.* ceket; kat, tabaka; palto, manto; hayvan postu; *v/t* kaplamak, örtmek; **~ of arms** arma; **~ing** kaplama; boya tabakası

coax [kɔuks] *v/t* kandırmak

cob [kɔb] BOT mısır koçanı

cobble ['kɔbl] arnavut kaldırım taşı

cobra ['kɔubrı] zoo kobra yılanı

cobweb ['kɔbweb] örümcek ağı

cocaine [kıˈkeyn] kokain

cock [kɔk] horoz; erkek kuş; musluk; tetik; **~chafer** zoo mayısböceği; **~ney** [-ni] Londralı adam; **~pit** AVIA pilot yeri; **~roach** ['-rıuʧ] zoo hamamböceği; **~scomb** ['-skıum] horoz ibiği; **~tail** kendinden fazla emin; **~tail** kokteyl

coco ['kıukıu] BOT Hindistan cevizi ağacı; **~a** ['kıukıu] kakao; **~nut** ['kıukınat] Hindistan cevizi

cocoon [kıˈkuun] koza

cod [kɔd] morina balığı

code [kɔud] *n.* kanun; şifre; *v/t* şifre ile yazmak

cod-liver oil balık yağı

co|-education ['kıuedyuˈkeyşın] karma öğretim; **~erce** [kıuˈɜs] *v/t* zorlamak;

~existence ['ig'zistıns] bir arada var oluş

coffee ['kofi] kahve; ~**bean** kahve çekirdeği; ~**grounds** kahve telvesi; ~**mill** kahve değirmeni; ~**pot** kahve ibriği; cezve

coffin ['kofin] tabut

cog ['kog] çark dişi

cognac ['kunyäk] kanyak

cog-wheel dişli çark

cohe|re [kuu'hiı] v/i yapışmak, tutmak; ~**rence**, ~**rency** tutarlık; ~**rent** yapışık; uygun; ~**sive** [-'hisiv] yapışık

coiffure [kwä'fyuı] saç biçimi

coil [koyl] n. kangal, roda; EL bobin; ~ (**up**) v/t sarmak; v/i kıvrılmak, burulmak

coin [koyn] n. maden para, sikke; v/t basmak; uydurmak; ~**age** para basma; para sistemi

coincide [kuin'sayd] v/i tesadüf etm., uymak (**with** ~e); ~**nce** [kıu'insidıns] tesadüf; rastlantı

coke [kıuk] kok kömürü; sl. kokain

cold [kıuld] soğuk; soğukkanlı; nezle; ümleç; **catch a** ~ nezle olm., üşümek; ~**ness** soğukluk; ~**storage room** soğuk hava deposu

colic ['kolik] MED sancı, kolik

collaborat|e [kı'läbıreyt] işbirliği yapmak; ~**ion** işbirliği

collapse|e [kı'läps] n. çökme, yıkılma; v/i çökmek, düş-

mek, yıkılmak; ~**ible** açılır kapanır

collar ['kolı] n. yaka; tasma; v/t yakalamak; ~**bone** ANAT köprücük

colleague ['koliğ] meslektaş

collect [kı'lekt] v/t toplamak, tahsil etm., biriktirmek; v/i birikmek, toplanmak; ~**ed** aklı başında; ~**ion** topla(n)-ma; koleksiyon; ~**ive** toplu; ~**or** koleksiyon sahibi, toplayan; tahsildar

college ['kolic] kolej; üniversite

collide [kı'layd] çarpmak (**with** ~e); çarpışmak (ile)

colliery ['kolyıri] maden kömürü ocağı

collision [kı'lijın] çarp(ış)ma

colloquial [kı'lukwiıl] konuşma diline ait

colon ['kuuln] GR iki nokta

colonel ['kınl] MIL albay

colonial [kı'lunyıl] sömürgelere ait; ~**ism** sömürgecilik

colon|ist ['kolinist] sömürgede yerleşen insan; ~**ize** v/t sömürge kurmak -de; yerleşmek -e; ~**y** sömürge; koloni

colo(u)r ['kalı] n. renk; boya; v/t boyamak; kızarmak; fig. olduğundan başka göstermek; ~ **bar** ırk ayrımı; ~**ed** renkli; zenci, beyaz ırka mensup olmıyan; ~**s** pl. bayrak, bandıra; ~**ful** renkli, canlı; ~**ing** renk; ~**less** renksiz

colt [kıult] zoo tay, sıpa

column ['kolım] sütun, direk; gazete sütunu; MIL kol

coma ['kumı] MED koma

comb [kıum] n. tarak; ibik; v/t taramak, taraklamak

combat ['kombıt] n. savaş, çarpışma; v/i dövüşmek, çarpışmak; ~ant savaşçı

combin|ation [kombi'neyşın] birleş(tir)me; kasa şifresi; ~er [kım'bayn] v/t birleştirmek; v/i birleşmek; ~e-harvester biçer-döver makinası

combusti|ble [kım'bastıbl] tutuşabilir; ~bles pl. yakacak, yakıt sg.; ~on [-stşın] yanma

come [kam] gelmek (to -e); to ~ gelecek; ~ about olmak; ~ across rast gelmek -e; ~ along ilerlemek; acele etm.; birlikte gelmek; ~ at varmak -e; ~ by geçmek; ~ for alıp götürmek -i; ~ in girmek; ~ loose çözülmek, gevşemek; ~ off kopmak; olmak; ~ on! Haydi gel!; ~ round ayılmak; uğramak; ~ upon rast gelmek -e; ~back THEA sahneye dönüş

comed|ian [kı'mıdyın] komik aktör; ~y ['komidi] komedi, komedya

comet ['komit] ASTR kuyruklu yıldız

comfort ['kamfıt] n. konfor, rahat(lık), refah; teselli; v/t teselli etm.; ~able rahat, konforlu

comic|(al) ['komik(ıl)] komik,

gülünç; ~ strips pl. karikatür şeklinde hikâye serisi sg.

comma ['komı] GR virgül

command [kı'mând] n. emir, komuta; otorite; v/t emretmek; kumanda etm.; hâkim olm. -e; ~er komutan, kumandan; ~er-in-chief başkumandan; ~ment REL Allahın emri

commemorat|e [kı'memı-reyt] v/t kutlamak -i, -in hatırasını anmak; ~ion kutlama, anma

commence [kı'mens] v/t başlamak -e; ~ment başlangıç

commend [kı'mend] v/t övmek; emanet etm. (to -e)

comment ['koment] n. düşünce; tefsir, yorum; v/i tefsir etm., yorumlamak (upon -i); ~ary ['-ıntıri] tefsir, şerh; ~ator [-ınteytı] yorumcu, eleştirmeci

commerc|e ['komäs] ticaret; ~ial ['komäşıl] ticarî

commiseration [kımızı-'reyşın] acıma

commission [kı'mişın] n. görev, vazife; emir, sipariş; komisyon; kurul; v/t yetki vermek -e; hizmete koymak -i; ~er [-,şnı] delege; komiser

commit [kı'mit] v/t teslim etm., tevdi etm.; işlemek; ~ment taahhüt; ~tee [-ti] komite, komisyon, kurul

commodity [kı'moditi] mal, ticaret eşyası

common ['komın] genel; ortak; bayağı; mutat; **in** ~ ortaklaşa; ~ **law** JUR örf ve âdete dayanan hukuk; ~ **market** ECON ortak pazar; ~ **sense** sağduyu; ~**er** burjuva; ~**place** adî, olağan; basma kalıp şey; **House of** ♀**s** Avam Kamarası; **the British** ♀**wealth** İngiliz Milletler Topluluğu

commotion [kı'mıuşın] heyecan, ayaklanma

commun|al ['komyunl] toplumsal; ~**e** ['♀yûn] komün

communicat|e [kı'myûnikeyt] v/t bildirmek; v/i haberleşmek (**with** ile); ~**ion** tebliğ, haber; pl. ulaştırma sg.; ~**ive** [♀tiv] konuşkan

communion [kı'myûnyın] cemaat, birlik; REL şarap içme ve yemek yeme ayini

communis|m ['komyunizım] komünizm; ~**t** komünist

community [kı'myûniti] topluluk, cemaat

commute [kı'myût] v/t değiştirmek; JUR hafifletmek

compact ['kompäkt] sıkı, kesif; pudralık; ~ **disc** compact disk, CD

companion [kım'pänyın] arkadaş; eş; ortak; ~**ship** arkadaşlık; ortaklık

company ['kampıni] grup; arkadaşlar, misafirler pl.; ECON kumpanya, ortaklık; MIL bölük

compar|able ['kompırbl] karşılaştırılabilir; ~**ative**

[kım'päritiv] orantılı; ~**e** v/t karşılaştırmak; **beyond** (**without, past**) ~**e** eşsiz, üstün; ~**ison** [♀'pärisn] mukayese

compartment [kım'pâtmınt] bölme; kompartıman

compass ['kampıs] çevre; hacim; pusula; (**pair of**) ~**es** pl. pergel sg.

compassion [kım'päşın] merhamet, acıma; ~**ate** [♀it] şefkatli

compatible [kım'pätibl] uygun

compatriot [kım'pätriıt] vatandaş, yurttaş

compel [kım'pel] v/t zorlamak

compensat|e ['kompenseyt] v/t tazmin etm., telâfi etm.; ~**ion** tazmin, telâfi; bedel, karşılık

compete [kım'pît] boy ölçüşmek, müsabakaya girmek (**for** için)

competen|ce ['kompıtıns], ~**cy** yetki; yeterlik; ~**t** yetkili; yeterli

competit|ion [kompi'tişın] yarışma, rekabet; ~**ive** [kım'petitiv] rekabet edilebilir; rakip olan; ~**or** rakip

compile [kım'payl] v/t derlemek, toplamak

complacent [kım'pleysnt] kendini beğenmiş

complain [kım'pleyn] v/i şikâyet etm. (**about, of** ~**den**); ~**t** şikâyet; hastalık

dert
complet|e [kım'plit] *adj.* tam, tamam; eksiksiz; *v/t* tamamlamak, bitirmek; **~ion** tamamlama, bitirme

complex ['kompleks] karışık; bileşik; kompleks; **~ion** [kım'plekşın] ten, cilt

compliance [kım'playıns] rıza

complicate ['komplikeyt] *v/t* karıştırmak, güçleştirmek

compliment ['komplimınt] *n.* kompliman, iltifat; *v/t* kompliman yapmak -*e*, övmek -*i*

comply [kım'play] razı olm. (with -*e*)

component [kım'pıunınt] parça, unsur

compos|e [kım'pıuz] *v/t* yazmak, bestelemek; dizmek; **~ed** kendi halinde; ibaret (of -*den*); **~er** MUS bestekâr; **~ition** [kompı'zişın] kompozisyon; terkip, bileşim; eser; **~ure** [kım'pıuji] sakinlik

compote ['kompot] komposto

compound [kım'paund] *adj.* bileşik; *n.* bileşim, alaşım; [kım'paund] *v/t* birleştirmek; **~ interest** ECON bileşik faiz

comprehen|d [komprı'hend] *v/t* anlamak, kavramak; içine almak; **~sible** anlaşılır; **~sion** anlayış, idrak; **~sive** şümullü, etraflı

compress [kım'pres] *v/t* sıkmak; *n.* MED kompres

comprise [kım'prayz] *v/t* kapsamak, ihtiva etm.

compromise ['komprımayz] *n.* uzlaşma; *v/t -in* şerefini tehlikeye atmak

compuls|ion [kım'palşın] zorlama; **~ory** mecburî

compunction [kım'pankşın] vicdan azabı; pişmanlık

compute [kım'pyût] *v/t* hesaplamak; **~r** TECH kompütür, bilgisayar

comrade [kı'mrid] arkadaş; yoldaş; **~ship** arkadaşlık

conceal [kın'sîl] *v/t* gizlemek, saklamak

conceit [kın'sît] kendini beğenmişlik, kibir; **~ed** kibirli

conceiv|able [kın'sîvıbl] düşünülebilir; akla gelecek; **~e** *v/t* düşünmek, kavramak; gebe olm. -*den*

concentrat|e ['konsıntreyt] *v/t* bir yere toplamak; *v/i* bir yere toplanmak; **~ion** topla(n)ma; **~ion camp** toplama kampı

conception [kın'sepşın] fikir, görüş; gebe olma

concern [kın'sın] *n.* ilgi; endişe; ECON firma, ortaklık; *v/t* ilgilendirmek; endişeye düşürmek; **~ed** ilgili; endişeli; **~ing** hakkında; dair -*e*

concert ['konsıt] konser

concession [kın'seşın] teslim; imtiyaz

conciliat|e [kın'silieyt] *v/t* uzlaştırmak, barıştırmak; **~ory**

[_ɪtɪrɪ] barıştırıcı
concise [kın'says] muhtasar, kısa
conclu|de [kın'kluud] v/t bitirmek; sonuçlandırmak; akdetmek; ~sion [_ʃın] sonuç; akdetme; ~sive [_siv] son, kesin
concord ['koŋkôd] uygunluk; barış
concrete ['konkrît] beton; somut; belirli
concur [kın'kз] uymak, razı olm. (with -e)
concussion [kın'kaʃın] (of the brain) MED sadme
condemn [kın'dem] v/t mahkûm etm.; ~ation [kondem'neyʃın] mahkûmiyet
condense [kın'dens] v/t koyulaştırmak; kısaltmak; ~r EL kondansatör
condescend [kondi'send] tenezzülde bulunmak; ~ing tenezzül eden
condition [kın'dişın] durum, hal; koşul, şart; ~al şartlı, şarta bağlı; ~al clause GR şart cümlesi; ~al (mood) GR şart kipi
condole [kın'diul] taziyede bulunmak (with -e); ~nce taziye
conduct ['kondakt] n. davranış, tavır; [kın'dakt] v/t idare etm., yürütmek; nakletmek; ~ oneself davranmak; ~or [kın'daktı] orkestra şefi; biletçi; kondoktör
cone [kıun] koni, mahrut; BOT kozalak

confection [kın'fekşın] şekerleme; ~er [_şnı] şekerci, pastacı; ~ery şekerlemeler pl.; pastahane
confedera|cy [kın'fedırısı] POL birlik; ~te [_it] adj. birleşmiş; [_eyt] v/i birleşmek; ~tion birlik, konfederasyon
confer [kın'fз] v/i danışmak, görüşmek; v/t vermek (on -e); ~ence ['konfırıns] müzakere, konferans
confess [kın'fes] v/t itiraf etm., ikrar etm.; ~ion itiraf, ikrar; REL günah çıkarma
confid|e [kın'fayd] v/t emanet etm. (to -e); v/i güvenmek (in -e); ~ence ['konfidens] güven; emniyet; ~ent emin, güvenli; ~ential [_'denşıl] gizli, mahrem
confine [kın'fayn] v/t sınırlamak; hasretmek; be ~d takta yatmak; loğusa olm.; ~ment hapis; loğusalık
confirm [kın'fзm] v/t teyit etm., saptamak; ~ation [konfı'meyşın] tasdik
confiscat|e ['konfiskeyt] v/t müsadere etm.; ~ion müsadere
conflagration [konflı'greyşın] yangın
conflict ['konflikt] n. aykırılık; çatışma; mücadele; [kın'flikt] v/i zıtlaşmak (with ile); muhalif olm. (-e)
conform [kın'fôm] v/t uydurmak (to -e); v/t uymak (to

-e); **~ity** uygunluk; **in ~ity with** uyarak -e; mucibince

confound [kın'faund] v/t karıştırmak; **~ it!** Allahın cezası!

confront [kın'frant] v/t karşılaştırmak

confuse [kın'fyûz] v/t karıştırmak; şaşırtmak; **~ed** karışık; şaşkın; **~ion** [-ʃın] karışıklık; şaşkınlık

congeal [kın'cîl] v/t dondurmak; v/i donmak

congestion [kın'cesçın] MED kan birikmesi; tıkanıklık

congratulate [kın'grätyuleyt] v/t tebrik etm.; **~ion** tebrik, kutlama

congregate [koŋrigeyt] v/i toplanmak, birleşmek; **~ion** REL cemaat; toplantı

congress [koŋgres] kongre; ♀ Am. Millet Meclisi; **~man** Am. Millet Meclisi üyesi

conjecture [kın'cekçı] n. zan, sanı; v/t tahmin etm.

conjugal [koncugıl] evlilikle ilgili

conjugate [koncugeyt] GR çekmek; **~ion** fiil çekimi

conjunction [kın'caŋkşın] birleşme; GR bağlaç; **~ive (mood)** GR şart kipi

conjuncture [kın'caŋkçı] hal, durum; ECON konjonktür

conjure[1] [kın'cuı] v/t yalvarmak -e

conjure[2] [kancı] (**up**) v/t büyü yolu ile çağırmak

connect [kı'nekt] v/t bağla-

mak, birleştirmek; **~ion** bağlantı; ilgi; **in this ~ion** bu münasebetle

connexion [kı'nekşın] s. con-nection

conquer [koŋkı] v/t fethetmek, zaptetmek; **~ror** fatih, galip; **~st** [-kwest] fetih; basarı

conscience [konşıns] vicdan; **~tious** [-ʃi'enşıs] vicdanının sesini dinliyen; temiz iş yapan; **~tious objector** POL askerlik hizmetini reddeden kimse

conscious [konşıs] bilinçli, şuurlu; ayık; **be ~ of** -in farkında olm.; **~ness** bilinç, şuur, idrak

conscription [kın'skripşın] askere çağırma

consecrate [konsikreyt] v/t takdis etm.

consecutive [kın'sekyutiv] art arda gelen, ardıl

consent [kın'sent] n. müsaade, muvafakat; v/t razı olm., muvafakat etm. (**to, in** -e)

consequence [konsikwıns] sonuç, akıbet; **~tly** adv. sonuç olarak

conservat|ion [konsı-'veyşın] komura, muhafaza; **~ive** [kın'sɜvıtiv] muhafazakâr

conserve [kın'sɜv] v/t muhafaza etm., korumak; **~s** pl. konserve sg.

consider [kın'sidı] v/t addetmek, saymak; hesaba alma-

düşünmek; incelemek; **~a-ble** hayli; çok; önemli; **~ably** *adv.* oldukça; **~ate** [-rit] saygılı, nazik; **~ation** itibar; saygı, nezaket; karşılık

consign [kın'sayn] *v/t* göndermek, teslim etm.; **~ment** sevk, teslim

consist [kın'sist] ibaret olm., mürekkep olm. (of *-den*); **~ency** koyuluk, kesafet; birbirini tutma; **~ent** birbirini tutan

consol|ation [konsı'leyşın] teselli; **~e** [kın'sıul] *v/t* teselli etm., avundurmak

consolidate [kın'solideyt] *v/t* sağlamlaştırmak; birleştirmek

consonant ['konsınınt] GR sessiz harf

consort ['kon'sôt] eş

conspicuous [kın'spikyuıs] göze çarpan, âşikâr

conspir|acy [kın'spirsi] JUR gizli anlaşma; **~ator** suikastçı; **~e** [-'spayı] fesat maksadı ile anlaşmak

constable ['kanstıbl] polis memuru

constant ['konstınt] devamlı, sabit

consternation [konstı-'neyşın] donup kalma, hayret

constipation [konsti'peyşın] MED peklik

constituen|cy [kın'stityuın-si] POL seçim çevresi, seçmenler *pl.*; **~t** seçmen; öğe, unsur

constitut|e ['konstityût] *v/t* teşkil etm.; tayin etm., atamak; kurmak; **~ion** terkip; bünye; POL anayasa; **~ional** anayasaya uygun

constrain [kın'streyn] *v/t* zorlamak; **~t** zorlama, cebir

construct [kın'strakt] *v/t* inşa etm., kurmak; **~ion** yapı, bina; **~ive** yapıcı; **~or** kurucu, yapıcı

consul ['konsıl] POL konsolos; **~ general** başkonsolos; **~ate** ['-yulit] konsolosluk

consult [kın'salt] *v/t* başvurmak, müracaat etm. *-e*; danışmak *-e*; **~ation** [konsıl-'teyşın] başvurma; MED konsültasyon; **~ing hours** *pl.* MED muayene saatleri

consume [kın'syûm] *v/t* yiyip bitirmek, yoğaltmak; **~r** yoğaltıcı; **~mate** ['-sa-mit] *adj.* tam, mükemmel; ['konsımeyt] *v/t* tamamlamak; **~ption** [kın'sampşın] yoğaltım; MED verem

contact ['kontâkt] *n.* temas, dokunma; *v/t* temasa geçmek (ile); **~ lense** kontakt mercek

contagious [kın'teycıs] bulaşıcı

contain [kın'teyn] *v/t* ihtiva etm., içine almak; **~er** kap, konteyner

contaminat|e [kın'tämineyt] *v/t* kirletmek; bulaştırmak; **~ion** bulaştırma

contemplat|e ['kontempleyt] v/t seyretmek; düşünmek, tasarlamak; ~ion düşünme; ~ive dalgın

contemporary [kın'tempırıri] çağdaş

contempt [kın'tempt] nefret, küçük görme; ~ible alçak, rezil; ~uous [-yuıs] küçük gören, kibirli

contend [kın'tend] çarpışmak; müsabakaya girmek (for için)

content [kın'tent] n. öz; hacim; adj. memnun, razı; v/t memnun etm.; be ~ yetinmek (with ile); ~ed memnun; ~s ['kontents] pl. içindekiler

contest ['kontest] n. yarışma, müsabaka; v/t itiraz etm. -e; v/i müsabakaya girmek

context ['kontekst] sözgelişi, münasebet

continent ['kontinınt] GEO kıta; ~al [-'nentl] kıtaya ait; Avrupa kıtasına ait

continu|al [kın'tinyuıl] devamlı, sürekli; ~ance devam; ~ation devam, uzatma; ~e [-û] v/t devam etm. -e; v/i devam etm., sürmek; to be ~ed arkası var; ~ous devamlı, sürekli

contort [kın'tôt] v/t burmak, bükmek

contour [ˌkontuı] dış hatlar pl.

contraband [kontrı'-] kaçak mal

contraceptive [kontrı'septiv] MED gebeliği önleyici

contract ['konträkt] n. sözleşme; [kın'träkt] v/t daraltmak, kısaltmak; disease: tutulmak -e; v/i daralmak, büzülmek; ~or [kın'träktı] müteahhit

contradict [kontrı'dikt] v/t yalanlamak, -in aksini söylemek; ~ion yalanlama; ~ory aykırı

contrary ['kontrıri] ters, zıt; aykırı; karşı (to -e); on the ~ bilakis, tersine

contrast ['konträst] n. tezat, ayrılık; [kın'träst] v/t karşılaştırmak; v/i ~ with -in tezadı olm.

contribut|e [kın'tribyut] v/t bağışlamak; v/i yazı vermek (to -e); ~ion [kontri'byûşın] yardım; iane; yazı; ~or [kın'tribyutı] yardım eden; yazı veren

contriv|ance [kın'trayvıns] buluş; biçer; tertibat, cihaz; ~e v/t icat etm., bulmak; başarmak

control [kın'trıul] n. kontrol, denetleme; v/t kontrol etm., denetlemek; ~ler murakıp

controvers|ial [kontrı'vösıl] çekişmeli; ~y ['-vösi] çekişme, münakaşa

contus|e [kın'tyûz] v/t berelemek; ~ion [-jın] bere, çürük

convalesce [konvı'les] iyileşmek; ~nce nekahet; ~nt iyileşen, şifa bulan

convenience [kın'vînyıns] uygunluk, rahatlık; **at your earliest ~** müsait ve yakın zamanınızda; **public ~** umumî helâ

convenient [kın'vînyınt] uygun; rahat

convent ['konvınt] manastır; **~ion** [kın'venşın] toplantı; anlaşma; **~ional** göreneksel

convers|ation [konvı'seyşın] konuşma, sohbet; **~e** [kın'vзs] konuşmak, görüşmek (**with** ile)

conver|sion [kın'vзşın] değiş(tir)me; REL ihtida; **~t** n. REL dönme, mühtedi; v/t değiştirmek; **~tible** değiştirilebilir; kabriyole

convey [kın'vey] v/t taşımak, götürmek; ifade etm.; **~ance** taşıma, nakil; taşıt; **~or** (**belt**) TECH taşıma bandı

convict [kın'konvîkt] n. mahkûm, suçlu; v/t suçlandırmak (**of** ile); **~ion** inanç; suçlandırma

convince [kın'vins] v/t inandırmak **~e** (**of -i**)

convoke [kın'vıuk] v/t toplantıya çağırmak

convoy ['konvoy] n. konvoy; v/t rehberlik etm.

convuls|ion [kın'valşın] ihtilâç, çırpınma; **~ive** ihtilâç gibi

cook [kuk] n. aşçı; v/t pişirmek; v/i pişmek; **~ing** pişirme (sanatı)

cool [kuul] adj. serin, soğuk; soğukkanlı; v/t soğutmak, serinletmek; v/i serinleşmek; **~er** TECH soğutma cihazı; **~ness** serinlik; soğukkanlılık

co-op ['kuop] s. **co-operative** (**society**)

co(-)operat|e [kıu'opıreyt] v/i işbirliği yapmak, birlikte çalışmak; **~ion** işbirliği; **~ive** [..ıtiv] n. kooperatif; adj. işbirliği yapan; **~ive society** tüketim kooperatifi; **~or** iş arkadaşı

co(-)ordinate [kıu'ôdineyt] v/t ayarlamak; düzeltmek

cop [kop] vulg. polis memuru

co-partner ['ku'pâtnı] ortak

cope [kıup] boy ölçmek (**with** ile)

co-pilot ['kıu'paylıt] AVIA ikinci pilot

copious ['kupyıs] bol, mebzul

copper ['kopı] bakır; kazan; bakır para

copy ['kopi] n. kopya, nüsha; örnek; v/t kopya etm., -in suretini çıkarmak; **~book** defter; **~right** telif hakkı

coral ['korıl] mercan

cord [kôd] n. ip, sicim, şerit; v/t iple bağlamak

cordial ['kôdyıl] samimî, candan; **~ity** [-'i'âliti] samimiyet

corduroy ['kôdıroy] fitilli kadife

core [kô] iç, öz; BOT göbek

cork [kôk] n. mantar, tapa; v/t

mantarla kapamak; **~screw**
tirbuşon, tapa burgusu

corn [kôn] *n.* hububat; buğday; *Am.* mısır; MED nasır;
v/t tuzlayıp kurutmak;
~cob mısır koçanı

corner ['kônı] *n.* köşe, köşebaşı; *v/t* çıkmaza sokmak;
~ed köşeli

cornet ['kônit] MUS kornet;
kâğıt külâh

coronation [korı'neyşın] taç giydirme

coroner ['korını] JUR şüpheli ölüm vakalarını tahkik eden memur

corpor|al ['kôpırıl] bedenî;
MIL onbaşı; **~ate** [_rıt] ortaklığa ait; birlik olmuş, toplu;
~ation birlik; JUR tüzel kişi;
anonim ortaklık

corps [kô] MIL kolordu; Diplomatic ♀ kordiplomatik

corpse [kôps] ceset

corpulent ['kôpyulınt]
şişman

corral [kô'râal, *Am.* kı'räl]
ağıl

correct [kı'rekt] *adj.* doğru,
sahih; dürüst; münasip; *v/t*
düzeltmek; cezalandırmak;
~ion tashih; cezalandırma

correspond [koris'pond]
mektuplaşmak (**with** ile);
uymak, uygun gelmek (**to**
-e); **~ence** mektuplaşma;
~ent muhabir

corridor ['koridô] koridor

corrigible ['koricıbl] düzeltilebilir

corroborate [kı'robıreyt] *v/t*
doğrulamak

corro|de [kı'rıud] *v/t* aşındırmak, çürütmek; **~sion**
[_jın] aşınma; paslanma;
~sive TECH aşındırıcı madde

corrugated iron ['korugeytid -] TECH oluklu demir levha

corrupt [kı'rapt] *adj.* çürümüş; rüşvet yiyen; *v/t* bozmak, ayartmak; **~ion** rüşvet
yeme

corset ['kôsit] korsa

cosmetic [koz'metik] makiyaja ait; kozmetik

cosm|ic ['kozmik] kozmik;
~onaut [_mınôt] kozmonot;
~os ['_mos] kozmos, acun

cost [kost] *n.* fiat, değer; zarar, masraf; *v/t* -*in* fiatı
olm., malı olm.; **~ly** değerli;
pahalı

costume ['kostyûm] kostüm,
elbise; kıyafet

cosy ['kuzi] rahat, keyifli

cot [kot] yatak, portatif karyola

cottage ['kotic] küçük ev,
köşk

cotton ['kotn] pamuk, pamuk
bezi; pamuklu; **~wool** hidrofil pamuk; *Am.* ham pamuk

couch [kauç] *n.* sedir; divan;
v/i uzanmak; çömelmek; **~potato** *n. coll.* oturduğu yerden
kalkmayan miskin kimse

cough [kof] *n.* öksürük; *v/i*
öksürmek

could [kud] *s.* can

council ['kaunsl] meclis, divan, konsey; ~(l)or ['-sılı] meclis üyesi

counsel ['kaunsıl] n. danışma; nasihat; JUR avukat, dava vekili; v/t öğüt vermek -e; ~(l)or ['-slı] müşavir

count¹ [kaunt] kont

count² n. sayma, hesap; v/t saymak, hesap etm., hesaba katmak; ~down hazırlık devresi

countenance ['kauntinıns] yüz, çehre

counter¹ ['kauntı] tezgâh; sayaç; marka

counter² adj. karşı, aykırı (to -e); v/t karşılamak, önlemek, ~act v/t [.'äkt] karşılamak, önlemek; ~balance ['-ba-lıns] v/t denkleştirmek; ~es-pionage karşı casusluk; ~feit ['-fit] adj. sahte; n. taklit; v/t taklit etm., ~foil ['-foyl] makbuz koçanı; ~intelli-gence ['-rintelicins] s. ~es-pionage

countess ['kauntis] kontes

counting-house ECON muhasebe dairesi; ~less sayısız, hesapsız

country ['kantri] memleket, yurt, vatan; taşra, kır; in the ~ kırda, köyde; ~house yazlık; ~man yurttaş, vatandaş; ~side kır, kırlık; ~town kasaba

county ['kaunti] kontluk; vilâyet, il; Am. kaza, ilçe

couple ['kapl] n. çift; v/t bir-

leştirmek, bağlamak; ~ing TECH kavrama

coupon ['kupon] kupon

courage ['karic] cesaret, mertlik; ~ous [kı'reycıs] cesur, yiğit

courier ['kuriı] haberci, kuriye

course [kôs] yol, rota; yön; pist; ECON rayiç; kurs, ders; in due ~ sırası gelince; of ~ tabiî, elbette; matter of ~ tabiîlik

court [kôt] n. avlu; alan, kort; JUR mahkeme; saray; v/t kur yapmak -e; ~ of justice mahkeme; ~eous ['kıstyıs] nazik, kibar; ~esy ['kıtisi] nezaket, saygı; ~ier ['kôtyı] saraylı; ~martial askerî mahkeme; ~ship kur yapma; ~yard avlu

cousin ['kazn] kuzen, kuzin, amca (veya) dayı, hala, teyze) çocuğu

cover ['kavı] n. kap, örtü, kılıf; zarf; sığınak, siper; v/t kaplamak, örtmek; saklamak; gizlemek; yazmak; distance: almak, katetmek; damage: karşılamak; ~age olayın takip edilip yazılması; ~ing örtü

covet ['kavit] v/t şiddetle arzu etm.; ~ous açgözlü

cow [kau] inek, dişi manda

coward ['kauıd] korkak, yüreksiz; ~ice ['-is] korkaklık; ~ly korkak, alçak

cowboy kovboy

cower ['kauı] v/i çömelmek

cow|-hide sığır derisi; **~slip** BOT çuhaçiçeği; *Am.* merzagi nergis

cox|comb ['kokskıum] züppe, hoppa; **~swain** ['~sweyn, 'koksn] dümenci

coy [koy] çekingen, ürkek

crab [kräb] ZOO yengeç

crack [kräk] *n.* çatlak, yarık; çatırtı, şaklama; darbe; *tütün gibi yakılıp içilmek üzere kristal haline getirilmiş kokain*; *v/t* kırmak, yamak; çatlatmak; şaklatmak; *v/i* kırılmak, çatlamak; şaklamak; **~er** gevrek bisküvit; patlangaç; **~le** *v/i* çatırdamak

cradle ['kreydl] *n.* beşik; *v/t* beşiğe yatırmak

craft [kräft] hüner; sanat; hile; *mar.* gemi; **~sman** sanat erbabı, sanatkâr, usta; **~y** kurnaz

crag [kräg] sarp kayalık

cram [kräm] *v/t* doldurmak, tıkmak

cramp [krämp] *n.* MED kramp; TECH mengene, kenet; *v/t* kenetlemek; kısıtlamak

cranberry ['kränbırı] BOT kırmızı yaban mersini

crane [kreyn] *n.* ZOO turna kuşu; TECH maçuna; *v/t boynunu* uzatmak

crank [kräŋk] TECH manivela, kol; garip adam; **~ up** *v/t* hareket ettirmek; **~shaft** TECH krank mili

crape [kreyp] krep; siyah tül

crash [kräş] *n.* çatırtı; şangırtı; AVIA düşüp parçalanma; ECON iflâs; *v/t* kırmak; *v/i* kırılmak; AVIA düşüp parçalanmak; **~hel**met motosikletçi miğferi; **~landing** AVIA mecburi iniş

crate [kreyt] kafesli sandık

crater ['kreytı] GEO krater; huni şeklinde çukur

crav|e [kreyv] şiddetle arzu etm. (**for-**i); **~ing** şiddetli arzu

crawl [kröl] sürünmek, emeklemek; krol yüzmek

crayfish ['kreyfiş] ZOO kerevides

crayon ['kreyın] renkli kalem

crazy ['kreyzi] çılgın, deli

creak [krîk] gıcırdamak

cream [krîm] *n.* krema, kaymak; krem; *fig.* kalbur üstü; *v/t -in* kaymağını almak; **~y** kaymaklı; krem gibi

crease [krîs] *n.* kırma; ütü çizgisi; *v/t* buruşturmak

creat|e [krî'eyt] *v/t* yaratmak, meydana getirmek; **~ion** yaradılış, yaratma; evren; **~ive** *adj.*, **~or** *n.* yaratıcı; **~ure** ['krîçı] yaratık

credentials [kri'denşılz] *pl.* itimatname *sg.*

credible ['kredibl] inanılabilir

credit ['kredit] *n.* ECON kredi; güven, itibar; *v/t* inanmak **-**e; ECON matluba geçirmek **-**i; **letter of ~** ECON akreditif;

on ~ veresiye; **~able** şerefli;
~ **card** kredi kartı; **~or** alacaklı

credulous ['kredyulıs] her
şeye inanan

creed [krîd] iman, itikat

creek [krîk] koy; *Am.* dere,
çay

creep [krîp] sürünmek; ürpermek; sarılmak; **~er** sürüngen; **~y** tüyler ürpertici

cremate [kri'meyt] *v/t ölüyü*
yakmak; **~ion** yakma

crept [krept] *s.* creep

crescent ['kresnt] dilim ay,
ayça

cress [kres] BOT tere

crest [krest] ibik; miğfer püs-
külü; tepe, zirve; **~fallen** üzgün, yılgın

Crete [krît] Girit adası

crevasse [kri'väs] buzul
yarığı; **~ice** [krevis] çatlak,
yarık

crew[1] [kruu] tayfa, takım

crew[2] *s.* crow

crib [krib] yemlik; çocuk yatağı

cricket ['krikit] zoo cırcırbö-
ceği; kriket oyunu

crime [kraym] cinayet, suç,
cürüm

Crimea [kray'mii] Kırım

criminal ['kriminl] *n.* suçlu,
cani; *adj.* ağır cezalarla ilgili

crimson ['krimzn] fes rengi

cringe [krinc] *v/i* köpeklemek

cripple [kripl] *adj.* sakat, topal, kötürüm; *v/t* sakatlamak

crisis [kraysis] *pl.* **~es** ['-îz]

buhran, kriz

crisp [krisp] kıvırcık; gevrek

criterion [kray'tiirin] ölçüt

critic ['kritik] eleştirici, mü-
nekkit; **~al** tenkitci; vahim,
tehlikeli; **~ism** ['-sizim] tenkit; **~ize** ['-sayz] *v/t* eleştirmek; kusur bulmak -*de*

croak [kruk] vak vak diye
bağırmak

Croat, **~ian** ['kruıt,
kruı'eyşın] Hırvat

crochet ['kruuşey] *v/i* kroşe
yapmak

crockery ['krokiri] çanak
çömlek

crocodile ['krokıdayl] zoo
timsah

crocus ['kruukıs] BOT çiğdem

crook [kruk] *n.* kanca; değnek; *sl.* dolandırıcı; *v/t* bükmek; **~ed** ['-id] eğri, çarpık

crop [krop] *n.* kursak; ekin,
ürün; *v/t* kesmek, biçmek; **~
up** meydana çıkmak

cross [kros] *n.* haç, salip;
çarmıh, istavroz; çapraz işareti; *v/t* geçmek, aşmak;
karıştırmak; çapraz koymak
-*e*; *adj.* dargın, öfkeli; **~
off** *or* **out** *v/t* çizmek, silmek; **~
oneself** istavroz çıkarmak;
~examination JUR sorgu;
~ing geçit; **~road** yol sırt;
pl. dört yol ağzı; **~word
(puzzle)** çapraz bilmece

crouch [krauç] çömelmek,
eğilmek

crow [kruu] zoo karga; *v/i* ötmek; **~bar** TECH kaldıraç

crowd [kraud] *n.* kalabalık; halk; yığın; *v/t* doldurmak, sıkıştırmak; *v/i* toplanmak, birikmek; **~ed** kalabalık; dolu

crown [kraun] *n.* taç; kuron; tepe; *v/t* taç giydirmek *-e*

crucial [ˈkruːʃl] kesin, önemli

cruci|fix [ˈkruːsifiks] çarmıh; **~fixion** [-ˈfikʃın] çarmıha ger(il)me; **~fy** *v/t* çarmıha germek

crude [kruud] ham; kaba

cruel [kruil] zalim, gaddar; **~ty** zulüm, gaddarlık

cruise [kruuz] *n.* deniz gezintisi; *v/i* gemi ile gezmek; **~r** kruvazör

crumb [kram] ekmek kırıntısı; **~le** [ˈ-bl] *v/t* ufalamak, parçalamak; *v/i* ufalmak

crumple [ˈkrampl] *v/t* buruşmak; **~ (up)** *v/t* buruşturmak

crunch [kranç] *v/t* çiğnemek, ezmek

crusade [kruuˈseyd] Haçlılar seferi; **~r** Haçlı

crush [kraş] *n.* kalabalık; ezme; *v/t* ezmek, sıkıştırmak

crust [krast] *n.* kabuk; *v/t* kabukla kaplamak; **~y** kabuklu; huysuz

crutch [kraç] koltuk değneği

cry [kray] *n.* bağırma; ağlama; *v/i* bağırmak; ağlamak

crypt [kript] ARCH yeraltı kemer *veya* türbe

crystal [ˈkristl] kristal, billur;

~lize *v/t* billurlaştırmak

cu [ˈsiyû] (= *see you*) (*kısa mesajda*) görüşmek üzere

cub [kab] ZOO hayvan yavrusu

cub|e [kyûb] küp; **~e root** MATH küp kök; **~ic** kübik

cubicle [ˈkyûbikl] odacık

cuckoo [ˈkukuu] ZOO guguk kuşu

cucumber [ˈkyûkambı] BOT hıyar, salatalık

cuddle [ˈkadl] *v/t* kucaklamak

cudgel [ˈkacıl] *n.* sopa, değnek; *v/t* dövmek

cue [kyuu] işaret; isteka

cuff [kaf] kolluk, yen; tokat; **~link** kol düğmesi

culminat|e [ˈkalmineyt] zirvesine ermek, sonuçlanmak; **~ion** en yüksek derece

culprit [ˈkalprit] suçlu, mücrim

cult [kalt] ibadet, tapınma; **~i-vate** [ˈ-iveyt] *v/t* işlemek, yetiştirmek; **~ivation** tarım; toprağı işleme; yetiştirme; **~ivator** çiftçi

cultur|al [ˈkalçırıl] kültürel; uygarlığa ait; **~e** [ˈ-çı] kültür; **~ed** kültürlü

cum(m)in [ˈkamin] BOT kimyon

cumul|ative [ˈkyûmyulıtiv] birikmiş, biriken; **~us** [ˈ-lıs] yığın; böyük

cunning [ˈkanin] kurnaz, açıkgöz; kurnazlık, şeytanlık

cup [kap] fincan, kâse, bardak; kupa; **~board** [ˈkabıd] dolap; ~ful fincan dolusu

cupola ['kyûpılı] kubbe

cura|ble ['kyuırıbl] tedavisi kabil; ~te ['_rit] papaz muavini; ~tor [._'reytı] müdür

curbstone [kɜb-] s. kerbstone

curd [kɜd] kesilmiş süt, beyaz peynir; ~le v/i v/t süt: kesilmek; v/t kesmek

cure [kyuı] n. tedavi, şifa; v/t tedavi etm.; tuzlamak, tütsülemek

curfew ['kɜfyû] JUR sokağa çıkma yasağı

curio|sity [kyuırı'ositi] merak; az bulunan veya tuhaf şey; ~us ['_ıs] meraklı; tuhaf

curl [kɜl] n. büküm; bukle; v/t kıvırmak; v/i kıvrılmak; ~y kıvırcık

currant ['kʌrınt] BOT frenküzümü

curren|cy ['kʌrınsi] revaç; döviz; ~t akıntı, cereyan; akım; cari; bugünkü

curriculum [kı'rikyulım] pl. ~a [_ı] müfredat programı; ~um vitae [_'vaytî] hal tercümesi

curse [kɜs] n. lânet, beddua, küfür; v/t lânetlemek

curt [kɜt] kısa, sert

curtail [kɜ'teyl] v/t kısaltmak, kısmak

curtain ['kɜtn] perde

curts(e)y ['kɜtsi] diz bükerek reverans

curve [kɜv] n. kavis, eğri; viraj; v/t eğmek; v/i eğilmek;

~d kavisli; virajlı

cushion ['kuşın] n. yastık; minder; v/t kıtıkla doldurmak

custody ['kastıdı] muhafaza; nezaret

custom ['kastım] âdet, örf, görenek; pl. gümrük; ~ary alışılmış, âdet olan; ~er müşteri; ~house gümrük dairesi

cut [kat] n. kesim, kesme; kesinti; tenzilât; yara; biçim; kalıp; adj. kesik, kesilmiş; v/t kesmek, biçmek; kısaltmak; selâm vermemek -e; power ~ EL akımın kesilmesi; short ~ kestirme yol; ~ down kesip devirmek; ~ off kesip koparmak; ayırmak; ~ out kesip çıkarmak ~ up doğramak; ~back kesinti

cute [kyût] açıkgöz; zarif, hoş

cuticle ['kyûtikl] ANAT üstderi; tırnakları çevreliyen ölüderi

cutlery ['katlıri] sofra takımı

cutlet ['katlit] pirzola

cut|off Am. kestirme yol; ~purse yankesici; ~ter kesici; NAUT kotra; ~ting keskin, kesici; kesilip çıkarılmış gazete makalesi

cyber... ['saybı] siber...

cycle ['saykl] n. devir, devre; bisiklet; v/i bisikletle gitmek; ~ist bisikletçi

cyclone ['sayklun] siklon, kiklon

cylinder ['silindı] silindir

cynic ['sinik] n., ~al adj. kötü

gözle gören, alaycı; ~ism kinizm

cypress ['saypris] BOT servi
Cypr|iot ['sipriot] Kıbrıslı;

~us ['saypris] Kıbrıs
cyst [sist] MED kist
Czech [çek] Çek; ~ Republic
Çek Cumhuriyeti

D

dab [däb] v/t hafifçe vurmak -e

dad|(dy) ['däd(ı)] baba, babacık; ~dy-longlegs ZOO sivrisinek; *Am. uzun bacaklı örümcek çeşidi*

daffodil ['däfıdil] BOT fulya, zerrin, nergis

dagger ['dägı] hançer, kama

dahlia ['deylyı] BOT dalya, yıldız çiçeği

daily ['deyli] günlük, her gün

dainty ['deynti] nefis; ince; lezzetli

dairy ['däiri] süthane; sütçü dükkânı

daisy ['deyzi] BOT papatya

dale [deyl] vadi, dere

dam [däm] *n.* baraj, bent; v/t bentle durdurmak

damage ['dämic] *n.* zarar; *pl.* tazminat; v/t zarar vermek -e, bozmak -i

Damas|cus [dı'mäskıs] Şam; **2k** ['dämısk] damasko

damn [däm] v/t lânetlemek; ~ation [-'neyşın] lânet, kargıma

damp [dämp] *adj.* rutubetli, nemli; *n.* rutubet; v/t ıslatmak; *pro.* söndürmek, azaltmak

danc|e [dâns] v/t, v/i dansetmek; *n.* dans; ~er danseden; dansöz

dandelion ['dändilayın] BOT kara hindiba

dandruff ['dändraf] ANAT kepek, konak

Dane [deyn] Danimarkalı

danger ['deyncı] tehlike; ~ous ['-crıs] tehlikeli

dangle ['dängl] v/i asılıp sallanmak; v/t sallamak

Danish ['deyniş] Danimarkalı

dar|e [däi] v/t, v/i (*inf.*) cesaret etm., kalkışmak -*(meğ)e*; I ~e say diyebilirim ki, her halde; ~ing cüretli; cesaret

dark [dâk] karanlık; koyu; ~ brown esmer; ~en v/t karartmak; v/i kararmak; ~ness karanlık; koyuluk

darling ['dâliñ] sevgili

darn [dân] v/t örerek tamir etm.

dart [dât] *n.* cirit, kargı; hızla atılma; v/t fırlatmak; v/i hızla atılmak (**at**, **on** -*e*)

dash [däş] *n.* saldırma; hamle; darbe, vuruş; az miktar; çizgi; *v/i* atılmak, fırlamak (**at** *-e*); *v/t* fırlatmak; *hope*: kırmak; **~board** TECH kontrol paneli; **~ing** atılgan

data ['deytı] *pl.* veriler; bilgi *sg.*

date[1] [deyt] BOT hurma

date[2] *n.* tarih, zaman; randevu; *v/t* tarih koymak *-e*; *v/i* tarihli olm.; **out of ~** modası geçmiş; **up to ~** modern, modaya uygun

dative ['deytiv] (**case**) GR *-e* hali, datif

daub [dôb] *v/t* bulaştırmak

daughter ['dôtı] kız, kız evlât; **~-in-law** gelin

dawdle ['dôdl] **~** (**away**) *v/t* avare geçirmek

dawn [dôn] *n.* fecir, tan, gün ağarması; *v/i* gün ağarmak

day [dey] gün; gündüz; zaman; **~ off** boş gün; **the other ~** geçenlerde; **~ by ~** günden güne; **~ spa** ['~spâ] (*büyük otellerde*) *bir günlüğüne kullanılabilen sağlık ve güzellik merkezi*; **~break** tan, şafak; **~labo(u)rer** gündelikçi; **~light** gün ışığı, aydınlık; **~time** gündüz

daze [deyz] *v/t* kamaştırmak, sersemletmek

dazzle ['dâzl] *v/t -in* gözünü kamaştırmak

dead [ded] ölü, ölmüş; solgun; duygusuz; **the ~** *pl.* ölüler; **~ tired** çok yorgun, bitkin; **~-end** çıkmaz yol; **~-line** son teslim tarihi; **~-lock**

çıkmaz; durgunluk; **~ly** öldürücü; ölüm derecesinde

deaf [def] sağır; **~en** *v/t* sağır etm.; **~ness** sağırlık

deal [dîl] *n.* miktar; alışveriş; anlaşma; *v/t* dağıtmak; *v/i* meşgul olm., uğraşmak (**with** ile); **~ in ...** ticareti yapmak; **a great ~ of** bir hayli; **~er** tüccar, satıcı; **~ings** *pl.* ilişkiler; **~t** [delt] *s.* **deal**

dean [dîn] dekan

dear [dî] sevgili; pahalı; ♀ **Sir** Sayın Bay ...

death [deth] ölüm, vefat; **~ly** öldürücü; **~rate** ölüm oranı

debar [di'bâ] *v/t* mahrum etm. (**from** *-den*)

debase [di'beys] *v/t* alçaltmak

debate [di'beyt] *n.* tartışma; *v/t* tartışmak

debauchery [di'bôçri] sefahat

debit ['debit] *n.* ECON borç, açık; *v/t -in* zimmetine geçirmek; **~ card** *yapılan harcamaların doğrudan banka hesabına borç kaydedilmesini sağlayan kart*; ATM kartı

debris ['deybrî] enkaz *pl.*

debt [det] borç; **~or** borçlu

decade ['dekeyd] on yıl

decadence ['dekıdıns] inhitat, çöküş

decapitate [di'kâpiteyt] *v/t -in* başını kesmek

decay [di'key] *n.* çürüme, bozulma; *v/i* çürümek, bozulmak

decease [di'sîs] *n.* vefat; *v/i* vefat etm.

deceit [di'sît] hile(kârlık), yalan; **~ful** aldatıcı, hilekâr

deceive [di'sîv] *v/t* aldatmak; yalan söylemek *-e*

decelerate [di'selıreyt] *v/i* yavaşlamak

December [di'sembı] aralık (ayı)

decen|cy ['dîsnsi] terbiye; iffet; **~t** edepli, terbiyeli

deception [di'sepşın] aldatma, hile

decide [di'sayd] *v/t* kararlaştırmak; karar vermek (hakkında); **~d** kesin

decimal ['desiml] MATH ondalık

decipher [di'sayfı] *v/t -in* şifresini çözmek

decisi|on [di'sijın] karar, hüküm; sebat; **~ve** [di'saysiv] katî, kesin

deck [dek] NAUT güverte; **~chair** şezlong

declar|ation [deklı'reyşın] beyanname; bildiri; **~e** [di-'klâr] *v/t* bildirmek, ilân etm., beyan etm.

declension [di'klenşın] GR isim çekimi

decline [di'klayn] *n.* inme; inhitat; *v/i* azalmak, kuvvetten düşmek; *v/t* reddetmek, kabul etmemek; GR çekmek

declivity [di'kliviti] iniş, meyil

decode ['dî'kıud] *v/t -in* şifresini çözmek

decorat|e ['dekıreyt] *v/t* süslemek, donatmak; nişan vermek *-e*, **~ion** süs; nişan, madalya; **~ive** ['~ıtiv] süsleyici; **~or** dekoratör

decoy ['dîkoy] *n.* tuzak, yem; *v/t* tuzağa düşürmek

decrease ['dîkrîs] *n.* azalma; [dî'krîs] *v/t* azaltmak; *v/i* azalmak

decree [di'krî] *n.* hüküm, karar; *v/t* kararlaştırmak

decrepit [di'krepit] dermansız, zayıf

dedicat|e ['dedikeyt] *v/t* vakfetmek, adamak (to *-e*); **~ion** tahsis, ithaf

deduce [di'dyûs] *v/t* anlamak, sonuç çıkarmak (from *-den*)

deduct [di'dakt] *v/t* hesaptan çıkarmak; **~ion** çıkarılan miktar; sonuç

deed [dîd] iş, eylem; hareket; belge

deep [dîp] *adj.* derin; koyu (*colour*); tok (*voice*); *n.* derinlik; **~en** *v/t* derinleştirmek; artırmak; *v/i* derinleşmek; **~freeze** dipfriz; **~ness** derinlik; tokluk

deer [di:] zoo geyik, karaca

deface [di'feys] *v/t* bozmak

defame [di'feym] *v/t* iftira etm. *-e*

defeat [di'fît] *n.* yenilgi, bozgun; *v/t* yenmek

defect [di'fekt] kusur, eksiklik; **~ive** kusurlu, noksan

defen|ce, *Am.* **~se** [di'fens]

müdafaa, savunma; ~d v/t müdafaa etm., savunmak; ~dant JUR davalı; ~er koruyucu; ~sive müdafaa; savunmalık

defer [di'fɜ:] v/t ertelemek

defian|ce [di'fayıns] meydan okuma; ~t karşı gelen, serkeş

deficien|cy [di'fişınsi] eksiklik; açık; ~t noksan, eksik

deficit ['defisit] ECON açık

defile [di'fayl] geçit, boğaz

defin|e [di'fayn] v/t tanımlamak; sınırlamak; ~ite ['definit] kesin; belirli; ~ition tarif; tanım; ~itive [di'finitiv] kesin; son

deflat|e [di'fleyt] v/t -in havasını boşaltmak; ~ion ECON deflasyon

deflect [di'flekt] v/t saptırmak, çevirmek

deform [di'fôm] v/t bozmak, çirkinleştirmek; ~ed biçimsiz, çirkin

defrost [di'frost] v/t -in buzlarını çözmek

defy [di'fay] v/t -in alnını karışlamak; dayanmak -e

degenerat|e [di'cenirit] adj. soysuzlaşmış; [~reyt] v/t soysuzlaşmak; ~ion [~'reyşın] soysuzlaşma

degrade [di'greyd] v/t alçaltmak; -in rütbesini indirmek

degree [di'gri] derece, mertebe; **by ~s** derece derece, gittikçe

dejected [di'cektid] kederli

delay [di'ley] n. gecikme, te-

hir; v/t geciktirmek; v/i gecikmek

delegat|e ['deligit] n. delege; [~geyt] v/t göndermek, delege etm.; ~ion [~'geyşın] delegasyon

deliberat|e [di'librit] adj. kastî, kasıtlı; [~eyt] v/t düşünmek, tartmak; ~ion [~'reyşın] düşünme; tartışma

delica|te [di'likit] nazik, ince; ~tessen [~'tesn] mezeci dükkânı

delicious [di'lişıs] nefis, hoş

delight [di'layt] n. zevk, sevinç; v/t sevindirmek; zevk vermek -e; v/i sevinmek; ~ful hoş, zevkli

delinquen|cy [di'liŋkwınsi] kabahat; suçluluk; ~t suçlu

deliver [di'livı] v/t kurtarmak; teslim etm., vermek; dağıtmak; **be ~ed of** doğurmak -i; ~ance kurtuluş; ~y teslim; dağıtım; doğurma

delude [di'luud] v/t aldatmak

deluge [di'delyuc] tufan, sel

delusi|on [di'luujın] aldatma, aldanma; vehim; ~ve [~siv] aldatıcı

demand [di'mând] n. talep, istem; istek; v/t istemek; gerektirmek

demeano(u)r [di'mînı] tavır, davranış

demi- ['demi] yarı

demilitarize [di:'militırayz] v/t askersiz hale getirmek

demise [di'mayz] JUR vefat, ölüm

demobilize [di'miubilayz] v/t
MIL terhis etm.

democra|cy [di'mokrısi] de-
mokrasi; **~t** ['demıkrät] de-
mocrat; **~tic** [.'krätik] de-
mokratik

demoli|sh [di'moliş] v/t
yıkmak; **~tion** [demı'lişın]
yıkma, tahrip

demon ['dîmın] şeytan, cin

demonstrat|e ['demınstreyt]
v/t ispat etm. göstermek; v/i
nümayiş yapmak; **~ion** ispat,
gösterme; nümayiş; **~ive**
[di'monstrıtiv] işaret eden,
gösteren; **~or** ['demınstrey-
tı] nümayişçi

demoralize [di'morılayz] v/t
-in ahlâkını bozmak

den [den] n, mağara; küçük
oda

denial [di'nayıl] inkâr, yalanlama; ret

Denmark ['denmâk] Danimarka

denomination [dinomi-
'neyşın] ad(landırma); REL
mezhep

denote [di'nıut] v/t göstermek

denounce [di'nauns] v/t suçlamak; -in feshini bildirmek

dens|e [dens] sık, kesif; **~ity**
kesafet, sıklık

dent [dent] n. çentik; v/t çentmek

dent|al ['dentl] dişlere ait, diş-
çiliğe ait; **~ist** dişçi, diş doktoru; **~ure** [-çı] takma dişler
pl.

deny [di'nay] v/t inkâr etm.,
yalanlamak; reddetmek

depart [di'pât] ayrılmak
(from -den); **~ment** şube,
daire; Am. bakanlık; **~ment
store** büyük mağaza; **~ure**
[di'pâçı] gidiş kalkış

depend [di'pend] bağlı olm.;
güvenmek (on, upon -e);
~ence bağlılık; **~ent** bağlı
(on, upon -e); bağımlı

deplor|able [di'plôribl] acına-
cak; **~e** v/t acımak -e

deport [di'pôt] v/t yurtdışı
etm.; **~ation** [.'teyşın]
yurtdışı etme

depose [di'pıuz] v/t azletmek

deposit [di'pozit] n. tortu;
ECON depozito; pey; v/t yatırmak, tevdi etm.; **~or** para
yatıran

depot ['depıu] depo, ambar

depraved [di'preyvd] ahlâkı
bozuk

depress [di'pres] v/t indirmek, alçaltmak; **~ed** kederli;
~ion ECON durgunluk; çukur;
alçak basınç bölgesi

deprive [di'prayv] v/t mahrum etm. (of -den)

depth [depth] derinlik

deputy ['depyuti] vekil; muavin; POL milletvekili

derail [di'reyl] v/t raydan
çıkarmak

derange [di'reync] v/t
karıştırmak

deri|de [di'rayd] v/t alay etm.
(ile); **~sion** [.'ijın] alay;
~sive [.'aysiv] alaylı

derive [di'rayv] *v/t* çıkarmak, türetmek (**from** *-den*)

derogatory [di'rogıtıri] zararlı (**to** *-e*)

descend [di'send] *v/i* inmek, alçalmak; **be** ~**ed** nesebi olm. (**from** *-den*); ~**ant** torun, hafit

descent [di'sent] iniş; yokuş; soy, nesil

descri|**be** [dis'krayb] *v/t* tanımlamak, vasıflandırmak; anlatmak; ~**ption** [~'kripşın] tanımlama, tarif

desert[1] ['dezıt] GEO çöl

desert[2] [di'zöt] *v/t* bırakmak, terketmek; *v/i* askerlikten kaçmak; ~**ed** ıssız; ~**er** asker kaçağı; ~**ion** terk; askerlikten kaçma

deserve [di'zöv] *v/t* ... hakkı olm.

design [di'zayn] *n* resim, plan, proje, model; maksat; *v/t* tasarlamak, hazırlamak; çizmek

designate ['dezigneyt] *v/t* belirtmek; seçmek

designer [di'zaynı] teknik ressam

desir|**able** [di'zayrıbl] istenilir; makbul; ~**e** [~ayı] *n* arzu, istek; *v/t* arzu etm., istemek; ~**ous** istekli

desk [desk] yazı masası; okul sırası

desolat|**e** ['desılıt] *adj.* harap; ıssız, tenha; perişan; [~'leyt] *v/t* perişan etm.; boş bırakmak; ~**ion** viranlık; pe-

rişanlık

despair [dis'päi] *n* ümitsizlik; *v/i* ümidi kesmek (**of** *-den*)

desperat|**e** ['despırit] ümitsiz; deliye dönmüş; ~**ion** ümitsizlik

despise [dis'payz] *v/t* hakir görmek

despite [dis'payt], **in** ~ **of** *-e* rağmen

despondent [dis'pondınt] ümitsiz

despot ['despot] despot, müstebit; ~**ism** istibdat

dessert [di'zöt] yemiş, tatlı

destin|**ation** [desti'neyşın] gidilecek yer; ~**e** ['-in] *v/t* ayırmak, tahsis etm. (**for** *-e*); ~**y** kader; talih

destitute ['destityût] yoksul, mahrum

destroy [dis'troy] *v/t* yıkmak, bertaraf etm.; ~**er** NAUT destroyer

destructi|**on** [dis'trakşın] yıkım, imha; ~**ve** yıkıcı

detach [di'täç] *v/t* ayırmak, kopmak; ~**ed** ayrı; tarafsız; ~**ment** ayırma; MIL müfreze, kol

detail ['dîteyl] ayrıntı; ~**ed** mufassal, ayrıntılı

detain [di'teyn] *v/t* alıkoymak; geciktirmek

detect [di'tekt] *v/t* meydana çıkarmak, keşfetmek; ~**ion** keşif, bulma; ~**ive** sivil polis; dedektif

detention [di'tenşın] alıkoyma; tevkif

deter [di'tö] *v/t* vazgeçirmek

detergent [di'töcınt] deterjan

deteriorat|e [di'tiıriıreyt] *v/t* fenalaştırmak; *v/i* fenalaşmak; **~ion** fenalaşma

determin|ation [ditʒmi'neyşın] tespit, sınırlama; azim; hüküm, karar; **~e** [di'tʒmin] *v/t* sınırlamak, belirtmek; kararlaştırmak

deterrent [di'terınt] caydıran

detest [di'test] *v/t* nefret etm. **-den;** **~able** iğrenç, berbat

detonation [detıu'neyşın] patlama, infilâk

detour [dîtuı] dolambaçlı yol

devalu|ation [dîvälyu'eyşın] ECON devalüasyon, para değerinin düşürülmesi; **~e** ['_'välyû] *v/t* **-in** değerini düşürmek

devastate ['devısteyt] *v/t* harap etm.

develop [di'velıp] *v/t* geliştirmek; PHOT develope etm.; *v/i* gelişmek; **~ment** gelişme; PHOT developman

deviat|e ['dîvieyt] sapmak (**from -den**); **~ion** sapma

device [di'vays] icat; cihaz; hile, oyun

devil ['devl] şeytan, iblis; **~ish** şeytanca

devise [di'vayz] *v/t* tasarlamak

devoid [di'voyd]: **~ of -den** mahrum

devolution devir, havale; terk

devot|e [di'vıut] *v/t* vakfet-

mek, adamak (**to -e**); **~ed** sadık, bağlı (**to -e**); **~ion** bağlılık, fedakârlık

devour [di'vauı] *v/t* yutmak

devout [di'vaut] dindar; sadık

dew [dyû] çig; **~y** çiğle kaplı

dexter|ity [deks'teriti] beceriklik, ustalık; **~ous** ['_ırıs] becerikli

diabetes [dayı'bîtîz] MED şeker hastalığı

diagnosis [dayıg'nıusis] MED teşhis

dial ['dayıl] *n* kadran; TEL kurs; *v/t* telefon numaralarını çevirmek

dialect ['dayılekt] şive, lehçe

dia|log(ue) ['dayılog] THEA diyalog; **~meter** [day'ämitr] çap

diamond ['dayımınd] elmas; (*pl.*) karo

diaper ['dayıpı] *Am.* kundak bezi

diaphragm ['dayıfräm] ANAT diyafram

diarrh(o)ea [dayı'rîı] MED ishal, amel

diary ['dayırı] muhtıra defteri

dice [days] **1.** *pl.* oyun zarları; **2.** *v/i* zar oynamak

dict|ate [dik'teyt] *v/t* yazdırmak, dikte etmek; zorla kabul ettirmek; **~ation** emir; dikte; **~ator** diktatör; **~atorship** diktatörlük

dictionary ['dikşnrı] sözlük

did [did] *s.* **do**

die¹ [day] zar

die² ölmek; şiddetle arzu etm.

diet 252

(for *sth.*, to *inf. -i*)

diet ['dayıt] *n* perhiz, rejim; POL diyet, meclis; *v/i* perhiz etm., rejim yapmak

differ ['difı] farklı olm., ayrılmak (**from** *-den*); ~**ence** ['difrıns] ayrılık, fark; ihtilâf; ~**ent** farklı, ayrı, başka; çeşitli; ~**ential** [difı'renşıl] TECH diferansiyel

difficult ['difikılt] zor, güç; titiz, inatçı; ~**y** güçlük

diffident ['difidınt] çekingen

diffuse [di'fyûz] *v/t* yaymak, dağıtmak

dig [dig] *v/t* kazmak

digest ['daycest] *n* özet; [di'cest] *v/t* hazmetmek, sindirmek; ~**ible** [di'cestibl] hazmı kolay; ~**ion** [di'cestşın] hazım, sindirim

digital ['dicitel] dijital; ~ **camera** dijital fotoğraf makinesi; ~ **photo** dijital fotoğraf

digni|**fied** ['dignifayd] ağırbaşlı, vakur; ~**ty** vakar; değer

digress [day'gres] ayrılmak (**from** *-den*); ~**ion** ayrılma

dike [dayk] set, bent; hendek

dilapidated [di'läpideytid] harap

dilate [day'leyt] *v/t* genişletmek; *v/i* genişlemek

diligen|**ce** ['dilicens] gayret; ~**t** gayretli, çalışkan

dill [dil] BOT dereotu

dilute [day'lyût] *v/t* sulandırmak

dim [dim] bulanık, donuk; *v/t* bulandırmak; *v/i* kararmak

dime [daym] *Am.* on sentlik para

dimension [di'menşın] ebat, boyut

dimin|**ish** [di'miniş] *v/t* azaltmak; *v/i* azalmak; ~**utive** [-yutiv] ufak; GR küçültme

dimple ['dimpl] çene *veya* yanak çukuru, gamze

dine [dayn] *v/i* akşam yemeğini yemek; ~**r** vagon restoran

dining-**car** ['daynin-] vagon restoran; ~**room** yemek odası

dinner ['dinı] esas yemek; akşam yemeği; ~**jacket** smokin

dip [dip] *n.* dal(dır)ma; yokuş, iniş; *v/t* daldırmak, batırmak; *ışıkları* körletmek; *v/i* dalmak

diphtheria [dif'thiırı] MED difteri

diphthong ['difthoŋ] GR diftong

diploma [di'plumı] diploma; ~**cy** diplomasi; ~**t** ['-imät] diplomat; ~**tic** [-ı'mätik] diplomatik

direct [di'rekt] *adj.* doğru, vasıtasız; *v/t* doğrultmak, yöneltmek; idare etm.; ~ **current** EL doğru akım; ~**ion** yön, cihet; emir; *pl.* tarifname, kullanış tarzı *sg.*; ~**ly** *adv.* doğrudan doğruya

director [di'rektı] müdür, direktör; **board of** ~**s** idare kurulu; ~**y** rehber, adres kitabı

dirigible ['diricıbl] güdümlü

dirt [dɜt] kir, pislik, çamur; ~-**cheap** sudan ucuz; ~**y** *adj.* kirli, pis; iğrenç; *v/t* kirletmek, pisletmek

disable [dis'eybl] *v/t* sakatlamak; ~**d** sakat, malul

disadvantage [disıd'vântic] mahzur, aleyhte oluş; ~**ous** [disâdvân'teycıs] mahzurlu, zararlı

disagree [dısı'grî] uyuşmamak; anlaşamamak (**with** ile); uygun gelmemek (**with** *-e*); ~**able** [-ııbl] hoş olmıyan; ~**ment** uyuşmazlık, çekişme

disappear [dısı'pıı] kaybolmak; ~**ance** gözden kaybolma

disappoint [dısı'poynt] *v/t* hayal kırıklığına uğratmak; ~**ment** hayal kırıklığı

disapprov|**al** [dısı'pruuvıl] beğenmeyiş, ayıplama; ~**e** *v/t* beğenmemek, uygun görmemek

disarm [dis'âm] *v/t* silâhsızlandırmak; ~**ament** [-mı-mınt] silâhsızlanma

disarrange ['dısı'reync] *v/t* karıştırmak, *-in* düzenini bozmak

disarray ['dısı'rey] karışıklık

disaste|**r** [di'zâstı] felâket, belâ; ~**rous** feci

disband [dis'bänd] *v/t* terhis etm., dağıtmak

disbelie|**f** ['disbi'lîf] imansızlık; güvensizlik; ~**ve** ['-'lîv] *v/t* inanmamak *-e*

disc [disk] disk; plak; ~ **jock-ey** diskcokey

discern [di'sön] *v/t* ayırt etm.

discharge [dis'câc] *n.* boşaltma, salıverme; terhis; işten çıkarılma; ateş etme; *v/t* boşaltmak; terhis etm., işten çıkarmak; ödemek; *duty:* yerine getirmek

discipl|**e** [di'saypl] öğrenci; REL havari; ~**ine** ['disiplin] disiplin

disclaim [dis'kleym] *v/t* inkâr etm.; feragat etm. *-den*

disclose [dis'kluz] *v/t* ifşa etm.

discolo(**u**)**r** [dis'kalı] *v/t -in* rengini bozmak

discomfort [dis'kamfıt] rahatsızlık

discompose [diskım'pıuz] *v/t* şaşırtmak

disconcert [diskın'söt] *v/t* şaşırtmak, karıştırmak

disconnect ['diskı'nekt] *v/t* ayırmak

discontent ['diskın'tent] hoşnutsuzluk; ~**ed** hoşnutsuz

discontinue [dis'kın'tinyu] *v/t* kesmek; devam etmemek *-e*

discord ['diskôd], ~**ance** ['-'kôdıns] anlaşmazlık, ahenksizlik; ~**ant** uygunsuz

discotheque ['diskıutek] diskotek

discount ['diskaunt] ECON iskonto; ~ **house** *Am.* uzuca mal satılan mağaza

discourage [dis'karic] *v/t -in*

cesaretini kırmak, vazgeçirmek -i (from -den)

discourse [dis'kôs] söylev, nutuk

discover [dis'kavı] v/t keşfetmek, bulmak; ~er bulucu; ~y keşif, buluş

discredit [dis'kredit] güvensizlik; şüphe; v/t kötülemek, itibardan düşürmek

discreet [dis'krît] ketum, ağzı sıkı

discrepancy [dis'krepınsi] ayrılık

discretion [dis'kreşın] ketumiyet; akıllılık; nazaklik; yetki

discriminat|e [dis'krimineyt] v/t ayırmak; v/i ayırım yapmak; ~ion [.krimi'neyşın] ayırım, temyiz

discuss [dis'kas] v/t görüşmek, müzakere etm.; ~ion görüşme, tartışma

disdain [dis'deyn] n hakaret; v/t aşağısamak

disease [di'zîz] hastalık; ~d hasta

disembark [disim'bâk] v/t karaya çıkarmak; v/i karaya çıkmak

disengage ['disin'geyc] v/t ayırmak, çözmek; ~d serbest, boş

disentangle ['disin'tängl] v/t çözmek

disfavo(u)r ['dis'feyvı] gözden düşme

disfigure [dis'fıgı] v/t çirkinleştirmek

disgrace [dis'greys] n gözden düşme, yüzkarası; v/t gözden düşürmek; ~ful ayıp, yüz kızartıcı

disguise [dis'gayz] n kıyafet değiştirme; v/i kıyafet değiştirmek; v/t gizlemek

disgust [dis'gast] n nefret, tiksinme (at -den); v/t tiksindirmek, bıktırmak A; ~ing iğrenç

dish [diş] tabak; yemek

dishevel|l)ed [di'şevild] karmakarışık

dishonest [dis'onist] namussuz; ~y namussuzluk

dishono(u)r [dis'onı] m namussuzluk, leke; v/t -in namusuna leke sürmek; -in ırzına geçmek; bill: kabul etmemek -i; ~able namussuz

dish-washer bulaşık yıkama makinesi

disillusion [disi'luujın] v/t hayal kırıklığına uğratmak

disinfect [disin'fekt] v/t dezenfekte etm.; ~ant antiseptik ilâç

disinherit ['disin'herit] v/t mirastan mahrum etm.

disintegrate [dis'intigreyt] v/t parçalara ayırmak; v/i parçalanmak

disinterested [dis'intristid] tarafsız, menfaat düşünmiyen

disk [disk] s. **disc**; ~ **drive** disk sürücü

dislike [dis'layk] n beğenmeyiş; v/t beğenmemek, sevme-

mek
dislocate ['dislıkeyt] v/t yerinden çıkarmak
dismal ['dizmıl] kederli; sönük
dismantle [dis'mäntl] v/t sökmek
dismay [dis'mey] korku,
dehşet
dismember [dis'membı] v/t
parçalamak
dismiss [dis'mis] v/t işten
çıkarmak; yol vermek -e;
~al yol verme
dismount ['dis'maunt] v/t
sökmek; v/i attan inmek
disobedience [disı'bidyıns]
itaatsizlik; ~t itaatsiz
disobey [dısı'bey] v/t itaat
etmemek -e
disobliging ['dısı'blayciŋ]
nezaketsiz
disorder [dis'ôdı] karışıklık;
hastalık; ~ly düzensiz; itaatsiz; çapaçul
disown [dis'ıun] v/t inkâr
etm., tanımamak
disparage [dis'päric] v/t kötülemek
dispassionate [dis'päşnit]
tarafsız
dispatch [dis'päç] n. acele;
gönderme; rapor, haber;
telgraf; v/t göndermek; tamamlamak
dispensable [dis'pensıbl]
vaz geçilebilir; ~ary dispanser; ~e v/t dağıtmak; v/i vazgeçmek (**with** -den)
disperse [dis'pos] v/t dağıt-

mak, yaymak; v/i dağılmak
displace [dis'pleys] v/t yerinden çıkarmak, götürmek
display [dis'pley] n. gösteriş,
nümayiş, teşhir; v/t göstermek, teşhir etm., sermek
displease [dis'plîz] v/t gücendirmek; ~ed dargın;
~ure [-_jı] gücenme
disposal [dis'pıuzıl] tertip,
düzen; tasarruf; bertaraf etme; ~e v/t düzenlemek; ~e
of -in tasarrufunda olm.;
kullanmak -i; bertaraf etm.
-i; ~ed hazır (**to** -e); ~ition
[-ı'zişın] düzen; eğilim; tabiat
disproportionate [disprı-
'pôşnit] nispetsiz
dispute [dis'pyût] n. münakaşa, tartışma; v/i tartışmak,
kabul etmemek
disqualify [dis'kwolifay] v/t
diskalifiye etm.
disregard [disri'gaad] v/t ihmal etm., saymamak
disreputable [dis'repyutıbl]
rezil; itibarsız
disrespectful [disris'pekt-
ful] hürmetsiz
disrupt [dis'rapt] v/t yarmak,
ayırmak
dissatisfaction['dissätisfäk-
şın] hoşnutsuzluk; ~y ['di-
'sätisfay] v/t memnun etmemek
disseminate [di'semineyt]
v/t saçmak, yaymak
dissension [di'senşın] ihtilâf, çekişme; ~t **bir hususta**

ayrılmak (from *-den*)
dissimilar ['di'simılı] farklı (to *-den*)
dissipate ['disipeyt] *v/t* dağıtmak; israf etm.; **~ion** [-'peyşın] sefahat
dissociate [dis'sıuşieyt]: ~ oneself ayrılmak (from *-den*)
dissol|ute ['disıluut] ahlâksız, sefih; **~ution** [-'luuşın] eri(t)me; **~ve** [di'zolv] *v/t* eritmek; feshetmek; *v/i* erimek
dissuade [di'sweyd] *v/t* vazgeçirmek, caydırmak (from *-den*)

distan|ce ['distıns] mesafe; uzaklık; ara; **~t** uzak; soğuk, mesafeli
distaste ['dis'teyst] tiksinme, nefret; **~ful** [-'teystful] iğrenç
distinct [dis'tiŋkt] ayrı, farklı; belli; **~ion** ayırma, ayırt etme, temayüz, üstünlük; nişan; **~ive** ayıran, özellik belirten
distinguish [dis'tiŋgwiş] *v/t* ayırmak, ayırt etm.; **~ed** seçkin, mümtaz, kibar
distort [dis'tôt] *v/t* bükmek, bozmak, tahrif etm.
distract [dis'träkt] *v/t* başka tarafa çekmek, **~ed** deli, çılgın; **~ion** karışıklık; eğlence; çılgınlık

ken
distribut|e [dis'tribyut] *v/t* dağıtmak, yaymak; **~ion** [-'byuşın] dağıtım; yayılma
district ['distrikt] bölge; ilçe, kaza
distrust [dis'trast] *n.* güvensizlik, şüphe; *v/t* güvenmemek *-e*
disturb [dis'tɜb] *v/t* karıştırmak; rahatsız etm.; **~ance** karışıklık; rahatsızlık
disuse ['dis'yûs] kullanılmayış; **~d** [-'yûzd] eski, vaktini doldurmuş
ditch [diç] hendek
dive [dayv] *n.* dalış; AVIA pike; *v/i* dalmak (into *-e*); pike yapmak; **~r** dalgıç
diverge [day'vɜc] birbirinden ayrılmak
divers|e [day'vɜs] çeşitli, değişik; **~ion** başka tarafa çevirme; eğlence; **~ity** fark, başkalık
divert [day'vɜt] *v/t* başka tarafa çevirmek; eğlendirmek
divide [di'vayd] *v/t* bölmek, ayırmak; *v/i* ayrılmak
divin|e [di'vayn] ilâhî, kutsal; **~ity** [di'viniti] tanrılık niteliği; ilâhiyat
division [di'vijın] bölme; ayrılma; kısım, daire; MIL tümen
divorce [di'vôs] *n.* boşanma; *v/t* boşamak; *v/i* boşanmak
DIY [diay'vay] (= *do-it-yourself*) kişinin bir işi, uzmanına başvurmak yerine, kendi-

sinin yapması

dizzy ['dizi] baş döndürücü

do [duu] *v/t* yapmak; etmek; hazırlamak; bitirmek; *that will* ~ yeter; *how* ~ *you* ~? nasılsınız?; ~ *you like London?* Londra hoşunuza gider mi?; *we* ~ *not know* bilmiyoruz; ~ *shut up!* sus yahu!; ~ *well isi iyi* gitmek; *iyi para kazanmak;* ~ *with* ihtiyacı olm. *-e*; ~ *without* muhtaç olmamak *-e*

docile ['dusayl] uslu, uysal

dock [dok] NAUT havuz, dok; ~er liman işçisi; ~yard tersane

doctor ['doktı] doktor; hekim; ~ate ['-rit] doktora

doctrine ['doktrin] doktrin, öğreti

document ['dokyumınt] belge; ~ary ['-mentıri] belgelere dayanan, yazılı

dodge [doc] *n.* oyun, kurnazlık; *v/i* kaçamak bulmak

doe [dıu] ZOO dişi geyik *veya* tavşan

dog [dog] köpek; ~eared kıvrılmış; ~ged ['-id] inatçı

dogma ['dogmı] dogma, inak

doings ['duuiŋz] *pl.* işler

dole [dıul] sadaka; işsizlere verilen haftalık

doll [dol] bebek, kukla

dollar ['dolı] dolar

dolorous ['dolırıs] kederli, elemli

dolphin ['dolfin] ZOO yunus-balığı

domain [dı'meyn] mülk, arazi; alan

dome [dıum] kubbe

domestic [dı'mestik] *adj.* eve ait, ehlî, evcil; yerli; *n.* hizmetçi; ~ *animal* evcil hayvan; ~ation [-mesti'keyşın] alıştırma

domicile ['domisayl] oturma yeri

domin|ant ['dominınt] hâkim, üstün; ~ate [-neyt] *v/t* hâkim olm. *-e*; ~ation [-'neyşın] egemenlik

domineer [domi'niı] *v/t* tahakküm altında tutmak; zorbalık etm.; ~ing otoriter

dominion [dı'minyın] POL dominyon

donat|e [dıu'neyt] *v/t* bağışlamak; ~ion bağış

done [dan] *s.* do; *be* ~ yapılmak; bitkin olm.

donkey ['donki] eşek

donor ['dıunı] veren, verici

doom [duum] *n.* kader; kıyamet; *v/t* mahkûm etm. (*to -e*); ~sday REL kıyamet günü

door [do] kapı; ~handle kapı mandalı; ~keeper, ~man kapıcı; ~way kapı yeri, giriş

dope [dıup] *n.* esrar, afyon; *v/t* ilâçla sersemletmek

dorm|ant ['dômınt] uyuyan; ~er (window) çatı penseresi; ~itory ['dômitri] yatakhane, koğuş

dose [dıus] doz

dot [dot] *n.* nokta; benek; *v/t* noktalamak

dote 258

dote [dιut] bunamak; düşkün olm. **(on, upon** *-e)*

double ['dʌbl] çift, iki misli, iki kat; *n.* eş; dublör; *v/i* iki misli olm.; *v/t* iki kat etm.; ~ **bed** iki kişilik yatak; ~ **room** çift yataklı oda; ~**click** *v/i* çift tıklamak; ~**cross** *v/t* aldatmak; ~**faced** ikiyüzlü

doubt [daut] *n.* şüphe; *v/i* şüphelenmek **(about** *-den)*; ~**ful** şüpheli, kararsız; ~**less** şüphesiz

douche [duuş] MED şırınga

dough [du] hamur; ~**nut** çörek

dove [dav] ZOO güvercin

down¹ [daun] GEO kumul, eksibe

down² hav, ince tüy

down³ *adv.* aşağı(ya); *v/t* indirmek; ~**cast** üzgün; ~**fall** düşüş; ~**hearted** cesareti kırılmış; ~**hill** yokuş aşağı; ~**load** *v/t* indirmek; *n.* indirilen dosya; ~**pour** sağanak; ~**right** kesin; tamamiyle; ~**stairs** aşağıda; aşağıya; ~**town** *Am.* şehrin merkezi; ~**ward** ['~wıd] aşağıya doğru

dowry [dauri] çeyiz

doze [diuz] *v/i* uyuklamak; *n.* hafif uyku

dozen ['dazn] düzine

drab [dräb] gri

draft [dräft] *n.* police; taslak; MIL mecburî askerliğe alma; *v/t* tasarlamak, çizmek; MIL silâh altına çağırmak; *s.*

draught; ~**sman** *s.* **draughtsman**

drag [dräg] *v/t* sürüklemek, çekmek

dragon ['drägın] ejderha; ~**fly** ZOO yusufçuk

drain [dreyn] *n.* lağım, su yolu; *v/t* akıtmak, kurutmak; ~**age** akaçlama, drenaj; kanalizasyon

drake [dreyk] ZOO erkek ördek

drama ['drāmı] dram, tiyatro eseri; ~**tic** [drı'mätik] dramatik; heyecanlı

drank [dränk] *s.* **drink**

drape [dreyp] *v/t* kumaşla kaplamak, *-in* kıvrımlarını düzeltmek; *r* kumaşçı

drastic ['drästik] şiddetli; açık

draught [dräft], *Am.* **draft** çekme, içme, yudum; hava cereyanı; ~**sman** teknik ressam; ~**y** cereyanlı

draw [drō] *n.* kur'a çekilişi; çok rağbetli şey; berabere biten oyun; *v/t* çekmek, celbetmek; germek; çizmek; *money:* çekmek; ~ **near** *v/i* yaklaşmak; ~ **out** *v/t* uzatmak; ~ **up** *v/t* tasarlamak, hazırlamak; *v/i* yaklaşıp durmak; ~**back** mahzur, engel; ~**er** çekmece, göz; ressam; *pl.* don

drawing ['drōiŋ] resim; çekme; ~**pin** pünez; ~**room** salon, misafir odası

drawn [drōn] *s.* **draw:** berabere

dread [dred] korku, dehşet;
v/t korkmak *-den*; **~ful** dehşet;
korkunç

dream [drim] *n.* rüya; hulya;
v/i rüya görmek; **~t** [dremt]
s. **dream**; **~y** dalgın

dreary ['driıri] can sıkıcı, ıssız

dredge [drec] *v/t* taramak; *n.*
tarak; **~r** tarak dubası

dregs [dregz] *pl.* tortu, telve
sg.

drench [drenç] *v/t* ıslatmak

dress [dres] *n.* elbise, kıyafet;
v/t giydirmek; süslemek;
hazırlamak; düzenlemek;
v/i giyinmek; **~ designer**
moda desinatörü

dressing ['dresiŋ] giy(in)me;
MED pansuman; salça, terbiye; **~cubicle** soyunma kabi-
nası; **~gown** sabahlık; **~ta-
ble** tuvalet masası

dress-maker kadın terzisi

drew [druu] *s.* **draw**

dried [drayd] *s.* **dry**; kuru

drift [drift] *n.* sürüklenme; kar
yığıntısı; hedef, eğilim; *v/t*
sürüklemek; *v/i* sürüklenmek

drill [dril] *n.* delgi, matkap;
MIL talim; tohum dizisi; *v/t*
delmek; talim etm.

drink [driŋk] *n.* içki; içecek;
v/t içmek; **~ing water** içecek
su

drip [drip] *n.* damlamak;
~dry buruşmaz; **~ping** erimiş yağ

drive [drayv] *n.* gezinti; işle-

me; teşebbüs, gayret; *v/t* sürmek; kullanmak; götürmek;
sevketmek; **~ away** *v/t* kovmak; **~ on** *v/i* gitmeğe devam
etm.; **~ out** kovmak, çıkarmak; **~in** müşterilerine araba içinde servis yapan

driven ['drivn] *s.* **drive**

driver ['drayvı] şoför

drive-thru ['drayvthruu] *Am.*
n. araçla bir ucundan girilip
yemek alındıktan sonra öbür
ucundan çıkılanrestoran

driving ['drayviŋ] sürme, kullanma; **~ license** şoförlük
ehliyetnamesi; **~ school**
şoförlük okulu

drizzle ['drizl] *n.* çiseleme; *v/i*
çiselemek

dromedary ['dramıdıri] zoo
hecin devesi

drone [drıun] zoo erkek arı

droop [druup] *v/t* indirmek;
v/i sarkmak, bükülmek

drop [drop] *n.* damla; düşme,
sukut; *v/t* düşürmek, atmak;
damlatmak; *v/i* damlamak; **~
a line** kısa bir mektup yazmak; **~ in** uğramak (**at** *-e*)

drought [draut] kuraklık

drove [drıuv] *s.* **drive**

drown [draun] *v/t* boğmak; *v/i*
boğulmak; **be ~ed** boğulmak

drowsy ['drauzi] uykusu
basmış; uyutucu

drudge [drac] ağır işler yapmak

drug [drag] *n.* ilâç; esrar; *v/t*
ilâçla uyutmak; **~ addict** es-
rarkeş; **~gist** ['~gist] eczacı

bakkal; ~store *Am.* bakkaliye; eczane

drum [dram] *n.* davul; trampete; *v/i* davul çalmak

drunk [draŋk] *s.* drink; sarhoş; ~ard ['-ıd] ayyaş, sarhoş; ~en sarhoş

dry [dray] *adj.* kuru, kurak; susuz; *v/i* kurutmak, kurulamak; *v/i* kurumak; ~ goods *pl. Am.* manifatura *sg.*; ~ up tamamen kurumak; ~cleaning kuru temizleme

dual ['dyuil] çift, iki kat

dubious ['dyûbyıs] şüpheli

duch|ess ['daçis] düşes; ~y dukalık

duck [dak] *n.* zoo ördek; *v/i* dalmak, başını eğmek; *v/t* daldırmak

dudgeon ['dacın] öfke

due [dyû] *adj.* gerekli; ödenmesi gerekli; *n.* hak; vergi; ~ to yüzünden, ~den dolayı; in ~ time zamanı gelince; be ~ -mesi gerekli olm.

duel ['dyuil] düello

dug [dag] *s.* dig; ~out MIL sığınak

duke [dyûk] duka, dük

dull [dal] donuk, sönük; sıkıcı; durgun; cansız

duly ['dyûli] *adv.* gereğince; tam zamanında

dumb [dam] dilsiz, sessiz; *Am.* aptal, budala; ~founded hayret içince; ~waiter seyyar masa; mutfak asansörü

dummy ['dami] taklit; man-

ken; kukla adam

dump [damp] *v/t* boşaltmak, atmak; ~ing ECON damping

dun [dan] *v/t* borçluyu sıkıştırmak

dune [dyûn] kumul, eksibe

dung [daŋ] *n.* gübre; *v/t* gübrelemek

dungeon ['dancın] zindan

dupe [dyûp] *v/t* aldatmak

dupl|ex ['dyûpleks] çift; ~icate ['-likit] *n.* eş; kopya, nüsha; ['-likeyt] *v/t -in* suretini çıkarmak

dura|ble ['dyuırıbl] dayanıklı, devamlı; ~tion [-'reyşın] devam, süre

duress(e) [dyu'res] cebir, baskı

during ['dyuriŋ] esnasında, zarfında

dusk [dask] akşam karanlığı

dust [dast] toz; çöp; *v/t -in* tozunu silkmek; ~bin çöp tenekesi; ~man çöpçü; ~pan faraş; ~y tozlu, toz gibi

Dutch [daç] Holandalı, Felemenkli; Felemenkçe; ~man Felemenkli

dutiful ['dyûtiful] görevini bilen

duty ['dyuti] ödev, görev, hizmet; gümrük resmi; off ~ izinli; on ~ vazife başında; ~free gümrüksüz

DVD [dîvî'dî] *n.* DVD; ~ROM DVD-ROM

dwarf [dwôf] cüce, bodur

dwell [dwel] *v/i* oturmak, durmak (on üzerinde); ~ing

oturma yeri
dwelt [dwelt] s. dwell
dye [day] n. boya; v/t boyamak
dying ['dayiŋ] s. die
dyke [dayk] s. dike
dynamic [day'nämik] dina-

mik; enerjik; ~ics dinamik;
~ite ['ımayt] dinamit; ~o
['ımıu] EL dinamo
dynasty ['dınısti] hanedan,
soy
dysentery ['dısntri] MED dizanteri, kanlı basur

E

each [iç] her biri, her; beher; ~
other birbiri
eager ['igı] hevesli; istekli,
sabırsız; ~ness istek, gayret
eagle ['igl] zoo kartal, karakuş
ear [iı] kulak; başak; ~drum
ANAT kulak zarı
earl [ɜl] kont
early ['ɜli] erken(den); eski,
ilk
earn [ɜn] v/t kazanmak
earnest ['ɜnist] ciddi; in ~ ciddî olarak
earnings ['ɜniŋz] pl. kazanç
sg.
ear|-phone EL kulaklık;
~ring küpe; ~shot kulak
erimi
earth [ɜth] n. toprak; kara;
yeryüzü; dünya; v/t EL toprağa bağlamak; ~en topraktan yapılmış; ~enware çanak
çömlek; ~quake GEO deprem; ~worm zoo yer solucanı
ease [iz] n. rahat; refah; kolaylık; v/t hafifletmek,
yatıştırmak; at ~ rahat, hoş

east [ist] doğu; Near 2 Yakın
Doğu
Easter ['istı] REL paskalya
east|ern ['istın] doğu(da);
~ward ['-wıd] doğuya doğru
easy ['izi] kolay, rahat,
sıkıntısız; take it ~! acele etmeyiniz!; darılmayınız!;
~-chair koltuk; ~-going
kayıtsız, kaygısız
eat [it] v/t yemek; ~ up v/t yiyip bitirmek; ~en s. eat
eaves [ivz] çıkıntı; ~drop v/i
gizlice dinlemek
ebb(-tide) ['eb('-)] GEO cezir
ebony ['ebni] abanoz
e-book ['ibuk] e-kitap
eccentric [ik'sentrik] eksantrik, dışmerkezli; fig. garip,
tuhaf
ecclesiastical [ikli:zi'ästikıl]
kiliseye ait
echo ['ekıu] n. yankı; v/i
yansımak; v/t yansıtmak
eclipse [i'klips] ay tutulması,
güneş tutulması
econom|ic [ikı'nomik] iktisadî; pl. iktisat bilimi; ~ical
idareli, tutumlu

econom|ist [i'konimist] ikti-
satçı; **~ize** idareli kullanmak
(**in, on** -*i*); **~y** iktisat, ekonomi; tutum, idare

ecstasy ['ekstısi] vecit

edge|e [ec] *n.* kenar, sırt; bıçak
ağzı; *v/t* bilemek; kenar geçirmek -*e*; **on ~e** sinirli;
~ing kenarlık, şerit; **~y** sinirli

edible ['edibl] yenir

edif|ice ['edifis] bina; **~ying**
['-fayiŋ] yüksek duygulara
ulaştıran

edit ['edit] *v/t* yayımlamak;
~ion [i'dişın] baskı; **~or** ['edi-
tı] yayımlayan; yazı işleri
müdürü; **~orial** [edi'tôrıl]
başyazı; yazı işleri müdür-
lüğüne ait

educat|e ['edyukeyt] *v/t* eğit-
mek, yetiştirmek; **~ed** oku-
muş, aydın; **~ion** eğitim,
öğretim; **~or** eğitmen

eel [il] zoo yılan balığı

effect [i'fekt] *v/t* başarmak;
etkilemek; *n.* sonuç, etki;
gösteriş; *pl.* mallar, eşya;
take ~ yürürlüğe girmek;
~ive etkili

effeminate [i'feminit] kadın
gibi, yumuşak

effervescent [efı'vesnt] kö-
püren

efficien|cy [i'fişınsi] kifayet,
ehliyet; etki; verim; **~ient** ehliyetli; verimli; etkili

effort ['efıt] gayret, çaba

effusive [i'fyûsiv] taşkın; bol

egg [eg] yumurta; **~-cup** yumurta kabı; **~-plant** BOT

patlıcan; **~-head** *Am. sl.*
aydın kimse; **~-shell** yumurta kabuğu

egois|m ['egıuizım] bencilik;
~t bencil, hodbin

egress ['îgrıs] çıkış

Egypt ['îcipt] Mısır; **~ian**
[i'cipşın] Mısırlı

eight [eyt] sekiz; **~een** ['ey-
'tîn] on sekiz; **~fold** sekiz
misli; **~y** seksen

either ['aydhı] ikisinden biri,
her iki; **~ ... or ...** ya ... yahut
...

ejaculation [icäkyu'leyşın]
ünlem

eject [i'cekt] *v/t* dışarı atmak,
kovmak

elaborate [i'läbırıt] *adj.* dikkatle işlenmiş, özenilmiş;
v/t incelikle işlemek

elapse [i'läps] *v/i* geçmek

elastic [i'lästik] elastikî, esnek; lastik bant

elbow ['elbıu] *n.* dirsek; *v/t*
dirsekle dürtmek

elder[1] ['eldı] BOT mürver
ağacı

elder[2] daha yaşlı, büyük; **~ly**
yaşlı

elect [i'lekt] *v/t* seçmek; *adj.*
seçkin; **~ion** seçim; **~or** seçmen

electric [i'lektrik] elektrik
(-li); **~al engineer** elektrik
mühendisi; **~ian** [.-'trışın]
elektrikçi; **~ity** [.-'trisiti]
elektrik

electrify [i'lektrifay] *v/t* elek-
triklemek

electrocution [ilektrı'kyûşın] elektrikle idam

electron [i'lektron] elektron

elegan|ce ['eligıns] zarafet, şıklık; **~t** zarif, şık

element ['elimınt] öğe; unsur; eleman; **~al** [_'mentl] temel, ilkel; **~ary** [_'mentıri] ilk, basit; **~ary school** ilkokul

elephant ['elifınt] zoo fil

elevat|e ['elyveyt] v/t yükseltmek; **~ion** yükseklik; yüksek yer; **~or** Am. asansör; AVIA irtifa dümeni

eleven [i'levn] on bir

eligible ['elicıbl] seçilebilir; uygun

eliminat|e [i'limineyt] v/t çıkarmak; bertaraf etm.; **~ion** çıkarma

elk [elk] bir geyik çeşidi

ellipse [i'lips] elips

elongate ['ilongeyt] v/t gerip uzatmak

elope [i'lıup] âşık ile kaçmak

eloquen|ce ['elıukwıns] belâgat; **~t** beliğ; dokunaklı

else [els] yoksa; başka; what **~?** bundan başka ne var?; **~where** başka yerde *veya* yere

elu|de [i'luud] v/t sakınmak, sıyrılmak -*den*; **~sive** tutulmaz, ele geçmez

emaciated [i'meyşieytid] çok zayıflanmış, sıska

e-mail ['îmayl] *n.* e-posta; **~** e-posta göndermek; **~ address** e-posta adresi

emanate ['emıneyt] çıkmak (from *-den*)

emancipat|e [i'mänsipeyt] v/t serbest bırakmak; **~ion** serbest bırakma, eşit hakları verme

embalm [im'bâm] v/t tahnit etm.

embankment [im'bäŋkmınt] set, bent; rıhtım

embargo [em'bâgıu] NAUT ambargo

embark [im'bâk] v/t gemiye bindirmek; v/i gemiye binmek; girişmek (**in**, **on** -*e*)

embarras [im'bäris] v/t şaşırtmak; utandırmak; **~ing** utandırıcı; nahoş; **~ment** sıkıntı, sıkılganlık

embassy ['embısi] POL büyük *veya* orta elçilik; sefarethane

embed [im'bed] v/t gömmek, yerleştirmek

embellish [im'beliş] v/t süslemek, güzelleştirmek

ember ['embı] kor

embezzle [im'bezl] v/t zimmetine geçirmek

embitter [im'bitı] v/t acılaştırmak

emblem ['em'blım] sembol, simge

embody [im'bodi] v/t temsil etm.

embolism ['embılizım] MED amboli

embrace [im'breyc] v/t kucaklamak; benimsemek; v/i kucaklaşmak; *n.* kucaklaşma

embroider [im'broydı] v/t -*in*

üzerine nakış işlemek; ~y
nakış, işleme

embryo ['embriu] cenin, dö-
lüt

emerald ['emərld] zümrüt

emerge [i'mɜc] ortaya
çıkmak, (from *-den*); ~nce
çıkma, zuhur

emergency [i'mɜcınsi] olağanüstü durum, tehlike; ~
brake imdat freni; ~ call istimdat; ~ exit ihtiyat kapı;
~ landing AVIA mecburî iniş

emery ['emıri] zımpara

emigra|nt ['emigrınt] göç-
men; ~te ['-eyt] göçmek;
~tion göçmenlik

eminen|ce ['eminıns] yüksek-
lik; yüksek rütbe; ~t yüksek;
seçkin; ~tly *adv.* pek, gayet

emission [i'mişın] yayma

emit [i'mit] *v/t* çıkarmak

emotion [i'muşın] heyecan,
his; ~al duygulu; heyecanlı

emperor ['empırı] imparator

empha|sis ['emfısis] şiddet,
vurgu, kuvvet; ~size *v/t*
önem vermek *-e*, vurgulamak *-i*; ~tic [im'fätik] etkili;
vurgulu

empire ['empayı] imparator-
luk

employ [im'ploy] *v/t* kullanmak, istihdam etm.; *n.* görev,
hizmet; ~ee [employ'i] işçi,
müstahdem, işalan; ~er işveren, patron; ~ment *n* iş verme;
memuriyet; ~ment agency
iş ve işçi bulma kurumu

empower [im'pauı] *v/t* yetki

emptiness ['emptinis] boşluk; ~y *adj.* boş; anlamsız;
v/t boşaltmak

enable [i'neybl] *v/t* muktedir
kılmak; kuvvet vermek *-e*

enact [i'näkt] *v/t* kararlaştırmak; THEA oynamak

enamel [i'nämıl] *n.* mine; *v/t*
mine ile kaplamak

encase [in'keys] *v/t* kılıfla-
mak

enchant [in'çânt] *v/t* büyülemek, teshir etm.

encircle [in'sɜkl] *v/t* kuşatmak

enclos|e [in'kluz] *v/t* kuşat-
mak; ilişikte göndermek;
~ure [-ʒı] çit; ilişik kâğıt

encompass [in'kampıs] *v/t*
-in etrafını çevirmek

encounter [in'kauntı] *n.*
karşılaşma; *v/t* karşılamak

encourage [in'karic] *v/t* teşvik etm.; cesaret vermek *-e*;
~ment teşvik

encroach [in'kruç] *v/i* el
uzatmak (on, upon *-e*)

encumber [in'kambı] *v/t* yüklemek; engel olm. *-e*

end [end] *n.* son; amaç, gaye;
v/t bitirmek; *v/i* bitmek;
stand on ~ *tüyleri* ürpermek; to this ~ bu amaçla

endanger [in'deyncı] *v/t* tehlikeye düşürmek

endear [in'diı] *v/t* sevdirmek
(to *-e*)

endeavo(u)r [in'devı] *n.*
emek, çaba; çalışmak

end|ing ['endiŋ] son; GR sonek; **~less** sonsuz

endorse [in'dôs] v/t. ECON ciro etm.; onaylamak; **~ment** ciro; tasvip

endow [in'dau] v/t donatmak

endur|ance [in'dyurins] tahammül; **~e** v/t tahammül etm., dayanmak -e

enemy ['enimi] düşman; hasım

energ|etic [enı'cetik] enerjik, faal; **~y** enerji, gayret

enervate ['enısveyt] v/t kuvvetten düşürmek

enfold [in'fıuld] v/t sarmak

enforce [in'fôs] v/t zorla kabul ettirmek; yürütmek

enfranchise [in'fränçayz] v/t POL seçim hakkı vermek -e

engage [in'geyc] v/t hizmete almak, tutmak; işgal olm. (in ile); **be ~d** nişanlı olm. (to ile); **~ment** söz, vaat; angajman, hizmete alma; nişanlanma; randevu

engine ['encin] makine, motor; lokomotif; **~-driver** makinist

engineer [enci'niı] makinist; mühendis; **~ing** mühendislik; makinistlik

England ['iŋglınd] İngiltere

English ['iŋgliş] İngiliz; İngilizce; **the ~** pl. İngilizler; **~man** İngiliz erkeği; **~woman** İngiliz kadını

engrav|e [in'greyv] v/t hakketmek, oymak; **~ing** hakkâk işi

engross [in'grıus] v/t zaptetmek, işgal etm.

enigma [i'nigmı] bilmece

enjoin [in'coyn] v/t emretmek, tembih etm.

enjoy [in'coy] v/t sevmek; hoşlanmak -den; **~ oneself** zevk almak; **~ment** eğlence, zevk

enlarge [in'lâc] v/t büyültmek, genişletmek; v/i genişlemek; **~ment** büyü(lt)me; büyüteç; randisman

enlighten [in'laytn] v/t aydınlatmak; **~ed** aydın

enlist [in'list] v/t MIL kaydetmek; v/i asker olm.

enliven [in'layvn] v/i canlandırmak

enmity ['enmiti] düşmanlık

enormous [i'nômıs] koca-man, iri

enough [i'naf] kâfi, yeter

enquire [in'kwayı] s. inquire

enrage [in'reyc] v/t kızdırmak

enrapture [in'räpçı] v/t kendinden geçirmek

enrich [in'riç] v/t zenginleştirmek

enrol(l) [in'rıul] v/t kaydetmek

enslave [in'sleyv] v/t köle yapmak

ensue [in'syû] v/i ardından gelmek; hâsıl olm.; gelmek (from -den)

ensure [in'şuı] v/t sağlamak

entangle [in'tängl] v/t dolaştırmak

enter ['entı] v/i girmek (into

-e); girişmek (-e); v/t kaydetmek, deftere geçirmek

enterpris|e ['entiprayz] teşebbüs, iş; **~ing** girişken, faal

entertain [enti'teyn] v/t eğlendirmek; misafirliğe kabul etm.; **~er** prezantatör; **~ment** eğlence; ağırlama

enthusias|m [in'thyûziâzm] coşkunluk; can atma; **~tic** [-'âstik] heyecanlı, coşkun

entic|e [in'tays] v/t ayartmak; **~ing** ayartıcı

entire [in'tayı] tam, bütün; **~ly** adv. büsbütün

entitle [in'taytl] v/t yetki vermek -e

entity ['entiti] varlık

entrails ['entreylz] pl. bağırsaklar

entrance [entrıns] giriş, girme; giriş yeri; **~ fee** girmelik, duhuliye

entreat [in'trît] v/t ısrarla rica etm. -den; **~y** yalvarma, rica

entrust [in'trast] v/t emniyet etm. (to -e)

entry ['entri] girme, giriş; kayıt; **~ permit** giriş müsaadesi

enumerate [i'nyûmıreyt] v/t birer birer saymak

envelop [in'velıp] v/t sarmak; **~e** ['envılıp] zarf

env|iable ['enviıbl] gıpta edilir; **~ious** gıpta eden, kıskanç

environment [in'vayırınment] muhit, çevre; **~al pol-**

lution çevre kirlenmesi; **~ally friendly** çevre dostu

environs ['envirınz] pl. civar, etraf

envoy ['envoy] elçi

envisage [in'vizic] v/t planlamak; tasavvur etm.

envy ['envi] n. gıpta, haset; v/t gıpta etm., imrenmek -e

epic ['epik] destan; destan gibi

epidemic [epi'demik] (disease) MED salgın hastalık

epidermis [epi'dımis] üstderi

epilepsy ['epilepsi] MED sara, tutarak

epilog(ue) ['epilog] sonsöz

episcopal [i'piskıpıl] REL piskoposa ait; **~te** [-_pit] piskoposluk

episode ['episıud] olay

epitah ['epitâf] mezar kitabesi

epoch ['îpok] devir, çağ

equal ['îkwıl] adj. eşit, denk; n. eş, emsal; v/t eşit olm. -e; **~ity** [î'kwoliti] eşitlik; **~ize** v/t eşitlemek

equanimity [ekwı'nimiti] ılım, vakar

equat|ion [i'kweyjın] MATH denklem; **~or** GEO ekvator

equilibrium [îkwi'libriım] denge

equip [i'kwip] v/t donatmak; **~ment** teçhizat, donatım

equity ['ekwiti] insaf, adalet

equivalent [i'kwivılınt] n. bedel, karşılık; adj. muadil eşit

(to ~e)

era ['ıırı] devir, çağ

erase [i'reyz] v/t silmek, çizmek

ere [âı] -den önce

erect [i'rekt] v/t dikmek, kurmak; adj. dik, dikili; ~ion dikme, kurma; bina

erosion [i'rıujın] erozyon

erotic [i'rotik] aşka ait; şehvanî

err [3] v/i yanılmak

errand ['erınd] iş, sipariş

erro|neous [i'rıunyıs] yanlış, hatalı; ~r ['erı] hata, yanlışlık

erudition [eru'dişın] âlimlik

erupt [i'rapt] v/i fışkırmak; ~ion fışkırma; MED kızartı

escalat|ion [eskı'leyşın] artış; ~or ['_tı] yürüyen merdiven

escape [is'keyp] n. kaçma; kurtuluş; v/i kaçmak, kurtulmak (from -den)

escort ['eskôt] n. muhafız; maiyet; kavalye; [is'kôt] v/t refakat etm. -e

especial [is'peşıl] özel, mahsus; ~ly adv. özellikle

espionage [espiı'nâj] casusluk

essay ['esey] makale, yazı; deneme

essen|ce ['esns] öz, esas, nitelik; CHEM esans; ~tial [i'senşıl] esaslı; elzem

establish [is'tâbliş] kurmak; ~ oneself yerleşmek; ~ment kurma; kurum; egemen çevreler, ileri gelenler pl.

estate [is'teyt] mal, mülk, arsa; ~ agency emlâk bürosu; ~ car pikap

esteem [is'tîm] n. itibar, saygı; v/t takdir etm.; hürmet etm. -e

estimat|e ['estimit] n. hesap; tahmin; ['estimeyt] v/t tahmin etm.; takdir etm.; ~ion tahmin; itibar; fikir

estrange [is'treync] v/t soğutmak, uzaklaştırmak

estuary ['estyuıri] GEO nehir ağzı

etern|al [i'tınl] ebedî, sonsuz; ezelî, öncesiz; ~ity ebediyet, sonsuzluk

ether ['îthı] eter; esir

ethic|al [i'ethikıl] ahlâkî; ~s pl. ahlâk

Ethiopia [îthi'ıupyı] Habeşistan

ethno|graphy [eth'nogrıfi] etnografya; ~logy [_lıci] etnoloji

eucalyptus [yûkı'liptıs] BOT okaliptüs

eunuch ['yûnık] hadım, harem ağası

Europe ['yuırıp] Avrupa; ~an [_'pıın] Avrupalı

evacuat|e [i'väkyueyt] v/t boşaltmak; ~ion boşaltma, tahliye

evade [i'veyd] v/t sakınmak -den

evaporate [i'väpıreyt] v/t buharlaştırmak; v/i buharlaşmak; ~d milk kondanse süt

evasi|on [i'veyjın] kaçınma; kaçamak; ~ve [_siv] kaça-

maklı
eve [ìv] arife
even [ìvın] *adj.* düz, pürüzsüz; tam; denk; *adv.* hatta, bile, dahi; ~ number çift sayı; ~ if, ~ though olsa bile
evening [ìvnìg] akşam; good ~! iyi akşamlar!
event [ìvent] olay; hal; at all ~s her halde; ~ful olaylarla dolu
eventual [ìvençuıl] sonraki; ~ly *adv.* ilerde
ever [ìevı] daima, her zaman; hiç; for ~ ebediyete kadar; hardly ~ hemen hemen hiç; ~ since *-den* beri; ~lasting sonsuz; devamlı
every [ìevrì] her, her bir; ~ now and then arasıra; ~ other day günaşırı; ~body herkes; ~day her günkü; ~one *s.* ~body; ~thing her şey; ~where her yer(d)e
evidence [ìevidıns] tanıklık, delil; ~t aşikâr, belli, açık
evil [ììvl] fena, kötü; fenalık, kötülük
evoke [ìvuık] *v/t* uyandırmak
evolution [ìvıluìşın] gelişme
ewe [yû] zoo dişi koyun
ex- [eks-] sabık, eski
exact [ìgzäkt] *adj.* tam, doğru; *v/t* icap etm.; talep etm.; ~itude [~ìtyûd] sıhhat, doğruluk; ~ly *adv.* tamamen; aynen; ~ness *s.* ~itude
exaggerate [ìgzäcıreyt] *v/t* mübalâğa etm., abartmak; ~ion mübalâğa

exalt [ìgzôlt] *v/t* yükseltmek; ~ation [egzôlìteyşın] heyecan
examination [ìgzämìineyşın] sınav, imtihan, muayene, yoklama; ~e [~ìzämìn] *v/t* sınavlamak, yoklamak; teftiş etm.
example [ìgzämpl] örnek, misal; for ~ meselâ, örneğin
exasperate [ìgzâspıreyt] *v/t* kızdırmak
excavate [ìekskıveyt] *v/t* kazmak; ~ion kazı
exceed [ìkìsìd] *v/t* aşmak, geçmek; ~ingly *adv.* son derece
excel [ìkìsel] *v/t* geçmek, üstün olm. *-den*; ~lence [ìeksılıns] üstünlük; His (*or* Your) ~lency Ekselans; ~lent mükemmel, çok iyi
except [ìkìsept] *v/t* hariç tutmak; *prp.* *-den* başka; ~ion istisna; ~ional müstesna; olağanüstü
excess [ìkìses] ifrat, aşırılık, fazla; ~ fare bilet ücretine yapılan zam; ~ luggage fazla bagaj; ~ postage taksa
exchange [ìks'çeync] *n.* değişme, trampa; kambiyo; borsa; *v/t* değiştirmek; foreign ~ döviz
exchequer [ìks'çekı] POL devlet hazinesi
excite [ìkìsayt] *v/t* kışkırtmak; heyecanlandırmak; ~ment heyecan; telâş
exclaim [ìks'kleym] *v/i*, *v/t*

bağırmak

exclamation [ekskle'meyşın] ünlem; ~ mark GR ünlem işareti

exclu|de [iks'kluud] v/t hariç tutmak; ~sion [-jın] hariç tutma; ~sive [-siv] has; tek; özel

excommunication ['ekskı-myûni'keyşın] REL aforoz

excursion [ıks'kɜşın] gezinti

excuse [iks'kyûs] n. özür, mazeret; bahane; [-z] v/t affetmek, mazur görmek; ~ me affedersiniz

execut|e ['eksikyût] v/t yapmak; yerine getirmek; idam etm.; ~ion yapma, icra; idam; ~ioner cellât; ~ive [ig'zekyutiv] icra eden; idareci, yetki sahibi; ~or vasiyeti tenfiz memuru

exemplary [ig'zemplıri] örnek verici; ibret verici

exempt [ig'zempt] adj. muaf; v/t muaf tutmak (from -den); ~ion muafiyet

exercise ['eksısayz] n. uygulama; idman; egzersiz, alıştırma; v/t kullanmak; v/i idman yapmak

exert [ig'zɜt] v/t sarfetmek, kullanmak; ~ oneself uğraşmak; ~ion kullanma; çaba

exhale [eks'heyl] v/t koku v.s. çıkarmak

exhaust [ig'zôst] n. TECH egzoz; v/t tüketmek, bitirmek; ~ion bitkinlik; ~-pipe egzoz borusu

exhibit [ig'zibit] v/t teşhir etm., sermek, göstermek; n. JUR delil olarak ibraz edilen şey; ~ion [eksi'bişın] sergi; burs; ~or sergiye katılan kimse

exhumation [eksyû'meyşın] mezardan çıkarma

exile ['eksayl] n. sürgün; v/t sürmek, sürgüne göndermek

exist [ig'zist] var olm.; bulunmak; yaşamak; ~ence varlık; hayat; ~ent mevcut, bulunan

exit ['eksit] çıkış; çıkış yeri; ~ visa çıkış vizesi

exorbitant [ig'zôbitınt] aşırı

exotic [eg'zotik] dıştan gelen

expan|d [iks'pänd] v/t genişletmek, yaymak; v/i yayılmak, açılmak; ~sion yayılma, genişleme; yayma, engin

expect [iks'pekt] v/t beklemek; ummak; ~ation [ekspek'teyşın] bekleme, ümit

expedi|ent [iks'pîdyınt] adj. yararlı, uygun; çare, tedbir; ~tion [ekspi'dişın] acele; sefer; gezi; ~tious süratli

expel [iks'pel] v/t kovmak, çıkarmak

expen|d [iks'pend] v/t sarfetmek, harcamak; ~se [-s] masraf, gider; at the ~se of -in zararına; ~sive masraflı, pahalı

experience [iks'pıırins] n. tecrübe, deneme, görgü; v/t görmek, tecrübe etm.; ~d tecrübeli, görgülü

experiment [iks'perimınt] n. tecrübe, deney; [.ment] v/t tecrübe etm., denemek

expert ['ekspət] usta, mahir; uzman, eksper

expir|ation [ekspayı'reyşn] nefes verme; son; ~e [iks-'payı] nefes vermek; ölmek; sona ermek

expl|ain [iks'pleyn] v/t açıklamak, anlatmak; ~anation [eksplı'neyşın] izah, açıklama

explicit [iks'plisit] açık, kesin

explode [iks'plıud] v/i patlamak; v/t patlatmak

exploit [iks'ployt] v/t sömürmek

explor|ation [eksplö'reyşın] araştırma, keşif; ~e [iks'plö] v/t araştırmak, keşfetmek; ~er kâşif, bulucu

explosi|on [iks'plıujın] patlama; ~ve [.siv] patlayıcı (madde)

export ['ekspôt] n. ECON ihraç malı; ihracat; [.'pôt] v/t ihraç etm.; ~ation ihraç; ~er ihracatçı

expose [iks'pıuz] v/t açığa vurmak; maruz bırakmak; teşhir etm.; ~ition [ekspıu-'zişin] sergi; ~ure [iks'pıuji] maruz olma; açığa vurma; PHOT poz; ~ure meter PHOT ışıkölçer, pozometre

express [iks'pres] adj. açık, sarih; süratli, hızlı; n. ekspres; v/t ifade etm.; ~ train

ekspres treni; ~ion ifade, deyim; ~ive anlamlı; etkileyici; ~way Am. otoyol

expropriation [ekspriu-pri'eyşn] kamulaştırma

expulsion [iks'palşın] kovma, çıkarma

exquisite ['ekskwizit] ince, seçkin

extant [eks'tänt] hâlâ mevcut

exten|d [iks'tend] uzatmak, genişletmek, yaymak; v/t uzanmak, büyümek; ~sion uzatma; uzanma; ek; munzam telefon; ~sive geniş; şümullü; ~t derece, had; büyüklük; mesafe; **to a certain** ~t bir dereceye kadar

exterior [eks'tiıriı] dış taraf; dış; zâhirî

exterminat|e [eks'tǝmineyt] v/t imha etm.

external [eks'tǝnl] dış, zâhirî

extinct [iks'tinkt] sönmüş; nesli tükenmiş

extinguish [iks'tiŋgwiş] söndürmek; ~er yangın söndürme aleti

extirpate [iks'tǝspeyt] v/t imha etm., yok etm.

extortion [iks'tôşın] zorla alma, şantaj

extra ['ekstrı] fazla; ekstra; ilâve, ek, zam

extract ['eksträkt] n. özet; esans; [iks'-] v/t çıkarmak; koparmak; ~ion çıkarma; nesil, soy

extraordinary [iks'trôdnri] olağanüstü; garip

extravagan|ce [iks'trävigıns] israf; aşırılık; ~t tutumsuz; aşırı

extreme [iks'trîm] son derece; son; aşırı, müfrit; ~ist aşırı giden kimse; ~ity [~emiti] uç; son; sınır; aşırı tehlike; *pl.* ANAT eller, ayaklar

extricate ['ekstrikeyt] *v/t* kurtarmak

exuberant [ig'zyûbırınt] coş-

kun; bol

exult [ig'zalt] çok sevinmek (**at** *-e*)

eye [ay] *n.* göz; delik, ilik; budak; *v/t* göz atmak *-e*; ~ball göz küresi; ~brow kaş; (a **pair of**) ~glasses gözlük; ~lash kirpik; ~lid göz kapağı; ~shot görüş mesafesi; ~sight görme kuvveti; ~witness JUR görgü tanığı

F

fable ['feybl] masal, efsane

fabric ['fäbrik] yapı; kumaş; ~ate ['~eyt] *v/t* yapmak, uydurmak

fabulous ['fäbyulıs] efsanevî; inanılmaz

face [feys] *n.* yüz, çehre; yüzey; kadran, mine; yüzsüzlük; *v/t* karşılamak; *-in* karşısında olm.; *-in* kenarını çevirmek; **make** ~**s** yüzünü gözünü oynatmak; ~ **value** itibarî değer

facilit|ate [fı'siliteyt] *v/t* kolaylaştırmak; ~**y** kolaylık; *pl.* imkânlar, tesisat

fact [fäkt] gerçek; durum; **in** ~ gerçekten

faction ['fäkşın] grup; ihtilâf

factor ['fäktı] âmil, sebep; ~**y** fabrika, imalâthane

faculty ['fäkılti] yetenek; güç; fakülte

fade [feyd] solmak, rengi uçmak

fag(g)ot ['fägıt] çalı demeti

fail [feyl] *v/i* başaramamak (**in** *-i*); yapamamak; zayıflamak; iflâs etm.; *v/t* bırakmak; **without** ~ mutlaka, elbette; ~**ure** [~yı] başarısızlık; iflâs; başarı kazanamıyan insan

faint [feynt] *adj.* baygın, zayıf; *v/i* bayılmak

fair[1] [fäı] ECON panayır, fuar

fair[2] insaflı, doğru; haklı; güzel; sarışın; şöyle böyle; ~ **copy** temiz kopya; ~ **play** temiz oyun; tarafsızlık; ~**ly** *adv.* oldukça; ~**ness** dürüstlük; güzellik

fairy ['fäıri] peri; ~**tale** peri masalı; yalan

faith [feyth] itikat, inanç; güven; vefa; sadakat; ~**ful** vefalı, sadık; ~**less** vefasız

fake [feyk] *n.* taklit; uydurma; şarlatan; *v/t* uydurmak

falcon ['fôlkın] ZOO doğan, şahin

fenc|e [fens] n. çit, parmaklık, tahta perde; v/t -in etrafını parmaklıkla çevirmek; v/i eskrim yapmak; ~ing çit; eskrim

fend [fend]: ~ for geçindirmek -i; ~ off v/t kovmak; ~er çamurluk

ferment ['fɜment] n. mayalanma; maya; [fə'-] v/t mayalamak; v/i mayalanmak; ~ation mayalanma

fern [fɜn] BOT eğreltiotu

ferocious [fɪ'rıuʃıs] yırtıcı, vahşi

ferry ['feri] n. NAUT feribot, araba vapuru; v/t -in nehirden geçirmek; ~boat feribot

fertil|e ['fɜtayl] bereketli, verimli; ~ity [-'tiliti] verimlilik; ~ize ['-ilayz] v/t gübrelemek; verimli hale getirmek; ~izer gübre

fervent ['fɜvınt] hararetli, ateşli

festival ['festivıl] bayram, festival; ~e [-.iv] şen, neşeli; ~ity [-'tiviti] şenlik, eğlenti

fetch [feç] v/t gidip getirmek

fetter ['fetı] zincir, köstek

feud¹ [fyûd] kan davası

feud² [fyûd] tımar, zeamet; ~al ['-dl] derebeyliğe ait; ~alism ['-dılızım] derebeylik

fever ['fîvı] ateş, humma; ~ish hararetli, ateşli

few [fyû] az; a ~ birkaç; quite a ~ birçok

fez [fez] fes

fiancé(e) [fi'ânsey] nişanlı

fib|re, Am. ~er ['faybı] lif, tel; ~rous lifli, telli

fickle ['fikl] kararsız

fiction ['fikʃın] roman; roman edebiyatı; hayal; yalan; ~tious [-'tiʃıs] hayalî, uydurma

fiddle ['fidl] n. keman; v/i keman çalmak

fidelity [fi'deliti] vefa

fidget ['ficit] v/t rahat oturamamak; v/i yerinde durmıyan

field [fîld] tarla, kır; alan, meydan; ~ events pl. atlama ve atma yarışları; ~glasses pl. çifte dürbün sg.; ~-marshal MIL mareşal

fiend [fînd] iblis, şeytan; fig. tiryaki

fierce [fîıs] vahşî, azgın

fiery ['fayırı] ateşli, alevli

fife [fayf] MUS fifre

fift|een ['fif'tîn] on beş; ~y elli

fig [fig] BOT incir

fight [fayt] n. dövüş, kavga; savaş; v/i savaşmak; dövüşmek; v/t defetmek; yapmak; ~er savaşçı; AVIA avcı uçağı

figurative ['figyurıtiv] mecazî

figure ['figı] n. şekil, endam, boy bos; şahsiyet; rakam; mecaz; v/t desenlerle süslemek; temsil etm.; tasavvur etm.; ~ out v/t hesaplamak

filament ['filımınt] tel, lif

file¹ [fayl] n. TECH eğe; v/t eğelemek

file² n. dizi; dosya, klasör; v/t

dosyaya koymak, tasnif etm.; *dilekçe v.s.* vermek

filigree ['filigri] telkâri

fill [fil] *v/i* dolmak, kabarmak; *v/t* doldurmak; işgal etm.; ~ **in** *soru kâğıdını* doldurmak; ~ **up** *v/t* tamamen doldurmak

fillet ['filit] fileto; dilim

filling ['filiŋ] doldurma; dolgu; ~ **station** benzin istasyonu

film [film] *n.* zar; film; *v/t* filme geçirmek; zarla kaplamak

filter ['filtı] *n.* süzgeç; *v/t* süzmek; *v/i* sızmak

filth [fildh] kir, pislik; ~**y** kirli, pis

fin [fin] zoo yüzgeç

final ['faynl] son; kesin; final, son yarış; ~**ly** *adv.* nihayet, sonunda

financ|e [fay'näns] *n.* maliye; *v/t -in* masraflarını karşılamak; ~**ial** [-ʃl] malî; ~**ier** [-sıı] sermayedar

finch [finç] zoo ispinoz

find [faynd] *n.* bulunmuş şey; keşif; *v/t* bulmak; öğrenmek; rastlamak *-e*; ~ **out** keşfetmek; öğrenmek; ~**ing** bulunan şey; *pl.* sonuç

fine[1] [fayn] *n.* JUR para cezası; *v/t* para cezasına mahkûm etm.

fine[2] ince; güzel, zarif; hoş, nazik; **I am** ~ iyiyim; ~**ry** gösteriş, süslü giyim

finger ['fiŋgı] parmak; ~**nail**

tırnak; ~**print** parmak izi

finish ['finiş] *n.* son; son iş, rötuş; *v/t* bitirmek, tamamlamak; *v/i* bitmek, sona ermek

Finland ['finlınd] Finlandiya

Finn(ish) [fin(iş)] Finlandiyalı

fir [fʒ] BOT köknar; ~**cone** köknar kozalağı

fire ['fayı] *n.* ateş, yangın; *v/t* tutuşturmak, yakmak; patlatmak; işinden çıkarmak; **cease** ~ ateş kesmek; **on** ~ tutuşmuş, yanan; ~**alarm** yangın işareti; ~**brigade**, *Am.* ~ **department** itfaiye; ~**engine** yangın tulumbası; ~**escape** yangın merdiveni; ~**extinguisher** yangın söndürme aleti; ~**man** itfaiyeci; ateşçi; ~**place** ocak, şömine; ~**proof** ateşe dayanır, yanmaz; ~**side** ocak başı; ~**wood** odun; ~**works** *pl.* donanma fişekleri

firm [fʒm] sabit, metin, bükülmez; ECON firma; ~**ness** sağlamlık, metanet

first [fʒst] birinci, ilk; *adv.* önce, ilkin; **at** ~ ilk önce; ~ **aid** ilk yardım; ~ **floor** birinci kat; *Am.* zemin kat; ~**aid box** ilk yardım kutusu; ~**class** birinci sınıfa ait; ~**rate** birinci sınıf, en iyi cinsten

fiscal ['fiskıl] malî

fish [fiş] *n.* balık; *v/i* balık tutmak; ~**bone** kılçık

fisher|man ['fişımın] balıkçı; ~**y** balıkçılık

fishing ['fişiŋ] balık avı; ~line olta; ~rod olta kamışı; ~tackle balıkçı takımı

fishmonger ['fişmaŋgı] balıkçı; balık satan

fissure ['fişı] yarık, çatlak

fist [fist] yumruk

fistula [fistyulı] MED fistül

fit [fit] n. tutarak, hastalık nöbeti; adj. uygun, yaraşır; lâyık; hazır; v/i uymak, yakışmak; v/t yerleştirmek; donatmak; ~ on v/t takmak, prova etm.; ~ out v/t donatmak; ~ness uygunluk; sağlık; ~ter boru işlerine bakan kimse; ~ting uygun; prova; pl. tertibat

five [fayv] beş; ~fold beş misli, beş kat

fix [fiks] v/t takmak; yerleştirmek; hazırlamak; tamir etm.; gözlerini dikmek (on -e); n. güç durum; ~ up v/t kurmak, düzeltmek; ~ed sabit; bağlı; ~tures ['-çız] pl. demirbaş eşya

fizz [fiz] v/i fışırdamak

flabbergast ['fläbıgaast] v/t şaşırtmak

flabby ['fläbi] gevşek

flag [fläg] n. bayrak, bandıra; kaldırım taşı; BOT süsen, susam; v/t bayraklarla donatmak

flail [fleyl] harman döveni

flake [fleyk] n. kuşbaşı, lapa; ince tabaka; ~ off v/i tabaka tabaka ayrılmak

flame [fleym] n. alev; v/i alevlenmek

flank [fläŋk] n. böğür; yan; v/t yandan kuşatmak; bitişik olm. -e

flannel ['flänl] fanila

flap [fläp] n. sarkık parça, kapak; vuruş; v/i kanatlarını çırpmak; v/t hafifçe vurmak -e

flare [flä] v/i alevlenmek; fig. birden hiddetlenmek

flash [fläş] ışıltı, parıltı; fig. an; bülten; v/i parlamak; birden gelmek; v/t (radyo ile) yayımlamak; ~bulb PHOT flaş ampulü; ~light PHOT flaş; cep feneri

flask [flâsk] küçük şişe; termos

flat [flät] düz, yassı; tatsız, yavan; MUS bemol; yüzey; apartman dairesi; ~iron ütü; ~ten v/t yassılatmak; v/i yassılaşmak

flatter ['flätı] v/t pohpohlamak, göklere çıkarmak; ~y dalkavukluk

flavo(u)r ['fleyvı] n. tat, lezzet, çeşni; v/t tat vermek -e; lezzet vermek -e

flaw [flô] çatlak, yarık; noksan, kusur; ~less kusursuz

flax [fläks] BOT keten

flea [flî] pire

fled [fled] s. flee

flee [flî] kaçmak

fleece [flîs] n. yapak, yünlü post; v/t aldatmak, kazıklamak

fleet [flît] NAUT donanma, filo;

süratli, hızlı

flesh [fleş] et; vücut, ten; ~y etli, şişman

flew [fluu] s. fly

flexible ['fleksıbl] bükülebilir; uysal

flick [flik] v/t hafifçe vurmak -e

flicker ['flikı] v/i titremek, oynamak

flight [flayt] uçma, uçuş; firar, kaçış; sıra

flimsy ['flimzi] ince, gevşek

flinch [flinç] v/i sakınmak, kaçınmak

fling [fliŋ] n. fırlatma, atma; v/t atmak, fırlatmak

flint [flint] çakmak taşı

flip [flip] n. fiske; v/i fiske vurmak

flippant ['flipınt] küstah

flipper ['flipı] balık kanadı

flirt [flöt] v/i flört yapmak; ~ation flört

flit [flit] v/i geçmek; çırpınmak

float [fluut] n. duba, şamandıra; olta mantarı; v/t yüzdürmek; v/i yüzmek, suyun yüzünde durmak; ~ing yüzen; değişen

flock [flok] n. sürü; yün veya saç yumağı; v/i toplanmak

floe [flu] buz kitlesi

flog [flog] kamçılamak; dövmek

flood [flad] n. sel, seylâp; met, kabarma; v/t taşmak; su basmak; ~gate bent kapağı; ~light projektör; ~tide

met, kabarma

floor [flô] n. döşeme; zemin; kat; v/t tahta veya parke döşemek -e; yere yıkmak -i; ~lamp ayaklı lâmba

flop [flop] v/i çöküvermek; v/t düşürmek

florist ['florist] çiçekçi

flour ['flaui] un

flourish ['flariş] v/t sallamak; v/i gelişmek, bayındır olm.; n. gösterişli hareket; paraf

flow [flu] n. cereyan, akıntı; met, kabarma; v/i akmak; kabarmak

flower ['flaui] çiçek; ~pot saksı

flown [flun] s. fly

flu [fluu] grip

fluctuate ['flaktyueyt] v/i değişmek; ~ion değişme

fluent ['fluint] akıcı (söz)

fluff [flaf] tüy, hav; ~y tüy gibi yumuşak

fluid ['fluid] akıcı; sıvı madde

flung [flaŋ] s. fling

flunk [flaŋk] v/t sınavda bırakmak; v/i başaramamak

flurry ['flari] anî rüzgâr; sağanak; telaş; v/t telaşa düşürmek

flush [flaş] birden akmak; (face) kızarmak; v/t akıtmak; kızartmak; n. galeyan; akıtma

fluster ['flastı] n. telaş; v/t telaşa düşürmek

flute [fluut] MUS flavta, flüt

flutter ['flatı] v/i çırpınmak; n. çırpınma; telaş

flux [flaks] akış; değişiklik

fly¹ [flay] sinek

fly² v/i uçmak; kaçmak; v/t uçurmak; ~ **into a rage** öfkelenmek; ~**er** pilot; ~**ing** uçma; uçan; ~**over** üstgeçit; ~**weight** sinekağırlık

foal [foul] zoo tay, sıpa

foam [fıum] n. köpük; v/i köpürmek; ~**y** köpüklü

focus ['fıukıs] n. odak, mihrak; v/t ayar etm.

fodder ['fodı] yem

foe [fıu] düşman

fog [fog] sis; ~**gy** sisli, dumanlı

foil¹ [foyl] foya, ince yaprak

foil² v/t engellemek

fold¹ [fuld] ağıl; sürü

fold² kat, kıvrım; v/t katlamak; **elleri** kavuşturmak; ~**er** dosya; ~**ing-chair** açılır kapanır sandalye

foliage ['fıuliic] ağaç yaprakları pl.

folk [fıuk] halk, ahali; pl. **fam.** aile; ~**lore** folklor

follow ['folıu] v/t takip etm., izlemek; riayet etm. -e; ~**er** taraftar

folly ['foli] ahmaklık

fond [fond] seven **(of** -i); düşkün (-e); ~**le** v/t okşamak

food [fuud] yiyecek, yemek, gıda; yem; ~**stuffs** pl. gıda maddeleri

fool [fuul] n. budala, enayi; v/t aldatmak; ~**hardy** delice cesur; ~**ish** sersem, akılsız; ~**proof** sağlam; kusursuz

foot [fut] pl. **feet** [fiit] ayak; kadem (30,48 cm); **on** ~ yaya; ~**ball** futbol; ~**hills** pl. dağ eteklerindeki tepeler; ~**hold** ayak basacak yer; ~**ing** ayak basacak yer; durum, hal; ~**note** dipnot; ~**path** keçi yolu, patika; ~**print** ayak izi; ~**step** ayak sesi; ayak izi

for [fô, fı] prep; için; olarak; zarfında; -**den** beri; yerine; yüzünden; **conj.** zira, çünkü; ~ **example**, ~ **instance** mesela, örneğin

foray ['forey] çapul

forbade [fı'bäd] s. **forbid**

forbid [fı'bid] v/t yasak etm.; ~**den** s. **forbid**; yasak; ~**ding** nahoş

forbo(r)e, ~**ne** [fô'bô, ~n] s. **forbear**

force [fôs] n. kuvvet, kudret; şiddet, zor; v/t zorlamak; sıkıştırmak; kırıp açmak; **armed** ~**s** pl. silahlı kuvvetler; **in** ~ yürürlükte; ~**d** mecburi

ford [fôd] n. nehir geçidi, sığ geçit; v/t sığ yerden geçmek

fore [fô] ön, ön taraf; ~**boding** [-'bıudiŋ] önsezi; ~**cast** n. tahmin; v/t önceden tahmin etm.; ~**finger** işaretparmağı; ~**ground** ön plan; ~**head** ['forid] alın

foreign ['forin] ecnebi, yabancı; dış; ~ **currency** ECON döviz; ~ **exchange** kambiyo; **♀ Office** Dışişleri Bakanlığı; ~ **trade** dış ticaret; ~**er** ecnebi, yabancı

fore|leg önayak; **~man** JUR jüri başkanı; işçi başı; **~most** en önde; ilk önce; **~ noon** öğleden önceki zaman; v/t **~see** önceden görmek; **~sight** basiret, önceden görme

forest ['forist] orman; **~ry** ormancılık

fore|taste önceden alınan tat; **~tell** önceden haber vermek (sth. hakkında)

forever [fı'revı] devamlı olarak

foreword önsöz

forfeit ['fôfit] n. ceza; v/t kaybetmek

forge [fôc] n. demirci ocağı; v/t demiri işlemek; uydurmak; **~ry** sahte şey; kalpazanlık

forget [fı'get] v/t unutmak; **~ful** unutkan; **~menot** BOT unutma beni

forgive [fı'giv] v/t affetmek, bağışlamak; **~ness** af, bağışlama

forgot [fı'got, _n.] s. **forget**

fork [fôk] n. çatal; bel; v/i çatallaşmak

forlorn [fı'lôn] kimsesiz; ümitsiz

form [fôm] n. şekil, biçim; kâğıt, formül; form; forma; sınıf (school); v/t teşkil etm., kurmak; şekil vermek -e; v/i şekil almak

formal ['fômıl] biçimsel; res-

mî; **~ity** [_'äliti] usul; formalite

formation [fô'meyşın] teşkil, kurma

former ['fômı] önceki, eski, sabık; **~ly** adv. eskiden

formidable ['fômidıbl] heybetli, korkulur

formula ['fômyulı] formül; reçete

formulate ['fômyuleyt] v/t açık olarak belirtmek

for|sake [fı'seyk] v/t terketmek; vazgeçmek -den; **~saken, ~sook** [fı'suk] s. **~sake**

fort [fôt] kale

forth [fôth] ileri, dışarı, açığa; sonra; **~coming** gelecek, çıkacak; **~right** açık; **~with** derhal, hemen

forti|fication [fôtifi'keyşın] tahkim, istihkâm; **~fy** ['_fay] v/t kuvvetlendirmek

fortnight ['fôtnayt] iki hafta

fortress ['fôtris] kale

fortunate ['fôçnit] talihli, şanslı; **~ly** adv. hamdolsun, çok şükür

fortune ['fôçın] baht; fal; ECON servet; **~teller** falcı

forty ['fôti] kırk

forward ['fôwıd] adv. ileri (-ye); adj. önde, ilerdeki; küstah; v/t sevketmek, göndermek (to -e)

foster ['fostı] v/t beslemek; **~child** evlâtlık; **~mother** analık

foul [faul] adj. pis, kirli; bozuk; iğrenç; v/t kirletmek;

found 280

dolaştırmak

found¹ [faund] *s.* find

found² *v/t* kurmak; TECH dökmek; ~**ation** kurma, tesis; kuruluş; temel; ~er kurucu; dökmeci; ~**ling** sokakta bulunmuş çocuk, buluntu; ~ry TECH dökümhane

fountain ['fauntın] çeşme; memba; fıskiye; ~-**pen** dolma kalem

four [fô] dört; ~**score** seksen; ~**teen** ['_'tîn] on dört

fowl [faul] tavuk; kuş; ~**ing** piece av tüfeği

fox [foks] zoo tilki

fract|ion ['fräkşın] kır(ıl)ma; parça; MATH kesir; ~**ure** ['_çı] *n.* kırma; kırık; *v/t* kırmak

fragile ['fräcayl] kolay kırılır

fragment ['frägment] kırılmış parça, kısım

fragran|ce ['freygrıns] güzel koku; ~t güzel kokulu

frail [freyl] zayıf, narin; ~ty zayıflık

frame [freym] *n.* çerçeve, gergef; beden, yapı; *v/t* şekil vermek *-e*, uydurmak *-i*; çerçevelemek *-i*; ~ of mind mizaç, hal; ~**work** çatı, iskelet

France [frâns] Fransa

franchise ['fränçayz] POL oy verme hakkı

frank [fränk] açık sözlü, samimî

frankfurter ['fränkfıtı] *bir çeşit* sosis

frankness ['fränknis] açık

sözlülük

frantic ['fräntik] çılgınca heyecanlanmış

fratern|al [frı'tsnl] kardeşçe; ~**ity** kardeşlik

fraud [frôd] hile, dolandırıcılık

fray [frey] *v/t* yıpratmak; *v/i* yıpranmak

freak [frîk] kapris; eksantrik kimse

freckle ['frekl] çil

free [frî] *adj.* serbest; parasız; muaf; cömert; *v/t* serbest bırakmak, kurtarmak; tahliye etm.; **set** ~ *v/t* serbest bırakmak; ~**dom** hürriyet, serbestlik; açıklık; ~**mason** mason; ~**way** *Am.* çevre yolu

freez|e [frîz] *v/i* donmak; *v/t* dondurmak; ~**ing-point** donma noktası

freight [freyt] *n.* hamule, navlun; *v/t* yükletmek; ~**er** NAUT yük vapuru, şilep

French [frenç] Fransız; Fransızca; ~ **window** balkona *v.s.* giden camlı kapı; ~**man** Fransız

frenzy ['frenzi] çılgınlık

frequen|cy ['frîkwınsi] sık sık olma; PHYS frekans; ~t *adj.* sık sık olan; [fri'kwent] *v/t* sık sık gitmek *-e*

fresh [freş] taze; yeni; dinç; acemi; ~**man** üniversitenin birinci sınıf öğrencisi; ~**ness** tazelik; acemilik; ~**water** tatlı suda olan

fret [fret] *v/t* rahatsız etm.; *v/i*

kızmak

friar ['frayı] rahip

friction ['friksın] sürtünme; friksiyon; *fig.* uyuşmazlık

Friday ['fraydi] cuma (günü)

fridge [fric] buzdolabı

fried [frayd] kızartılmış

friend [frend] dost, arkadaş, ahbap; ~ly dostça, samimi; ~ship dostluk, arkadaşlık

fright [frayt] dehşet, korku; ~en *v/t* korkutmak, ürkütmek; ~ful korkunç

frigid ['fricid] soğuk, buzlu

frill [fril] fırfır, farbala

fringe [frinc] saçak; kenar

frisk [frisk] sıçramak, oynamak; ~y neşeli, oynak

fro [frıu]: to and ~ öteye beriye

frock [frok] kadın elbisesi, rop; REL rahip cüppesi

frog [frog] zoo kurbağa

frolic ['frolik] *n.* neşe; *v/i* oynamak; ~some ['-sım] oynak, neşeli

from [from, frım] -den, -dan; -den itibaren

front [frant] ön, yüz; cephe; in ~ of -*in* önünde; ~ door ön kapı; ~ page ön sayfa; ~ wheel ön tekerlek

frontier ['frantiı] sınır

frost [frost] *n.* don, ayaz, kırağı; *v/t* dondurmak; ~bitten donmuş; ~ed glass buzlu cam; ~y ayazlı; soğuk

froth [froth] *n.* köpük; *v/i* köpürmek

frown [fraun] *v/i* kaşlarını çat-

mak; hoş görmemek (upon -*i*)

froze, ~n [friuz, _n] *s.* freeze; ~n meat dondurulmuş et

frugal ['fruugıl] tutumlu, idareli

fruit [fruut] meyva, yemiş; *fig.* verim, sonuç; ~erer manav, yemişçi; ~ful verimli; ~less verimsiz; faydasız

frustrat|e ['fras'treyt] *v/t* önlemek, bozmak; hüsrana uğratmak; ~ion önleme; hüsran

fry [fray] *v/t* tavada kızartmak; *v/i* kızarmak; ~-ing-pan tava

fuchsia ['fyûşi] BOT küpe çiçeği

fuel [fyuıl] yakacak, yakıt

fugitive ['fyûcitiv] kaçak, mülteci

fulfil [ful'fil] *v/t* yerine getirmek, yapmak; bitirmek; ~ment icra, yapma

full [ful] dolu; dolgun; olgun; tam, bütün; tok; ~ moon dolunay; ~ stop GR nokta

ful(l)ness ['fulnis] dolgunluk; olgunluk

full-time tam günlük

fumble ['fambl] *v/i* el yordamıyla aramak (for -*i*)

fume [fyûm] *n.* duman, buhar; *v/t* tütsülemek; *v/i* hiddetlenmek

fun [fan] eğlence; şaka, alay; for ~ şakadan; make ~ alay etm. (of ile)

function ['fankşın] *n.* görev.

tören, merasim; MATH fonksiyon; v/i işlemek, iş görmek; ~ary görevli

fund [fʌnd] kapital, stok; fon

fundamental [fʌndɪ'mentl] esaslı; önemli

funeral ['fyûnɪrɪl] cenaze alayı, gömme

funicular (railway) [fyu'nikyulı] füniküler, kablolu demiryolu

funnel ['fanl] baca; huni; boru

funny ['fani] eğlenceli; tuhaf, acayip

fur [fɜ] kürk, post; pas, kir

furious ['fyuɪrıs] öfkeli; şiddetli

furl [fʌl] v/t sarmak

furnace ['fɜnis] ocak

furnish ['fɜniş] v/t döşemek, teçhiz etm. ~ed möbleli, mobilyalı

furniture ['fɜnıçı] mobilya

furrier ['farı] kürkçü

furrow ['faru] sapan izi; tekerlek izi; v/t sabanla açmak

further ['fɜdhı] adj. daha fazla, daha öte, yeni; adv. ayrıca; v/t ilerletmek; ~more bundan başka, ayrıca

furtive ['fɜtiv] sinsi, gizli

fury ['fyuıri] kızgınlık; şiddet

fuse [fyûz] n. MIL tapa; EL sigorta; v/t eritmek; v/i erimek

fuselage ['fyûzilâj] AVIA gövde

fusion ['fyûjın] eri(t)me; birleşme

fuss [fas] n. telâş; v/i meraklanmak, sızlanmak; make a ~ about mesele yapmak -i

futile ['fyûtayl] beyhude, boş

future ['fyûçı] gelecek; gelecekteki

G

gab [gäb] palavra; gift of ~ konuşkanlık

gable ['geybl] çatı altındaki üç köşeli duvar

gad-fly ['gädflay] ZOO atsineği

gadget ['gäcit] hünerli alet, cihaz

gag [gäg] ağız tıkacı; şaka

gage [geyc] s. gauge

gaiety ['geyıti] neşe, şenlik; ~ly s. gay

gain [geyn] n. kâr, kazanç; yarar; artış; v/t kazanmak; var-

mak -e; ~say v/t inkâr etm.

gait [geyt] yürüyüş, gidiş; ~er tozluk, getir

galaxy ['gälıksi] ASTR gökada; samanyolu

gale [geyl] bora, fırtına

gall [gôl] ANAT safra

gallant ['gälınt] cesur; gösterişli; nazik, kibar

gallery ['gälıri] galeri; üstü kapalı balkon

galley ['gäli] NAUT kadırga; gemi mutfağı

gallon ['gälın] galon (4,54 l,

Am. 3,78 l)

gallop ['gälıp] *n.* dörtnala gidiş; *v/i* dörtnala koşmak

gallows ['gäluz] darağacı

gamble ['gämbl] *n.* kumar; *v/i* kumar oynamak; **~ing-house** kumarhane

gambol ['gämbl] *n.* sıçrama; *v/i* sıçrayıp oynamak

game [geym] oyun, parti; av; **~keeper** avlak bekçisi

gander ['gändı] zoo erkek kaz

gang [gäŋ] güruh, takım, ekip; **~ster** ['~stı] gangster

gangway ['gäŋwey] geçit; NAUT iskele tahtası

gaol [ceyl] *n.* cezaevi; *v/t* tutuklamak; **~er** gardiyan

gap [gäp] yarık, aralık, boşluk; eksiklik

gape [geyp] *v/i* esnemek; hayretten ağzı açık kalmak; açık olm.

garage ['gäräj] *n.* garaj; *v/t* garaja koymak

garbage ['gäabic] süprüntü; çöp

garden ['gaadn] bahçe; **~er** bahçıvan

gargle ['gaagl] *v/t* gargara etm.

garland ['gaalınd] çelenk

garlic ['gaalik] BOT sarmısak

garment ['gaamınt] elbise, giysi

garnet ['gaanit] lâl taşı

garnish ['gaaniş] *v/t* süslemek

garret ['gärıt] çatı arası

garrison ['gärisn] MIL garnizon

garrulous ['gärulıs] geveze

garter ['gaatı] çorap bağı; **Order of the** ♀ Dizbağı nişanı

gas [gäs] gaz, havagazı; *Am.* benzin; **~-burner** havagazı memesi

gash [gäş] uzunca bıçak *v.s.* yarası

gasket ['gäskit] TECH conta

gasoline ['gäsılîn] *Am.* benzin

gasp [gaasp] *n.* soluma; *v/i* solumak, soluyarak konuşmak

gate [geyt] kapı; su yolu kapağı; **~way** giriş yeri, kapı

gather ['gädhı] *v/t* toplamak; anlamak, kavramak; *v/i* toplanmak; çoğalmak; **~ speed** hızlanmak; **~ing** toplantı

gaudy ['gôdi] zevksizce süslenmiş

gauge [geyc] *n.* ölçü, ayar; çap; *v/t* ayar etm.

gaunt [gônt] zayıf; kasvetli

gauze [gôz] gaz, tül

gave [geyv] *s.* give

gay [gey] neşeli, şen; zevk düşkünü; parlak (*renk*); **~ly** neşe ile

gaze [geyz] dik dik bakmak (**at** *-e*)

gazelle [gı'zel] zoo ceylan

gear [gıa] eşya, giyim; TECH dişli takımı; şanjman; vites; **~change** şanjman; **~lever, ~shift** vites kolu

gem [cem] kıymetli taş

gender ['cendı] GR cins

gene ['cîn] biyoloji: gen

general ['cenırıl] MIL general; genel; ~ize v/t genelleştirmek; ~ly adv. genellikle

generate ['cenıreyt] v/t husule getirmek, doğurmak; ~ion nesil, döl; meydana getirme; ~or EL jeneratör, dinamo

generosity [cenı'rositi] cömertlik, âlicenaplık; ~ous cömert, eli açık

genetic [cîn'ätik] bir şeyin aslına ait; genetiğe ait, genetik; ~ engineering genetik mühendisliği; ~ fingerprinting suçluların bulunması ya da hastalıkların önlenmesi için bir kimsenin genetik kimliğinin saptanması; ~ally engineered genetik mühendisliği yoluyla elde edilmiş; ~ally modified genetik olarak değiştirilmiş GM

Geneva [ci'nîvı] Cenevre

genial ['cînyıl] güleryüzlü, hoş

genitive (case) ['cenitiv] GR -in hali, tamlayan

genius ['cînyıs] deha; dâhi; cin, ruh

Genoa ['cenıuı] Cenova

gentle ['centl] nazik; yumuşak; kibar; ~man centilmen; ~manlike centilmence; ~ness kibarlık, nezaket

gentry ['centri] küçük derebeylik sınıfı

genuine ['cenyuin] sahih,

taklit olmıyan

geography [ci'ogrıfi] coğrafya; ~logy [.'olıci] jeoloji; ~metry [.'omitri] geometri

Georgia [ci'ôcı] Kafkasya'da Gürcüstan; A.B.D. de Georgia devleti

germ [cɜm] mikrop; tohum

German ['cɜmın] Alman; Almanca; ~y Almanya

germinate [cɜnimeyt] v/i filizlenmek

gerund ['cerınd] GR ulaç, gerundium

gesture ['cɜscı] hareket, jest

get [get] v/t elde etm., almak, sağlamak, kazanmak; yakalamak; anlamak, kavramak; yaptırmak; ~ about v/i yayılmak; dolaşmak; ~ along ilerlemek; geçinmek (with ile); ~ away kurtulmak, kaçmak; ~ in içeri girmek; ~ off inmek; kurtulmak; ~ out dışarı çıkmak; ~ to varmak -e; başlamak -e; ~ to know v/t tanımak; have got to inf. -meğe mecbur olm.; ~ together bir araya gelmek; ~ up kalkmak

geyser ['gayzı] GEO gayzer

ghastly ['gaastli] korkunç; ölü gibi

ghost [gust] hayalet, hortlak; Holy ~ REL Ruhulkudüs

giant ['cayınt] dev; dev gibi iri

gibbit ['cibit] darağacı

gibe [cayb] v/i alay etm (with ile)

giblets ['ciblıts] pl. tavuk sakatatı

giddy ['gidi] başı dönmüş; hoppa

gift [gift] hediye, armağan; Allah vergisi, hüner; ~ **card** hediye çeki; ~ed hünerli

gigantic [cay'gäntik] kocaman

giggle ['gigl] v/i kıkır kıkır gülmek

gild [gild] v/t yaldızlamak

gill [gil] zoo solungaç

gilt [gilt] s. gild; yaldız

gin ['cin] cin, ardıç, rakısı

ginger ['cıncı] BOT zencefil; sl. canlılık; ~bread zencefil pastası; ~ly ihtiyatla, dikkatle

gipsy ['cipsi] Çingene

giraffe [ci'râf] zoo zürafa

gird [gзd] v/t sarmak, kuşatmak

girder ['gзdı] kiriş; direk

girdle ['gзdl] kemer; kuşak; korsa

girl [gзl] kız; sevgili; ~hood kızlık çağı; ~ish genç kız gibi

girt [gзt] s. gird

girth [gзth] kolan, çevre

give [giv] v/t vermek, bağışlamak; ~ **away** v/t vermek; açığa vurmak; ~ **in** v/i vazgeçmek; ~ **rise** sebebiyet vermek (to -e); ~ **up** v/t terketmek; teslim etm.; vazgeçmek -den; ~ **way** çekilmek; çökmek; ~n s. give; düşkün (to -e)

glacier ['gläsyı] GEO buzul

glad [gläd] memnun (of -den); ~ness memnunluk, sevinç

glam|orous ['glämırıs] göz alıcı; ~o(u)r parlaklık; cazibe

glance [glâns] n. bakış; göz atma; parıltı; v/i bakmak, göz atmak (at -e)

gland [gländ] ANAT bez, gudde

glare [gläı] n. kamaştırıcı ışık; dargın bakış; v/i parıldamak; ters ters bakmak (at -e)

glass [glâs] cam; bardak; ayna; dürbün; pl. gözlük; ~y cam gibi

glaz|e [gleyz] n. sır, cilâ; v/t cilâlamak; cam geçirmek -e; ~ier camcı

gleam [glîm] n. parıltı; v/i parıldamak

glee [glî] neşe; birkaç sesle söylenen şarkı

glen [glen] vadi, dere

glib [glib] süratli konuşan; çevik

glide [glayd] n. kayma; v/i kaymak; AVIA motoru işletmeden inmek; ~r AVIA planör

glimmer ['glimı] v/i parıldamak; n. parıltı

glimpse [glimps] n. kısa bakış; v/t bir an için görmek

glint [glint] parlamak

glisten ['glisn] parlamak, parıldamak

glitter ['glitı] n. parıltı, ışıltı; v/i parıldamak

gloat [glıut] v/i şeytanca bir zevkle seyretmek (upon, over -i)

global ['glıubıl] küresel; ~ **warming** küresel ısınma; ~i-

globe 286

zation [gluıbıl'ayzeyşın] küreselleşme

globe [glub] küre, top; dünya

gloom [gluum] karanlık; üzgünlük, hüzün; **~y** kapanık; kederli, endişeli

glor|ify ['glôrifay] v/t yüceltmek, methetmek; **~ious** şanlı, parlak; **~y** şan, şeref, ihtişam

gloss [glos] cilâ, perdalı

glossary ['glosırı] ek sözlük

glossy ['glosi] parlak

glove [glav] eldiven

glow [glou] n. kızıllık; hararet; v/i hararet saçmak, yanmak, parlamak; **~worm** zoo ateşböceği

glue [gluu] n. tutkal; v/t tutkallamak, yapıştırmak

glutton ['glatn] obur; **~ous** obur gibi; **~y** oburluk

gnarled [naald] budaklı, boğumlu

gnash [näş] v/t gıcırdatmak

gnat [nät] zoo sivrisinek

gnaw [nô] v/t kemirmek

go [gıu] n. gayret; başarı; v/i gitmek; hareket etm., kalkmak; çıkmak; gezmek; işlemek; olmak; **let ~** v/t bırakmak; **~ by** geçmek; **~ for -i** almaya gitmek; sayılmak -e; **~ in for -in** meraklısı olm.; **~ mad** çıldırmak, delirmek; **~ on** devam etm. (-ing -meğe); **~ through** geçmek -den; uğramak -e; **~ up** çıkmak, yükselmek

goad [gıud] v/t dürtmek

goal [gıul] hedef, gaye; gol, kale; **~keeper** kaleci

goat [gıut] zoo keçi

go-between aracı

goblet ['goblit] kadeh

goblin ['goblin] gulyabani, cin

god [god] tanrı, ilâh; put; ♀ Tanrı, Allah; **~child** vaftiz çocuğu; **~dess** tanrıça, ilâhe; **~father** vaftiz babası; **~less** dinsiz; **~mother** vaftiz anası

goggle ['gogl] v/i şaşı bakmak; n. pl. gözlük sg.

going ['gıuin] gidiş; **be ~ to** inf. -mek üzere olm.

gold [gıuld] altın; **~en** altından yapılmış; altın renkli; **~smith** kuyumcu

golf [golf] golf oyunu; **~course**, **~links** pl. golf alanı sg.

gone [gon] s. go; mahvolmuş

good [gud] adj. iyi, güzel; edepli, nazik; uygun; n. iyilik; fayda, yarar; pl. eşya, mallar; **~afternoon!** iyi günler (öğleden sonra kullanılır); **~evening!** iyi akşamlar!, tünaydın!; ♀ **Friday** REL paskalya yortusundan önceki cuma (İsanın çarmıhta öldüğüne inanılan gün); **~morning!** günaydın!; **~night!** iyi geceler!; **~by!** Allaha ısmarladık!, güle güle!; **~for-nothing** yaramaz, serseri; **~natured** iyi tabiatlı, halim; **~ness** iyilik; **thank ~ness!** Allaha şükür!;

~will iyi niyet, hayırhahlık

goose [guus] *pl.* **geese** [gîs] zoo kaz; ~**berry** ['guzbıri] bot bektaşîüzümü

gorge [gôc] *n.* boğaz, dar geçit; gırtlak; *v/t* yutmak, tıka basa yemek

gorgeous ['gôcıs] parlak, tantanalı

gospel ['gospıl] rel İncil

gossip ['gosip] *n.* dedikodu; dedikoducu; *v/i* dedikodu etm.

got, ~**ten** [got, '_n] *s.* get

gourd [guıd] bot kabak

gout [gaut] med gut, nıkris

govern ['gavın] *v/t* yönetmek, idare etm.; hâkim olm. *-e*; ~**ess** mürebbiye; ~**ment** hükümet; idare; ~**or** vali

gown [gaun] rop; cüppe

grab [gräb] *v/t* kapmak, ele geçirmek

grace [greys] lütuf; nezaket; rahmet; econ mühlet, vade; rel şükran duası; ~**ful** zarif, latif

gracious ['greyşıs] şirin, nazik; inayetkâr; **good** ~! Allah Allah!

grade [greyd] *n.* derece; rütbe; mertebe; sınıf; *v/t* sınıflandırmak; tesviye etm.; ~ **crossing** *Am.* hemzemin geçit; ~ **school** *Am.* ilkokul

gradient ['greydıynt] yokuş

gradua|**l** ['gräcuıl] tedricî, derece derece; ~**te** ['_cuıt] *n.* mezun, diplomalı;

['_dyueyt] *v/i* mezun olm.; *v/t* diploma vermek *-e*; derecelere ayırmak *-i*; ~**tion** [-dyu'eyşın] mezun olma

graft [grâft] *n.* ağaç aşısı; *v/t* aşılamak; med transplante etm.

grain [greyn] tane, habbe; damar; hububat

gramma|**r** ['grämi] gramer; ~**tical** [grı'mätikıl] gramere ait; dilbilgisinin kurallarına uygun

gram(me) [gräm] gram

gramophone ['grämıfıun] gramofon

granary ['gränırı] tahıl ambarı

grand [gränd] büyük; muhteşem, şahane; ~**child** ['-nç-] torun; ~**daughter** ['-ndô-] kız torun; ~**eur** ['-ncı] azamet; ~**father** ['-df-] büyükbaba; ~**mother** ['-nm-] büyükanne; ~**son** ['-ns-] erkek torun; ~**stand** tribün

granite ['gränit] granit

granny ['gräni] *fam.* nineciğim

grant [graant] *n.* bağış; hibe; tahsisat; *v/t* vermek, bağışlamak; kabul etm.; **take for** ~**ed** *v/t* olmuş gibi kabul etm.

granula|**r** ['gränyulı] taneli; ~**te** ['_eyt] *v/t* tanelemek

grape [greyp] bot üzüm; ~**fruit** greypfrut, altıntop; ~**sugar** dekstroz

graphic ['gräfik] çizgili; canlı

grasp [graasp] *n.* tutma; kavrayış; *v/t* tutmak; kavramak

grass [graas] ot; çimen; çayır; ~hopper zoo çekirge; ~y çimenlik

grate [greyt] *n.* demir parmaklık, ızgara; *v/t* rendelemek; gıcırdatmak

grateful ['greytful] minnettar

grater ['greytı] rende

gratification [grätifi'keyşın] memnuniyet; ~fy ['-fay] *v/t* memnun etm.

grating ['greytin] parmaklık, ızgara

gratitude ['grätitiyûd] minnettarlık, şükran

gratuitous [grı'tyuitıs] bedava, parasız; ~y bahşiş; bağış

grave[1] [greyv] ağır, ciddî

grave[2] mezar, kabir

gravel ['grävil] çakıl

graveyard mezarlık

gravitation [grävi'teyşın] PHYS yerçekimi; ~y ['-ti] ağırbaşlılık; önem; yerçekimi

gravy ['greyvi] etsuyu, salça

gray [grey] *Am. s.* grey

graze [greyz] *v/i* otlamak; *v/t* otlatmak

grease [grîs] *n.* yağ; [-z] *v/t* yağlamak; ~y ['-zi] yağlı

great [greyt] büyük, iri; şöhretli; ♀ Britain Büyük Britanya; ~coat palto; ~grandfather büyük dede; ~ly pek çok; ~ness büyüklük; şöhret; önem

Greece [grîs] Yunanistan

greed [grîd] hırs, açgözlülük; ~y obur, açgözlü

Greek [grîk] Yunan(lı); Yunanca; Rum; Rumca

green [grîn] yeşil; ham, taze; tecrübesiz; çimen; ~grocer manav, yemişçi; ~horn toy, acemi; ~house limonluk

greet [grît] *v/t* selâmlamak; selâm vermek *-e*; ~ing selâm

grew [gruu] *s.* grow

grey [grey] boz, gri, kır; ~hound zoo tazı

grid [grid] ızgara; şebeke; ~iron ızgara

grief [grîf] keder, acı

grievance ['grîvıns] keder verici şey, dert; ~e *v/i* kederlenmek, üzülmek; *v/t* üzüntü vermek *-e*; ~ous kederli, acıklı

grill [gril] *n.* ızgara; *v/t* ızgarada pişirmek

grim [grim] haşin; korkunç

grimace [gri'meys] *n.* yüz buruşturma; *v/i* yüzünü ekşitmek

grime [graym] kir, pis; ~y kirli

grin [grin] *n.* sırıtma; *v/i* sırıtmak

grind [graynd] *v/t* öğütmek, ufalamak; bilemek; *teeth:* gıcırdatmak; ~stone bileği taşı

grip [grip] *n.* sıkı kavrama; kabza; *v/t* sıkı tutmak, kavramak; *fig. -in* dikkatini çekmek

gripes [graips] *pl.* MED sancı

gristle ['grisl] ANAT kıkırdak

grit [grit] çakıl, iri taneli kum

groan [grıun] n. inilti; v/i inlemek

grocer ['grıusı] bakkal; ~y bakkaliye

groin [groyn] ANAT kasık

groom [grum] n. seyis; güvey; v/t tımar etm.; bir işe hazırlamak

groove [gruuv] yiv, oluk

grope [grıup] v/t, v/i el yordamıyla aramak (for -i)

gross [grıus] on iki düzine; kaba, şişko, hantal; toptan

grotesque [grıu'tesk] acayip, tuhaf

ground¹ [graund] s. grind

ground² n. yer, zemin; toprak, arsa; dip; meydan; neden, sebep; v/t kurmak; EL toprağa bağlamak; ~ crew AVIA hava meydanı tayfası; ~ floor zemin katı; ~less sebepsiz; ~ nut BOT yerfıstığı

group [gruup] n. grup; v/t grup halinde toplanmak; v/i toplamak

grove [grıuv] koru, ormancık

grow [grıu] v/i olmak; büyümek, gelişmek; v/t yetiştirmek; ~ up büyümek

growl [graul] v/i hırlamak; homurdanmak

grow|n [grıun] s. grow; ~th [~th] büyüme, artma, gelişme

grub [grab] zoo sürfe, kurt; ~by kirli, pis

grudge [grac] n. kin, garaz;

v/t esirgemek, kıskanmak

gruel [gruıl] pişirilmiş yulaf ezmesi

gruesome ['gruusım] ürkütücü

gruff [graf] sert; boğuk sesli

grumble ['grambl] mırıldanmak; şikâyet etm. (at -den)

grunt [grant] domuz gibi hırıldamak

guarant|ee [gärın'tî] n. kefalet, garanti, teminat; kefil; v/t garanti etm.; ~or [~'tô] kefil; ~y ['~ti] garanti, kefalet

guard [gaad] n. muhafız; korucu, bekçi; koruma; v/t korumak, beklemek, muhafaza etm.; ~ian ['~yın] bekçi, muhafız; JUR veli, vasi

guess [ges] n. zan, tahmin; v/t tahmin etm., zannetmek

guest [gest] misafir, davetli; müşteri; ~room misafir yatak odası

guidance ['gaydıns] rehberlik, yol gösterme

guide [gayd] n. rehber, kılavuz; v/t yol göstermek -e; sevketmek, idare etm. -i; ~book seyahat rehberi; ~line prensip, tüzük

guild [gild] lonca; ℚhall Londra belediye dairesi

guileless ['gayllis] saf, riyasız

guilt [gilt] suç, kabahat; ~y suçlu, mücrim

Guinea ['gini] GEO Gine; ℚ-pig zoo kobay

guitar [gi'tâ] MUS gitar

gulf [galf] körfez; uçurum; ≈ **Stream** GEO golfstrim

gull [gal] zoo martı

gullet ['galit] ANAT boğaz, gırtlak

gulp [galp] *n.* yudum; *v/t* yutmak

gum [gam] *n.* zamk; ANAT dişeti; *v/t* zamklamak, yapıştırmak

gun [gan] tüfek; top; *Am.* tabanca; ~**ner** topçu; ~**powder** barut

gurgle ['gəgl] *v/i* fokurdamak

gush [gaş] *n.* fışkırma; *v/i* fışkırmak

gust [gast] anî rüzgâr, bora

guts [gats] *pl.* bağırsaklar; *sl.* cesaret *sg.*

gutter ['gatı] oluk, su yolu

guttural ['gatırıl] gırtlaktan çıkarılan (*ses*)

guy [gay] *Am. sl.* adam, herif

gymnas|ium [cim'neyzyım] cimnastik salonu; ~**tics** [-'nästiks] *pl.* cimnastik *sg.*

gyn(a)ecologist [gayni'kolıcist] kadın hastalıkları hekimi, jinekolog

gypsum ['cipsım] alçı taşı

gypsy ['cipsi] *s.* **gipsy**

H

haberdasher ['häbıdäşı] tuhafiyeci; *Am.* erkek giyimi satan mağaza

habit ['häbit] âdet, alışkanlık, huy; ~**ation** ev, ikametgâh; ~**ual** [hı'bityuıl] alışılmış, âdet olmuş

hack [häk] *v/t* çentmek, yarmak; ~**saw** demir testeresi

had [häd] *s.* **have**

haddock ['hädık] zoo mezgit balığı

haemorrh|age ['hemıric] kanama; ~**oids** ['-roydz] *pl.* basur *sg.*

hag [häg] acuze, cadı

haggard ['hägıd] bitkin görünüşlü

Hague [heyg]: **the** ~ Lâhey

hail[1] [heyl] *n.* dolu; *v/i* dolu yağmak

hail[2] *v/t* çağırmak; alkışlarla karşılamak

hair [häı] saç, kıl, tüy; ~**cut** saç kesme; ~**do** saç şekli; ~**dresser** berber, ku(v)aför; ~**pin** firkete; ~**y** kıllı, tüylü

half [hâf] yarım; yarı; buçuk; **three and a** ~ üç buçuk; ~ **past six** saat altı buçuk; ~**breed** melez (adam); ~**moon** yarımay; ~**penny** ['heypni] yarım peni; ~**time** haftaym; ~**way** yarı yolda

hall [hôl] salon; hol; koridor; resmî bina

hallo! [hı'lıu] hey!; alo!

halo ['heylıu] ağıl, hale

halt [hôlt] *n.* duruş; durak; *v/i* duraklamak; *v/t* durdurmak

halter ['hôltı] yular; idam ipi

halve [hâv] v/t yarıya bölmek

ham [häm] jambon

hamburger ['hämbıgı] sığır kıyması; köfte; köfteli sandviç

hamlet ['hämlit] küçük köy

hammer ['hämı] n. çekiç; tüfek horozu; v/t çekiçle işlemek

hammock ['hämık] hamak

hamper ['hämpı] n. büyük sepet; v/t engel olm. -e

hand [händ] n. el; akrep, ibre; işçi; v/t el ile vermek; teslim etm.; **at ~** yanında; **on the other ~** diğer taraftan; **on the right ~** sağ tarafta; **~ back** geri vermek; **~ over** teslim etm. (**to** -e); **~bag** el çantası; **~cuff** kelepçe; **~ful** avuç dolusu

handi|cap ['händikäp] n. engel; v/t engel olm. -e; **~craft** el sanatı

handkerchief ['hänkıçif] mendil

handle ['händl] n. sap, kulp, tokmak; v/t ellemek, ele almak, kullanmak; **~bar** gidon

hand|-made elişi; **~rail** tırabzan; **~s-free** adj. hands-free (araba telefonu); **~shake** el sıkma; **~some** ['hänsım] yakışıklı, güzel; **~writing** el yazısı; **~y** kullanışlı; elverişli

hang [häŋ] v/t asmak, takmak; v/i asılı olm.; sarkmak; **~ about** avare dolaşmak; **~ out** v/t sarkıtmak; **~ up** v/t asmak

hangar ['häŋı] AVIA hangar

hang|man cellât; **~over** içkiden gelen baş ağrısı

haphazard ['häp'häzıd] rasgele, gelişigüzel

happen ['häpın] olmak, vuku bulmak; **~ to** inf. rasgele olm.; **~ on** bulmak -i; **~ing** olay

happi|ness ['häpinis] saadet, bahtiyarlık; **~y** bahtiyar, talihli; neşeli; yerinde

harass ['härıs] v/t taciz etm., tedirgin etm.

harbo(u)r ['hâbı] n. liman; fig. barınak; v/t barındırmak; beslemek

hard [hâd] sert, katı; zor, güç, ağır; çetin; şefkatsiz; **~ by** pek yakın; **~ up** eli dar; try **~** çok uğraşmak; **~boiled** hazırlop; fig. pişkin; **~en** v/t katılaştırmak, sertleştirmek; v/i sertleşmek, katılaşmak; **~ly** adv. hemen hiç; ancak; **~ness** sertlik, katılık; **~ship** güçlük; sıkıntı; **~ware** madenî eşya; **~y** cesur, dayanıklı

hare [häı] zoo tavşan; **~bell** BOT çançiçeği; **~lip** tavşandudağı

hark [hâk] v/t dinlemek

harm [hâm] n. zarar; kötülük; v/t vermek -e; **~ful** zararlı; **~less** zararsız

harmony [hâ'mını] uyum, ahenk

harness ['hânis] n. koşum; v/t

horse; koşmak

harp [hâp] MUS harp; ~ on üzerinde durmak

harpoon [hâ'puun] *n.* zıpkın; *v/t* zıpkınlamak

harrow ['hârıu] *n.* sürgü; *v/t* sürgü geçirmek -*e*

harsh [hâş] sert, haşin, merhametsiz; ~ness sertlik

harvest ['hâvist] *n.* hasat; ürün, rekolte; *v/t ürünü* toplamak; biçmek; ~er orakçı; orak makinesi

has [hâz] *s.* have

hash [hâş] *n.* kıymalı yemek; *v/t* doğramak, kıymak

hast|e [heyst] acele; ~en ['sn] *v/i* acele etm.; *v/t* hızlandırmak; ~y acele, çabuk, üstün körü

hat [hât] şapka

hatch [hâç] *n.* kaporta; üstü açık kapı; *v/t fig.* kurmak; *v/i* yumurtadan çıkmak

hatchet ['hâçit] küçük balta

hat|e [heyt] *n.* nefret, kin; *v/t* nefret etm. -*den*, kin beslemek -*e* karşı; ~eful nefret verici, iğrenç; ~red ['rid] kin

haught|iness ['hôtinis] gurur, kurum; ~y kibirli, mağrur

haul [hôl] *n.* çekme; bir ağda çıkarılan balık mikdarı; *v/t* çekmek

haunch [hônç] kalça, but; sağrı

haunt [hônt] *n.* uğrak; *v/t* sık sık uğramak -*e*; sık görünmek -*de*; ~ed perili, tekin

olmıyan

have [hâv, hıv] *v/t* malik olm., sahip olm. -*e*; (*yardımcı fiil olarak bileşik fiil şekillerine katılır*); yaptırmak -*i*; ~ to *inf.* -*meğe* mecbur olm.; we had better finish now artık bitirsek iyi olur; ~not fakir, yoksul

haven ['heyvn] liman; sığınak

havoc ['hâvık]: make ~ çok zarar vermek (of -*e*)

hawk [hôk] zoo doğan

hawthorn ['hôthôn] BOT yabani akdiken

hay [hey] kuru ot; ~ fever MED saman nezlesi; ~cock, ~rick, ~stack ot yığını

hazard ['hâzıd] *n.* riziko, talih; tehlike; *v/t* talihe bırakmak; ~ous tehlikeli

haze [heyz] sis, pus

hazel ['heyzl] BOT fındık (ağacı); ~nut fındık

H-bomb ['eyçom] hidrojen bombası

he [hi] o (*eril*)

head [hed] *n.* baş, kafa; başkan; şef; baş taraf; *v/t* -*in* başında olm.; *v/i* gitmek, yönelmek (for -*e* doğru); ~ache baş ağrısı; ~band baş örtüsü; ~ing serlevha, başlık; ~light ön ışık, far; ~line başlık; ~long baş önde; ~master okul müdürü; ~mistress okul müdürü; ~quarters *pl.* MIL karargâh *sg.*; merkez; ~way ilerleme

heal [hîl] *v/t* iyileştirmek; şifa

vermek *-e*; *v/i* iyileşmek; ~ up *v/i yara*; kapanmak

health [helth] sağlık, sıhhat; ~ **resort** ılıca; ~**y** sağlıklı

heap [hîp] *n.* yığın, küme; *v/t* yığmak

hear [hiı] *v/t* işitmek, duymak, dinlemek; haber almak (about, from, of *-den*); ~**d** [hɜd] *s.* hear; ~**ing** dinleme, sorgu; ses erimi; ~**say** söylenti

hearse [hɜs] cenaze arabası

heart [hât] kalp, yürek, gönül; iç; cesaret; *pl.* kupa; **by** ~ ezber; ~**breaking** son derece keder verici; ~**burn** mide ekşimesi

hearth [hâth] ocak

heart|less [hâtlis] kalpsiz, merhametsiz; ~**y** içten, samimî; bol

heat [hît] *n.* hararet, sıcaklık, ısı; *v/t* ısıtmak; *v/i* ısınmak

heath [hîth] fundalık, BOT funda, süpürgeotu

heathen [hîdhın] dinsiz, kâfir

heat|ing [hîtig] ısıtma; central ~**ing** kalorifer; ~**stroke** MED güneş çarpması

heave [hîv] *n.* kaldırma; *v/t* atmak; kaldırmak; *v/i* kabarıp inmek

heaven [hevn] gök, sema; **for** ~**'s sake!** Allah aşkına!; **good** ~**s!** Allah Allah!, aman aman!; ~**ly** göksel; tanrısal

heav|iness [hevinis] ağırlık, sıklet; ~**y** ağır; güç; şiddetli;

üzgün; ~**y-weight** ağır sıklet(li)

Hebrew [hîbruu] İbranî, Yahudi; İbranîce

hectic [hektik] heyecanlı, telâşlı

hedge [hec] çit, çalı; *fig.* mania; ~**hog** zoo kirpi

heed [hîd] *n.* dikkat; *v/t* dikkat etm., kulak vermek *-e*; ~**less** dikkatsiz

heel [hîl] topuk, ökçe; *sl. Am.* alçak herif; **take to one's** ~**s** kaçmak

he-goat zoo teke, erkeç

heifer [hefı] zoo düve

height [hayt] yükseklik; tepe; ~**en** *v/t* yükseltmek, artırmak

heinous [heynıs] iğrenç, kötü

heir [äı] varis, mirasçı; ~**ess** kadın varis

held [held] *s.* **hold**

helicopter [helikoptı] AVIA helikopter

hell [hel] cehennem

hello! [he'luu] merhaba!, selam!; TEL alo!

helm [helm] NAUT dümen

helmet [helmit] miğfer, tolga

help [help] *n.* yardım, imdat; yardımcı, hizmetçi; *v/t* yardım etm. *-e*; **not** ~ *-ing* *-mekten* alamamak; ~ **yourself!** buyurunuz! (*yemek için*); ~**er** yardımcı; ~**ful** faydalı, işe yarar; ~**less** çaresiz, gücü yetmez

helter-skelter [heltı'skeltı]

aceleyle

hem¹ [hem] *n.* kenar; *v/t -in* kenarını kıvırıp dikmek

hem² *v/i* hafifçe öksürmek; sesi tutulmak

hemisphere ['hemisfıı] yarımküre

hemline etek ucu

hemp [hemp] вот kenevir

hen [hen] zoo tavuk; dişi kuş

hence [hens] buradan; bundan dolayı; ~forth, ~forward bundan sonra

henna ['henı] kına

hen-pecked kılıbık

her [hз] ona, onu; onun (*dişil*)

herald ['herıld] *n.* haberci, müjdeci; *v/t* ilân etm.; ~ry armacılık

herb [hзb] ot, bitki

herd [hзd] sürü; ~sman çoban

here [hiı] burada, buraya; ~ you are! buyurun alınız!; işte!; ~after bundan sonra, gelecekte; ~by bu vesile ile

heredit|ary [hi'reditırı] kalıtsal; ~y kalıtım

heresy ['herisı] REL bir akideye aykırı mezhep

here|upon bunun üzerine; ~with bununla

heritage ['heritic] miras, tereke

hermit ['hзmit] münzevi

hero ['hiıru] kahraman; ~ic [hi'ruik] kahramanca

heroin ['heruin] eroin

heron ['herın] zoo balıkçıl

herring ['heriŋ] zoo ringa

her|s [hзz] onun(ki) (*dişil*)

~self kendisi (*dişil*)

hesita|nt ['hezitınt] tereddüt eden, kararsız; ~te ['-teyt] tereddüt etm., duraksamak; ~tion tereddüt

heterogeneous ['hetıru-'cinyıs] heterogen, ayrı cinsten

hew [hyû] *v/t* yontmak, yarmak; ~n *s.* hew

heyday ['heydey] en enerjik çağ

hi! [hay] hey!; *Am.* merhaba!

hicc|ough, ~up ['hikap] *n.* hıçkırık; *v/i* hıçkırık tutmak

hid [hid] *s.* hide

hide¹ deri, post

hide² *v/t* saklamak, gizlemek; *v/i* saklanmak (**from** *-den*)

hideous ['hidiıs] çirkin, iğrenç

hi-fi ['hay'fay] *coll. s.* **high-fidelity**

high [hay] yüksek, yukarı; pahalı; şiddetli; kibirli; dolgun; esrarın etkisi altında; *n.* yüksek basınç bölgesi; ~ **school** lise; ~ **spirits** *pl.* neşe *sg.*; ~ **time** tam vakit; ~ **treason** JUR vatan hainliği; ~brow *fig.* fikir adamı; ~fidelity sesi çok tabii şekilde veren; ~land dağlık bölge; ~light ilgi çekici olay; ~ly *adv.* çok; ~ness yükseklik; **His** (*or* **Your**) ☓ness fehametlü; ~road anayol; ~way karayol

hijack ['haycäk] *v/t* kuvvet zoru ile çalmak; kaçırmak; ~er yolkesici; uçak korsanı

hike [hayk] *v/i* yürümek

hilarious [hi'lâıriıs] neşeli ve gürültülü

hill [hil] tepe; yokuş; ~**billy** ['-bili] *Am.* orman köylüsü; ~**y** tepelik

hilt [hilt] kabza

him [him] onu, ona; ~**self** kendisi (*eril*)

hind [haynd] arka; ~ **leg** arka ayak

hind|er ['hindı] *v/t* engellemek; mâni olm. -*e*; ~**rance** ['hindrıns] engel

hinge [hinc] menteşe, reze

hinny ['hini] *zoo* at ile dişi eşekten hâsıl olan katır

hint [hint] *n.* ima, üstü kapalı söz; *v/i* ima etm., çıtlatmak (**at** -*i*)

hip [hip] kalça, kaba et.

hippo|drome ['hipıdrıum] hipodrom, at meydanı; ~**potamus** [-'potımıs] *zoo* suaygırı

hire ['hayı] *n.* kira; *v/t* kiralamak, ücretle tutmak; **for ~** kiralık, serbest

his [hiz] onun(ki) (*eril*)

hiss [his] *n.* tıslama; *v/i* tıslamak; ıslık çalmak

histor|ian [his'tôrıın] tarihçi; ~**ical** [-'torikıl] tarihî; ~**y** ['-ıri] tarih

hit [hit] *n.* vuruş, darbe; isabet; başarı; *v/t* vurmak, çarpmak -*e*; isabet etm. -*e*; rasgele bulmak (**upon** -*i*); ~**and-run** çarpıp kaçan (*şöför*)

hitch [hiç] *n.* çekiş; engel, arı-

za; *v/t* bağlamak, takmak; *v/i* takılmak; ~**hike** otostop yapmak; ~**hiker** otostopçu

hither ['hidhı] buraya; ~**to** şimdiye kadar

hive [hayv] kovan; arı kovanı gibi kaynaşan yer

hoard [hôd] *n.* saklanan stok; *v/t* biriktirmek, saklamak

hoarfrost ['hô'-] kırağı

hoarse [hôs] boğuk, kısık

hoax [huks] *n.* şaka, muziplik; *v/t* aldatmak

hobble ['hobl] *v/i* topallamak; *v/t* kösteklemek

hobby ['hobi] merak

hobgoblin ['hobgoblin] gulyabani

hobo ['hıubıu] serseri, aylak

hockey ['hoki] hokey

hoe [hıu] *n.* çapa; *v/t* çapalamak

hog [hog] *zoo* domuz

hoist [hoyst] *n.* kaldıraç; yük asansörü; *v/t* yükseltmek; *bayrağı* çekmek

hold [huld] *n.* tutma; dayanak; otorite; *v/t* tutmak, kavramak; dayanmak -*e*; sahip olm. -*e*; içine almak -*i*; işgal etm. -*i*; **get (lay, take)** ~ **of** *v/t* yakalamak; ~ **the line** telefonda beklemek; ~ **on** devam etm.; ~ **to** *v/t* tutmak; devam etm. -*e*; ~ **up** *v/t* tutmak; durdurmak; ~**er** sahip, hamil; ~**ing** tutma; mülk; ECON holding; ~**up** gecikme; yol kesme

hole [hul] delik, çukur

holiday ['holıdi] tatil günü; bayram günü

Holland ['holınd] Hollanda, Felemenk

hollow ['holuı] adj. içi boş, oyuk; n. çukur, boşluk; v/t oymak, çukurlatmak

holly ['holi] BOT çobanpüskülü

holy ['hıuli] kutsal; 2 Week paskalyadan önceki hafta

homage ['homic] biat

home [hıum] ev, aile ocağı; vatan, yurt; yerli; adv. eve; at ~ evde; see ~ v/t evine kadar refakat etm. -e; 2 Office POL İçişleri Bakanlığı; ~ Secretary İçişleri Bakanı; ~less evsiz, yurtsuz; ~ly basit, sade, gösterişsiz; ~made evde yapılmış; ~sick yurt hasreti çeken; ~ward eve doğru

homicide ['homisayd] JUR adam öldürme

homosexual [humıu'seksyuıl] homoseksüel

honest ['onist] doğru, dürüst, namuslu; ~y namusluluk, dürüstlük

honey ['hani] bal; ~moon bal ayı

honk [hoŋk] v/i klakson çalmak

honorary ['onırıri] fahrî

hono(u)r ['onı] n. şeref, onur, namus; v/t şereflendirmek; ECON -in karşılığını ödemek; have the ~ to inf. -mek şerefine nail olm.; ~able şerefli, namuslu; sayın

hood [hud] kukulete; Am. motor kapağı

hoodlum ['huudlım] serseri, kabadayı

hoodwink ['hudwiŋk] v/t aldatmak

hoof [huuf] zoo at v.s. tırnağı

hook [huk] n. çengel, kanca; v/t kancaya takmak; yakalamak

hooligan ['huuligın] serseri, külhanbeyi

hoop [huup] kasnak, çember

hooping-coug ['huupiŋ-] MED boğmaca

hoot [huut] v/i baykuş gibi ötmek; yuha çekmek

hop[1] [hop] BOT şerbetçiotu

hop[2] n. sekme, sıçrama; v/i sıçramak, sekmek

hope [hıup] n. umut, ümit; v/i ümit etm., ummak (for -i); ~ful ümitli, ümit verici; ~less ümitsiz

horizon [hı'rayzn] çevren, ufuk; ~tal [hori'zontl] yatay

horn [hôn] boynuz; MUS boru; korna, klakson

hornet ['hônit] zoo büyük sarı arı

horny ['hôni] boynuzdan; boynuzlu; nasırlanmış

horoscope ['horıskıup] yıldız falı

horrible ['horıbl] dehşetli, korkunç; iğrenç; ~id ['-id] korkunç; iğrenç; ~ify ['-ifay] v/t korkutmak; ~or dehşet, korku; nefret

horse [hôs] at; on ~back ata

binmiş; ~**power** TECH beygir gücü; ~**race** at yarışı; ~**radish** BOT acırga; ~**shoe** at nalı

horticulture ['hôtikalçı] bahçıvanlık

hos|le [hıuz] hortum; çorap; ~**iery** ['-ıiri] çorap ve iç çamaşırı

hospitable ['hospitıbl] misafirperver

hospital ['hospitl] hastane; ~**ity** [-'tâliti] konukseverlik

host [hıust] ev sahibi, mihmandar; otelci; kalabalık; REL takdis edilen fodla

hostage ['hostic] rehine, tutak

host|el ['hostıl] talebe yurdu; ~**ess** ['hıustis] ev sahibesi; hostes

hostil|e ['hostayl] düşmanca; ~**ity** [-'tâliti] düşmanlık

hot [hot] sıcak, kızgın; acı; şiddetli; ~ **dog** sıcak sosisli sandviç; ~**bed** camlık

hotel [hıu'tel] otel

hot|headed ateşli, kızgın; ~**house** camlık

hound [haund] n. av köpeği; v/t takip etm., izlemek

hour ['auı] saat (60 dakika); zaman; ~**ly** saatte bir, her saat başı

house [haus] n. ev; hanedan; seyirciler pl.; v/t barındırmak; ♀ of Commons Avam Kamarası; ♀ of Lords Lordlar Kamarası; ~**hold** ev halkı, aile; eve aid; ~**keeper** kâhya kadın; ~**warming** ye-

ni eve taşınanların verdikleri ziyafet; ~**wife** ev kadını

hove [hıuv] s. **heave**

hover ['hovı] v/i dolaşmak, sallanmak; ~**craft** tazyikli hava üzerinde gidebilen taşıt

how [hau] nasıl; ~ **are you?**, ~ **do you do?** nasılsınız?; ~ **much (many)?** nekadar?; ~**ever** mamafih, bununla beraber; nekadar ... olursa olsun

howl [haul] n. uluma, bağırma; v/i ulumak

hub [hab] poyra

hubbub ['habab] gürültü

huddle ['hadl] v/i sıkı halde toplanmak; v/t toplamak

hue [hyû] renk

hug [hag] n. kucaklama; v/t kucaklamak

huge [hyûc] pek büyük, kocaman

hull [hal] n. BOT kabuk; NAUT tekne, gövde; v/t -in kabuğunu soymak

hullabaloo [halıbı'luu] gürültü

hallo! ['ha'lu] s. **hello!**

hum [ham] v/i vınlamak, vızıldamak

human ['hyûmın] insana ait; insan; ~ **being** insanoğlu; ~**e** [-'meyn] insana, merhametli; ~**ity** [-'mâniti] beşeriyet; insanlık

humble ['hambl] adj. alçak gönüllü; v/t -in kibrini kırmak, aşağılatmak

humbug ['hambag] n. şarlatanlık, yalan; v/t aldatmak

humdrum ['hamdram] can sıkıcı, tekdüzen

humid ['hyûmid] rutubetli, nemli; **~ity** [-'miditi] rutubet

humili|ate [hyû'milieyt] v/t küçültmek; **-in** kibrini kırmak; **~ation** küçültme; **~ty** [-'militi] alçak gönüllülük

humming-bird zoo sinek kuşu

humorous ['hyûmırıs] mizahî, komik

humo(u)r ['hyûmı] mizah, nükte; huy, tabiat; **good-~ed** iyi huylu

hump [hamp] hörgüç; kambur; tümsek

hunch [hanç] kambur; **~back** kambur adam

hundred ['handrıd] yüz; **~weight** (50.8 kilo, Am. 45.4 kilo)

hung [hang] s. hang

Hungar|ian [han'gäiriın] Macar; Macarca; **~y** ['-gırı] Macaristan

hunger ['hangı] n. açlık; v/i şiddetle arzulamak (after, for -i); **~ry** aç; pek istekli

hunt [hant] n. av; arama; v/t avlamak; **~er** avcı; **~ing** avcılık

hurdle ['hɜdl] çit, mânia; **~race** mânialı koşu

hurl [hɜl] v/t fırlatmak

hurra|h! [hu'râ], **~y!** [-'rey] yaşa!

hurricane ['harikın] kasırga

hurried ['harid] acele ile, telâşlı

hurry ['hari] n. acele; telâş; v/i acele etm.; v/t aceleleştirmek; **be in a ~** acelesi olm.; **~ up** acele etm.

hurt [hɜt] n. yara; zarar; v/t yaralamak; incitmek; v/i ağrımak

husband ['hazbınd] koca, eş; **~ry** ziraat, tarım

hush [haş] n. susma, sessizlik; v/i susmak; v/t susturmak; **~ up** v/t örtbas etm.

husk [hask] n. kabuk, kılıf; v/t -in kabuğunu soymak; **~y** kısık, boğuk; dinç, gürbüz

hustle ['hasl] n. itip kakma; falliyet; v/t itip kakmak; v/i itişip kakışmak

hut [hat] kulübe, baraka

hutch [haç] tavşan kafesi; kulübe

hyacinth ['hayısinth] BOT sümbül

hybrid ['haybrid] melez

hydr|ant ['haydrınt] yangın musluğu; **~aulic** [-'drôlik] hidrolik

hydro- ['haydrıu-] su ile ilgili; **~carbon** hidrokarbon; **~gen** [-'cın] idrojen; **~phobia** MED kuduz

hyena [hay'în] zoo sırtlan

hygien|e ['haycîn] sağlık bilgisi, hıfzıssıhha; **~ic** sağlıkla ilgili

hymn [him] REL ilâhi

hyphen ['hayfın] tire, çizgi

hypno|sis [hip'nıusis] ipnoz;

~tic [-'notik] uyutucu
hypo|crisy [hi'pokrısi] iki-
yüzlülük; ~crite ['hipıkrit]
ikiyüzlü; ~thesis [hay'pothi-
sis] varsayım, hipotez
hyster|ia [his'tirıı] MED isteri;
~ical [-'terikıl] isterik

I

I [ay] ben
ice [ays] n. buz; v/i buzlan-
mak; v/t buz ile kaplan-
mak; soğutmak; ~berg ['-bəg]
buzdağı, aysberk; ~breaker
buzkıran; ~ cream dondur-
ma; ≗land İzlanda
ic|icle ['aysikl] buz parçası; ~y
buz gibi, soğuk
idea [ay'diı] fikir, düşünce;
sanı, tahmin; ~l n. ideal, ülkü; adj. ülküsel; ~list ülkücü,
idealist
identi|cal [ay'dentikıl] aynı;
~fication [aydentifi'keyşın]
hüviyet; ~fy [-'dentifay] v/t
-in hüviyetini göstermek;
~ty [-'dentiti] aynılık; hüviyet; ~ty card kimlik cüzdanı
ideology [aydi'olıci] ideoloji
idiom ['idiım] şive, lehçe; deyim
idiot ['idiıt] anadan doğma
deli; aptal; ~ic [-'otik] ahmak
idle ['aydl] adj. aylak, boş; v/i
vaktini boş geçirmek; boşta
çalışmak; ~ness tembellik
idol ['aydl] put; tapılan kimse;
~ater [-'dolıtı] putperest;
~ize ['-dılayz] v/t tapınmak
-e

idyl|(l) ['idil] idil; ~ic [ay'di-
lik] pastoral; saf ve sevimli
if [if] eğer, şayet; ise; as ~ sanki, güya
ignition [ig'nişın] ateşleme;
marş
ignoble [ig'nıubl] alçak
ignor|ance ['ignırıns] cahil-
lik; ~ant cahil, bilmez; ~e
[ig'nô] v/t önem vermemek
-e
ill [il] hasta, rahatsız; fena, kötü; uğursuz; kötülük, fenalık;
fall ~, be taken ~ hastalanmak; ~ at ease huzursuz;
~advised tedbirsiz; ~bred
terbiyesiz
ill|legal [i'ligıl] kanuna aykırı;
~legible okunmaz; ~legiti-
mate kanuna aykırı; evlilik
dışı
ill-humo(u)red fena huylu;
huysuz
il|licit [i'lisit] kanuna aykırı;
caiz olmıyan; ~literate [i'li-
tırit] okuma yazma bilmiyen
ill|ness ['ilnıs] hastalık; ~tem-
pered huysuz; ~timed za-
mansız; ~treat v/t kötü davranmak -e
illuminat|e [i'lyûmineyt]
aydınlatmak; ~ion aydınlat-

ma, tenvir

illusi|on [i'luujin] hayal, kuruntu, aldanma; ~ve aldatıcı

illustrat|e ['iləstreyt] v/t tasvir etm., anlatmak, resimlerle süslemek; ~ion resim; izah; örnek

illustrious [i'lastriɪs] ünlü, meşhur

imag|e ['imic] şekil, suret; heykel; hayal; ~inary [i'mäcinɪri] hayalî; ~ination tasavvur; imgelem; ~inative yaratıcı; ~ine v/t tasavvur etm.; hayal etm.

imbecile ['imbisil] ahmak, budala

imitat|e ['imiteyt] v/t taklit etm., benzetmek; ~ion taklit, yapma

im|maculate [i'mäkyulit] lekesiz; ~material [im'tiiriıl] önemsiz; ~mature olgunlaşmamış; ~measurable ölçülemez

immediate [i'mîdyıt] doğrudan doğruya; derhal olan; ~ly derhal, hemen

immense [i'mens] çok büyük, engin

immerse [i'mɜs] v/t daldırmak

immigra|nt [i'imigrɪnt] göçmen; ~te [i'.eyt] göçmek; ~tion göçmenlik

imminent ['imininnt] yakında olan

im|mobile [i'mıubayl] hareketsiz; ~moderate ölçüsüz, ifrata kaçan; ~modest açık

saçık; haddini bilmez; ~moral ahlâkı bozuk, ahlâksız

immortal [i'môtl] ölümsüz, ölmez; ~ity [-'tältti] ölmezlik

immovable [i'muuvɪbl] kımıldamaz

immun|e [i'myûn] muaf (from -den); ~ity JUR dokunulmazlık

imp [imp] küçük şeytan

impact ['impäkt] vuruş; etki

impair [im'päı] v/t bozmak

impart [im'pât] v/t vermek; bildirmek; ~ial [-şɪl] tarafsız; ~iality [- şi'älitt] tarafsızlık

im|passable geçilmez; ~passive duygusuz

impatien|ce sabırsızlık; ~t sabırsız; çok arzu eden (for -i)

impeach [im'pîç] v/t suçlamak

impediment [im'pedimɪnt] mânia, engel

impend [im'pend] v/i asılı olm., vuku bulmak üzere olm.

impenetrable [im'penitrıbl] girilemez

imperative [im'perɪtiv] mecburî; ~ (mood) GR emir kipi

imperceptible hissolunamaz

imperfect [im'pɜfikt] eksik, kusurlu; tamam olmayan; ~ (tense) GR geçmiş zaman

imperial [im'piırıl] şahane; imparatora ait; ~ism emperyalizm

imperil v/t tehlikeye düşür-

mek
imperious [im'piiriis] zorba; zarurî
impermeable [im'pəmyıbl] *su ve hava* geçirmez
impersonal|l [im'pəsnl] şahşî olmayan; ~te [-'pəsineyt] *v/t* temsil etm.
impertinen|ce [im'pətinins] küstahlık; ~t arsız, küstah
imperturbable [impı'tɜbıbl] ağırbaşlı
impetuous [im'petyuıs] coşkun, atılgan
impinge [im'pinc] *v/i* çarpmak (on, upon -e)
implacable [im'pläkıbl] teskin edilemez, amansız
implant *v/t* dikmek; aşılamak
implement ['implimınt] *n.* alet, araç; *v/t* yerine getirmek
implicate ['implikeyt] *v/t* sokmak, karıştırmak
implicit [im'plisit] zimnî, altık
implore [im'plô] *v/t* yalvarmak -e
imply [im'play] *v/t* içine almak; ima etm.
impolite nezaketsiz
import ['impôt] *n.* ECON ithal, ithalât; mana; önem; [-'pôt] *v/t* ithal etm.; belirtmek; ~ance [-'pôtıns] önem; ~ant önemli; ~ation ithal (malı)
importune [im'pôtyûn] *v/t* sıkıştırmak
impos|e [im'pıuz] *v/t* yükle-

mek; *v/i* aldatmak (on, upon -i); ~ing heybetli
impossib|ility olanaksızlık; ~le imkânsız, olamaz
impostor [im'postı] sahtekâr
impotent [im'pıtınt] kudretsiz; MED iktidarsız
impoverish [im'povıriş] *v/t* fakirleştirmek
impracticable yapılamaz; kullanışsız
impregnate ['impregneyt] *v/t* döllemek, doyurmak
impress ['impres] *n.* basma, damga; *v/t* basmak; etkilemek; ~ion basma; izlenim; etki; ~ive etkili, müessir
imprint *n.* damga; *v/t* basmak; etkilemek
imprison [im'prizn] *v/t* hapsetmek; ~ment hapis, tutukluluk
improbable [im'probıbl] ihtimal dahilinde olmıyan
improper yersiz, yakışıksız
improve [im'pruuv] *v/t* düzeltmek; *v/i* düzelmek; ~ment ıslah, düzelme
improvise ['imprıvayz] *v/t* doğaçtan söylemek *veya* yapmak
imprudent [im'pruudınt] tedbirsiz
impuden|ce ['impyudıns] yüzsüzlük, arsızlık; ~t arsız, saygısız
impuls|e ['impals] itici kuvvet, tahrik, içtepi; ~ive itici; atılgan
impunity [im'pyûniti] ceza-

dan muaf olma
impure [im'pyuı] pis, kirli
imput|ation [impyu'teyşın]
suçlama; ~e v/t [-'pyût] itham etm., suçlamak (to ile)
in [in] -de, -(y)e; -*in* içinde, içine; içerde, içeriye; evde
inability ehliyetsizlik
inaccessible [inäk'sesıbl]
erişilemez
inaccurate [in'äkyurit]
yanlış, kusurlu
inactive hareketsiz
inadequate [in'ädıkwıt] ye-
tersiz
inadvertent [inıd'vзtınt] dikkatsiz; kasıtsız
inalienable satılamaz
inalterable değişmez
inanimate [in'änimit] cansız
inappropriate münasebetsiz
inapt beceriksiz; uygun olmıyan
inarticulate anlaşılmaz
inasmuch as [ınız'maç -] mademki
inattentive dikkatsiz
inaudible işitilemez
inaugura||l [i'nôgyrıl] açılışa
ait; ~**te** [-'eyt] v/t açmak; başlamak -*e*; ~**tion** açılış (töreni)
inborn [in'bôn] doğuştan,
fıtrî
incalculable [in'kälkyulıbl]
hesap edilemez
incapa|ble [in'keypıbl] yete-
neksiz; beceriksiz; ~**city**
[ınkı'päsiti] kabiliyetsizlik;
yetkisizlik
incarnation [inkaa'neyşın]

tecessüm
incautious düşüncesiz
incendiary [in'sendyiri] kun-
dakçı; yangın çıkarıcı
incense[1] [in'sens] buhur
incense[2] [in'sens] v/t öfke-
lendirmek
incentive [in'sentiv] dürtü,
saik
incessant [in'sesnt] sürekli
incest ['insest] JUR akraba
arasında cinsî temas
inch [inç] pus (*2,54 cm*)
incident ['insidınt] olay; ~**al**
[-'dentl] tesadüfî
incinerate [in'sinıreyt] v/t kül
etm.
incis|e [in'sayz] v/t oymak,
hakketmek; ~**ion** [-ıjın] yar-
ma, deşme; ~**or** ANAT ön diş
incite [in'sayt] v/t teşvik etm.,
kışkırtmak
inclin|ation [inkli'neyşın]
meyil; istek; ~**e** [-'klayn] *n.*
meyil, yokuş; *v/i* eğilmek,
meyletmek (**to** -*e*); *v/t* eğmek
inclos|e [in'kluz], ~**ure** [-_jı]
s. enclose, enclosure
inclu|de [in'kluud] *v/t* içine
almak; ~**sion** [-_jın] dahil olma; ~**sive** dahil, kapsayan
incognito [in'kognitu] takma adla; takma ad
incoherent anlaşılmaz, manasız
income ['inkam] gelir, irat;
~**tax** ['inkımtäks] gelir vergisi
incomparable emsalsiz
incompatible birbirine uy-

maz

incompetent ehliyetsiz

incomplete tam olmıyan

incomprehensible anlaşılamaz

inconceivable tasavvur olunamaz

inconsequent mantıksız, birbirini tutmaz

inconsidera|ble önemsiz; **~te** saygısız; düşüncesiz

inconsistent kararsız; uyuşmaz

inconspicuous önemsiz

inconvenien|ce n. zahmet, rahatsızlık; v/t rahatsız etm.; **~t** zahmetli

incorporate [in'kôpıreyt] v/t birleştirmek; v/i birleşmek; **~d** ECON anonim

incorr|ect yanlış; **~igible** düzelmez

increase ['inkrîs] n. çoğalma; [in'krîs] v/i artmak, çoğalmak; v/t artırmak, çoğaltmak; **~ingly** gittikçe artarak

incred|ible inanılmaz; **~ulous** inanmaz; kuşkusu olan

incriminate [in'krimineyt] v/t suçlamak

incubator [in'kyubeytı] kuluçka makinesi

incur [in'kə] v/t uğramak -e, yakalanmak -den

incurable şifa bulmaz

indebted borçlu (**to** -e)

indecen|cy ahlâksızlık; **~t** utanmaz; yüzsüz

indecisi|on kararsızlık; **~ve** kararsız; kesin olmıyan

indeed gerçekten; intj. öyle mi?

indefatigable [indi'fätigıbl] yorulmaz

indefinite belirsiz

indelible [in'delibl] silinmez

indelicacy kabalık, uygunsuzluk

indemni|fy [in'demnifay] v/t -in zararını ödemek; **~ty** tazminat

indent ['indent] n. çentik; [.'dent] v/t çentmek; -in kenarını oymak; **~ure** [in'dençı] sözleşme

independen|ce bağımsızlık; **~t** bağımsız

indescribable [indis'kraybıbl] anlatılmaz

indestructible [indis'traktıbl] yıkılmaz

index [in'deks] n. indeks; fihrist; ibre; işaret; v/t -in indeksini yapmak; **~ (finger)** işaret parmağı

India ['indıy] Hindistan; **~n** Hint, Hintli; (Red) **~n** kırmızı derili; **~n corn** BOT mısır; **~n summer** pastırma yazı

indicate [in'dikeyt] v/t göstermek; -ın belirti, delil; **~ive (mood)** [in'dikitiv] GR bildirme kipi; **~or** ['~eytı] ibre, gösterge

indict [in'dayt] v/t suçlamak; **~ment** JUR iddianame

indifferen|ce aldırmazlık; **~t** kayıtsız; orta derecede

indigestible hazmolunmaz;

~ion hazımsızlık
indigna|nt [in'dignınt]
dargın, öfkeli; ~tion
dargınlık, öfke
indirect dolaşık; dolaylı
indiscre|et boşboğaz, düşün-
cesiz; ~tion boşboğazlık,
düşüncesizlik
indiscriminate [indis'krimi-
nit] gelişigüzel
indispensable zarurî
indispos|ed [indis'pıuzd] ra-
hatsız; ~ition rahatsızlık
indisputable ['indis'pyûtıbl]
söz götürmez
indistinct iyice görülmez
individual [indi'vidyuıl] bi-
rey, fert, kimse; bireysel, ferdî; ~ist bireyci; ~ity ferdiyet
indivisible bölünmez
indolen|ce ['indılıns] tembel-
lik; ~t tembel
indomitable [in'domitıbl] boyun eğmez
indoor ['indô] ev içinde olan;
~ aerial oda anteni; ~s [in-
'dôz] ev içinde
indorse [in'dôs] s. endorse
induce [in'dyûs] v/t teşvik
etm.; sebep olm. -e
indulge [in'dalc] v/t müsamaha etm.; v/i düşkün olm.,
kapılmak (in -e); ~nce müsamaha; düşkünlük; ~nt müsa-
mahakâr
industri|al [in'dastriıl] sınaî,
endüstri ile ilgili; ~alize v/t
sanayileştirmek; ~ious çalışkan; ~y ['indıstri] sanayi, endüstri; çalışkanlık

ineff|ective, ~icient etkisiz
inept [i'nept] yersiz; hünersiz
inequ|ality eşitsizlik; ~itable
insafsız
inert [i'nıt] hareketsiz; tembel; ~ia [-şyı] atalet
inestimable [in'estimıbl] hesaba sığmaz
inevitable [in'evitıbl] kaçını-
lamaz
inex|cusable affedilemez;
~haustible tükenmez; ~pen-
sive ucuz; ~perienced tecrübesiz, acemi; ~plicable
[-'eksplikıbl] izah edilemez;
~pressible [iniks'presıbl]
ifade edilemez; ~pressive
anlatımsız; ~tricable söküle-
mez
infallible [in'fälıbl] yanılmaz;
şaşmaz
infam|ous ['infımıs] ahlâkı
bozuk, rezil; ~y rezalet
infan|cy ['infınsi] çocukluk,
bebeklik; ~t küçük çocuk,
bebek; JUR ergin olmıyan
kimse; ~tile [-tayl] çocuğa
ait, çocukça; ~tile paralysis
MED çocuk felci
infantry ['infıntri] MIL piyade,
yaya
infatuate [in'fätyuеyt] v/t
çıldırtmak; ~d meftun (with
-e)
infect [in'fekt] v/t bulaştırmak; ~ion bulaşma; ~ious
bulaşık, bulaşan
infer [in'fı] v/t anlamak,
çıkarmak; ~ence [in'fırıns]
sonuç, çıkarma

inferior [in'fiıriı] aşağı, alt; ikinci derecede, adi; ast; ~ity [-'oriti] aşağılık

infernal [in'fɔnl] cehenneme ait, şeytanca

infest [in'fest] v/t sarmak; zarar vermek -e

infidel ['infidıl] kâfir, imansız

infiltrate ['infiltreyt] v/t girmek -e; v/i süzülmek

infinite ['infinit] sonsuz; ~esimal [infini'tesimıl] bölünemiyecek kadar küçük; ~ive (mood) [in'finitiv] GR mastar; ~y sonsuzluk

infirm [in'fɔm] zayıf; hastalıklı; ~ary hastane; ~ity sakatlık, zayıflık

inflame [in'fleym] v/i tutuşmak; v/t alevlendirmek

inflammable [in'flämıbl] tutuşur; ~tion [-'meyşın] MED yangı, iltihap

inflate [in'fleyt] v/t şişirmek; ~ion ECON enflasyon

inflect [in'flekt] v/t GR çekmek

inflexible [in'fleksıbl] eğilmez; sarsılmaz; ~ion [-kşın] bükülme; GR çekim

inflict [in'flikt] v/t getirmek, uğratmak (on -e); ~ion [-kşın] ceza; sıkıntı

influence [in'fluıns] n. etki, nüfuz; v/t etkilemek; ~tial [-'enşıl] sözü geçer, nüfuzlu

influenza [influ'enzı] MED grip, enflüanza

inform [in'fɔm] v/t haber vermek -e (of hakkında), bildir-

mek (-i); ~al resmî olmıyan, teklifsiz

information [infı'meyşın] bilgi; danışma; ~ bureau, ~ office danışma bürosu

informative [in'fɔmıtiv] aydınlatıcı; ~er jurnalcı

infringe [in'frinc] v/t bozmak; ~ment bozma, ihlâl

infuriate [in'fyuırieyt] v/t çıldırtmak

infuse [in'fyûz] v/t aşılamak; fig. telkin etm.

ingenious [in'cînyıs] hünerli; usta; ~uity [-i'nyuiti] hüner, marifet

ingot ['iŋgıt] külçe

ingratiate [in'greyşieyt]: ~ oneself yağcılık yaparcasına sokulmak (with -e)

ingratitude [in'grätityûd] nankörlük

ingredient [in'grîdyınt] cüz, parça

inhabit [in'häbit] v/t oturmak, ikamet etm. -de; ~able oturulabilir; ~ant oturan, sakin

inhale [in'heyl] v/t içine çekmek

inherent [in'hiırınt] tabiî, doğal

inherit [in'herit] v/t miras almak; ~ance miras, kalıt

inhibit [in'hibit] v/t engel olm. -e; ~ion yasak

inhospitable misafir sevmez; barınılmaz

inhuman gaddar, kıyıcı

initial [i'nişıl] n. ilk harf; büyük harf; adj. ilk, baştaki;

initiate
306

~te [-şieyt] başlamak *-e;* başlatmak *-i;* **~tive** [-şiitiv] öncecilik, inisiyatif

inject [in'cekt] *v/t* şırınga etm.; iğne ile içine sokmak; **~ion** enjeksiyon, iğne yapma

injur|e [incı] *v/t* zarar vermek, dokunmak *-e;* bozmak *-i;* **~ious** [in'cuiriıs] zararlı; **~y** [' ..ırı] zarar; haksızlık; yara

injustice adaletsizlik

ink [ink] mürekkep

inkling [inkliŋ] ima; seziş

ink-pot mürekkep hokkası

inlaid [in'leyd] kakma

inland ['inlınd] *n.* memleket içi; *adj.* iç, dahilî

inlay [in'ley] *v/t* kakma ile süslemek

inlet ['inlet] giriş yolu; GEO koy

inmate ['inmeyt] oturan

inmost ['inmıust] en içerdeki

inn [in] otel, han

innate [i'neyt] fıtrî, doğuştan olan

inner ['inı] iç; **~ tube** iç lastik; **~most** en içerdeki

innkeeper otelci, hancı

innocen|ce ['inısns] suçsuzluk; **~t** suçsuz, günahsız

innovation [inıu'veyşın] yenilik

innumerable [i'nyûmırıbl] sayısız

inoculate [i'nokyuleyt] *v/t* aşılamak; **~ion** aşılama

inoffensive zararsız

inopportune vakitsiz

input ['input] ECON girdi

inquest ['inkwest] JUR resmî soruşturma

inquietude endişe

inquir|e [in'kwayı] *v/t* sormak; *v/i* soruşturmak **(about, after, for** *-i);* araştırmak **(into** *-i);* **~y** sorgu, soruşturma; araştırma

inquisitive [in'kwizitiv] çok sual soran, meraklı

insan|e [in'seyn] deli; **~ity** [in'säniti] akıl hastalığı, delilik

insatiable [in'seyşyıbl], **~te** [-şiit] doymak bilmez

inscri|be [in'skrayb] *v/t* kaydetmek, yazmak; hakketmek; **~ption** [-ipşın] kayıt; yazıt

insect ['insekt] böcek, haşere

insecure emniyetsiz

insensi|ble hissiz, duygusuz; kayıtsız; **~tive** duygusuz

inseparable ayrılmaz

insert [in'sıt] *v/t* sokmak, sıkıştırmak; **~ion** ekleme; ilân

inside ['in'sayd] *n., adj.* iç; *adv.* içerde, içeriye; *prp.* -in içerisinde, içerisine

insight ['insayt] anlayış

insignificant önemsiz

insincere ikiyüzlü

insinuat|e [in'sinyueyt] *v/t* ima etm.; **~ion** ima, üstü kapalı itham

insipid [in'sipid] yavan, lezzetsiz

insist [in'sist] ısrar etm. **(on,**

upon üzerinde); ~ent ısrarlı, inatçı

insolent ['insılınt] küstah, terbiyesiz

insoluble [in'solyubl] erimez; çözülemez

insolvent müflis

insomnia [in'somniı] uykusuzluk

insomuch [insu'maç] that o kadar ki

inspect [in'spekt] v/t teftiş etm.; muayene etm.; ~ion teftiş, yoklama; ~or müfettiş; kontrol memuru

inspir|ation [inspı'reyşın] nefes alma; ilham; ~e [in'spayı] v/t ilham etm., esinlemek

instability sebatsızlık

instal|(l) [in'stôl] v/t yerleştirmek, kurmak; ~lation [.ı'leyşın] yerleştirme; tesisat; ~(l)ment [.ı'stôlmınt] taksit

instance ['instıns] misal, örnek; for ~ meselâ, örneğin

instant ['instınt] n. an; adj. hemen olan; ~aneous [.'teynıyıs] anî; ~ly adv. hemen, derhal

instead [in'sted] yerinde, yerine; ~ of -in yerine

instep ['instep] ayağın üst kısmı

instigat|e ['instigeyt] v/t kışkırtmak; ~or kışkırtıcı

instinct ['instinkt] içgüdü, insiyak; ~ive [.'stinktiv] içgüdülü

institut|e ['instityût] n. ensti-

tü; kuruluş; kurum; v/t kurmak; ~ion kuruluş, müessese

instruct [in'strakt] v/t eğitmek; talimat vermek -e; ~ion eğitim, talim; pl. emir, direktif sg.; ~ive öğretici; ~or eğitmen, okutman

instrument ['instrumınt] alet; MUS çalgı, saz; JUR belge

insubordinate [insı'bôdnit] itaatsiz

insufferable tahammül olunamaz

insufficient eksik

insula|r [in'syulı] adaya ait, adada yaşıyan; ~te [.eyt] v/t izole etm., yalıtmak

insult ['insalt] n. hakaret; v/t -in şerefine dokunmak

insur|ance [in'şuırıns] sigorta; ~e [.'şuı] v/t sigorta etm.; sağlamak

insurmountable [insı'maun-tıbl] geçilemez

insurrection [insı'rekşın] ayaklanma

intact [in'täkt] dokunulmamış, eksiksiz

integral [in'tigrıl] gerekli; tam, bütün; ~ate v/t tamamlamak, bütünlemek; ~ity [in'tegriti] bütünlük; dürüstlük

intellect ['intilekt] akıl; anlık; ~ual [.'lektyuıl] akla ait; bilgili, zekâ sahibi

intellig|ence [in'telicıns] akıl, anlayış, haber; ~ence service istihbarat dairesi; ~ent akıllı, zeki, anlayışlı; ~ible anlaşılır

intemperate taşkın; şiddetli

intend [in'tend] v/t niyet etm., tasarlamak

intense|e [in'tens] keskin, şiddetli, gergin; ~ify [~ifay] v/t -in şiddetini artırmak; v/i şiddetlenmek; ~ity keskinlik, şiddet; ~ive şiddetli

intent [in'tent] n. niyet, maksat; adj. gayretli; meşgul (on ile); ~ion niyet, maksat; ~ional kasıtlı

inter [in'tə] v/t gömmek

inter|**cede** [intə'sid] aracılık etm.; ~cept [~'sept] v/t durdurmak; -in yolunu kesmek; ~cession [~'seşin] şefaat, iltimas

interchange [intə'çeync] n. mübadele; v/t değiştirmek

intercourse ['intıkôs] münasebet

interdict [intə'dikt] v/t yasak etm.

interest ['intrist] n. ilgi, merak; menfaat; ECON faiz; v/t ilgilendirmek; ~ed ilgili (in ile); meraklı (-e); ~ing ilgi çekici, ilginç

interfere [intı'fii] karışmak, mâni olm. (with -e); ~nce karışma, müdahale

interior [in'tiiriı] iç; içerdeki

inter|**jection** [intı'ceksın] ünlem; ~lude [~'luud] ara faslı

intermedia|**ry** [intı'mîdyıri] aracı; aracılık eden; ~te [~yıt] ortadaki; aradaki

inter|**mission** aralık, fasıla; ~mittent fever [intı'mitınt -] MED sıtma

intern ['intən] v/t enterne etm.; n. Am. stajyer doktor; ~al [~'tənl] iç

inter|**national** uluslararası; ~net internet; ~pellation [intəpe'leyşın] POL gensoru; ~pose [~'pouz] v/t -in arasına koymak; v/i araya girmek

interpret [in'tə:prit] v/t -in manasını açıklamak; ~ation yorum, tefsir; ~er tercüman, çevirmen

interrogat|**e** [in'terıugeyt] v/t sorguya çekmek; ~ion sorgu; note (mark, point) of ~ion GR soru işareti; ~ive [intı'rogıtiv] pronoun GR soru zamiri

interrupt [intı'rapt] v/t kesmek; ara vermek -e; ~ion ara, fasıla

intersect [intı'sekt] v/t ikiye bölmek; v/i kesişmek; ~ion kesişme, kavşak

interurban [intır'əbın] şehirlerarası

interval ['intıvıl] ara, fasıla; müddet

interven|**e** [intı'vîn] araya girmek; ~tion [~'venşın] araya girme; aracılık

interview ['intıvyû] n. görüşme, mülâkat; v/t görüşmek b. ile

intestine [in'testin] ANAT bağırsak

intima|**cy** ['intimısi] sıkı dostluk; ~te ['_it] *adj.* sıkı fıkı; içten; ['_eyt] *v/t* üstü kapalı anlatmak, ima etm.; ~tion ima

intimidate [in'timideyt] *v/t* korkutmak

into ['intu, 'inti] -e, *-in* içerisine

intolera|ble tahammül olunmaz; ~nce taassup; ~nt hoşgörüsüz

intoxicate [in'toksikeyt] *v/t* sarhoş etm.

intransitive GR geçişsiz

intrepid [in'trepid] yılmaz

intri|cate ['intrikit] karışık; ~gue [in'tríg] *n.* entrika; *v/i* entrika çevirmek

introduc|e [intri'dyûs] *v/t* tanıştırmak, tanıtmak (to *-e*); ~tion [_'dakşın] takdim; önsöz; ~tory [_'daktıri] tanıtma maksadıyle yapılan

intru|de [in'truud] *v/t* zorla sokmak; *v/i* zorla sokulmak (into *-e*); ~der davetsiz misafir; zorla sokulan biri; ~sion [_jın] içeri sokulma

intuition [intyu'işın] sezgi, içine doğma

invade [in'veyd] *v/t* saldırmak, istilâ etm. *-e*; ~r saldıran

invalid [in'inválid] JUR hükümsüz; MED hasta, sakat; ~ate [_eyt] *v/t* hükümsüz kılmak

invaluable para biçilmez

invariab|le değişmez; ~ly *adv.* değişmeyerek; her zaman

invasion [in'veyjın] akın,

saldırış, istilâ

invent [in'vent] *v/t* icat etm.; uydurmak; ~ion icat; uydurma; ~or mucit, türeten

inver|se [in'v3s] ters; ~sion ters dönme; ters çevirme; ~t *v/t* tersine çevirmek; ~ted commas *pl.* GR tırnaklar

invest [in'vest] *v/t* ECON yatırmak; *authority:* vermek *-e*; MIL kuşatmak *-i*

investigat|e [in'vestigeyt] *v/t* araştırmak; ~ion araştırma

investment [in'vestmınt] ECON yatırma; yatırılan para

invincible [in'vinsıbl] yenilmez

inviolable [in'vayılıbl] dokunulmaz; bozulamaz

invisible [in'vizıbl] görülmez

invit|ation [invi'teyşın] davet, çağrı; davetiye; ~e [in'vayt] *v/t* davet etm., çağırmak

invoice [in'voys] ECON fatura

invoke [in'vuuk] *v/t* yalvarmak *-e*; çağırmak *-i*

involuntary tasarlanmamış

involve [in'volv] *v/t* sarmak; sokmak, karıştırmak (in *-e*); gerektirmek

invulnerable yaralanamaz

inward ['inwıd] iç; ~(s) içe doğru

iodine ['ayudîn] CHEM iyot

irascible [i'räsibl] çabuk öfkelenir

Ir|eland ['ayılınd] İrlanda; ~ish [_riş] İrlandalı; İrlanda dili irksome ['ɔksım] usandırıcı

iron ['ayın] *n.* demir; ütü; *adj.* demirden, demir gibi; *v/t* ütülemek

ironic(al) [ay'ronik(ıl)] alay eden

iron|ing ütüleme; ~monger hırdavatçı; ~works *pl.* demirhane *sg.*

irony ['ayırni] alay, istihza

irradiate [i'reydieyt] *v/t* aydınlatmak

irrational akla uymaz

irreconcilable barıştırılamaz

irrecoverable geri alınamaz, telâfi edilemez

irredeemable ıslah olunamaz; ECON nakde tahvil olunamaz

irregular düzensiz, usule aykırı; GR kural dışı

irrelevant konu, dışı

irreparable [i'repırıbl] telâfisi imkânsız; tamir olunamaz

irreplacable yeri doldurulamaz

irresistible karşı konulamaz

irrespective of -*e* bakmaksızın

irresponsible sorumsuz, güvenilemez

irretrievable telâfi edilemez, bir daha ele geçmez

irreverent [i'revırınt] saygısız

irrevocable [i'revıkıbl] değiştirilemez, geri alınamaz

irrigat|e ['irigeyt] *v/t* sulamak; ~ion sulama

irrita|ble ['iritıbl] çabuk kızan, titiz; ~te ['–eyt] *v/t* gücendirmek, sinirlendirmek; ~tion sinirlilik, dargınlık

is [iz] -dir, -tir

Islam ['izlâm] İslâm, müslümanlık; ~ic [–'lämik] İslâma ait

island ['aylınd], isle [ayl] ada

isolat|e ['aysıleyt] *v/t* ayırmak, tecrit etm.; ~ion ayırma, tecrit

Israel ['izreyıl] İsrail

issue ['işuu] *n.* çıkış; akma; sonuç; döl, zürriyet; yayım, dağıtma; *v/i* çıkmak; *v/t* çıkarmak, dağıtmak, yayınlamak

isthmus ['ismıs] GEO berzah

it [it] o, onu, ona *(cinssiz)*

Ital|ian [i'tälyın] İtalyan; İtalyanca; ~y ['itıli] İtalya

itch [iç] *n.* kaşıntı; *v/i* kaşınmak

item ['aytım] parça; fıkra, madde

itinerary [ay'tinırıri] yol; yolcu rehberi

its [its] onun(ki) *(cinssiz)*

itself [it'self] bizzat, kendi; by ~ kendi kendine

ivory ['ayvıri] fildişi

ivy ['ayvi] BOT sarmaşık

J

jab [cäb] *v/t* dürtmek, itmek
jack [cäk] TECH kriko; bacak, vale (*cards*); *v/t* bocurgat ile kaldırmak
jackal ['cäköl] ZOO çakal
jack|ass ['cäkäs] erkek eşek; *fig.* ['kaas] ahmak; **~daw** ['-dô] küçük karga
jacket ['cäkit] ceket; kitap zarfı; kaplama
jack|-knife ['cäk-] çakı; **~pot** *oyunda* pot
jag [cäg] diş, uç; **~ged** ['-gid] dişli, çentik
jail [ceyl] *n.* cezaevi; *v/t* tutuklamak; **~er** gardiyan
jam [cäm] **1.** reçel, marmelat; **2.** *n.* sıkışma, kalabalık; *v/t* sıkıştırmak; *v/i* sıkışmak
janitor ['cänitı] kapıcı
January ['cänyuırı] ocak ayı
Japan [cı'pän] Japonya; **~ese** [cäpı'nîz] Japon(yalı); Japonca
jar [câ] kavanoz
jaundice ['côndis] MED sarılık
javelin ['cävlin] cirit
jaw [cô] çene; **~bone** çene kemiği
jazz [cäz] caz
jealous ['celıs] kıskanç; **~y** kıskançlık, haset
jeep [cîp] cip
jeer [cıı] *a.* alay, yuha; *v/i* yuhalamak (**at** *-i*)

peltelеştirmek; *v/i* pelteleşmek; **~fish** ZOO denizanası, medüz
jeopardize ['cepıdayz] *v/t* tehlikeye koymak
jerk [cık] *n.* ani çekiş; *v/i* birdenbire çekmek; *v/t* atmak; **~y** sarsıntılı
jersey ['cızi] jarse
jest [cest] *n.* şaka; *v/i* şaka söylemek; **~er** şakacı
Jesu|it ['cezyuit] REL cizvit; **~s** ['cîzıs] Hazreti İsa
jet [cet] meme; tepki; AVIA jet uçağı; *v/i* fışkırmak; **~ lag** *uçakla kısa bir süre içinde birçok saat dilimi geçmiş olmaktan kaynaklanan yorgunluk ve benzeri belirtiler*
jetty ['ceti] dalgakıran; iskele
Jew [cuu] Yahudi
jewel ['cuuıl] kıymetli taş, mücevher; **~(l)er** kuyumcu; **~(le)ry** kuyumculuk; mücevherat *pl.*
Jew|ish ['cuuiş] Yahudi, Musevi; **~ry** ['-ırı] Yahudilik
jiggle ['cigıl] *v/i* sallanmak; *v/t* sallamak
jingle ['cingıl] *n.* çıngırtı; *v/t* çıngırdatmak
jingo ['cingıu] POL şoven
job [cob] iş, görev; **out of ~**, **~less** işsiz; **~work** götürü iş
jockey ['coki] cokey
jog [cog] *v/t* sarsmak; *v/i* yavaş

gezinmek

join [coyn] *n.* bitişim noktası; *v/t* birleştirmek, bağlamak; katılmak *-e*; ~**er** doğramacı, marangoz; ~**t** *n.* ek; ANAT eklem, mafsal; *Am. sl.* esrarlı sigara; *adj.* birleşik, ortaklaşa; ~**t-stock company** ECON anonim ortaklık

joke [cıuk] *n.* şaka; *v/i* şaka yapmak; ~**r** *oyunda* koz, coker

jolly ['coli] şen, neşeli

jolt [cıult] *n.* sarsıntı; *v/t* sarsmak

Jordan ['côdn] Ürdün

jostle ['cosl] *v/t* itip kakmak

jot [cot] *n.* zerre; ~ **down** *v/t* yazıvermek

journal ['cɜnl] gazete; dergi; yevmiye defteri; ~**ism** ['-lizım] gazetecilik; ~**ist** gazeteci

journey ['cɜni] *n.* yolculuk, seyahat; *v/i* seyahat etm.; ~**man** kalfa

jovial ['cıuvyıl] şen, keyifli

joy [coy] sevinç, neşe; ~**ful**, ~**ous** neşeli, sevinçli

jubilant ['cuubilınt] büyük neşe içinde; ~**ee** ['-lî] ellinci yıldönümü; neşeli kutlama

Judaic [cuu'deyik] Yahudilere ait; ~**sm** Yahudilik

judge [cac] *n.* hâkim, yargıç; hakem; *v/t* yargılamak; tenkit etm.; karar vermek (hakkında); ~**(e)ment** hüküm, yargı; mahkeme kararı; 2**(e)ment Day** REL kıya-

met günü

judicial [cu'dişıl] mahkemeye ait, adlî; ~**ious** tedbirli, akıllı

jug [cag] testi, çömlek

juggle ['cagl] *n.* hokkabazlık; *v/i* hokkabazlık yapmak; ~**r** hokkabaz

Jugoslav ['yûgu'slâv] *hist.* Yugoslav(yalı); ~**ia** [-yı] *hist.* Yugoslavya

juice [cuus] özsu, usare; ~**y** sulu, özlü

juke-box ['cuuk-] otomatik pikap

July [cu'lay] temmuz

jump [camp] *n.* atlama, sıçrama; *v/t* atlamak, sıçramak; *v/t* atlamak (*-den*, *-i*); ~**er** atlayıcı; ~**y** sinirli

junction ['cankşın] birleşme; kavşak; ~**ure** birleşme yeri; nazik zaman, önemli an

June [cuun] haziran

jungle ['cangl] cengel

junior ['cuunyı] yaşça küçük; ast

junk [cank] pılı pırtı, çöp; ~ **food** *gıdasal değeri az abur cubur*

juridical [cuı'ridikıl] adlî, kanunî; ~**isdiction** [-ris'dikşın] yargılama hakkı; kaza dairesi; ~**isprudence** ['-rispruudıns] hukuk ilmi; ~**or** ['-rı] jüri üyesi; ~**y** ['-ri] jüri

just [cast] *adj.* âdil, insaflı; haklı; *adv.* sadece; tam; hemen; ancak; şimdi; ~ **now** hemen şimdi

justice ['castis] adelet, insaf; hâkim, yargıç

justif|ication [castifi'keyşın] haklı çık(ar)ma; mazur gösterme; ~**y** ['-fay] v/t haklı çıkarmak

justly ['castli] adv. haklı olarak

jut [cat]: ~ **out** dışarı çıkmış olm.

juvenile ['cuuvinayl] genç; gençlikle ilgili

K

kangaroo [kängı'ruu] zoo kanguru

keel [kîl] NAUT omurga

keen [kîn] keskin; canlı; şiddetli; düşkün (on -e)

keep [kîp] n. geçim; v/t tutmak, korumak; işletmek; sürdürmek; devam etm. (-ing -meğe); v/i kalmak; ~ **away** v/i uzak durmak; v/t uzak tutmak; ~ **off** v/t uzak tutmak (from -den); v/i uzak kalmak; ~ **on** v/t çıkarmamak, söndürmemek; devam etm. (-ing -meğe); ~ **up** geri kalmamak (with -de); ~**er** bakıcı; bekçi; ~**ing** koruma; geçim; in ~**ing** uygun (with -e); ~**sake** hatıra, andaç

kennel ['kenl] köpek kulübesi

kerb(stone) ['kɜːb(-)] yaya kaldırımının kenar taşı

kerchief ['kɜːcif] baş örtüsü

kernel ['kɜːnl] çekirdek

kettle ['ketl] çaydanlık; ka-zan; ~**drum** MUS dümbelek

key [kî] anahtar; tuş; ~**board** klavye; ~**hole** anahtar deliği; ~**note** ana nota; fig. temel, ilke

khaki ['kaaki] toprak rengi,

hakî

khan [kaan] han

kick [kik] n. tekme, tepme; v/t tekmelemek, çiftelemek

kid [kid] n. zoo oğlak; sl. çocuk; v/t takılmak -e; ~**nap** ['-näp] v/t zorla kaçırmak

kidney ['kidni] ANAT böbrek

kill [kil] v/t öldürmek; time: geçirmek; ~**er** adam öldüren

kiln [kiln] kireç ocağı, fırın

kilo|gram(me) ['kiluɡräm] kilo(gram); ~**metre** Am. ~**meter** kilometre; ~**watt** kilovat

kilt [kilt] İskoç erkeklerinin giydiği eteklik

kin [kin] akraba

kind [kaynd] n. cins, çeşit; adj. sevimli, nazik

kindergarten ['kindıɡaatn] anaokulu

kindle ['kindl] v/t tutuşturmak, yakmak; v/i tutuşmak

kindness ['kayndnis] şefkat, yumuşaklık

kindred ['kindrid] akraba; akrabalık

king [kiŋ] kıral; şah; ~**dom** kırallık, kıraliyet; ~**size** normalden büyük

kinship ['kinşip] akrabalık

kipper ['kipı] tuzlanmış isli ringa balığı

kiss [kis] *n.* buse, öpücük; *v/t* öpmek

kit[1] [kit] avadanlık; takım

kit[2] yavru kedi

kitchen ['kiçin] mutfak; ~ette [-'net] ufak mutfak

kite [kayt] uçurtma

kitten ['kitn] yavru kedi

knack [näk] hüner, ustalık

knapsack ['näpsäk] sırt çantası

knave [neyv] herif, düzenbaz; *oyunda* bacak; ~ry ['-ıri] hilekârlık

knead [nîd] *v/t* yoğurmak; masaj yapmak

knee [nî] ANAT diz; ~cap, ~pan diz kapağı; ~l [-l] *v/i* diz çökmek

knelt [nelt] *s.* kneel

knew [nyû] *s.* know

knife [nayf], *pl.* knives [-vz] *n.* bıçak; *v/t* bıçaklamak

knight [nayt] silâhşor; şövalye

knit [nit] *v/t* örmek; ~ the eyebrows kaşlarını çatmak

knob [nob] topuz; pürtük

knock [nok] *n.* vuruş, çalma, darbe; *v/t* vurmak; çarpmak *-e*; *v/i* çalmak (**at** *-i*); ~ down *v/t* yere sermek; ~out nakavt; oyun dışı etme; ~er kapı tokmağı

knoll [nıul] tepecik

knot [not] *n.* düğüm, bağ; küme; güç durum; *v/t* düğümlemek, bağlamak; ~ty düğümlü; budaklı

know [nıu] *v/t* bilmek; tanımak; **make** ~n *v/t* tanıtmak; bildirmek; ~ing akıllı, açıkgöz; ~ingly *adv.* bilerek; ~ledge ['nolic] bilgi, malumat

knuckle ['nakl] ANAT parmak orta eklemi; ~bone aşıkkemiği

L

label ['leybl] *n.* etiket, yafta; *v/t* etiketlemek

labo|ratory [lı'borıtırı] laboratuvar; ~rious [-'bôriıs] çalışkan; yorucu

labo(u)r ['leybı] *n.* iş, çalışma; emek; işçi sınıfı; MED doğum ağrıları *pl.*; zahmet; *v/i* çalışmak, uğraşmak; **Ministry of** 2 **Çalışma Bakanlığı**; **forced** ~ angarya; 2 **Party İşçi Parti-**si; ~ **union** işçi sendikası; ~er işçi, rençper

lace [leys] *n.* bağ, şerit; dantel(a); *v/t* bağlamak; dantel ile süslemek

lack [läk] *n.* noksan, eksiklik; ihtiyaç; *v/i* eksik olm.; *v/t* muhtaç olm. *-e*

lackey ['läki] uşak, hizmetçi

laconic [lı'konik] kısa ve öz

lacquer ['läkı] *n.* vernik; *v/t*

vernik ile kaplamak

lad [läd] genç, delikanlı

ladder ['lädı] el merdiveni; **~proof** çözülmez (*corap*)

lad|e [leyd] *v/t* yüklemek; **~en** ['-n] *s.* **lade**; **~ing** yük

ladle ['leydl] kepçe

lady ['leydi] bayan, hanım; asılzade kadın, leydi; **~bird** zoo gelinböceği; **~like** hanıma yakışır

lag [läg] *n.* geçikme; *v/i* geri kalmak

lager(beer) ['lâgı(-)] Alman birası

lagoon [lı'guun] GEO deniz kulağı

laid [leyd] *s.* **lay**

lain [leyn] *s.* **lie**

lair [läı] in, yatak

lake [leyk] göl

lamb [läm] kuzu

lame [leym] *adj.* topal, ayağı sakat; *v/t* topallamak

lament [lı'ment] *n.* inilti; *v/i* inlemek; *v/t* ağlamak *b.* için; **~able** ['lämıntıbl] acınacak; **~ation** [lämen'teyşın] ağlayış, inleme

lamp [lämp] lamba; **~post** sokak feneri direği; **~shade** abajur

lance [lâns] *n.* mızrak; *v/t* deşmek, yarmak

land [länd] *n.* toprak, kara; ülke; arsa; arazi; *v/i* karaya çıkmak, yere inmek; *v/t* karaya çıkarmak; indirmek; **~ed property** arazi, mülk; **~holder** mülk sahibi

landing ['ländiŋ] iniş, karaya çıkma; sahanlık; **~gear** AVIA iniş takımı; **~stage** NAUT iskele

land|lady ['länleydi] pansiyoncu kadın; ev sahibesi; **~lord** ['län-] mal sahibi; **~mark** ['länd-] sınır taşı; **~scape** ['län-] manzara; peyzaj; **~slide** ['länd-] GEO, *fig.*, **~slip** ['länd-] GEO kayşa, heyelân

lane [leyn] dar sokak, dar yol; otomobil yolu

language ['läŋgwic] dil, lisan

langu|id ['läŋgwid] gevşek, cansız; **~ish** *v/i* gevşemek, zayıf düşmek; **~or** ['-gı] gevşelik, cansızlık

lank [läŋk] uzun ve zayıf; **~y** sırık gibi

lantern ['läntın] fener

lap [läp] *n.* diz üstü; kucak; etek; *v/t* üst üste bindirmek; yalıyarak içmek

lapel [lı'pel] klapa

lapse [läps] kusur; geçme, mürur

laptop ['läptop] dizüstü bilgisayar

larceny ['lâsıni] hırsızlık

lard [lâd] domuz yağı; **~er** kiler

large [lâc] büyük, iri, bol, geniş; **at ~** serbest; ayrıntılı olarak; **~scale** büyük çapta

lark [lâk] zoo tarla kuşu; *fig.* şaka

larva ['lâvı] zoo kurtçuk, sürfe

larynx ['lärinks] ANAT hançere, gırtlak

lascivious [lı'siviıs] şehvetli

lash [läş] *n.* kamçı darbesi; kamçı; kirpik; *v/t* kamçılamak; iple bağlamak

lass [läş] kız

lassitude ['läsityûd] yorgunluk

last[1] [lâst] son, sonuncu; son defa, son olarak; **at ~** sonunda; **~ (but) not least** özellikle

last[2] *v/i* devam etm., sürmek; dayanmak; **~ing** sürekli; dayanıklı

latch [läç] *n.* mandal, sürgü; *v/t* mandallamak

late [leyt] geç; gecikmiş; ölü, rahmetli; **as ~ as** ancak; artık; **at (the) ~st** en geç olarak; **of ~** son zamanlarda; **~ly** geçenlerde; **~r on** daha sonra

lath [lâth] lata

lathe [leydh] torna tezgâhı

lather ['lâdhı] *n.* sabun köpüğü; *v/i* köpürmek; *v/t* sabunlamak

Latin ['lätin] Latin(ce)

latitude ['lätityûd] GEO enlem, arz

latter ['lätı] son, sonraki

lattice ['lätis] kafes

laudable ['lôdıbl] övgüye değer

laugh [lâf] *n.* gülme, gülüş; *v/i* gülmek; alay etm. (**at** ile); **~ter** gülüş; kahkaha

launch [lônç] *v/t* NAUT kızaktan suya indirmek; atmak,

fırlatmak; **~ing-pad** atış rampası

laundr|ess ['lôndris] çamaşırcı kadın; **~y** çamaşır; çamaşırhane

laurel ['lorıl] BOT defne

lavatory ['lävıtıri] yıkanma yeri; tuvalet, helâ

lavender ['lävındı] lavanta

lavish ['läviş] *adj.* savurgan, müsrif; *v/t* bol bol harcamak

law [lô] kanun, yasa; nizam; hukuk; **~ful** kanuna uygun, meşru; **~less** kanuna aykırı; kanunsuz

lawn [lôn] çimen(lik)

law|suit dava; **~yer** ['lôyı] avukat, dava vekili

lax [läks] gevşek; ihmalci; **~ative** ['_ıtiv] MED sürgün ilâcı

lay[1] [ley] *s.* lie

lay[2] REL layik; işin ehli olmıyan

lay[3] *n.* durum; *v/t* koymak, yatırmak, yaymak, sermek; *table:* kurmak; **~ out** yaymak; tasarlamak; düzenlemek; **~er** kat, tabaka

layman ['leymın] meslek sahibi olmıyan kimse

layout düzen, tertip

lazy ['leyzi] tembel

lead[1] [led] kurşun

lead[2] [lîd] *n.* kılavuzluk, öncülük; THEA baş rol; tasma kayışı; EL ana tel; *v/t* yol göstermek -*e*; kumanda etm. -*i*; götürmek -*i*; idare etm. -*i*

leaden ['ledın] kurşun(dan)

leader ['lîdı] önder, lider, öna-

yak; ~ship önderlik, liderlik
leading ['lîdîŋ] önde olan, baş, başlıca
leaf [lif] *pl.* **leaves** [~vz] BOT yaprak; (*door*) kanat; ~let ['~lit] yaprakçık; ufak risale
league [lîg] lig; birlik
leak [lîk] *n.* delik, akıntı; *v/i* sızmak; ~age sızıntı; ~y sızıntılı
lean¹ [lîn] zayıf
lean² *v/t* dayamak; *v/i* dayanmak (against *-e*)
leant [lent] *s.* **lean**²
leap [lîp] *n.* atlama, sıçrayış; *v/i* atlamak, sıçramak; *v/t* atlatmak; ~t [lept] *s.* **leap**; ~-**year** artık yıl
learn [lən] *v/t* öğrenmek; ~ed ['~nid] âlim, bilgili; ~ing öğrenme, bilgi; ~t [lənt] *s.* **learn**
lease [lîs] *n.* kira(lama); *v/t* kiralamak; kiraya vermek
leash [lîş] tasma zinciri
least [lîst] en az, en ufak; at ~ hiç olmazsa
leather ['ledhı] kösele, meşin
leave [lîv] *n.* müsaade; izin; *v/t* bırakmak, terketmek; ayrılmak *-den*
leaven ['levn] maya
Lebanon ['lebının] Lübnan
lecture ['lekçı] *n.* konferans; umumî ders; azarlama; *v/i* konferans vermek, ders vermek; *v/t* azarlamak; ~r konferans veren kimse; doçent
led [led] *s.* **lead**
ledge [lec] düz çıkıntı; kaya

tabakası
leech [lîç] zoo sülük
leek [lîk] BOT pırasa
leer [lii] kötü niyetle bakmak (at *-e*)
left¹ [left] *s.* **leave**
left² sol, sol taraf; ~-**handed** solak
leg [leg] bacak; but; **pull** *someone's* ~ takılmak *-e*
legacy ['legısi] miras, kalıt
legal ['lîgıl] kanunî, meşru; ~**ize** *v/t* kanunlaştırmak, meşru kılmak
legation [li'geyşın] POL orta elçilik
legend ['lecınd] masal, hikâye; yazı; ~ary efsanevî
legible ['lecıbl] okunaklı
legion ['lîcın] eski Roma alayı; birçok; kalabalık
legislat|ion [lecis'leyşın] JUR yasama; ~ive ['~lıtiv] yasamalı; ~or ['~leyti] kanun yapan
legitimate [li'citimit] kanuna uygun, meşru
leisure ['leji] boş vakit; ~ly rahatça
lemon ['lemın] limon; ~ **squash** limon suyu; ~ade [~'neyd] limonata
lend [lend] *v/t* ödünç vermek; ~ **help** yardım etm. (to *-e*)
length [length] uzunluk; boy; süre; at ~ nihayet; ~en *v/t* uzatmak; *v/i* uzamak; ~**wise** ['~wayz] uzunluğuna
lenient ['lînyınt] yumuşak huylu

lens [lenz] PHYS mercek, adese

Lent[1] [lent] REL büyük perhiz

lent[2] [lent] *s.* lend

lentil ['lentil] BOT mercimek

leopard ['lepid] ZOO pars

lep|er ['lepı] MED cüzamlı; **~rosy** ['-rısı] cüzam, miskin hastalığı

less [les] daha az, daha küçük; MATH eksi; **~en** *v/t* küçültmek, azaltmak; *v/i* azalmak; **~er** daha az

lesson ['lesn] ders; ibret

lest [lest] olmasın diye; belki

let [let] *v/t* bırakmak; kiraya vermek; müsaade etm. *-mesine*; **~ alone** şöyle dursun; **~ down** *v/t* indirmek; hayal kırıklığına uğratmak; **~ go** elinden bırakmak

lethal ['lîdhıl] öldürücü

lethargy ['ledhıci] uyuşukluk

letter ['letı] harf; mektup; *pl.* edebiyat; **~box** mektup kutusu; **~head** mektup başlığı

lettuce ['letis] BOT salata

leuk(a)emia [lyû'kîmii] MED lösemi, kan kanseri

level ['levl] *n.* seviye, hiza; tesviye aleti; *adj.* düz, düzlem; ufkî, yatay; *v/t* düzlemek, tesviye etm.; **~ crossing** *yolun* demiryolundan aynı seviyede geçmesi

lever ['lîvı] manivela

levity ['leviti] hoppalık

levy ['levi] *n.* toplama, tarh; *v/t* tarhetmek; **~ war** harp açmak (**on** *-e* karşı)

lewd [luud] şehvet düşkünü

liab|ility [layı'biliti] sorumluluk, mükellefiyet; **~le** ['-bl] sorumlu (**for** *-den*), mükellef (ile); maruz (**to** *-e*)

liar ['layı] yalancı

libel ['laybıl] JUR iftira

liber|al ['libırıl] serbest düşünceli; POL liberal; **~ate** ['-reyt] *v/t* kurtarmak, özgür kılmak; **~ation** kurtuluş, serbest bırakma; **~ty** ['-ti] hürriyet, serbestlik

librar|ian [lay'brärirın] kütüphane memuru; **~y** ['-briri] kitaplık, kütüphane

lice [lays] *pl., s.* louse

licen|ce, *Am.* **~se** ['laysıns] *n.* ruhsat; müsaade; çapkınlık; *v/t* ruhsat vermek; yetki vermek *-e*; **~see** [-'sî] ruhsat sahibi; **~tious** [-'senşıs] şehvete düşkün

lick [lik] *v/t* yalamak; dayak atmak *-e*

lid [lid] kapak

lie[1] [lay] *n.* yalan; *v/i* yalan söylemek

lie[2] *v/i* yatmak, uzanmak

lieutenant [lef'tenınt, NAUT le'tenınt, *Am.* luu'tenınt] MIL teğmen; **~colonel** yarbay; **~general** korgeneral

life [layf] *pl.* lives [-vz] hayat; ömür; **~ assurance, ~ insurance** hayat sigortası; **~ expectancy** ortalama ömür uzunluğu; **~ support** yaşam destek (*ünitesi/makinesi*); **~belt** cankurtaran kemeri;

~**guard** cankurtaran yüzücü-sü; ~**less** cansız; ~**like** canlı gibi görünen; ~**time** hayat süresi, ömür

lift [lift] *n.* asansör; kaldırma gücü; *v/t* kaldırmak, yükselt-mek; *v/i* yükselmek; **give** *so.* **a** ~ arabasına almak -*i*

ligament ['ligımınt] ANAT bağ; ~**ture** [-çu] MED kanı durduran bağ

light[1] [layt] *n.* ışık, aydınlık; *adj.* açık; ~ (**up**) *v/t* yakmak; aydınlatmak; *v/i* parılda-mak; **give** *so.* **a** ~ ateş ver-mek -*e*

light[2] hafif

lighten[1] ['laytn] *v/t* aydınlat-mak

lighten[2] *v/t* hafifletmek

lighter ['laytı] çakmak; ~**house** fener kulesi; ~**ning** şimşek, yıldırım

lightweight *adj.* hafif; *n.* tüysüklet

like[1] [layk] *v/t* sevmek, beğen-mek

like[2] gibi; benzer -*e*; ~**lihood** ['layklihud] ihtimal; ~**ly** muhtemel; ~**ness** benzerlik; ~**wise** [-wayz] dahi, keza

liking ['laykin] beğenme, me-yil

lilac ['laylık] BOT leylak; *adj.* açık mor

lily ['lili] BOT zambak; ~ **of the valley** inciçiçeği

limb [lim] uzuv, örgen; dal

lime [laym] **1.** kireç; **2.** BOT ıhlamur; **in the** ~**light** *fig.*

göz önünde, halkın dilinde; ~**stone** kireç taşı

limit ['limit] *n.* had, sınır; *v/t* sınırlamak; hasretmek; **off** ~**s** *Am.* yasak bölge; ~**ation** tahdit; kayıtlama; ~**ed** mah-dut, sayılı; ECON limitet

limp [limp] *adj.* gevşek, yu-muşak; *v/i* topallamak

line [layn] *n.* sıra, dizi; çizgi; satır; hat; ip, olta; *v/t* dizmek, sıralamak; çizgilerle göster-mek; astarlamak; **hold the** ~ telefonu kapatmamak; **stand in** ~ kuyrukta bekle-mek

lineament ['liniımınt] yüz hattı

linear ['liniı] doğrusal

linen ['linin] keten bezi; iç ça-maşır

liner ['laynı] NAUT transatlan-tik; AVIA yolcu uçağı

linger ['lingı] *v/i* gecikmek, ayrılamamak

linguistics [lin'gwistiks] *pl.* dilbilim, lengüistik sg.

lining ['laynin] astar

link [link] *n.* zincir halkası; *bil-gisayar:* bağlantı; *fig.* bağ; *v/t* bağlamak; *v/i* bağlanmak

links [links] *pl.* kumurlar; golf oyunu alanı *sg.*

lion ['layın] aslan; ~**ess** dişi aslan

lip [lip] dudak; ~**stick** ruj

liposuction ['lipusaksın] li-posuction

liquid ['likwid] sıvı, mayi; ~**ate** ['-eyt] *v/t* tasfiye etm..

~ity [li'kwiditi] ECON likidite
liquor ['likı] içki; sıvı madde
lisp [lisp] peltek konuşmak
list [list] *n.* liste, cetvel; *v/t* listeye yazmak, kaydetmek
listen ['lisn] dinlemek (to *-i*), kulak vermek (-*e*); ~er dinleyici
listless ['listlis] kayıtsız
lit [lit] *s.* light[1]
literall ['litırıl] harfi harfine; sözlü; ~ry ['-rırı] edebî; ~ture [' ̗riçı] edebiyat
lithe [laydh] elastikî
lit|**re**, *Am.* ~er ['litı] litre
litter ['litı] sedye; teskere; ZOO bir batında doğan yavrular *pl.*; ~ bag çöp torbası
little ['litl] küçük, ufak; az, önemsiz; *n.* ufak miktar, az zaman
live[1] [liv] yaşamak; oturmak, ikamet etm.; geçinmek (on ile)
live[2] [layv] diri, canlı; direkt, doğrudan
live|**lihood** ['layvlihud] geçim, geçinme; ~**liness** canlılık; ~**ly** canlı
liver ['livı] ANAT karaciğer
livery ['livırı] hizmetçi üniforması
livestock ['layv-] çiftlik hayvanları *pl.*
livid ['livid] mavimsi; solgun
living ['liviŋ] hayatta, canlı; yaşayış, geçim; ~**room** oturma odası
lizard ['lizıd] ZOO kertenkele
load [lıud] *n.* yük, hamule; EL

şarj; *v/t* yüklemek; doldurmak
loaf[1] [luf], *pl.* **loaves** [-vz] bütün bir ekmek, somun
loaf[2] *v/i* vaktini boş geçirmek; ~er haylaz, aylak
loam [lıum] balçık
loan [lıun] *n.* ödünç verme, ödünç alma; *v/t* ödünç vermek
loath [lıudh] isteksiz; ~e *v/t* iğrenmek, nefret etm. *-den*; ~**ing** nefret; ~**some** iğrenç, nefret verici
lobby ['lobi] koridor; antre; POL kulis yapanlar *pl.*
lobe [lıub] ANAT kulak memesi
lobster ['lobstı] ZOO ıstakoz
local ['lıukıl] mahallî, yöresel; ~**ity** ['-kâliti] yer, yöre; ~**ize** *v/t* sınırlamak
locate [lıu'keyt] *v/t* yerleştirmek; bulmak; be ~d in *-de* bulunmak
lock [lok] *n.* kilit; yükseltme havuzu; bukle; *v/t* kilitlemek; ~ up kilit altında saklamak; ~**et** [' ̗it] madalyon; ~**out** lokavt; ~**smith** çilingir
locomotive ['lıukımıutiv] lokomotif
locust ['lıukıst] ZOO çekirge
lodge|**e** [loc] *n.* kulübe; in; loca; *v/t* yerleştirmek, barındırmak; *v/i* yerleşmek, kirada oturmak; ~er kiracı; ~**ing** kiralık oda; geçici konut
loft [loft] çatı arası; ~y yüksek; kibirli

log [log] kütük; *bilgisayar:* ~ **in** *a.* **on** *v/i.* oturum açmak; *bilgisayar:* ~ **out** *v/i.* oturum kapamak;
~**book** NAUT rota defteri; ~**cabin** kütüklerden yapılmış kulübe

logic ['locik] mantık; ~**al** mantıkî, makul

loin [loyn] bel; fileto

loiter ['loytı] *v/i* gezmek, aylak dolaşmak

loll [lol] *v/i* sallanmak

lonely ['lunli] yalnız, kimsesiz; tenha

long[1] [loŋ] uzun; çok; **before** ~ **yakında**; **so** ~! Allaha ısmarladık!

long[2] *v/i* can atmak (**for** -*e*), çok istemek (**to** *inf. meği*)

long-distance şehirlerarası

longing ['loŋiŋ] *n.* özlem, iştiyak

longitude ['loncityûd] GEO boylam, tul

look [luk] *n.* bakış, nazar; görünüş, güzellik; *v/i* bakmak (**at** -*e*); görünmek; ~ **after** bakmak -*e*; ~ **for** aramak -*i*; ~ **forward to** beklemek, ummak -*i*; ~ **into** araştırmak -*i*; ~ **out!** dikkat et!; ~ **over** gözden geçirmek -*i*; ~ **up** yukarıya bakmak; *v/t* sözlükte aramak; ~**ing glass** ayna

loom[1] [luum] dokuma tezgâhı

loom[2] *v/i* hayal gibi görünmek

loop [luup] *n.* ilmik, düğüm; *v/t* ilmik yapmak; *v/t* ilmikle-

mek

loose [luus] çözük, gevşek; hafifmeşrep, başıboş; ~**n** ['.-sn] *v/t* gevşetmek, çözmek; *v/i* gevşemek, çözülmek

loot [luut] *n.* yağma, ganimet; *v/i* yağma etm.

lop [lop] *v/t* budamak, kesmek; *v/i* sarkmak; ~**-sided** bir tarafa yatkın

lord [lôd] sahip; lord; **the** 2 Allah, Tanrı; **House of** 2**s** POL Lordlar kamarası; 2 **Mayor** Londra belediye başkanı; 2'**s Prayer** REL İsa'nın öğrettiği dua; 2'**s Supper** kudas, liturya

lorry ['lori] üstü açık yük arabası; kamyon

lose [luuz] *v/t* kaybetmek; kaçırmak; ~**r** kaybeden *veya* yenilen kimse

loss [los] kayıp; zarar; **at a** ~ şaşırmış; zararına

lost [lost] *s.* **lose**; ~**-property office** kayıp eşya bürosu

lot [lot] hisse, pay; talih; çok miktar; **a** ~ **of** çok; **draw** ~**s** kur'a çekmek

loth [luth] *s.* **loath**

lotion ['luşın] losyon

lottery ['lotırı] piyango

loud [laud] (*voice*) yüksek; gürültülü; (*colour*) çiğ; ~**speaker** hoparlör

lounge [launc] *n.* dinlenme salonu; hol; şezlong; *v/i* tembelce uzanmak; avare dolaşmak

louse 322

louse [laus], *pl.* **lice** bit, kehle; ~**y** bitli; alçak

lout [laut] kaba adam

love [lav] *n.* sevgi; aşk; sevgili; *v/t* sevmek; **fall in** ~ **with** âşık olm. -*e*; **send one's** ~ **to** selâm söylemek -*e*; ~**ly** sevimli, güzel; ~**r** sevgili; meraklı

low[1] [lıu] *v/i* böğürmek

low[2] aşağı, alçak; bayağı; düşük; (*voice*) yavaş; ~ **tide** GEO cezir, inik deniz; ~**er** *adj.* daha alçak; *v/t* indirmek, alçaltmak; düşürmek, azaltmak; 2**er House** Avam Kamarası; ~**fat** az yağlı; ~**land** GEO düzarazi; ova; ~**necked** dekolte; ~**pressure** alçak basınçlı; ~**spirited** kederli

loyal ['loyıl] sadık; ~**ty** sadakat

lozenge ['lozinc] eşkenar dörtgen; pastil

lubber ['labı] acemi kimse

lubricate ['luubrikeyt] *v/t* yağlamak

lucid ['luusid] vazıh, berrak

luck [lak] talih, uğur, şans; **bad** ~ talihsizlik, fena talih; ~**y** talihli, şanslı

ludicrous ['luudikrıs] gülünç

lug [lag] *v/t* sürüklemek

luggage ['lagic] bagaj; ~**rack** bagaj filesi; ~**van** furgon

lukewarm ['luukwôm] ılık; *fig.* kayıtsız

lull [lal] *v/t* uyuşturmak; *v/i* uyuşmak; ara, fasıla; ~**aby** ['~ıbay] ninni

lumbago [lam'beygıu] MED lumbago

lumber ['lambı] lüzumsuz eşya; kereste

luminous ['luuminıs] parlak; açık

lump [lamp] topak, yumru, küme; **in the** ~ toptan; ~ **sugar** kesme şeker

lunar ['luunı] aya ait

lunatic ['luunitik] deli; ~ **asylum** tımarhane

lunch [lanç] *n.* öğle yemeği; *v/i* öğle yemeğini yemek; ~**eon** öğle yemeği; ~**hour** öğle tatili

lung [laŋ] ANAT akciğer

lunge [lanc] *v/i* ileri atılmak **(at** -*e*)

lurch [lɜç] *v/i* sallanmak

lure [lyuı] *n.* cazibe, tuzak; *v/t* cezbetmek

lurk [lɜk] *v/i* gizlenmek

luscious ['laşıs] pek tatlı, nefis

lust [last] şhvet; hırs

lustre, *Am.* ~**er** ['lastı] perdah; avize

lusty ['lasti] dinç, kuvvetli

lute [luut] MUS ut, lavta

luxate ['lakseyt] MED *v/t* mafsaldan çıkarmak

luxuriant [lag'zyuırıınt] bol; ~**ious** [~rııs] süslü, tantanalı; ~**y** ['lakşıri] lüks; süs

lying ['layiŋ] *s.* **lie**[1], **lie**[2]

lynch [linç] *v/t* linç etm.

lynx [liŋks] ZOO vaşak

lyric ['lirik] lirik

M

ma'am [mäm, mım] *s.* **madam**

macaroni [mäkı'rıuni] makarna

machine [mı'şîn] makina; **~gun** makinalı tüfek; **~made** makina işi; **~ry** makinalar *pl.*

mack [mäk] *s.* **~intosh**

mackerel ['mäkrıl] zoo uskumru

mackintosh ['mäkintoş] yağmurluk

mad [mäd] deli, çılgın; kuduz; öfkeli; **drive ~** *v/t* çıldırtmak; **go ~** delirmek

madam ['mädım] hanımefendi, bayan

madden ['mädn] *v/t* çıldırtmak

made [meyd] *s.* **make**

mad|man deli; **~ness** delilik, çılgınlık

magazine [mägı'zîn] depo; TECH şarjör; dergi

maggot ['mägıt] kurt, sürfe

magic ['mäcik] sihir, büyü; sihirbazlık; **~(al)** sihirli; **~ian** [mı'cişın] sihirbaz

magistrate ['mäcistreyt] sulh yargıcı

magnanimous [mäg'nänimıs] yüce gönüllü, âlicenap

magnet ['mägnit] mıknatıs; **~ic** [-'netik] manyetik;

~ism manyetizma

magnificen|ce [mäg'nifisns] azamet, ihtişam; **~t** muhteşem

magnify ['mägnifay] *v/t* büyütmek; **~ing glass** büyüteç, pertavsız

magpie ['mägpay] zoo saksağan

mahogany [mı'hogıni] mahun

maid [meyd] kadın hizmetçi; kız; **old ~** gençliği geçmiş kız; **~en** kız; evlenmemiş; bakir; **~en name** kızlık adı

mail¹ [mayl] zırh

mail² *n.* posta; *v/t* posta ile göndermek; **~bag** posta torbası; **~box** *Am.* mektup kutusu; **~man** *Am.* postacı; **~-order** posta ile sipariş

maim [meym] *v/t* sakatlamak

main [meyn] ana, asıl, esas, başlıca, ana; **~land** GEO kara; **~ly** başlıca

maint|ain [meyn'teyn] *v/t* sürdürmek, muhafaza etm.; iddia etm.; **~enance** ['-tınıns] bakım; muhafaza

maize [meyz] BOT mısır

majest|ic [mı'cestik] muhteşem, heybetli; **~y** ['mäcisti] haşmet, azamet; **His (Her) 2y** Majeste

major ['meycı] daha büyük, daha önemli; MUS majör

mıl binbaşı; başlıca konu; ~**general** tümgeneral; ~**ity** [mı'coriti] çoğunluk

make [meyk] *n.* şekil; yapı; marka; *v/t* yapmak; meydana getirmek; teşkil etm.; sağlamak; kazanmak; ~ **for** *-in* yolunu tutmak; ~ **out** anlamak, çözmek; yazmak; ~ **over** devretmek; ~ **up** teşkil etm.; uydurmak; telâfi etm., tamamlamak (for *-i*); ~ **up one's mind** karar vermek; ~**r** yapan, fabrikatör; ~**shift** eğreti; ~**up** makyaj

malady ['mälıdi] hastalık

malaria [mı'lärıı] MED sıtma

male [meyl] erkek

male|diction [mäli'dikşın] lânet; ~**factor** [' ..fäktı] kötülük eden; ~**volence** [mı'levılıns] kötü niyet

malic|e ['mälis] garaz, kötü niyet; ~**ious** [mı'lişıs] kötü niyetli

malignant [mı'lignınt] kötü yürekli; MED habis

malnutrition ['mälnyu'trişın] gıdasızlık

malt [môlt] malt

Malt|a ['môltı] Malta adası; ~**ese** [' .'tîz] Maltız

mam(m)a [mı'mâ] *fam.* anne

mammal ['mämıl] *n.* memeli hayvan

man [män, mın], *pl.* **men** *n.* erkek, adam; insan; insan türü; *v/t* kadro koymak *-e*

manage ['mänic] *v/t* idare etm.; kullanmak; *-in* yolunu

bulmak; ~**able** idare edilebilir; ~**ment** idare, yönetim; müdürlük; ~**r** müdür, yönetmen

mandate ['mändeyt] vekillik; POL manda

mane [meyn] yele

maneuver [mı'nuuvı] *Am. s.* manoeuvre

manger ['meyncı] yemlik

mangle ['mängl] *n.* ütü cenderesi; *v/t* cendereden geçirmek; *fig.* parçalamak

manhood ['mänhud] erkeklik; mertlik

mania ['meynyı] tutku, mani, manya; ~**c** [' .iäk] manyak

manicure ['mänikyuı] manikür

manifest ['mänifest] *adj.* belli, anlaşılır; *v/t* açıkça göstermek; ~**ation** gösteri, izhar

manifold ['mänifuıld] *adj.* türlü türlü, çok; *v/t* çoğaltmak

manipulate [mı'nipyuleyt] *v/t* hünerle kullanmak; hile karıştırmak *-e*

man|kind [män'kaynd] insanlık; ~**ly** mert, yiğit

mannequin ['mänikin] manken

manner ['mänı] tarz, yol, usul; *pl.* terbiye

manoeuvre [mı'nuuvı] *n.* MIL manevra; düzen, hile; *v/i* manevra yapmak; *v/t* sokmak (into *-e*)

manor ['mänı] tımar, malikâne; ~**house** toprak ağası konağı

man|power el emeği; insan gücü; **~servant** erkek hizmetçi

mansion ['mänşin] konak

manslaughter JUR kasıtsız adam öldürme

mantelpiece ['mäntlpîs] şömine rafı

manual ['mänyuıl] el ile yapılan; el kitabı

manufacture ['mänyu'fäkçı] n. imal, yapım; v/t imal etm.; **~r** [-rı] fabrikatör

manure [mı'nyuı] n. gübre; v/t gübrelemek

manuscript ['mänyuskript] yazma; el yazması

Manx [mänks] Man adasına ait

many ['meni] çok, birçok; **how ~?** kaç tane?; **a good ~, a great ~** hayli

map [mäp] n. harita; v/t -in haritasını yapmak

maple ['meypl] BOT akçaağaç

marble ['mâbl] mermer; bilya, bilye

March¹ [mâç] mart ayı

march² n. marş; yürüyüş; v/i yürümek

mare [mäı] kısrak

margarine [mâcı'rîn] margarin

margin ['mâcin] kenar, ara; kazanç; **~al** kenarda olan

marine [mı'rîn] denize ait; deniz kuvvetleri pl.; silâhendaz; **~r** ['märini] gemici

marionette [märiı'net] kukla

marital [mı'raytl] evlenmeğe ait

maritime ['märitaym] denizciliğe ait

mark [mâk] n. işaret, alâmet; iz; leke; marka; hedef; numara, not; v/t işaretlemek; not vermek **-e**; dikkat etm. **-e**; **~ out** -in sınırlarını çizmek; **~ed** işaretlenmiş; göze çarpan

market ['mâkit] n. çarşı; pazar; piyasa; v/t satmak, satışa çıkarmak; **~ing** ECON pazarlama

marksman ['mâksmın] nişancı

marmalade ['mâmıleyd] portakal marmelatı

marmot ['mâmıt] ZOO dağ sıçanı

marque|ess, ~is ['mâkwis] marki

marriage ['märic] evlenme; evlilik; **~ certificate** evlenme cüzdanı; **~able** evlenecek yaşta

married ['märid] evli

marrow ['märıu] ilik, öz

marry ['märi] v/t evlenmek (so. ile); evlendirmek (so. to -i ile)

Mars [mârz] ASTR Merih, Sakıt

marsh [mâş] bataklık

marshal ['mâşıl] n. polis müdürü; MIL mareşal; v/t dizmek, sıralamak

marshy ['mâşi] bataklık

marten ['mâtin] ZOO zerdava

martial ['mâşıl] harbe ait; ~ law sıkıyönetim

martyr ['mâtı] şehit

marvel ['mâvıl] *n.* mucize, harika; *v/i* hayret etm. (**at** *-e*); ~(l)ous hayret verici, şaşılacak

mascot ['mäskıt] maskot

masculine ['mäskyulin] erkeğe ait; erkeksi; GR eril

mash [mäş] *v/t* ezmek; ~ed potatoes patates ezmesi

mask [mâsk] *n.* maske; *v/t* maskelemek

mason ['meysn] duvarcı; ℥ farmason; ~ry duvarcılık; duvarcı işi

mass [mäs] kütle, yığın, küme; REL kilise ayini; *v/t* yığmak, bir araya toplamak

massacre ['mäsıkı] *n.* katliam; *v/t* kılıçtan geçirmek

massage ['mäsâjl] *n.* ovma; masaj; *v/t* ovmak

massif ['mäsîf] GEO dağ kitlesi; ~ve ['-siv] som; kütle halinde

mast [mâst] direk

master ['mâstı] *n.* usta, üstat; öğretmen; amir; kolej rektörü; *v/t* idare etm.; yenmek; ℥ **of Arts** (*edebiyat fakültesi diploması ile doktora arasında bir derece*); ~ful zorba; ustaca; ~ly ustaca; ~piece şaheser; ~ship yönetim; ustalık; ~y üstünlük; maharet

mat [mät] hasır; paspas; altlık; donuk, mat

match¹ [mäç] kibrit

match² denk; eş; maç; *v/t* uymak, denk olm. *-e*; karşılaştırmak *-i*; ~less eşsiz, emsalsiz; ~maker çöpçatan

mate [meyt] *n.* eş; arkadaş; *v/i* evlenmek; *v/t* çiftleştirmek

material [mı'tiriıl] *n.* madde; malzeme; kumaş; *adj.* maddî; önemli; ~ism materyalizm

maternal [mı'tɜn!] anaya ait; ana tarafından; ~ity analık

mathematics [mäthi'mätiks] *pl.* matematik *sg.*

matriculate [mı'trikyuleyt] *v/t* kaydetmek; *v/i* kaydedilmek

matrimony ['mätrimıni] evlilik

matron ['meytrın] ana kadın; amir kadın

matter ['mätı] *n.* madde; mesele; konu; MED irin; *v/i* önemi *olm.*; **no** ~ zararı yok; önemi yok; **what's the** ~? ne var?; **what's the** ~ **with you?** neyiniz var?; ~ **of course** işin tabiî gidişi; ~ **of fact** hakikat

mattress ['mätris] şilte

mature [mı'tyuı] *adj.* olgun, ergin; reşit; *v/i* olgunlaşmak; vadesi gelmek; *v/t* olgunlaştırmak; ~ity olgunluk, erginlik; vade

mausoleum [môsı'liım] türbe

mauve [mıuv] leylak rengi

maxim ['mäksim] vecize; kural; ~um ['-ım] maksimum;

azamî
May¹ [mey] mayıs ayı
may² -ebilmek, *-meğe* izinli
olm.; **~be** belki
may-bug zoo mayısböceği
mayor [mäi] belediye başkanı
maze [meyz] lâbirent
me [mî, mi] bana, beni
meadow ['medıu] çayır
meagre, *Am.* **~er** ['mîgı]
zayıf, yavan
meal¹ [mîl] yemek
meal² un
mean¹ [mîn] bayağı, adî, alçak
mean² orta; *pl.* vasıtalar; gelir, servet *sg.*; **by all ~s** şüphesiz; **by no ~s** asla; **by ~s**
of vasıtasıyle
mean³ *v/t* düşünmek; demek
istemek; kastetmek; demek;
~ing mana, anlam; **~ingless**
manasız; **~t** [ment] *s.* mean
mean|time, **~while** bu aralık,
bu sırada
measles ['mîzlz] *pl.* MED
kızamık *sg.*
measure ['mejı] *n.* ölçü; tedbir; ölçme; *v/t* ölçmek;
~ment ölçü; ölçme
meat [mît] et
mechani|c [mi'känik] maki-
nist, makinacı; mekanik; *pl.*
mekanik, teknik *sg.*; **~cal**
makinaya ait, makanik;
~sm ['mekınızım] mekanizma; **~ze** *v/t* MIL motorlu taşıt-
larla donatmak
medal ['medl] madalya
meddle ['medl] *v/i* karışmak

(**in**, **with** *-e*)
mediaeval [medi'îvıl] *s.* **me-**
dieval
mediate ['mîdieyt]   *v/i*
aracılık etm. **~ion** aracılık;
~or aracı
medic|al ['medikıl] tıbbî; **~i-**
nal [.'disinl] şifa verici;
~ine ['medsin] ilâç; tıp
medieval [medi'îvıl] ortaçağa
ait
mediocre [mîdi'ıukı] orta derecede
meditate ['medieyt]   *v/i*
düşünceye dalmak; *v/t* tasarlamak;   **~ion**   düşünme;
dalgınlık,   **~ive**   ['-tıtiv]
düşünceli
Mediterranean (Sea) [medi-
tı'reynyın(-)] Akdeniz
medium ['mîdyım] orta, ortalama; medyum; **~ wave** TECH
orta dalga
medley ['medli] karışık şey;
MUS potpuri
meek [mîk] alçak gönüllü, uysal
meet [mît] *v/t* rastlamak *-e*;
karşılamak *-i*; tanışmak, görüşmek (*so.* ile *-e*); ödemek *-i*;
v/i toplanmak; uğramak
(**with** *-e*); rastlamak (*-e*);
~ing miting, toplantı
melancholy ['melınkıli] melankoli, karasevda; karasev-
dalı
mellow ['melıu] olgun; yumuşak
melod|ious [mi'lıudyıs]
ahenkli; **~y** ['melıdi] melodi,

melon 328

ezgi

melon ['melın] BOT kavun

melt [melt] v/i erimek; v/t eritmek; *fig.* yumuşatmak

member ['membı] üye; organ,
uzuv; ~ship üyelik; üyeler pl.

membrane ['membreyn] zar

memoirs ['memwâs] pl. hatı-
ralar

memor|able ['memırıbl]
hatırlanmağa değer; ~an-
dum [.'rândım] POL memo-
randum; ~ial [mi'môrıl]
anıt, abide; hatırlatıcı; ~ize
['memırayz] v/t ezberlemek;
~y hafıza; hatıra

menace ['menıs] n. tehdit; v/t
tehdit etm.

mend [mend] v/t onarmak,
yamamak

menial ['mînyıl] hizmetçiye
ait, bayağı

menstruation [menstru-
'eyşın] MED aybaşı

mental ['mentl] akılla ilgili;
zihnî; ~ity [.'tâliti] zihniyet

mention ['menşın] n. anma;
v/t anmak, zikretmek; don't
~ it! bir şey değil!; estağfurullah!

mercantile ['mɔkıntayl] tica-
rete ait

mercenary ['mɔsınıri] ücretli;
ücretli asker

merchan|dise ['mɔçındayz]
ticaret eşyası, emtia; ~t
['.ınt] tüccar

merci|ful ['mɔsiful] merha-
metli; ~less merhametsiz

mercury ['mɔkyuri] CHEM

cıva

mercy ['mɔsi] merhamet

mere [mii] saf, sade; ~ly adv.
sadece, ancak, yalnız

merge [mɔc] v/t birleştirmek;
v/i birleşmek

meridian [mı'ridiın] GEO meridyen

merit ['merit] değer; fazilet;
v/t lâyık olm. -e; ~orious
[.'tôrııs] değerli; medhe
değer

mermaid ['mɔmeyd] de-
nizkızı

merriment ['merimınt] neşe

merry ['meri] şen, neşeli; ~
andrew [.'ândruu] soytarı;
~-go-round atlıkarınca

mesh [mes] ağ gözü

mess [mes] karışıklık; sofra
arkadaşları pl.; v/t (up) kirletmek; karıştırmak

mess|age ['mesic] haber,
mesaj; ~enger ['.ıncı] haberci, kurye

met [met] s. meet

metal ['metl] maden, metal;
~lic [mi'tâlik] madenî

meteor ['mîtyıl] ASTR
akanyıldız, meteortaşı; ~olo-
gy [.'rolıci] meteoroloji

meter ['mîtı] 1. sayaç; 2. s. metre

method ['methıd] usul, yöntem, metot; ~ical [mi'thodi-
kıl] yöntemli

meticulous [mi'tikyulıs] çok
titiz

met|re Am. ~er ['mîtı] metre;
vezin

metropoli|s [mi'tropilis] başkent; **~tan** [metrı'politın] başşehre ait

mew [myü] *v/i* miyavlamak

Mexico ['meksikıu] Meksika

miaou, miaow [mî'au] *s.* mew

mice [mays] *s.* mouse

micro|be ['maykrıub] mikrop; **~chip** ['~çip] mikroçip; **~phone** ['~krıfıun] mikrofon; **~scope** ['~krıskıup] mikroskop

mid [mid] orta; **~day** öğle

middle ['midl] orta, merkez; 2 **Ages** *pl.* ortaçağ *sg.*; **~ class** orta sınıf; **~ weight** orta sıklet; **~aged** orta yaşlı

midge [mic] tatarcık; **~t** ['~it] cüce

mid|night ['midnayt] gece yarısı; **~st**: in the **~st** of *-in* ortasında; **~summer** yaz ortası; yaz dönemi; **~way** yarı yolda; **~wife** ebe

might¹ [mayt] *s.* may

might² [mayt] kuvvet, kudret; **~y** kuvvetli, güçlü

migrate [may'greyt] *v/i* göçmek

mild [mayld] hafif; yumuşak

mildew ['mildyû] küf

mildness ['mayldnis] hafiflik, yumuşaklık

mile [mayl] mil *(1,609 km)*; **~(e)age** ['~lic] mil hesabiyle mesafe; **~estone** kilometre taşı

milit|ant ['militınt] saldırgan; **~ary** ['~tıri] askerî; **~ia** ['~şı] milis

milk [milk] *n.* süt; *v/t* sağmak; **~man** sütçü; **~sop** ['~sop] korkak; **~y** sütlü; **~y Way** ASTR samanyolu

mill [mil] *n.* değirmen; fabrika; *v/t* öğütmek; TECH frezelemek; **~er** değirmenci

millet ['milit] BOT darı

milli- ['mili-] mili-

milliner ['milinı] kadın şapkacısı

million ['milyın] milyon; **~aire** [~'näıl] milyoner

milt [milt] ANAT dalak

mimic ['mimik] *n.* taklitçi; *v/t* taklit etm.

minaret ['minırıt] minare

mince [mins] *v/t* kıymak; **~d meat** kıyma; **~meat** tatlı börek dolgusu

mind [maynd] *n.* akıl, beyin; hatır; fikir; istek; *v/t* dikkat etm., bakmak *-e*; önem vermek *-e*; karşı çıkmak *-e*; never **~**! zararı yok!; out of one's **~** deli; would you **~** opening the window? pencereyi açar mısınız?; **~** your own business! sen kendi işine bak!; **~ful** dikkatli (of *-in*)

mine¹ [mayn] benim(ki)

mine² maden ocağı; MIL mayın; *v/t* kazmak, çıkarmak; **~r** madenci

mineral [minırıl] maden, mineral; madenli

mingle ['miŋgl] *v/t* karıştırmak; *v/i* karışmak (in *-e*); katılmak (with *-e*) mini|ature ['minyıçı] minyatür; küçük; ~mal ['miniml] asgarî; ~mize ['-nimayz] v/t küçümsemek; ~mum ['-nimum] minimum; asgarî

minist|er ['ministı] n. REL papaz; POL bakan; orta elçi; v/i bakmak (to -e); ~ry bakanlık

mink [miŋk] ZOO Amerika sansarı, vizon

minor ['maynı] daha küçük; önemsiz; ikinci konu; MUS minör; ~ity [-'noriti] azınlık

minstrel ['minstrıl] halk şairi; zenci şarkıcısı

mint¹ [mint] BOT nane

mint² n. darphane; v/t madenî parayı basmak

minus ['maynıs] MATH eksi

minute ['minit] dakika; [may'nyût] an; ufak, minimini; pl. tutanak sg.; to the ~ ['minit] tam zamanında

mirac|le ['mirıkl] mucize, harika; ~ulous [-'räkyulıs] mucize gibi

mirage ['mirâj] ılgım, serap

mire ['mayı] çamur, pislik

mirror ['mirı] n. ayna; v/t yansıtmak

mirth [mз:th] neşe

miry ['mayırı] çamurlu

mis- [mis-] yanlış; kötü

misadventure aksilik, kaza

mis|apply v/t yerinde kullanmamak; ~apprehension yanlış anlama; ~behaviour yaramazlık; ~calculate v/t yanlış, hesap etm.

miscarr|iage başarısızlık;

MED çocuk düşürme; ~y başaramamak; çocuk düşürmek

miscellaneous [misi'leynyıs] çeşitli

mischie|f ['misçif] yaramazlık; fesat; ~vous ['-vıs] yaramaz; zarar verici

mis|conduct kötü davranış; ~deed kötülük; ~demeano(u)r JUR hafif suç

miser ['mayzı] hasis, cimri

miser|able ['mizırıbl] sefil; ~y sefalet

mis|fortune talihsizlik, bedbahtlık; ~giving şüphe; korku; ~government kötü idare; ~guide v/t yanlış yola sapmak; ~hap ['-häp] kaza, aksilik; ~inform v/t yanlış bilgi vermek -e; ~lay v/t kaybetmek; ~lead v/t yanlış yola sevketmek; aldatmak; ~place v/t yanlış yere koymak; ~print ['-'print] n. baskı hatası; [-'print] v/t yanlış basmak; ~pronounce v/t yanlış söylemek; ~represent v/t yanlış anlatmak

miss¹ [mis] bekâr bayan

miss² n. nişanı vuramayış; başarısızlık; v/t vuramamak; kaçırmak

missile ['misayl] mermi

missing ['misiŋ] eksik; kaybolmuş

mission ['mişın] görev; misyon; ~ary ['-şnırı] REL misyoner

mis-spell v/t yanlış yazmak

mist [mist] sis, duman

mistake [mis'teyk] *n.* yanlış(lık), hata; *v/t* yanlış anlamak; benzetmek (for *-e*); **by ~** yanlışlıkla; **be ~n** yanılmak

mister [misti] bay

mistletoe [misltiu] BOT ökseotu

mistress ['mistris] bayan; metres

mistrust *v/t* güvenmemek *-e*

misty ['misti] sisli; bulanık

misunderstand *v/t* yanlış anlamak; **~ing** anlaşmazlık

misuse ['mis'yûs] suiistimal; *v/t* ['_'yûz] suiistimal etm.

mitigate ['mitigeyt] *v/t* hafifletmek

mitten ['mitn] kolçak, parmaksız eldiven

mix [miks] *v/t* karıştırmak; *v/i* karışmak, birleşmek (**with** *-e*); **~ed up** karmakarışık; **~ture** ['_çı] karışım

moan [mıun] *n.* inilti; *v/i* inlemek

moat [mıut] kale hendeği

mob [mob] ayaktakımı

mobile ['mubayl] oynak; seyyar; **~ize** [_bilayz] *v/t* seferber etm.

mock [mok] *adj.* sahte, taklit; *v/i* alay etm. (**at** ile); *v/t* taklit etm. **~ery** alay

mode [mıud] tarz, usul; moda

model ['modl] *n.* örnek, nümune, model; *v/t -in* modelini yapmak

moderate ['modırit] *adj.*

ılımlı; ['_eyt] *v/t* hafifletmek; *v/i* azalmak; **~ion** itidal, ölçülülük

modern ['modın] yeni, modern; **~ize** *v/t* modernleştirmek

modest ['modist] alçak gönüllü, mütevazı; **~y** alçak gönüllülük

modification [modifi'keyşın] değişiklik; **~y** ['_fay] *v/t* değiştirmek

module ['modyûl] TECH feza gemisinin kısmı

moist [moyst] nemli, rutubetli; **~en** ['_sn] ıslatmak; **~ure** ['_sçı] nem, rutubet

molar (tooth) ['mıuh] azı (dişi)

mole¹ [mıul] ZOO köstebek

mole² ben, leke

mole³ dalgakıran

molekule ['molikyûl] PHYS molekül

molest [mıu'lest] *v/t* rahatsız etm.

mollify ['molifay] *v/t* yumuşatmak

moment ['mıumınt] an; önem; **~ary** anî; geçici; **~ous** [_'mentıs] önemli; **~um** ['_'mentım] PHYS moment; *fig.* hız

monarch ['monık] hükümdar, kıral; **~y** kırallık

monastery ['monıstıri] manastır

Monday ['mandi] pazartesi

monetary ['manitıri] paraya ait

money ['mani] para, nakit; ~ order posta havalesi

Mongolia [mon'gıulyı] Moğolistan

monk [maŋk] rahip

monkey ['maŋki] zoo maymun

monogamy [mo'nogımi] tekeşlilik

mono|polize [mı'nopılayz] v/t tekeline almak; ~poly tekel; ~tonous [-tnıs] monoton, tekdüzen; ~tony [-tni] tekdüzenlik

monst|er ['monstı] canavar, dev; ~rous canavar gibi; anormal

month [manth] ay; ~lay aylık, ayda bir; aylık dergi

monument ['monyumınt] anıt, abide

moo [muu] böğürmek

mood [muud] mizaç, ruh haleti; ~y dargın, küskün

moon [muun] ay, kamer; ~light mehtap

moor¹ [muı] kır

moor² NAUT v/t palamarla bağlamak

mop [mop] n. silme bezi; v/t silip süpürmek, temizlemek

moral ['morıl] adj. ahlâkî, törel; n. ahlâk dersi; pl. ahlâk; ~e [mo'râl] maneviyat, manevî güç; ~ity [mı'râliti] ahlâk

morass [mı'räs] bataklık

morbid ['môbid] hastalıklı

more [mô] daha, daha çok, fazla; once ~ bir daha;

~over bundan başka

morgue [môg] morg

morning [mı'môniŋ] sabah; good ~! günaydın!

Morocco [mı'roku] Fas

morose [mı'rus] somurtkan

morphi|a ['môfyı], ~ne ['-fîn] CHEM morfin

morsel ['môsıl] lokma, parça

mortal ['môtl] ölümlü; öldürücü; insan; ~ity [-'tâliti] ölümlülük; ölüm oranı

mortar ['môtı] harç; MIL havan topu

mortgage n. ['môgic] ipotek; v/t rehine koymak

mortify ['môtifay] v/t alçaltmak

mortuary ['môtyuıri] morg

mosaic¹ [mıu'zeyik] mosaik

Mosaic² Musa'ya ait

Moslem ['mozlim] Müslüman

mosque [mosk] cami

mosquito [mıs'kîtıu] zoo sivrisinek

moss [mos] BOT yosun; ~y yosunlu

most [mıust] en, en çok, son derecede; en çoğu; at (the) ~ olsa olsa; ~ly ekseriya

motel [mıu'tel] motel

moth [moth] güve; pervane; ~-eaten güve yemiş

mother ['madhı] anne, ana; ~country anayurt; ~hood analık; ~-in-law kaynana; ~-of-pearl sedef

motion ['mıuşın] n. hareket; önerme; v/t işaret etm. -e; ~ picture film; ~less hareketsiz

motiv|ate ['mıutiveyt] v/t sevketmek; ~e saik, güdü

motor ['mıutı] n. motor; v/i otomobille gitmek; v/t otomobille götürmek; ~car otomobil; ~coach otobüs; ~cycle motosiklet; ~ing otomobilcilik; ~ist otomobil kullanan; ~ize v/t motorla donatmak; ~lorry kamyon; ~scooter skuter; ~way oto yolu

motto [mıtu] vecize; parola

mo(u)ld¹ [mıuld] küf

mo(u)ld² n. kalıp; v/t kalıba dökmek; şekil vermek -e; ~er v/i çürümek

mo(u)ldy ['mıuldi] küflü

mo(u)lt [mıult] tüylerini dökmek

mound [maund] höyük; tepecik

mount [maunt] n. dağ, tepe; binek; v/t binmek, çıkmak -e; kurmak -i; v/i artmak, yükselmek

mountain ['mauntin] dağ, tepe; pl. dağ silsilesi; ~eer [-'niı] dağlı; dağcı; ~ous dağlık

mourn [môn] v/i yas tutmak; v/t -in matemini tutmak; ~er yaslı; ~ing matem, yas; matem elbiseleri pl.

mouse [maus] fare

moustache [mıs'tâş] bıyık

mouth [mauth] ağız; ~ful ağız dolusu; ~piece ağızlık; fig. sözcü; ~wash gargara

mov|able ['muuvıbl] taşınabilir; JUR menkul; ~e n. hareket; tedbir; göç, nakil; v/i hareket etm., ilerlemek; taşınmak; v/t harekete getirmek, yürütmek; tahrik etm.; önermek; ~e in eve taşınmak; ~e out çıkmak; ~ement hareket; ~ies ['-viz] pl. sinema sg.; ~ing oynar; fig. dokunaklı

mow [mıu] v/t biçmek; ~n s. mow

much [maç] çok, hayli; how ~? ne kadar?; **make** ~ önem vermek (of -e); **too** ~ pek çok, pek fazla

mucus ['myûkıs] sümük

mud [mad] çamur

muddle ['madl] n. karışıklık; ~ (up, together) v/t karıştırmak

mud|dy ['madi] çamurlu; ~guard çamurluk

muff [maf] manşon; TECH boru bileziği

muffle ['mafl] v/t sarmak; voice: boğmak; ~r boyun atkısı

mug [mag] maşrapa, bardak

mulberry ['malbıri] BOT dut

mule [myûl] zoo katır; ~teer [-'li'tiı] katırcı

mullet ['malit], **red** ~ zoo barbunya

multi|cultural [malti'kalçırıl] çok kültürlü; ~ple ['maltipl] katmerli, çeşitli; ~plex ['-pleks] multipleks (sinema); ~plication [-pli'keyşın]

MATH çarpma; çoğalma; ~ply ['~play] v/t çarpmak; çoğaltmak; v/i çoğalmak; ~tasking [~'tâskiŋ] *birden fazla görevi aynı anda yerine getirebilen*; ~tude [~'tyûd] kalabalık

mumble ['mambl] v/t, v/i mırılda(n)mak

mummy ['mami] mumya

mumps [mamps] MED kabakulak

munch [manç] v/t kıtır kıtır yemek

municipal [myu'nisipıl] belediyeye ait; ~ity [~'pâliti] belediye

mural ['myuırıl] duvara ait

murder ['mədı] n. katil, adam öldürme; v/t öldürmek, katletmek; ~er katil; ~ous öldürücü

murmur ['məmı] n. mırıltı; v/i mırılda(n)mak; homurdanmak (**against, at** *-e karşı*)

muscle ['masl] adale, kas; ~bound kas tutukluğu olan

muscular ['maskyulı] adaleli; kuvvetli

muse [myûz] v/i düşünceye dalmak

museum [myu'zîım] müze

mush [maş] *Am.* mısır unu lapası

mushroom ['maşrum] BOT mantar

music ['myûzik] müzik, musiki; ~al müzikal; müziğe ait; ahenkli; ~hall varyete; ~ian [~'zişın] çalgıcı; ~stand nota sehpası

musk [mask] misk

musket ['maskit] asker tüfeği

Muslim ['muslim] Müslüman

muslin ['mazlin] muslin

mussel ['masl] midye

must¹ [mast] şıra

must² küf (kokusu)

must³ -meli, -malı; n. zorunluk; **I ~ not** izinli değilim

mustard ['mastıd] hardal

muster ['mastı] v/t toplamak

musty ['masti] küflü

mute [myût] sessiz, dilsiz

mutilate ['myûtileyt] v/t kötürüm etm.

mutin|eer [myûti'niı] isyan eden asker; ~y ['~ni] *n.* isyan; v/i ayaklanmak

mutter ['matı] mırıltı; v/i mırıldanmak

mutton ['matn] koyun eti; ~ chop koyun pirzolası

mutual ['myûçuıl] karşılıklı; ortak

muzzle ['mazl] *n.* hayvan burnu; burunsalık; top *veya* tüfek ağzı; v/t burunsalık takmak *-e*

my [may] benim

myrtle ['mətl] BOT mersin

myself [may'self] ben, kendim

myster|ious [mis'tiriıs] esrarengiz, gizemli; ~y ['~turi] gizem, sır

mysti|cism ['mistisizım] mistisizm; tasavvuf; ~fy v/t şaşırtmak

myth [mith] efsane, mit

N

nag [näg] dırlanmak; ~ **at** *-in* başının etini yemek

nail [neyl] *n.* TECH çivi; ANAT, ZOO tırnak; *v/t* çivilemek, mıhlamak

naive [nâ'iv] saf, bön

naked ['neykid] çıplak

name [neym] *n.* isim, ad; nam, şöhret; *v/t* adlandırmak; tayin etm., atmak; **call** *so.* ~**s** sövmek *-e*; ~**less** isimsiz; bilinmiyen; ~**ly** yani, şöyle ki; ~**sake** adaş

nanny ['näni] dadı; ~ **(goat)** dişi keçi

nap [näp] şekerleme

nape [neyp] ense

napkin ['näpkin] peçete; kundak bezi

narcissus [nâ'sisis] BOT nergis

narco|sis [nâ'kıusis] narkoz; ~**tic** [-'kotik] narkotik, uyuşturucu (ilâç)

narrat|e [nä'reyt] *v/t* anlatmak; ~**ion** hikâye; ~**ive** ['-ıtiv] rivayet

narrow ['närıu] *adj.* dar, ensiz; *v/i* daralmak; *v/t* daraltmak; ~**-minded** dar fikirli

nasty ['nâsti] pis, fena kokulu, iğrenç; yaramaz

nation ['neyşın] millet, ulus

national ['näşınl] ulusal, millî; *n.* vatandaş; ~**ist** [-'şnilist] milliyetçi; ~**ity** [-'näliti] mil-

liyet; vatandaşlık; ~**ize** ['-şnılayz] *v/t* kamulaştırmak

native ['neytiv] yerli; doğma; ♀ **American** *adj. & n.* Amerikan yerlisi; ~ **language** ana dil

natural ['näçrıl] tabiî, doğal; doğuştan; sunî olmıyan; ~**ize** *v/t* vatandaşlığa kabul etm.

nature ['neyçır] tabiat; mizaç

naught [nôt] sıfır; ~**y** yaramaz, haylaz

nausea ['nôsyı] bulantı; iğrenme; ~**ting** ['-ieytiŋ] bulandırıcı; iğrenç

nautical ['nôtikıl] gemiciliğe ait; ~ **mile** deniz mili

naval ['neyvıl] bahriye ile ilgili; ~ **base** deniz üssü

nave [neyv] tekerlek yuvası

navel ['neyvıl] göbek

naviga|ble ['nävigıbl] gidiş gelişe elverişli; ~**te** ['-eyt] *v/t gemiyi, uçağı:* kullanmak; *v/i* gemi ile gezmek; ~**tion** denizcilik; dümencilik

navy ['neyvi] deniz kuvvetleri *pl.*; donanma

nay [ney] hayır; hatta

near [niı] *adj.* yakın; bitişik; samimî; sımrî; *adv.* yakın (-da); *v/i* yaklaşmak; ~**ly** hemen bemen, âdeta; ~**-sighted** miyop

neat [nît] temiz; zarif

necessary ['nesisiri] gerekli; zaruri; ~itate [ni'sesiteyt] v/t gerektirmek; ~ity [ni'sesiti] lüzum, zaruret, ihtiyaç

neck [nek] n. boyun, gerdan; şişede boğaz; v/i sl. öpüşmek; ~lace ['~lis] kolye; ~tie kravat

née [ney] kızlık adı

need [nîd] n. ihtiyaç, lüzum, gereklik; v/t ihtiyacı olm. -e istemek -i

needle ['nîdl] iğne; ibre

needless ['nîdlis] lüzumsuz; ~y muhtaç

negate [ni'geyt] v/t inkâr etm.; ~ion inkâr

negative ['negtiv] negatif; olumsuz

neglect [ni'glekt] v/t ihmal etm., savsaklamak; n. ihmal

negligent ['neglicint] kayıtsız, ihmalci

negotiate [ni'guşieyt] v/t müzakere etm.; ~ion müzakere, görüşme

negress ['nîgris] zenci kadın; ~o ['~ıu] zenci

neigh [ney] n. kişneme; v/i kişnemek

neighbou(u)r ['neybı] komşu; ~hood komşuluk; civar; ~ing komşu, bitişik

neither ['naydhı] hiç biri; ve ne de; ~ ... nor ... ne ... ne de ...

nephew ['nevyu] erkek yeğen

nerve [nɜv] n. sinir; cesaret; v/t cesaret vermek -e; ~ one-self to inf. -meğe cesur olm.

nervous ['nɜvıs] sinirli; ~ness sinirlilik

nest [nest] n. yuva; v/i yuva yapmak; ~le ['nesl] v/i sokulmak (to -e); v/t barındırmak

net¹ [net] ağ, tuzak; internet

net² adj. net, safi; v/t kazanmak

Netherlands ['nedhılındz]: the ~ pl. Holanda sg.

nettle ['netl] n. BOT ısırgan; v/t kızdırmak

network ['netwɜk] şebeke

neurosis ['nyu'rıusis] MED nevroz

neuter ['nyûtı] GR cinssiz

neutral ['nyûtrıl] yansız, tarafsız; ~ gear TECH boş vites; ~ity ['~trâliti] tarafsızlık; ~ize ['~trılayz] v/t etkisiz bırakmak; yansız kılmak

neutron ['nyûtron] nötron

never ['nevı] asla, hiç bir zaman; ~theless bununla beraber, mamafih

new [nyû] yeni; taze; acemi; 2 Year yılbaşı; ~born yeni doğmuş

news [nyûz] pl. haber sg.; ~cast haber yayını; ~paper gazete; ~reel aktüalite filmi; ~stand gazete tezgâhı

next [nekst] en yakın; sonraki, gelecek; sonra

nibble ['nibl] v/i kemirmek (at -i)

nice [nays] güzel, hoş, sevimli; ince; ~ty ['~iti] incelik

niche [niç] duvarda hücre

nick [nik] *n.* çentik, kertik;
tam zaman; *v/t* çentmek
nickel ['nikl] *n.* nikel; *Am.* beş
sentlik para; *v/t* nikel ile kaplamak
nickname ['nikneym] *n.*
takılmış ad; *v/t* lakap takmak
-e
niece [nîs] kız yeğen
niggard ['nigıd] cimri adam
night [nayt] gece; **good** ~! iyi
geceler!; ~ **cap** *yatmadan ön-*
ce içilen içecek; ~**club** gece
kulübü; ~**dress,** ~**gown** gecelik; ~**ingale** ['~ingeyl]
zoo bülbül; ~**mare** ['~mäı]
karabasan, kâbus; ~**y** *fam.*
gecelik
nil [nil] hiç, sıfır
nimble ['nimbl] çevik, tez
nine [nayn] dokuz; ~**pins** *pl.*
kiy oyunu *sg.*; ~**ty** doksan
nip¹ [nip] *n.* ayaz; çimdik; *v/t*
çimdiklemek; *v/i* hızlı git-
mek
nip² *n.* azıcık içki; *v/t* azıcık içmek
nipple ['nipl] meme başı
nit|**re,** *Am.* ~**er** ['naytı] CHEM
güherçile; ~**rogen** azot, ni-
trojen
no [nıu] hayır, öyle değil; hiç
(bir); ~ **one** hiç kimse
nobility [nıu'biliti] asalet;
asılzadeler sınıfı
noble ['nıubl] asıl, soylu; asılzade; ~**man** asılzade
nobody ['nıubıdi] hiç kimse
no-brainer [nıu'breynı] *n.*
coll. çok kolay, apaçık bir

şey
nocturnal [nok'tɜnl] geceye
ait
nod [nod] *n.* baş sallama; *v/i*
kabul ifade etmek için başını
sallamak; uyuklamak
nois|**e** [noyz] gürültü, patırdı;
~**y** gürültülü
nomad ['nomıd] göçebe
nomina|**l** ['nominl] sözde;
saymaca; ~**te** ['~eyt] *v/t* atamak, görevlendirmek; ~**tion**
tayin, aday gösterme; ~**tive**
['~nıtıv] (case) GR yalın hal
non-aggression [~] POL
saldırmazlık; ~**alcoholic** alkolsuz; ~**commissioned** officer MIL erbaş; ~**descript**
['~diskript] kolay tanımla-
namaz
none [nan] hiç biri
non-existence yokluk, varol-
mayış
nonsense ['nonsıns] saçma
non-stop doğru giden;
aralıksız
noodle ['nuudl] şeriye
nook [nuk] bucak, köşe
noon [nuun] öğle
noose [nuus] ilmik
nor [nô] ne de
norm [nôm] kural, norm, örnek; ~**al** normal; düzgülü
north [nôth] kuzey; kuzeye
doğru; ♀ **Sea** GEO Kuzey Denizi; ♀ **Star** ASTR kutup
yıldızı; ~**east** kuzeydoğu;
~**ern** ['~dhın] kuzeye ait;
~**ward(s)** ['~wıd(z)] kuzeye
doğru; ~**west** kuzeybatı

Norway ['nôwey] Norveç; **~egian** [~'wîcin] Norveçli

nose [niuz] *n.* burun; uç; *v/t -in* kokusunu almak; arayıp bulmak *-i;* **~gay** ['~gey] çiçek demeti

nostril ['nostril] burun deliği

not [not] değil; ~ **at all** asla

notable ['niutibl] tanınmış; dikkate değer; **~ry** ['~tırı] noter; **~tion** [~'teyşın] not; sistem; kayıt

notch [noç] *n.* çentik, kertik; *v/t* çentmek, kertmek

note [niut] *n.* not; işaret; MUS, POL nota; pusula; *v/t* kaydetmek; ~ **down** deftere yazmak; ~**d** tanınmış; ~**book** not defteri; ~**worthy** önemli, dikkate değer

nothing ['nathiŋ] hiçbir şey; sıfır; **say ~ of** bile değil, şöyle dursun

notice ['nıutis] *n.* haber; ilân; dikkat; *v/t -in* farkına varmak; görmek *-i,* dikkat etm. *-e;* **until further ~** yeni bir habere kadar; **without ~** mühlet vermeden; **~able** görülebilir

notification [nıutifi'keyşın] bildirme; ihbar; **~fy** ['~fay] *v/t* ilân etm.; bildirmek

notion ['nıuşın] sanı, zan; *Am.* tuhafiye

notorious [nıu'tôriıs] adı çıkmış; dile düşmüş

notwithstanding [notwith-'ständiŋ] *-e* rağmen

nought [nôt] sıfır

noun [naun] GR isim, ad

nourish ['nariş] *v/t* beslemek; **~ing** besleyici; **~ment** yemek, gıda

novel ['novıl] roman; yeni, tuhaf; **~ist** romancı; **~ty** yenilik

November [nıu'vembı] kasım (ayı)

novice ['novis] çırak

now [nau] şimdi, bu anda; işte; **just ~** demin(cek), şimdi; ~ **and again,** (every) ~ **and then** arasıra; **~adays** ['~ıdeyz] bugünlerde

nowhere ['nıuwäı] hiçbir yerde

noxious ['nokşıs] zararlı

nozzle ['nozl] TECH ağızlık, meme

nuclear ['nyûklıı] nükleer; ~ **power plant,** ~ **station** nükleer elektrik santralı

nude [nyûd] çıplak; nüd

nudge [nac] *n.* dürtme; *v/t* dirsek ile dürtmek

nugget ['nagit] (altın) külçe

nuisance ['nyûsns] sıkıcı şey *veya* kimse

null [nal] **(and void)** hükümsüz, geçersiz

numb [nam] uyuşuk, duygusuz

number ['nambı] *n.* sayı; miktar; numara; *v/t* saymak; numara koymak *-e;* ~ **plate** plaka; **~less** sayısız

numeral ['nyûmırıl] sayı, rakam; **~ous** birçok

nun [nan] REL rahibe

nuptials ['napşılz] *pl.* düğün,

nikâh sg.

nurse [nɜs] n. sütnine; hasta-
bakıcı; dadı; v/t emzirmek;
beslemek; bakmak -e

nursery ['nɜsiri] çocuk odası;
fidanlık; ~ **school** anaokulu

nursing ['nɜsiŋ] hasta-
bakıcılık; ~ **home** özel sağlık
yurdu

nut [nat] fındık, ceviz; TECH

vida somunu; **drive** ~s v/t
sl. çıldırtmak; ~**cracker**
fındıkkıran

nutri|ment ['nyûtrimɪnt]
gıda, besin; ~**tion** besleme;
~**tious** besleyici

nutshell fındık kabuğu; **in a** ~
kısaca

nylon ['naylın] naylon

nymph [nimf] peri

O

oak [ıuk] BOT meşe ağacı

oar [ô] kürek; ~**sman** kürekçi

oasis [u'eysis] vaha

oat [ıut] BOT yulaf (tanesi)

oath [ıuth] yemin; küfür; **take
an** ~ ant içmek

oatmeal yulaf unu

obe|dience [ı'bîdyıns] itaat;
~**dient** itaatli

obey [ı'bey] v/t itaat etm. -e

obituary [ı'bityuıri] ölüm
ilânı; anma yazısı

object ['obcikt] n. şey; GR nesne; amaç, hedef; v/i razı olmamak, itiraz etm. (**to** -e);
~**ion** itiraz; ~**ive** n. PHYS mercek, objektif; amaç; adj. objektif; tarafsız

obligat|ion [obli'geyşın] mec-
buriyet, yüküm; borç; ~**ory**
[o'bligıtıri] mecburî

oblig|e [ı'blayc] v/t zorunlu
kılmak; minnettar kılmak;
be ~**ed** minnettar olm.; mecbur olm. (**to** inf. -meğe); ~**ing**
nazik

oblique [ı'blîk] eğri, meyilli

obliterate [ı'blitıreyt] v/t silmek, yoketmek

obli·vi|on [ı'bliviın] unutma;
~**ous** unutkan

oblong ['obloŋ] boyu enin-
den fazla

obscene [ıb'sîn] açık saçık

obscure [ıb'skyuı] adj. çapraşık; karanlık; v/t karartmak

obsequies ['obsikwız] pl. cenaze törenleri

observ|ance [ıb'zɜvıns] yeri-
ne getirme; usul; ~**ant** dikkatli; ~**ation** gözetleme; göz-
lem; fikir; ~**atory** [_tri] rasat-
hane; ~**e** v/t yerine getirmek;
gözlemek; ~**er** gözliyen

obsess [ıb'ses] v/t musallat
olm. -e; ~**ed** musallat (**by**,
with -e); ~**ion** musallat fikir

obsolete ['obsılît] eskimiş

obstacle ['obstıkl] engel, mâni

obstina|cy   ['obstinısi]

inatçılık; ~te ['~it] inatçı, dik kafalı

obstruct [ıb'strakt] v/t tıkamak; engel olm. -e

obtain [ıb'teyn] v/t bulmak, ele geçirmek; ~able bulunabilir

obtrusive [ıb'truusiv] sokulup sıkıntı veren

obvious ['obviıs] belli, açık

occasion [ı'keyjın] n. fırsat, vesile; sebep; v/t sebep olm. -e; on the ~ of dolayısıyla; ~al arasıra olan

occident ['oksidınt] batı; ~al batı(lı)

occupant ['okyupınt] işgal eden; ~ation işgal; meslek, iş; ~y ['~pay] v/t işgal etm.

occur [ı'kö] v/r bulmak; ~ to -in aklına gelmek; ~rence ['ı'karıns] olay

ocean ['uşın] okyanus, deniz

o'clock [ı'klok] saate göre

October [ok'tıubı] ekim (ayı)

ocular ['okyulı] göze ait; gözle görülür; ~ist göz doktoru

odd [od] tuhaf, acayip; MATH tek; seyrek; pl. fark, eşit olmayış sg.; menfaat; the ~s are that ihtimali var ki; at ~s aralan açık; ~s and ends pl. ufak tefek şeyler

odo(u)r ['ıudı] koku; fig. şöhret

of [ov, ıv] -in; -den; the city ~ London Londra şehri; ~ wood tahtadan

off [of] -den; -den uzak; kesilmiş; kopuk; görev dışında;

intj. defol!; **be ~** ayrılmak

offence [ı'fens], Am. ~se suç, kabahat; hakaret; hücum; ~d v/t gücendirmek, darıltmak; v/i suç işlemek; ~sive taarruz, saldırı; çirkin; yakışmaz

offer ['ofı] n. teklif; sunu; v/t sunmak, teklif etm.; ~ing teklif; REL kurban

office ['ofis] büro, yazıhane; daire; bakanlık; ~er subay; polis memuru; memur; ~ial [ı'fişıl] resmî; memur; ~ious [ı'fişıs] el sokan

offset n. ofset; v/t denkleştirmek; ~side ofsayt; ~spring döl, ürün

often ['ofn] çok defa, sık sık

oh! [ıu] intj. ya!; öyle mi?

oil [oyl] n. yağ; petrol; v/t yağlamak; ~cloth muşamba; ~y yağlı

ointment ['oyntmınt] merhem

O.K., okay ['ıu'key] peki

old [ıuld] eski, kohne; yaşlı; ~ age yaşlılık; ~-fashioned modası geçmiş

oleander [ıuli'ändı] BOT zakkum

olive ['oliv] BOT zeytin

Olympic games [ıu'limpik -] pl. olimpiyat oyunları

omelet(te) ['omlit] omlet, kaygana

ominous ['ominıs] uğursuz

omission [ı'mişın] atlama, ihmal; ~t v/t atlamak, ihmal etm.

omni|bus ['omnibıs] otobüs; antoloji; **~potent** her şeye kadir

on [on] *-in* üzerine, üzerinde, üstüne, üstünde; -de; *-e* doğru; **and so ~** ve saire; **turn ~** *v/t* açmak

once [wans] bir defa; bir zamanlar; **at ~** derhal, hemen

one [wan] bir, tek; biri(si); **~ another** birbirine, birbirini; **the little ~s** *pl.* küçük çocuklar; **~self** kendisi; **~sided** tek taraflı; **~way street** tek yönlü sokak

onion ['anyın] soğan

online ['onlayn] *adj. & adv.* online; **~ banking** online bankacılık; **~ dating** karşı cinsten kimselerle online olarak tanışıp arkadaşlık kurmak; **~ shopping** online alışveriş

onlooker ['onlukı] seyirci

only ['ıunli] tek, biricik; yalnız, ancak, sadece

onto ['ontu,'_ı] *-in* üstün(d)e

onward ['onwıd] ileri

ooze [uuz] *n* sızıntı; balçık; *v/i* sızmak

opaque [ıu'peyk] ışık geçirmez

open ['ıupen] *adj.* açık, meydanda; *v/i* açılmak; *v/t* açmak; başlamak *-e;* **in the ~** air açıkta; **~er** açacak; **~ing** açıklık; fırsat; münhal görev; **~minded** açık fikirli

opera ['ıpırı] opera

operat|e ['opıreyt] *v/i* iş gör-

mek, işlemek; *v/t* kullanmak, işletmek; *v/t* kullanmak, işletmek; **MED** ameliyat etm.; **~ion** ameliyat; işleme, işletme; **MIL** harekât *pl.;* **~or** **TECH** operatör; **TEL** telefon memuru

ophthalmic [of'thälmik] göze ait

opinion [ı'pinyın] fikir, düşünce; tahmin

opium ['ıupyım] afyon

opponent [ı'pıunınt] muhalif, karşıki

opportunity [opı'tyûniti] fırsat

oppos|e [ı'pıuz] *v/t* direnmek, engel olm. *-e;* karşıla(ştır)mak *-i;* **~ite** ['opızit] karşıda, karşı karşıya; zıt, aksi; *-e* karşı; **~ition** [opı'zişın] muhalefet; zıtlık; **POL** muhalif parti

oppress [ı'pres] *v/t* sıkıştırmak; zulmetmek *-e;* **~ion** baskı, zulüm; sıkıntı; **~ive** ezici; sıkıcı

optic ['optik] görme duyusuna ait; **~al** optikle ilgili; **~ian** [.'tişn] gözlükçü

optimis|m ['optimizm] iyimserlik; **~t** iyimser

option ['opşın] seçme (hakkı)

or [ô] yahut, veya; yoksa; ya; **~ else** yoksa

oral ['ôrıl] sözlü

orange ['orinc] **BOT** portakal; **~ade** ['-'eyd] portakal suyu

orator ['orıtı] hatip, söyleyici

orbit ['ôbit] *n.* **ASTR** yörünge; *v/t -in* etrafında dönmek orchard ['ôçıd] meyva bahçesi

orchestra ['ôkistrı] MUS orkestra

orchid ['ôkid] BOT orkide

ordeal [ô'dîl] büyük sıkıntı

order ['ôdı] n. düzen; dizi; emir, sipariş; tabaka, sınıf; REL tarikat; v/t emretmek; düzenlemek; ısmarlamak; in ~ to -mek için; out of ~ bozuk; düzensiz; ~ly düzenli; MIL emir eri

ordinal number ['ôdinl] MATH sıra sayısı

ordinary ['ôdnri] adî; bayağı

ore [ô] maden cevheri

organ ['ôgın] organ, örgen, uzuv; araç, vasıta; MUS org; ~ic [ô'gänik] organik; canlı

organiz|ation [ôgınay-'zeyşın] teşkilât, örgüt; düzen (-leme); ~e ['-ayz] v/t düzenlemek, örgütlemek

orient ['ôrint] doğu; ~al [-'entl] doğu ile ilgili

origin ['ôrîn] asıl, köken; soy; ~al [ı'rîcınl] aslî, yaratıcı; orijinal; ~ate [ı'rîcıneyt] v/i meydana gelmek (from -den); v/t yaratmak, türetmek

ornament ['ônımınt] n. süs; ['-mınt] v/t süslemek; ~al süs kabilinden

orphan ['ôfın] öksüz, yetim; ~age ['-ic] öksüzler yurdu

ortho|dox ['ôthıdoks] REL ortodoks; ~graphy [ô'thogrıfi] imlâ

oscillate ['osileyt] v/i sallanmak, sarsılmak

ostrich ['ostriç] ZOO devekuşu

other ['adhı] başka, diğer, sair; the ~ day geçen gün; every ~ day her gün aşırı; ~wise ['-wayz] başka türlü; yoksa

Ottoman ['otımın] Osmanlı

ought [ôt] to inf. -meli

ounce [auns] ons (28,35 g)

our ['auı] bizim; ~s bizimki; ~selves [-'selvz] kendimiz

oust [aust] v/t yerinden çıkarmak

out [aut] dışarı, dışarıda; sönmüş; intj. defol!; ~ of -den dışarı; -den yapılmış; -den dolayı; için; ~balance v/t geçmek; ~board motor takma motor; ~break, ~burst patlama, fışkırma; ~cast toplumdan atılmış, serseri; ~come sonuç; ~do v/t üstün gelmek -e; ~door(s) açık havada; ~er dış, dışarıdaki; ~fit gereçler pl.; v/t donatmak; ~grow v/t -den daha çabuk büyümek; ~last v/t -den daha çok dayanmak; ~law v/t kanun dışı adam; v/t kanun dışı etm.; ~let çıkış (yeri); delik; ~line n. taslak; v/t -in taslağını çizmek; ~live v/t -den fazla yaşamak; ~look görünüş; ~number sayıca üstün gelmek -e; ~put verim

outrage ['autreyc] n. zulüm, zorbalık; v/t kötü davranmak

-e; ~**ous** gaddar, insafsız
out|right büsbütün; açıkça;
~**side** dış; dış taraf, dış görünüş; ~**sider** bir grubun
dışında olan kimse; ~**source** *v/t*
(*işi*) başkasına devretmek;
~**spoken** sözünü sakınmaz;
~**standing** göze çarpan;
(*debt*) kalmış; ~**ward** dış; görünüşte; ~**weigh** *v/t -den* daha ağır gelmek; ~**wit** *v/t -den*
daha kurnazca davranmak
oval ['ıuvıl] oval, beyzî
oven ['avn] fırın
over ['ıuvı] karşı tarafa; fazla,
artık; bitmiş; *-in* üstüne, üstünde, üzerine, üzerinde; yu-
karısında; (**all**) ~ **again** bir
daha; ~ **there** karşıda; ~**all**
baştan başa; iş tulumu;
~**board** gemiden denize;
~**burden** *v/t* fazla yük yüklemek *-e*; ~**cast** bulutlu;
~**charge** *v/t* aşırı fiat istemek
-den; EL fazla doldurmak *-i*;
~**coat** palto; ~**come** *v/t* yenmek; ~**crowd** *v/t* fazla kalabalık etm.; ~**do** *v/t* abartmak;
fazla pişirmek; ~**draw** *v/t*
bankadaki hesabından fazla
para çekmek; ~**due** vadesi
geçmiş; ~**estimate** *v/t* fazla
tahmin etm.; ~**flow** *n.* taşma;
v/t su basmak; *v/i* taşmak;
~**haul** *v/t* elden geçirmek,
kontrol etm.; ~**head** baştan
geçen; yukarıda; ~**hear** *v/t*
rastlantılı olarak işitmek;
~**land** karadan; ~**lap** *v/i* üst

üste kaplanmak; ~**load** *v/t*
fazla yüklemek; ~**look** *v/t*
gözden kaçırmak; yukarıdan
bakmak *-e*; ~**night** gecele-
yin; bir gece için; ~**rate** *v/t*
fazla önem vermek *-e*; ~**rule**
v/t JUR geçersiz kılmak; ~**run**
v/t kaplamak; ~**sea(s)** deni-
zaşırı
over|see *v/t* yönetmek; ~**r** mü-
fettiş; ustabaşı
over|shadow *v/t* gölgelemek;
~**sight** kusur; ~**size** fazla büyük; ~**sleep** *v/t* uykuda
kaçırmak; ~**strain** *v/t* fazla
yormak; ~**take** *v/t* yetişmek
-e; ~**throw** ['ıuvıthrıu] *n.* de-
virme; [-'thru] *v/t* devir-
mek; ~**time** fazla çalışma süresi; ~**top** *v/t -in* tepesini
aşmak
overture ['ıuvıtyuı] teklif;
MUS uvertür
over|turn *v/t* devirmek; *v/i*
devrilmek; ~**weight** fazla
ağırlık; ~**whelm** [ıuvı'welm]
v/t yenmek; bunaltmak;
~**work** *v/i* fazla çalışmak;
v/t fazla çalıştırmak
ow|e [ıu] borcu olm., borçlu
olm. (*so. sth. -e -den* dolayı);
~**ing** to sebebiyle, yüzünden
owl [aul] ZOO baykuş, puhu
own [ıun] *adj.* kendi; özel; *v/t*
malik olm., sahip olm. *-e*;
tanımak, itiraf etm. *-i*; ~**er** sahip, mal sahibi
ox [oks], *pl.* ~**en** ['ˌın] öküz;
sığır
oxidation [oksi'deyşın] oksit-

lenme
oxygen ['oksicın] oksijen

oyster ['oystı] zoo istiridye
ozone ['ıuzıun] CHEM ozon

P

pace [peys] n. adım, yürüyüş; v/t adımlamak
Pacific Ocean [pı'sifik] GEO Büyük Okyanus; ~ist ['päsi-fist] barışçı; ~y ['päsifay] v/t yarıştırmak
pack [päk] n. bohça; sürü; (is-kambilde) deste; balya; Am. paket (sigara); v/t istif etm.; sarmak; ~age paket; amba-laj; ~et ['_it] paket; deste; ~ing bağlama; ambalaj
pact [päkt] anlaşma, sözleş-me
pad [päd] n. yastık; TECH ram-pa; v/t -in içini doldurmak
paddle ['pädlok] n. kısa kü-rek, pala; v/i suda oynamak
padlock ['pädlok] asma kilit
pagan ['peygın] putperest
page[1] [peyc] ulak, uşak
page[2] sayfa
paid [peyd] s. pay
pail [peyl] kova
pain [peyn] n. ağrı, sızı; acı; v/t acı vermek -e; take ~s to inf. -e özenmek; ~ful acı veren, zahmetli; ~staking özenli
paint [peynt] n. boya; v/t bo-yamak; tasvir etm.; ~box bo-ya kutusu; ~brush boya fırçası; ~er ressam; ~ing res-samlık; resim, tablo
pair [päı] n. çift; v/i çiftleş-

mek; v/t çiftleştirmek
pajamas [pı'cämız] pl. Am. pijama sg.
palace ['pälis] saray
palate ['pälit] ANAT damak
pale[1] [peyl] kazık
pale[2] adj. soluk, solgun; v/i sa-rarmak; ~ness solgunluk
Palestine ['pälistayn] Filistin
pallor ['pälı] solgunluk
palm[1] [pâm] BOT palmiye
palm[2] el ayası
palpitation [pälpi'teyşın] çarpıntı
pamper ['pämpı] v/t şımart-mak
pamphlet ['pämflit] risale, broşür
pan [pän] tava; ~cake gözle-me
pane [peyn] pencere camı
panel ['pänl] n. kapı aynası; pano; heyet; v/t tahta ile kap-lamak
pang [päŋ] anî sancı
panic ['pänik] panik, korku
panorama [pänı'râmı] pano-rama, manzara
pansy ['pänzi] BOT hercaî me-nekşe
pant [pänt] v/i solumak
panther ['pänthı] zoo pars, panter
pantry ['päntri] kiler

pants [pänts] *pl.* pantolon *sg.*; don

pap [päp] lapa

papa [pı'pâ] baba

papacy ['peypısi] REL papalık

paparazzi [pıpı'rıtsi] *n. pl.* paparazzi *sg.* (*pl.* = paparazziler)

paper ['peypı] *n.* kâğıt; gazete; *pl.* evrak; hüviyet cüzdanı *sg.*; *v/t* duvar kâğıdı ile kaplamak; ~**back** cep kitabı; ~**bag** kese kâğıdı; ~**hanger** duvar kâğıdı yapıştıran; ~**mill** kâğıt fabrikası

paprika [pı'prîkı] kırmızı biber

parachute ['pärışuut] paraşüt; ~**ist** paraşütçü

parade [pı'reyd] *n.* gösteri, nümayiş; *v/i* gösteriş yapmak; yürümek

paradise ['pärıdays] cennet

paragraph ['pärıgrâf] satır başı; paragraf

parallel ['pärılel] paralel

paralyse, *Am.* ~**ze** ['pärılayz] *v/t* felce uğratmak; ~**sis** [pı'rälisis] felç

paramount ['pärımaunt] üstün, en önemli

parasite ['pärısayt] parazit, asalak

parcel ['pâsl] *n.* paket, koli; parsel; *v/t* parsellemek

parch [pâç] *v/t* kavurup kurutmak; ~**ment** parşömen, tirşe

pardon ['pâdn] *n.* af, bağışlama; *v/t* affetmek; **I beg your** ~ affedersiniz; ~**able** affolunabilir

pare [päı] *v/t* yontmak; *-in* kabuğunu soymak

parent ['pärırnt] baba; anne; *pl.* ana baba, ebeveyn; ~**age** soy, nesil; ~**al** [pı'rentl] ana babaya ait

parenthesis [pı'renthisis] GR parantez, ayraç

parings ['pärinız] *pl.* kırpıntı, döküntü *sg.*

parish ['päriş] REL cemaat

park [pâk] *n.* park; otopark; *v/t* park etm.

parking ['pâkin] park yapma; ~ **lot** *Am.* park yeri; ~ **meter** otopark sayacı

parliament ['pâlımınt] parlamento, millet meclisi; **Member of** ♀ İngiliz parlamento üyesi; ~**ary** [‿'mentıri] parlamentoya ait

parlo(u)r ['pâlı] oturma odası, salon

parole [pı'rıul] şeref sözü

parquet ['pâkey] parke

parrot ['pärıt] ZOO papağan

parsley ['pâsli] BOT maydanoz

parson ['pâsn] papaz; ~**age** papaz evi

part [pât] *n.* parça, bölüm; pay; taraf; *v/t* parçalara ayırmak; *v/i* ayrılmak (**with** *-den*); **for my** ~ bence, bana kalırsa; **take** ~ katılmak (**in** *-e*)

partake [pâ'teyk] *v/i* katılmak (**of** *-e*)

partial ['pâşıl] eksik, tam

olmıyan; taraflı; ~ity [-şi'äli-
ti] tarafgirlik; beğenme

particip|ant [pâ'tisipınt] katı-
lan; paylaşan; ~ate [-eyt] v/i
katılmak (in -e)

participle [pâtisipl] GR ortaç,
sıfat-fiil

particle [pâtikl] cüz, zerre;
GR edat, takı

particular [pı'tikyulı] belirli;
özel; titiz; pl. ayrıntılar;
~ity [-läriti] özellik; titizlik;
~ly adv. özellikle

parting [pâtiŋ] ayrılma; ayıran, bölen

partisan [pâti'zän] taraftar;
partizan, çeteci

partition [pâ'tişın] n. taksim;
bölme; v/t bölmek

partly [pâtli] adv. kısmen

partner [pâtnı] ortak; eş;
dans arkadaşı; ~ship or-
taklık

partridge [pâtric] zoo keklik

part-time yarım günlük

party [pâti] grup; taraf; parti;
toplantı, şölen

pass [pâs] n. GEO boğaz, geçit;
pasaport; paso; v/t geçmek,
aşmak; geçirmek; v/i bitmek;
sayılmak (as, for olarak); ~
away v/i ölmek; geçmek;
v/t geçirmek; ~ by v/i geçmek; ~ round v/t elden ele
geçirmek; ~able geçilebilir;
oldukça iyi

passage [pâsic] yol; geçit;
pasaj; yolculuk

passenger [pâsıncı] yolcu

passer-by [pâsı'bay] yoldan

gelip geçen

passion [pâşın] ihtiras, tutku; aşk; hiddet; ~ate ['-it]
heyecanlı, ateşli

passive [pâsiv] eylemsiz, uysal, pasif; GR edilgen; ~
smoking pasif sigara kul-
lanımı

pass|port [pâspôt] pasaport;
~word parola

past [pâst] geçmiş, bitmiş; -in
yanından; geçmiş zaman (GR
~ tense); quarter ~ two ikiyi
çeyrek geçiyor

paste [peyst] n. macun; çiriş,
kola; v/t yapıştırmak;
~board mukavva

pasteurize [pâstrayz] v/t
pastörize etm.

pastime [pâstaym] eğlence

pastry [peystri] hamur işi,
pasta

pasture [pâsçı] n. otlak,
çayır; v/t otlatmak

pat [pât] n. el ile hafif vuruş;
v/t hafifçe vurmak -e

patch [pâç] n. yama; arazi
parçası; v/t yamamak; ~work
yama işi

patent [peytınt] n. patent; v/t
-in patentini almak

patent leather rugan

patern|al [pı'tönl] babaya ait;
~ity baba aşkı

path [pâth] keçi yolu, patika

pathetic [pı'thetik] acıklı, dokunaklı

patien|ce [peyşıns] sabır; ~t
sabırlı; hasta

patriarch [peytriâk] REL patrik

patriot ['peytriıt] *n.*, **~ic** [pä-tri'otik] *adj.* yurtsever; **~ism** ['pätriıtizım] yurtseverlik

patrol [pi'trıul] *n.* devriye; *v/t* devriye gezmek

patron ['peytrın] velinimet; patron; **~age** ['pätrınic] himaye, koruma

patter ['pätı] *v/i* pıtırdamak

pattern ['pätın] örnek, model, nümune, mostra

paunch [pônç] göbek

pause [pôz] *n.* fasıla, mola, teneffüs; *v/i* durmak, duraklamak

pave [peyv] *v/t* kaldırım *v.s.* ile döşemek; *fig. yolu* açmak; **~ment** kaldırım

paw [pô] *n.* pençe; *v/t* kabaca ellemek

pawn [pôn] *n.* rehin; *v/t* rehine koymak; **~broker** rehinci

pay [pey] *n.* maaş, ücret; *v/t* ödemek; **~ for** *b.ş.* için para vermek; **~in** cezasını çekmek; **~-in** cezasını çekmek; **~ attention** dikkat etm.; **~ a visit** görmeğe gitmek (**to** -*i*); **~able** ödenmesi gereken; **~day** ücretlerin verildiği gün; **~ee** [-'i] alacaklı; **~ment** ödeme; ücret; **~roll** ücret bordrosu

pea [pî] *bot* bezelye

pease [pîs] barış, sulh; rahat; **~ful** sakin; uysal

peach [pîç] *bot* şeftali

peacock ['pîkok] *zoo* tavus

peak [pîk] zirve, tepe; *kaskette* siper; **~ load** azami sıklet

peal [pîl] *n.* gürültü; *v/i* gürlemek

peanut ['pînat] *bot* American fıstığı, yerfıstığı

pear [päı] *bot* armut

pearl [pöl] inci

peasant ['pezınt] köylü

peat [pît] turba

pebble ['pebl] çakıl taşı

peck [pek] *v/i* gaga ile vurmak (**at** -*e*)

peculiar [pi'kyûlyı] özel; tuhaf, garip; **~ity** [-li'äriti] özellik

pedal ['pedl] *n.* pedal; *v/t* ayakla işletmek

pedestal ['pedistl] ARCH taban; temel

pedestrian [pi'destrıın] yaya giden; **~ precinct, ~ zone** yaya bölgesi

pedigree ['pedigrî] şecere; soy

pedlar ['pedlı] seyyar satıcı

peel [pîl] *n.* kabuk; *v/t* -*in* buğunu soymak; *v/i* soyulmak

peep [pîp] *n.* **1.** civciv gibi ötme; **2.** azıcık bakış; *v/i* gizlice bakmak (**at** -*e*)

peer [pıı] eş; asılzade; **~age** [-'ric] asalet; **~less** eşsiz

peevish ['pîviş] titiz, densiz

peg [peg] *n.* tahta çivi; askı; *v/t* mıhlamak; ECON -*de* istikrar sağlamak

pelt [pelt] *bot* atmak; *v/i* üzerine boşanmak

pen[1] [pen] yazı kalemi

pen[2] kümes, ağıl

penal ['pînl] cezaya ait; ~ **servitude** ağır hapis cezası; ~**ty** ['penltɪ] ceza; penaltı

penance ['penɪns] REL kefaret

pence [pens] *pl.* pensler

pencil ['pensl] kurşun kalem; ~ **sharpener** kalemtıraş

pendant ['pendɪnt] askı; ~**ing** henüz karara bağlanmamış; zarfında, -*e* kadar

penetrat|e ['penitreyt] *v/t* delip girmek; ~, -*in* içine girmek; ~**ion** sokuluş; etki

penguin ['peŋgwin] zoo penguen

penholder kalem sapı

penicillin [peni'silin] penisilin

peninsula [pi'ninsyulı] GEO yarımada

penitent ['penitınt] pişman, tövbekâr; ~**iary** [.'tenşıri] *Am.* hapishane, cezaevi

penknife çakı

penn|iless ['penilis] parasız; ~**y** pens, peni

pension ['penşın] pansiyon; emekli aylığı; ~**er** emekli

pensive ['pensiv] dalgın, düşünceli

penthouse ['penthaus] çatı katı

people ['pîpl] *n.* halk, ahali; millet, ulus; akrabalar *pl.*; *v/t* insanla doldurmak

pepper ['pepı] *n.* biber; *v/t* biberlemek; ~**mint** nane

per [pɜ] vasıtasiyle

perambulator ['prämbyuleytı] çocuk arabası

perceive [pı'sîv] *v/t* görmek, anlamak

percent [pı'sent] yüzde; ~**age** yüzdelik

percept|ible [pı'septıbl] duyulur, farkına varılır; ~**ion** idrak, anlayış

perch [pɜç] tünek

percussion [pı'kaşın] vurma, çarpma

peremptory [pı'remptıri] kesin, katî

perfect ['pɜfikt] *adj.* tam; kursursuz; *n.* GR (~ **tense**) geçmiş zaman; [pı'fekt] *v/t* tamamlamak; ~**ion** kusursuzluk; ikmal

perforate ['pɜfıreyt] *v/t* delmek

perform [pı'fôm] *v/t* yapmak, yerine getirmek; THEA oynamak; ~**ance** yerine getirme; THEA temsil, gösteri

perfume ['pɜfyûm] *n.* güzel koku; parfüm, esans; *v/t* lavanta sürmek -*e*

perhaps [pı'häps] belki

peril ['peril] tehlike; ~**ous** tehlikeli

period ['piırıd] çağ, devir, süre; ~**ic** [.'odik] belirli aralıklarla yer bulan; ~**ical** belli zamanlarda çıkan; dergi

perish ['periş] *v/i* ölmek; mahvolmak; ~**able** kolay bozulur

perjury ['pɜcıri] JUR yalan yere yemin

perm [pɜm] *coll.* perma (-nant); ~anent sürekli, devamlı; ~anent wave perma (-nant)

permeable ['pɜmyıbl] geçirgen

permi|ssion [pı'mişın] müsaade; ruhsat; ~t [-t] *v/t* müsaade etm.; kabul etm.; ['pɜmit] *n.* permi, ruhsatname

perpendicular [pɜpın'dikyulı] dikey; düşey

perpetual [pı'peçuıl] sürekli, ebedî

persecut|e ['pɜsikyût] *v/t* sıkıştırmak; zulmetmek -*e*; ~ion zulüm; ~or zulmelden

persever|ance [pɜsi'viırıns] sebat; ~e [.'viı] *v/i* sebat göstermek (in -*de*)

Persia ['pɜşı] İran; ~n İranlı; Farsça

persist [pı'sist] ısrar etm., sebat etm. (in -*de*); ~ence, ~ency sebat; ısrar; ~ent ısrarlı

person ['pɜsn] şahıs, kimse; ~age şahsiyet, zat; ~al özel; şahsî, zatî; ~ality [.sı'näliti] şahsiyet; ~ify [.'sonifay] *v/t* cisimlendirmek; ~nel [.sı'nel] kadro, takım

perspective [pı'spektiv] perspektif

perspir|ation [pɜspı'reyşın] ter(leme); ~e [pıs'payı] *v/i* terlemek

persua|de [pı'sweyd] *v/t* kandırmak; ~sion [.jın]

kandırma; inanç; ~sive [.siv] kandırıcı

pert [pɜt] şımarık, arsız

pertain [pɜ'teyn] ait olm. (to -*e*)

perturb [pı'tɜb] *v/t* altüst etm.

perus|al [pı'ruuzıl] dikkatle okuma; ~e *v/t* incelemek

pervade [pɜ'veyd] *v/t* kaplamak; yayılmak -*e*

perverse [pı'vɜs] ters, aksi; sapık

pessimis|m ['pesimizım] kötümserlik; ~t ['.mist] *n.* kötümser

pest [pest] veba, taun; ~er *v/t* sıkmak, usandırmak

pet [pet] *n.* evde beslenen hayvan; sevgili; *v/t* okşamak

petal ['petl] BOT çiçek yaprağı

petition [pı'tişın] *n.* dilekçe; *v/t* dilekçe vermek -*e* (for için)

petrify ['petrifay] *v/t* taş haline getirmek; *v/i* taş haline gelmek

petrol ['petrıl] benzin; ~ station benzin istasyonu

petticoat ['petikıut] iç etekliği

petty ['peti] küçük, önemsiz

pew [pyû] *kilisede* oturacak sıra

phantom ['fäntım] hayal; görüntü

pharma|ceutic(al) [fâmı'syûtikıl] eczacılığa ait; ~y ['.si] eczane

phase [feyz] safha, faz

pheasant ['feznt] zoo sülün

philanthropist [fi'länthrı-pist] hayırsever

philately [fi'lätıli] pul merakı

philology [fi'lolıci] filoloji

philosoph|er [fi'losıfı] filozof; **~y** felsefe

phone [fıun] *coll. n.* telefon; *v/t* telefon etm. *-e*; **~card** telefon kartı

phon(e)y ['fıuni] *sl.* sahte, düzme

photo ['fıutıu] *n.* fotoğraf; **~copy** fotokopi

photograph ['fıutıgrâf] *n.* fotoğraf; *v/t* fotoğrafını çekmek; **~er** [fı'togrıfı] fotoğrafçı; **~y** fotoğrafçılık

phrase [freyz] ibare; deyim; cümle

physic|al ['fizikıl] fiziksel; maddî; bedene ait; **~ian** [fi'zişın] doktor, hekim; **~ist** ['-sist] fizikçi; **~s** *pl.* fizik *sg.*

physique [fi'zîk] beden yapısı

piano [pi'änıu] MUS piyano

piast|er, ~re [pi'yästı] kuruş

pick [pik] *n.* sivri kazma; seçme; *v/t* gagalamak; kazmak; delmek; toplamak, koparmak; seçmek; **~ out** seçmek, ayırmak; **~ up** kaldırmak, toplamak

picket ['pikit] *n.* kazık; grevciler nöbetçisi; *v/i* nöbet beklemek

pickle ['pikl] *n.* turşu, salamura; *v/t -in* turşusunu kurmak

pick|pocket yankesici; **~up** pikap kolu

picnic ['piknik] piknik

pictorial [pik'tôrıl] resimli; resimlerle ilgili; resimli dergi

picture ['pikçı] *n.* resim; tablo; *pl.* sinema; *v/t* tasavvur etm.; *-in* resmini yapmak; tanımlamak; **~ postcard** resimli kartpostal; **~sque** [.'resk] pitoresk, canlı

pie [pay] börek, tarta

piece [pîs] parça, bölüm; **by the ~** parça başına; **~meal** parça parça; **~work** parça başına ücret

pier [pıı] NAUT iskele, rıhtım

pierce [pııs] *v/t* delmek; nüfuz etm. *-e*

piety ['payıti] dindarlık

pig [pig] domuz

pigeon ['picin] güvercin; **~hole** *yazı masasında v.s.* göz

pig-headed inatçı; **~tail** saç örgüsü

pike [payk] zoo turna balığı

pile [payl] *n.* yığın, küme; *v/t* yığmak, istif etm.; *v/i* birikmek

pilfer ['pilfı] *v/t* aşırmak

pilgrim ['pilgrim] hacı; **~age** hacca gitme

pill [pil] hap

pillar ['pilı] direk, sütun; **~box** mektup kutusu

pillory ['pilıri] teşhir direği

pillow ['pilıu] yastık; **~case, ~slip** yastık yüzü

pilot ['paylıt] *n.* kılavuz; pilot; *v/t* kılavuzluk etm. *-e*

pimp [pimp] pezevenk

pimple ['pimpl] sivilce

pin [pin] *n.* toplu iğne; çivi; *v/t* iğnelemek

pincers ['pinsız] *pl.* kerpeten, kıskaç *sg.*

pinch [pinç] *n.* çimdik; tutam; sıkıntı; *v/t* çimdiklemek; kısırmak; *sl.* ele geçirmek

pine¹ [payn] *v/i* zayıflamak; ~ for *-in* hasretini çekmek

pine² BOT çam; ~-apple ananas

pink [piŋk] BOT karanfil; pembe

pinnacle ['pinıkl] kule; zirve, tepe

PIN number [pin-] PIN numarası, kart şifresi

pint [paynt] galonun sekizde biri *(0,57 l, Am. 0,47 l)*

pioneer [payı'niı] öncü; MIL istihkâm eri

pious ['payıs] dindar

pip [pip] çekirdek

pipe [payp] *n.* boru; çubuk; pipo; künk; *v/t* borularla iletmek; çalmak; *v/t* düdük çalmak; ~line petrol borusu

pira|cy ['payırısi] korsanlık; ~te ['-rıt] korsan

pistachio [pis'tâşiu] BOT fıstık

pistol ['pistl] tabanca

piston ['pistın] TECH piston

pit¹ [pit] çukur

pit² *Am.* çekirdek

pitch¹ [piç] zift

pitch² *n.* fırlatma; yükseklik; MUS perde; derece; *v/t tent:* kurmak; atmak, fırlatmak;

high-~ed MUS perdesi ince; ~ed battle meydan savaşı

pitcher ['piçı] testi

piteous ['pitiıs] acınacak

pitfall ['pitfôl] tuzak olarak kazılan çukur; tuzak

pith [pith] ANAT, ZOO, BOT öz, ilik

piti|able ['pitiıbl] acınacak; acıklı; ~ful acınacak; aşağılık; ~less merhametsiz

pity ['piti] *n.* acıma, merhamet; it is a ~ yazık

pivot ['pivıt] mil; eksen; mihver

placard ['pläkaad] *n.* yafta, duvar ilânı; *v/t* afiş ile bildirmek

place [pleys] *n.* yer; meydan; görev; *v/t* koymak, yerleştirmek; in ~ of yerine; out of ~ yersiz; take ~ yer bulmak

placid ['pläsid] sakin, halim

plague [pleyg] *n.* veba; belâ, musibet; *v/t* eziyet vermek -e

plaice [pleys] ZOO pisi balığı

plain [pleyn] ova; düz, sade, sarih, süssüz; ~clothes man sivil polis

plaint [pleynt] şikâyet; ~iff ['-tif] JUR davacı; ~ive ['-tiv] iniltili, kederli

plait [plät] kırma; örgü; *v/t hair:* örmek

plan [plän] *n.* plan, taslak; niyet; *v/t* tasarlamak

plane [pleyn] *adj.* düz, düzlem; *n.* TECH planya, rende; AVIA uçak; *v/t* rendelemek

planet ['plänit] ASTR gezeğen

seyyare

plank [plǎŋk] uzun tahta, kalas

plant [plǎnt] *n.* bitki, nebat; fabrika; *v/t* dikmek, kurmak; ~ation [plǎn'teyşın] fidanlık; büyük çiftlik; ~**er** ['plǎntı] ekici; çiftlik sahibi

plaque [plǎk] levha

plaster ['plǎstı] *n.* sıva; alçı; yakı; *v/t* sıvamak, yakı yapıştırmak *-e*

plastic ['plǎstik] *adj.*, ~**s** *pl.* plastik

plate [pleyt] *n.* tabak; levha; plaka; fotoğraf camı; *v/t* kaplamak

platform ['plǎtfôm] sahanlık; peron; POL parti programı

platinum ['plǎtinım] platin

platoon [plı'tuun] MIL takım

plausible ['plôzıbl] akla sığan, makul

play [pley] *n.* oyun; piyes; *v/t* oynamak; MUS çalmak; ~**er** oyuncu; ~**fellow** oyun arkadaşı; ~**ful** oyunbaz, şakacı; ~**ground** oyun sahası; ~**thing** oyuncak; ~**time** tatil zamanı; ~**wright** ['~rayt] THEA piyes yazarı

plea [plî] müdafaa; rica; bahane

plead [plîd] *v/t* ileri sürmek; savunmak; *v/i* yalvarmak; ~ **guilty** suçu kabul etm.

pleasant ['pleznt] hoş, latif

please [plîz] *v/t* sevindirmek, *-in* hoşuna gitmek; *intj.* lütfen; **be** ~**d** memnun olm.

(with *-den*)

pleasure ['plejı] zevk, keyif

pleat [plît] pli

plebiscite ['plebisit] plebisit

pledge [plec] *n.* rehin; söz, vaat; *v/t* rehin olarak vermek

plent|**iful** ['plentiful] bol, çok; ~**y** bolluk, zenginlik; ~**y of** çok

pleurisy ['pluırisi] MED zatülcenp

pliable ['playıbl] bükülür; *fig.* uysal

pliers ['playız] *pl.* kıskaç, pens(e)

plight [playt] kötü durum

plod [plod] ağır yürümek *veya* çalışmak

plot [plot] *n.* arsa, parsel; entrika, suikast; plan; *v/t -in* haritasını çıkarmak; *v/i* kumpas kurmak

plough, *Am.* **plow** [plau] saban, pulluk; *v/t* sabanla işlemek; ~**share** saban demiri

pluck [plʌk] *n.* cesaret, yiğitlik; *v/t* koparmak, yolmak; ~**y** cesur, yılmaz

plug [plʌg] *n.* tapa, tıkaç; EL fiş; buji; *v/t* tıkamak; ~ **in** EL prize sokmak

plum [plʌm] BOT erik; kuru üzüm; ~ **pudding** baharatlı Noel pudingi

plumage ['pluumic] kuşun tüyleri *pl.*

plumb [plʌm] *n.* şakul; *v/t* iskandil etm.; ~**er** lehimci, muslukçu

plume [pluum] gösterişli tüy,

sorguç

plump [plamp] *adj.* şişman, tombul; *v/i* birdenbire düşmek; oy vermek (for *-e*); yardım etm. (*-e*)

plunder ['plandı] *n.* yağma; *v/t* yağma etm., soymak

plunge [planc] *v/t* daldırmak; *v/i* dalmak, atılmak (into *-e*)

pluperfect (tense) ['pluu'pɜfikt] GR geçmiş zamanın hikâye şekli

plural ['plurıl] GR çoğul

plus [plas] ve, ilâvesiyle; MATH artı

plush [plaş] pelüş

ply [play] *n.* kat; *v/t* eğmek; ~wood kontrplak

pneumatic [nyû'mätik] TECH hava basıncı ile ilgili; ~onia [-'mıunyı] MED zatürree

poach [piuç] *v/i* gizlice avlanmak; ~er ruhsatsız avlanan kimse

pocket ['pokıt] *n.* cep; *v/t* cebe sokmak; ~book cep kitabı; ~knife çakı

pod [pod] kabuk, zarf

poem ['puim] şiir

poet ['puit] şair; ~ic(al) [-'etik(ıl)] şiire ait; manzum; ~ry ['-itri] şiir sanatı

poignant ['poynınt] acı, keskin

point [poynt] *n.* nokta; uç; puvan; derece; pl. demiryolunda makaslar; *v/t* yöneltmek, sivriltmek; *v/i* göstermek (at *-i*); silâhı doğrultmak (*-e*); **beside the** ~ konu

dışında; **on the** ~ of *-ing* *-mek* üzere; ~ **of view** görüş noktası; ~ **out** *v/t* belirtmek; ~blank doğrudan doğruya; ~ed uçlu; manalı; ~er işaret değneği; gösterge

poise [poyz] *n.* denge; istikrar; *v/t* -in dengesini sağlamak; *v/i* sarkmak

poison ['poyzn] *n.* zehir; *v/t* zehirlemek; ~ous zehirli

poke [puk] *v/t* dürtmek, karıştırmak; ~r ocak demiri

Poland ['pulınd] Polonya

polar ['pulı] GEO kutba ait; ~ **bear** ZOO kutup ayısı

pole[1] [pıul] kutup; direk, kazık

Pole[2] Polonyalı, Lehli

police [pı'lîs] polis; ~man polis memuru; ~station karakol

policy ['polisi] siyaset; poliçe

polio ['pıuliıu] MED çocuk felci

polish[1] ['poliş] *n.* cilâ, perdah; boya; *v/t* cilâlamak, parlatmak

Polish[2] ['pıuliş] Polonyalı; Lehçe

polite [pı'layt] nazik, kibar; ~ness nezaket, kibarlık

political [pı'litikıl] siyasî; ~ **sciences** *pl.* siyasal bilgiler

politics ['politiks] *pl.* siyaset, politika *sg.*

poll [pıul] *n.* oy; anket; *pl.* seçim bürosu *sg.*

pollut|e [pı'luut] *v/t* kirletmek; ~ion pisletme

polygamy [po'ligimi] çok-
karılılık, poligami
pomegranate ['pomgränit]
BOT nar
pomp [pomp] gösteriş, tantana; ~ous tantanalı, debde-
beli
pond [pond] havuz, gölcük
ponder ['pondı] v/i uzun boylu düşünmek (on, over -i);
v/t zihninde tartmak; ~ous
ağır; can sıkıcı
pony ['pıuni] ZOO midilli
poodle ['puudl] ZOO kaniş köpeği
pool [puul] n. gölcük, su birikintisi; havuz; ortaya konulan para; toto; v/t ortaklaşa
toplamak
poor [puı] fakir, yoksul; az; fena; the ~ pl. yoksullar
pop [pop] n. pat, çat; patlama
sesi; v/i patlamak; v/t patlatmak; ~ out v/i fırlamak
pope [pıup] REL papa
poplar ['poplı] BOT kavak
poppy ['popi] BOT gelincik,
haşhaş
populace ['pópyulıs] halk,
avam; ~ar halka ait; herkesçe sevilen; ~arity [-'läriti]
halk tarafından tutulma;
rağbet; ~ate ['-.eyt] v/t şe-
neltmek; ~ation nüfus, ahali;
~ous nüfusu çok, kalabalık
porcelain ['pôslin] porselen
porch [pôç] kapı önünde sun-
durma; Am. veranda
porcupine ['pôkyupayn] ZOO
oklukirpi

pore [pô] n. ANAT gözenek,
mesame; v/i derin düşün-
mek (over -i)
pork [pôk] domuz eti
pornography [pô'nogrıfi]
pornografi, müstehcen yazı-
lar pl.
porous ['pôrıs] göznekli
porphyry ['pôfiri] somaki,
porfir
porridge ['poric] yulaf lapası
port¹ [pôt] liman
port² NAUT lombar
port³ porto şarabı
portable ['pôtıbl] taşınabilir,
portatif
porter ['pôtı] hamal; kapıcı
portion ['pôşın] n. hisse, pay;
parça; porsiyon; çeyiz; v/t
ayırmak
portly ['pôtli] iri yapılı; heybetli
portrait ['pôtrit] portre, resim
Portugal ['pótyugıl] Portekiz; ~uese [-'gîz] Portekizli;
Portekizce
pose [pıuz] n. tavır; duruş;
poz; v/i poz almak; taslamak
(as -i)
position [pı'zişın] yer; durum, vaziyet
positive ['pozitiv] olumlu;
pozitif
possess [pı'zes] v/t malik
olm., sahip olm. -e; ~ed deli;
düşkün (with -e); ~ion tasarruf; mal, mülk; iyelik; ~ive
pronoun GR iyelik zamiri;
~or mal sahibi
possibility [posı'biliti] im-

kân, ihtimal; **~le** ['posibl]
mümkün, muhtemel; **~ly**
adv. belki

post [pıust] *n.* direk, kazık;
görev, memuriyet; posta; *v/t*
postaya vermek; koymak,
yerleştirmek; **~age** posta ücreti; **~age stamp** posta pulu;
~card kartpostal; **~e res-
tante** [-'restant] postrestant

poster ['pıustı] yafta, afiş

posterity [pos'teriti] gelecek
nesiller *pl.*

post-free posta ücretine tabi
olmıyan

post|-graduate üniversite
mezunu; **~humous** ['postyu-
mıs] ölümden sonra olan

post|man postacı; **~mark** pos-
ta damgası; **~master** postane
müdürü; **~(-)office** postane;
~(-)office box posta kutusu

postpone [pıust'pıun] *v/t* ertelemek, sonraya bırakmak

postscript ['pıusskript] derkenar, not

posture ['posçı] duruş, poz

post-war ['pıust'wô] savaş
sonrası

posy ['pıuzi] çiçek demeti

pot [pot] *n.* çömlek, kavanoz;
saksı; *v/t* saksıya dikmek; ka-
vanozda konserve etm.

potato [pı'teytıu] patates; **~es
in their jackets** *pl.* kabuğiyle
haşlanan patates

potent ['pıutınt] kuvvetli, etkili; **~ial** güç; potansiyel

potter[1] ['potı] *v/i* oyalanmak

potter[2] çömlekçi; **~y** çanak

çömlek; çömlekçilik

pouch [pauç] kese

poulterer ['pıultırı] tavukçu

poultice ['pıultis] lapa

poultry ['pıultri] kümes hayvanları *pl.*

pounce [pauns] *v/i* atılmak
(on -*in* üzerine)

pound[1] [paund] libre (*454 g*);
sterlin, İngiliz lirası

pound[2] *v/t* dövmek; yumruklamak

pour [pô] *v/i* akmak, dökülmek; *v/t* dökmek, akıtmak

pout [paut] *v/t* dudaklarını
sarkıtmak; *v/i* somurtmak

poverty ['poviti] yoksulluk

powder ['paudı] *n.* toz; pudra;
barut; *v/t* toz *veya* pudra sürmek -*e*

power ['pauı] kudret, kuvvet,
güç; yetki; **~ful** kuvvetli,
kudretli; etkili; **~less** kuv-
vetsiz; **~-plant**, **~-station**
elektrik santralı

practi|cable ['präktikıbl]
yapılabilir; elverişli; **~cal**
pratik; kullanışlı; **~ce**, *Am.*
~se ['-tis] uygulama;
alışıklık; pratik; müşteriler
pl.; **~se** *v/t* yapmak; uygulamak; talim etm.; **~tioner**
[-'tişnı] doktor; avukat

prairie ['präuri] *Kuzey Amerika'da* bozkır

praise [preyz] *n.* övgü; *v/t* övmek; **~worthy** övülmeğe
değer

pram [präm] çocuk arabası

prank [pränk] kaba şaka,

oyun

prattle ['prätl] gevezelik etm.

prawn [prôn] zoo karides, deniz tekesi

pray [prey] v/i dua etm.; yalvarmak (to -e); çok rica etm. (for -i); ~er [präı] dua; ibadet

preach [prîç] v/i va'zetmek (to -e); ~er vaiz

preamble [pri'âmbl] önsöz

precarious [pri'käriıs] kararsız; tehlikeli

precaution [pri'kôşın] ihtiyat, tedbir

precede [pri'sîd] v/t -den önce gelmek; -in önünden yürümek; ~nce önce gelme, üstünlük; ~nt ['presidınt] emsal, örnek

precept ['prîsept] hüküm; kural

precinct ['prîsiŋkt] bölge, çevre

precious ['preşıs] kıymetli, çok sevilen

precipi|ce ['presipis] uçurum; ~tate** [pri'sipiteyt] v/t zamanından önce meydana getirmek; hızlandırmak; [pri'sipitit] adj. aceleci; düşüncesiz; ~tation** [prisipi'teyşin] acelecilik, telâş; yağış (miktarı); ~tous** [pri'sipitıs] dik, sarp

précis ['preysî] özet

precis|e [pri'says] tam; kesin; ~ion** [-'sijın] dikkat; kesinlik

precocious [pri'kıuşıs] vak-

tinden önce gelişmiş

preconception ['prîkın'sepşın] önyargı

predatory ['preditıri] yağmacılıkla geçinen; yırtıcı

predecessor ['prîdisesı] öncel, selef

predetermine ['prîdi'tзmin] v/t önceden tayin etm.

predicament [pri'dikımınt] kötü durum

predicate ['predikit] GR yüklem

predict [pri'dikt] v/t önceden bildirmek; ~ion** önceden haber

predisposition ['prîdispı'zişın] eğilim, meyil

predomina|nt [pri'dominınt] üstün; ~te** [-eyt] v/i hâkim olm.

preface ['prefis] önsöz

prefer [pri'fз] v/t tercih etm. (to -e); ~able** ['prefırıbl] daha iyi; ~ence** ['prefırıns] öncelik, üstünlük; ~ment** [pri-'fзmınt] terfi, yükselme

prefix ['prîfiks] GR önek

pregnan|cy ['pregnınsi] gebelik; ~t** gebe

prejudice ['precudis] n. önyargı, peşin hüküm; v/t haksız hüküm verdirmek -e (against -e karşı)

preliminary [pri'liminıri] hazırlayıcı, ilk

prelude ['prelyûd] başlangıç, giriş

premature [premı'tyuı] mevsimsiz, erken

premeditate [pri'mediteyt] *v/t* tasarlamak

premier ['premyı] baştaki; POL başbakan

premises ['premisiz] *pl.* mülk, ev ve müştemilâtı *sg.*

premium ['prîmyım] prim, mükâfat; ikramiye

preoccupied [pri'okyupayd] zihni meşgul

prepar|ation [prepı'reyşın] hazırlama; hazırlık; ~atory [pri'pärıtıri] hazırlayıcı; ~e [pri'päı] *v/t* hazırlamak; *v/i* hazırlanmak

prepay ['prî'pey] *v/t* peşin ödemek

preposition [prepı'zişın] GR edat

prepossess [prîpı'zes] *v/t* lehinde fikir hâsıl ettirmek; ~ing elıcı, cazibeli

preposterous [pri'postırıs] akıl almaz, mantıksız

Presbyterian [prezbı'tiriyn] REL İskoçya Protestan kilisesine ait

prescri|be [pris'krayb] *v/t* emretmek; *ilâcı* vermek; ~ption [-'kripşın] MED reçete

presence ['prezns] huzur, varlık; ~ of mind soğukkanlılık

present[1] ['preznt] hazır; şimdiki; hediye, armağan; ~ (tense) GR şimdiki zaman

present[2] [pri'zent] *v/t* sunmak; tanıştırmak; göstermek

presentation [prezen'teyşın]

sunma, takdim; hediye; temsil

presentiment [pri'zentimınt] önsezi

presently ['prezntli] *adv.* derhal; *Am.* şimdi

preserv|ation [prezз'veyşın] saklama, koruma; ~e [pri'zзv] *v/t* korumak, saklamak; dayandırmak; -*in* konservesini yapmak; *n. pl.* reçel *sg.*

preside [pri'zayd] *v/t* başkanlık etm. -*e*

president ['prezidınt] başkan

press [pres] *n.* baskı; basın; matbaa; mengene; *v/t* sıkmak, sıkıştırmak; basmak; zorlamak; ütülemek; ~ing acele; ~ure ['-şı] basınç; baskı

prestige [pres'tîj] ün; nüfuz

presum|e [pri'zyûm] *v/t* tahmin etm.; cesaret etm. -*e*; ~ing haddini aşan

presumpt|ion [pri'zampşın] farz, tahmin; küstahlık; ~uous [-'tyuıs] küstah

preten|ce, *Am.* ~se [pritens] bahane; iddia; ~d *v/t* yalandan yapmak; taslamak (**to** *inf.* -*i*); *v/i* yapar gibi görünmek; iddia etm. (**to** -*i*); ~der hak iddia eden; ~sion hak iddiası; haksız iddia

preterit(e) (**tense**) ['pretirit] GR geçmiş zaman kipi

pretext ['prîtekst] bahane

pretty ['priti] güzel, sevimli; *adv.* oldukça, hayli

prevail [pri'veyl] hâkim olm.; yürürlükte olm.; ~alent ['previlınt] hüküm süren, yaygın

prevent [pri'vent] v/t önlemek; durdurmak; ~ion önleme; ~ive önleyici

previous ['prîvyıs] önceki, sabık; önce (to -den)

pre-war [prî'wô] savaş öncesi

prey [prey] n. av; v/i soymak, yağma etm. (upon -i)

price [prays] n. fiat, bedel; v/t fiat koymak -e; ~less paha biçilmez

prick [prik] n. iğne veya diken batması; v/t sokmak, delmek; ~ up one's ears kulak kabartmak; ~le diken; ~ly dikenli

pride [prayd] kibir, gurur, iftihar

priest [prîst] papaz

primary ['praymıri] ilk, asıl; başlıca; ~ school ilkokul

prime [praym] birinci; başlıca; olgunluk çağı; ~ minister POL başbakan; ~r okuma kitabı

primitive ['primitiv] iptidaî, ilkel; basit; kaba

primrose ['primrıuz] BOT çuhaçiçeği

prince [prins] prens; hükümdar; ~ss ['-ses] prenses

principal ['prinsipıl] başlıca, en önemli; şef, müdür, patron; sermaye; ~le ['-ıpl] prensip, ilke

print [print] n. damga; empri-

me, basma kumaş; matbua, basma; v/t basmak; out of ~ baskısı tükenmiş; ~ed matter matbua; ~er başımcı; ~ing matbaacılık; baskı; ~ing-office basımevi, matbaa

prior ['prayı] önce (to -den); ~ity [-'oriti] öncelik

prison ['prizn] cezaevi, hapishane; ~er tutuklu; esir; take ~er v/t esir etm.

privacy ['privisi, 'pray-] özellik; gizlilik

private ['prayvit] özel; şahsî; gizli; MIL er; ~ion ['veyşın] yoksunluk, sıkıntı

privilege ['privilic] imtiyaz; ~d imtiyazlı

prize [prayz] n. mükâfat, ödül; v/t değer vermek -e

pro- [prıu-] lehinde, ... tarafı; profesyonel

probability [probı'biliti] ihtimal; ~able ['-ıbl] muhtemel

probation [prı'beyşın] deneme süresi; JUR gözaltı

probe [prub] n. sonda; v/t araştırmak

problem ['problım] sorun, mesele

procedure [prı'sîcı] işlem, muamele

proceed [prı'sîd] v/i ilerlemek; çıkmak (from -den); n. pl. kazanç, gelir sg.; ~ing muamele, usul

process ['prıuses] n. yöntem, metot, işlem; gidiş, gelişme; JUR dava; celpname; v/t işlemek; **~ion** [prɪ'seʃın] alay

proclaim [prɪ'kleym] *v/t* ilân etm.; beyan etm.; **~mation** [proklı'meyʃın] ilân; bildiri

procure [prɪ'kyu] *v/t* elde etm., tedarik etm.

prodigious [prɪ'dıcıs] kocaman, şaşılacak; **~y** ['prodici] olağanüstü şey; dâhi

produce [prɪ'dyûs] *v/t* meydana getirmek; üretmek; çıkarmak; ['prodyûs] *n.* ürün, mahsul; **~r** [prɪ'dyûsı] üretici; THEA prodüktör

product ['prodakt] ürün, mahsul; sonuç; **~ion** [prɪ'dakʃın] imal, üretim; THEA sahneye koyma; **~ive** [prɪ'daktiv] verimli

profess [prɪ'fes] *v/t* açıkça söylemek; ikrar etm.; **~ed** açıklanmış; **~ion** meslek; iddia, söz; **~ional** mesleğe ait; meslekî, profesyonel; **~or** profesör

proffer ['profı] *v/t* sunmak

proficiency [prɪ'fiʃınsı] ehliyet, beceriklilik; **~t** ehliyetli, usta

profile ['prıufayl] profil

profit ['profit] *n.* kazanç; yarar; *v/t* kazanç getirmek *-e*; *v/i* yararlanmak (**by**, **from** *-den*); **~able** kazançlı; faydalı; **~eer** [-'ti] vurguncu

profound [prɪ'faund] derin, engin

profusion [prɪ'fyûjın] bolluk

progeny ['procini] soy, nesil

prognosis [prog'nıusis] tah-

min, prognoz

program(me) ['prıugräm] program; düzen

progress ['prıugres] *n.* ilerleme, gelişme; *v/i* ilerlemek; **~ive** ilerleyen; ilerici

prohibit [prɪ'hibit] *v/t* yasak etm.; mâni olm. *-e*; **~ed area** yasak bölge; **~ion** [prıui-'biʃın] yasak; içkilerin yasak olması

project ['prockt] *n.* plan, proje, tasarı; *v/t* tasarlamak; perdede göstermek; *v/i* çıkık olm.; **~ion** PHYS projeksiyon; gösterim; çıkıntı; **~or** projektör, ışıldak

proletaria|n [prıule'täırın] proleter; **~t** [-ıit] proletarya

prolog(ue) ['prıulog] THEA prolog, önsöz

prolong [prıu'loŋ] *v/t* uzatmak

promenade [promi'nâd] gezinti; gezme yeri

prominent ['prominınt] tanınmış; çıkıntılı

promiscuity [promis'kyûiti] karışıklık; **~ous** [prımis-'kyuıs] rasgele cinsel ilişkide bulunan

promis|e ['promis] *v/t* söz vermek; *n.* söz, vaat; **~ing** ümit verici

promontory ['promıntri] GEO gağlık burun

promot|e [prɪ'mut] *v/t* ilerletmek; terfi ettirmek; **~ion** terfi

prompt [prompt] *adj.* hemen,

çabuk; *v/t* tahrik etm., sevketmek

prong [proŋ] çatal dişi

pronoun ['prıunaun] GR zamir

pro|nounce [prı'nauns] *v/t* söylemek, telaffuz etm.; **~nunciation** [_nansi'eyşın] söylemiş

proof [pruuf] delil; deneme; prova; dayanıklı

prop [prop] *n.* destek; *v/t* desteklemek

propaga|nda [propı'gändı] propaganda; **~te** [‑'geyt] *v/i* çoğalmak; *v/t* çiftleştirmek; yaymak; **~tion** [‑'geyşın] üreme; yayım

propel [prı'pel] *v/t* sevketmek; **~ler** TECH pervane, uskur

proper ['propı] uygun; özel; yakışıklı; **~ty** mal, mülk; özellik

prophe|cy ['profisi] önceden haber verme, kâhinlik; **~sy** ['‑say] *v/t* önceden haber vermek (*sth.* hakkında); **~t** peygamber; kâhin

proportion [prı'pôşın] oran(tı), nispet; **~al** orantılı

propos|al [prı'puzıl] önerme, teklif; evlenme teklifi; **~e** *v/t* önermek; *v/i* evlenme teklifi yapmak (**to** *-e*); **~ition** [propı'zişın] teklif; mesele

propriet|ary [prı'prayıtıri] ECON sicilli, markalı; **~or** sahip

propulsion [prı'palşın] itici güç

prose [prıuz] nesir

prosecut|e ['prosikyût] *v/t* takip etm.; kovuşturmak; **~ion** JUR takibat; **~or** davacı; savcı

prospect ['prospekt] *n.* manzara, görünüş; ümit; ihtimal; [prıs'pekt] *v/i* araştırmak (**for** *-i*); **~ive** [prıs'pektiv] muhtemel; beklenen; **~us** [prıs'pektıs] prospektüs

prosper ['prospı] *v/i* başarılı olm.; gelişmek; **~ity** [‑'periti] refah, gönenç; **~ous** ['‑pırıs] bayındır; başarılı

prostitute ['prostityût] fahişe

prostrate ['prostreyt] yere uzanmış; takati kesilmiş

protect [prı'tekt] *v/t* korumak (**from** *-den*); **~ion** koruma; **~ive** koruyucu; **~or** hami, koruyucu

protest ['prıutest] *n.* protesto, itiraz; [prı'test] *v/i* protesto etm. (**against** *-i*); *v/t* protesto etm.; iddia etm.; **~ant** ['protistınt] REL Protestan; **~ation** [prıutes'teyşın] itiraz

protocol ['prıutıkol] tutanak; POL protokol

protract [prı'träkt] *v/t* uzatmak

protrude [prı'truud] *v/i* dışarı çıkmak; *v/t* çıkarmak

proud [praud] kibirli; kıvanç duyan (**of** *-e*)

prove [pruuv] *v/t* tanıtlamak, göstermek; *v/i* çıkmak

proverb ['provɜb] atasözü

~ial [prı'vɔbyıl] herkesçe bilinen

provide [prı'vayd] v/t tedarik etm.; donatmak; v/i sağlamak (for -i); ~d (that) -si şartıyla

providence ['providıns] REL takdir; basiret

provinc|e ['provins] il, vilâyet; taşra; yetki alanı; ~al [prı'vinşıl] taşralı; dar düşünceli

provision [prı'vijın] tedarik; şart, koşul; pl. erzak; ~al geçici

provo|cation [provı'keyşın] kışkırtma; gücendirme; ~cative [prı'vokıtiv] kışkırtıcı; kızdırıcı; ~ke [prı'viuk] v/t kışkırtmak, tahrik etm.; sebep olm. -e

prowl [praul] v/t dolaşmak; v/i gezinmek

proximity [prok'simiti] yakınlık

proxy ['proksi] vekillik

prude [pruud] fazilet taslayıcı

pruden|ce ['pruudıns] ihtiyat, basiret; ~t ihtiyatlı, tedbirli

prune [pruun] n. kuru erik; v/t budamak

pry [pray] burnunu sokmak (into -e)

psalm [sâm] REL ilâhi

pseudonym ['psyûdınim] takma ad

psych|iatry [say'kayıtri] psikiyatri, ruh hekimliği; ~ology [say'kolıci] psikoloji

pub [pab] birahane

puberty ['pyûbıti] ergenlik çağı

public ['pablik] halk; halka ait; devletle ilgili; alenî; genel; ~ house lokanta, birahane; ~ school özel okul; Am. resmî okul; 2 Works pl. Bayındırlı İşleri; ~ation yayım(lama); yayın; ~ity [-'lisiti] aleniyet; reklam

publish ['pabliş] v/t yayımlamak; bastırmak; ~er yayınlayıcı; ~ing-house yayınevi

pudding ['pudiŋ] puding

puddle ['padl] su birikintisi

puff [paf] n. üfleme, püf; hafif yumuşak börek; pudra pomponu; v/i üflemek, püflemek; v/t şişirmek; ~y şişkin

pull [pul] n. çekme, çekiş; v/t çekmek; koparmak; ~ down indirmek, yıkmak; ~ out v/t çekip çıkarmak; v/i ayrılmak; ~ oneself together kendine gelmek

pulley ['puli] TECH makara

pull-over ['puluvı] kazak, süveter

pulp [palp] meyva veya sebze eti; lapa

pulpit ['pulpit] mimber

pulpy ['palpi] etli, özlü

puls|ate [pal'seyt] v/i nabız gibi kımıldamak; ~e nabız

pulverize ['palvırayz] v/t ezmek, toz haline getirmek

pump [pamp] n. TECH tulumba, pompa; iskarpin; v/t tulumba ile çekmek; ~ up pompa ile şişirmek

pumpkin ['pampkin] BOT helvacı kabağı

pun [pan] cinas, söz oyunu

punch [panç] *n.* punç; TECH zımba; yumrukla vuruş; *v/t* yumruklamak; zımbalamak

Punch [panç] **and Judy** ['cuudi] *İngiliz kukla oyununda iki başfigür*

punctual ['paŋktyuıl] tam zamanında olmuş

punctuat|e ['paŋktyueyt] *v/t* noktalamak; **~ion** GR noktalama

puncture ['paŋkçı] delik, lastik patlaması

pungent ['pancınt] keskin, dokunaklı

punish ['paniş] *v/t* cezalandırmak; **~ment** ceza(landırma)

pup [pap] köpek yavrusu

pupil¹ ['pyûpl] öğrenci, talebe

pupil² ANAT gözbebeği

puppet ['papit] kukla

puppy ['papi] köpek yavrusu

purchase ['pɜçis] *n.* satın alma; satın alınan şey; *v/t* satın almak; **~r** müşteri

pure [pyuı] saf, halis; temiz

purée ['pyurey, pü're] püre, ezme

purgat|ive ['pɜgıtiv] müshil, sürgün ilâcı; **~ory** REL araf

purge [pɜc] *n.* MED müshil; POL tasfiye; *v/t* temizlemek

puri|fy ['pyuırifay] *v/t* temizlemek; **~tan** [-tın] Püriten, mutaassıp Protestan; **~ty** temizlik, saflık

purloin [pɜ'loyn] *v/t* aşırmak

purple ['pɜpl] mor

purpose ['pɜpıs] *n.* maksat, niyet; *v/t* niyet etm.; **on ~** kasten, istiyerek; **to no ~** faydasızca; **~ful** maksatlı; **~less** manasız; **~ly** bile bile

purr [pɜ] *v/t* mırlamak

purse¹ [pɜs] *n.* para kesesi; *Am.* el çantası; haz(i)ne

purse² *v/t* dudakları büzmek

pursu|e [pı'syû] *v/t* takip etm., kovalamak; **~it** [-yût] takip, arama; iş, uğraşma

purvey [pɜ'vey] *v/t* tedarik etm.; **~or** satıcı

pus [pas] irin

push [puş] *n.* itiş, dürtüş; teşebbüs; *v/t* itmek, dürtmek; saldırmak; **~ on** devam etm.

puss [pus], **~y** kedi

put [put] *v/t* koymak, yerleştirmek; ifade etm.; **~ away** saklamak; **~ down** indirmek; bastırmak; yazmak; **~ forth**, **~ forward** ileri sürmek; **~ off** sonraya bırakmak; vazgeçirmek; çıkarmak; **~ on** giymek; açmak; takınmak; **~ out** söndürmek; çıkarmak; **~ through** TEL bağlamak; **~ up with** katlanmak *-e*

putr|efy ['pyûtrifay] *v/i* çürümek; *v/t* çürütmek, bozmak; **~id** [-id] çürük, bozuk

putty ['pati] çamcı macunu

puzzle ['pazl] *n.* bilmece, bulmaca; mesele; *v/t* şaşırtmak; *v/i* şaşırmak

pyjamas [pı'câmız] *pl.* pijama *sg.*

pyramid ['pırımid] piramit, ehram

Q

quack [kwäk] *n.* ördek sesi; *fig.* doktor taslağı, şarlatan; *v/i* ördek gibi bağırmak

quadr|angle ['kwodrängl] dörtgen; avlu; **~ate** [_.it] kare; dört köşeli; **~ipartite** [_.i'pâtayt] dört taraflı

quadrup|ed ['kwodruped] dört ayaklı; **~le** *adj.* dört kat, dört misli; *v/t* dört misli çoğaltmak

quail [kweyl] *zoo* bıldırcın

quaint [kweynt] tuhaf, garip ve hoş

quake [kweyk] *n.* titreme, deprem; *v/i* titremek; 2r Kuveykır mezhebinin üyesi

qualif|ication [kwolifi'keyşın] ehliyet; **~ed** ['-fayd] ehliyetli; nitelik; **~y** ['-fay] *v/t* nitelendirmek; sınırlamak; hafifletmek; *v/i* ehliyet göstermek

quality ['kwoliti] nitelik; kalite

qualm [kwâm] azap; bulantı

quantity ['kwontiti] nicelik, miktar

quarantine ['kworıntîn] karantina

quarrel ['kworıl] *n.* kavga; *v/i* kavga etm., çekişmek; **~some** kavgacı, huysuz

quarry[1] ['kwori] av

quarry[2] taş ocağı

quart [kwôt] galonun dörtte biri *(1,136 l, Am. 0,946 l)*

quarter ['kwôtı] *n.* dörtte biri, çeyrek; üç aylık süre; etraf, semt; aman, hayatını bağışlama; *mıl pl.* kışla, ordugâh *sg.*; *v/t* dörde ayırmak; *mıl* yerleştirmek; **a ~ past** *-i* çeyrek geçe; **a ~ to** *-e* çeyrek kala; **~ly** üç ayda bir

quartet(te) [kwô'tet] *mus* kuartet

quaver ['kweyvı] *v/i* titremek *(ses)*

quay [kî] rıhtım, iskele

queen [kwîn] kıraliçe

queer [kwiı] acayip, tuhaf

quell [kwel] *v/t* bastırmak

quench [kwenç] *v/t* söndürmek; soğutmak

querulous ['kwerulıs] şikâyetçi

query ['kwiıri] *n.* soru; *v/t* sormak *-e*; şüphelenmek *-den*

quest [kwest] arama

question ['kwesçın] *n.* soru; mesele; şüphe; *v/t* sual sormak *-e*; şüphe etm. *-den*; sorguya çekmek *-i*; **be out of the ~** olamamak; **~able** şüpheli; **~mark** GR soru işareti; **~naire** [_.stiı'näi] soru kâğıdı

queue [kyû] bekliyen halk di-

zisi, kuyruk; ~ **up** v/i kuyruğa
girmek

quick [kwik] çabuk, tez, süratli; keskin; çevik; ~**en** v/t
canlandırmak; çabuklaştır-
mak; v/i hızlanmak; ~**ness**
çabukluk, sürat; ~**sand** bataklık kumu; ~**silver** civa;
~**witted** çabuk anlıyan

quid [kwid] sl. bir sterlin

quiet ['kwayıt] adj. sakin, sessiz; gösterişsiz; n. sessizlik;
v/t susturmak; ~**ness**, ~**ude**
['~ityûd] sessizlik, rahat

quill [kwil] tüy kalem; kirpi
dikeni

quilt [kwilt] yorgan

quince [kwins] BOT ayva

quinine [kwi'nîn] CHEM kinin

quintal ['kwintl] yüz kiloluk
ağırlık

quit [kwit] v/t terketmek,
bırakmak; adj. serbest

quite [kwayt] tamamen; gerçekten; hayli

quiver ['kwivı] n. ok kılıfı; titreme; v/i titremek

quiz [kwiz] n. sorgu, test; v/t
sorguya çekmek

quota ['kwıutı] hisse, pay, kota

quotation [kwıu'teyşın] aktarma; ECON fiat ~ **marks**
pl. GR tırnaklar

quote [kwıut] v/t (aktarma
yolu ile) söylemek

R

rabbi ['räbay] REL haham

rabbit ['räbit] ZOO adatavşanı

rabble ['räbl] ayaktakımı

rabid ['räbid] kudurmuş; öfkeli; ~**es** ['reybîz] MED kuduz

race[1] [reys] ırk, soy; nesil

race[2] n. yarış; koşu; akıntı; v/i
yarışmak, koşmak

racial ['reysıl] ırksal

racing ['reysın] yarış; yarışla-
ra ait

rack [räk] n. parmaklık; raf;
yemlik; v/t yormak, işkence
etm.; ~ **one's brains** kafa
patlatmak

racket ['räkit] raket; velvele,
gürültü; haraççılık; ~**eer**

[~'tii] şantajcı, haraççı

racy ['reysi] canlı; açık saçık

radar ['reydı] radar (aygıtı)

radia|nce ['reydyıns] par-
laklık; ~**nt** parlak; ~**te**
['~ieyt] v/i ışın yaymak; v/t
yaymak; ~**tion** yayılma; ~**tor**
radyatör

radical ['rädikıl] kökten, radi-
kal; köksel

radio ['reydiu] n. radyo; telsiz telgraf; v/t yayımlamak;
~**activity** radyoetkinliği;
~**therapy** radyoterapi

radish ['rädiş] BOT turp

radius ['reydyıs] yarıçap; fig.
çevre

raffle ['räfle] piyango

raft [râft] sal; ~er kiriş

rag [räg] paçavra; değersiz şey

rage [reyc] *n.* öfke, hiddet; düşkünlük (for *-e*); *v/i* kudurmak, köpürmek

ragged ['rägid] yırtık; pürüzlü

raid [reyd] *n.* akın, baskın; *v/t* baskın yapmak *-e*

rail¹ [reyl] sövüp saymak

rail² *n.* tırabzan, parmaklık; TECH ray; *v/t* parmaklıkla çevirmek; run off the ~s raydan çıkmak; ~ing parmaklık; ~road *Am.*, ~way demiryolu

rain [reyn] *n.* yağmur; *v/i* yağmur yağmak; *v/t* yağmak; ~bow alkım, gökkuşağı; ~coat yağmurluk; ~y yağmurlu

raise [reyz] *v/t* kaldırmak, yükseltmek, artırmak; *parayı* toplamak; yetiştirmek, büyütmek; ileri sürmek

raisin [reyzn] kuru üzüm

rake [reyk] *n.* tarak, tırmık; sefih adam; *v/t* taramak, tırmıklamak

rally ['räli] *n.* toplama; ralli; *v/i* düzene girmek; *v/t* düzeltmek, canlandırmak

ram [räm] zoo koç; TECH şahmerdan; *v/t* vurmak; vurarak yerleştirmek

ramble ['râmbl] *n.* gezinme; *v/i* boş gezinmek

ramify ['râmifay] *v/i* dallanmak; *v/t* kollara ayırmak

ramp [râmp] rampa; ~art

['_ât] sur

ran [rän] *s.* run

ranch [rânç] *Am.* hayvan çiftliği; büyük çiftlik; ~er çiftlik sahibi

rancid ['ränsid] ekşimiş, kokmuş

ranco(u)r ['rängkı] kin, hınç

random ['rändım]: at ~ rasgele

rang [räng] *s.* ring

range [reync] *n.* sıra, dizi; erim, menzil; uzaklık; alan; mutfak ocağı; atış yeri; *Am.* otlak; *v/t* sıralamak, dizmek; dolaşmak; *v/i* uzanmak; yetişmek; ~r korucu

rank [rängk] *n.* rütbe, derece; sıra, dizi; *v/t* sıralamak, tasnif etm.; saymak; *v/i* katılmak (among, with *-e*); *adj.* uzun büyümüş; koşmuş

ransack ['ränsäk] *v/t* araştırmak; yağma etm.

ransom ['ränsım] *n.* fidye, kurtulmalık; *v/t* fidye ile kurtarmak

rap [räp] *n.* hafif vuruş; rap (*müzik*); *v/t* hafifçe vurmak *-e*

rapacious [rı'peyşıs] haris, açgözlü

rape [reyp] *n.* ırzına geçme; *v/t* -*in* ırzına geçmek

rapid ['räpid] çabuk, hızlı; *n. pl.* GEO ivinti yeri *sg.*; ~ity [rı'piditi] sürat, hız

rapt [räpt] dalgın, esri(k); ~ure ['_çı] esrilik, vecit

rar|e ['räı] seyrek, nadir; az bu-

lunur; ~ity nadirlik; kıymetli
şey

rascal ['râskıl] çapkın, serseri

rash¹ [râş] MED isilik

rash² sabırsız, düşüncesiz

rasp [râsp] n. raspa, kaba törpü; v/t törpülemek; v/i törpü
gibi ses çıkarmak

raspberry ['râzbırı] BOT ahududu

rat [rät] ZOO sıçan

rate [reyt] n. nispet, oran; fiyat; ücret; belediye vergisi;
sürat; sınıf, çeşit; v/t saymak;
değerlendirmek; v/i sayılmak; at any ~ her halde; ~
of exchange ECON kambiyo
sürümdeğeri; ~ of interest
faiz oranı

rather ['râdhı] oldukça; tersine; ~ than -den ziyade

ratif|ication [rätifi'keyşın]
tasdik; ~y ['-fay] v/t tasdik
etm., onaylamak

ration ['räşın] n. pay; tayın;
miktar; v/t karneye bağlamak; ~al ['-nl] akıl sahibi;
akıllı; ~alize ['-şnılayz] v/t
akla uydurmak; ölçülü şekle
sokmak

rattle ['rätl] n. takırtı, çıtırtı;
çıngırak; v/i takırdamak; v/t
takırdatmak; ~snake ZOO
çıngıraklı yılan

ravage ['rävic] v/t tahrip etm.

rave [reyv] v/i sayıklamak;
bayılmak (about, of -e)

raven ['reyvn] zoo kuzgun;
kuzguni; ~ous ['rävınıs] haris, doymak bilmez

ravine [rı'vîn] çukur

ravish ['räviş] v/t esritmek

raw [rô] ham, çiğ; fig. acemi,
tecrübesiz; ~ material hammadde

ray [rey] ışın, şua

rayon ['reyon] suni ipek

raz|e [reyz] v/t temelinden
yıkmak; ~or ustura; tıraş makinesi

re- ['rî-] geri(ye)

reach [riç] n. uzatma; alan;
menzil; erim; v/t varmak, yetişmek, ulaşmak -e; uzatmak
-i; out of ~ erişilmez; within
~ erişilebilir

react [ri'äkt] v/i tepkimek; etkilemek (to -i); ~ion tepki;
reaksiyon; POL gericilik;
~ionary [-şnırı] gerici; ~or
reaktör

read [rîd] v/t okumak; göstermek; ~able okunaklı; ~er
okuyucu

readi|ly ['redıli] seve seve;
~ness hazır olma

ready ['redi] hazır (to do sth.
-i yapmağa); istekli; get ~
hazırlanmak; ~ money hazır
para, nakit; ~-made hazır

real [riıl] gerçek; asıl; ~ estate
JUR gayri menkul mal, mülk;
~ism gerçekçilik, realizm;
~istic gerçeğe uygun; ~ity
[-'äliti] gerçeklik, realite; ~ization farketme; gerçekleştirme; ECON paraya çevirme;
~ize v/t anlamak, -in farkına
varmak; gerçekleştirme -i;
ECON paraya çevirmek -i

~ly adv. gerçekten
realm [relm] kırallık; alan
realty ['rıılti] mülk, gayri menkul mal
reap [rîp] v/t biçmek, toplamak; **~er** orakçı; biçerdöver
reappear ['rîı'pîı] v/i tekrar görünmek
rear[1] [rîı] v/t dikmek; yetiştirmek; v/i yükselmek; şahlanmak
rear[2] geri, arka; **~ view mirror** dikiz aynası; **~admiral** NAUT tuğamiral; **~lamp**, **~light** arka feneri
rearmament ['rî'âmımınt] silâhlandırma
reason ['rîzn] n. akıl, idrak; sebep; mantık; v/t düşünmek; uslamlamak, muhakeme etm.; v/i kandırmağa çalışmak (**with** -e); **by ~ of** sebebiyle; **~able** akla uygun, makul
reassure [rîı'şuı] v/t tekrar güven vermek -e
rebel ['rebl] adj.,n. isyan eden, ayaklanan; [ri'bel] v/i isyan etm., ayaklanmak; **~lion** [-'belyın] isyan, ayaklanma; **~lious** [-'belyıs] serkeş
rebound [ri'baund] v/i geri tepmek
rebuff [ri'baf] ters cevap
rebuild ['rî'bild] v/t tekrar inşa etm.
rebuke [ri'byûk] n. azar, paylama; v/t azarlamak
recall [ri'kôl] n. geri çağırma; v/t geri çağırmak; hatırla-

mak; feshetmek
recede [ri'sîd] v/i geri çekilmek
receipt [ri'sît] reçete; alındı; pl. gelir sg.
receive [ri'sîv] v/t almak; kabul etm.; **~r** alıcı; ahize
recent ['rîsnt] yeni (olmuş); **~ly** adv. son zamanlarda, geçenlerde
reception [ri'sepşın] alma; kabul; resepsiyon; **~ist** resepsiyon memuru
recess [ri'ses] ARCH girinti; Am. paydos, teneffüz; pl. iç taraf sg.; **~ion** ECON durgunluk
recipe ['resipi] yemek tarifi; reçete
recipient [ri'sipint] alıcı
reciprocal [ri'sipnkıl] karşılıklı
recit|al [ri'saytl] ezberden okuma; MUS resital; **~e** v/t ezberden okumak; anlatmak
reckless ['reklis] dikkatsiz, pervasız
reckon ['rekın] v/t hesap etm., saymak; tahmin etm.; v/i güvenmek (**on** -e); hesaba katmak (**with** -i); **~ing** ['-kniŋ] hesaplama
reclaim [ri'kleym] v/t geri istemek; elverişli hale koymak
recline [ri'klayn] v/i uzanmak; dayanmak
recogni|tion [rekıg'nişın] tanıma; **~ze** v/t tanımak
recoil [ri'koyl] v/i geri çekilmek; geri tepmek

recollect [rekɪ'lekt] *v/t* hatırlamak; **~ion** hatıra

recommend [rekɪ'mend] *v/t* tavsiye etm.; **~ation** tavsiye

recompense ['rekɪmpens] *v/t* mükâfatlandırmak; telâfi etm.

reconcil|e ['rekɪnsayl] *v/t* barıştırmak; mutabık kılmak; **~iation** [-sili'eyşın] barışma, uzlaşma

reconsider ['rîkın'sidı] *v/t* tekrar düşünmek

reconstruct ['rîkın'strakt] *v/t* yeniden inşa etm.; yinelemek; **~ion** tekrar inşa; yeniden kalkınma

record ['rekôd] kayıt; sicil; tutanak; rekor; plak; [ri'kôd] *v/t* kaydetmek, yazmak; plaka almak; **~er** kayıt aygıtı; **~player** pikap

recourse [ri'kôs]: **have ~ to** başvurmak *-e*

recover [ri'kavı] *v/t* tekrar ele geçirmek; geri almak; *v/i* iyileşmek; kendine gelmek; **~y** geri alma; iyileşme; kendine gelme

recreation [rekri'eyşın] dinlenme, eğlence

recruit [ri'kruut] *n.* MIL acemi asker; *v/t* toplamak

rect|angle ['rektängl] dik dörtgen; tatil; **~ify** ['-ifay] *v/t* düzeltmek

rector ['rektı] REL papaz; rektör; **~y** papaz evi

recur [ri'kə] *v/i* tekrar dönmek (**to** *-e*); tekrar olmak;

~rent [ri'karınt] tekrar olan

red [red] kırmızı, kızıl, al; ♀ **Crescent** Kızılay; ♀ **Cross** Kızılhaç; **~ tape** kırtasiyecilik; **~den** *v/t* kırmızılaştırmak; *v/i* kızıllaşmak, kızarmak

redeem [ri'dîm] *v/t* fidye vererek kurtarmak; yerine getirmek; REL halâs etm.; ♀**er** REL Kurtarıcı, Halâskâr

redemption [ri'dempşın] halâs; kurtar(ıl)ma

red|-handed JUR suçüstü; **~-hot kızgın; ~-letter day** yortu günü; önemli gün

redouble [ri'dabl] *v/t* tekrarlamak; *v/i* iki misli olm.

reduc|e [ri'dyûs] *v/t* azaltmak, indirmek, küçültmek; **~tion** [-'dakşın] azaltma, indirme

reed [rîd] kamış, saz

re-education ['rîedyu'keyşın] yeniden eğitme

reef [rîf] kayalık, resif

reek [rîk]: **~ of, with** *-in* kokusunu yaymak

reel [rîl] *n.* makara; *v/t* makaraya sarmak; *v/i* sendelemek; dönmek

re|-elect ['rîi'lekt] *v/t* POL tekrar seçmek; **~-enter** *v/t* tekrar girmek *-e*; **~-establish** *v/t* yeniden kurmak

refer [ri'fə] *v/t* göndermek (**to** *-e*); *v/i* göstermek (**to** *-i*); ilgili olm. (**ile**); **~ee** [refı'rî] hakem

reference ['refrıns] ilgi; başvuruş; referans; bonservis; with ~ to -e gelince

refill ['rifil] n. yedek takım; ['_'fil] v/t tekrar doldurmak

refine [ri'fayn] v/t tasfiye etm.; inceleştirmek; v/i incelmek, zarifleşmek; ~ment incelik, zariflik; ~ry rafineri; şeker fabrikası

reflect [ri'flekt] v/t yansıtmak; v/i düşünmek (on, upon -i); ~ion yansıma; düşünme; fikir

reflex ['rifleks] refleks, tepke, yansı; ~ive [ri'fleksiv] GR dönüşlü

reform [ri'fôm] n. reform, ıslah; v/t ıslah etm., düzeltmek; v/i iyileşmek, ℒation [refi'meyşın] REL Reformasyon, dinsel devrim; ~er reformcu

refract [ri'fräkt] v/t ışınları kırmak; ~ory inatçı

refrain¹ [ri'freyn] MUS nakarat

refrain² v/i çekinmek, sakınmak (from -den)

refresh [ri'freş] v/t canlandırmak; ~ oneself dinlenmek; ~ment canlan(dır)ma; canlandırıcı şey

refrigerator   [ri'fricireytı] buzdolabı, soğutucu

refuel ['ri'fyuıl] v/t yakıtı doldurmak

refuge ['refyûc] sığınak, barınak; ~e [_'cî] mülteci

refund [ri'fand] v/t parayı geri vermek

refus|al [ri'fyûzıl] ret, kabul etmeyiş; ~e v/t reddetmek; istememek; ['refyûs] n. süprüntü

refute [ri'fyût] v/t yalanlamak

regain [ri'geyn] v/t tekrar ele geçirmek

regal ['rîgıl] kırala ait

regard [ri'gaad] n. bakış, nazar; saygı; v/t dikkatle bakmak -e; dikkat etm. -e; saymak -i (as ...); as ~s hakkında, hususunda; kind ~s pl. saygılar; selâmlar; with ~ to -e gelince; ~ing hakkında, -e gelince; ~less of -e bakmayarak

regent ['rîcınt] saltanat vekili

regiment ['recimınt] MIL alay

region ['rîcın] bölge; ~al bölgesel

regist|er ['recistı] n. kütük; sicil; fihrist; v/t kaydetmek; taahhütlü olarak göndermek; v/i kaydolunmak; ~ered taahhütlü; kaydolunmuş; ~ration kayıt, tescil

regret [ri'gret] n. teessüf; pişmanlık; v/t teessüf etm., acınmak -e; pişman olm. -e; ~table acınacak

regular ['regyulı] kurallı, düzenli; MIL nizamî; ~ity [_'lärıti] düzen, intizam

regulat|e ['regyuleyt] v/t düzenlemek; ayar etm.; yoluna koymak; ~ion düzen, nizam; pl. kurallar; tüzük sg.

rehears|al [ri'hösıl] THEA prova; ~e v/t prova etm.; tekrarlamak

reign [reyn] *n.* hükümdarlık (devri); *v/i* hüküm sürmek

rein [reyn] dizgin

reindeer ['reyndiı] zoo ren

reinforce [riin'fôs] *v/t* kuvvetlendirmek; ~d concrete betonarme

reiterate [ri'itıreyt] *v/t* tekrarlamak

reject [ri'cekt] *v/t* reddetmek; atmak; ~ion ret, reddedilme

rejoice [ri'coys] *v/i* sevinmek (at *-e*); *v/t* sevindirmek; ~ing sevinç; şenlik

rejoin [ri'coyn] *v/t* tekrar kavuşmak *-e*; [ri'coyn] cevap vermek *-e*

relapse [ri'läps] *n.* eski hale dönme; *v/i* tekrar fenalaşmak; tekrar sapmak (into *-e*)

relate [ri'leyt] *v/t* anlatmak; *v/i* ilgili olm. (to ile); ~d to *-in* akrabası olan

relation [ri'leyşın] ilişki; ilgi; akraba; hikâye; *pl.* ilişkiler; in ~ to *-e* gelince; ~ship akrabalık; ilişki

relative [re'lıtiv] göreli, nispî; bağlı, ilişkin (to *-e*); akraba; ~ (pronoun) GR ilgi adılı; ~ly *adv.* nispeten

relax [ri'läks] *v/t* gevşetmek; *v/i* gevşemek; dinlenmek

relay ['ri'ley] *n.* değiştirme atı; EL düzenleyici; *v/t* nakletmek, yaymak; ~ race bayrak koşusu; ~ station EL ara istasyonu

release [ri'lîs] *n.* kurtarma,

salıverme; PHOT deklanşör; *v/t* kurtarmak; serbest bırakmak; harekete geçirmek

relent [ri'lent] *v/i* yumuşamak; ~less merhametsiz

relevan|ce ~cy ['relivns, -i] ilgi; uygunluk; ~t uygun, ilgili

relia|ble [ri'layıbl] güvenilir; ~nce güven, itimat

relic ['relik] kalıntı; REL mukaddes emanet

relie|f [ri'lîf] yardım, imdat; nöbet değiştirme; ferahlama; rölyef, kabartma; ~ve [-v] *v/t* hafifletmek; yardım etm. *-e*; kurtarmak *-i*

religi|on [ri'licin] din; ~ous dinî, dinsel; dindar; dikkatli

relinquish [ri'linkwiş] *v/t* terketmek; vazgeçmek *-den*

relish ['reliş] *n.* tat, lezzet; çeşni; *v/t* hoşlanmak *-den*

reluctant [ri'laktınt] isteksiz, gönülsüz

rely [ri'lay] güvenmek (on, upon *-e*)

remain [ri'meyn] *v/i* kalmak; durmak; *n. pl.* kalıntılar; cenaze *sg.*; ~der kalıntı; artan

remand [ri'mând] *v/t* geri göndermek; *n.* JUR tutukevine geri gönderme

remark [ri'mâk] *n.* söz; mülâhaza; *v/t* söylemek, demek; ~able dikkate değer

remedy ['remidi] *n.* çare; ilâç; *v/t* düzeltmek; *-in* çaresini bulmak

remem|ber [ri'membı] *v/t* hatırlamak; anmak; ~rance

hatırlama; andaç
remind [ri'maynd] v/t hatırlatmak -e (of -i); **~er** hatırlatma

reminiscent [remi'nisnt] hatırlayan, hatırlatan (of -i)
remit [ri'mit] v/t affetmek, bağışlamak; havale etm.; **~tance** para gönderme

remnant ['remnınt] artık
remodel ['ri'modl] v/t -in şeklini değiştirmek

remonstrate ['remınstreyt] v/i protesto etm. (against -i); v/t itiraz etm. (that -e)

remorse [ri'môs] pişmanlık, nedamet; **~less** merhametsiz

remote [ri'muut] uzak; **~ control** uzaktan kumanda

remov|al [ri'muuvıl] kaldır(ıl)ma; yol verme; taşınma; **~e** v/t kaldırmak; uzaklaştırmak; v/i taşınmak; **~er** leke v.s. gideric; nakliyeci

Renaissance [rı'neysıns] Rönesans

rend [rend] v/t yırtmak; v/i yırtılmak

render ['rendı] v/t kılmak, yapmak; geri vermek; teslim etm.; tercüme etm., çevirmek (into -e)

renew [ri'nyû] v/t yenile(ştir)mek; **~al** yenile(n)me

renounce [ri'nauns] v/t terketmek; vazgeçmek -den; reddetmek -i

renovate ['renıuveyt] v/t ye-

nileştirmek

renown [ri'naun] şöhret, ün; **~ed** ünlü

rent¹ [rent] s. rend; yırtık, yarık

rent² n. kira; v/t kiralamak

reorganize ['ri'ôgınayz] v/t düzenlemek

repair [ri'päı] n. tamir, onarım; v/t tamir etm., onarmak; **in good ~** iyi halde; **~shop** tamir evi

reparation [repı'reyşın] tazminat pl.

repartee [repâ'tî] hazırcevap sözlerle konuşma

repatriation ['rîpätri'eyşın] kendi vatanına dönme

repay [rî'pey] v/t ödemek; -in karşılığını vermek

repeat [ri'pît] v/t tekrarlamak

repel [ri'pel] v/t püskürtmek, defetmek; **~lent** uzaklaştırıcı

repent [ri'pent] v/t pişman olm. -e. **~ance** pişmanlık

repetition [repi'tişın] tekrarla(n)ma

replace [ri'pleys] v/t tekrar yerine koymak; ödemek; -in yerini almak; **~ment** yerine geçen şey

replenish [ri'pleniş] v/t tekrar doldurmak

reply [ri'play] n. cevap, karşılık; v/i cevap vermek (to -e)

report [ri'pôt] n. rapor, not karnesi; söylenti; patlama sesi; v/t anlatmak; bildirmek; söylemek; **~er** muhabir, muhbir

repose [ri'pıuz] *n.* rahat, istirahat; *v/t* yatırmak; *v/i* yatmak; dayanmak (on -*e*)

represent [repri'zent] *v/t* göstermek; temsil etm.; ~ation temsil; göster(il)me; itiraz; ~ative temsil eden, nümune olan; POL milletvekili; **House of** ℒatives *Am.* Temsilciler Meclisi

repress [ri'pres] *v/t* bastırmak

reprieve [ri'prîv] geçici olarak erteleme

reprimand ['reprimând] *n.* azar, paylama; *v/t* azarlamak

reprint ['rî'print] yeni baskı

reproach [ri'prıuç] *n.* ayıp (-lama); *v/t* azarlamak; ~ful sitem dolu

reproduc|e [rîpri'dyûs] *v/t* kopya etm.; tekrar meydana getirmek; *v/i* çoğalmak, üremek; ~tion [-'dakşın] üreme; kopya

reproof [ri'pruuf] azar, paylama

reprove [ri'pruuv] *v/t* ayıplamak

reptile ['reptayl] sürüngen; yılan

republic [ri'pablik] cumhuriyet; ~an cumhuriyete ait; cumhuriyetçi

repudiate [ri'pyûdieyt] *v/t* tanımamak

repugnan|ce [ri'pagnıns] nefret, tiksinme; ~t iğrenç, çirkin

repuls|e [ri'pals] *n.* kovma; ret; *v/t* püskürtmek, kovmak; ~ive iğrenç

reput|able ['repyutıbl] saygıdeğer; ~ation ün, şöhret; ~e [ri'pyût] ad, şöhret

request [ri'kwest] *n.* dilek; rica; *v/t* rica etm., dilemek (**from** -*den*); **by** ~, **on** ~ istenildiği zaman; ~ **stop** ihtiyarî durak

require [ri'kwayı] *v/t* istemek; muhtaç olm. -*e*; ~ment gerek, ihtiyaç

requisite ['rekwizit] gerekli, elzem (şey)

requite [ri'kwayt] *v/t* mükafatlandırmak; -*in* karşılığını vermek

rescue ['reskyû] *n.* kurtuluş, kurtarış; *v/t* kurtarmak

research [ri'sıç] araştırma; ~er araştırıcı

resembl|ance [ri'zemblıns] benzeyiş; ~e *v/t* andırmak; benzemek -*e*

resent [ri'zent] *v/t* gücenmek -*e*; ~ful gücenik; ~ment gücenme

reserv|ation [rezı'veyşın] yer ayırtma, rezervasyon; JUR ihtiraz kaydı; POL yerlilere ayrılmış bölge; ~e [ri'zıv] *n.* yedek olarak saklanan şey; ağız sıkılığı; *v/t* saklamak; ayırtmak; *hakkını* muhafaza etm.; ~ed ağzı sıkı; mahfuz; ~oir [-'vwâ] su haznesi; havza

reside [ri'zayd] *v/i* oturmak,

ikamet etm.; ~nce ['rezi-
dıns] ikamet(gâh); ~nce
permit ikamet tezkeresi;
~nt oturan, sakin

residue ['rezidyû] artık

resign [ri'zayn] v/t bırakmak;
vazgeçmek -den; ~ oneself
to baş eğmek -e; ~ation [re-
zig'neyşın] istifa, çekilme;
uysallık; ~ed baş eğmiş

resin ['rezin] sakız, reçine

resist [ri'zist] v/t karşı durmak -e; dayanmak -e; ~ance
direniş, PHYS direniş, rezis-
tans; ~ant direnen (to -e)

resolut|e ['rezuluut] kararlı;
cesur; ~ion kararlılık; POL
önerge

resolve [ri'zolv] v/t çözmek;
kararlaştırmak (to inf. -i);
v/i tasarlamak, kararlaştırmak (on, upon -i)

resonance ['reznıns] yankı-
lama

resort [ri'zôt] n. dinlenme yeri; barınak; v/i sık sık gitmek
(to -e); başvurmak (-e)

resound [ri'zaund] v/i çınlamak

resource [ri'sôs] kaynak, çare; pl. imkânlar, olanaklar;
~ful becerikli

respect [ris'pekt] n. münasebet; saygı, itibar; v/t saygı
göstermek -e; riayet etm.
-e; in ~ to, with ~ to -e gelince; ~able namuslu; epeyce;
~ful saygılı; ~ing bakımın-
dan, -e gelince; ~ive ayrı ayrı,
kendisinin olan; ~ively sırası

ile

respiration [respı'reyşın] nefes (alma); soluk

respite ['respayt] mühlet; geçici erteleme

resplendent [ris'plendınt]
parlak, göz alıcı

respond [ris'pond] v/i cevap
vermek (to -e); ~ent JUR sa-
vunan

respons|e [ris'pons] cevap;
~ibility sorumluluk; ~ible
sorumlu, mesul (for -den,
to -e)

rest¹ [rest] v/i dinlenmek;
yatmak; oturmak; dayan-
mak (on, upon -e); v/t dayamak, koymak (on -e); n. rahat; istirahat; dayanak

rest² geri kalan, artan

restaurant [ri'restirörğ] restoran, lokanta

rest|ful rahat (verici); ~house
dinlenme evi; ~less yerinde
durmaz; uykusuz

restor|ation [restı'reyşın] ye-
nileme; eski haline getirme;
restore etme; ~e [ris'tô] v/t
geri vermek; eski haline koymak; restore etm.; ~e to
health iyileştirmek

restrain [ris'treyn] v/t geri
tutmak; sınırlamak; ~t
sınırlılık; çekinme

restrict [ris'trikt] v/t kısıtlamak, sınırlamak; ~ion
sınırlama, kısıtlama

result [ri'zalt] n. sonuç; son;
v/i meydana gelmek (from
-den); sonuçlamak (in -i)

resum|e [ri'zyûm] *v/t* yeniden başlamak -*e*; geri almak -*i*; **~ption** ['-'zampşın] yeniden başlama

resurrection [rezi'rekşın] yeniden diril(t)me

retail ['rîteyl] *n.* ECON perakende satış; [-'teyl] *v/t* perakende olarak satmak; **~er** [-'t-] perakendeci

retain [ri'teyn] *v/t* alıkoymak; tutmak

retaliat|e [ri'tälieyt] *v/t* dengiyle karşılamak; *v/i* intikam almak (**upon** -*den*); **~ion** misilleme

retard [ri'tâd] *v/t* geciktirmek

retell ['rî'tel] *v/t* tekrar anlatmak

retention [ri'tenşın] alıkoyma

retinue ['retinyû] maiyet, heyet

retire [ri'tayı] *v/i* çekilmek; emekliye ayrılmak; *v/t* geri çekmek; **~d** emekli; münzevi; **~ment** emeklilik; inziva

retort [ri'tôt] sert cevap vermek

retrace [ri'treys] *v/t* -*in izini* takip ederek kaynağına gitmek

retract [ri'träkt] *v/t* geri çekmek; geri almak

retreat [ri'trît] *v/i* geri, çekilmek; *n.* geri çek(il)me

retribution [retri'byûşın] karşılıkta bulunma; ceza

retrieve [ri'trîv] *v/t* tekrar ele geçirmek; bulup getirmek

retrospect ['retriuspekt] geç-

mişe bakış; **~ive** geçmişi hatırlayan; önceyi kapsayan

return [ri'tın] *n.* geri dönüş; tekrar olma; resmî rapor; ECON kazanç, kâr; *v/i* geri dönmek; cevap vermek; *v/t* geri vermek; geri göndermek; **by ~** hemen; **in ~** karşılık olarak; **~ match** revanş maçı; **~ ticket** gidiş dönüş bileti; *Am.* dönüş bileti

reunion ['rî'yûnyın] yine birleşme

revaluation [rîvälyu'eyşın] yeniden değerlendirme

reveal [ri'vîl] *v/t* açığa vurmak; göstermek

revel ['revl] *v/i* eğlenmek; mest olm. (**in** -*de*); *n.* şenlik, eğlenti

revelation [revi'leyşın] açığa vurma; REL ilham, vahiy

revenge [ri'venc] *n.* öç, intikam; revanş; intikam almak (**on** -*den*); **~ful** kinci

revenue ['revinyû] gelir; **~ office** maliye tahsil şubesi

revere [ri'vii] *v/t* saymak; saygı göstermek -*e*; **~nce** ['revirıns] *n.* saygı, hürmet; *v/t* yüceltmek; saygı göstermek -*e*; **~nd** ['revirınd] muhterem (*papazın lakabı*)

reverse [ri'vœs] *n.* ters; arka taraf; aksilik; *adj.* ters; aksi; *v/t* tersine çevirmek; JUR iptal etm.; **~ gear** geri vites; **~ side** ters taraf

review [ri'vyû] *n.* resmî teftiş; geçit töreni; eleştiri; dergi;

v/t yeniden incelemek; teftiş etm.; eleştirmek; tekrar gözden geçirmek; **~er** eleştirici

revis|e [ri'vayz] *v/t* tekrar gözden geçirip düzeltmek; değiştirmek; **~ion** [‿ijın] düzeltme, tashih

reviv|al [ri'vayvıl] yeniden canlanma; **~e** *v/t* canlandırmak; *v/i* yeniden canlanmak

revocation [revı'keyşın] geri alınma, iptal

revoke [ri'vıuk] *v/t* geri almak, iptal etm.

revolt [ri'vıult] *v/i* ayaklanmak; *fig.* tiksinmek (**against**, *at -den*); *n.* isyan, ayaklanma

revolution [revı'luuşın] dönme, devir; POL devrim, inkılâp; ihtilâl; **~ary** devrimci; ihtilâlci; **~ize** *v/t* tamamen değiştirmek

revolve [ri'volv] *v/i* dönmek; **~r** revolver, altıpatlar

reward [ri'wôd] *n.* mükâfat, ödül; *v/t* mükâfatlandırmak

rheumati|c [ruu'mätik] romatizmalı; **~sm** ['‿mıtizm] romatizma

rhubarb ['ruubâb] BOT ravent

rhyme [raym] *n.* kafiye; şiir; *v/t* kafiyeli olarak yazmak

rhythm ['ridhım] ritim; vezin; **~ic(al)** ahenkli, ritmik

rib [rib] ANAT kaburga kemiği

ribbon ['ribın] kurdele; şerit

rice [rays] BOT pirinç

rich [riç] zengin; verimli, bol; dolgun (*ses*); **the ~** *pl.* zengin-

ler; **~es** ['‿iz] *pl.* zenginlik, servet *sg.*; **~ness** zenginlik

rickets ['rikits] *pl.* MED raşitizm *sg.*

rid [rid] *v/t* kurtarmak; **get ~** başından atmak (**of** *-i*)

ridden ['ridn] *s.* ride

riddle[1] ['ridl] bilmece, bulmaca

riddle[2] kalbur

ride [rayd] *n.* binme; gezinti; *v/t* binmek *-e*; sürmek *-i*; **~ out** *fig.* atlatmak; **~r** atlı, binici

ridge [ric] sırt; çatı sırtı

ridicul|e ['ridikyûl] *n.* alay; *v/t* alay etm. (*so.* ile); **~ous** ['‿dikyulıs] gülünç

rifle ['rayfl] tüfek

rift [rift] yarık, açıklık

right [rayt] *n.* sağ (taraf); hak; yetki; *adj.* doğru; sahih; haklı; insaflı; *adv.* hemen; doğruca; **all ~** iyi; *intj.* peki; **be ~** haklı olm.; **put ~**, **set ~** *v/t* düzeltmek; **turn ~** *v/i* sağa dönmek; **~ angle** dik açı; **~ away** hemen; **~ of way** önden geçme hakkı; **~eous** dürüst; **~ful** haklı

rig|id ['ricid] eğilmez, sert; **~orous** ['‿ırıs] sert, şiddetli; **~o(u)r** sertlik, şiddet

rim [rim] kenar; jant

rind [raynd] kabuk

ring[1] [riŋ] yüzük, halka; çember; halka

ring[2] *n.* zil sesi, çan sesi; çınlama; *v/i* çalmak, çınlamak; *v/t* çalmak; **~ up** telefon etm. *-e*;

~leader elebaşı

rink [riŋk] patinaj alanı

rinse [rins] v/t çalka(la)mak

riot ['rayıt] n. kargaşalık, ayaklanma; v/i kargaşalık yapmak; ~ous gürültülü

rip [rip] n. yarık; sökük dikiş; v/t sökmek; yarmak

ripe [rayp] olgun(laşmış); yetişmiş; ~n v/i olgunlaşmak, v/t olgunlaştırmak

ripple ['ripl] n. ufacık dalga; v/i hafifçe dalgalanmak

rise [rayz] n. yükseliş, artış; çıkış; v/i kalkmak, yükselmek, artmak; kabarmak; ayaklanmak; ~n ['rizn] s. rise

rising ['rayziŋ] yükselen; yükseliş; ayaklanma

risk [risk] n. tehlike, riziko; v/t tehlikeye koymak, göze almak; ~y tehlikeli

rite [rayt] REL ayin, tören

rival ['rayvıl] n. rakip; v/t rekabet etm., çekişmek (so. ile); ~ry rekabet

river ['rivı] nehir, ırmak

rivet ['rivit] n. perçin; v/t perçinlemek

rivulet ['rivyulit] dere, çay

road [rud] yol, şose; ~ sign trafik işareti

roam [rum] dolaşmak, gezinmek

roar [rô] n. gürleme, gümbürtü; v/i gürlemek, gümbürdemek

roast [rust] adj. kızarmış; v/t kızartmak; kavurmak; ~

beef rozbif

rob [rob] v/t soymak; çalmak; ~ber hırsız, haydut; ~bery hırsızlık; soyma

robe [rub] rop; kaftan, üstlük giysi

robin (redbreast) ['robin] zoo kızıl gerdan (kuşu)

robot ['rubot] makine adam, robot

robust [rıu'bast] dinç, kuvvetli

rock¹ [rok] kaya

rock² v/i sallanmak, sarsılmak; v/t sallamak

rocket ['rokit] roket; havaî fişek

rocking-chair salıncaklı koltuk

rocky ['roki] kayalık

rod [rod] çubuk, değnek

rode [rud] s. ride

rodent ['rıudınt] zoo kemirgen

roe¹ [rıu] balık yumurtası

roe² (deer) karaca

rogue [rıug] çapkın; dolandırıcı; ~ish çapkın; kurnaz

rôle, role [rıul] rol

roll [rıul] n. makara, silindir; tomar; sicil, kayıt; küçük ekmek; v/t yuvarlamak, tekerlemek; sarmak; v/i yuvarlanmak; dalgalanmak; ~ film makaralı film; ~ up v/t sarmak, sıvamak; ~call yoklama; ~er silindir; ~er-skate tekerlekli paten; ~ing-mill haddehane

Roman ['rumın] Romalı
roman|ce [rıu'mäns] macera; aşk macerası; macera romanı; **~tic** romantik
Rome [rıum] Roma
romp [romp] v/i gürültü ile oynamak; **~er(s** pl.) çocuk tulumu
roof [ruuf] n. dam, çatı; v/t çatı ile örtmek
room [ruum] yer; oda; **make ~** yer açmak (for -e); **~y** geniş
rooster ['ruustı] horoz
root [ruut] n. kök; v/t kökleştirmek; v/i kökleşmek; **~ out** v/t kökünden sökmek
rope [rıup] n. halat; ip; v/t halatla bağlamak; **~off** ip çevirerek sınırlamak
ros|ary ['ruzıri] tesbih; **~e¹** [rıuz] gül
rose² s. **rise**
rosy ['ruzi] gül gibi; fig. ümit verici
rot [rot] n. çürüme; v/i çürümek; v/t çürütmek
rota|ry ['rutırı] dönen, dönel; **~te** [-'teyt] v/i dönmek; v/t döndürmek; **~tion** dönme
rotor ['rutı] rotor; helikopter pervanesi
rotten ['rotn] çürük, bozuk
rotund [rıu'tand] yuvarlak; dolgun (ses)
rough [raf] pürüzlü; kaba; sert; **~ copy** taslak, müsvedde; **~ness** kabalık, sertlik
round [raund] adj. yuvarlak, toparlak; prp. -in etrafın(d)a; n. parti; devriye; dö-

nem; ravnt; v/t yuvarlak hale getirmek; dönmek -den; v/i yuvarlaklaşmak; **~ trip** gidiş dönüs, tur; **~ up** v/t bir araya toplamak; **~about** dolambaçlı; dolaşık; **~table conference** yuvarlak masa konferansı
rouse [rauz] v/t uyandırmak, canlandırmak; v/i uyanmak
rout|e [ruut] yol; rota; **~ine** [.'tîn] usul, iş programı
rove [rıuv] dolaşmak, gezinmek
row¹ [rau] kavga, patırtı
row² [rıu] sıra, dizi
row³ [rıu] v/t kürek çekmek; v/t kürek çekerek götürmek
rowdy ['raudi] külhanbeyi
rowing-boat ['ruuıŋ -] kayık, sandal
royal ['royıl] kırala ait; şahane; **~ty** hükümdarlık, kırallık; ECON kâr hissesi
rub [rab] v/t sürtmek, ovmak; n. ovalama, sürt(ün)me; **~ in** ovarak yedirmek; **~ out** silmek
rubber ['rabı] lastik, kauçuk; silgi
rubbish ['rabiş] süprüntü, çöp; saçma
rubble ['rabl] moloz
ruby ['ruubi] yakut, lâl
rucksack ['ruksäk] sırt çantası
rudder ['radı] dümen
ruddy ['radi] kırmızı yanaklı
rude [ruud] kaba; terbiyesiz; **~ness** kabalık

ruffian   378

ruffian ['rafyın] kavgacı, gaddar

ruffle ['rafl] v/t buruşturmak; rahatsız etm.; n. kırma, farbala

rug [rag] halı, kilim; ~ged ['._id] engebeli; sert

ruin [ruin] n. harabe; yıkım; perişanlık; v/t yıkmak, tahrip etm.; perişan etm.; ~ous yıkıcı; yıkık

rul|e [ruul] n. kural; usul; yönetim; cetvel; v/t idare etm., yönetmek; v/i saltanat sürmek; ~ out v/t çıkarmak, silmek; ~er cetvel; hükümdar; ~ing yönetim; JUR yargı; çizme, çizgi

rum [ram] rom

Rumania [ru'meynyı] Romanya; ~n Romanyalı; Romen(ce)

rumble ['rambl] n. gümbürtü; v/i gümbürdemek

ruminant ['ruuminınt] zoo gevişgetiren

rummage ['ramic] v/t araştırmak

rumo(u)r ['ruumı] şayia, söylenti

run [ran] v/i koşmak; akmak; gitmek; TECH işlemek, çalışmak; adaylığınıkoymak (for için); v/t işletmek; yönetmek; sürmek; n. koşu; rağbet; sıra; süre **in the long ~** eninde sonunda; ~ **across** rast gelmek -e; ~ **down** v/i

bitmek; v/t kötülemek; ~ **into** rast gelmek, çarpmak -e; ~ **out** bitmek, tükenmek; ~ **short of** sth. -si azalmak, tükenmek; ~ **up to** erişmek -e

rung[^1] [ran] s. ring

rung[^2] portatif merdiven basamağı

runner ['ranı] koşucu; kızak ayağı; ~**up** ikinciliği kazanan

running koşu; sürekli; akan; ~**board** marşpiye

runway ['ranwey] pist

rupture ['rapçı] kır(ıl)ma; kesilme

rural ['ruırıl] köye ait; tarımsal

rush [raş] n. namle, saldırış; sıkışıklık; v/i koşmak; saldırmak (**at** -e); v/t acele ettirmek; püskürtmek

Russia ['raşı] Rusya; ~**n** Rus (-yalı); Rusça

rust [rast] n. pas; v/i paslanmak

rustic ['rastik] köye ait; kaba; köylü

rustle ['rasl] n. hışırtı; v/i hışırdamak; v/t hışırdatmak

rusty ['rasti] paslı

rut[^1] [rat] n. kösnüme

rut[^2] tekerlek izi

ruthless ['ruuthlis] merhametsiz

rutty ['rati] tekerlek izleriyle dolu

rye [ray] BOT çavdar

S

sable ['seybl] zoo samur

sabotage ['sɑbɪtâj] *n.* sabo-taj; *v/t* baltalamak

sabre ['seybɪ] kılıç

sack [säk] *n.* çuval, torba; yağma; *v/t* yağma etm.; işin-den çıkarmak

sacr|ament ['säkrɪmɪnt] REL Hıristiyanlıkta kutsal ayin; **~ed** ['seykrid] kutsî, kutsal; **~ifice** ['säkrifays] *n.* kurban; fedakârlık; *v/t* kurban etm.; feda etm.

sad [säd] kederli, üzgün; acı-nacak; **~den** *v/i* acınmak; *v/t* kederlendirmek

saddle ['sädl] *n.* eyer; sırt; *v/t* eyerlemek; **~r** saraç

sadness ['sädnis] keder, üz-günlük

safe [seyf] emin (**from** -den); sağlam; kasa; **~guard** *n.* ko-ruma; *v/t* korumak

safety ['seyfti] güvenlik; em-niyet; **~belt** emniyet kemeri; **~pin** çengelli iğne

saffron ['säfrɪn] BOT safran

sag [säg] *v/i* sarkmak; çök-mek

sagacity [sɪ'gäsiti] akıllılık

said [sed] *s.* say

sail [seyl] *n.* yelken; NAUT yola çıkmak; **~ing-ship** yelkenli; **~or** gemici, denizci

saint [seynt] REL aziz, evliya

sake [seyk]: **for the ~ of** *-in*

hatırı için

salad ['sälɪd] salata

salary ['säliri] maaş, aylık

sale [seyl] satış; **for ~** satılık; **~sman** satıcı; **~swoman** satıcı kadın

salient ['seylyɪnt] göze çar-pan

saliva [sɪ'layvɪ] salya, tükü-rük

sallow ['sälu] soluk yüzlü

sally ['säli] *v/i* dışarı fırlamak

salmon ['sämɪn] som balığı

saloon [sɪ'luun] salon; bar; *Am.* meyhane

salt [sôlt] *n.* tuz; *v/t* tuzlamak; **~cellar** tuzluk; **~y** tuzlu

salut|ation [sälyu'teyşɪn] se-lâm (verme); **~e** [sɪ'luut] *v/t* selâmlamak; *n.* selâm

salvage ['sälvic] tahlisiye (ücreti)

salvation [säl'veyşɪn] kurtu-luş, kurtarma; ♀ **Army** selâ-met ordusu

salve [sâv] merhem

same [seym] aynı, tıpkı; **all the ~** bununla beraber

sample ['sâmpl] örnek, nü-mune; mostra

sanatorium [sänɪ'tôrɪm] sa-natoryum

sanct|ify ['säŋktifay] *v/t* kut-sallaştırmak; **~ion** *n.* tasdik, tasvip; *v/t* uygun bulmak; **~u-ary** ['-tyuɪri] tapınak;

sand 380

sığınak

sand [sänd] kum

sandal ['sändl] çarık, sandal

sandwich ['sänwic] sandviç; ~man sırtında ve göğsünde reklam yaftaları dolaştıran adam

sandy ['sändi] kumlu; kumsal

sane [seyn] aklı başında, akıllı; makul

sang [säŋ] s. **sing**

sanit|ary ['sänitəri] sıhhî; ~tion hıfzıssıhha; sağlık işleri pl.; sıhhî tertibat; ~y akıl sıhhati

sank [säŋk] s. **sink**

Santa Claus [säntı'klôz] Noel baba

sap [säp] BOT özsu, usare

sapling ['säpliŋ] fidan

sarcasm ['sâkäzım] dokunaklı alay

sardine [sâ'din] sardalya

sash [säş] kuşak; ~ **window** sürme pencere

Satan ['seytın] REL Iblis, şeytan

satchel [säçl] okul çantası

satellite ['sätılayt] ASTR, POL peyk; ~ **dish** çanak anten

satin ['sätin] saten, atlas

satir|e ['sätayı] hiciv, yergi; ~ical [sı'tirikıl] hicivli

satis|faction [sätis'fäkşın] hoşnutluk; tarziye; tazmin; ~factory tatmin edici; memnunluk verici; ~fy ['~fay] v/t memnun etm.; tatmin etm.; tazmin etm.

Saturday ['sätıdi] cumartesi

sauce [sôs] salça; ~r fincan tabağı; ~pan uzun saplı tencere

saucy ['sôsi] arsız, saygısız

saunter ['sôntı] gezinmek

sausage ['sosic] sucuk, salam; sosis

savage ['sävic] vahşî, yabanî; yırtıcı

sav|e [seyv] v/t kurtarmak; biriktirmek, tasarruf etm.; prp. -den başka; ~ings pl. biriktirilen paralar

savio(u)r ['seyvyı] kurtarıcı, halâskâr; ♀ Hazreti Isa

savo(u)r ['seyvı] n. tat, lezzet, çeşni; v/i andırmak (of -i); ~y lezzetli

saw[1] [sô] s. **see**

saw[2] n. testere, bıçkı; v/t testere ile kesmek; ~dust bıçkı tozu; ~mill kereste fabrikası; ~n s. **saw**[2]

Saxon ['säksn] Sakson(yalı)

say [sey] v/t söylemek, demek; beyan etm.; **he is said to** inf. onun -diği söyleniyor; **that is to** ~ yani; **have a** ~ **in** -de söz sahibi olm.; ~ing söz; atasözü; **it goes without** ~ing kendisinden anlaşılır

scab [skäb] yara kabuğu

scaffold ['skäfıld] yapı iskelesi

scald [skôld] v/t kaynar su ile haşlamak; kaynatmak

scale[1] [skeyl] n. balık pulu; v/t pullarını çıkarmak

scale[2] terazi gözü; ölçek; ıskala; ölçü; derece

scalp [skälp] *n.* kafatasını kaplayan deri; *v/t -in* başının derisini yüzmek

scan [skän] *v/t* incelemek; gözden geçirmek; taramak; *n.* tarama

scandal [skändl] rezalet; dedikodu; **~ous** ['-dılıs] rezil, iftiralı

Scandinavia [skändi'neyvı] Skandinavya; **~n** Skandinav

scanner tarayıcı

scant(y) ['skänt(i)] az, kıt, dar

scapegoat ['skeypgıut] başkalarının suçlarını yüklenen kimse

scar [skaa] *n.* yara izi; *v/t -in* üstünde yara izi bırakmak

scarce [skäıs] az bulunur, nadir, seyrek; kıt; **~ely** *adv.* ancak, hemen hemen hiç; **~ity** azlık kıtlık

scare [skäı] *v/t* korkutmak, ürkütmek; **be ~d** korkmak, ürkmek (**of** *-den*); **~crow** bostan korkuluğu

scarf [skaaf] boyun atkısı; eşarp

scarlet ['skaalit] al, kırmızı; **~ fever** MED kızıl hastalığı

scarred [skaad] yara izi olan

scathing ['skeydhiŋ] sert; yakıcı

scatter ['skätı] *v/t* saçmak, dağıtmak; *v/i* dağılmak, yayılmak

scavenger ['skävincı] çöpçü

scene [sîn] sahne; dekor; manzara; **~ry** manzara, dekor

scent [sent] *n.* güzel koku; iz; *v/t -in* kokusunu almak; koku ile doldurmak *-i*

sceptic ['skeptik] *n.*, **~al** *adj.* şüpheci, septik

schedule ['şedyûl] *n.* liste, program; *Am.* ['skecûl] tarife; *v/t -in* listesini yapmak; tarifeye geçirmek *-i*

scheme [skîm] *n.* plan, proje, tasarı; entrika; *v/t* tasarlamak

scholar ['skolı] âlim, bilgin; **~ship** burs

school [skuul] *n.* okul; mezhep; balık sürüsü; *v/t* alıştırmak; **~fellow** okul arkadaşı; **~ing** terbiye; **~master** öğretmen; **~mate** s. **~fellow**; **~mistress** kadın öğretmen

scien|ce ['sayıns] ilim, bilgi, bilim; fen; **~tific** [-'tifik] ilmî; bilimsel, fennî; **~tist** ilim adamı; fen adamı

scissors ['sizız] *pl.* makas *sg.*

scoff [skof] alay etm. (**at** ile)

scold [skuld] *v/t* azarlamak paylamak

scoop [skuup] *n.* kepçe; *vt* kepçe ile çıkarmak

scooter ['skuutı] trotinet; küçük motosiklet

scope [skup] saha, alan; faaliyet alanı

scorch [skôç] *v/t* kavurmak, yakmak

score [skô] *n.* sıyrık, kertik; hesap; puvan sayısı; yirmi; MUS partisyon; *v/t* çent mek; hesap etm.; *puvanları* saymak; *puvan* kazanmak

scorn [skôn] *n.* küçümseme; tahkir; *v/t* küçümsemek; **~ful** tahkir edici

scorpion ['skôpyın] zoo ak rep

Scot [skot] Iskoçyalı

Scotch [skoç] Iskoçya ile ilgili; **~man** Iskoçyalı

Scotland ['skotlınd] Iskoç ya; **~ Yard** Londra Emniyet Müdürlüğü

Scots|man Iskoçyalı; **~woman** Iskoçyalı kadın

scoundrel ['skaundrıl] kötu adam, herif

scour ['skauı] *v/t* ovalayarak temizlemek

scout [skaut] *n.* izci; *v/t* keşfetmek, taramak

scowl [skaul] *v/i* kaşlarını çatıp bakmak; *n.* tehditkâ bakış

scrabble ['skräbl] *v/t* sıyırmak; acele ile yazmak

scramble ['skrämbl] *v/t* tırmanmak -e; karıştırmak -i; **~d eggs** *pl.* karıştırılıp yağda pişirilmiş yumurtalar

scrap [skräp] parça; döküntü, kırıntı

scrape [skreyp] *n.* kazıma, sıyırma; kazımak, sıyırmak; **~ away**, **~ off** kazıyarak silmek

scrap-iron hurda demir

scratch [skräç] *n.* çizik, sıyrık; *v/t* kaşımak, tırnaklamak

scrawl [skrôl] *v/t* acele ile

yazmak; *n.* dikkatsiz yazı

scream [skrîm] *n.* feryat, çığlık; *v/i* feryat etm.

screech [skriç] *s.* **scream**

screen [skrîn] *n.* paravana, bölme; perde; *v/t* gizlemek, korumak; elemek, kalburdan geçirmek

screw [skruu] *n.* vida; pervane; *v/t* vidalamak; **~driver** tornavida

scribble ['skribl] *n.* dikkatsiz yazı; *v/t* dikkatsiz yazmak

script [skript] yazı; THEA senaryo; **~ure** ['-pçı] REL Kutsal Kitap

scroll [skruul] tomar

scrub [skrab] *n.* çalılık, fundalık; *v/t* fırçalayarak yıkamak

scruple ['skruupl] vicdan; tereddüt; endişe; **~ulous** ['-pyulıs] dikkatli, titiz

scrutin|ize ['skruutinayz] *v/t* incelemek; **~y** tetkik, inceleme

scuffle ['skafl] *v/i* çekişmek, dövüşmek

sculpt|or ['skalptı] heykeltıraş; **~ure** ['-çı] *n.* heykel tıraşlık; heykel; *v/t* oymak, hakketmek

scum [skam] pis köpük; *fig.* ayaktakımı

scurf [skâf] kepek, konak

scurvy [s'kxvi] MED iskorbüt

scuttle ['skatl] kömür kovası

scythe [saydh] tırpan

sea [sî] deniz; yüksek dalga; **at ~** denizde, gemide; **~far-**

ing denizcilikle uğraşan; **~gull** zoo martı
seal¹ [sîl] zoo fok
seal² *n.* mühür; *v/t* mühürlemek; kapatmak, tıkamak
seam [sîm] dikiş (yeri)
seaman ['sîmın] denizci
seamstress ['semstris] dikişçi kadın
sea|plane deniz uçağı; **~port** liman
search [sɜç] *n.* arama, araştırma; *v/t* aramak, araştırmak, yoklamak; **~light** ışıldak, projektör
sea|shore sahil; **~sick** deniz tutmuş; **~side** sahil
season ['sîzn] *n.* mevsim; zaman; *v/t* çeşnilendirmek; kurutmak; alıştırmak; *v/i* kurumak; **in ~** zamanında; kullanılabilir; **~able** tam vaktinde olan, uygun; **~al** mevsimlik; **~ing** çeşni veren şey
seat [sît] *n.* oturulacak yer, iskemle, sandalye; THEA koltuk; merkez; *v/t* oturtmak; **take a ~** oturmak; **be ~ed!** oturunuz!; **~belt** emniyet kemeri
seaweed yosun
secession [si'seşın] ayrılma
seclu|de [si'kluud] *v/t* ayırmak, tecrit etm.; **~sion** [-jın] inziva
second ['sekond] saniye; ikinci; **~ary** ikinci derecede, ikincil; **~ary school** ortaokul, lise; **~class** ikinci sınıf; **~hand** kullanılmış, elden

düşme; **~rate** ikinci derecede
secre|cy ['sîkrisi] gizlilik, ketumiyet; **~t** gizli, mahrem; sır, gizli şey
secretary ['sekrıtri] sekreter, kâtip; 2 **of State** *Am.* Dışişleri Bakanı
secret|e [si'krît] *v/t* MED salgılamak, ifraz etm.; **~ion** salgı, ifraz
sect [sekt] REL mezhep; **~ion** ['~kşın] kesme; kesilmiş şey; kısım, parça; bölge; şube; MATH kesit; **~or** bölge
secular ['sekyulı] layik; dünyevî
secur|e [si'kyuı] *adj.* emin emniyetli, sağlam; *v/t* sağlamak; bağlamak; elde etm.; **~ity** emniyet, güven; rehin; *pl.* ECON tahviller, senetler
sedan [si'dän] kapalı otomobil; **~ (chair)** sedye
sedative ['sedıtiv] teskin edici, yatıştırıcı (ilâç)
sediment ['sedimınt] tortu, telve
sedition [si'dişın] ayaklanma(ya teşvik)
seduc|e [si'dyûs] *v/t* baştan çıkarmak, ayartmak; **~tive** [-'daktiv] çekici
see [sî] *v/t* görmek; anlamak, kavramak; bakmak *-e*; **home** eve götürmek; **~ off** uğurlamak; **~ to** bakmak *-e* meşgul olm. ile
seed [sîd] tohum
seek [sîk] *v/t, v/i* (**after, for**)

aramak -i

seem [sîm] görünmek, gelmek (like gibi); ~ing görünüşte; ~ly yakışır, münasip

seen [sîn] s. see

seep [sîp] v/i sızmak

seesaw ['sîsô] tahterevalli

segment ['segmınt] parça, kısım

segregat|e ['segrigeyt] v/t ayırmak; ~ion ayrım

seismic(al) ['sayzmik(ıl)] depremsel

seiz|e [sîz] v/t yakalamak, tutmak; kavramak; müsadere etm.; ~ure ['sîjı] müsadere, el koyma

seldom ['seldım] nadiren, seyrek

select [si'lekt] adj. seçme, güzide; v/t seçmek; ~ion seçme (şeyler pl.)

self [self] zat, kişi; kendi; kendi kendine; ~command kendini tutma, nefsini yenme; ~confidence kendine güven; ~conscious utangaç, sıkılgan; ~control kendini yenme; ~defence nefsini koruma; ~evident aşikâr, belli; ~government özerklik, muhtariyet; ~ish becerikli, hodbin; ~made kendini yetiştirmiş; ~possession kendine hâkim olma; ~reliant kendine güvenir; ~respect onur, öz saygısı; ~service selfservis

sell [sel] v/t satmak; v/i satılmak; ~ out bütün stoku satmak; ~er satıcı

semblance ['semblıns] benzerlik

sem|ester [si'mestı] sömestr; ~icolon ['semi'kıulın] noktalı virgül

Semitic [si'mitik] Samî

senat|e ['senit] senato; ~or ['..ıtı] senatör

send [send] v/t yollamak, göndermek; ~ for çağırmak, getirtmek -i; ~er gönderen

senior ['sînyı] yaşça büyük; kıdemli

sensation [sen'seyşın] his, duygu; heyecan uyandıran olay

sense [sens] n. mana; his, duyu; anlayış; akıl; v/t sezmek; anlamak; ~less baygın; duygusuz; manasız

sensi|bility [sensi'biliti] duyarlık; seziş inceliği; ~ble hissedilir; aklı başında; be ~ble of sezmek -i; ~tive hassas, içli, duygulu

sensual ['sensyuıl] şehvanî

sent [sent] s. send

sentence ['sentıns] n. GR cümle; JUR hüküm, karar; v/t mahkûm etm.

sentiment ['sentimınt] his, duygu; düşünce; ~al [..'mentl] hissi, duygusal, içli

sentry ['sentri] nöbetçi

separa|ble ['sepırıbl] ayrılabilir; ~te ['..yet] adj. ayrı; v/t ayırmak; v/i ayrılmak; ~tion ayırma, ayrılma

September [sep'tembı] eylül

septic ['septik] MED bulaşık, mikroplu

sepulch|re, *Am.* ~**er** ['sepılkı] kabir, mezar

seque|l ['sîkwıl] devam; sonuç; ~**nce** sıra; ardılık

seren|ade [seri'neyd] MUS serenat; ~**e** [si'rîn] sakin; açık

serf [sзf] serf, köle

sergeant ['sâcınt] MIL çavuş; polis komiseri muavini

seri|al ['sîırıl] seri halinde olan; tefrika; ~**es** ['-rîz] *sg.*, *a. pl.* sıra, seri

serious ['sîırıs] ciddî

sermon ['sзmın] vaız

serpent ['sзpınt] yılan

serv|ant ['sзvınt] hizmetçi, uşak; ~**e** *v/t* hizmet etm. *-e*; sofraya koymak *-i*; yerine getirmek *-i*; yaramak *-e*; *v/i* işini görmek; ~**e out** *v/t* dağıtmak

service ['sзvis] hizmet; servis; görev; yarar; MIL askerlik; REL ayin, tören; ~ **station** benzin istasyonu; ~**able** işe yarar, faydalı

session ['seşın] oturum, celse

set [set] *n.* takım; koleksiyon; seri; cihaz; grup; *v/t* koymak, yerleştirmek, dikmek, kurmak; düzeltmek, tanzim etm.; *v/i* katılaşmak; *sun:* batmak; *adj.* belirli; düzenli; değişmez; ~ **about** başlamak (*-ing -e*); ~**free** *v/t* serbest bırakmak; ~ **off** yola çıkmak; ~ **to** başlamak *-e*; ~ **up** *v/t*

dikmek, kurmak; ~**back** aksilik

settee [se'tî] kanepe

setting ['setiŋ] yuva; batma (*güneş*); ortam

settle ['setl] *v/i* oturmak, yerleşmek; durulmak; *v/t* yerleştirmek; kararlaştırmak; halletmek; *account:* görmek, ödemek; *quarrel:* yatıştırmak; ~ **down** yerleşmek; ~**ment** yerleş(tir)me; sömürge; yeni iskân edilmiş yer; ECON hesap görme, tasfiye; halletme; ~**r** yeni yerleşen göçmen

seven ['sevn] yedi; ~**teen** ['-'tîn] on yedi; ~**ty** yetmiş

sever ['sevı] *v/t* ayırmak, koparmak; *v/i* ayrılmak

several ['sevrıl] birkaç; çeşitli

sever|e [si'vi] şiddetli, sert; ~**ity** [-eriti] şiddet, sertlik

sew [sıu] *v/t dikiş* dikmek

sew|age ['syuic] pis su; ~**er** lağım

sex [seks] cins; cinsiyet; ~**ual** ['-yuıl] cinsî, cinsel

shabby ['şäbi] kılıksız; alçak

shack [şäk] kulübe

shade [şeyd] *n.* gölge; siper; abajur; renk tonu; *v/t* ışıktan korumak; gölgelemek

shadow ['şädu] *n.* gölge; *v/t* gölgelemek; gizlice gözetlemek

shady ['şeydi] gölgeli; *fig.* şüpheli

shaft [şâft] sap; sütun; şaft; maden kuyusu

shaggy ['şägi] kaba tüylü

shake [şeyk] v/t silkmek, sallamak, sarsmak; v/i sallanmak, titremek; n. çalkalanmış şey; sarsıntı; ~ hands el sıkışmak; ~n s. shake; sarşılmış

shaky titrek; zayıf

shall [şäl] -ecek; -meli

shallow ['şälu] sığ; üstünkörü; sığyer

sham [şäm] yapma; v/t yalandan yapmak

shame [şeym] n. utanç; rezalet; v/t utandırmak; ~ful utandırıcı, ayıp; ~less utanmaz, arsız

shampoo [şäm'puu] n. şampuan; v/t başı yıkamak

shank [şänk] ANAT incik, baldır

shape [şeyp] n. şekil, biçim; v/t şekil vermek -e; düzenlemek -i; ~less biçimsiz, şekilsiz; ~ly yakışıklı

share¹ [şii] saban demiri

share² n. pay, hisse; ECON hisse senedi, aksiyon; v/t paylaşmak; katılmak -e; ~holder hissedar

shark [şâk] ZOO köpek balığı

sharp [şâp] keskin, sivri; ekşi; sert; zeki; tam; ~en v/t bilemek, sivriltmek; v/i keskinleşmek; ~ener ['-pnı] kalemtıraş; ~ness keskinlik, sivrilik; şiddet; ~witted zeki

shatter ['şätı] v/t kırmak, parçalamak; v/i kırılmak

shave [şeyv] n. tıraş; v/t tıraş etm.; sıyırıp geçmek; v/i tıraş olm.; ~en s. shave; ~ing tıraş; pl. talaş sg.

shawl [şôl] omuz atkısı; şal

she [şi] o (dişil); dişi

sheaf [şif] demet

shear [şii] v/t kırkmak, kesmek; ~s n. pl. büyük makas sg.

sheath [şith] kın, kılıf, zarf

shed¹ [şed] n. baraka, kulübe

shed² v/t dökmek, akıtmak; dağıtmak

sheep [şip] koyun(lar pl.); ~ish sıkılgan, utangaç

sheer [şii] halis, saf; tamamıyla

sheet [şit] çarşaf; yaprak, tabaka; levha; ~ iron saç; ~ing çarşaflık bez

shelf [şelf] raf; GEO şelf, sığlık

shell [şel] n. kabuk; top mermisi; v/t kabuğundan çıkarmak; ~fish ZOO kabuklu hayvan

shelter ['şeltı] sığınak, barınak, siper; v/t barındırmak

shepherd ['şepıd] çoban

sherbet ['şäbıt] şerbet; dondurma

sheriff ['şerif] ilce veya bucakta polis müdürü

shield [şild] n. kalkan; siper; v/t korumak

shift [şift] n. değiş(tir)me; nöbet; çare; hile; v/t değiştirmek; v/i değişmek; ~y hilekâr

shilling ['şilin] şilin

shin(-bone) ['şin(-)] ANAT in-

cik kemiri
shine [şayn] *n.* parlaklık; *v/i* parlamak; *v/t* parlatmak
shingle ['şingıl] padavra, tahta kiremit
shiny ['şayni] parlak
ship [şip] *n.* gemi; *v/t* gemiyle sevketmek, yollamak; **~ment** gemiye yükleme; hamule; **~ping** gemiye yükleme; deniz nakliyesi; **~wreck** gemi enkazı; deniz kazası; **~wright** tersane işçisi; **~yard** tersane
shire ['şayı] kontluk
shirk [şık] *v/t* kaçınmak -*den*
shirt [şıt] gömlek; **~sleeve** gömlek kolu
shiver[1] ['şivı] ufak parça
shiver[2] *n.* titreme; *v/i* titremek
shock [şok] *n.* sarsma, sarsıntı; darbe; *v/t* sarsmak; iğrendirmek; **~absorber** TECH amortisör; **~ing** korkunç; iğrenç; **~proof** sarsıntıya dayanır
shoe [şuu] *n.* kundura, ayakkabı; nal; *v/t* nallamak; **~maker** ayakkabıcı; **~string** ayakkabı bağı; **on a ~string** az pata ile
shone [şon] *s.* shine
shook [şuk] *s.* shake
shoot [şuut] *n.* atış; filiz; *v/t* atmak; silâhla vurmak; öldürmek; filme almak; *v/i* fışkırmak; filiz sürmek; **~ at** ateş etmek -*e*; **~down** düşürmek; **~er** nişancı; **~ing** atış;

avcılık; **~ing star** ASTR göktaşı
shop [şop] dükkân, mağaza; fabrika; **talk ~** iş konusunda konuşmak; **~keeper** dükkâncı; **~lifter** dükkân hırsızı; **~ping** alışveriş; **~window** vitrin
shore [şô] kıyı, sahil
shorn [şôn] *s.* shear
short [şôt] kısa; bodur, kısa boylu; az; ters; *pl.* şort, kısa pantolon *sg.*; **~ cut** kestirme yol; **in ~** kısaca; **~ of** *adv.* -*den* başka; **be ~ of** -*si* eksik olm.; **~age** yokluk, kıtlık; **~cirkuit** kısa devre; **~coming** kusur, noksan; **~en** *v/t* kısaltmak; *v/i* kısalmak; **~hand** stenografi; **~ness** kısalık, eksiklik; **~sighted** miyop; *fig.* kısa görüşlü; **~term** kısa vadeli; **~winded** nefes darlığı olan
shot [şot] atış; gülle; erim; silâh sesi; *s.* shoot; **big ~** pop. önemli şahıs; **~gun** saçma tüfeği
should [şud] *s.* shall
shoulder ['şuldı] *n.* omuz; *v/t* omuzlamak; **~ blade** ANAT kürek kemiği
shout [şaut] *n.* bağırma; *v/t* bağırmak
shove [şav] *v/t* itmek, dürtmek
shovel ['şavl] *n.* kürek; *v/t* kürelemek
show [şu] *n.* gösteriş; THEA temsil, oyun; sergi; *v/t* göstermek; sergilemek; tanıtla-

mak; *v/i* görünmek; ~ off
gösteriş yapmak; ~ up *v/i* gözükmek

shower ['şauı] *n.* sağanak;
duş; *v/i* sağanak halinde yağmak; *v/t* bol vermek; yağdırmak

show|n [şıun] *s.* show; ~y gös-
terişli

shrank [şräŋk] *s.* shrink

shred [şred] *n.* dilim, paçavra;
v/t parçalamak

shrewd [şruud] kurnaz, becerikli

shriek [şrîk] *n.* feryat, yaygara; *v/i* çığlık koparmak

shrill [şril] keskin sesli

shrimp [şrimp] zoo karides

shrink [şrinp] *v/i* ürkmek; çekinmek, büzülmek; *v/t* daraltmak

shrivel ['şrivl] *v/i* büzülmek

Shrovetide ['şruvtayd] rel
etkesimi, apukurya

shrub [şrab] küçük ağaç; çalı;
~bery çalılık

shrug [şrag] *n.* omuz silkme;
v/t omuzlarını silkmek

shrunk [şrank] *s.* shrink; ~en
büzülmüş

shudder [şadı] *n.* titreme; *v/i*
ürpermek, titremek

shuffle ['şafl] *v/t* karıştırmak;
v/i ayak sürümek

shun [şan] *v/t* sakınmak,
kaçınmak *-den*

shut [şat] *v/t* kapa(t)mak; *v/i*
kapanmak; ~ down *v/t* işye-
rini kapamak; ~ up! *intj.*
sus!; ~ter kepenk; phot ka-

pak

shuttle ['şatl] mekik

shy [şay] *adj.* korkak, ürkek;
v/i ürkmek; ~ness çekingen-
lik

sick [sik] hasta; midesi bu-
lanmış; bıkmış (of -*den*);
~en *v/i* hastalanmak; *v/t*
bıktırmak

sickle ['sikl] orak

sick|-leave hastalık izni;
~ness hastalık; kusma

side [sayd] yan, taraf; kenar;
~ with -*in* tarafını tutmak;
~board büfe; ~-car yan arabası, sepet; ~walk *Am.* yaya
kaldırımı; ~ways yandan;
yan

siege [sîc] muhasara, kuşat-
ma

sieve [siv] *n.* kalbur, elek; *v/t*
elemek

sift [sift] *v/t* kalburdan geçirmek, elemek; *fig.* incelemek;
ayırmak

sigh [say] *n.* iç çekme; *v/i* iç
çekmek

sight [sayt] *n.* görme; manzara; *v/t* görmek; at first ~ ilk
görüşte; know by ~ *v/t* yüzünden tanımak; ~seeing
seyredecek yerleri görmeğe
gitme, gezme

sign [sayn] *n.* işaret, alâmet;
iz, belirti; levha; *v/t* imzalamak; işaret etm. -*e*

signal [['signl] *n.* işaret; ihtar;
v/t işaretle bildirmek; ~tory
['_nıtıri] imza eden; ~ture
['_niçi] imza

signboard tabela, afiş

significa|nce ['sig'nifikıns] mana; önem; ~nt manalı; önemli; ~tion mana

signify ['signifay] v/t belirtmek

signpost işaret direği

silen|ce ['saylıns] n. sessizlik; v/t susturmak; ~t sessiz, sakin

silk [silk] ipek; ~en ipekli; ~y ipek gibi

sill [sil] eşik; denizlik

silly ['sili] budala, aptal

silver ['silvı] n. gümüş; v/t gümüş kaplamak -e; ~y gümüş gibi, parlak

similar ['similı] benzer (to -e), gibi; ~ity [,~'läriti] benzerlik

simmer ['simı] v/i yavaş yavaş kaynamak

simpl|e ['simpl] basit, sade; kolay; safdil; ~icity [,~'plisiti] sadelik; saflık; ~ify ['~lifay] v/t kolaylaştırmak; ~y adv. sadece, sırf, ancak

simulate ['simyuleyt] v/t yalandan yapmak; ... gibi görünmek

simultaneous [siml'teynyıs] aynı zamanda olan, eşzamanlı

sin [sin] n. günah; v/i günah işlemek

since [sins] prp. -den beri; mademki, zira, çünkü

sincer|e [sin'siı] samimî, içten; Yours ~ely saygılarımla; ~ity [,~'seriti] samimiyet, içtenlik

sinew ['sinyû] kiriş; ~y kiriş gibi; fig. kuvvetli, dinç

sing [sin] v/i şarkı söylemek; ötmek; v/t söylemek, okumak

singe [sinc] v/t yakmak

singer ['sinı] şarkıcı

single ['singl] tek, bir; yalnız; tek kişilik; bekâr; ~ out v/t seçmek, ayırmak; ~handed tek başına

singular ['singyulı] acayip; tek; eşsiz; gr tekil; ~ity [,~'läriti] özellik

sinister ['sinistı] uğursuz

sink [sink] n. musluk taşı, bulaşık oluğu; v/i batmak, düşmek, inmek; v/t batırmak

sinner ['sinı] günahkâr

sip [sip] v/t azar azar içmek

siphon ['sayfın] sifon

sir [sı] beyefendi, efendim; 2 sör (bir asalet unvanı)

siren ['sayırın] canavar düdüğü

sirloin ['sıloyn] sığır filetosu

sister ['sustı] kızkardeş, hemşire; abla; ~-in-law görümce, baldız, yenge, elti

sit [sit] v/i oturmak; ~ down (yerine) oturmak; ~up dik oturmak; yatmamak

site [sayt] yer, mahal

sitting ['sitin] oturum; ~room oturma odası

situat|ed ['sityueytid]: be ~ed bulunmak (in -de); ~ion yer; durum

six [siks] altı; ~teen ['~'tîn] on altı; ~ty altmış

size [sayz] hacim, oylum; büyüklük

sizzle ['sizl] *v/i* cızırdamak

skate|**e** [skeyt] paten; ~er patinaj yapan; ~ing patinaj

skeleton ['skelitn] iskelet; çatı

sketch [skeç] *n.* kroki, taslak; skeç; *v/t* -in taslağını çizmek

skewer ['skyûı] kepap şişi

ski [skî] *n.* kayak; *v/i* kayak yapmak

skid [skid] *n.* takoz; kayma; *v/i* yana kaymak

ski|**er** ['skî] kayakçı; ~ing kayakçılık

skil|**ful** ['skilful] hünerli, mahir; ~l hüner, ustalık; ~led tecrübeli; kalifiye; ~lful *Am. s.* skilful

skim [skim] *v/t* -in köpüğünü almak; *fig.* göz gezdirmek -e; ~(med) mâlih kagnağı alınmış süt

skin [skin] *n.* deri; post; kabuk; *v/t* yüzmek, -in kabuğunu soymak; ~deep sathî, yüzeysel; ~ny sıska

skip [skip] *n.* sekme, zıplama; *v/i* zıplamak; *v/t* atlamak

skipper ['skipı] kaptan

skirmish ['skımiş] MIL hafif çarpışma

skirt [skıt] *n.* etek(lik); kenar; *v/t* -in kenarından geçmek

skittles ['skitlz] *pl.* kiy oyunu *sg.*

skull [skal] kafatası

sky [skay] gök; ~jacker ['cäkı] hava korsanı; ~lark zoo

tarlakuşu, toygar; ~light dam penceresi, kaporta; ~scraper gökdelen

slab [släb] kalın dilim, tabaka

slack [släk] gevşek; kayıtsız; *pl.* pantolon; ~en *v/i* gevşemek; *v/t* gevşetmek

slain [sleyn] *s.* slay

slake [sleyk] *v/t thirst:* gidermek; *lime:* söndürmek

slam [släm] *v/t* çarpıp kapamak; yere vurmak

slander ['slândı] *n.* iftira; *v/t* iftira etm. -e

slang [släng] argo

slant [slânt] *n.* eğim; meyilli düzey; *v/i* eğilmek; *v/t* eğmek

slap [släp] *n.* şamar, tokat; *v/t* avuçla vurmak -e; ~stick THEA güldürü; gürültülü

slash [släş] *n.* uzun yara; yarık; kamçı vuruşu; *v/t* yarmak; kamçılamak

slate [sleyt] arduvaz, kabayağantaş

slattern ['slätın] pasaklı kadın

slaughter ['slôtı] *n.* kesim, katliam; *v/t* kesmek, boğazlamak; ~house mezbaha

slave [sleyv] *n.* köle, esir; *v/i* köle gibi çalışmak; ~ry kölelik, esirlik

slay [sley] *v/t* öldürmek

sled(**ge**) [sled (slec)] *n.* kızak; *v/i* kızakla gitmek

sledge-hammer balyoz

sleek [slîk] *adj.* düzgün, parlak; *v/t* düzlemek

sleep [slîp] *n.* uyku; *v/i* uyumak; **go to ~** yatağa yatmak; **~ on, ~ over** *v/t* ertesi güne bırakmak; **~er** uyuyan kimse; yataklı vagon; travers; **~ing-bag** uyku tulumu; **~ing-car** yataklı vagon; **~less** uykusuz; **~walker** uyurgezer; **~y** uykusu gelmiş

sleet [slît] sulu sepken kar

sleeve [slîv] yen, elbise kolu; TECH manşon, kol, bilezik

sleigh [sley] *n.* kızak; *v/i* kızakla gitmek

slender [′slendı] ince, zayıf; az

slept [slept] *s.* **sleep**

slew [sluu] *s.* **slay**

slice [slays] *n.* dilim, parça; balık bıçağı; *v/t* dilimlemek

slick [slik] kaygan; kurnaz

slid [slid] *s.* **slide**

slide [slayd] *v/i* kaymak; *v/t* kaydırmak; *n.* kayma; TECH sürme; diyapozitif; **~rule** hesap cetveli

slight [slayt] *adj.* zayıf, önemsiz; *v/t* önem vermemek -*e*, küçümsemek -*i*

slim [slim] *adj.* ince, zayıf; *v/i* incelmek

slime [slaym] sümük; balçık; **~y** sümüksü, pis

sling [sliŋ] *n.* sapan; askı; *v/t* sapanla atmak; askı ile kaldırmak

slip [slip] *n.* kayma; söz kaçırma; hata; kâğıt, pusula; yastık yüzü; *v/i* kaymak; kaçmak; **~ on** *v/t* kaydırmak; **~ on**

giyivermek; **~ out** *v/i* ağzından kaçmak; **~per** terlik; **~pery** kaygan, kaypak

slit [slit] *n.* kesik, yarık; *v/t* yarmak

slogan [′slugın] parola, slogan

sloop [sluup] NAUT şalopa

slop [slop] *n.* sulu çamur; *v/t* dökmek; **~ over** *v/i* taşmak

slope [slup] *n.* bayır; meyilli düzey; *v/t* meyletmek

sloppy [′slopi] çamurlu; *fig.* şapşal

slot [slot] delik, kertik

sloth [sluuth] tembellik

slot-machine oyun makinası

slough [slau] bataklık

sloven [′slavn] hırpani, şapşal

slow [slu] *adj.* ağır, yavaş; geri kalmış; aptal; **~ down** *v/t* yavaşlatmak; *v/i* ağırlaşmak; **~motion** yavaşlatılmış hareket; **~ness** ağırlık, yavaşlık

sluggish [′slagiş] tembel, cansız

sluice [sluus] savak

slum [slam] teneke mahallesi

slumber [′slambı] *n.* uyku, uyuklama; *v/i* uyumak, uyuklamak

slung [slaŋ] *s.* **sling**

slush [slaş] eriyen kar; çamur

slut [slat] pasaklı kadın

sly [slay] kurnaz, şeytan gibi

smack[1] [smäk] *n.* şapırtı; şamar; *v/t* şaplatmak

smack[2] hafif çeşni; **~ of** -*in* çeşnisi olm.

small [smôl] küçük, ufak, az;

~ change bozuk para; ~ hours pl. gece yarısından sonraki saatler; ~ talk önemsiz sohbet; ~pox MED çiçek hastalığı

smart [smât] şık, zarif; akıllı; kurnaz; çevik; şiddetli

smash [smäş] v/t ezmek, parçalamak; v/i ezilmek; ~ing fig. çok güzel

smattering ['smätırın] çat pat bilgi

smear [smiı] n. leke; v/t bulandırmak, lekelemek; sürmek

smell [smel] koku; v/t -in kokusunu almak; v/i kokmak

smelt¹ [smelt] s. smell

smelt² v/t eritmek

smile [smayl] n. gülümseme, tebessüm; v/i gülümsemek

smith [smith] demirci, nalbant

smitten ['smitn] çarpılmış; fig. vurgun (with -e)

smock [smok] iş kıyafeti

smog [smog] dumanlı sis

smoke [smuuk] n. duman; v/i tütmek; v/t tütsülemek; cigarette, etc.: içmek; ~e-free sigara içilmeyen (bina); ~er tütün içen; tütün içenlere mahsus vagon; ~ing tütün içme; ~ing-car(riage) tütün içenlere mahsus vagon; ~y dumanlı, tüten

smooth [smuudh] düz, düzgün, pürüzsüz; akıcı; nazik; v/t düzlemek, yatıştırmak

smother ['smadhı] v/t boğ-

mak; v/i boğulmak

smo(u)lder ['smuldı] alevsiz yanmak

smudge [smac] n. leke; v/t kirletmek

smuggle ['smagl] v/t kaçırmak; ~r kaçakçı

smut [smat] is, kurum; pis laf

snack [snäk] çerez, hafif yemek

snail [sneyl] zoo salyangoz

snake [sneyk] zoo yılan

snap [snäp] n. ısırma; çatırtı, şıkırtı; gayret, enerji; v/i ısırmak, kopmak (at -i); çatırdayıp kırılmak; v/t kırmak; cold ~ soğukluk dalgası; ~py çevik, çabuk; ~shot enstantane fotoğraf

snare [snäı] tuzak, kapan

snarl [snâl] v/i hırlamak; n. hırlama

snatch [snäç] v/t kapmak, koparmak; n. kapma; parça

sneak [snîk] v/i sinsi sinsi dolaşmak

sneer [sniı] n. alay, istihza; v/i küçümsemek (at -i), alay etm. (ile)

sneeze [snîz] n. aksırma; v/i aksırmak

sniff [snif] v/i burnuna hava çekmek; burnunu buruşturmak; v/t koklamak; ~le ['-fl] nezle

snipe [snayp] zoo çulluk; ~r pusuya yatan nişancı

snivel ['snivl] v/i burnu akmak; burnunu çekerek ağlamak

snob [snob] snop, züppe

snoop [snuup] burnunu sokan

snooze [snuuz] *n.* şekerleme; *v/i* kısaca uyumak

snore [snô] *n.* horlama; *v/i* horlamak

snort [snôt] at gibi horuldamak

snout [snaut] zoo burun, hortum

snow [snıu] *n.* kar; *v/i* kar yağmak; ~ball kar topu; ~drift kar yığıntısı; ~drop BOT kardelen; ~y karlı, kar gibi

snub [snab] *v/t* küçümsemek; *n.* hiçe sayma; ~nose ucu kalkık burun

snuff [snaf] enfiye

snug [snag] rahat, konforlu; ~gle [-.gl] *v/i* yerleşmek, sokulmak

so [sıu] öyle, böyle; bu kadar; bundan dolayı; ~ far şimdiye kadar; ~ long! hoşça kalın!

soak [sıuk] *v/t* ıslatmak; *v/i* ıslanmak

so-and-so filanca

soap [sıup] *n.* sabun; *v/t* sabunlamak

soar [sô] yükselmek

sob [sob] *n.* hıçkırık; *v/i* hıçkıra hıçkıra ağlamak

sober [sıubı] *adj.* ayık; ağırbaşlı; *v/i* ayılmak

so-called diye anılan, sözde

soccer [sokı] futbol

sociable [sıuşıbl] girgin; nazik

social [sıuşıl] hoş sohbet; toplumsal, sosyal; ~ insurance sosyal sigorta; ~ism sosyalizm; ~ist sosyalist; ~ize *v/t* kamulaştırmak

society [sı'sayıti] kurum; ortaklık; sosyete

sociology [sıusi'olıci] sosyoloji

sock [sok] kısa çorap, şoset

socket [sokit] sap deliği, oyuk; yuva

sod [sod] çimen parçası

soda [sıudı] soda; soda suyu

sofa [sıufı] kanepe

soft [soft] yumuşak; uysal; (*voice*) yavaş; ~ drink alkolsuz içecek; ~en [sofn] *v/t* yumuşatmak; *v/i* yumuşamak; ~ness yumuşaklık

soil [soyl] *n.* toprak; *v/t* kirletmek; *v/i* kirlenmek

sojourn [socın] *v/i* kalmak; *n.* konukluk

solar [sulı] güneşe ait

sold [sıuld] *s.* sell

soldier [sulcı] asker, er

sole¹ [sıul] *n.* taban, pençe; *v/t* pençe vurmak -*e*

sole² zoo dilbalığı

sole³ yalnız, biricik

solemn [solım] törenli; ağırbaşlı

solicit [sı'lisit] *v/t* istemek, rica emt.; ~or avukat; ~ous endişeli; istekli

solid [solid] sağlam; sağlam; katı; som; ~arity [_'däriti] dayanışma, tesanüt; ~ity katılık

solit|ary [solitıri] tek, yalnız

tenha; ~ude ['-tyûd]
yalnızlık

solo ['suːlu] solo; ~ist solist

solstice ['solstis] ASTR gün-dönümü

solu|ble ['solyubl] eriyebilir, çözülebilir; ~tion [sı'luːşın] erime; çözüm; çare

solve [solv] v/t halletmek, çözmek; ~nt ECON borcunu ödeyebilir

somb|re, Am. ~er ['sombı] loş, karanlık

some [sam] bazı, birkaç; biraz; ~body ['-bıdi] biri (-si); ~how nasılsa; ~one biri(si)

somersault ['samısôlt] taklak

some|thing bir şey; ~times bazan, arasıra; ~what bir dereceye kadar; ~where bir yer(d)e

son [san] oğul

song [soŋ] şarkı; ötme; ~bird ötücü kuş

sonic ['sonik] sesle ilgili

son-in-law damat

soon [suun] biraz sonra; hemen; erken; as ~ as -ince; no ~er ... than -ir-mez

soot [suut] n. is, kurum; v/t ise bulaştırmak

soothe [suudh] v/t yatıştırmak, teskin etm.

sophisticated [sı'fistikeytid] hayata alışmış; kültürlü; yapmacık

soporific [sopı'rifik] uyutucu ilâç

sorcer|er ['so'sırı] büyücü, sihirbaz; ~y büyü(cülük)

sordid ['sôdid] alçak, sefil; kirli

sore [sô] acı veren; kırgın; şiddetli; ~ throat boğaz ağrısı

sorrow ['soru] keder, acı; ~ful kederli, elemli

sorry ['sori] üzgün; pişman; **be** ~ acımak, üzülmek **(for** -e)

sort [sôt] n. çeşit, nevi; v/t sınıflandırmak, ayıklamak

sought [sôt] s. **seek**

soul [sul] ruh, can

sound¹ [saund] sağlam; emin

sound² GEO boğaz

sound³ v/t iskandil etm.

sound⁴ n. ses; v/i ses vermek; gelmek, görünmek **(like** gibi); v/t çalmak; ~proof ses geçirmez; ~wave PHYS ses dalgası

soup [suup] çorba

sour ['saul] ekşi(miş); somurtkan, asık

source [sôs] kaynak

south [sauth] güney; ~east güney doğu

souther|ly ['sadhıli] güneye doğru; ~ern güneyde olan; ℚner Am. güneyli

south|ward(s) ['sauthwıd(z)] güneye doğru; ~west güney-batı

souvenir ['suuvnıı] hatıra, andaç

sovereign ['sovrin] hükümdar; ~ty ['-rınti] egemenlik

Soviet Union ['sıuviet -] hist.

Sovyetler Birliği
sow¹ [sau] zoo dişi domuz
sow² [siu] v/t ekmek; ~n s.
  sow²
soya, soybean ['soyi] BOT soya (fasulyesi)
spa [spâ] ılıca, kaplıca
space [speys] alan, yer; uzay;
  ~**craft**, ~**ship** uzay gemisi
spacious ['speyşıs] geniş, engin
spade [speyd] bel; maça
Spain [speyn] Ispanya
spam (mail) [späm] spam
span¹ [spän] n. karış; süre;
  ARCH açıklık; v/t ölçmek;
  boydan boya uzatmak
span² s. **spin**
spangle ['spängl] n. pul; v/t
  pullarla süslemek
Spani|ard ['spänyıd] Ispan-
  yol; ~**sh** Ispanyol(ca)
spank [spänk] v/t -in kıçına
  şaplak vurmak; ~**ing** şaplak
  atma
spanner ['spänı] somun
  anahtarı
spare [späı] adj. dar; boş; yedek; v/t esirgemek; vazgeçmek -den; tutumlu kullanmak -i; ~ **part** TECH yedek
  parça; ~**room** misafir odası;
  ~ **time** boş vakit
spark [spâk] n. kıvılcım; v/i
  kıvılcım saçmak; ~(**ing**)-
  plug TECH buji; ~**le** n.
  kıvılcım; parlayış; v/i parıldamak
sparrow ['späriu] zoo serçe
sparse [spâs] seyrek

spasm ['späzım] MED ıspaz-
  moz; ~**odic** [-'modik] ıspaz-
  moz kabilinden
spat [spät] s. **spit**
spatter ['spätı] v/t serpmek
spawn [spôn] balık yumurtası
speak [spîk] v/i konuşmak (**to**
  ile); bahsetmek (**about, of**
  -den); v/t söylemek; **out,** ~
  up v/t açıkça söylemek; ~**er**
  sözcü
spear [spiı] n. mızrak; v/t
  mızrakla vurmak -e
special ['speşıl] özel; mahsus;
  özellik; ~**ist** uzman, mütehassıs; ~**ity** [-'äliti] özellik;
  ~**alize** in -in ihtisas sahibi
  olm.; ~**ty** özellik
species ['spîşîz] tür, çeşit
speci|fic [spi'sifik] has, özgü;
  özel; belirli; ~**fy** v/t belirtmek; ~**men** ['spesimin] örnek, nümune
specta|cle ['spektıkl] manza-
  ra; pl. gözlük sg.; ~**cular**
  [-'täkyulı] görülmeye değer;
  ~**tor** [-'teytı] seyirci
speculate ['spekyuleyt] v/i
  ECON borsada oynamak;
  düşünmek, mütalâa etm.
  (**on, upon** -i); ~**ion** spekülasyon; kurgu
sped [sped] s. **speed**
speech [spîç] dil; söz, söylev;
  ~**less** dili tutulmuş
speed [spîd] n. hız, sürat, çabukluk; v/i hızla gitmek; v/t
  hızlandırmak; ~**dial button**
  hızlı çağrı tuşu; ~**limit** azamî

sürat; ~ometer [spi'domıtı] hızölçer; ~y çabuk, hızlı

spell¹ [spel] nöbet; süre

spell² v/t hecelemek; belirtmek

spell³ büyü; ~bound büyülenmiş

spelling ['speliŋ] imlâ, yazım

spelt [spelt] s. spell²

spend [spend] v/t harcamak, sarfetmek, israf etm.; time: geçirmek

spent [spent] s. spend

sperm [spɜm] sperma, belsuyu

sphere [sfir] küre; alan, saha

spice [spays] n. bahar; v/t çeşni vermek -e; ~y baharatlı; fig. açık saçık

spider ['spaydı] örümcek

spike [spayk] ʙoʈ başak; uclu demir, çivi

spill [spil] v/t dökmek; v/i dökülmek

spilt [spilt] s. spill

spin [spin] v/t eğirmek; döndürmek; v/i dönmek

spinach ['spinic] ʙoʈ ıspanak

spinal ['spaynl] ᴀɴᴀᴛ belkemiğine ait; ~ column omurga, belkemiği; ~ cord omurilik

spindle ['spindl] iğ, eğirmen; mil

spine [spayn] ᴀɴᴀᴛ omirga, belkemiği; diken

spinning eğirme; ~wheel çıkrık

spinster ['spinstı] kalık, yaşı geçmiş kız

spiny ['spayni] dikenli

spiral ['spayırıl] helis, helezon; helezonî

spire ['spayı] kule tepesi

spirit ['spirit] ruh; cin, peri; canlılık; alkol; ispirto; high ~s pl. keyif, neşe; low ~s keder, gam; ~ed cesur, canlı; ~ual ['_tyuıl] ruhanî; ruhî; ᴍᴜs Amerikan zencilerine has ilâhî

spit¹ [spit] kebap şişi

spit² n. tükürük; v/i tükürmek (on -e); cat: tıslamak

spite [spayt] kin, garaz; in ~ of -e rağmen; ~ful garazkâr

spittle ['spitl] salya, tükürük

splash [släş] n. zifos; v/t zifos atmak, su sıçratmak -e; v/i suya çarpmak; ~ down su içine inmek

spleen [splin] ᴀɴᴀᴛ dalak; fig. terslik; kin

splendid ['splendid] parlak, gösterişli; mükemmel; ~o(u)r parlaklık; tantana

splint [splint] ᴍᴇᴅ cebire, süyek; ~er n. kıymık; v/i parçalanmak

split [split] n. yarık, çatlak; v/t yarmak, bölmek, ayırmak; v/i yarılmak, ayrılmak; ~ting şiddetli, keskin

splutter ['splatı] v/t fışkırtmak

spoil [spoyl] n. yağma, çapul; v/t bozmak; şımartmak; ~sport oyunbozan; ~t s. spoil

spoke¹ [spuık] tekerlek parmağı

spoke² s. speak; ~sman sözcü

sponge [spanc] n. sünger; ~ away, ~ off v/t silmek

sponsor ['sponsi] n. REL vaftiz babası; JUR kefil; v/t desteklemek

spontaneous [spon'teynyıs] kendiliğinden olan

spook [spuuk] hayalet

spool [spuul] n. makara; v/t makaraya sarmak

spoon [spuun] kaşık; ~ful kaşık dolusu

sporadic [spı'rädik] arasıra olan

sport [spôt] n. spor; eğlence; alay; v/i takılmak (at, over -e); v/t övünmek ile; ~sman sporcu, sportmen

spot [spot] n. nokta, benek; yer; v/t beneklemek; görmek, bulmak; on the ~ yerinde; derhal; ~less leziz; ~light projektör ışığı

spouse [spauz] eş, koca, karı

spout [spaut] n. oluk ağzı, emzik; v/t fışkırtmak; v/i fışkırmak

sprain [spreyn] n. burkulma; v/t burkmak

sprang [spräŋ] s. spring

sprawl [sprôl] yerde uzanmak

spray [sprey] n. serpinti; püskürgeç; v/t serpmek, püskürtmek

spread [spred] n. yayılma; örtü; v/t yaymak, sermek; sürmek; v/i yayılmak

sprig [sprig] ince dal

sprightly ['spraytli] canlı, şen

spring [spriŋ] (ilk)bahar; TECH yay, zemberek; kaynak; sıçrayış; v/i fırlamak, sıçramak; çıkmak (from -den); ~board tramplen, sıçrama tahtası; ~time ilkbahar

sprinkle ['spriŋkl] v/t serpmek; ~r serpme makinası

sprint [sprint] v/i koşmak; n. kısa koşu; ~er kısa mesafe koşucusu

sprout [spraut] n. filiz; v/i filizlenmek

spruce [spruus] şık

sprunk [spraŋ] s. spring

spun [span] s. spin

spur [spɜ] n. mahmuz; fig. saik; güdü; v/t kışkırtmak (into -e)

sputter ['spatı] v/t saçmak; v/i tükürük saçmak

spy [spay] n. casus; hafiye; v/i gizlice gözetlemek (on -i)

squabble ['skwobl] v/i kavga etm.

squad [skwod] takım

squall [skwôl] bora, kasırga

squander ['skwondı] v/t israf etm., savurmak

square [skwäi] n. dördül, kare; meydan; adj. dürüst, doğru; eşit; pop. eski kafalı; v/t MATH ~in karesini almak; doğrultmak -i; ödemek -i; ~ mile mil kare (259 hektar)

squash¹ [skwoş] n. ezme; v/t ezmek; bastırmak

squash² BOT kabak

squat [skwot] *v/i* çömelmek; boş topraklara yerleşmek

squeak [skwîk] cırlamak; gıcırdamak

squeal [skwîl] domuz gibi ses çıkarmak

squeamish ['skwîmiş] çabuk tiksinen; titiz

squeeze [skwîz] *v/t* sıkmak, sıkıştırmak

squint [skwint] şaşı bakmak; yan bakmak

squire ['skwayı] asilzade; kavalye

squirm [skwɜm] kıvranmak

squirrel ['skwirıl] *zoo* sincap

squirt [skwɜt] *v/t* fışkırtmak

stab [stäb] *n.* bıçak yarası; *v/t* bıçaklamak

stabili|ty [stı'biliti] denge; sağlamlık; ~**ze** ['steybilayz] *v/t* dengelemek; saptamak

stable[1] ['steybl] sağlam, sabit

stable[2] ahır

stack [stäk] *n.* tınaz; yığın; *v/t* yığmak

stadium ['steydyım] stadyum

staff [stâf] değnek, asa; personel, kadro; MIL kurmay

stag [stäg] *zoo* erkek geyik

stage [steyc] *n.* sahne; tiyatro; merhale; konak; safha; *v/t* sahneye koymak; ~**coach** menzil arabası

stagger ['stägı] *v/i* sendelemek, sersemlemek

stagna|nt ['stägnınt] durgun; ~**tion** durgunluk

stain [steyn] *n.* leke, boya; *v/t* lekelemek; ~**ed** lekeli; renk-

li; ~**less** lekesiz; paslanmaz

stair [stäı] basamak; ~**case**, ~**way** merdiven

stake [steyk] *n.* kazık; kumarda ortaya konan para; *v/t* tehlikeye koymak; **be at** ~ tehlikede olm.

stale [steyl] bayat

stalk [stôk] *n.* sap; *v/i* azametle yürümek

stall [stôl] *n.* kulübe; ahır bölmesi; THEA koltuk; *v/t* durdurmak; *v/i* durmak

stallion ['stälyın] aygır, damızlık at

stalwart ['stôlwıt] kuvvetli; sadık

stammer ['stämı] *n.* kekemelik; *v/i* kekelemek

stamp [stämp] *n.* damga; posta pulu; *v/t* damgalamak; pul yapıştırmak -*e*; ayağını vurmak -*e*

stanch [stânç] *s.* **staunch**

stand [ständ] *n.* duruş; ayaklık; tezgâh; *v/i* durmak; ayakta durmak; *v/t* dayanmak -*e*; ~**by** hazır beklemek; ~ **for** manası olm.; ~ (**up**)**on** -*in* üzerinde ısrar etm.; -*in* tarafını tutmak; ~ **up** ayağa kalkmak; taraftarı olm. (**for** -*in*)

standard ['ständıd] **1.** bayrak; **2.** standart; ayar; mikyas, ölçü; seviye; ~**ize** *v/t* belirli bir ölçüye uydurmak

standing ayakta duran; şöhret; süreklilik; **of long** ~ eski

stand|point görüş noktası;

bakım; **~still** durma
stank [stäŋk] s. **stink**
star [stâ] yıldız; v/i fig. birinci
rolü oynamak
starboard ['stâbıd] NAUT sancak (tarafı)
starch [stâç] n. nişasta; kola;
v/t kolalamak
stare [stäı] n. sabit bakış; v/i
dik bakmak (**at** -e)
starling ['stâliŋ] ZOO sığırcık
start [stât] n. başlangıç;
kalkış; sıçrama; v/i hareket
etm., yola çıkmak; ürkmek;
v/t başlamak (**at** -e); çalıştırmak
-i; **~er** TECH marş
startl|e ['stâtl] v/t ürkütmek,
korkutmak; **~ing** şaşırtıcı
starv|ation [stâ'veyşın]
açlık(tan ölme); **~e** v/i açlıktan ölmek; v/t açlıktan öldürmek
state [steyt] n. durum, hal;
POL devlet; v/t beyan etm.,
belirtmek; **~ Department**
Am. Dışişleri Bakanlığı; **~ly**
haşmetli; heybetli; **~ment**
ifade; demeç; rapor; **~room**
NAUT tek kişilik kamara; **~s-**
man devlet adamı
static ['stätik] PHYS statik
station ['steyşın] n. yer; makam, rütbe; istasyon; kara-
bol; v/t yerleştirmek; **~ary**
sabit; **~ery** kırtasiye; **~mas-**
ter istasyon müdürü
statistics [stı'tistiks] pl. istatistik sg.
statue ['stäçuu] heykel
status ['steytıs] durum, hal

statute ['stätyût] kanun; kural
staunch [stônç] adj. sadık;
kuvvetli; v/t durdurmak
stay [stey] n. kalış, ikamet;
destek; v/i durmak, kalmak;
v/t durdurmak; **~ away** gelmemek; **~ up** yatmamak
stead [sted]: **in his ~** onun yerine; **~fast** sabit, sarsılmaz;
~y adj. devamlı, düzenli; sabit, sarsılmaz; v/t sağlamlaştırmak; v/i yatışmak
steak [steyk] fileto; kontrfile
steal [stîl] v/t çalmak, aşırmak; v/i gizlice hareket etm.
stealth [stelth]: **by ~** gizlice;
~y sinsi, gizli
steam [stîm] n. buhar, istim;
v/i buhar salıvermek; v/t bu-
harda pişirmek; **~ engine**
buhar makinesi; **~er**, **~ship**
vapur
steel [stîl] çelik; **~works** pl.
çelik fabrikası sg.
steep [stîp] n. dik, sarp; v/t suya batırmak
steeple ['stîpl] çan kulesi;
~chase engelli yarış
steer[1] [stiı] boğa; öküz
steer[2] v/t dümenle idare etm.,
yönetmek; **~ing-gear** dümen
donanımı; **~ing-wheel** direk-
siyon
stem [stem] sap; gövde
stench [stenç] pis koku
stenography [ste'nogrıfi]
stenografi
step[1] [step] n. adım; basamak; kademe, derece; v/i

adım atmak; basmak (on -e)

step² üvey; ~**father** üvey baba; ~**mother** üvey ana

steppe [step] bozkır

steril|e ['sterayl] kısır; verimsiz; ~**ize** ['-ilayz] v/t kısırlaştırmak; sterilize etm.

sterling ['stǝliŋ] sterlin; değerli

stern [stɜn] sert, haşin; NAUT kıç; ~**ness** sertlik

stew [styû] n. güveç; v/t hafif ateşte kaynatmak

steward ['styuıd] kâhya; NAUT kamarot; ~**ess** hostes

stick [stik] n. değnek, sopa; baston; v/t saplamak; yapıştırmak; v/i yapışmak, takılmak (to -e); ~**y** yapışkan

stiff [stif] katı, sert; bükülmez; alkolü çok; ~**en** v/i katılaşmak; v/t katılaştırmak

stifle ['stayfl] v/t boğmak; v/i boğulmak

still [stil] adj. sakin, durgun; v/t durdurmak; yatıştırmak; adv. hâlâ, henüz; mamafih; ~**born** ölü doğmuş

stimula|nt ['stimyulınt] uyandırıcı (ilâç); ~**te** ['-eyt] v/t uyarmak; ~**tion** uyarım, teşvik

sting [stiŋ] n. sokma; iğne; v/t sokmak, yakmak; v/i acımak

stingy ['stinci] cimri

stink [stiŋk] pis koku; ~ **of** -in kokusunu çıkarmak

stipulat|e ['stipyuleyt] v/i şart koymak; v/t anlaşmak -de; ~**ion** şart (koyma)

stir [stɜ] v/i harekete geçmek; v/t karıştırmak; harekete geçirmek; ~**rup** ['stirp] üzengi

stitch [stiç] n. dikiş; ilmik; v/t dikmek

stock [stok] n. soy; çiftlik hayvanları pl.; ECON stok; kapital; sermaye hisseleri pl.; v/t yığmak; in ~ mevcut; out of ~ mevcudu tükenmiş; ♀ **Exchange** borsa; ~**breed**er büyükbaş yetiştiren çiftçi; ~**broker** borsacı; ~**holder** hissedar

stocking ['stokiŋ] (uzun) çorap

stock|-market borsa; ~**y** bodur

stole [stıul] n. s. steal

stomach ['stamık] n. mide; karın; v/t hazmetmek

ston|e [stıun] n. taş; çekirdek; v/t taşlamak; -in çekirdeğini çıkarmak; ~**y** taşlık; taş gibi

stood [stud] s. stand

stool [stuul] iskemle, tabure; MED büyük aptes

stoop [stuup] v/i eğilmek; alçalmak

stop [stop] n. dur(dur)ma; durak; engel; nokta; v/t durdurmak, önlemek, kesmek, engellemek; tıkamak; v/i durmak, kesilmek; ~ **over** yolculukta mola vermek; ~**page** durdurma, kes(il)me; ECON stopaj; ~**per** tapa, tıkaç; ~**ping** MED dolgu

storage ['stôric] depoya koyma; ardiye (ücreti)

store [stô] *n.* depo, ambar; *Am.* dükkân, mağaza; stok; *v/t* saklamak; ambara koymak; biriktirmek; **~house** ambar, depo

storey ['stôri] bina katı

stork [stôk] zoo leylek

storm [stôm] *n.* fırtına; MIL hücum; *v/t* hücumla zaptetmek; **~y** fırtınalı

story¹ ['stôri] *s.* storey

story² hikâye, masal; roman

stout [staut] sağlam; şişman

stove [stıuv] soba; fırın

stow [stıu] *v/t* saklamak, istif etm.; **~away** kaçak yolcu

straggle ['strägl] *v/i* yoldan sapmak; **~r** arkada kalan

straight [streyt] doğru; dürüst; saf; **~ away**, **~ off** hemen; **~ ahead**, **~ on** doğru; **~en** *v/t* saklamak, düzeltmek; *v/i* doğrulmak; **~forward** doğru sözlü, dürüst

strain [streyn] *n.* ger(il)me, gerginlik; MED burkulup incinme; *v/t* germek, zorlamak; süzmek; *v/i* çabalamak; süzülmek; **~er** süzgeç

strait [streyt] GEO boğaz; sıkıntı; **~en** *v/t* sıkıştırmak; **~-laced** tutucu

strand [stränd] *n.* sahil; halat kolu; *v/i* karaya oturmak

strange [streync] yabancı; tuhaf, acayip; **~r** yabancı

strangle ['strängl] *v/t* boğmak

strap [sträp] *n.* kayış; atkı; *v/t* kayışla bağlamak

strateg||ic [strı'tîcik] stratejik; **~y** ['strätici] strateji

straw [strô] saman; **~berry** BOT çilek

stray [strey] *adj.* başı boş; *v/i* yoldan sapmak

streak [strîk] *n.* çizgi; iz; *v/t* çizgilemek; **~y** çizgili

stream [strîm] *n.* çay, dere; ırmak; akıntı; *v/i* akmak; dalgalanmak

street [strît] sokak, cadde; **~car** *Am.* tramvay

strength [strenth] kuvvet, güç; **~en** *v/t* kuvvetlendirmek; desteklemek

strenuous ['strenyuıs] faal gayretli

stress [stres] *n.* baskı; tazyik; gayret; GR vurgu; *v/t* vurgulamak

stretch [streç] *n.* uzanma; geniş yer; süre; *v/t* germek, uzatmak; *v/i* gerilmek, uzanmak; **~er** teskere, sedye

strew [struu] *v/t* serpmek, dağıtmak; **~n** *s.* strew

stricken ['strıkın] uğramış (with **-e**); *s.* strike

strict [strikt] sıkı; kesin

strid||den ['stridn] *s.* stride; **~e** [strayd] *v/i* uzun adımlarla yürümek; *n.* uzun adım

strife [strayf] çekişme

strike [strayk] *n.* vurma; grev; *v/i* grev yapmak; çalmak; *v/t* vurmak, çarpmak; **~er** *flag:* indirmek **-i match:** çakmak **-i;** coin kesmek **-i;** oil, etc.: bulmak **-i; ~ off, out** *v/t* listeden çıkarmak; **~r** grevci

striking ['straykiŋ] göze çarpan, şaşılacak

string [striŋ] *n.* ip, sicim, kordon; dizi; tel; *v/t* dizmek; tel takmak *-e*; **~bean** fasulye; **~y** ['-ŋi] lifli; kılçıklı

strip [strip] *n.* şerit; *v/t* soymak, sıyırmak; *v/i* soyunmak

stripe [strayp] *n.* çizgi, kumaş yolu; *v/t* çizgilemek

strive [strayv] uğraşmak, çalışmak (**for** *-meğe*); **~n** ['strivn] *s.* **strive**

strode [strud] *s.* **stride**

stroke [struk] *n.* vuruş, çarpma; çizgi; MED inme; *v/t* okşamak

stroll [strul] *v/i* gezinmek; *n.* gezme

strong [stroŋ] sağlam; kuvvetli; şiddetli; **~hold** kale; *fig.* merkez; **~room** hazine odası

strove [struv] *s.* **strive**

struck [strak] *s.* **strike**

structure ['strakçı] yapı; yapılış

struggle ['stragl] *n.* savaş; çaba; *v/i* çabalamak; uğraşmak (**against** ile)

strung [straŋ] *s.* **string**

strut [strat] *v/i* baba hindi gibi gezmek

stub [stab] kütük

stubble ['stabl] anız; uzamış tıraş

stubborn ['stabın] inatçı; sert

stuck [stak] *s.* **stick**

stud [stad] *n.* çivi; düğme; *v/t* çivilerle süslemek

student ['styûdınt] öğrenci; araştırıcı; **~io** ['-diıu] stüdyo; **~ious** ['-dıys] çalışkan; dikkatli; **~y** ['stadi] *n.* tahsil, öğrenim; tetkik; çalışma; çalışma odası; *v/t* tahsil etm.; araştırmak

stuff [staf] *n.* madde; malzeme; kumaş; boş laf; *v/t* doldurmak; **~ing** dolma (içi); **~y** havasız, küf kokulu

stumble ['stambl] *n.* sürçme; hata; *v/i* sürçmek; rastlamak (**across, upon** *-e*)

stump [stamp] *n.* kütük; *v/i* tahta ayaklı gibi yürümek

stun [stan] *v/t* sersemletmek

stung [staŋ] *s.* **sting**

stunk [staŋk] *s.* **stink**

stunning ['staniŋ] hayret verici

stunt [stant] hüner gösterisi; **~ man** dublör

stupefy ['styûpifay] *v/t* sersemletmek

stupid ['styûpid] budala, akılsız; **~ity** aptallık

stupor ['styûpı] uyuşukluk

sturdy ['stıdi] kuvvetli

stutter ['statı] *n.* kekeleme; *v/i* kekelemek

sty[1] [stay] domuz ahırı

sty[2] MED arpacık

style [stayl] tarz, üslûp; moda; **~ish** zarif, modaya uygun

suave [swâf] tatlı, nazik

sub|- [sab, sıb] ast, alt; **~conscious** ['sab-] bilinçaltı

subdivision ['sab-] parselleme; alt bölüm

subdue [sıb'dyû] *v/t* zaptetmek; hafifletmek

subject ['sabcikt] *n.* konu; POL uyruk, tebaa; GR özne; *adj.* tabi, bağlı (**to** *-e*); [sıb-'cekt] *v/t* maruz kılmak (**to** *-e*); **~ion** [sıb'cekşın] hüküm altına alma

subjunctive (**mood**) [sıb-'cantiv] GR şart kipi

sublime [sı'blaym] yüce, ulu

submarine [sab-] NAUT denizaltı

submerge [sıb'mɜc] *v/t* batırmak; *v/i* batmak

submissi|on [sıb'mişın] boyun eğme; **~ve** uysal, boyun eğen

submit [sıb'mit] *v/t* teslim etm. (**to** *-e*); sunmak (*-e*); *v/i* boyun eğmek, itaat etm. (**to** *-e*)

subordinate [sı'bôdnit] ikincil; ast memur; **~ clause** GR bağımlı cümlecik

subpoena [sıb'pînı] JUR mahkemeye davet

subscribe [sıb'skrayb] *v/t* imzalamak; bağışlamak; *v/i* abone olm. (**to** *-e*); **~r** abone (olan)

subscription [sıb'skripşın] imza; abone; üye aidatı

subsequent ['sabsikwınt] sonra gelen; **~ly** sonradan

subsid|e [sıb'sayd] *v/i* inmek; yatışmak; bağlı; **~ize** ['sabsidayz] *v/t* para vermek -*e*; **~y**

['sabsidi] para yardımı

subsist [sıb'sist] *v/i* beslenmek (**on** ile); **~ence** geçinim; nafaka

substance ['sabstıns] madde, cevher; öz

substantial [sıb'stänşıl] gerçek; önemli; zengin

substantive ['sabstıntiv] GR isim, ad

substitut|e ['sabstityût] *n.* bedel; vekil; *v/t* yerine koymak (**for** *-in*); *v/i* yerine geçmek; **~ion** ikame, yerine koyma

subterrane|an, **~ous** [sabtı'reynyın, -yıs] yeraltı; gizli

subtle ['satl] ince; kurnaz

subtract [sıb'träkt] *v/t* MATH çıkarmak

suburb ['sabıb] varoş, banliyö; **~an** [sı'bɜbın] banliyö ile ilgili

subvention [sıb'venşın] para yardımı

subversi|on [sab'vɜşın] devirme; ifsat; **~ve** yıkıcı

subway ['sabwey] tünel; *Am.* yeraltı metro

succeed [sık'sîd] *v/i* başarmak (**in** *-i*); vâris olm. (**to** *-e*), (*-in*) yerine geçmek

success [sık'ses] başarı; **~ful** başarılı; **~ive** ardıl, müteakip; **~or** halef, ardıl

succumb [sı'kam] dayanamamak (**to** *-e*)

such [saç] böyle, öyle; bu gibi; **~ as** gibi; örneğin

suck [sak] *v/t* emmek, içine

çekmek; ~le v/t emzirmek;
meme vermek -e; ~ling me-
mede çocuk

sudden ['sʌdn] anî, birden;
all of a ~, ~ly birdenbire,
ansızın

suds [sʌdz] pl. sabun köpüğü
sg.

sue [syû] v/i istemek (for -i);
v/t dava açmak (so. -in aley-
hine)

suède [sweyd] (podü)süet

suet ['syut] iç yağı

suffer ['sʌfı] v/t katlanmak -e;
v/i tutulmuş olm. (from -e);
~ance müsamaha; ~ing acı,
ıstırap

suffic|e [sı'fays] kâfi gelmek,
yetmek; ~ient [-'fişınt] kâfi,
yeterli

suffix ['safiks] GR sonek

suffocate ['safıkeyt] v/t boğmak; v/t boğulmak

suffrage ['safric] oy kullanma (hakkı)

sugar ['şugı] n. şeker; v/t
şeker katmak -e; ~cane
şekerkamışı

suggest [sı'cest] v/t telkin
etm.; ileri sürmek; önermek;
~ion teklif; ima; ~ive manalı;
müstehcen

suicide ['syuisayd] intihar;
kendini öldüren kimse

suit [syût] n. takım; erkek elbisesi; tayyör; JUR dava; v/t
uygun gelmek, yaramak -e;
~able uygun, elverişli (for,
to -e); ~case bavul, valiz;
~e [swît] maiyet; oda takımı;

~or ['syûtı] JUR davacı; âşık

sulk [salk] somurtmak; ~y somurtkan

sullen ['salın] asık yüzlü, somurtkan; kapanık

sulphur ['salfı] CHEM kükürt

sultry ['saltri] sıcak, boğucu;
tutkulu

sum [sam] tutar; yekûn; miktar; ~ up v/t özetlemek; hüküm vermek (so. b. hakkında)

summar|ize ['samırayz] v/t
özetlemek; ~y özet, hulâsa

summer ['samı] yaz; ~resort
sayfiye

summit ['samit] zirve, doruk

summon ['samın] v/t çağırmak; ~s ['-z] pl. JUR celpname, çağrı

sumptuous ['samtyus] tan-
tanalı

sun [san] n. güneş; v/t güneş-
lendirmek; v/i güneşlenmek;
~bath güneş banyosu;
~beam güneş ışını; ~burn
güneşten yanma; 2day
['-di] pazar (günü)

sundry ['sandri] çeşitli

sunflower BOT ayçiçeği

sung [saŋ] s. sing

sun-glasses pl. güneş göz-
lüğü sg.

sunk [saŋk] s. sink; ~en gö-
mülmüş; çökmüş

sun|ny ['sani] güneşli; neşeli;
~rise gün doğuşu; ~set güneş batması; ~shine güneş
ışığı; ~stroke güneş çarp-
ması

super|- ['syu:pɪ] üst; fazla; **~a-bundant** bol

superb [syu'pɔb] muhteşem

super|**ficial** [syüpɪ'fiʃl] sathî, üstünkörü; **~fluous** [.'pɔfluɪs] fazla, lüzumsuz; **~highway** *Am.* oto yolu; **~human** insanüstü; **~intend** *v/t* kontrol etm.; **~intendent** müfettiş; müdür

superior [syu'pɪɪrɪ] üstün, daha iyi; üst, âmir; **~ity** [.'orɪti] üstünlük

superlative [syu'pɔltiv] GR enüstünlük

super|**man** üst insan; **~market** büyük mağaza; **~natural** doğaüstü; **~scription** yazıt; adres; başlık; **~sonic** PHYS sesten hızlı; **~stition** [.'stɪʃn] boş inan, hurafe; **~stitious** boş şeylere inanan; **~vise** ['.vayz] *v/t* nezaret etm. *-e*; idare etm. *-i*; **~visor** murakıp, denetçi

supper ['sapɪ] akşam yemeği; **the Lord's** ♀ REL kudas

supple ['sapl] kolayca eğilir; uysal

supplement ['saplimɪnt] *n.* ek, zeyil; ['.ment] *v/t* eklemek; **~ary** eklenen; bütünleyici

supplication [sapli'keyʃın] yalvarış

supply [sɪ'play] *n.* gereç, malzeme; ECON arz, sunu; *v/t* sağlamak (*sth. -i*; *so.* with *-e -i*)

support [sɪ'pôt] *n.* dayanak,

destek; yardım; geçim; *v/t* desteklemek; yardım etm. *-e*; beslemek *-i*

suppos|**e** [sɪ'puz] *v/t* farzetmek, zannetmek; **~ition** [sapɪ'zişn] farz; varsayım, ipotez

suppress [sɪ'pres] *v/t* bastırmak; **~ion** bastırma; baskı

suppurate ['sapyuɪreyt] *v/i* cerahat bağlamak

supra- ['syüpɪ] üst; öte

suprem|**acy** [syu'premɪsɪ] üstünlük; egemenlik; **~e** [.'prîm] en yüksek

surcharge ['sɔçâç] *n.* sürşarj; [.'çâc] *v/t* fazla yüklemek, fazla doldurmak; sürşarj basmak *-e*

sure [ʃuɪ] emin (of -*den*): sağlam; muhakkak; **make ~** kanaat getirmek (of, that *-e*); **~ly** elbette; **~ty** [.'.rɪtı] kefil; rehine

surf [sɔf] *n.* çatlayan dalgalar *pl.*; *v/t* **~ the net** internette gezinmek

surface ['sɔfis] yüz, düzey görünüş

surge [sɔc] *n.* büyük dalga; *v/i* dalgalanmak

surg|**eon** ['sɔcɪn] cerrah, operatör; **~ery** cerrahlık; **~ical** cerrahî

surly ['sɔli] gülmez, ters

surmise ['sɔmayz] *n.* zan, sanı; [.'mayz] *v/t* sanmak, zannetmek

surmount [sɔ'maunt] *v/t* üstün gelmek *-e*

surname ['sɜneym] soyadı
surpass [sɜ'pâs] v/t geçmek; üstün olm. *-e*
surplus ['sɜplɪs] fazla, artk
surprise [sɪ'prayz] n. sürpriz; hayret; v/t hayrete düşürmek, şaşırtmak
surrender [sɪ'rendɪ] n. teslim, feragat; v/t teslim etm.; v/i teslim olm. (**to** *-e*)
surround [sɪ'raund] v/t kuşatmak; **~ings** pl. çevre, muhit *sg.*
surtax ['sɜtæks] ek vergi
survey ['sɜvey] n. teftiş; gözden geçirme; mesaha; [*_*'vey] v/t teftiş etm.; yoklamak; mesaha etm.; **~or** [*_*'v-'] mesaha memuru
surviv|al [sɪ'vayvıl] kalım; hayatta kalma; **~e** v/i hayatta kalmak; v/t fazla yaşamak *-den*; **~or** hayatta kalan, kurtulan
susceptible [sɪ'septıbl] has sas, alıngan
suspect ['saspekt] adj., n. şüpheli; [sɪs'pekt] v/t şüphelenmek, kuşkulanmak *-den*
suspend [sɪs'pend] v/t asmak; ertelemek; geçici olarak durdurmak; tart etm.; **~ed** asılı, muallak; **~er** çorap askısı; Am. pantolon askısı
suspens|e [sɪs'pens] muallak kalma; merak; **~ion** asma; (*of payment*) tatil, durdurma
suspici|on [sɪs'pişın] şüphe; **~ous** şüpheli; şüphe verici
sust|ain [sɪs'teyn] v/t destek

lemek; beslemek; katlanmak *-e*; kuvvet vermek *-e*; **~enance** ['sastinıns] besleme, gıda, geçim
SUV [sɪv] (= *sports utility vehicle*) SUV
swagger ['swägı] caka satmak, horozlanmak
swallow[1] ['swolıu] zoo kırlangıç
swallow[2] v/t yutmak, emmek
swam [swäm] s. **swim**
swamp [swämp] n. bataklık; v/t batırmak
swan [swon] zoo kuğu
swarm [swôm] n. sürü, küme; v/i toplanmak; kaynaşmak
swarthy ['swôdhi] esmer
swathe [sweydh] v/t sarmak
sway [swey] n. sallanma; nüfuz; v/i sallanmak; v/t sallamak; etkilemek
swear [swäı] v/i yemin etm.; küfretmek (**at** *-e*); **~ in** v/t yeminle işe başlatmak
sweat [swet] n. ter; v/i terlemek; v/t terletmek; **~er** kazak
Swede [swîd] İsveçli; **~en** İsveç; **~ish** İsveçli; İsveççe
sweep [swîp] n. süpürme; alan; ocakçı; v/t süpürmek, temizlemek; taramak; geçmek; **~er** sokak süpürücü, çöpçü; **~ing** genel, şümullü; **~ings** pl. süprüntü *sg.*
sweet [swît] tatlı, şekerli; hoş; pl. tatlılar, bonbonlar; **~en** v/t tatlılaştırmak; **~heart** sevgili; **~ness** tatlılık

swell [swel] v/i şişmek, kabarmak; v/t şişirmek, kabartmak; *Am. adj.* güzel, âlâ; ~ing kabarık, şişlik

swept [swept] *s.* sweep

swerve [swɜv] yoldan sapmak

swift [swift] çabuk, hızlı; ~ness çabukluk, hız

swim [swim] v/i yüzmek; *head:* dönmek; ~mer yüzücü; ~ming-pool yüzme havuzu

swindle ['swindl] *n.* dolandırıcılık; v/t dolandırmak; ~r dolandırıcı

swine [swayn] domuz

swing [swiŋ] *n.* sallanma; salıncak; v/i sallanmak, salınmak; dönmek; v/t sallamak; ~door iki tarafa açılır kapanır kapı

swirl [swəl] girdap

Swiss [swis] İsviçreli

switch [swiç] *n.* EL düğme; şalter; anahtar; (*rail*) makas; ince değnek; v/t çevirmek; ~ off EL kapamak; ~ on EL açmak; ~board EL anahtar tablosu

Switzerland ['switsılınd] İsviçre

swivel ['swivl] fırdöndü; ~ chair döner iskemle

swollen [swoulın] *s.* swell

swoon [swuun] *n.* bayılma; v/i bayılmak

sword [sôd] kılıç

swor|e [swô], ~n *s.* swear

swum [swam] *s.* swim

swung [swaŋ] *s.* swing

syllable ['silıbl] hece

symbol ['simbıl] sembol, simge; ~ic(al) [-'bolik(ıl)] sembolik, simgesel

symmetry ['simitri] simetri, bakışım

sympath|etic [simpı'thetik] sempatik, sevimli; ~ize yakınlık duymak (**with** -*e*); ~y sempati

symphony ['simfını] MUS senfoni

symptom ['simptım] alâmet, belirti

synagogue ['sinıgog] REL havra

synchronize ['siŋkrınayz] v/t aynı zamana uydurmak

synonym ['sinınim] GR eşanlam, anlamdaş kelime; ~ous [-'nonimıs] anlamdaş

syntax ['sintäks] GR sözdizimi, sentaks

synthe|sis ['sinthisis] bireşim, sentez; ~tic [-'thetik] sentetik

syphilis ['sifilis] MED frengi

Syria ['sirıı] Suriye; ~n Suriyeli

syringe ['sirinc] şırınga

syrup ['sirıp] şekerli sos

system ['sistım] sistem, usul; ~atic [-'mätik] sistemli, usule göre

T

tab [täb] askı; etiket

table ['teybl] masa; sofra; liste, cetvel; tarife; ~**land** GEO plato, yayla; ~**spoon** yemek kaşığı

table ['täblit] komprime, tablet; levha

tacit ['täsit] zimnî; ~**urn** ['‿ǝn] az konuşur

tack [täk] *n.* pünez; teyel dikişi; *v/t* teyellemek

tackle ['täkl] *n.* takım, cihaz; TECH palanga; *v/t* uğraşmak (*sth.* ile)

tact [täkt] incelik, nezaket; ~**ful** ince(likli); ~**ics** *pl.* taktik *sg.*; ~**less** nezaketsiz, kaba

tadpole ['tädpıul] ZOO iribaş

tag [täg] *n.* etiket; *v/t* etiketlemek; *v/i* takılmak (after -*e*)

tail [teyl] kuyruk; arka; son; ~**coat** frak

tailor ['teylı] terzi

taint [teynt] *n.* leke; kusur; *v/t* lekelemek, bozmak

take [teyk] *v/t* almak; kabul etm.; götürmek; yapmak; sürmek; uğramak -*e*; ihtiyacı olm. -*e*; ~ **account** hesaba katmak (of -*i*); ~ **advantage** faydalanmak (of -*den*); ~ **care** bakmak (of -*e*); ~ **hold** tutmak (of -*i*); ~ **in** *v/t* almak; daraltmak; *pop.* aldatmak; ~ **off** *v/t* çıkarmak; *v/i* AVIA ha-

valanmak; ~ **pains** uğraşmak (with ile); ~ **place** vuku bulmak; ~ **to** kendini vermek -*e*, hoşlanmak -*den*; ~**n** *s.* take; ~**off** AVIA havalanma

tale [teyl] masal, hikâye

talent ['tälnt] kabiliyet, yetenek; ~**ed** kabiliyetli, hünerli

talk [tôk] *n.* konuşma; görüşme; laf; *v/i* konuşmak (to ile); *v/t* söylemek, konuşmak; ~ **big** övünmek; ~**ative** ['‿ıtiv] konuşkan

tall [tôl] uzun (boylu); yüksek

tallow ['tälu] donyağı

talon ['täln] ZOO pençe

tame [teym] *adj.* evcil, ehlî; uysal; *v/t* alıştırmak

tamper ['tämpı] karışmak (with -*e*), karıştırmak -*i*

tan [tän] *n.* güneş yanığı; *adj.* açık kahverengi; *v/t* tabaklamak; karartmak

tangent ['täncınt] MATH teğet; ~**ible** dokunulur; gerçek

tangerine [täncı'rîn] BOT mandalina

tangle ['täŋgl] *n.* karışıklık; *v/t* karıştırmak

tank [täŋk] MIL tank; depo, sarnıç

tankard ['täŋkıd] içki maşrapası

tanner ['tänı] tabak, sepici

tantalize ['täntılayz] *v/t* hayal

kırıklığına uğratmak

tantrum ['täntrım] hiddet (nöbeti)

tap [täp] *n.* musluk; fıçı tapası; hafif vuruş; *v/t* hafifçe vurmak *-e*; akıtmak *-i*

tape [teyp] şerit, bant, kurdele; ~ **recorder** teyp; ~ **cording** teype alma; ~**measure** mezür, mezura

taper ['teypı]: ~ **off** *v/i* sivrilmek

tapestry ['täpistri] *n.* goblen

tapeworm bağırsak kurdu

tar [tâ] *n.* katran; *v/t* katranlamak

tare [täı] ECON dara

target ['tâgit] hedef, nişangâh

tariff ['tärif] gümrük tarifesi; fiat listesi

tarnish ['tâniş] *v/i* donuklaşmak; *v/t* donuklaştırmak

tart [tât] ekşi; keskin; turta

task [tâsk] ödev; görev; **take to** ~ *v/t* azarlamak

tassel ['täsıl] püskül

taste [teyst] *n.* tat, lezzet, çeşni; zevk; *v/t -in* tadına bakmak; denemek *-i*; ~**ful** lezzetli; zevkli; ~**less** tatsız; zevksiz

tasty ['teysti] tatlı; zevkli

tatter ['tätı] paçavra

tattoo [tı'tuu] *n.* dövme; MIL yat borusu; *v/t* dövme yapmak *-e*

taught [tôt] *s.* teach

taunt [tônt] *n.* hakaret, alay; *v/t* alay etm. ile

tavern ['tävın] meyhane

tax [täks] *n.* vergi, resim; *v/t* vergi koymak *-e*; ~**ation** vergi tarhı

taxi|(-**cab**) ['täksi(-)] taksi; ~**driver** taksi şoförü

tax|**payer** vergi mükellefi; ~**return** vergi beyannamesi

tea [tî] çay

teach [tîç] *v/t* öğretmek, okutmak; ders vermek *-e*; ~**er** öğretmen

team [tîm] takım, ekip; ~**work** takım halinde çalışma

teapot çaydanlık

tear¹ [tâı] gözyaşı

tear² *n.* yırtık; *v/t* yırtmak, koparmak; *v/i* yırtılmak

tease [tîz] *v/t* tedirgin etm.; takılmak *-e*

teaspoon çay kaşığı

teat [tît] meme, emcik

techni|**cal** ['teknikıl] teknik; resmî; kurallara uygun; ~**cian** [..'nişın] teknisyen, teknikçi; ~**que** [..'nîk] teknik, yapma usulü

tedious ['tîdyıs] usandırıcı, can sıkıcı

teen|**ager** ['tîneycı] on üçten on dokuz yaşlar arasındaki kimse, delikanlı; ~**s** [-z] *pl.* on üç ile on dokuz arasındaki yaşlar

teeny ['tîni] ufak

teetotal(**l**)**er** [tî'tıutıl] içki içmiyen kimse

tele|**gram** ['teligräm] telgraf (-name); ~**graph** ['..grâf] *n.* telgraf; *v/i* telgraf çekmek

telephone ['telifıun] *n.* telefon; *v/t* telefon etm. *-e;* ~ **call** telefon çağırması; ~ **exchange** santral

tele|printer ['teliprinti] teleks; ~**scope** [‑'skıup] teleskop; ~**vision** ['‑vijın] televizyon

tell [tel] *v/t* söylemek, anlatmak, bildirmek (*so. -e*); ~**er** veznedar; ~**tale** dedikoducu; belli eden

temper ['tempı] *n.* tabiat; huy, mizaç; öfke; *v/t* ayarlamak, hafifletmek; TECH tavlamak; **lose one's ~** hiddetlenmek; ~**ament** ['‑rımınt] mizaç, tabiat; ~**ance** ölçülülük; içkiden kaçınma; ~**ate** ['‑rit] ılımlı; içkiden kaçınan; ~**ature** ['‑priçi] sıcaklık; ısı derecesi

tempest ['tempist] fırtına, bora; ~**uous** [‑'pestyuıs] fırtınalı

temple¹ ['templ] REL mabet, tapınak

temple² ANAT şakak

temporal ['tempırıl] geçici; REL dünyevi; ~**ary** geçici

tempt [tempt] *v/t* baştan çıkarmak, ayartmak; ~**ation** günaha teşvik; ~**ing** çekici

ten [ten] on

tenacious [ti'neyşıs] inatçı, vazgeçmez

tenant ['tenınt] kiracı

tend [tend] *v/t* bakmak *-e;* *v/i* meyletmek, yönelmek (**to** *-e*); ~**ency** meyil, eğilim

tender¹ ['tendı] tender

tender² *n.* teklif; *v/t* sunmak

tender³ nazik, şefkatli; ~**loin** fileto; ~**ness** şefkat

tendon ['tendın] ANAT veter, kiriş

tendril ['tendril] BOT asma filizi

tenement ['tenimınt] apartman; kiralık daire

tennis ['tenis] tenis; ~**court** kort, tenis alanı

tenor ['tenı] gidiş; yön; MUS tenor

tens|e [tens] gergin, gerili; gr. fiil zamanı; ~**ion** gerginlik; EL gerilim

tent [tent] çadır

tentacle ['tentıkl] ZOO kavrama uzvu

tentative ['tentıtiv] deneme, tecrübe

tepid ['tepid] ılık

term [tım] *n.* terim; süre; şart; sömestr; dönem; *v/t* adlandırmak; **bring to ~s** *v/t* razı etm.; **on good ~s** araları iyi

termin|al ['tımınl] son; terminal; ~**ate** ['‑eyt] *v/t* bitirmek; sınırlamak; ~**ation** son, bitirme; ~**us** ['‑nıs] terminal

terrace ['terıs] taraça, teras

terri|ble ['terıbl] korkunç, dehşetli; ~**fic** [ri'rifik] korkunç; *pop.* çok güzel; ~**fy** ['terıfay] *v/t* korkutmak, dehşete düşürmek

territor|ial [teri'törııl] karaya ait; belirli bir bölgeye ait; ~**y** ['‑tırı] ülke; bölge; arazi

terror ['terı] korku, dehşet; **~ism** tedhişçilik; **~ist** tedhişçi

test [test] *n*. deney, tecrübe; test; *v/t* denemek, prova etm.; imtihan etm.

testament ['testımınt] vasiyetname

testify ['testifay] *v/i* şehadette bulunmak; *v/t* kanıtlamak

testimon|ial [testi'miunyıl] bonservis; belge; **~y** ['.mini] tanıklık, şahadet

testy ['testi] ters, hırçın

text [tekst] metin; konu; kısa mesaj; *v/t* kısa mesaj göndermek; **~book** ders kitabı

textile ['tekstayl] dokuma; tekstil; *pl.* mensucat

text-message ['tekst.] kısa mesaj

texture ['-çı] doku; örgü; yapı

than [dhän, dhın] *-den* daha

thank [thänk] *v/t* teşekkür etm. *-e*; **~ God** Allaha şükür; **~s** *pl.* teşekkür; şükür; **~s to** sayesinde; **~ful** minnettar; **Ҫsgiving Day** *Am.* şükran yortusu

that [dhät, dhıt] şu, o; ki; **~ is** yani

thatch [thäç] *n.* dam örtüsü olarak kullanılan saman veya saz; *v/t* sazla kaplamak

thaw [thô] *n.* erime; *v/t* eritmek; *v/i* erimek

the [dhı, dhî] (*belirtme edatı*)

~ ... ~ ne kadar ... o kadar

theat|re, *Am.* **~er** ['thiıtı] tiyatro

thee [dhî] seni; sana

theft [theft] hırsızlık

their [dhäı] onların; **~s** [.z] onlarınki

them [dhem, dhım] onları, onlara

theme [thîm] konu

themselves [dhım'selvz] kendileri (ni, -ne, -nde)

then [dhen] ondan sonra; o zaman; şu halde; **by ~** o zamana kadar; **~ce** oradan; bundan dolayı

theology [thi'olıci] ilâhiyat, teoloji

theor|etic(al) [thiı'retik(ıl)] kuramsal, nazarî; **~y** ['.ri] teori, kuram

therapy ['therıpi] MED tedavi

there [dhäı] ora(sı); orada; oraya; **~ is**, *pl.* **~ are** vardır; **~about(s)** o civarda; **~after** ondan sonra; **~by** o suretle; **~fore** onun için, bundan dolayı; **~upon** onun üzerine; **~with** onunla

therm|al ['thımıl] sıcağa ait; termal; **~ometer** [thı'momitı] termometre; **~os** ['thımos] (*bottle, flask*) termos

these [dhîz] bunlar

thesis ['thîsis] tez; dava

they [dhey] onlar

thick [thik] kalın; sık; kesif; **~en** *v/t* kalınlaştırmak; *v/i* kalınlaşmak; **~et** ['.it] çalılık; **~ness** kalınlık; sıklık

thief [thîf] hırsız

thigh [thay] ANAT uyluk, but

thimble ['thimbl] yüksük

thin [thin] *adj.* ince, zayıf; az; *v/t* inceltmek; *v/i* incelmek

thing [thiŋ] şey, nesne

think [thiŋk] *v/i* düşünmek (about *-i*); *v/t* düşünmek; zannetmek; tasavvur etm.; ~ of hatırlamak *-i*; saymak *-i*; ~ over *v/t -in* üzerinde düşünmek

third [thəd] üçüncü; üçte bir

thirst [thəst] *n.* susuzluk; *v/i* susamak (after, for *-e*); ~y susuz, susamış

thirteen [thəˈtin] on üç; ~y otuz

this [dhis] bu

thistle [ˈthisl] вот devedikeni

thither [ˈdhidhə] oraya

thorn [thôn] diken; ~y dikenli

thorough [ˈthar] tam, mükemmel; ~bred saf kan, soylu; ~fare cadde; geçit

those [dhuz] şunlar, onlar

thou [dhau] sen

though [dhau] gerçi, her ne kadar, -diği halde; as ~ -miş gibi

thought [thôt] düşünme; düşünce; fikir; s. think; ~ful düşünceli; saygılı; ~less düşüncesiz; dikkatsiz

thousand [ˈthauzınd] bin

thrash [thräş] *v/t* dövmek; dayak atmak -*e*; ~ing dayak

thread [thred] *n.* iplik, tire; тесн yiv; *v/t* ipliğe dizmek; yol bulup geçmek; ~bare eskimiş, yıpranmış

threat [thret] tehdit; tehlike; ~en *v/t* tehdit etm.; ~ening tehdit edici

three [thrî] üç; ~fold üç misli; ~score altmış

thresh [threş] *v/t* harman dövmek; ~er, ~ing-machine harman dövme makinası

threshold [ˈthreshuld] eşik

threw [thruu] s. throw

thrice [thrays] üç kere

thrifty [ˈthrifti] tutumlu, idareli

thrill [thril] *n.* titreme; heyecan; *v/t* heyecanlandırmak; *v/i* heyecanla titremek; ~er heyecanlı kitap *veya* piyes

thrive [thrayv] iyi gitmek, gelişmek; ~n [ˈthrivn] s. thrive

throat [thrut] boğaz, gırtlak

throb [throb] *v/i* çarpmak; titreşmek

throne [thrun] that

throng [throŋ] *n.* kalabalık; *v/i* toplanmak

throstle [ˈthrosl] zoo ardıçkuşu

throttle [ˈthrotl] *v/t* boğmak; kısmak; ~(-valve) тесн kısma valfı; kelebek

through [thruu] arasından, içinden; bir yandan öbür yana; baştan başa; bitirmiş; ~ carriage direkt vagon; ~out *-in* her tarafında; baştan başa

throve [thruv] s. thrive

throw [thru] *n.* atış; *v/t* atmak, fırlatmak; ~ off çıkarmak, üstünden atmak; ~ up yukarı atmak; kusmak

thrush [thraş] zoo ardıçkuşu

thrust [thrast] *n.* itiş; hamle; *v/t* itmek, dürtmek

thud [thad] *n.* gümbürtü; *v/i* güm diye ses çıkarmak

thumb [tham] başparmak; *v/t* aşındırmak; ~ a ride otostop yapmak; ~tack *Am.* pünez

thump [thamp] *n.* vuruş; ağır düşüş; *v/t* vurmak -*e*; *v/i* hızla çarpmak

thunder ['thandı] *n.* gök gürlemesi; *v/i* gürlemek; ~storm gök gürültülü yağmur fırtınası; ~struck *fig.* hayrete düşmüş

Thursday ['thɜzdi] perşembe

thus [dhas] böyle(ce), bu suretle

thwart [thwôt] *v/t* bozmak, önlemek

thy [dhay] senin

thyme [taym] вот kekik

tick¹ [tik] zoo kene

tick² *n.* tıkırtı; *v/i* tıkırdamak; ~ off *v/t* işaretliyerek saymak

tick³ kılıf

ticket ['tikit] *n.* bilet; aday listesi; etiket; *v/t* etiketlemek; ~-office *Am.*, ~-window bilet gişesi

tickle ['tikl] *v/i* gıdıklanmak; *v/t* gıdıklamak; ~ish gıdıklanır; *fig.* nazik

tidal ['taydl] GEO gelgite bağlı; ~e [tayd] gelgit, met ve cezir; *fig.* akış

tidy ['taydi] temiz, düzenli; *pop.* epey; ~ up *v/t* düzeltmek

tie [tay] *n.* bağ; kravat; travers;

v/t bağlamak

tier [tiı] sıra, kat

tiger ['taygı] zoo kaplan

tight [tayt] sıkı; su geçirmez; müşkül; *pop.* sarhoş; ~en *v/t* sıkıştırmak; *v/i* sıkışmak; ~rope sıkı gerilmiş ip; ~s *pl.* sıkı giysi *sg.*; külotlu çorap

Tigris ['taygris] Dicle

tile [tayl] *n.* kiremit; çini; *v/t* kiremit kaplamak -*e*

till¹ [til] -*e* kadar, -*e* değin

till² para çekmecesi

till³ *v/t* toprağı işlemek

tilt¹ [tilt] tente

tilt² devrilmek; *v/t* eğmek

timber ['timbı] kereste; kerestelik orman

time [taym] *n.* vakit, zaman; süre; defa; mus tempo; *v/t* ayarlamak; uydurmak; ölçmek; for the ~ being şimdilik; in ~ vaktinde; in no ~ bir an evvel; on ~ tam zamanında; ~ly uygun, yerinde; ~table tarife

timid ['timid], ~orous ['~ırıs] sıkılgan, ürkek

tin [tin] *n.* teneke; kalay; teneke kutu; *v/t* kalaylamak; kutulara doldurmak

tinge [tinc] *n.* hafif renk, iz; *v/t* hafifçe boyamak

tingle ['tingl] sızlamak

tinkle ['tinkl] *v/i* çınlamak; *v/t* çıngırdatmak

tint [tint] *n.* hafif renk; *v/t* hafif boyamak

tiny ['tayni] ufak, minicik

tip 414

tip [tip] n. uç; ağızlık; bahşiş; tavsiye; v/t bahşiş vermek -e; eğmek -i; v/i devrilmek; ~ **off** v/t imada bulunmak -e

tipsy ['tipsi] çakırkeyf

tiptoe ['tiptou] ayak parmağının ucu; **on** ~ ayak parmaklarının ucuna basarak

tire[1] ['tayı] s. **tyre**

tire[2] v/t yormak; usandırmak; v/i yorulmak; ~**d** yorgun; bıkmış (**of** -den); ~**some** yorucu

tissue ['tişuu] doku; ince kâğıt

tit[1] [tit] baştankara

tit[2]: ~ **for tat** kısasa kısas

titbit ['titbit] lezzetli lokma

title ['taytl] unvan; isim; hak

titmouse ['titmaus] zoo baştankara

to [tuu, tu, tı] **1.** (*mastar edatı*); **2.** -e (-a, -ye, -ya); -mek için; ~ **and fro** öteye beriye

toad [tud] zoo kara kurbağa

toast[1] [tıust] n. kızartılmış ekmek; v/t ekmek kızartmak

toast[2] n sıhhatine içme; v/t -in şerefine içmek

tobacco [tı'bäkıu] tütün; ~**nist** [_-kınist] tütüncü

toboggan [tı'bogın] kızak

today [tı'dey] bugün

toe [tıu] ayak parmağı; uç

together [tı'gedhı] birlikte; aralıksız

toil [toyl] n. zahmet; v/i zahmet çekmek

toilet ['toylit] tuvalet, aptes-

hane; ~**paper** tuvalet kâğıdı

token ['tuukın] belirti; hatıra

told [tuuld] s. **tell**

tolera|ble ['tolırıbl] dayanılabilir; ~**nce** müsamaha; ~**nt** müsamahakâr; ~**te** ['-eyt] v/t müsamaha etm. -e; katlanmak -e; ~**tion** müsamade; hoşgörü

toll[1] [tuul] v/t, v/i çalmak

toll[2] yol *veya* köprü parası, resim; ~**bar**, ~**gate** bariyer

tomato [tı'mâtu] domates

tomb [tuum] kabir; türbe; ~**stone** mezar taşı

tomcat ['tom'kät] erkek kedi

tomorrow [tı'moru] yarın

ton [tan] ton (*1016 kilo, Am. 907 kilo*)

tone [tıun] ses; mus ton

tongs [tonz] pl. maşa *sg.*

tongue [tan] dil, lisan

tonic ['tonik] ilâç, tonik

tonight [tı'nayt] bu gece

tonnage ['tanic] tonilato, tonaj

tonsil ['tonsl] ANAT bademcik; ~**itis** [_-si'laytis] MED bademcik iltihabı

too [tuu] dahi, keza; (haddinden) fazla

took [tuk] s. **take**

tool [tuul] alet

tooth [tuuth] diş; ~**ache** diş ağrısı; ~**brush** diş fırçası; ~**paste** diş macunu; ~**pick** kürdan

top [top] n. üst, zirve, tepe; en yüksek nokta; v/t kapamak; üstün gelmek -den, -in birin-

cisi olm.; **on (the)** ~ **of** -*in* üstünde; ~ **secret** çok gizli
topic ['topik] konu
topple ['topl] *v/i* devrilmek;
v/t devirmek
topsy-turvy ['topsi'tɜvi] altüst; karmakarışık
torch [tɔtʃ] meşale; cep feneri
tore [tɔ] *s*. tear²
torment ['tɔment] *n*. cefa,
eziyet; *v/t* eziyet etm. -*e*
torn [tɔn] *s*. tear²
tornado [tɔ'neydıu] kasırga
torpedo [tɔ'pîdıu] *n*. torpil;
v/t torpillemek
torpid ['tɔpid] uyuşuk
torrent ['torınt] sel
tortoise ['tɔtıs] zoo kaplumbağa
torture ['tɔtʃı] *n*. işkence; *v/t*
işkence etm. -*e*
Tory ['tɔri] POL tutucu parti
üyesi
toss [tos] *n*. atma, fırlatma;
v/t atmak, fırlatmak; ~ **about**
v/i çalkanmak
total ['tiutl] *n*. tutar, yekûn;
adj. tam, bütün; *v/t* toplamak; tutmak; ~**itarian** [_tä-
li'täriın] POL totaliter
totter ['totı] sendelemek
touch [tatʃ] *n*. dokunma; temas; iz; *v/t* dokunmak -*e*, ellemek -*i*; ~ **down** *v/i* inmek;
~**ing** dokunaklı; ~**y** alıngan;
titiz
tough [taf] sert; çetin; dayanıklı
tour [tuı] *n*. gezi; tur; *v/i*, *v/t*
gezmek; ~**ism** ['_rizım] tu-

---

rizm; ~**ist** turist; ~**nament**
['_nımınt] turnuva, yarışma
tousle ['tauzl] *v/t* saçı karıştırmak
tow [tıu] *n*. yedekte çek(il)-
me; *v/t* çekmek; **have, take
in** ~ *v/t* yedekte çekmek
toward(s) [tı'wɔd(z)] -*e* doğru; -*e* karşı
towel ['tauıl] havlu
tower ['tauı] *n*. kule, burç; *v/i*
yükselmek
town [taun] şehir, kasaba; ~
hall belediye binası
tow-rope yedek halatı
toy [toy] *n*. oyuncak; *v/i* oynamak
trace [treys] *n*. iz; *v/t* izlemek;
kopya etm.
track [träk] *n*. iz; pist; yol; ray;
v/t izlemek; ~ **down**, ~ **out** iz-
liyerek bulmak; ~**-and-field**
atletizm
tract [träkt] risale; bölge; alan
tract|ion [ä'träksın] çekme;
~**or** traktör
trade [treyd] *n*. ticaret; meslek, iş; *v/i* ticaret yapmak
(**in** ile); ~**mark** alâmeti farika, marka; ~**r** tüccar; ~**union**
sendika; ~**unionist** sendikacı
tradition [trı'dişın] gelenek,
anane; ~**al** geleneksel
traffic ['träfik] *n*. gidişgeliş,
trafik; ticaret, trampa; *v/i* ticaret yapmak; ~ **jam** trafik
tıkanıklığı; ~ **sign** trafik işareti
trag|edy ['träcidi] trajedi; fa-

cia; ~ic(al) feci; acıklı

trail [treyl] n. kuyruk; iz; yol; v/t peşinden sürüklemek; izlemek; v/i sürüklenmek; ~er römork; treyler

train [treyn] n. tren; maiyet; sıra; yerde sürünen uzun etek; v/t öğretmek, alıştırmak; talim etm.; ~er antrenör; talim; antrenman

trait [trey] özellik

traitor ['treytı] hain

tram(-car) [träm(-)] tramvay (vagonu)

tramp [trämp] n. serseri; NAUT tarifesiz işliyen yük gemisi; avare gezme; ağır adım ve sesi; v/i avare dolaşmak; v/t ayak altında çiğnemek; ~le v/t çiğnemek, ezmek

tramway tramvay

tranquil ['tränkwil] sakin, asude; ~(l)ity sükûn; ~(l)izer yatıştırıcı (ilâç)

transact [trän'zäkt] v/t bitirmek, iş görmek; ~ion iş, muamele

transalpine ['tränz'älpayn] GEO Alplerin ötesinde bulunan; ~atlantic Atlantık aşırı; ~continental kıtayı kateden

transcribe [träns'krayb] v/t kopya etm.

transcript ['tränskript] ikinci nüsha, kopya; ~ion transkripsiyon

transfer [träns'fö:] n. nakil; transfer; aktarma bileti; [-'fö:] v/t nakletmek; devretmek; havale etm.; v/i aktarma yapmak; ~able [-'förıbl] devredilebilir

transform [träns'fôm] v/t başka kalıba sokmak; -in şeklini değiştirmek; tahvil etm. -i; ~ation dönüş(tür)üm; şekil değişmesi; ~er EL transformatör

transfuse [träns'fyûz] v/t aktarmak; ~ion [-_jın] aktarma; MED kan nakli

transgress [träns'gres] v/t bozmak; çiğnemek; aşmak; ~ion haddi aşma; suç; ~or tecavüz eden

transient ['tränziınt] geçici; kısa zaman kalan misafir

transistor [trän'sistı] EL transistor

transit ['tränsit] geçme; ECON transit; ~ion [-'sijın] geçiş; ~ive GR geçişli

translate [träns'leyt] v/t çevirmek, tercüme etm.; ~ion çeviri, tercüme; ~or çevir(m)en

translucent [trä nz'luusnt] yarı şeffaf

transmission [tränz'mişın] nakil; intikal; yayım

transmit [tränz'mit] v/t geçirmek; göndermek; yayımlamak; ~ter yayım istasyonu

transparent [träns'päırınt] şeffaf, saydam

transpire [träns'payı] v/i terlemek; fig. duyulmak, sızmak

transplant [träns'plânt] v/t başka yere dikmek veya yerleştirmek; ~(ation) nakil

transport [träns'pôt] v/t götürmek, nakletmek, taşımak; ['_] n. nakil; taşınma; taşıt; ulaştırma; ~ation nakil; taşıt

trap [träp] n. tuzak; kapanca; v/t tuzağa düşürmek, yakalamak; ~door kapak şeklinde kapı; ~pet tuzakçı

trash [träş] değersiz şey, süprüntü; değersiz adam; ayaktakımı

travel [′trävl] n. yolculuk, seyahat; v/i seyahat etm.; v/t dolaşmak; ~(l)er yolcu; ~(l)er's cheque (Am. check) seyahat çeki

traverse [′trävəs] v/t karşıdan karşıya geçirmek; katetmek

trawl [trôl] n. tarak ağı; v/i tarak ağı ile balık tutmak

tray [trey] tepsi; tabla

treacherlous [′treçırıs] hain, güvenilmez; ~y hainlik

treacle [′trîkl] şeker pekmezi

tread [tred] n. ayak basışı; v/i ayakla basmak (on -e); çiğnemek (-i); ~le pedal; ~mill ayak değirmeni; fig. sıkıcı iş

treason [′trîzn] hainlik

treasure [′treji] n. hazine; v/t biriktirmek; değerli tutmak; ~r haznedar

treasury [′trejiri] hazne; ♀ Department Am. Maliye Bakanlığı

treat [trît] n. zevk; ikram; v/t ikram etm. -e (to sth. -i); muamele etm. -e (to); tedavi etm. -i;

v/i bahsetmek (of -den); ~ise [′_iz] risale; ~ment muamele; tedavi; ~y antlaşma

treble [′trebl] üç kat, üç misli; v/i üç misli olm.; v/t üç kat etm.

tree [trî] ağaç

trefoil [′trefoyl] BOT yonca

trellis [′trelis] kafes işi

tremble [′trembl] titremek (with -den)

tremendous [tri'mendıs] kocaman; heybetli

tremlor [′tremı] titreme; sarsıntı; ~ulous [′_yulıs] titrek; ürkek

trench [trenç] hendek, siper

trend [trend] yön, eğilim (towards -e)

trespass [′trespıs] n. günah, suç; v/i tecavüz etm. (on, upon -e), bozmak (-i)

tress [tres] bukle; saç örgüsü

trestle [′tresl] sehpa

trial [′trayıl] deneme, tecrübe; JUR muhakeme, duruşma

triang|le [′trayängl] üçgen; ~ular [_′ängyulı] üçgen şeklinde

tribe [trayb] kabile, aşiret

tribulation [tribyu'leyşın] keder, sıkıntı

tribun|al [tray'byûnl] mahkeme; ~e [′tribyûn] **1.** halkı savunan; **2.** tribün

tributlary [′tribyutıri] nehir kolu; ~e [′_yût] haraç, vergi; takdir

trick [trik] n. oyun, hile, düzen; v/t aldatmak; **play a ~**

oyun oynamak (**on** -*e*)

trickle ['trikl] *v/i* damla damla akmak; *v/t* akıtmak

tricky ['triki] hileli

trif|le ['trayfl] *n.* önemsiz şey; az miktar; *v/i* oynamak; **~ing** önemsiz

trigger ['trigı] tetik

trill [tril] *n.* ses titremesi; *v/i* sesi titretmek

trillion ['trilyın] trilyon; *Am.* bilyon

trim [trim] *adj.* biçimli, şık; *v/t* düzeltmek; süslemek; kısaltmak; denkleştirmek

Trinity ['triniti] REL teslis

trinket ['trinkit] değersiz süs

trip [trip] *n.* gezinti, kısa seyahat; tur; *v/i* sürçmek; hata yapmak

tripe [trayp] işkembe

triple ['tripl] üç misli; üçlü; **~ts** ['-its] *pl.* üçüzler

tripod ['traypod] sehpa

Tripoli ['triplī] Trablusgarp; Trablusşam

triumph ['trayımf] *n.* zafer, galebe; zafer alayı; *v/i* yenmek (**over** -*i*); **~ant** galip, muzaffer

trivial ['trivil] ufak tefek, önemsiz

trod [trod], **~den** *s.* **tread**

troll(e)y ['troli] yük arabası; tekerlekli servis masası; troleybüs

troop [truup] *n.* takım, sürü; *pl.* askerler; *v/i* bir araya toplanmak

trophy ['trıufi] ganimet; hatı-ra

tropic ['tropik] GEO tropika, dönence; *pl.* sıcak ülkeler; **~al** tropikal

trot [trot] *n.* tırıs; *v/i* tırıs gitmek; koşmak

trouble ['trabl] *n.* sıkıntı, zahmet; dert, keder; rahatsızlık; *v/t* rahatsız etm.; sıkmak; *v/i* zahmet çekmek; **ask for ~** belâ aramak; **~maker** mesele çıkaran; **~some** zahmetli, sıkıntılı

through [trof] tekne, yalak

trousers ['trauzız] *pl.* pantolon *sg.*

trousseau ['truusıu] çeyiz

trout [traut] ZOO alabalık

truant ['truınt] dersi asan

truce [truus] ateşkes, mütareke

truck[1] [trak] el arabası; üstü açık yük vagonu; kamyon

truck[2] *Am.* sebze

trudge [trac] zahmetle yürümek

true [truu] doğru, gerçek; sahih; halis; sadık; **come ~** gerçekleşmek

truly ['truuli] *adv.* gerçekten; samimî olarak

trump [tramp] *n.* koz; *v/i* koz çıkarmak

trumpet ['trampit] MUS boru; boru sesi

truncheon ['trançın] polis sopası

trunk [trank] bavul; gövde; ZOO hortum; TEL ana hat; *Am.* kısa don; erkek mayosu;

~call şehirlerarası telefon

trust [trast] *n.* güven; emanet; ECON tröst; *v/t* güvenmek *-e;* emanet etm. *-e* (**with** *-i*); **~ee** [.'tî] mutemet, vekil; **~ful,** **~ing** güvenen; **~worthy** güvenilir

truth [truuth] doğruluk, hakikat; **~ful** doğru; gerçek

try [tray] *v/t* denemek, tecrübe etm.; JUR yargılamak, muhakeme etm.; *v/i* uğraşmak; *n.* deneme, tecrübe; **~ing** yorucu

tub [tab] tekne; fıçı; küvet

tube [tyûb] boru; tüp; iç lastik; yeraltı metro

tuberculosis [tyubəkyû'luusis] tüberküloz, verem

tuck [tak] *v/t* sokmak, sıkıştırmak; **~ up** sıvamak

Tuesday [tyûzdi] salı

tuft [taft] küme; sorguç; püskül

tug [tag] *n.* kuvvetli çekiş; NAUT römorkör; *v/t* şiddetle çekmek

tuition [tyû'işın] öğretim

tulip [tyûlip] BOT lâle

tumble [tambl] *v/i* düşmek, devrilmek; *v/t* düşürmek; **~r** bardak

tummy [tami] *fam.* karın; mide

tumo(u)r [tyûmı] MED tümör, ur

tumult [tyûmalt] kargaşalık, gürültü; **~uous** [.'maltyuıs] gürültülü

tun [tan] fıçı

tuna [tuunı] ZOO ton balığı, orkinos

tune [tyûn] *n.* nağme, melodi; akort; *v/t* akort etm.

tunnel [tanl] tünel

turban [tɜbın] sarık

turbine [tɜbin] türbin

turbulent [tɜbyulınt] serkeş; çalkantılı

turf [tɜf] *n.* çimen(lik); hipodrom; *v/t* çimen döşemek *-e*

Turk [tɜk] Türk

Turkey¹ [tɜki] Türkiye

turkey² [tɜki] ZOO hindi

Turkish [tɜkiş] Türk; Türkçe; **~ delight** lokum

turmoil [tɜmoyl] kargaşa, gürültü

turn [tɜn] *n.* dönme; devir; nöbet; viraj; tarz; sıra; yön; *v/i* olmak; dönmek; sapmak, yönelmek (**to** *-e*); *v/t* döndürmek, çevirmek; **take ~s** sıra ile yapmak (**at** *-i*); **~ back** *v/i* geri dönmek; *v/t* geri çevirmek; **~ down** *v/t* indirmek; reddetmek; **~ off** *v/t* kapatmak, kesmek; **~ on** *v/t* açmak; çevirmek; **~out** *v/t* kovmak; *v/i* meydana çıkmak (**to** *inf. -diği*); **~ up** *v/i* çıkmak; görünmek; *v/t* yukarı çevirmek; açmak; **~coat** POL dönek adam; **~er** tornacı; **~ing** dönen; dönüş

turnip [tɜnip] BOT şalgam

turn|-out ECON ürün, verim; **~over** devrilme; ECON satış; **~pike** *Am.* geçiş parası alınan yol; **~stile** turnike

turquoise ['t3kwâz] firuze

turret ['tarit] küçük kule; MIL taret

turtle ['t3tl] ZOO kaplumbağa; ~-dove kumru

tusk [task] ZOO fildişi; azıdişi

tutor ['tyûtı] öğretmen; JUR vasi

tuxedo [tak'sidıu] smokin

twang [twäŋ] n. tıngırtı; genizden çıkan ses; v/i tıngırdamak; genizden konuşmak

tweed [twîd] tüvit

tweezers ['twîzız] pl. cımbız sg.

twelve [twelv] on iki

twenty ['twenti] yirmi

twice [tways] iki kere, iki defa

twiddle ['twidl] v/t döndürmek

twig [twig] ince dal

twilight ['twaylayt] alaca karanlık

twin [twin] ikiz; çift, çifte

twine [twayn] n. sicim; v/t bükmek, sarmak; v/i sarılmak

twinkle ['twiŋkl] n. pırıltı; v/i

pırıldamak; göz kırpıştırmak

twirl [twɔl] n. dönüş; kıvrım; v/i fırıldanmak

twist [twist] n. bük(ül)me; burma dönüş; ibrişim; v/t bükmek, burmak; v/i bükülmek, burulmak

twitch [twiç] v/i seğirmek; v/t seğirtmek

twitter ['twitı] cıvıldamak

two [tuu] iki; ~fold iki kat; ~pence ['tapıns] iki pens; ~-way iki taraflı; iki yollu

type [tayp] n. çeşit, tip; model; basma harf; v/t daktilo ile yazmak; ~writer yazı makinesi, daktilo

typhoid (fever) ['tayfoyd] MED tifo

typhoon [tay'fuun] tayfun

typhus ['tayfıs] MED tifüs

typical ['tipikıl] tipik

typist ['taypist] daktilo(da yazan)

tyrann|ic(al) [ti'ränikıl] zalim, gaddar; ~y ['-rıni] istibdat, zulüm

tyrant ['tayırınt] zalim, zorba

tyre ['tayı] dış lastik

U

udder ['adı] ZOO inek memesi

ugly ['agli] çirkin; korkunç

ulcer ['alsı] MED ülser, karha

ultimat|e ['altimit] son, nihaî; ~um [.'meytım] POL ültimatom

ultra- ['altrı] aşırı, son derece

umbrella [am'brelı] şemsiye

umpire ['ampayı] hakem

un- [an-] -siz, gayri

un|abashed küstah, arsız; ~able gücü yetmez; beceriksiz;

~acceptable kabul edilemez; ~accountable anlatılmaz; olağanüstü; ~affected etkilenmemiş; samimî; ~alterable değişmez
unanim|ity [yûni'nimiti] oy birliği; ~ous [-'nänimıs] aynı fikirde
un|approachable yanına varılamaz; ~armed silâhsız; ~asked sorulmamış, davetsiz; ~assuming gösterişsiz; ~authorized yetkisiz; ~avoidable kaçınılmaz; ~aware ['anı'wä] habersiz; ~balanced dengesiz; ~bar v/t -in sürgüsünü açmak; ~bearable dayanılmaz; ~becoming yakışıksız; ~believable inanılmaz; ~bending sabit, eğilmez; ~bias(s)ed tarafsız; ~bidden davetsiz; ~born henüz doğmamış; ~bounded sınırsız; ölçüsüz; ~breakable kırılamaz; ~broken kırılmamış; sürekli; ~button v/t -in düğmelerini çözmek; ~called-for lüzumsuz, yersiz; ~canny [-'känl] tekin olmayan; ~cared-for bakımsız; ~ceasing durmıyan, aralıksız; ~certain şüpheli; kararsız, belirsiz; ~changing değişmez; ~checked durdurulmamış, serbest; ~civil nezaketsiz; ~civilized medenileşmemiş; ~claimed sahibi çıkmamış
uncle ['aŋkl] amca, dayı; teyze *veya* halanın kocası

un|clean pis, kirli; ~comfortable rahatsız (edici); ~common olağanüstü; nadir; ~communicative az konuşur; ~complaining şikâyet etmiyen; ~compromising uzlaşmaz, eğilmez; ~concerned ilgisiz; kayıtsız; ~conditional şartsız; ~confirmed doğrulanmamış; ~conscious bilinçsiz; baygın; ~constitutional anayasaya aykırı; ~conventional göreneklere uymayan; ~couth [an'kuuth] kaba; ~cover v/t -in örtüsünü kaldırmak; ~damaged zarar görmemiş; ~decided kararsız; kararlaştırılmamış; asıda; ~deniable inkâr olunamaz
under ['andı] -in altın(d)a; -den aşağı, -den eksik; ~carriage şasi; AVIA iniş takımı; ~clothes *pl.*, ~clothing iç çamaşır; ~developed az gelişmiş; -do v/t gerektiğinden az pişirmek; ~estimate v/t gerektiğinden az değer vermek -e; ~fed gıdasız; ~go v/t katlanmak, uğramak -e; ~graduate üniversite öğrencisi; ~ground yeraltı; metro; ~line v/t -in altını çizmek; -in önemini belirtmek; ~mine v/t -in temelini çürütmek; ~most en alttaki; ~neath -in altın(d)a; ~privileged imkânları kıt olan; ~rate s. ~estimate; ~shirt iç gömleği, fa-

nila; ~**signed** imza sahibi; ~**sized** normalden küçük; ~**stand** v/t anlamak, kavramak; ~**standing** anlayış; anlaşma; anlayışlı; ~**statement** olduğundan hafif gösteren ifade; ~**take** v/t üzerine almak; ~**taker** cenaze işleri görevlisi; ~**taking** iş, teşebbüs; ~**value** s. ~**estimate**; ~**wear** s. ~**clothes**; ~**world** ölüler diyarı; kanunsuzlar âlemi

un|**deserved** lâyık olmıyan; ~**developed** gelişmemiş; ~**diminished** azalmamış; ~**disputed** karşı gelinmemiş; ~**disturbed** karıştırılmamış, rahatsız edilmemiş; ~**do** v/t açmak; çözmek; telâfi etm.; bozmak; ~**dreamt-of** akla gelmeyen; ~**dress** v/i elbiselerini çıkarmak, soyunmak; ~**due** aşırı; kanunsuz; uygunsuz; ~**dying** ölmez; ~**earth** v/t topraktan çıkarmak; ~**easy** huzursuz; ~**educated** okumamış

un**employ|ed** işsiz; ~**ment** işsizlik

un**ending** sonsuz, bitmez tükenmez

un**equal** eşit olmıyan; ~(**l)ed** eşsiz; üstün

un|**erring** yanılmaz; ~**even** düz olmıyan, MATH tek; ~**eventful** olaysız; ~**expected** beklenilmedik; ~**failing** tükenmez; şaşmaz; ~**fair** haksız; hileli; ~**familiar** iyi bilmiyen (**with** -*i*); alışıl-

mamış (-*e*); ~**fasten** v/t çözmek, açmak; ~**favo(u)rable** müsait olmıyan; elverişsiz; ~**feeling** hissiz; merhametsiz; ~**finished** bitmemiş, tamamlanmamış; ~**fit** uymaz (**for** -*e*); ehliyetsiz; ~**fold** v/t açmak, yaymak; v/i açılmak; ~**foreseen** beklenmedik; ~**forgettable** unutulmaz; ~**forgiving** uzlaşmaz

un**fortunate** talihsiz, bahtsız; ~**ly** adv. maalesef, yazık ki

un|**founded** temelsiz, asılsız; ~**friendly** dostça olmıyan; ~**furl** v/t açmak; ~**furnished** mobilyasız; ~**gainly** hantal, biçimsiz; ~**governable** yönetilmez; ~**gracious** nezaketsiz; ~**grateful** nankör; ~**happy** kederli; şanssız; ~**harmed** zararsız; ~**healthy** sıhhate zararlı; ~**heard-of** işitilmemiş

un**heed|ed** aldırış edilmiyen; ~**ing** dikkat etmiyen

un|**hesitating** tereddüt etmiyen; ~**hurt** zarar görmemiş

uni|**fication** [yūnifi'keyşn] birleş(tir)me; ~**form** ['yūnifôm] üniforma, resmî elbise; tekdüzen, yeknesak; ~**fy** ['yūnifay] v/t birleştirmek; ~**lateral** ['yūni'lätırıl] tek taraflı

un|**imaginative** yaratma kabiliyeti olmıyan; ~**impaired** zarar görmemiş; ~**important** önemsiz; ~**inhabited** oturulmamış; ıssız; ~**intelligible** anlaşılmaz; **~intentional** istemiyerek yapılan; **~interrupted** aralıksız

union ['yûnyın] birleşme; birlik; anlaşma; sendika; ♀ Jack İngiliz bayrağı; **~ist** sendikacı

unique [yû'nîk] tek, biricik

unison ['yûnizn] birlik, ahenk

unit ['yûnit] birlik; ünite; **~e** [.'nayt] v/i birleşmek; v/t birleştirmek; ♀ed **Kingdom** Britanya Kırallığı; **~ed Nations** pl. Birleşmiş Milletler; **~ed States** pl. **of America** Amerika Birleşik Devletleri; **~y** birlik; birleşme

univers|al [yûni'vısıl] genel; evrensel; **~e** ['-ɜs] evren, kâinat; **~ity** [-'vɜsiti] üniversite

un|just haksız; **~kempt** taranmamış; **~kind** dostça olmıyan, sert; **~known** bilinmez; yabancı; **~lace** v/t -in bağlarını çözmek; **~lawful** kanuna aykırı; **~learn** v/t ögrendiğini unutmak

unless [ın'les] -medikçe, meğerki

unlike -e benzemiyen, -den farklı; **~ly** umulmaz, olasısız

un|limited sınırsız; sayısız; **~load** v/t boşaltmak; **~lock** v/t -in kilidini açmak; **~loose** (-n) v/t çözmek; **~lucky** talihsiz, bahtsız; **~manageable** idare edilemez; **~manly** erkekçe olmıyan; **~married** evlenmemiş; **~mistakable** açık, belli; **~moved** sarsılmaz; **~natural** tabiata aykırı; anormal; **~necessary** lüzumsuz; **~noticed**, **~observed** gözden kaçmış; **~obtrusive** göze çarpmaz; alçak gönüllü; **~occupied** boş, serbest; **~offending** kusursuz, zararsız; **~official** resmî olmayan; **~pack** v/t boşaltmak; açmak; **~paid** ödenmemiş; ücretsiz; **~paralleled** essiz, emsalsiz; **~pardonable** affedilemez; **~perturbed** ['-pɜ-'tɜbd] sakin, soğukkanlı; **~pleasant** nahoş; **~polished** parlatılmamış; fig. kaba; **~popular** rağbet görmeyen; gözden düşmüş; **~practical** elverişli olmayan; **~precedented** emsali görülmemiş; **~prejudiced** tarafsız; **~prepared** hazırlıksız; **~principled** karaktersiz, ahlâksız; **~productive** verimsiz

unprovided yoksun (**with** -den); **~ for** ihtiyacı karşılanmamış

un|qualified ehliyetsiz; şartsız; **~questionable** şüphe götürmez

unreal gerçek olmıyan, hayalî; **~istic** gerçekçi olmıyan

un|reasonable makul olmayan; aşırı; **~recognizable** tanınmaz; **~refined** tasfiye edilmemiş; inceliksiz; **~reliable** güvenilmez; **~reserved** sınırlanmamış; samimî;

~rest kargaşa; rahatsızlık; ~restrained frenlenmemiş; ~restricted sınırsız; ~ripe ham; erken gelişmiş; ~rival(l)ed eşsiz, rakipsiz; ~roll v/t açmak; v/i açılmak; ~ruly azılı; itaatsiz; ~safe emniyetsiz; tehlikeli; ~satisfactory memnuniyet vermeyen; tatmin etmiyen; ~screw v/t -in vidalarını sökmek; çevirerek açmak -i; ~scrupulous vicdansız; prensipsiz; ~seemly yakışıksız; ~seen görülmemiş; gizli; ~selfish kendini düşünmiyen; ~settled kararlaştırılmamış; belirsiz; boş; ödenmemiş

unshave|d, ~n tıraşı uzamış
unshrink|able çekmez, büzülmez; ~ing çekinmesiz
un|sightly çirkin; ~skilled becerIksiz; ehliyetsiz; ~sociable çekingen, konuşmayan; ~sophisticated saf, sade; ~sound sağlam olmıyan; hastalıklı; ~spoiled bozulmamış; şımarmamış; ~stable sağlam olmıyan; kararsız; ~steady oynak; kararsız; ~successful başarısız; ~surpassed eşsiz
unsuspect|ed şüphelenilmeyen; ~ing saf, masum
un|thinkable düşünülemez, akla gelmez; ~tidy düzensiz; ~tie v/t çözmek
until [ın'til] -e kadar, -e değin
un|timely vakitsiz; uygunsuz; ~tiring yorulmak bilmez;

~told hesapsız; ~touched dokunulmamış; ~tried denenmemiş; yargılanmamış; ~true yalan, doğru olmıyan; ~trustworthy güvenilmez
unus|ed ['an'yûzd] kullanılmamış; ~ual nadir; olağandışı
un|utterable ağza alınmaz, söylenmez; ~veil v/t -in örtüsünü açmak; ~wanted istenilmez; ~warranted [.'worıntıd] haksız; ~wholesome sıhhate zararlı; ~willing isteksiz; ~wind v/t çözmek; v/i açılmak; ~wise akılsız; ~worthy yakışmaz; lâyık olmıyan (of -e); ~wrap v/t açmak, çözmek; ~yielding boyun eğmez
up [ap] yukarı(ya); yukarıda; ~ to -e kadar; be ~ to -e bağlı olm., -in işi olm.; be ~ to inf. -mekte olm.; ~ and about hastalıktan kurtulmuş; ~s and downs pl. iniş çıkışlar, iyi ve kötü günler
up|bringing yetiş(tir)me; ~heaval karışıklık; devrim; ~hill yokuş yukarı; ~hold v/t tutmak; desteklemek; ~holstery döşemecilik; ~keep bakım; bakım masrafı
upon [ı'pon] s. on
upper ['apı] üst; üstteki; yukarıdaki; ~ class zenginler sınıfı; ♀ House pol Lortlar kamarası; ~most en üst
up|right dik, dikey; dürüst; ~rising ayaklanma; ~roar

şamata; ~set v/t devirmek, altüst etm.; v/i devrilmek; adj. altüst; ~side-down altüst; ~stairs yukarıya; yukarıda; üst kat; ~start türedi, sonradan görme; ~stream akıntıya karşı; ~to-date modern, asrî; ~ward(s) ['~wıd(z)] yukarıya doğru

uranium [yu'reynıym] uranyum

urban ['ıbın] şehre ait

urbane [ı'beyn] nazik, kibar

urchin ['ıçin] afacan çocuk

urge v/t ileri sürmek, sevketmek; sıkıştırmak; ~ncy acele; ~nt acele olan

urine ['yurin] ANAT idrar, sidik

urn [ın] (ayaklı) kap; semaver

us [as, ıs] bizi; bize

usage [yu'sôc] kullanış; usul; âdet

use [yûs] n. fayda; kullanma; âdet; [yûz] v/t kullanmak; yararlanmak -den; he ~d

[yûst] to inf. eskiden -erdi; ~ up v/t tüketmek; ~d [yûzd] kullanılmış; alışık (to -e); ~ful faydalı, yararlı; ~less faydasız

usher ['aşı] n. mübaşir; kapıcı; THEA yer gösteren kimse; v/t yol göstermek -e

usual ['yûjuıl] her zamanki, olağan, ~ly adv. çoğunlukla

usurer ['yûjırı] tefeci

usurp [yû'zıp] v/t gaspetmek, zorla almak

usury ['yûjuri] murabaha

utensil [yu'tensl] kap; alet

utility [yu'tiliti] yarar(lık); kamu hizmeti; ~ze v/t kullanmak; faydalanmak -den

utmost ['atmıust] en uzak; son derece

utter ['atı] adj. tam; sapına kadar; v/t ağza almak, söylemek; ~ance ifade; söz

uvula ['yûvyulı] ANAT küçük dil

V

vacancy ['veykınsi] boşluk; boş yer; ~t boş; açık; münhal

vacate [vı'keyt] v/t boş bırakmak; boşaltmak; ~ion tatil

vaccinate ['väksineyt] v/t aşılamak; ~ion aşı(lama)

vacuum ['väkyum] boşluk, vakuum; ~ bottle termos; ~ cleaner elektrik süpürgesi

vagabond ['vägıbond] serse-

ri, avare

vagary ['veygıri] kapris

vagina [vı'caynı] ANAT dölyolu, mehbil

vague [veyg] belirsiz, müphem

vain [veyn] boş, nafile; kendini beğenmiş; in ~ adv. boşuna, beyhude (yere)

vale [veyl] vadi, dere

valentine ['välıntayn] sevgili; Saint 2's Day 14 şubat

valerian [vı'lıirin] BOT kediotu

valiant ['välyınt] yiğit, cesur

valid ['välid] yürürlükte olan, geçerli

valise [vı'liz] valiz, bavul

valley ['väli] vadi, dere

valo(u)r ['väli] yiğitlik, cesaret

valu|able ['välyuıbl] değerli; değerli şey; **~ation** değer biçme; **~e** ['_û] n. değer; v/t takdir etm.; değer vermek -e

valve [välv] TECH supap, valf; radyo lambası

vamp [vämp] pop. fındıkçı kadın; **~ire** ['_ayı] vampir, hortlak

van [vän] üstü kapalı yük arabası; furgon

vane [veyn] yelkovan, fırıldak; pervane kanadı

vanilla [vı'nili] vanilya

vanish ['väniş] gözden kaybolmak

vanity ['väniti] nafilelik; kendini beğenme; **~ bag**, **~ case** makyaj çantası

vanquish ['vänkwiş] v/t yenmek

vantage ['väntic] üstünlük

vap|orize ['veypırayz] v/t buharlaştırmak; v/i buharlaşmak; **~orous** buharlı; **~o(u)r** buhar

variable ['väiriıbl] değişken; kararsız

variance ['väiriins] değişik-

lik; ayrılık; **at ~** aykırı (**with** -**e**)

varia|nt ['väiriint] farklı; varyant; **~tion** değişme; değişiklik

varicose ['värikıus] (**vein**) MED varisli (damar)

varie|d ['väirid] çeşitli, türlü; **~ty** [vı'rayti] değişiklik; varyete

various ['väiriıs] çeşitli; birkaç

varnish ['väniş] n. vernik; v/t verniklemek

vary ['väiri] v/t değiştirmek; v/i değişmek; farklı olm. (**from** -**den**)

vase [vâz] vazo

vast [vâst] engin, geniş, vâsi

vat [vät] tekne, fıcı

vault [vôlt] n. tonoz; kemer; kasa; atlayış; v/t atlamak

veal [vil] dana eti

vegeta|ble ['vecitibl] bitkilere ait; bitki; sebze; **~rian** [_'täirin] et yemez kimse; **~tion** bitkiler pl.

vehemen|ce ['viimıns] şiddet; **~t** şiddetli

vehicle ['viikl] taşıt; vasıta

veil [veyl] n. peçe, yaşmak; örtü; v/t örtmek; v/i örtünmek

vein [veyn] damar

velocity [vı'lositi] hız, sürat

velvet ['velvit] kadife

venal ['vinl] satın alınır

vend [vend] v/t satmak; **~er**, **~or** satıcı

venera|ble ['venırıbl] muhterem, saygıdeğer; **~te** ['_eyt] *v/t* saygı göstermek *-e;* tapmak *-e*

venereal ['vi'nıırııl] MED zührevî

Venetian ['vi'nişın] Venedikli; ~ **blind** jaluzi

vengeance ['vencıns] öç, intikam; **with a** ~ son derecede

Venice ['venis] Venedik

venison ['venzn] geyik *veya* karaca eti

venom ['venım] zehir; *fig.* düşmanlık; ~**ous** zehirli

vent [vent] delik, menfez; kıç; **give a** ~ **to** *-i* açığa vurmak

ventilat|e ['ventileyt] *v/t* havalandırmak; ~**ion** havalandırma; ~**or** vantilatör

ventr|al ['ventrıl] karna ait; ~**iloquist** [-'trilıkwist] vantrlok

venture ['vençı] *n.* tehlikeli iş, şans işi; *v/t, v/i* (**to** *inf.*) tehlikeye atmak *-i;* ~**some** atılgan; tehlikeli

Venus ['vîıus] REL Venüs; ASTR Çulpan, Venüs

veranda(h) [vı'rändı] veranda, çamlı taraça

verb [vıb] GR fiil; ~**al** GR fiile ait; sözlü; harfiyen

verdant ['vıdınt] yeşil, taze

verdict ['vıdikt] JUR jüri kurulu hükmü; karar

verdure ['vıcı] yeşillik

verge [vıc] *n.* kenar; sınır; *v/i* yaklaşmak (**on** *-e*)

verifi|cation [verifi'keyşın] tahkik; ~**y** ['-fay] *v/t* doğrulamak; tahkik etm.

vermicelli [vımi'seli] *pl.* tel şehriye *sg.*

vermiform ['vımifôm] **appendix** ANAT apandis

vermin ['vımin] haşarat

vernacular [vı'näkyulı] bölgesel; günlük dil

vers|atile ['vısıtayl] çok iş bilen; ~**e** [vıs] mısra; beyit; ~**ed** iyi bilen (**in** *-i*); ~**ion** tercüme; okunuş tarzı; ~**us** *-e* karşı

vertebra ['vıtıbrı] ANAT omur(ga kemiği)

vertical ['vıtikıl] dikey, düşey

very ['veri] çok, pek; tam; aynı; bile; **this** ~ **day** bugünkü gün

vessel ['vesl] kap; gemi; ANAT damar

vest [vest] iç gömleği; *Am.* yelek

vestige ['vestic] iz

vestry ['vestri] REL giyinme odası; yönetim kurulu

vet [vet] *pop.* veteriner

veteran ['vetırın] kıdemli; emekli; emekli asker

veterinary (**surgeon**) ['vetırinri] veteriner, baytar

veto ['vîtu] *n.* veto; *v/t* reddetmek, veto etm.

vex [veks] *v/t* incitmek, kızdırmak; ~**ation** kızma; sıkıntı; ~**atious** gücendirici; aksi

via ['vayı] yolu ile

viaduct ['vayıdakt] ARCH köprü, viyadük

vibrat|e [vay'breyt] *v/i* titre-

mek, sallanmak; ~ion tit-
reşim

vicar ['vıkı] REL papaz; vekil;
~age papazın evi

vice¹ [vays] kötü huy; leke

vice² mengene, sıkmaç

vice versa ['vaysi'vɔsı] tersine

vice|-admiral [vays-] korami-
ral; ~consul konsolos
yardımcısı; ~president başkan yardımcısı

vicinity [vi'siniti] civar, çevre

vicious ['vişıs] kötü; ahlâkî
bozuk

victim ['viktim] kurban; mağdur kimse

victor ['viktı] galip; Qian
[-'tôrın] Kıralıçe Viktorya
zamanına ait; ~ious galip,
muzaffer; ~y zafer

victuals ['vitlz] pl. yemekler,
erzak

Vienna [vi'enı] Viyana

view [vyû] n. bakış; manzara;
görüş; v/t bakmak -e; tetkik
etm. -i; düşünmek -i; in ~
of -in karşısında; point of
~, ~point bakım, görüş noktası

vigil ['vicil] gece nöbet tutma;
~ance uyanıklık; ~ant
uyanık

vigo|rous ['vigırıs] dinç, kuv-
vetli; ~(u)r kuvvet, dinçlik

vile [vayl] kötü, iğrenç; rezil

village ['vilic] köy; ~r köylü

villain ['vilın] alçak veya
çapkın adam; ~ous çirkin,
habis; ~y kötülük, rezalet

vindicat|e ['vindikeyt] v/t -in
doğruluğunu ispat etm.; korumak -i; ~ion koruma

vindictive [vin'diktiv] kinci

vine [vayn] asma (çubuğu);
~gar ['vinigı] sirke; ~yard
bağ

vintage ['vintic] bağ bozumu;
kaliteli şarap

violat|e ['vayıleyt] v/t boz-
mak; tecavüz etm. -e; ~ation
ihlâl; tecavüz

violen|ce ['vayılıns] zor; şid-
det; ~t şiddetli, sert

violet ['vayılit] BOT menekşe;
mor

violin [vayı'lin] MUS keman

viper ['vaypı] ZOO engerek;
yılan

virgin ['vɔcin] kız, bakire; bakir; ~ity kızlık, bakirelik

viril|e ['virayl] erkekçe; ~ity
[-'riliti] erkeklik

virtual ['vɔtyuıl] gerçek kuvveti olan; ~ly adv. gerçekte

virtue ['vɔtyû] fazilet, iffet; by
~ of -e dayanarak

virtuous ['vɔtyuıs] iffetli

virus ['vayırıs] virüs

visa ['vîzı] vize

viscount ['vaykaunt] vikont

vise [vays] s. vice²

visib|ility [vizi'biliti] görüş;
görünürlük; ~le görünebilir;
belli

vision ['vijın] görme; görüş;
hayal, kuruntu

visit ['vizit] n. ziyaret; vizita;
v/t ziyaret etm., görmeğe gitmek; pay a ~ to -i ziyaret

etm.; ~or ziyaretçi, misafir

visual ['vizyuıl] görmekle ilgili; görülebilir; ~ize v/t gözünde canlandırmak

vital ['vaytl] hayatî; esaslı, zarurî; ~ity [-'täliti] dirilik; canlılık

vitamin ['vitımin] vitamin

viv|acious [vi'veyşıs] canlı, neşeli; ~id ['-vid] canlı; parlak

vocabulary [vıu'käbyulıri] sözlük; kelime bilgisi

vocal ['vıukıl] sesle ilgili; sesli; ~ist şarkıcı

vocation [vıu'keyşın] davet; meslek; ~al meslekle ilgili

vogue [vıug] moda; rağbet

voice [voys] ses; GR etken *veya* edilgen şekil; çati; ~ mail telesekreter; ~d sesli

void [voyd] boş; hükümsüz; mahrum (of *-den*)

volcan|ic [vol'känik] volkanik; ~o [-'keynıu] volkan, yanardağ

volley ['voli] yaylım ateş; yağmur; (*tennis*) topa yere değmeden geri vurma

volt [vıult] EL volt; ~age voltaj, gerilim

voluble ['volyubl] konuşkan; çenebaz

volum|e ['volyum] hacim, oylum; cilt; ~inous [vı'lyûmi-

nıs] büyük, hacimli

volunt|ary ['volıntıri] istemli, ihtiyarî, gönüllü; ~eer [-'tiı] *n*. gönüllü; v/t kendi isteği ile teklif etm.; v/i gönüllü yazılmak (for *-e*)

voluptuous [vı'lapçuıs] şehvetli

vomit ['vomit] v/i kusmak; v/t kusturmak

voodoo ['vuuduu] zenci büyücü

voracious [vı'reyşıs] doymak bilmez

vote [vıut] *n*. oy (hakkı); v/i oy vermek (for lehine); v/t seçmek; ~r seçmen

voting ['vıutiŋ] seçme; seçim; ~-paper oy pusulası

vouch [vauç] temin etm. (for *-i*); kefil olm. (için); ~er belgit, tanıt; ~safe [-'seyf] v/t ihsan etm.

vow [vau] *n*. adak, yemin; v/t yemin etm. *-e*; adamak, nezretmek *-i*

vowel ['vauıl] GR sesli harf

voyage ['voyic] yolculuk, seyahat

vulcanize ['valkınayz] v/t vulkanize etm.

vulgar ['valgı] kaba; bayağı

vulnerable ['valnırıbl] kolayca yaralanır

vulture ['valçı] zoo akbaba

W

wad [wod] *n.* tıkaç; tampon; *v/t* pamukla beslemek; **~ding** pamuk *v.s.* kaplaması, vatka

waddle ['wodl] badi badi yürümek

wade [weyd] su içinde yürümek

wafer ['weyfı] bisküvit, kağıt helvası; REL mayasız ince ekmek

wag [wäg] *v/t* sallamak; *v/i* sallanmak

wage¹ [weyc] ~ **war** savaşmak (**on** ile)

wage², *pl.* **~s** ['weyciz] ücret; **~earner** ['-ını] ücretli kimse

wager ['weycı] *n.* bahis; *v/i* bahis tutuşmak

wag(g)on ['wägın] yük arabası

wail [weyl] *n.* çığlık; *v/i* hayıflanmak (**over** -*e*)

wainscot ['weynskıt] tahta kaplama

waist [weyst] ANAT bel; **~coat** ['weyskıut] yelek; **~line** bel yeri

wait [weyt] *v/i* beklemek (**for** -*i*); hizmetçilik yapmak (**on** -*e*); ~**er** garson; **keep** ~**ing** *v/t* bekletmek; **~ing-room** bekleme salonu; **~ress** kadın garson

waive [weyv] *v/t* vazgeçmek,

feragat etm. -*den*

wake¹ [weyk] dümen suyu; *fig.* peşinde

wake²: ~ (**up**) *v/i* uyanmak; *v/t* uyandırmak; **~n** *s.* wake²

walk [wôk] *n.* yürüyüş; gezinti; *v/i* yürümek; *a. v/t* gezmek; ~ **out** *pop.* grev yapmak; terk etm. (**on** -*i*); **~er** gezen; yürüyücü; **~ie-talkie** ['wôki'tôki] portatif telsiz telefon; **~ing-stick** baston; **~out** grev

wall [wôl] *n.* duvar; sur; *v/t* duvarla çevirmek; ~ **up** duvarla kapamak

wallet ['wolit] cüzdan

wallpaper duvar kâğıdı

walnut ['wôlnat] BOT ceviz (ağacı)

walrus ['wôlrıs] ZOO mors

waltz [wôls] *n.* vals; *v/i* vals yapmak

wan [won] solgun, soluk

wand [wond] değnek, çubuk

wander ['wondı] *v/i* dolaşmak, gezmek; sayıklamak; **~er** ['-rı] çapagayisizce dolaşan

wane [weyn] *v/i moon:* küçülmek; azalmak

want [wont] *n.* yokluk; ihtiyaç; zaruret; *v/t* istemek; gereksemek; gerektirmek; **~ed** aranan; **~ing** eksik; yoksun (**in** -*den*)

war [wô] savaş; ♀ **Department**

Am. Millî Savunma Bakanlığı

warble ['wôbl] *v/i* ötmek, şakımak

ward [wôd] vesayet; vesayet altında bulunan kimse; koğuş; bölge; ~ **off** *v/t* savuşturmak; ~**en**, ~**er** bekçi; müdür

wardrobe ['wôdrıub] giysi dolabı, gardırop; elbiseler *pl.*

ware [wäı] mal, emtia; ~**house** ambar

war|fare ['wôfäı] savaş; ~**like** savaşçı; savaşla ilgili

warm [wôm] *adj.* sıcak; hararetli; *v/t* ısıtmak; *v/i* ısınmak; ~**th** [_th] sıcaklık

warn [wôn] *v/t* ihtar etm. -*e* (**of** -*i*); ~**ing** ihtar; ihbar

warp [wôp] *v/t* eğriltmek; *v/i* eğrilmek

warrant ['worınt] *n.* yetki; ruhsat; tevkif müzekkeresi; geranti; *v/t* temin etm.; izin vermek -*e*; kefil olm. -*e*; ~**y** kefalet, garanti

warrior ['woriı] savaşçı

wart [wôt] siğil

wary ['wäri] uyanık, ihtiyatlı

was [woz, wız] *z.* be

wash [woş] *v/t* yıkamak; *wave:* yalamak; *v/i* yıkanmak; *n.* yıkama; çamaşır; ~ **up** *v/t* bulaşık yıkamak; ~**basin**, *Am.* ~**bowl** lavabo; ~**ed-out** soluk; ~**er** yıkama makinesi; ~**ing** yıkama; çamaşır

wasp [wosp] zoo yabanarısı

waste [weyst] *n.* savurma; boş arazi; çöp; *adj.* boş; ıssız; *v/t* boşuna sarfetmek; harap etm.; ~ **away** *v/i* eriyip gitmek; ~**paperbasket** kâğıt sepeti; ~**pipe** künk

watch [woç] *n.* gözetleme; nöbet; nöbetçi; cep *veya* kol saati; *v/t* gözetlemek; bakmak -*e*; *v/i* beklemek (**for** -*i*); ~ **out** *v/i* dikkat etm.; ~**dog** bekçi köpeği; ~**ful** uyanık; ~**maker** saatçi; ~**man** bekçi

water ['wôtı] *n.* su; *v/t* sulamak, sulandırmak; ~**buffalo** manda; ~**closet** apteshane; ~**colour** sulu boya (resim); ~**fall** çağlayan; ~**ing-can** emzikli kova, sulama ibriği; ~**level** su seviyesi; ~**melon** karpuz; ~**proof** su geçirmez; yağmurluk; ~**ski** su kayağı; ~**works** *pl.* su dağıtım tesisatı; ~**y** sulu

watt [wot] EL vat

wave [weyv] *n.* dalga; sallama; *v/t* dalgalanmak; sallanmak; *v/t* sallamak

waver ['weyvı] *v/i* kararsızlık göstermek; sallanmak

wavy ['weyvi] dalgalı

wax¹ [wäks] *n.* balmumu; *v/t* mum sürmek -*e*

wax² [wäks] *v/i* büyümek, artmak

way [wey] yol; yön, cihet; mesafe; tarz, usul; çare, vasıta; **by the** ~ sırası gelmişken; **by** ~ **of** yolu ile; **give** ~ geri çekilmek; öncelik vermek (**to** -*e*); **on the** ~ yolunda;

out of the ~ sapa; yerinde olmayan; ~ of life yaşama tarzı; ~lay v/i -in yolunu kesmek; ~side yol kenarı; ~ward ['-wıd] ters, inatçı

we [wî, wi] biz

weak [wîk] zayıf; dayanıksız; ~en v/i zayıflamak; v/t zayıflatmak; ~ness kuvvetsizlik

wealth [welth] bolluk, servet; ~y zengin

wean [wîn] v/t sütten kesmek

weapon ['wepın] silâh

wear [wäı] v/t giymek, takınmak; taşımak; takmak; dayanmak -e; n. giysi, elbise; aşınma; ~ (away, down, off, up) v/t aşındırmak; v/i aşınmak; ~ out v/t tüketmek

wear|isome ['wıirısım] usandırıcı; yorucu; ~y adj. yorgun; yorucu; v/t yormak

weasel ['wîzl] zoo gelincik

weather ['wedhı] n. hava; v/t aşındırmak; v/i aşınmak, solmak; ~ out v/t geçiştirmek; ~beaten fırtına yemiş; yanık; ~cock yelkovan; ~forecast hava raporu

weave [wîv] v/t dokumak; basket: örmek; ~r dokumacı, çulha

web [web] ağ; doku; örgü; internet: net; ~site web sitesi

wed [wed] evlenmek (so. b. ile); ~ding evlenme, düğün, nikâh; ~ding-ring nikâh yüzüğü

wedge [wec] n. kama, takoz; v/t sıkmak, sıkıştırmak

wedlock ['wedlok] evlilik

Wednesday ['wenzdi] çarşamba

weed [wîd] n. yabanî ot; v/t ayıklamak, temizlemek

week [wîk] hafta; ~day iş günü; ~end hafta sonu; ~ly haftalık, haftada bir

weep [wîp] ağlamak; ~ing willow bot salkımsöğüt

weigh [wey] v/t tartmak; ölçünmek; ağırlığı olm.; ~t ağırlık, sıklet; ~t-lifting haltercilik; ~ty ağır; önemli

welcome ['welkım] n. karşılama; v/t hoş karşılamak; hoş geldiniz demek -e; (you are) ~! Bir şey değil!

weld [weld] v/t kaynak yaparak birleştirmek

welfare ['welfäı] refah; (yoksullara) yardım; ~ state refah devleti

well¹ [wel] kuyu

well² iyi, iyice, tamamiyle; işte; neyse; as ~ dahi, bile; as ~ as hem ... hem de ...; I am not ~ rahatsızım; ~ off varlıklı; ~being saadet, refah; ~known tanınmış, meşhur; ~mannered terbiyeli; ~timed zamanlı; ~to-do hali vakti yerinde; ~worn eskimiş; bayatlamış

Welsh [welş] Gal dili; ~man Galli; ~ rabbit, ~ rarebit [' räbit] kızarmış ekmeğe sürülen peynir

wench [wenç] kız

went [went] s. go

wept [wept] *s.* weep

were [wɜ] *s.* be

west [west] batı, batıya doğru; ∼erly, ∼ern batıya ait; ∼ward(s) ['∼wıd(z)] batıda; batıya

wet [wet] *adj.* ıslak, rutubetli; *v/t* ıslatmak; ∼ through sırs klam; ∼ nurse sütnine

whack [wäk] *n.* şaklama; *v/t* dövmek

whale [weyl] zoo balina

wharf [wôf] iskele, rıhtım

what [wot] ne; nasıl; hangi; ∼ for? niçin?; ∼(so)ever her ne, her hangi

wheat [wit] buğday

wheel [wiːl] *n.* tekerlek; çark; *v/i* dönmek; *v/t* döndürmek; tekerlekli bir taşıtla götürmek; ∼barrow tekerlekli el arabası; ∼chair tekerlekli sandalye

whelp [welp] zoo enik

when [wen] ne zaman?; *-diği* zaman; iken; ∼ever her ne zaman

where [wäl] nerede?; nereye?; *-diği* yerde; ∼about(s) nerelerde; ∼as halbuki; ∼by vasıtasiyle; mademki; ∼(up)-on bunun üzerine; ∼ver her nereye; her nerede

whet [wet] *v/t* bilemek

whether ['wedhı] *-ip -mediği-*ni

which [wiç] hangi(si); ki; ∼(so)ever her hangi(si)

whiff [wif] esinti; püf

Whig [wig] POL İngiliz liberal partisi üyesi

while [wayl] müddet, zaman, süre; *conj.* iken, *-diği* halde

whim [wim] geçici istek, heves

whimper ['wimpı] *v/i* ağlamak, inlemek

whimsical ['wimzikıl] tuhaf, kaprisli

whine [wayn] *v/i* sızlanmak

whip [wip] *n.* kırbaç, kamçı; *v/t* kamçılamak; çalkamak; ∼ped cream kremşanti

whirl [wɜl] *n.* hızla dönme; *v/i* hızla dönmek; *v/t* hızla döndürmek; ∼pool burgaç, girdap

whir(r) [wɜ] *v/i* vızlamak

whisk [wisk] *n.* yumurta teli; tüy süpürge; *v/t* çalkamak

whiskers ['wiskız] *pl.* favori, bıyık

whisk(e)y ['wiski] viski

whisper ['wispı] *n.* fısıltı; *v/i* fısıldamak

whistle ['wisl] *n.* ıslık; düdük; *v/i* ıslık çalmak

white [wayt] beyaz, ak; 2 House *Am.* Beyaz Saray; ∼ lie zararsız yalan; 2hall *Londra'da resmî dairelerin bulunduğu cadde*; ∼n *v/t* beyazlatmak; *v/i* beyazlanmak, ağarmak; ∼ness beyazlık; ∼wash *n.* badana; *v/t* badana etm.; *fig.* temize çıkarmak

Whitsun(day) ['witsn; 'wit-'sandi] REL pantekot yortusunun pazar günü; ∼tide REL pantekot

whiz(z) [wiz] v/i vızıldamak
who [huu] kim?; o ki, onlar ki;
~dunit [-'danit] sl. dedektif
romanı; ~ ever kim olursa olsun
whole [hıul] bütün, tam; tam
şey; toplam; on the ~ genellikle; ~sale ECON toptan;
~some sıhhate yararlı
wholly ['hulli] büsbütün
whom [huum] kimi?; ki onu
whoop [huup] n. bağırma; v/i
bağırmak; ~ing cough MED
boğmaca öksürüğü
whore [hô] fahişe, orospu
whose [huuz] kimin?
why [way] nicin?, niye?
wick [wik] fitil
wicked ['wikid] fena, kötü;
~ness kötülük; günahkârlık
wicker ['wikı] hasır; sepet işi;
~ chair hasır koltuk
wicket ['wikit] ufak kapı;
krikette kale
wide [wayd] geniş, enli; açık;
~ awake tamamen uyanık;
~n v/t genişletmek; v/i genişlemek; ~spread yaygın
widow ['widıu] dul kadın; ~er
dul erkek
width [width] genişlik, en(lilik)
wife [wayf] karı, eş
wig [wig] peruka, takma saç
wild [wayld] yabanî; vahşi;
şiddetli; yun ~ v/i yabanîleş-
mek; ~cat ZOO yaban kedisi;
fig. düzensiz; ~erness
['wildnis] kır, sahra; ~ness
['wayldnıs] yabanîlik, vahşet

wil(l)ful ['wilful] inatçı; kasıtlı
will [wil] n. istek, arzu; vasi-
yet(name); (auxiliary verb)
istemek; -ecek; ~ing razı,
hazır (to inf. -meğe)
willow ['wilıu] BOT söğüt
wilt [wilt] v/i solmak
win [win] v/t kazanmak
wince [wins] v/i birdenbire
ürkmek
wind[1] [wind] n. rüzgâr, yel;
hava; osuruk; nefes; v/t -in
kokusunu almak
wind[2] [waynd] v/t çevirmek,
dolamak; v/i bükülmek; dolaşmak; ~ up v/t watch: kurmak; ~ing dolambaç(lı)
windlass ['windlıs] TECH ırgat
windmill ['winmill] yeldeğir-
meni
window ['windıu] pencere;
vitrin; ~pane pencere camı;
~shop v/i vitrin gezmek
wind|pipe ANAT nefes borusu;
~screen, Am. ~shield ön
cam; ~screen wiper silgiç;
~y rüzgârlı
wine [wayn] şarap
wing [wiŋ] kanat; kol
wink [wiŋk] n. göz kırpma; v/i
göz kırpmak; gözle işaret
vermek (at -e)
winn|er ['winı] kazanan; ~ing
kazanma; kazanan
wint|er ['wintı] n. kış; v/i
kışlamak; ~ry ['-tri] kış gibi,
pek soğuk
wipe [wayp] v/t silmek, silip
kurutmak; ~ off silip gidermek; ~ out silip yoketmek

wire ['wayı] *n.* tel; *pop.* telgraf; *v/t* telle bağlamak; *v/i* telgraf çekmek; **∼less** telsiz; radyo; **∼less phone** telsiz telefon

wiry ['wayırı] tel gibi

wisdom ['wizdım] akıl(lılık), hikmet; **∼ tooth** akıl dişi

wise [wayz] akıllı; tedbirli; tecrübeli

wish [wiş] *n.* istek, arzu; *v/t* istemek, arzu etm.

wistful ['wistful] hasretli; dalgın

wit [wit] akıl; anlayış; nükte; nükteci; **be at one's ∼'s end** tamamen şaşırmak

witch [wiç] büyücü kadın; **∼craft**, **∼ery** büyücülük

with [widh] ile; *-e* karşı; *-den* dolayı; *-in* yanında

withdraw [widh'drô] *v/t* geri almak; *v/i* çekilmek (**from** *-den*); **∼al** geri çek(il)me

wither ['widhı] *v/i* kurumak, solmak; *v/t* kurutmak

with|hold [widh'hıuld] *v/t* tutmak; vermemek; **∼in** ['dhin] *-in* içinde; içeride; **∼out** [‐'dhaut] *-siz*, *-in* dışında; **∼stand** *v/t* dayanmak *-e*

witness ['witnis] *n.* tanık, şahit; delil; şahitlik; *v/t* şahit olm. *-e*; şehadet etm. *-e*; **∼box**, *Am.* **∼stand** JUR tanık kürsüsü

witty ['witi] nükteci; nükteli

wizard ['wizıd] büyücü, sihirbaz

wobble ['wobl] *v/i* sallanmak; titremek

woe [wıu] keder, dert; **∼begone**, **∼ful** kederli

woke [wıuk], **∼n** *s.* **wake**

wolf [wulf] kurt

woman ['wumın] kadın; **∼doktor** kadın doktoru; **∼hood** kadınlık; **∼kind** kadınlar *pl.*; **∼ly** kadına yakışır

womb [wuum] ANAT rahim, dölyatağı

won [wan] *s.* **win**

wonder ['wandı] *n.* harika, şaşılacak şey; hayret; *v/i* hayrette kalmak, hayran olm.; merak etm. (**if**, **whether** *-ip -mediğini*); **∼ful** hayret verici, şaşılacak

won't [wıunt] = **will not**

wont [wıunt] âdet; alışmış (**to** *inf. -meğe*)

woo [wuu] *v/t* kur yapmak *-e*

wood [wud] orman; odun, tahta; **∼cutter** baltacı; **∼ed** ağaçlı; **∼en** tahtadan yapılmış, ahşap; **∼pecker** ZOO ağaçkakan; **∼work** doğrama(cılık), dülgerlik; **∼y** ormanlık; ağaç; cinsinden

wool [wul] yün; **∼(l)en** yünden, yünlü; **∼(l)y** yünlü; yumuşak

word [wıd] *n.* kelime; söz; laf; haber; *v/t* ifade etm.; **∼ing** yazılış tarzı

wore [wô] *s.* **wear**

work [wık] *n.* iş, çalışma; emek; eser; *pl.* fabrika *sg.*;

mekanizma; v/i çalışmak, uğraşmak; işlemek; v/t çalıştırmak; işletmek; zorlamak (into -e); at ~ iş başında; out of ~ işsiz, boşta; **able** ~s pl. bayındırlık sg.; **able** işlenebilir; pratik; **~day** iş günü; **~er** işçi, amele

working iş gören, çalışan; işliyen; ~ **class** işçi sınıfı; ~ **hours** pl. iş saatleri

workman işçi; **~ship** usta işi

workshop atelye

world ['wǝld] dünya, cihan, âlem; evren; uzay; ~ **war** dünya savaşı; **~ly** dünyevî; **~-wide** âlemşümul, dünyaya yaygın

worm [wǝm] kurt, solucan; **~-eaten** kurt yemiş

worn [wôn] s. wear; **~-out** bitkin; eskimiş

worried ['warid] endişeli; **~y** n. üzüntü, endişe, merak; v/i üzülmek, tasalanmak (about -e)

worse [wǝs] daha fena, daha kötü; **~n** v/i fenalaşmak; v/t fenalaştırmak

worship ['wǝşip] n. tapınma, ibadet; v/t tapmak, tapınmak -e; **~(p)er** tapan, ibadet eden

worst [wǝst] en fena, en kötü

worsted ['wustid] yün ipliği

worth [wǝth] n. değer, kıymet; adj. değer, lâyık (-ing -e); ~ **seeing** görmeğe değer; **~less** değersiz; **~while** (zahmetine) değer; faydalı; **~y** ['wǝdhi] değerli;

lâyık (of -e)

would [wud] -ecek(ti); istedi ~ **rather** inf. -meyi tercih edecekti

wound[1] [wuund] n. yara; v/t yaralamak; -in gönlünü kırmak

wound[2] [waund] s. wind[2]

wove [wıuv], **~n** s. weave

wrangle ['ræŋgl] n. kavga, ağız dalaşı; v/i kavga etm., çekişmek

wrap [ræp] n. örtü; atkı; v/t sarmak, örtmek; ~ **up** v/t sarmak (in -e); **~ped up** sarılmış (in -e); **~per** sargı; **~ping** ambalaj

wrath [roth] öfke, hiddet

wreath [rîth] çelenk

wreck [rek] n. gemi enkazı pl.; kazaya uğrama; harap olmuş kimse; v/t kazaya uğratmak; yıkmak; **~age** enkaz pl.; **~ing service** Am. yedeğe alma servisi

wren [ren] zoo çalıkuşu

wrench [renç] n. burk(ul)ma; TECH İngiliz anahtarı; v/t burkmak

wrest [rest] v/t zorla elde etm.

wrestle ['resl] v/i güreşmek; uğraşmak; **~er** pehlivan; **~ing** güreş

wretch [reç] herif; **~ed** ['_id] alçak, sefil; bitkin

wriggle ['rigl] v/i kıvranmak, sallanmak

wring [riŋ] v/t burup sıkmak

wrinkle ['rinkl] n. kırışık; v/t kırıştırmak; v/i kırışma

wrist [rist] ANAT bilek; ~ watch kol saati
writ [rit] yazı; ferman
write [rayt] v/t yazmak; ~ out yazıya dökmek; ~r yazar
writhe [raydh] v/i kıvranmak
writing ['raytiŋ] yazı; el yazısı; ~paper yazı kâğıdı
written ['ritn] s. write
wrong [roŋ] adj. yanlış; ters; n. haksızlık; v/t haksız muamele etm. -e; -in hakkını yemek; be ~ yanılmak; yanlış olm
wrote [rut] s. write
wrought [rôt] işlenmiş; iron dövme demir
wrung [raŋ] s. wring
wry [ray] çarpık, eğri

X, Y

Xmas ['krismıs] = Christmas
X-ray ['eks'rey] n. röntgen ışını; v/t röntgen ışınları ile muayene etm.
yacht [yot] NAUT yat; ~ing kotracılık
Yank(ee) ['yäŋki] Amerikalı; A.B.D.'nin kuzey eyaletlerinde oturan kimse
yap [yäp] havlamak
yard¹ [yâd] yarda (0,914 m)
yard² avlu
yarn [yân] iplik; pop. hikâye, masal
yawn [yôn] n. esneme; v/i esnemek
yeah [yey] evet
year [yз] yıl, sene; ~book yıllık; ~ly yıllık, yılda bir
yearn [yзn] v/i çok istemek (for -i)
yeast [yîst] maya
yell [yel] n. çığlık, bağırma; v/i çığlık koparmak
yellow ['yelıu] sarı
yelp [yelp] kesik kesik havlamak
yes [yes] evet
yesterday ['yestıdi] dün
yet [yet] henüz, daha, hâlâ; bile; as ~ şimdiye kadar
yew [yû] BOT porsukağacı
yield [yîld] n. mahsul, ürün; v/t vermek, meydana çıkarmak; v/i razı olm., teslim olm. (to -e); ~ing yumuşak, uysal
yoke [yıuk] n. boyunduruk; çift; v/t boyunduruğa koşmak
yolk [yıuk] yumurta sarısı
yonder ['yondı] ötedeki; ötede
you [yû, yu] sen; siz; sana, seni; size, sizi
young [yaŋ] genç; yavru; ~ster ['.stı] çocuk; delikanlı
your [yô] senin; sizin; ~s [.z] seninki; sizinki; ~self kendin(iz); ~selves kendiniz
youth [yûth] genç, delikanlı; gençlik; ~ hostel gençlik

yurdu, hostel; **~ful** genç, dinç
Yugoslav ['yûgıu'slâv] *hist.*

Yugoslav(yalı); **~ia** ['-'slâ-vyı] *hist.* Yugoslavya

Z

zap [zæp] v/t *coll. bilgisayar:* silmek; *bilgisayar oyununda:* öldürmek, vurmak; *TV* zapping yapmak

zeal [zîl] gayret; **~ous** ['zelıs] gayretli

zebra ['zîbrı] zoo zebir; **~ crossing** çizgili yaya geçidi

zenith ['zenith] ASTR başucu; *fig.* zirve

zephyr ['zefı] hafif rüzgâr, meltem

zeppelin ['zepılın] AVIA zeplin

zero ['zîırıu] sıfır

zest [zest] tat, lezzet; zevk

zigzag ['zigzäg] zikzak

zinc [zıŋk] çinko, tutya

Zionis|m ['zayınizım] siyonizm; **~t** siyonist

zip [zip] vızıltı; **~ code** *Am.* posta bölgesi numarası; **~fastener, ~per** fermuar

zodiac ['zıudiäk] ASTR zodyak

zone [zıun] bölge

zoo [zuu], **~logical garden** [zıu'lockıl -] hayvanat bahçesi; **~logy** [zıu'olıcı] zooloji, hayvanlar bilimi

Appendices

British and American Abbreviations
İngilizce'de Kullanılan Kısaltmalar

A.D.	anno Domini = Christian era *Milâttan sonra*
a.m.	ante meridiem = before noon *öğleden önce*
AP	Associated Press (*Amerikan haber ajansı*)
B.A.	Bachelor of Arts *edebiyat fakültesi diploması başöyelik*
BBC	British Broadcasting Corporation *İngiliz Radyo Kurumu*
B.C.	Before Christ *Milâttan önce*
Bros.	Brothers *ec. Kardeşler*
CIA	Central Intelligence Agency (*A.B.D. istihbarat bürosu*)
CID	Criminal Investigation Department (*İngiliz cinayet zabıtası*)
Co.	company *ec. ortaklık, şirket*
c/o	care of *eliyle*
COD	cash (*Am.* collect) on delivery *tesliminde ödenecek ödemeli*
Dept.	Department *kısım, şube; bakanlık*
doz.	dozen *düzine*
E	east *doğu*
Ed., ed.	edition *baskı*; edited *hazırlanmış*; editor *hazırlayan*
e.g.	exempli gratia = for instance *örneğin*
encl.	enclosed *ilişikte*
Esq.	Esquire (*isimden sonra*) *Bay*
F	Fahrenheit *fahrenhayt*
FBI	Federal Bureau of Investigation (*A.B.D. cinayet zabıtası örgütü*)
ft	foot, feet *kadem*
GB	Great Britain *Büyük Britanya*
GMT	Greenwich Mean Time *Greenwich orta saati*
GP	General Practitioner *pratisyen hekim*
GPO	General Post Office *merkez postanesi*
HMS	His (Her) Majesty's ship (*İngiliz donanmasına ait gemi*)
hr.	hour(s) *saat(ler)*
i.e.	id est = that is to say *yani*

IMF	International Monetary Fund *Uluslararası Para Fonu*
Inc.	Incorporated *ec. anonim*
£	pound sterling *İngiliz lirası, sterlin*
lb.	pound(s) *yarım kilo, libre*
Ltd.	limited *ec. limitet*
M.A.	Master of Arts *edebiyat fakültesi yüksek diploması*
M.D.	Doctor of Medicine *tıp doktoru*
MP	Member of Parliament *parlamento üyesi*; Military Police *askerî inzibat*
m.p.h.	miles per hour *saatte … mil*
Mr	Mister *Bay*
Mrs	Mistress *Bayan*
Ms	miss *Bayan*
Mt.	Mount *geo. dağ*
N	north *kuzey*
NE	northeast *kuzeydoğu*
NW	northwest *kuzeybatı*
oz, oz.	ounce(s) *ons*
p	new penny (pence) *yeni pens*
Ph.D.	Doctor of Philosophy *felsefe* (= *edebiyat*) *doktoru*
p.m.	post meridiem = after noon *öğleden sonra*
PO	Post Office *postane*; Postal Order *posta havalesi*
POB,	
PoBox	Post Office Box *posta kutusu*
RAF	Royal Air Force (*İngiliz hava kuvvetleri*)
Rd	Road *cadde*
S	south *güney*
$	dollar *dolar*
SE	southeast *güneydoğu*
Sq	Square *meydan, alan*
St	Saint *rel. aziz, sen*; Street *cadde, sokak*
SW	southwest *güneybatı*
TV	television *televizyon*
UK	United Kingdom *Britanya Kırallığı*
UN	United Nations *Birleşmiş Milletler*
UPI	United Press International (*Amerikan haber ajansı*)
US(A)	United States (of America) *Amerika Birleşik Devletleri*
V.A.T.	value-added tax *ec. katma değer vergisi*
W	west *batı*

Irregular English Verbs
İngilizce' deki Kuralsız Fiiller

(*) işaretli kuralsız fiil biçimlerinin yerlerine kurallı fiil biçimleri kullanılabilir.

abide (*kalmak*) – abode* – abode*

awake (*uyan[dır]mak*) – awoke – awoke*

be (*olmak*) – was – been

bear (*taşımak; doğurmak*) – bore – taşı(n)mış: borne – doğmuş: born

beat (*vurmak*) – beat – beaten

begin (*başlamak*) – bagan – begun

bend (*bük[ül]mek*) – bent – bent

bereave (*çalmak*) – bereft* – bereft*

bet (*bahse girmek*) – bet* – bet*

bid (*emretmek*) – bade, bid – bid(den)

bind (*bağlamak*) – bound – bound

bite (*ısırmak*) – bit – bitten

bleed (*kanamak*) – bled – bled

blend (*karış[tır]mak*) – blent* – blent*

blow (*üflemek, esmek*) – blew – blown

break (*kır[ıl]mak*) – broke – broken

breed (*üretmek*) – bred – bred

bring (*getirmek*) – brought – brought

build (*inşa etm.*) – built – built

burn (*yakmak; yanmak*) – burnt* – burnt*

burst (*patla[t]mak*) – burst – burst

buy (*satın almak*) – bought – bought

cast (*atmak*) – cast – cast

catch (*yakalamak*) – caught – caught

choose (*seçmek*) – chose – chosen

cleave (*yar[ıl]mak*) – cleft, clove* – cleft, cloven*

cling (*yapışmak*) – clung – clung

clothe (*giydirmek*) – clad* – clad*

come (*gelmek*) – came – come

cost (*fiatı olm.*) – cost – cost

creep (*sürünmek*) – crept – crept

crow (*ötmek*) – crew* – crowed

cut (*kesmek*) – cut – cut

deal (*uğraşmak*) – dealt – dealt

dig (*kazmak*) – dug – dug

do (*yapmak*) – did – done

draw (*çekmek*) – drew – drawn

dream (*rüya görmek*) –

dreamt* – dreamt*

drink (*içmek*) – drank – drunk

drive (*sürmek*) – drove – driven

dwell (*oturmak*) – dwelt – dwelt

eat (*yemek*) – ate, eat – eaten

fall (*düşmek*) – fell – fallen

feed (*yedirmek*) – fed – fed

feel (*duymak*) – felt – felt

fight (*savaşmak*) – fought – fought

find (*bulmak*) – found – found

flee (*kaçmak*) – fled – fled

fling (*fırlatmak*) – flung – flung

fly (*uçmak*) – flew – flown

forbid (*yasak etm.*) – forbade – forbidden

forget (*unutmak*) – forgot – forgotten

forsake (*vazgeçmek*) – forsook – forsaken

freeze (*don[dur]mak*) – froze – frozen

get (*elde etm.*) – got – got, Am. gotten

gild (*yaldızlamak*) – gilt* – gilt*

gird (*kuşatmak*) – girt* – girt*

give (*vermek*) – gave – given

go (*gitmek*) – went – gone

grind (*öğütmek*) – ground – ground

grow (*büyümek; yetiştirmek*) – grew – grown

hang (*asmak; asılı olm.*) –

hung – hung

have (*sahip olm.*) – had – had

hear (*işitmek*) – heard – heard

heave (*kaldırmak*) – hove* – hove*

hew (*yontmak*) – hewed – hewn*

hide (*sakla[n]mak*) – hid – hid(den)

hit (*vurmak*) – hit – hit

hold (*tutmak*) – held – held

hurt (*yaralamak*) – hurt – hurt

keep (*tutmak*) – kept – kept

kneel (*diz çökmek*) – knelt* – knelt*

knit (*örmek*) – knit* – knit*

know (*bilmek*) – knew – known

lay (*yatırmak*) – laid – laid

lead (*yol göstermek*) – led – led

lean (*daya[n]mak*) – leant* – leant*

leap (*atlamak*) – leapt* – leapt*

learn (*öğrenmek*) – learnt* – learnt*

leave (*ayrılmak*) – left – left

lend (*ödünç vermek*) – lent – lent

let (*bırakmak*) – let – let

lie (*yatmak*) – lay – lain

light (*yakmak*) – lit* – lit*

lose (*unutmak*) – lost – lost

make (*yapmak*) – made – made

mean (*kastetmek*) – meant – meant

meet (*rastlamak*) – met – met

mow (*biçmek*) – mowed – mown*

pay (*ödemek*) – paid – paid

put (*yerleştirmek*) – put – put

read (*okumak*) – read – read

rend (*yırt[ıl]mak*) – rent – rent

rid (*kurtarmak*) – rid* – rid

ride (*binmek*) – rode – ridden

ring (*çalmak*) – rang – rung

rise (*kalkmak*) – rose – risen

run (*koşmak*) – ran – run

saw (*testere ile kesmek*) – sawed – sawn*

say (*demek, söylemek*) – said – said

see (*görmek*) – saw – seen

seek (*aramak*) – sought – sought

sell (*satmak*) – sold – sold

send (*göndermek*) – sent – sent

set (*koymak*) – set – set

sew (*dikmek*) – sewed – sewn*

shake (*sallamak*) – shook – shaken

shave (*tıraş etm. veya olm.*) – shaved – shaven*

shear (*kırkmak*) – sheared – shorn

shed (*dökmek*) – shed – shed

shine (*parla[t]mak*) – shone – shone

shoot (*ateş etm.*) – shot – shot

show (*göstermek*) – showed – shown*

shred (*parçalamak*) – shred* – shred*

shrink (*daral[t]mak*) – shrank – shrunk

shut (*kapa[t]mak*) shut – shut

sing (*şarkı söylemek*) – sang – sung

sink (*bat[ır]mak*) – sank – sunk

sit (*oturmak*) – sat – sat

slay (*öldürmek*) – slew – slain

sleep (*uyumak*) – slept – slept

slide (*kaymak*) – slid – slid

sling (*sapanla atmak*) – slung – slung

slit (*yarmak*) – slit – slit

smell (*kokmak; kokusunu almak*) – smelt* – smelt

sow (*ekmek*) – sowed – sown*

speak (*konuşmak*) – spoke – spoken

speed (*hızlan[dır]mak*) – sped* – sped

spell (*hecelemek*) – spelt* – spelt

spend (*harcamak*) – spent – spent

spill (*dök[ül]mek*) – spilt* – spilt*

spin (*eğirmek*) – spun, span – spun

spit (*tükümek*) – spat – spat

split (*yar[ıl]mak*) – split – split

spoil (*bozmak*) – spoilt* – spoilt*

spread (*yay[ıl]mak*) – spread – spread

spring (*sıçramak*) – sprang – sprung

stand (*durmak*) – stood – stood

steal (*çalmak*) – stole – stolen

stick (*yapış[tır]mak*) – stuck – stuck

sting (*sokmak*) – stung – stung

stink (*koku çıkarmak*) – stank, stunk – stunk

strew (*serpmek*) – strewed – strewn*

stride (*yürümek*) – strode – stridden

strike (*vurmak*) – struck – struck, stricken

string (*dizmek; germek*) – strung – strung

strive (*uğraşmak*) – strove – striven

swear (*yemin etm.*) – swore – sworn

sweat (*terlemek*) – sweat* – sweat*

sweep (*süpürmek*) – swept – swept

swell (*şiş[ir]mek*) – swelled – swollen

swim (*yüzmek*) – swam – swum

swing (*salla[n]mak*) – swung – swung

take (*almak*) – took – taken

teach (*öğretmek*) – taught – taught

tear (*çekmek*) – tore – torn

tell (*söylemek*) – told – told

think (*düşünmek*) – thought – thought

thrive (*gelişmek*) – throve* – thriven*

throw (*atmak*) – threw – thrown

thrust (*dürtmek*) – thrust – thrust

tread (*basmak, çiğnemek*) – trod – trodden

wake (*uyan[dır]mak*) – woke* – woke(n)*

wear (*giymek*) – wore – worn

weave (*dokumak*) – wove – woven

weep (*ağlamak*) – wept – wept

wet (*ıslatmak*) – wet* – wet*

win (*kazanmak*) – won – won

wind (*dola[ş]mak*) – wound – wound

work (*çalışmak*) – wrought* – wrought*

wring (*burup sıkmak*) – wrung – wrung

write (*yazmak*) – wrote – written

Numbers
Sayılar

Cardinal Numbers
Asıl sayılar

0	nought, zero, cipher *sıfır*	21	twenty-one *yirmi bir*
1	one *bir*	22	twenty-two *yirmi iki*
2	two *iki*	23	twenty-three *yirmi üç*
3	three *üç*	30	thirty *otuz*
4	four *dört*	40	forty *kırk*
5	five *beş*	50	fifty *elli*
6	six *altı*	60	sixty *altmış*
7	seven *yedi*	70	seventy *yetmiş*
8	eight *sekiz*	80	eighty *seksen*
9	nine *dokuz*	90	ninety *doksan*
10	ten *on*	100	a (one) hundred *yüz*
11	eleven *on bir*	101	a hundred and one *yüz bir*
12	twelve *on iki*		
13	thirteen *on iki*	572	five hundred and seventy-two *beş yüz yetmiş iki*
14	fourteen *on dört*		
15	fifteen *on beş*		
16	sixteen *on altı*	1,000	a (one) thousand *bin*
17	seventeen *on yedi*	1,000,000	a (one) million *bir milyon*
18	eighteen *on sekiz*		
19	nineteen *on dokuz*	1,000,000,000	a (one) billion *bir milyar*
20	twenty *yirmi*		